D1565961

Speculative Bubbles, Speculative Attacks, and Policy Switching

Speculative Bubbles, Speculative Attacks, and Policy Switching

Robert P. Flood and
Peter M. Garber

The MIT Press
Cambridge, Massachusetts
London, England

To Petrice and Deborah

This book was set in Palatino by Asco Trade Typesetting Ltd., Hong Kong and was printed and bound in the United States of America.

Library of Congress Cataloging-in-Publication Data

Flood, Robert P.
  Speculative bubbles, speculative attacks, and policy switching /
  Robert P. Flood and Peter M. Garber.
    p. cm.
  Includes bibliographical references and index.
  ISBN 0-262-06169-4
  1. Monetary policy—United States. 2. Foreign exchange rates—United States.
  3. Speculation—United States. I. Garber, Peter M. II. Title.
  HG540.F57 1994
  332.4'937—dc20
                                                                93—40692
                                                                    CIP

Contents

Contents

Introduction

Speculative bubbles, currency reforms, speculative attacks on fixed exchange rate regimes, and metallic monetary standards—these tumultuous events are fixed in the minds of both the public and research economists as key markers of economic change. The studies in this volume are representative of our joint and separate research in these areas during the 1980s. They are bound together in several ways that reflect both our interests and our deficiencies. First, on a doctrinal level, they expose our fixation on understanding extreme events, for such events contain the few true disturbances that exist in our long series of macroeconomic data. Second, on a technical level, they employ primarily the forward-looking method of analysis with simple money-demand decision rules that emerged in the heyday of the rational expectations revolution of the 1970s, notably in the Sargent and Wallace's 1973 *Econometrica* article. Third, on an empirical level, they generally represent attempts at a first pass over new empirical propositions.

Our studies of speculative bubbles arose from the potential of multiple explosive price equilibria in forward-looking models of monetary or asset markets. This result was treated as a technical artifact by the principal architects of the rational expectations revolution in the 1970s, and the explosive solutions were assumed away by researchers who were focused on the unique, stable price solutions that might be produced for price dynamics by generalizations of the method of undetermined coefficients. The adhesion to stable solutions also had normative and policy dimensions in that to assume otherwise might invite market regulation aimed at controlling speculative instabilities. Many such prescriptions were made frequently during the 1980s by numerous researchers who could not square observable financial market data with their models of market fundamentals, concluding therefore that the markets must be dominated by rational or irrational speculative bubbles. Our initial research on bubbles was principally aimed at turning the inconclusive theoretical dispute into a simple empirical test. We examined the possibility of price level bubbles in an explosive hyperinflationary context in which we thought there was some possibility of observing them and in which theoretical research was unable to exclude them on a priori grounds.[1] In this context, we accepted the hypothesis of no bubbles. In doing this research we realized that acceptance or rejection of the existence of a bubble was contingent on the model of fundamentals one proposed—indeed, the conclusion that a bubble existed in the data could emerge only from adhering to a specific model of fundamentals as a maintained hypothesis.

Although approached from different directions, our work on bubbles is intimately related to that on process switching. In particular, as discussed in our first bubbles paper, there is no way to disentangle bubbles from anticipated policy switching. Empirical work on bubbles, therefore, requires taking a stand on on the model of fundamentals; this made us somewhat evangelical on insisting that the model of fundamentals be explored deeply before embracing the bubble explanation. A cursory examination of murkily understood episodes that formed part of everyone's litany of historical bubbles convinced us that better fundamental explanations could be formulated and led to several historical studies on bubbles.

The methods of the policy-switching approach achieved popularity because they permitted investigators studying macroeconomic data to come to grips with the "peculiar" behavior that surrounds crises and other discrete events. One of the most valuable products of the approach is that it has allowed economists to combine economic behavior in times of crisis with behavior during more normal times in a continuous series of observations.

One of the most fruitful applications of policy switching to date has been in the area of speculative attacks on asset price-fixing regimes. Our work in this area followed on Salant and Henderson's and Krugman's seminal work: as simplifications of their results on speculative attacks on exchange rates; applications to different institutional arrangements such as a collapse of a gold standard; demonstrations that fixed exchange rate regimes do not preclude arbitrary speculative activity in exchange markets in the form either of bubbles or of multiple equilibria from endogenously triggered monetary policy shifts; and efforts to find empirical support for the theory in both recent and historical speculative attacks.

From the start, the primary focus of our joint research was on the problem of a switch in government policy triggered by events generated by the operation of the economic system rather than directly by exogenous forces. The task then was to determine the timing and magnitude of the event. The potential for application of this view is rich, and the studies published here are a few examples of the kinds of applications of the method that have emerged in the past decade or more. For example, the initial article is a study of the the exchange rate dynamics of a country currently operating a floating exchange rate that will switch to a fixed exchange rate when the exchange rate reaches some par value, the salient example being Britain's return to gold in 1925. The underlying model has since been applied by Krugman to provide the most influential model of exchange rate target zones. In the context of monetary reform, the policy switch methods can explain the anomalous observations of Cagan's original study that money demand increased dramatically at the end of hyperinflations when the inflation rates reached their maximum values—points at which money demand should have been at its lowest.

This research program was begun at the University of Virginia. As assistant professors neither of us could embrace standard research methods requiring agents to believe that particular linear economic policies would last into the indefinite future and that rationally viable price solutions should be disregarded on the basis of neither theoretical reasoning nor empirical investigation. It seemed to us that standard assumptions, adopted for mathematical expediency, excluded all interesting and informative macroeconomic data.

We are grateful for the early and continuing input received from Bennett McCallum, Kenneth Singleton, Dale Henderson, Paul Krugman, and Steven Salant. We owe special thanks to coauthors of articles included in this volume, Herminio Blanco, Edwin Burmeister, Vittorio Grilli, Robert Hodrick, Peter Isard, Paul Kaplan, Nancy Marion, and Louis Scott.

Note

1. The work of W. Brock (1974, 1978, 1979 referenced in chapter 1) demonstrated that real price bubbles could be excluded on theoretical grounds but nominal price bubbles could not.

I

Speculative Bubbles

1

Market Fundamentals versus Price-Level Bubbles: The First Tests

Robert P. Flood and Peter M. Garber

The possibility of a market's launching itself onto a price bubble exists when the expected rate of market price change is an important factor determining current market price. While, for years, such a possibility has simultaneously confounded and intrigued economists,[1] the recent adoption of the rational-expectations assumption has clarified considerably the nature of price bubbles and has focused widespread professional attention on the problem. The rational-expectations assumption has stimulated progress because its application imposes a precise mathematical structure on the relationship between actual and expected price movements.

With expectations rational in the sense of Muth (1961), agents' anticipations of actual price movements are mathematical expectations, conditional on an information set which may include some structural knowledge of a particular economic model. Thus, a researcher can determine an expression for agents' expectations by manipulating a proposed model. However, if the expected rate of market price change influences the current market price, the researcher using the rational-expectations assumption often cannot produce a unique expression for agents' expectations. In its simplest form, the indeterminacy arises because only one market-equilibrium condition exists; but the researcher requires solutions for two endogenous variables—market price and the expected rate of market price change.

A bubble can arise when the actual market price depends positively on its own expected rate of change, as normally occurs in asset markets. Since agents forming rational expectations do not make systematic prediction errors, the positive relationship between price and its expected rate of change implies a similar relationship between price and its actual rate of change. In such conditions, the arbitrary, self-fulfilling expectation of price changes may drive actual price changes independently of *market fundamentals*; we refer to such a situation as *a price bubble*. An explicit definition of market fundamentals depends on a particular model's structure; indeed, the very notion of a bubble can make no sense in the absence of a precise model detailing a market's operation. Without such a model, it is impossible both to define market fundamentals and to isolate the trajectory characteristic of a bubble. We employ a specific model to advance an exact definition in section I.

Judging whether a price bubble or market fundamentals determine current market price is a difficult problem both for agents in an economy and for economists who model agents' behavior. Brock (1974, 1975, 1979) made progress on the problem by finding sets of conditions for both discrete-time and continuous-time models such that price-level bubbles may be excluded from the class of equilibrium price paths.[2]

Our approach in this chapter is complementary to such theoretical work. We test the hypothesis that price-level bubbles did not exist in a particular historical episode. We show that the existence of a price-level bubble places such extraordinary restrictions on the data that such bubbles are not an interesting research problem during normal times. However, since hyperinflations generated series of data extraordinary enough to admit the existence of a price-level bubble, we believe that the German episode is an appropriate and interesting period to search for bubbles. Furthermore, since hyperinflation provides the environment in which the link between price and its expected rate of change has received the strongest emphasis in recent literature, an inability to reject the hypothesis that price-level bubbles were not partly responsible for the German hyperinflation will provide strong evidence that markets avoid such bubbles even in the most extreme situations.

We wish to emphasize that our results concern only a single historical episode's price-level bubble. The rejection of such a bubble does not imply the nonexistence of bubbles in more specialized asset markets, such as the markets for equities or gold. Because these assets may have many substitutes, probing for specific asset price bubbles requires more complex market models; however, our basic technique remains generally applicable to tests for asset price bubbles.

We present the results of our investigation in two main sections. In section I we build a theoretical model of hyperinflation in which we allow price-level bubbles. In section II we translate the theoretical model into data restrictions and use these restrictions to test the hypothesis that price-level bubbles were not partly responsible for Germany's massive inflation during the early 1920s. The results reported in section II support the hypothesis of no price-level bubbles. Section II is followed by some concluding remarks and technical and data appendices.

I Market Fundamentals versus Price-Level Bubbles in the Monetary Model of Hyperinflation

Deriving a Price-Level Solution in a Simple Money Market

Cagan (1956) used the following monetary model in his study of seven hyperinflations:

$$m_t - p_t = \gamma + \alpha \pi_t^* + \varepsilon_t; \qquad \alpha < 0 \qquad t = 1, 2, 3, \ldots . \qquad (1)$$

The quantities m_t and p_t are the natural logarithms of money and price, respectively, at time t. We assume that m_t is determined by the government in accord with a process which is independent of current and past p. The anticipated rate of inflation between t and $t + 1$ is π_t^*, and ε_t is a stochastic disturbance term. Sargent and Wallace (1973a) combined this model with Muth's assumption that anticipations are formed rationally,[3] and we impose the same assumption. The rational-expectations assumption requires

$$\pi_t^* = E(\pi_t | I_t), \qquad (2)$$

where $\pi_t = p_{t+1} - p_t$, E is the mathematical expectations operator, and I_t is the information set available for use at time t. We assume that I_t contains current and past values of m, p, and ε, as well as knowledge of the structure described by equation (1).[4]

Using (2), we rewrite (1) as

$$m_t - p_t = \gamma + \alpha E(\pi_t | I_t) + \varepsilon_t. \qquad (3)$$

In Appendix A we describe the standard methods of solving equation (3) for $E(\pi_t | I_t)$. This solution is

$$E(\pi_t | I_t) = A_0 \psi^t - \frac{\psi^{-1}}{\alpha} \sum_{i=0}^{\infty} E(\mu_{t+i} - w_{t+i} | I_t) \psi^{-i}, \qquad (4)$$

where $\psi \equiv (\alpha - 1)/\alpha > 1$, $\mu_{t+i} = m_{t+i+1} - m_{t+i}$, $w_{t+i} = \varepsilon_{t+i+1} - \varepsilon_{t+i}$, and A_0 is an *arbitrary* constant.

Given that agents form expectations of inflation according to equation (4), the solution of (3) for price is

$$p_t = -\alpha A_0 \psi^t + \left[m_t - \gamma + \psi^{-1} \sum_{i=0}^{\infty} E(\mu_{t+i} - w_{t+i} | I_t) \psi^{-i} - \varepsilon_t \right]. \qquad (5)$$

For this model we define market fundamentals to be

$$\left[m_t - \gamma + \psi^{-1} \sum_{i=0}^{\infty} E(\mu_{t+i} - w_{t+i}|I_t)\psi^{-i} - \varepsilon_t \right];$$

price-level bubbles are then captured by the term $-\alpha A_0 \psi^t$.

Rational-expectations models normally contain the assumption $A_0 = 0$, which prevents bubbles. Notice the if $A_0 \neq 0$, then price will change with t *even if market fundamentals are constant.*

The definition of a price-level bubble as a situation in which $A_0 \neq 0$ is appropriate for two reasons. First, A_0 is an arbitrary and self-fulfilling element in expectations. The other components of expectations are unbiased predictors of future events determined exogenously to the money market. Therefore, we find in unrewarding to associate them with bubbles, since we could otherwise characterize all market prices as bubbles. Second, if $A_0 \neq 0$, then agents expect prices to change through time at an ever-accelerating rate, even if market fundamentals do not change. Since economists usually consider price bubbles to be episodes of explosive price movement which are unexplained by the normal determinants of market price, $A_0 \neq 0$ will produce a price-level bubble.[5]

An Identification Problem

A researcher who could measure p_t and all of the elements which make up market fundamentals could obtain an exact measurement of A_0, the bubble parameter. Unfortunately, such direct measurement is impossible since market fundamentals are comprised in part of agents' expectations, which are not directly observable. In this circumstance, measurement error can lead to a potentially serious identification problem.

To illustrate the nature of the problem, it is helpful to consider an ideal research environment with samples of unlimited size so that there is no problem in measuring α or γ. Further, suppose that ε_{t+i} is generated by a random walk so that $E(w_{t+i}|I_t) \equiv E(\varepsilon_{t+i+1} - \varepsilon_{t+i}|I_t) = 0$, $i = 0, 1, 2, \ldots$. Finally, assume that money growth has been constant at zero for a very long time. In such a situation, a researcher who uses standard forecasting techniques to estimate agents' expectations of future money growth will forecast zero money growth into the indefinite future, and he will estimate $E(\mu_{t+i} - w_{t+i}|I_t) = 0$, $i = 0, 1, 2, \ldots$.

Thus, the researcher's estimates of agents' beliefs, when substituted into equation (5), yield

$$p_t = -\alpha A_0 \psi^t + (m_t - \gamma - \varepsilon_t). \tag{6}$$

However, suppose agents do not actually expect money to remain constant; for example, they expect an alteration in the money supply at time $T > t$. Assuming, for simplicity, that they expect money to start growing at the constant rate $\bar{\mu} \neq 0$ at time T,[6] and substituting this expectation into (5), we obtain:[7]

$$p_t = -\alpha(A_0 + \bar{\mu}\psi^{-T})\psi^t + (m_t - \gamma - \varepsilon_t), \qquad T \geq t. \qquad (7)$$

The nature of the identification problem is apparent. If the researcher bases his estimation of agents' money-growth expectations on past money growth alone, while agents expect a future change in the money-supply process, then he will confound his measure of the arbitrary solution constant with market fundamentals: He will measure $(A_0 + \bar{\mu}\psi^{-T})$ instead of A_0.

This example is only an illustration of a problem which may assume a much more complex form. The problem is important in the context of the German hyperinflation, since previous work (e.g., Cagan 1956; Flood and Garber 1980a) has indicated that agents in Germany expected an alteration in the money-supply process during the hyperinflation's final five months (July–November 1923). Such as expectation by agents will seriously undermine the validity of the estimation procedures that we employ in the next section. We have not discovered a satisfactory method for resolving this identification problem. Therefore, we have been forced to ignore the final months of the hyperinflation and to examine only the period for which agents apparently did not strongly believe in a future money-supply process change. The data series we usually employ terminates in June 1923; thus, it is not much different from that used by other researchers, including Cagan, who also truncated the data around this date. Since the identification problem forces us to assume that agents' money forecasts are formed in a manner similar to those which we will use, it also restricts our sample to a period for which this assumption has not been refuted.[8]

II Some Tests

In this section we will use data generated in the German hyperinflation to implement the theoretical price-bubble model described in section I. For two reasons a hyperinflationary period is an appropriate environment for an initial examination of the question of market fundamentals versus price-level bubbles. First, if price-level bubbles occur, they are associated with self-fulfilling expectations; therefore, such bubbles should be most clearly observable when expectations play a dominant role in price determination, which occurs during hyperinflation.[9] Second, the existence of a positive price-level bubble implies that inflation and its higher-order rates of change must be accelerating through time. This is a very strong restriction on the data, and we doubt that data from normal times which conform to such a restriction will ever be found. However, hyperinflationary Germany experienced massive accelerations of inflation; thus, the episode should provide interesting results to tests of the existence of price-level bubbles.

In all our tests, we assume that money is exogenous with respect to the inflation rate. Though controversial, this assumption is appropriate in a first investigation of price bubbles:[10] We should conduct our first search for bubbles in order to detect the form of bubble most likely to inhabit the data.

The interaction of money demand and the money-supply process determines a bubble's form; in particular, all money-supply processes for which money is exogenous to inflation yield bubbles whose form is derived in section I.[11] Thus, the probability that our Section I bubble is the form relevant to our investigation equals the probability that money is exogenous to inflation.

On the other hand, when money is endogenous with respect to inflation, the form of bubble relevant to our investigation is sensitive both to money's functional relationship to inflation and to our assignment of initial conditions contingent on a given functional form.[12] In principle, there are an indefinitely large number of functional relationships between inflation and the money supply; for any given functional relationship, a variety of ways to assign initial conditions can exist. Consequently, the probability that a particular bubble form drives the inflation rate when money is endogenous equals (a) the probability that money is endogenous multiplied by (b) the probability that the given functional form is correct (conditional on endogeneity) multiplied by (c) the probability that we have correctly assigned the initial conditions. Therefore, it is not obvious to us that the bubble form produced by a particular endogenous money-supply process is a priori more likely than the form associated with an exogenous money supply.[13]

We will use three related techniques to test for a price-level bubble. Two methods are efficient in the sense of Salemi and Sargent (1979) and Hansen and Sargent (1979) because cross-equation restrictions are used in jointly estimating money-demand, anticipated, inflation, and money-supply parameters. With the third method, we first estimate the money-supply process parameters; then we employ the implied money predictions in estimating the money-demand parameters. While this method forgoes the efficiency of joint estimation, we can use more observations in estimating the money-supply process.[14]

Joint Estimation of Money-Demand and Inflation-Prediction Parameters

The direct estimation of the equation (1) parameters is difficult because we cannot observe the expectational variable π_t^*. In different models, McCallum (1976, 1977) and Abel et al. (1979) have proposed the use of the actual inflation rate π_t in place of π_t^*; in the context of a rational-expectations model, this creates a classical errors-in-variables problem which can be estimated by means of instrumental variables. If the instruments are lagged growth rates of money and a function of time, then we can interpret the regressor in the second stage of the instrumental variable technique as the resultant of a prediction equation for π_t. However, the McCallum technique is inefficient because the parameters of the inflation-prediction equation are not estimated jointly with the money-demand equation parameters.

Singleton (1979) has proposed a simple and computationally tractable generalization of McCallum's method to remedy the efficiency problem. In the current model, the inflation equation can be written as

$$\pi_t = \delta + \beta_1 \mu_{t-1} + \beta_2 \mu_{t-2} + \cdots + \beta_K \mu_{t-K} + A_0 \psi^t + v_{1t}. \tag{8}$$

If an $AR(K)$ model is sufficient to describe the μ_t process, the rational-expectations assumption guarantees that the parameters $(\delta, \beta_1, \ldots, \beta_K)$ are functions of both the money-supply process parameters and α. If $E(w_{t+j}|I_t) = 0, j = 0, 1, \ldots$, an assumption imposed by Salemi and Sargent (1979), then equation (4) and the rational-expectations assumption imply that v_{1t} is white noise. Rewriting the money-demand equation (1) with the predicted π_t from equation (8) substituted for π_t^*,

$$m_t - p_t = \gamma + \alpha(\delta + \beta_1 \mu_{t-1} + \beta_2 \mu_{t-2} + \cdots + \beta_K \mu_{t-K} + A_0 \psi^t) + \varepsilon_t. \tag{9}$$

Equations (8) and (9) can be estimated jointly with a nonlinear seemingly unrelated regression (SUR) model which imposes the cross-equation restrictions. Based on the Salemi and Sargent assumption that $E(w_{t+j}|I_t) = 0$, Singleton has shown that his method will produce estimates of the relevant parameters which have the same asymptotic distribution as those produced by the Hansen and Sargent (1979) technique.

The assumption that $E(w_{t+j}|I_t) = 0$ holds if ε_t is a random walk. Since preliminary estimates of (8) and (9) indicated that ε_t is autocorrelated, we report here the joint estimates for (8) and a first differenced version of (9).[15]

Table 1.1
Joint estimates of money-demand and inflation-prediction parameters

Period of bubble	θ	α	δ	β_1	β_2	β_3	β_4	$\hat{A}$	R^2	D-W	SEE
July 1920–June 1923	−0.284	−1.615	.0718	.921	−.162	.0565	.172	$.126 \times 10^{-7}$	.375	2.007	.162
	(.0299)	(.583)*	(.0546)	(.313)*	(.239)	(.188)	(.213)	$(.617 \times 10^{-7})$	.268	1.578	.260
July 1920–June 1923	⋯	−1.687	.0464	.891	−.140	.0672	.170	$.272 \times 10^{-7}$	.363	1.981	.164
		(.567)*	(.0481)	(.289)*	(.227)	(.183)	(.209)	$(.119 \times 10^{-6})$	.275	1.569	.259
Jan.–June 1923	−.0288	−1.598	.0717	.928	−.162	.0552	.170	$.113 \times 10^{-7}$	.377	1.996	.162
	(.0296)	(.572)*	(.0545)	(.315)*	(.247)	(.193)	(.217)	$(.516 \times 10^{-7})$	.268	1.573	.260
Jan.–June 1923	⋯	−1.682	.0457	.897	−.138	.0673	.171	$.262 \times 10^{-7}$	.366	1.976	.163
		(.573)*	(.0481)	(.290)*	(.229)	(.184)	(.209)	$(.118 \times 10^{-6})$	.272	1.556	.259

Note: No. monthly observations = 35; standard errors in parentheses. First line in R^2, D-W, SEE columns is for money-demand equation; second line is for inflation-prediction equation.
*Significantly different from zero at standard significance levels.

The price data are the monthly wholesale price indexes used by Cagan; however, we have recently discovered an improved money-supply series which we discuss in detail in Appendix B.

We investigated the existence of a bubble of three different possible durations: from July 1920 to June 1923; from June 1922 to June 1923; and from January 1923 to June 1923. To do this we multiplied the $A_0\psi^t$ term in each equation by a dummy variable whose value equaled one for the months of possible bubbles and zero for all other months; for each potential bubble period we produced a separate estimate of the parameters.[16]

We report the results in table 1.1. We do not include the estimates for the June 1922–June 1923 bubble because they are identical, except for the least significant digits, with those of the July 1920–June 1923 bubble. The θ parameter is simply a constant that we added to the first differenced equation (9); a nonzero θ indicates that a time trend should be included in (9).[17] Finally, we have used four lagged money-growth rates, to be consistent with Salemi and Sargent (1979).

In each case the results are the same. The quantity $\hat{A}_0$ is not significantly different from zero.[18] Therefore, the evidence does not contradict the hypothesis that only market fundamentals drove the German hyperinflation; that is, no price-level bubble existed in this episode.

Joint Estimation of Money-Demand and Money-Supply Parameters

Hansen and Sargent (1979) have proposed a different technique for estimating the model's parameters. Instead of substituting from (8) into the money-demand equation, we may substitute from (4) for π_t^* in money demand (assuming $E[w_{t+j}|I_t] = 0$) to derive:[19]

$$m_t - p_t = \gamma + \alpha\left[A_0\psi^t - \frac{\psi^{-1}}{\alpha}\sum_{i=0}^{\infty}E(\mu_{t+i}|I_t)\psi^{-i}\right] + \varepsilon_t. \qquad (10)$$

The infinite sum in (10) can be solved analytically as a function of currently available information, once we know the parameters of the money-supply process. If μ_t follows an $AR(K)$ process,

$$\mu_t = \eta + \phi_1\mu_{t-1} + \phi_2\mu_{t-2} + \cdots + \phi_K\mu_{t-K} + v_{2t}, \qquad (11)$$

then (10) and (11) can be estimated jointly, once suitable prediction formulas have been substituted into (10). Here, we identify the AR process on μ_t, solve for

$$\frac{\psi^{-1}}{\alpha}\sum_{i=0}^{\infty}E(\mu_{t+i}|I_t)\psi^{-i}$$

Table 1.2
Identification of the money-supply process, $(1 - L)\mu_t$, December 1918–August 1923*

Lags	Autocorrelations†												SE for row
1–12	.36	.10	−.19	−.17	−.06	.10	−.08	.09	.10	.08	.11	.03	.13
13–24	.01	.02	.00	.02	−.02	−.07	−.02	.00	.02	−.02	.01	−.03	.17
Partial autocorrelations													
1–12	.36	−.03	−.25	−.01	.05	.09	−.24	.20	.12	−.08	.11	.01	.13
13–24	.08	−.05	.04	.08	−.14	−.01	.03	−.01	−.05	−.08	.12	−.12	.13

*No. of observations = 56; units = %/month.
†Mean of series = .0261; variance = .0157. Box-Pierce Q-statistics; $Q(12) = 16.3$; $Q(24) = 19.3$; $Q(36) = 23.4$. Critical values: $P(Q > \text{c.v.}) = .05$; $\chi^2(10) = 18.3$; $\chi^2(22) = 33.9$.

as a function of the unknown money-supply process parameters, α, and lagged μ_t, and jointly estimate the parameters of (10) and (11). Our purpose in implementing a Hansen-Sargent procedure is to compare its results with those of the Singleton method.

As a first step we report the results of a standard Box and Jenkins (1970) identification routine in table 1.2. We identified the μ_t process as an AR (1) on the first difference of μ_t, and in table 1.3 we report estimates for the parameters of this process for the period December 1918—August 1923.[20]

The money-supply process then specializes to

$$\mu_t = \eta + (1 + \rho)\mu_{t-1} - \rho\mu_{t-2} + v_{2t}. \tag{12}$$

With this process, the infinite sum in (10) can be solved analytically as

$$-\frac{\psi^{-1}}{\alpha} \sum_{i=0}^{\infty} E(\mu_{t+i}|I_t)\psi^{-i}$$

$$= \mu_{t-1} - \frac{\eta(\alpha - 1)}{1 - \rho} + \left[\frac{\rho(\alpha - 1)}{\alpha - 1 - \rho\alpha}\right]\left(\mu_{t-1} - \mu_{t-2} - \frac{\eta}{1 - \rho}\right). \tag{13}$$

Substituting from (13) into (10) and first differencing, we can use restricted SUR to estimate the resulting equation's parameters jointly with those of (12). The problem is then a special case of the Hansen-Sargent method, based on the Salemi-Sargent assumption.

We report our estimates for the full-period bubble in table 1.4. Note that the $\hat{\alpha}$ and $\hat{A}_0$ estimates are almost identical with those of the Singleton method.

The $\hat{\rho}$ estimate is much different from the estimate produced by univariate time-series methods; the extra observations included at the beginning and end of the μ_t series used in the univariate method have produced markedly different results. The use of a higher-order AR process for the μ_t series may remedy this difficulty at the cost of a much more complicated formula for the infinite sum. However, since we wish only to indicate that, for the parameters of interest, the Singleton and Hansen-Sargent methods yield similar results, we did not continue along this line.

A Two-Step Procedure

As a final attempt at finding the track of a bubble, we substituted the parameter estimates reported in table 1.3 into equations (4) and (10) and jointly estimated the remaining unknown parameters contained in these two equations. The procedure is asymptotically inefficient in that cross-

Table 1.3
Estimation of AR(1) process on $(1 - L)\mu_t$

Parameters	Estimate	SE	t-Statistic
Constant	.0141	.0142	.995
AR(1)	.725	.163	4.453

Note: $R^2 = .263$; variance $= .0113$. Box-Pierce Q-statistic of residuals: $Q(12) = 6.8$; $Q(24) = 9.4$; $Q(36) = 11.9$. Critical values: $P(Q \geq$ c.v.$) = .05$; $\chi^2(9) = 16.9$; $\chi^2(21) = 32.7$.

Table 1.4
Hansen-Sargent joint estimation technique of money-demand and money-supply parameters

Period of bubble	$\hat{\eta}$	$\hat{\rho}$	$\hat{\alpha}$	$\hat{A}$	R^2	D-W	SEE
July 1920–	.01198	−.09186	−1.699	$.2372 \times 10^{-7}$	.3520	2.0733	.1651
June 1923	(.01381)	(.1507)	(.4722)	$(.7673 \times 10^{-7})$	.7727	2.0966	.0817

Note: Standard errors in parentheses. First line in R^2, D-W, SEE columns is for money-demand equation; second line is for money-supply equation.

equation restrictions are not used in estimating the money-supply parameters. However, a benefit is that more observations are available for estimating this process separately.

We report the results both for equation (10) and for a first differenced version of equation (10) in table 1.5. Once again, we cannot reject the hypothesis that $A_0 = 0$ at standard significance levels.

III Conclusions and Extensions

When expectations are endogenous, the potential for multiple solutions often arises in economic models; the selection of a price path which depends only on market fundamentals is arbitrary in such models. However, in many areas of economics, descriptions of behavior are widely accepted, although they have no basis in theory—for example, the downward-sloping consumers' demand curve and the fractional marginal propensity to consume. That these descriptions are widely accepted stems not from their theoretical priority but rather from the enormous body of empirical evidence supporting them. Similarly, the problem of the existence of bubbles in dynamic systems is inherently an empirical question: Is the potential for bubbles simply an artifact of a model which may otherwise predict well, or do bubbles actually exist?

Table 1.5
Nonlinear joint estimation of money-demand and inflation parameters for given money-supply process

A. Level of money-demand equation

Period of bubble	$\hat{\gamma}$	$\hat{\alpha}$	$\hat{A}$	R^2	D-W	SEE
July 1920–June 1923	8.599	−2.833	$.6728 \times 10^{-5}$	.6629	1.7553	.486
	$(.1135)^*$	$(.2575)^*$	$(.4556 \times 10^{-5})$	−.0597	2.214	.3096
June 1922–June 1923	8.597	−2.831	$.6605 \times 10^{-5}$	.6620	1.7465	.4868
	$(.1132)^*$	$(.2578)^*$	$(.4492 \times 10^{-5})$	−.0597	2.213	.3096
Jan.–June 1923	8.596	−2.871	$.6512 \times 10^{-5}$	.648	1.702	.4968
	$(.1157)^*$	$(.2621)^*$	$(.4782 \times 10^{-5})$	−.0588	2.198	.3095

B. First difference of money-demand equation

Period of bubble	$\hat{\gamma}$	$\hat{\alpha}$	$\hat{A}$	R^2	D-W	SEE
July 1920–June 1923	...	−.7117	$.2112 \times 10^{-13}$	.3629	2.0991	.163
		$(.1053)^*$	$(.6218 \times 10^{-13})$	.1054	2.1589	.2872
June 1922–June 1923	Same as July 1920–June 1923 (except for low-significance digits)					
Jan.–June 1923	...	−.7121	$.214 \times 10^{-13}$	.3679	2.0987	.163
		$(.1053)^*$	$(.6259 \times 10^{-13})$	.1059	2.1585	.2871

Note: Standard errors in parentheses. First line in R^2, D-W, SEE columns is for money-demand equation; second line is for inflation-prediction equation.
* Significantly different from zero at standard significance levels.

If bubbles actually exist, then explaining both their paths and their termi-nations is important, and dynamic models which ignore bubbles are clearly inadequate. Thus, to verify empirically that a bubble existed in an impor-tant market is to demonstrate that current dynamic economic models do not predict well the behavior which they are intended to explain.

However, if bubbles do not exist, then this artifact of dynamic models is unimportant; a special case of these models adequately predicts behavior, and further elaboration of the model to explain unobserved phenomena is unnecessary. To require such elaboration is analogous to requiring a biolo-gist to explain the nonexistence of unicorns or a chemist to explain why there is no philosopher's stone.

To our knowledge, the results reported in this paper represent the first empirical test of the existence of a price bubble; the profession's classifica-tion of various phenomena as bubbles has been based only on arbitrary, prior beliefs until now. Our test concerns only *price-level* bubbles in one extreme period. We intend to explore other periods to determine whether such bubbles existed in more normal times,[21] but our rejection of the existence of a bubble in the German hyperinflation raises doubt that such an instability will be found elsewhere. Thus, our results provide support for the assumption that only market fundamentals determine price solutions (see, e.g., Lucas 1972, 1973, 1975; Sargent and Wallace 1973b; Barro 1976).

That we doubt the existence of price-level bubbles does not imply that we have formed strong opinions about the existence of price bubbles in specialized asset markets. Indeed, the profession's folklore on the existence of bubbles emphasizes such markets, for example, the Tulip Bubble, the South Sea Bubble, the Mississippi Bubble, the crash of 1929. However, no one has verified that a bubble of the type defined in the current rational-expectations literature has ever existed.[22] We believe that the standard bubble catalog now requires reexamination. Economists can no longer as-sert that a particular event is a bubble; instead, we must provide empirical evidence that the event conforms to a strict, standard definition of a bubble.

Appendix A

Solution Technqiues

In this appendix we derive text equation (4) and we discuss an alternative solution technique.

Equation (3) may be first differenced to yield

$$\mu_t - \pi_t = \alpha[E(\pi_{t+1}|I_{t+1}) - E(\pi_t|I_t)] + w_t. \tag{A1}$$

Operate on both sides of (A1) with $E(\quad |I_t)$ and obtain

$$E(\mu_t|I_t) - E(\pi_t|I_t) = \alpha[E(\pi_{t+1}|I_t) - E(\pi_t|I_t)] + E(w_t|I_t), \qquad (A2)$$

where the law of iterated expectations (see Sargent 1979) allows us to substitute

$E(\pi_{t+1}|I_t)$ for $E[E(\pi_{t+1}|I_{t+1})|I_t]$.

Equation (A2) is in the form of a first-order linear difference equation in $E(\pi_{t+j}|I_t)$. Lag operator techniques for solving (A2) are explained in Sargent, and they yield the solution

$$E(\pi_t|I_t) = A_t - \left(\frac{\psi^{-1}}{\alpha}\right) \sum_{i=0}^{\infty} E(\mu_{t+i} - w_{t+i}|I_t)\psi^{-i}, \qquad (A3)$$

where A_t is an arbitrary solution constant whose t subscript indicates that it is determined at time t. For each point in time we obtain an arbitrary solution constant, yielding a time series of such terms $(\ldots A_{t-1}, A_t, A_{t+1}, \ldots)$. This is a point emphasized by Shiller (1978). It can be shown that the rational-expectations assumption places the following restriction on these solution constants:

$$E(A_{t+j}|I_t) = A_t\psi^j, \qquad j = 0, 1, 2, \ldots, \qquad (A4a)$$

$$A_{t+j} = A_t\psi^j + \sum_{i=1}^{j} z_{t+i}\psi^{j-i}, \qquad j = 0, 1, 2, \ldots, \qquad (A4b)$$

where $z_{t+i}, i = 0, 1, 2, \ldots$, is a white noise disturbance term. Other than the white noise requirement, there is no other condition on the z's; in particular, the variances of the z's may grow through time to allow a growing probability that the bubble may collapse. In the text we have chosen a particular deterministic process on the A's which will fulfill (A4). That process is

$$A_t = A_0\psi^t, \qquad (A5)$$

where time zero is the point in time chosen for the beginning of our test for bubbles. When (A5) is substituted into (A3), the result is text equation (4).

An alternate solution procedure to the above is a method of repeated substitutions in (A2), which is familiar from Sargent and Wallace (1973b), Mussa (1975), and Evans (1978). The method consists of substituting the $t + 1$ difference equation involving $E(\pi_{t+1}|I_t)$ for that term in (A2). The result involves $E(\pi_{t+2}|I_t)$, which in turn may be substituted for , and so on. In the limit this procedure yields

$$E(\pi_t|I_t) = \lim_{n\to\infty} E(\pi_{t+n}|I_t)\psi^{-n} - \left(\frac{\psi^{-1}}{\alpha}\right) \sum_{i=0}^{\infty} E(u_{t+i} - w_{t+i}|I_t)\psi^{-i}. \tag{A6}$$

The equivalence of (A6) and text equation (4) requires

$$\lim_{n\to\infty} E(\pi_{t+n}|I_t)\psi^{-n} = A_t = A_0\psi^t. \tag{A7}$$

The second equality in (A7) is true by assumption. Further, (A3) generalizes to

$$E(\pi_{t+n}|I_t) = A_t\psi^n - \left(\frac{\psi^{-1}}{\alpha}\right) \sum_{i=0}^{\infty} E(u_{t+n+i} - w_{t+n+i}|I_t)\psi^{-i}, \tag{A8}$$

and when (A8) is substituted into (A6) we find that the solution techniques are equivalent only if

$$\lim_{n\to\infty} \psi^{-1} \sum_{i=n}^{\infty} E(\mu_{t+i} - w_{t+i}|I_t)\psi^{-i} = 0. \tag{A9}$$

But this condition is required if the infinite sums in (A6) and (4) are to be finite, a condition which we impose.

Appendix B

Data

Cagan (1956) and most other researchers have used Statistisches Reichsamt (1925) as their source for German money-supply data. In this source, money-supply totals are reported for the end of each month through December 1922 and weekly thereafter. The apparent lack of weekly data forces researchers to interpolate the monthly data to the middle of the month to coincide with the price-level data. Such interpolation can cause well-known problems for some investigations in time-series analysis such as exogeneity tests.

We have recently discovered sources which allow us to construct a weekly series for the total of Reichsbanknotes in circulation from December 1918 through the end of 1992. The source for the pre-1922 data is the weekly report on central bank balance sheets contained in relevant volumes of *Economist*. The source for the 1992 data is Statistisches Reichsamt (1922, 1923). Since putting the series together is laborious and since such a series may be of independent interest to researchers of this period, we report it in table 1.B1

Table 1.B1
Weekly reichsbanknotes in circulation

Date	Total (million marks)	Date	Total (million marks)
December 1918:		September 1919:	
14	20,006	6	28,408
23	21,124	15	28,411
31	22,188	23	28,619
January 1919:		30	29,784
7	22,337	October 1919:	
15	22,526	7	29,862
23	23,393	14	29,987
30	23,648	23	30,223
February 1919:		31	30,929
7	23,666	November 1919:	
15	23,761	7	31,075
22	23,747	15	31,123
28	24,103	23	31,219
March 1919:		29	31,906
7	24,248	December 1919:	
15	24,351	7	32,460
22	24,502	15	32,876
31	25,490	23	34,127
April 1919:		31	35,698
7	25,495	January 1920:	
15	25,871	7	35,764
23	25,875	15	35,684
30	26,629	22	35,985
May 1919:		31	37,444
7	26,722	February 1920:	
15	26,958	7	37,989
23	27,286	15	38,779
31	28,245	23	39,520
June 1919:		28	41,034
7	28,218	March 1920:	
14	28,275	6	41,468
23	29,100	15	†
30	29,960	23	43,347
July 1919:		31	45,170
7	29,820	April 1920:	
15	29,600	7	45,617
23	29,340	15	45,706
31	29,260	23	46,228
August 1919:		30	47,940
7	28,860	May 1920:	
14	28,555	7	48,373
23	28,254	15	48,948
30	28,492	21	49,128
		31	50,017*

Table 1.B1 (continued)

Date	Total (million marks)	Date	Total (million marks)
June 1920:		March 1921:	
7	50,649	7	67,908
15	50,809	15	†
23	51,657	22	67,485
30	53,975	31	69,417*
July 1920:		April 1921:	
7	54,045	7	69,235
15	54,040	15	68,736
23	53,983	23	68,379
31	55,769*	30	70,840
August 1920:		May 1921:	
7	56,060	7	71,115
14	56,462	14	70,834
23	56,653	23	69,724
31	58,401	31	71,839
September 1920:		June 1921:	
7	58,752	7	72,145
14	58,928	15	71,884
23	59,264	22	71,987
30	61,735	30	75,321
October 1920:		July 1921:	
7	62,078	7	75,839
15	62,129	15	75,353
23	62,066	23	74,997
30	63,596	30	77,391
November 1920:		August 1921:	
6	63,600	6	77,655
15	64,095	14	77,396
23	63,583	23	77,191
30	64,284	31	80,073
December 1920:		September 1921:	
7	64,685	7	80,728
15	65,147	14	81,470
23	67,126	23	82,179
31	68,805	30	86,384
January 1921:		October 1921:	
7	67,976	7	87,462
15	66,547	15	87,728
22	66,018	23	88,144
31	66,621	31	91,528
February 1921:		November 1921:	
7	66,483	7	92,610
15	65,934	14	95,186
23	65,520	23	96,186
28	67,427	30	100,944

Table 1.B1 (continued)

Date	Total (million marks)	Date	Total (million marks)
December 1921:		July 1922:	
7	102,780	7	172,737
15	104,568	15	175,437
23	108,996	22	177,027
31	113,639	31	189,795
January 1922:		August 1922:	
7	113,140	7	198,464
14	112,594	15	205,275
23	111,890	23	215,168
31	115,375	31	238,147
February 1922:		September 1922:	
7	116,606	7	252,374
14	115,756	15	271,598
23	115,797	23	290,678
28	120,026	30	316,870
March 1922:		October 1922:	
7	121,930	7	344,172
15	122,120	14	374,506
23	122,904	23	409,973
31	130,671	31	469,457
April 1922:		November 1922:	
7	131,837	7	517,036
15	134,064	15	582,105
22	132,628	23	643,750
29	140,420	30	754,086
May 1922:		December 1922:	
6	142,464	7	846,894
15	142,904	15	970,202
23	144,138	23	1,136,910
31	151,949	30	1,280,095
June 1922:			
7	154,915		
15	155,345		
23	157,935		
30	169,212		

*For these dates the data reported by *Economist* did not agree with the end-of-month figures reported by Statistisches Reichsamt (1925). We have used the latter source for these three observations. The reports in *Economist* were 49,128, 53,998, and 64,382 (million marks), respectively.
†No report.

Table 1.B2
Mid-month money totals, December 1918–August 1923

Date	Total (million marks)	Date	Total (million marks)	Date	Total (million marks)
1918:		1921:		1923:	1,438,000
December	30,627	January	78,781	January	2,704,000
1919:		February	78,023	February	4,273,000
January	33,303	March	79,194	March	5,838,000
February	34,697	April	79,123	April	7,113,000
March	35,714	May	80,656	May	10,906,000
April	37,600	June	81,287	June	25,492,000
May	38,648	July	84,424	July	116,403,000
June	40,384	August	86,036	August	
July	42,188	September	89,732		
August	40,969	October	95,731		
September	40,761	November	103,050		
October	42,379	December	112,932		
November	44,011	1922:			
December	46,762	January	121,304		
1920:		February	124,278		
January	49,625	March	131,005		
February	52,177	April	143,797		
March	56,209	May	152,954		
April	60,034	June	165,835		
May	63,188	July	187,331		
June	64,965	August	218,723		
July	68,073	September	286,134		
August	70,316	October	389,623		
September	72,788	November	597,401		
October	75,865	December	985,451		
November	77,340				
December	77,897				

The possession of the weekly series does not completely solve the interpolation problem. Although Reichsbanknotes were the principal components of the money supply, other currencies—for example, Darlehnskassenscheine, Reichskassenscheine—also circulated, and only end-of-month reports for these currencies are available. However, the nominal total of these currencies changed very slowly and very little during the hyperinflation, and the proportion of the money supply which they represented fell from 34.6 percent in December 1918 to 1.5 percent in December 1922. Therefore, interpolation of only this component to the middle of the month should produce only a small error in the total mid-month money-supply measure. To produce our new mid-month money series through the end of 1922, we added the interpolated other currencies to the mid-month Reichsbanknote total. For 1923 we use the mid-month figure in Statistisches Reichsame (1925).

In table 1.B2 we present the new mid-month series of the monthly money supply used in our estimation.

Notes

We would like to thank O. Blanchard, W. Brock, B. McCallum. T. Sargent, K. Singleton, and H. White, the participants in the Macroeconomics Workshop at the University of Virginia, a Graduate School of Industrial Administration Seminar at Carnegie-Mellon University, the NBER Summer Institute in International Economics, the Macroeconomics Workshop at Columbia University, and the Macroeconomics Workshop at the University of Rochester, and an anonymous referee, for many useful comments.

1. Prominent among previous investigations involving bubbles are Heckscher (1931), Keynes (1936, chap. 12), Samuelson (1957, 1967), and Hahn (1966).

2. Other theoretical investigations involving the bubble phenomenon include those of Black (1974), Calvo (1976, 1977), Becker (1978), and Brock and Scheinkman (1979).

3. Other papers which assume rational expectations in Cagan's model are Sargent and Wallace (1973a, 1973b), Mussa (1975, 1978), Frenkel (1977), Sargent (1977), Evans (1978), Friedman (1978), La Haye (1978), Blanchard (1979), Salemi and Sargent (1979), and Flood and Garber (1980a, 1980b).

4. In the empirical part of this chapter, we retain the assumption of no time lag in agents' acquisition of information.

5. Aside from the arbitrary constant, A_0, three other types of potential indeterminacy have been noted in the context of rational-expectations models. Samuelson (1967, p. 230), in discussing the tulip-mania (bubble) phenomenon, pointed out that, if agents believe that tulips will rise in price at an arbitrary percentage rate, then these agents will be motivated to act so that tulips' prices actually rise at this particular rate. While this is a perfectly self-consistent example, Samuelson's concept of a bubble in general is inapplicable to situations where agents' information sets include a standard model of the market in question. The problem with completely arbitrary self-fulfilling expectations in a model is that the model places a structure on the expected time path of market price. For example, in the model of the present paper it would be impossible, in the absence of money creation, for prices to rise period after period at the annual rate of 10 percent just because agents expect prices to rise. This scenario is ruled out because the present model requires that a period-after-period inflation which is due to arbitrary self-fulfilling expectations be generated by an accelerating expectation of inflation. Taylor (1977) noted that in some cases agents may choose to add spurious variables into price solutions, with rationality preserved. Also, Blanchard (1979) pointed out that agents may rationally choose to base their price expectations partly on past money even when such data do not help forecast future money. In Flood and Garber (1980b) we show that, for the model used currently, the Taylor and Blanchard indeterminacies are equivalent to the bubble indeterminacy that we study.

6. The expectation may arise because of a government-announced money process change, which standard univariate time-series techniques could not predict based only on past money data. Note that the certainty of the future change in the money-growth rate makes

the money-supply process partly deterministic. If the process were purely indeterministic, there would be no identification problem.

7. This exercise is very similar to those used by Sargent and Wallace (1973b) and Brock (1974).

8. Interestingly, if A_0 is zero and if an expectation of monetary reform existed in Germany during July–November 1923, then data from this period should reveal a pattern indistinguishable from a negative price-level bubble. We are currently testing this implication of the theory. La Haye (1978) makes use of this theoretical pattern on prices to test for expectations of currency reform during the German experience. In her work A_0 is assumed to be zero, thereby avoiding the identification problem.

9. Cagan's (1956) model of inflation consisted of eq. (1) and the assumption that agents revise inflation expectations adaptively. Cagan noted that, if expectations revisions take place too quickly, then his model would exhibit explosive inflation without explosive monetary growth. Subsequently, Mussa (1978) showed that, if adaptive expectations are rational, Cagan's type of instability is ruled out, and the only type of potentially explosive behavior in the model is that captured by the present concept of a price-level bubble. Furthermore, if expectations are adaptive but not rational, then it is not possible for a price explosion generated by unstable adaptive expectations to be associated with self-fulfilling expectations. In fact, instability due to unstable adaptive expectations must be associated with expectational errors, of a single sign, which are systematically increasing through time. Thus, in conceptual contrast to a price-level bubble with its self-fulfilling expectations, unstable adaptive expectations are increasingly self-deluding.

10. The assumption that money was exogenous with respect to inflation has been criticized by Sargent and Wallace (1973a) and Evans (1978), who both use interpolated data, and by McAuliffe (1979), who used our new money data (see Appendix B) along with some new point in time price data. Such studies are useful in gaining knowledge about the probability of money's being exogenous. However, these studies are not designed to provide information about the probabilities attached to each money-supply process within the class of processes with money endogenous to inflation. Also, they are not designed to provide information about the assignment of initial conditions in agents' solutions for the expected rate of inflation.

11. By *form of a bubble*, we are referring to the specific function of time which generates a bubble.

12. If monetary policy is, e.g., $\mu_t = \gamma_0 + \gamma_1 \pi_{t-1} + \gamma_2 \pi_t + \gamma_3 E(\pi_{t+1}|\bar{I}_t) + v_t$, where $\bar{I}_t$ is the monetary authority's information set at t and v_t is a disturbance term, then the complete model which describes agents' formation of expectations involves a second-order difference equation. (We assume $\bar{I}_t \subseteq I_t$.) This second-order equation will, in general, have two roots, but the problem involves only one initial condition, π_{t-1}. We may test for bubbles in such a circumstance by "attaching" π_{t-1} to one root and testing to see whether the constant attached to the remaining root is zero.

13. Sometimes with endogenous money it is also necessary to specify additional arbitrary identifying restrictions (see, e.g., Sargent 1977).

14. If we can assume that the money-supply process remained unchanged during the postwar period which we examine, then we can employ observations from as far back as 1918 in determining the money process. For the inflation process we are not so blessed, because of the official controls on prices which were not entirely lifted until 1920 (for a description of the controls on consumer prices, see International Labour Office 1925).

15. We used the LSQ routine available in the TSP package.

16. Our choice of periods for the estimation of bubbles is arbitrary. The technique we have used for estimation is general enough to be used for testing hypotheses of bursting as well as nonbursting bubbles. For example, we could test the hypothesis of the existence of a price-level bubble from January through December 1992 with the bubble bursting in January 1923. In all three estimations t was normalized at unity in July 1920. The choice of normalization date will be reflected in the size of $\hat{A}_0$, but normalization will not affect the ratio of $\hat{A}_0$ to its standard error.

17. For example, the time trend may arise from income growth, which is ignored in the model.

18. Since one of our regressors is a vector whose jth element is ψ^j and whose maximum value is ψ^T, where T is the number of observations, and $\psi > 1$, our estimators will be consistent as $T \to \infty$. However, we must take care in the design of our hypothetical method of increasing our sample size in pressing to the limiting distribution for our estimators. If we allow $T \to \infty$, then it is well known that the asymptotic distribution of $\hat{A}_0$ will be degenerate (see, e.g., Anderson 1971). Even if we were to attempt to normalize $(\hat{A}_0 - A_0)$ by multiplying it by the quantity ψ^T, we still would not satisfy the sufficient conditions for normality of the asymptotic distribution listed by Anderson (p. 572). The problem is that the variance of the Tth observation does not become small relative to the summed and weighted variances of all previous observations. The conceptual experiment which we perform in finding an asymptotic distribution of $\hat{A}_0$ consists of repeating the hyperinflationary experience from 1920 through 1923, given the events through 1920 and the behavioral parameters, including A_0, of agents in the hyperinflation. Thus, for the full-period estimation we will always have 35 observations on ψ^j. However, new drawings on the random disturbances will be taken for each repetition of the hyperinflation. If the hyperinflation experiment is repeated K times, then we will have $35K$ observations and the maximum value of any regressor will be ψ^{35}. For $K \to \infty$, the restricted SUR estimators which we use are asymptotically equivalent to jointly and normally distributed random variables with mean $(\alpha, \delta, \beta_1, \beta_2, \beta_3, \beta_4, A_0)$ and variance-covariance matrix Ω. In addition the $\hat{\Omega}$ estimated by the SUR method is a consistent estimator of Ω. Thus, we use the normal distribution in testing our hypothesis. Hal White has pointed out that the parallel bubble concept will produce a nondegenerate normal asymptotic distribution only if we actually carry out the bubble test for a cross section of economies. Since we have performed the estimation only for the German economy, in essence we have only a pair of observations and cannot comfortably invoke asymptotic results. To address this issue, we are currently engaged in testing whether a bubble passed through the parallel hyperinflations of the 1920s. Finally, Ken Singleton has pointed out that if the parameters of our system were such that $|\psi| < 1$, then $A_0 \neq 0$ implies the existence of a bubble which converges to zero. The problems for testing this case are even more serious; the bubble converges so fast that the asymptotic distribution becomes diffuse if the conceptual experiment is to let $T \to \infty$. Then the estimator would not even be consistent.

19. The Hansen-Sargent technique is more general than is indicated by our description. The assumption that $E(w_{t+j}|I_t)$ produces a special case that is easily handled through existing statistical packages. Without this assumption, we would have to use the less accessible techniques proposed by Hansen and Sargent.

20. We also estimated an $AR(3)$ process for $(1 - L)\mu_t$, to be consistent with Salemi and Sargent. Since the estimated variance of the disturbance terms was almost identical with that of the $AR(1)$ process, we selected the $AR(1)$ process because of its simplicity.

21. For a model in which the problems generated by bubbles are explored for normal times, see Flood and Garber (1978).

22. The Dutch Tulip Bubble, a favorite example of an unstable market, is remarkable for the sparse information available on price series for particular kinds of tulips. The steady rise in prices through the early decades of the seventeenth century was a reflection of market fundamentals—taste changes increased the demand for bulbs for consumption purposes among upper-class flower fanciers. The mania began only with the advent of a tulip futures market in 1635–36, and the largest rise in prices occurred between growing seasons in 1636–37. After the collapse of that year, quality tulips continued to command high and rising prices. Thus, there is a basis for believing that a bubble existed in this market for one year, although no data are available for an explicit test of the hypothesis (see Posthumus [1929] for a more detailed account). The Mississippi Bubble seems to have been based on a money-printing scheme which generated expectations of a money-supply process which failed to materialize (see Thiers 1859; Mackay 1932). Similarly, the ultimate collapse of the Ponzi schemes and chain letters mentioned by Samuelson (1957) is based on the realization that expectations of future payments were erroneous. Thus, they are based on market fundamentals. If agents have mistaken expectations about the future stream of payments to be received from an asset, then the price of the asset will jump either up or down when the expected event fails to occur. If a collapse of an asset's price arising from agents' learning about their error were classified as a bursting bubble, then we must claim that most assets follow a bubble path because their prices are based on erroneous expectations with probability one.

References

Abel, A.; Dornbusch, Rudiger; Huizinga, J.; and Marcus, A. "Money Demand during Hyperinflation." *J. Monetary Econ.* 5 (January 1979): 87–104.

Anderson, T. W. *The Statistical Analysis of Time Series.* New York: Wiley, 1971.

Barro, Robert J. "Rational Expectations and the Role of Monetary Policy." *J Monetary Econ.* 2, no. 1 (January 1976): 1–33.

Becker, R. "Simple Dynamic Models of Equilibrium." Ph.D. dissertation, Univ,. Rochester, 1978.

Black, Fischer. "Uniqueness of the Price Level in Monetary Growth Models with Rational Expectations." *J. Econ. Theory* 7 (January 1974): 53–65.

Blanchard, Olivier J. "Forward and Backward Solutions for Economies with Rational Expectations." *A. E. R. Papers and Proc.* 69 (May 1979): 114–18.

Box, George E. P., and Jenkins, Gwilym M. *Time Series Analysis: Forecasting and Control.* San Francisco: Holden-Day, 1970.

Brock, William A. "Money and Growth: The Case of Long-Run Perfect Foresight." *Internat. Econ. Rev.* 15 (October 1974): 750–77.

———. "A Simple Perfect Foresight Monetary Model." *J. Monetary Econ.* 1 (April 1975): 133–50.

———. "A Note on Hyperinflationary Equilibria in Long-Run Perfect Foresight Monetary Models: A Correction." Working Paper, Univ. Chicago, Dept. Econ., 1979.

Brock, William A., and Scheinkman, Jose. "Rational Expectations in Overlapping Generations Models: The Problem of Tulip Mania." Working Paper, Univ. Chicago, Dept. Econ., 1979.

Cagan, Phillip. "The Monetary Dynamics of Hyperinflation." In *Studies in the Quantity Theory of Money*, edited by Milton Friedman. Chicago: Univ. Chicago Press. 1956.

Calvo, Guillermo. "On Models of Money and Perfect Foresight." Working Paper, Columbia Univ., Dept. Econ., 1976.

―――. "On the Indeterminacy of Interest Rates and Wages with Perfect Foresight." Working Paper, Columbia Univ., Dept. Econ., 1977.

Economist, vols. 89–97 (January 1919–December 1923).

Evans, P. "Time Series Analysis of the German Hyperinflation." *Internat. Econ. Rev.* 19 (February 1978): 195–209.

Flood, Robert P., and Garber, Peter M. "The Relation between Instability of Expectations and Agents' Beliefs about the Stability of Expectations: An Integration of Rational Expectations Solution Techniques." Working Paper, Univ. Virginia, Dept. Econ., 1978.

―――. "An Economic theory of Monetary Reform." *J. P. E.* 88, no. 1 (February 1980): 24–58. (*a*)

―――. "A Note on the Equivalence of Solution Indeterminacies in Rational Expectations Models." Working Paper, Univ. Virginia, Dept. Econ., 1980. (*b*).

Frenkel, Jacob A. "The Forward Exchange Rate, Expectations, and the Demand for Money: The German Hyperinflation." *A. E. R.* 67 (September 1977): 653–70.

Friedman, B. M. "Stability and Rationality in Models of Hyperinflation." *Internat. Econ. Rev.* 19 (February 1978): 45–64.

Hahn, F. H. "Equilibrium Dynamics with Heterogeneous Capital Goods." *Q. J. E.* 80 (November 1966): 633–46.

Hansen, L., and Sargent, Thomas J. "Formulating and Estimating Dynamic Linear Rational Expectations Models. I." Working Paper, Carnegie-Mellon Univ., Graduate School Indus. Admin., 1979.

Heckscher, Eli F. "A Note on South Sea Finance." *J. Econ. and Bus. Hist.* 3 (February 1931): 321–28.

International Labour Office. *The Workers' Standard of Life in Countries with Depreciated Currencies.* Studies and Reports, series D, no. 15. Geneva: International Labour Office, 1925.

Keynes, John Maynard. *The General Theory of Employment, Interest and Money.* London: Harcourt Brace, 1936.

La Haye, Laura. "Inflation and Currency Reform: A Study of the Effects of Anticipated Policy Switching." Working Paper, Univ. Chicago, Dept. Econ., 1978.

Lucas, Robert E., Jr. "Expectations and the Neutrality of Money." *J. Econ. Theory* 4 (April 1972): 103–24.

―――. "Some International Evidence on Output-InflationTradeoffs." *A. E. R.* 63 (June 1973): 326–34.

————. "An Equilibrium Model of the Business Cycle." *J. P. E.* 83, no. 6 (December 1975): 1113–44.

McAuliffe, R. "Causality and Estimating Money Demand in Hyperinflation." Working Paper, Univ. Virginia, Dept. Econ., 1979.

McCallum, Bennett T. "Rational Expectations and the Natural Rate Hypothesis: Some Consistent Estimates." *Econometrica* 44 (January 1976): 43–52.

————. "The Role of Speculation in the Canadian Forward Exchange Market: Some Estimates Assuming Rational Expectations." *Rev. Econ. and Statis.* 9, no. 2 (May 1977): 145–51.

Mackay, Charles. *Memoirs of Extraordinary Popular Delusions and the Madness of Crowds.* New York: Farrar, Straus & Giroux, 1932.

Mussa, Michael. "Adaptive and Regressive Expectations in a Rational Model of the Inflationary Process." *J. Monetary Econ.* 1 (October 1975): 423–42.

————."On the Inherent Stability of Rationally Adaptive Expectations." *J. Monetary Econ.* 4, no. 2 (April 1978): 307–14.

Muth, John F. "Rational Expectations and the Theory of Price Movements." *Econometrica* 29 (July 1961): 315–35.

Posthumus, Nicolaas W. "The Tulip Mania in Holland in the Years 1636 and 1637." *J. Econ. and Bus. Hist.* 1, no. 3 (May 1929): 434–55.

Salemi, M., and Sargent, Thomas J. "The Demand for Money during Hyperinflation under Rational Expectations. II." *Internat. Econ. Rev.* 20 (October 1979): 741–58.

Samuelson, Paul A. "Intertemporal Price Equilibrium: A Prologue to the Theory of Speculation." *Weltwirtschaftliches Archiv* 79 (December 1957): 181–219.

————. "Indeterminacy of Development in a Heterogeneous-Capital Model with Constant Saving Propensity." In *Essays on the Theory of Optimal Economic Growth,* edited by Karl Shell. Cambridge, Mass.: M. I. T. Press, 1967.

Sargent, Thomas J. "Rational Expectations, the Real Rate of Interest, and the Natural Rate of Unemployment." *Brookings Papers Econ. Activity,* no. 2 (1973), pp. 249–72.

————. "The Demand for Money during Hyperinflation under Rational Expectations. I." *Internat. Econ. Rev.* 18 (February 1977): 59–82.

————. *Macroeconomic Theory.* New York: Academic Press, 1979.

Sargent, Thomas J., and Wallace, Neil. "Rational Expectations and the Dynamics of Hyperinflation." *Internat. Econ. Rev.* 14 (June 1973): 328–50. (a)

————."The Stability of Models of Money and Growth with Perfect Foresight." *Econometrica* 41 (November 1973): 1043–48 (b)

————. "Rational Expectations and the Theory of Economic Policy." *J. Monetary Econ.* 2 (April 1976): 169–84.

Shiller, Robert J. "Rational Expectations and the Dynamic Structure of Macroeconomic Models: A Critical Review." *J. Monetary Econ.* 4 (January 1978): 1–44.

Singleton, K. "On the Estimation of Linear Macroeconomic Models with Rational Expectations." Working paper, Univ. Virginia, Dept. Econ., 1979.

Statistisches Reichsamt. *Wirtschaft und Statistik*, vol. 2 (1922).

————. *Wirtschaft und Statistik*, vol. 3 (1923).

————. *Zahlen zur Geldenwertung in Deutschland 1914 bis 1923*. Berlin: Hobbing, 1925.

Taylor, John B. "Conditions for Unique Solutions in Stochastic Macroeconomic Models with Rational Expectations." *Econometrica* 45 (September 1977): 1377–86.

Thiers, Adolphe. *The Mississippi Bubble: A Memoir of John Law*. New York: W. A. Townsend, 1859.

2

Famous First Bubbles

Peter M. Garber

The jargon of economics and finance contains numerous colorful expressions to denote a market-determined asset price at odds with any reasonable economic explanation. Such words as "tulip mania," "bublle," "chain letter," "Ponzi scheme," "panic," "crash," and "financial crisis" immediately evoke images of frenzied and probably irrational speculative activity. Many of these terms have emerged from specific speculative episodes which have been sufficiently frequent and important that they underpin a strong current belief among economists that key capital markets sometimes generate irrational and inefficient pricing and allocational outcomes.

Before economists relegate a speculative event to the inexplicable or bubble category, however, we must exhaust all reasonable economic explanations. While such explanations are often not easily generated due to the inherent complexity of economic phenomena, the business of economists is to find clever fundamental market explanations for events; and our methodology should always require that we search intensively for market fundamental explanations before clutching the "bubble" last resort.

Thus, among the "reasonable" or "market fundamental" explanations I would include the perception of an increased probability of large returns. The perception might be triggered by genuine economic good news, by a convincing new economic theory about payoffs or by a fraud launched by insiders acting strategically to trick investors. It might also be triggered by uninformed market participants correctly inferring changes in the distribution of dividends by observing price movements generated by the trading of informed insiders. While some of these perceptions might in the end prove erroneous, movements in asset prices based on them are fundamental and not bubble movements.

I aim in this chapter to propose market fundamental explanations for the three most famous bubbles: the Dutch tulipmania (1634–37), the Mississippi bubble (1719–20), and the closely connected South Sea bubble (1720).

Though several authors have proposed market fundamental explanations for the well-documented Mississippi and South Sea bubbles, these episodes are still treated in the modern literature as outbursts of irrationality. This may be attributable to the influence of Mackay's (1852) graphic descriptions of the frenzied speculative crowds which materialized in Paris and London in 1719 and 1720; from our current perspective, though, such "irrational" speculation probably looked a lot like a normal day in a pit of the Board of Trade.

As a justification for concentrating on these three bubbles, I will briefly explore the modern bubble literature to show that these episodes are frequently invoked as motivation for adopting bubble explanations. Next, I will briefly describe the nature of the asset markets and financial manipulations which occurred in these episodes and provide market fundamental explanations.

The Three Bubbles in the Modern Literature

Standard reference sources in economics typically refer to one or more of these events in defining the term *bubble*. For example, Palgrave's *Dictionary* (1926, p. 181) defines a bubble as "any unsound commercial undertaking accompanied by a high degree of speculation." It then provides histories of tulipmania, the Mississippi bubble and the South Sea Bubble as examples. In his article on bubbles in *The New Palgrave* (1987), Kindleberger includes the tulipmania as one of the two most famous manias. (His other example is the British railway mania of the 1840s.) Curiously, the entry on tulipmania in the *The New Palgrave* does not refer to the seventeenth-century Dutch speculative episode. Instead, Calvo defines *tulipmania* generically, as a situation in which asset prices do not behave in ways explainable by economic fundamentals, and then develops examples of rational bubbles.

In the past few decades, these historical episodes have passed into the common lore of economics. Samuelson (1957, 1967) refers to the tulipmania and associates it (1967, p. 230) with "the purely financial dream world of indefinite group self-fulfillment," though he is skeptical that such phenomena are important in real markets. Students of Samuelson like Shell and Stiglitz (1967) state, "The instability of the Hahn model is suggestive of the economic forces operating during 'speculative booms' like the Tulip Bulb mania."[1]

The "sunspot" literature has revived references to thee famous bubbles. For example, Azariadis (1981, p. 380) states that, "The evidence on the influence of subjective factors is ample and dates back several centuries;

the Dutch 'tulip mania,' the South Sea bubble in England, the collapse of the Mississippi Company in France are three well-documented cases of speculative price movements which historians consider unwarranted by 'objective' conditions."[2] In a more recent motivational argument for the importance of sunspots, Azariadis and Guesnerie (1986) state, "And the reading of economic historians may suggest that these factors (sunspots) have some pertinence for the explanation of phenomena like the Dutch tulipmania in the seventeenth century and the Great Depression in our own."

J. van Horne (1985), influenced by mounting evidence of financial market anomalies, accepts the possibility of bubbles and manias and refers to the tulipmania, where a "single bulb sold for many years' salary." With a reference to the tulipmania, Shiller (1986) argues that asset markets are driven by capricious investors acting on the basis of fads and bubbles. In papers related to this literature, Cutler, Poterba, and Summers (1989) refer to the tulipmania, the Mississippi bubble and the South Sea bubble as examples of how trading dynamics may affect asset prices. Finally, in the exchange rate literature, Meese (1986) refers to tulipmania and Krugman (1985) conjures up the images of both the tulipmania and the South Sea bubble while building a case for a bubble interpretation of the movements of the dollar exchange rate during the 1980s.

The reader can probably provide other cases where these episodes are cited as clear evidence of bubbles in the past. In contrast, I will argue that none of these episodes should actually qualify as bubbles.

The Fundamentals of Tulipmania

Mackay (1852) passed on to economists the standard description of the tulipmania as a speculative bubble.[3] In this description, the Netherlands became a center of cultivation and development of new tulip varieties after the tulip's entry into Europe from Turkey in the mid-1500s. Professional growers and wealthy flower fanciers created a market for rare varieties in which bulbs sold at high prices. For example, a Semper Augustus bulb sold for 2000 guilders in 1625, an amount of gold worth about $16,000 at $400 per ounce. Common bulb varieties, on the other hand, received very low prices.

By 1636, the rapid price rises attracted speculators, and prices of many varieties surged upward from November 1636 through January 1637. In February 1637, prices suddenly collapsed, and bulbs could not be sold at 10 percent of their peak values. By 1739, the prices of all the most prized bulbs of the mania had fallen to no more than 0.1 guilder. This was 1/200 of 1 percent of Semper Augustus's peak price. The story concludes by asserting that the collapse led to economic distress in the Netherlands for years afterwards.

The standard version of the tulipmania neglects discussion about what the market fundamental price of bulbs should have been. Mackay did not report transaction prices for the rare bulbs immediately after the collapse. Instead, he recorded tulip bulb prices from 60 or 200 years after the collapse, interpreting these much lower prices as ones justified by market fundamentals. Yet the dynamics of bulb prices during the tulip episode were typical of any market for rare bulbs, even those existing today. The tulip market involved only bulbs affected by a mosaic virus which had the effect of creating beautiful, feathered patterns in the flowers. Only diseased bulbs were valued by traders and collectors, because a particular pattern could not be reproduced through seed propagation. Only through budding of the mother bulb would a pattern breed true.

A standard pricing pattern arises for new varieties of flowers, even in modern markets. When a particularly prized variety is developed, its original bulb sells for a high price. As the bulbs accumulate, the variety's price falls rapidly; after less than 30 years, bulbs sell at their reproduction cost. This pattern raises two questions. First, why did the price of bulbs increase rapidly? Second, did prices decline faster than should have been expected?

The price increases prior to February 1637 occurred as the status of a variety become clear; and as its renown increased, so would its price. After all, most new varieties were not considered particularly beautiful. This would explain the steady increase in the price of Semper Augustus. Similarly, a shift in fashion toward the appreciation of tulips in general over a shorter period would generate rising prices for all the rare bulbs.

To form an expectation about a typical rate of price decline of tulip bulbs, I collected data on eighteenth-century bulb price patterns for various highly valued tulip bulbs. The level of eighteenth-century prices was much lower than during the mania. By 1707, an enormous variety of tulip bulbs had been developed; and the tulip itself had been replaced as the most fashionable flower by the hyacinth. Nonetheless, as table 2.1 shows, bulb prices still were falling sharply. The average annual rate of depreciation for these bulbs was 28.5 percent before bulb prices reached floor values.

Table 2.2 reports prices of those bulbs for which I have been able to gather price data for years immediately after the mania. February 5, 1637 was the day on which peak prices were attained. For these bulbs from February 1637 to 1642, the average annual rate of price depreciation was

Table 2.1
Guilder prices of tulip bulbs, 1707, 1722, and 1739

Bulb	1707	1722	1739
1. Premier Noble	409	—	1.0
2. Aigle Noir	110	0.75	0.3
3. Roi de Fleurs	251	10.0	0.1
4. Diamant	71	2.5	2.0

Source: Garber (1989).

Table 2.2
Postcollapse bulb prices in guilders

Bulb	Feb. 5, 1637	1642 or 1643
1. English Admiral (bulb)	700	210
2. Admirael van Eyck (bulb)	1345	220
3. General Rotgans	805	138

32 percent, not greatly different from the eighteenth-century depreciation rate. If the more rapid annual rate of decline for the tulipmania bulbs was attributed entirely to the crash, and not to factors which materialized in the succeeding five years, the crash can have accounted for no more than a 16 percent price decline: large, but hardly the stuff that legends are made of.

Strangely enough, if one is to speak of tulipmania, it would be more accurate to speak of the rapid price rise and collapse in common bulbs in the last week of January and first week of February 1637. Common bulbs became objects of speculation among the lower classes in a future market which emerged in November 1636. These markets were located in local taverns, and each sale was associated with a payment of "wine money." In January 1637, prices for some common bulb varieties increased by as much as 25 times. For example, the peak price for a bulb called Switser of .17 guilders/ass was attained on February 5, the apparent peak of the market (1 ass = 1/20 gram). Data from notarized contracts on February 6 and 9 indicate a sudden decline to .11 guilders/aas. This represents a substantial decline from prices in the first five days of February, but it still exceeds the price of .035 guilders/aas attained on January 23. Price increases through mid-January, while rapid, were not as great as in the final two weeks of the speculation; and there is no evidence that they were out of line. Since serious traders ignored this market and participants in this market had almost no wealth, it can have been little more than a mid-winter diversion among tavern regulars mimicking more serious traders.

Finally, there is no evidence of serious economic distress arising from the tulipmania. All histories of the period treat it as a golden age in Dutch development.

A Preliminary View: The Mississippi and South Sea Bubbles

The financial dynamics of these speculations assumed remarkably similar forms. Each involved a company that sought a rapid expansion of its balance sheet through corporate takeovers or acquisition of government debt, financed by successive issues of shares. The new waves of shares marketed were offered at successively higher prices. The purchasers of the last wave of shares took the greatest losses when stock prices fell, while the initial buyers generally gained.

Adam Anderson (1787, pp. 123–124) presents a remarkably lucid description of such speculative dynamics in which a sequence of investors buys equal shares in a venture:

A, having one hundred pounds stock in trade, though pretty much in debt, gives it out to be worth three hundred pounds, on account of many privileges and advantages to which he is entitled. B, relying on A's great wisdom and integrity, sues to be admitted partner on those terms, and accordingly buys three hundred pounds into the partnership. The trade being afterwords given out or discovered to be very improving, C comes in at five hundred pounds; and afterwards D, at one thousand one hundred pounds. And the capital is then completed to two thousand pounds. If the partnership had gone no further than A and B, then A had got and B had lost one hundred pounds. If it had stopped at C, then A had got and C had lost two hundred pounds; and B had been where he was before: but D also coming in, A gains four hundred pounds, and B two hundred pounds; and C neither gains nor loses: but D loses six hundred pounds. Indeed, if A could show that the said capital was intrinsically worth four thousand and four hundred pounds, there would be no harm done to D; and B and C would have been obliged to him. But if the capital at first was worth but one hundred pounds, and increased only by subsequent partnership, it must then be acknowledged that B and C have been imposed on in their turns, and that unfortunate thoughtless D paid the piper.

Should we, as outside observers, interpret such a sequence of transactions and prices as a bubble? The intrinsic value of the venture from the point of view of the new investors is the crux of the matter.

First, if the original investor falsely claimed that the venture promised great dividends, though as yet unrealized, he would be committing fraud. The new investors, however, would be basing their decisions on their perception of market fundamentals. This is a situation of asymmetric information in which one player has an incentive to dissemble.

Second, the original investor might use some of the proceeds from the stock sales to pay high dividends to the early investors. This would provide concrete evidence of the great prospects of the venture to new investors. Of course, this twist on the original fraud is known as a Ponzi scheme; but since the "pidgeons" are acting on their view of market fundamentals, there is still no bubble.

Third, the great future earnings may actually materialize, thereby satisfying all investors. This result is typical of the early stages of successful companies; and the sequence of stock issues at increasing prices would neither surprise a modern investment banker nor raise the eyebrows of the SEC. In this case, the promised market fundamentals would actually materialize.

Fourth, the projected future earnings, though based on the best available evidence, may fail to materialize. If the evidence of failure appears suddenly, the share price will suffer a precipitous decline causing late buyers vociferously to regret their purchases. Hindsight will readily identify the blind folly of the investors and, if it is extreme enough, perhaps categorize the event as a bubble. In fact, the traditional definition of a bubble, as in Palgrave (1926, p. 181) is "any unsound commercial undertaking accompanied by a high degree of speculation." If the undertaking appeared sound at the start, however, and only looks foolish in hindsight, economists should classify this event as being driven by market fundamentals.

Finally, all investors may perfectly understand that the venture has no chance of paying large dividends, but that a sequence of share buyers at ever increasing prices is available. Investors buy in on a gamble that they will not be in the last wave of buyers. The modern economics literature refers to this scenario as a bubble or chain letter. We now consider if the Mississippi and South Sea episodes can fit only in the last category.

John Law and the Fundamentals of the Mississippi and South Sea Bubbles

John Law's Financial System

Both the Mississippi and South Sea Bubbles can be best understood in the context of the monetary theory and system created by John Law. Law is not well known today, but Schumpeter (1954, p. 295), for example, is unreserved in praising him: "He worked out the economics of his projects with a brilliance and, yes, profundity which places him in the front ranks of monetary theorists of all times."

Law (1705) sketched a monetary theory in an environment of unemployed resources. In such an environment, he argued (1760, pp. 190–91), an emission of paper currency would expand real commerce permanently, thereby increasing the demand for the new currency sufficiently to preclude pressure on prices. To finance a great economic project, an entrepreneur needed only the power to create claims which served as a means of payment. Once financed, the project would profit sufficiently from the employment of previously wasted resources to justify the public's faith in its liabilities.

Economic policy advocates and their ideas, good or bad, float to the surface only when they provide a convenient pretext for politicians to impose their preferred schemes. Law's idea got its chance in France in 1715. France had been bankrupted by the wars of Louis XIV. In a situation similar to the current debt problems of less developed countries, it had repudiated part of its debt, forced a reduction in interest due on the remainder, and was still in arrears on its debt servicing. High taxes, combined with a tax system full of privileges and exemptions, had seriously depressed economic activity.

The French economic environment was well-suited for Law's scheme, and he quickly convinced the Regent to permit him to open a conventional, note-issuing bank in June 1716, the Banque Generale. In August 1717, Law organized the Compagnie d'Occident to take over the monopoly on trade with Louisiana and on trade in Canadian beaver skins. (This line of business is the source of the word "Mississippi" in characterizing Law's system.) To finance the company, Law took subscriptions on shares to be paid partly in cash but mostly in government debt. He then converted the government's debt into *rentes*, offering the government an interest rate reduction. The idea was to establish a solid "fund of credit," a certain cash inflow which, when capitalized, could be leveraged to undertake the grand commercial schemes which lay at the heart of Law's economic theory. The nature of Law's scheme was that finance of the operation came first; expanded commercial activity would result naturally once the financial structure was in place.

In effect, the French privatized the treasury under Law's plan, and had only to wait for the general commercial expansion promised by Law's theory to materialize and to support the market prices of the company's shares.

John Law's Finance Operations

The Company d'Occident did increase its commercial activity, obtaining the tobacco monopoly in September 1718 and the Senegalese Company (trade with Africa) in November 1718.[4] In January 1719, the Banque General was taken over by the regent and renamed the Banque Royale, with a note issue guaranteed by the crown. Law remained in control of the new bank. In May 1719, he acquired the East India Company and the China Company; and he reorganized the entire conglomerate as the Compagnie des Indes, an organization which monopolized all French trade outside Europe.

On July 25, 1719, the Compagnie purchased the right to mint new coinage for 50 million livres tournois to be delivered in fifteen monthly payments.[5] To finance this expenditure, Law issued 50,000 shares at 1000 livres per share to cover this acquisition, requiring share buyers to hold five previously issued shares. Share prices rose to 1800 livres.

In August 1719, Compagnie bought the right to collect all French indirect taxes for a payment of 53 million livres per year. The takeover of the administration of the tax system was in line with Law's views that a simplified fiscal regime would benefit commerce and reduce the costs of collection. Law thought that taxes should be broad-based and few, with no exemptions or privileges. He set about reorganizing the personnel of the tax system, since a reduced collection cost would be a source of company profit. In October 1719, he took over the collection of direct taxes. Share prices rose to 3000 livres.

Finally, Law determined to refund most of the national debt through the Compagnie des Indes, an amount with a face value of 1500 million livres. The face value of the entire debt was estimated by Harsin (1928) at about 2000 million livres; the market value of the debt was well below the par value because of previous defaults and arrearages.

To finance the debt acquisiton, Law undertook a sequence of three stock sales on September 12, September 28, and October 2, 1719. In each offering, the Compagnie sold 100,000 shares at 5000 livres per share payable in ten equal monthly payments. Payment could be made either at par in *rentes* or in the notes of the Banque Royale. Thus, by August 1720, enough would have been raised to acquire the face value of the debt.

Acquiring the debt would create a huge "fund of credit," a steady income flow from the government, which could be used as equity against any potential commercial venture of the Compagnie. Simultaneously, the Compagnie would reduce the interest paid by the state to 3 percent per year. Afer these operations, share prices rose to 10,000 livres in October 1719.[6]

Law attained maximum power in January 1720 when he was made France's Controller General and Superintendant General of Finance. As an official he now controlled all government finance and expenditure and the money creation of the Banque Royale. Simultaneously, he was the chief executive officer of a private firm that controlled France's overseas trade and the development of its colonies, that collected France's taxes, that minted its coins, and that held the bulk of France's national debt. The king was a principal shareholder of the firm. It must have been obvious to all that the Compagnie would find no government or financial obstacle to its undertaking any commercial scheme that it chose. Surely no economist has since had as perfect a set of conditions for testing a major economic theory as those possessed by Law. Figure 2.1 illustrates the Mississippi bubble. The phase of price increase is associated with the expanding activity of the company at this time.

In the end, however, the commercial scheme chosen was to print money. Starting with the July 1719 stock issue, the Banque Royale had increased its note issue to facilitate the stock sales. Each government authorization of a share expansion simultaneously authorized a note emission. For example, with only 159 million livres in notes previously authorized, the Banque received authorization to emit 240 million livres on July 25, 1719. A further 240 million livre expansion was associated with the September and

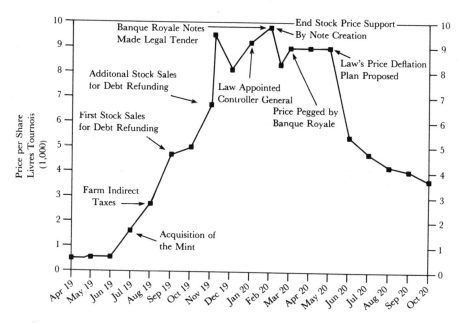

Figure 2.1
Compagnie des Indes stock price

October share sales. Additional note issues of 360 million and 200 million livres occurred on December 29, 1719 and February 6, 1720, respectively, without new share issues. For comparison, Harsin (1928) estimates the total specie stock of France at about 1.2 billion livres.

By the end of January 1720, share prices had begun to fall below 10,000 livres because of increasing attempts to convert capital gains into a gold form. The falling price of shares threatened Law's ability to use his "fund of credit" to begin a commercial expansion.

In January 1720, Law began to act against the use of specie in payments by prohibiting payments above 100 livres in metallic money. On February 22, 1720, the Compagnie took over direct control of the management of the Banque Royale; and the Banque Royale's notes were made legal tender for payments above 100 livres.[7] Simultaneously, the compagnie ceased supporting the price of its shares with banknotes, precipitating a sharp price decline.

Law criticized unsophisticated share holders trying to convert shares to the concrete form of gold because there was not enough gold in the kingdom to satisfy such an attempt. He believed that the high share value was justified by the Compagnie's prospects. Law stated that the shares had high value only if they were regarded as a capital investment, to be bought and sold infrequently, held by people content to receive their yields as a flow of dividends which he claimed was somewhat higher than the prevailing interest rate.[8]

On March 5, 1720, share prices were pegged at 9000 livres: the Banque Royale now intervened directly to exchange its notes for Compagnie stock. Effectively converting shares into banknotes with a denomination of 9000 livres, this policy was a realization of Law's theory that a commercial enterprise could finance itself with emissions of circulating debt. Until its termination on May 21, 1720, the pegging scheme generated legal tender note expansions of 300 million, 390 million, 438 million, and 362 million livres on March 25, April 5, April 19, and May 1, respectively, to absorb sales by shareholders. Thus, the Banque's legal tender note circulation doubled in about one month.

This also was a doubling in the money stock, since the metallic stock had disappeared. In an effort to drive out metallic currency and to maintain the facade of note convertibility, Law had simultaneously imposed a series of drastic devaluations of specie in terms of livre tournois. As a result of this dramatic monetary expansion, the average monthly inflation rate from August 1719 through September 1720 was 4 percent, with a peak of 23 percent in January 1720. The index of commodity prices increased from

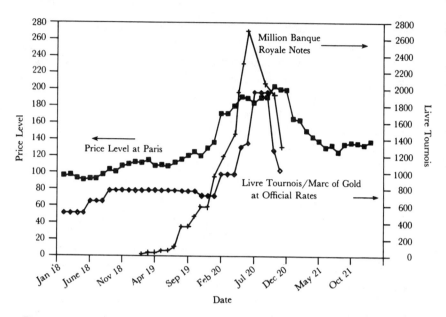

Figure 2.2
Mississippi bubble money and price data

116.1 in July 1719 to 203.7 in September 1720 (Hamilton, 1936). See figure 2.2 for a time series of the price level and the Bank Royale notes in circulation.

Deciding that he had fixed the price of shares at too high a level, Law proposed a drastic deflation on May 21, 1720. Share prices would be reduced from 9000 to 5000 livres in seven stages ending on December 1. Notes would be reduced in value to 50 percent of their face value. Thus, by December, there would remain only 2.3 billion livres in paper (1.3 billion in notes and 1 billion in stock). This reduction was actually accomplished by various other means. Law's plan simply to write down the value of the notes in terms of livre tournois was abandoned when he was thrown from office at the end of May 1720. He was, however, quickly reappointed and presided over the deflation.

By October 1720, only 1.2 billion livres of notes remained in circulation (of a peak of 2.7 billion) and 1.2 billion livres of specie reappeared. Specie was rapidly revalued to the definition that it had at the start of 1720. By December 1720, the price level had fallen to 164.2. Thus, the share price decline starting in 1720 represents a period of share price pegging by the bank—that is, the monetization of shares—and the purposeful monetary deflation undertaken by Law.

The price of the Compagnie's shares fell to 2000 livres in September 1720 and to 1000 livres by December. Law's enemies were now in a position to impose policies hostile to the Compagnie, notably a confiscation of two-thirds of the shares outstanding. The share price fell to 500 livres by September 1721, approximately its value in May 1719.

A Rehash of Mississippi Market Fundamentals

Should economists sum up the increasing stock prices of the Compagnie des Indes only as the "Mississippi bubble"? After all, behind the price rise lies Law's program to revitalize the French economy through financial innovation and fiscal reform. Law's theory was plausible and even has many modern manifestations, and he was an effective propagandist. Investors also could readily observe Law's astounding rise to power. At each stage, as the implementation of the economic experiment became ever more likely, they had to factor the possibility of success into the share prices of the Compagnie de Indes.

The downward slide of share prices is even easier to understand, given the radical shifts in monetary policy and the intimate connection of Compagnie shares to Banque Royale note emissions. The final fall to original share values was driven by Law's fall from power and the accession of his enemies, who aimed to dismantle the Compagnie.

That Law's promised expansion never materialized does not imply that a bubble occurred in the modern sense of the word. After all, this was not the last time that a convincing economic idea would fracture in practice. One respectable group of modern economists or another have described Keynesian economics, supply side economics, monetarism, fixed exchange rate regimes, floating exchange rate regimes, and the belief in rational expectations in asset markets as disastrously flawed policy schemes. Indeed, elements of the first three were primary components in Law's scheme.

Only after the experiment had been run could investors have known that the idea was flawed. That they referred to the ensuing collapse and their after-the-fact foolishness as a bubble should not confuse economists' interpretation of the event. According to the modern definition, the event is easily explainable on the basis of market fundamentals. For a finance operation to be successful always requies a certain degree of sustained confidence from investors. Finance serves as the spearhead of corporate rationalization. In any leveraged buyout or corporate acquisition, high securities prices come first and are followed only gradually by expanded revenues. If investors suddenly lose confidence, they may turn a potentially profitable restructuring into a bankruptcy.

Law's scheme was more audacious than the normal Wall Street operation in that he was attempting a corporate takeover of France. But Law's principle was also that finance came first; the financial operation and the expansion of circulating credit was the driving force for economic expansion. From a modern perspective, this idea is not flawed. It is the centerpiece of most money and macroeconomics textbooks produced in the last two generations and the *lingua franca* of economic policymakers concerned with the problem of underemployed economics.

Law's Shadow: The South Sea Bubble

Following Law's scheme to refinance the French debt, the South Sea Company launched a similar plan to acquire British government debt in January 1720.[9] The financial operations of the British scheme, however, were much simpler than those of Law: the South Sea Company was not involved in large-scale takeovers of commercial companies nor in government functions such as the mint, the collection of taxes, or the creation of paper money.

The British debt in 1720 amounted to approximately 50 million pounds. Of this, 18.3 million was held by the three largest corporations: 3.4 million by the Bank of England, 3.2 million by the East India Company, and 11.7 million by the South Sea Company. Redeemable government bonds held privately amounted to 16.5 million; these could be called by the government on short notice. About 15 million pounds of the debt was in the form of irredeemable annuities: long annuities of between 72 and 87 years and short annuities of 22 years in maturity. Neal (1988) discusses the nature of these annuities.

The Refunding Agreement

In 1720, the assets of the South Sea Company consisted of monopoly rights on British trade with the South Seas—that is, the Spanish colonies of South America—and its holdings of government debt. It was well known that British trade with the South Americas was effectively blocked by the Spanish, so only the holdings of government debt are important to the economic story. After competitive bidding between the South Sea

Company and the Bank of England, the bill permitting the South Sea
Company to refund the debt had its first passage in parliament on March
21, 1720. To acquire this right, the company agreed to pay the government
up to 7.5 million pounds if it managed to acquire the 31 million pounds of
debt in noncorporate hands.

To finance the debt acquisition, the Company was permitted to expand
the number of its shares, each of which had a par value of 100 pounds. For
each 100 pounds per year of the long and short annuities acquired the
company could increase the par value of its shares outstanding by 2000
pounds and by 1400 pounds, respectively. For each 100 pound par value
of redeemables acquired, it could increase its stock issue by 100 pounds.[10]
The interest to be paid by the government on the debt acquired by the
Company was 5 percent per year until 1727 and 4 percent per year thereafter. This would imply a substantial reduction in the annual debt servicing
costs of the government.

The Purchase of Parliament

Conditional on the passage of the refunding act, the South Sea Company
paid bribes to leading members of Parliament and favorites of the king
totaling 1.3 million pounds (Scott, 1911, p. 315). Also, in the sequence of
stock subscriptions through August 1720, numerous members of Parliament and of the government participated; and most received large cash
loans from the Company on their shares. For example, 128 members of
Parliament acquired shares in the first cash subscriptions for shares, 190 in
the second subscription, 352 in the third subscription, and 76 in the fourth
subscription. The total par value of shares acquired by them was 1.1 million
pounds. For peers, the participation was 58 in the first subscription, 73 in
the second subscription, 119 in the third subscription, and 56 in the fourth
subscription. The total par value for peers was 548,000 pounds. Prior to the
refunding operation, the par value of South Sea shares outstanding was
11.7 million pounds; and this was increased to 22.8 million pounds by the
end of the speculation. Thus, people in powerful positions in Parliament
took 17 percent of the additional shares created. In addition, as Dickson
(1967, pp. 108–109) explains, 132 members of Parliament received 1.1
million pounds and 64 Peers received 686,000 pounds in loans against
shares. Members of the government acquired 75,000 pounds of shares at
par value in these subscriptions.

While these bribes add a sinister appearance to the episode, they were
not themselves a signal of impending fraud. At the time, bribery was not

an unusual practice for a company seeking favors from a Parliament well positioned to block any profitable venture unless its members received their cut.

Indeed, that Parliament and the government supported the refunding so enthusiastically must have served as a signal that official cooperation in South Sea's ventures had been purchased. To the extent that members of Parliament held shares, they would have no interest in thwarting any commercial projects that the Company might propose in the future. Given Law's influential theories of commercial expansion, the equity in the South Sea Company could then have been leveraged to undertake those commercial projects that would drive the economy to a higher employment equilibrium. The income generated, accruing to the Company without hindrance of Parliament, could then have justified the initial value of the equity.

South Sea Finance Operations

Figure 2.3 depicts the movement of South Sea share prices during the speculation. Starting at about 120 pounds per 100 pound par value share

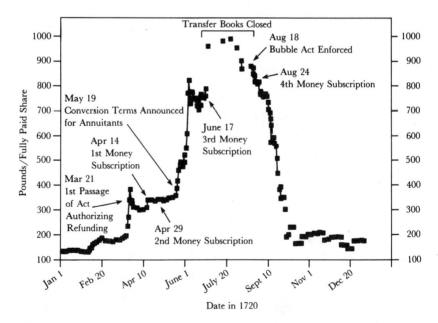

Figure 2.3
South Sea shares

in January 1720, prices moved upward as the refunding proposal was negotiated. With the passage of the refunding act on March 21, prices jumped from about 200 to 300.

To finance the contracted bribes and to make loans to shareholders, the Company offered two subscriptions of shares for cash on April 14 and April 29. In the first subscription, 22,500 shares were issued at a price of 300 pounds per share; one-fifth of the price was required immediately in cash with the remainder due in eight bimonthly installments. In the second, 15,000 shares were subscribed at a price of 400 pounds; one-tenth was required immediately in cash with the remainder due in nine payments at three or four month intervals. From these issues, the Company immediately realized about 2 million pounds to pay its bribe commitments.

The first debt conversion aimed at convincing the holders of the irredeemable annuities to agree to an exchange for South Sea shares. Subscriptions began on April 28. The Company announced its conversion terms on May 19, allowing holders of the debt one week to accept or reject the offer.

Scott (1911, Vol. III, pp. 308–314) extensively discusses the conversion terms, which depended on the type of annuity. As an example, the holders of 100 pound long annuities were offered 700 pounds par value of stock (7 shares) and 575 pounds in bonds and cash. At the time of the offer, South Sea shares were selling for about 400 pounds, so the value of the offer was about 3375 pounds for a long annuity. Scott (p. 310) estimates the market value of the annuity at about 1600 pounds prior to the conversion attempt. Since annuity holders would not lose unless share prices fell below 146 pounds, the offer was highly attractive.

All government creditors who had subscribed prior to the announcement assented to the Company's terms. According to Dickson (1967, pp. 130–132) the Company therefore absorbed about 64 percent of the long annuities and 52 percent of the short annuities outstanding in this subscription. As it became clear that the Company would succeed in accumulating most of the outstanding debt, share prices rose rapidly to 700 pounds.

To permit it sufficient cash to engage in market price manipulation and to make loans to its shareholders, the Company undertook a third cash subscription on June 17, 1720, in which it sold a par value of 5 million pounds (50,000 shares) for a market price of 1000 pounds per share. Purchasers had to pay one-tenth down in cash (5 million pounds), with the remainder to be paid in nine semi-annual payments. Share prices immediately jumped from 745 to 950. the final cash subscription occurred on August 24. The Company sold shares with a par value of 1.25 million pounds at a price of 1000 pounds per share. One-fifth was required immediately in cash, with four additional payments at nine-month intervals.[11]

Finally, the Company offered two additional bond subscriptions; terms for subscribing the remaining irredeemables and the redeemables were announced on August 4 and August 12, respectively. Of the outstanding 16.5 million pounds in redeemables, 14.4 million pounds were exchanged for 18,900 shares of stock. At market prices of 800 pounds per share, this amounted to a price of 105 pounds per 100 pound bond. The remaining irredeemables were to be exchanged for varying amounts of stock and cash. By means of all the debt conversions, the South Sea Company acquired 80 percent of the public's holdings of the irredeemables and 85 percent of the redeemables.

The Price Collapse

South Sea share prices collapsed from about 775 on August 31 to about 290 on October 1, 1720. Shares outstanding or to be issued to the public after subscribers were entered on Company registers numbered 212,012. Thus, the market value of all shares on August 31 was 164 million pounds and about 103 million pounds of that total evaporated in one month, an amount exceeding twice the value of the original, burdensome government debt.

Researchers of the episode like Dickson (1967, pp. 148–152), Scott (1911, vol. III, pp. 324–328) and Neal (1988) are vague about the reason for the speed and magnitude of the decline, though they generally attribute it to the appearance of a liquidity crisis. The South Sea speculation had triggered a simultaneous upsurge in the prices of other Companies along with the creation of numerous "bubble companies." The emergence of these companies, many of which were fraudulent, generated most of the amusing anecdotes that have been transmitted to us about this speculation. Many of the companies born in the 1720 speculation were quite sound, however, notably the Royal Assurance Company and the London Assurance Company. The channeling of capital into these companies alarmed the directors of the South Sea Company, who, having paid a high price to buy the Parliament, did not wish to see potential South Sea profits dissipated by the entry of unauthorized commercial corporations. Consequently, Parliament passed the Bubble Act in June 1720 to ban the formation of unauthorized corporations or the extension of existing corporate charters into new, unauthorized ventures.

When the act was enforced against some of the Company's competitors on August 18, 1720, immediate downward pressure was placed on the price of shares of the affected companies. Since the shares were mostly held on margin, general selling hit the shares of all companies, including South Seas, in a scramble for liquidity. Simultaneously, there was an international scramble for liquidity with the final collapse of Law's Compagnie des Indes in September 1720 and of a Dutch speculation. Liquidity may have been drained from English markets by these international events. Neal and Schubert (1985) provide evidence on large scale capital movements during this period.

With the collapse of share prices, the Company faced the hostility of its shareholders who had participated in its debt and cash subscriptions. Parliament quickly turned against the Company, eventually forcing it to sell off part of its debt holdings to the Bank of England. Parliament eventually stripped the Directors of the Company and several government officials of their wealth (2 million pounds) and directed the payment of the proceeds to the company. Also, adjustments were made to redistribute shares among the different waves of subscribers, so that losses to later subscribers were reduced. Finally, Parliament forgave payment of the 7.1 million pounds which the Company had contracted on receipt of the conversion privilege.

Fundamentals of the South Sea Company

At the beginning of September 1720, the market value of South Sea shares was 164 million pounds. The visible asset supporting this price was a flow of revenue from the Company's claim against the government of 1.9 million pounds per year until 1727 and 1.5 million pounds thereafter. At a 4 percent long term discount rate, this asset had a value of about 40 million pounds. Against this, the Company had agreed to pay 7.1 million pounds for the conversion privilege and owed 6 million pounds in bonds and bills for a net asset value of 26.1 million pounds. In addition, the Company's cash receivables were 11 million pounds due on loans to stockholders and 70 million pounds eventually due from cash subscribers. Thus, share values exceeded asset values by more than 60 million pounds. Given the dubious value of the company's cash claims, share values exceeded tangible net assets by five times or more.

What intangible assets could have justified this value of the Company? Again, the answer lies in Law's prediction of a commercial expansion associated with the accumulation of a fund of credit. The Company succeeded in gathering the fund and obviously had the support of Parliament in its ventures. On this basis, Scott (1911, p. 313–314) believed that a price of 400 was not excessive:

It may be added too that the great need of commerce in the first quarter of the eighteenth century was a sufficiency of capital, and so it is scarcely possible to estimate adequately, under the different conditions of the present time, the many promising outlets there were then for the remunerative employment of capital. In fact capital, organized in one single unit, might be utilized in many directions, where no single fraction of the same capital could find its way, and therefore some premium on South Sea stock was justified and maintainable.... Thus, it will be seen that the investor, who in 1720 bought stock at 300 or even 400, may have been unduly optimistic, but there was at least a possibility that his confidence would be rewarded in the future.

The experiment was terminated with the liquidity crisis and the withdrawal of parliamentary support while it was still in its finance stage. In retrospect, anyone projecting commercial returns high enough to justify the higher prices of South Sea shares was probably too optimistic. Nevertheless, the episode is readily understandable as a case of speculators working on the basis of the best economic analysis available and pushing prices along by their changing view of market fundamentals.

Conclusions

Fascinated with the brilliance of grand speculative events, economists have huddled in the bubble interpretation and have neglected an examination of potential market fundamentals. The ready availability of a banal explanation of the tulipmania, compared to its dominant position in he speculative pantheon of economics, is stark evidence of how bubble and mania characterizations have served to divert economists from understanding those outlying events highest in informational content. The bubble interpretation has relegated the far more important Mississippi and South Sea episodes to a description of pathologies of group psychology. Yet these events were a vast macroeconomic and financial experiment, imposed on a scale and with a degree of control by their main theoretical architects which has not since been experienced. True, the experiment failed, either because its theoretical basis was fundamentally flawed or bacause its managers lacked the complex financial skills required to undertake the day-to-day tactics necessary for its consummation. Nevertheless, investors *had* to take positions on its potential success. It is curious that economists have accepted the failure of the experiments as proof that the investors were foolishly and irrationally wrong.

Notes

I have benefited from several conversations with Herschel Grossman and comments of the editors.

1. Burmeister (1980, pp. 264–286) summarizes the research activity about "the Hahn problem."

2. Actually, the company involved was not called the Mississippi Company. Initially, it was the *Compagnie d'Occident*; and after a series of corporate takeovers, it became the *Compagnie des Indes*.

3. Mackay plagiarized his description from Beckmann (1846). Beckmann refers to a long sequence of research about the episode, but all sources are ultimately based on a set of three anonymously written pamphlets in dialogue form published in 1637. These pamphlets were among dozens written just after the collapse by anti-speculative partisans launched by the economic oligarchy which wished to assure that speculative capital was channeled through markets which it controlled.

4. This necessarily brief outline of Law's experiment is based on descriptions in Harsin (1928), Faure (1977), and Murphy (1986).

5. The livre tournois was the unit of account and was officially valued at weights of gold or silver which varied during Law's regime. See Figure 2 for changes in the offical gold definition of the livre tournois.

6. The approximately 540,000 shares outstanding would then have had a market value of 5.4 billion livres, somewhat less than four times the face value of the rentes which were the most tangible assets of the Compagnie. For perspective, Law himself estimated the national wealth of France at 30 billion livres. Of the shares outstanding, the king held 100,000 shares. In addition, the Compagnie held 100,000 shares which it could sell. Researchers of the Mississippi and South Sea episodes treat the quantity of own shares held by the companies as significant.

7. Simultaneously, the king sold his 100,000 shares back to the company at 9000 livres per share. Three hundred million livres would be deposited in the king's accounts in the Banque immediately with the rest to be paid over 10 years.

8. See Harsin's (1928, p. 180) citation of Law's *Deuxieme Lettre sur le nouveau system des finances.*

9. I have taken the factual information in this section primarily from Scott (1911) and Dickson (1967).

10. Quantities of shares were designated in terms of total par value issued. Most research on the episode has continued this convention and has emphasized the difference between the market and par value of shares. The company was free to set the exchange rate between shares and debt. It valued the shares exchanged at well above the par value, leaving it an excess of authorized shares which it was free to market. Scott (1911) labelled these surplus shares the company's "profits" from the conversion. The curious view that a company's holdings of its own shares represents an asset has been replicated in recent examinations of South Seas; for instance, Dickson (1967, p. 160) lists the company's holdings of its own stock among its assets.

11. From June 24 to August 22, the transfer books of the Company were closed in prepara- tion for a dividend payment, so the market prices depicted in Figure 3 for this period were future prices. Neal (1988) argues that the peak price was 950 on July 1. Scott (1911) indicates a peak price of 1050, but this apparently includes the announced stock dividend of 10 percent. Following Neal, I have used the peak price of 950.

References

Anderson, A., *An Historical and chronological Deduction of the Origin of Commerce*, vol. 3. London: J. Walter, 1787.

Azariadis, Costas, "Self-Fulfilling Prophecies," *Journal of Economic Theory*, December 1981, 25, 380–96.

Azariadis, Costas and Roger Guesnerie, "Sunspots and Cycles," *Review of Economic Studies*, October, 1986, 53, 725–37.

Beckmann, Johann, *History of Inventions, Discoveries, and Origins*. London: Harry G. Bohn, 4th edition, vol. 1, 1846.

Burmeister, Edwin, *Capital Theory and Dynamics*. Cambridge: Cambridge University Press, 1980.

Carswell, John, *The South Sea Bubble*. London: Cresset Press, 1960.

Cutler, David, James Poterba, and Lawrence Summers, "Speculative Dynamics," Working Paper, June, 1989.

Dickson, P. G. M., *The Financial Revolution in England: A Study in the Development of Public Credit*. London: Macmillan, 1967.

Faure, Edgar, *La Banqueroute de Law*. Paris, 1977.

Garber, Peter, "Tulipmania," *Journal of Political Economy*, June 1989, 97, 535–560.

Hamilton, Earl, "Prices and Wages at Paris under John Law's System," *Quarterly Journal of Economics*, 1936–7, 51, 42–70.

Harsin, Paul, *Les Doctrines Monetarires et Financieres en France*. Paris: Librairie Felix Alcan, 1928.

Kindleberger, Charles, *Manias, Panics, and Crashes*, New York: Basic Books, 1978.

Krugman, Paul, "Is the Strong Dollar Sustainable?" *The U.S. Dollar—Recent Developments, Outlook, and Policy Options*, Federal Reserve Bank of Kansas City, 1985.

Law, John, *Money and Trade Considered: with a Proposal for Supplying the Nation with Money*, 1st ed., 1705. Glasgow: Foulis, 1760.

Mackay, Charles, *Extraordinary Popular Delusions and the Madness of Crowds*, Vol. I, 2nd Edition. London: Office of the National Illustrated Library, 1852.

Malkiel, Burton, "The Madness of Crowds," Chapter Two in *A Random Walk Down Wall Street*, 4th Edition. New York: Norton, 1985, pp. 28–45.

Meese, Richard, "Testing for Bubbles in Exchange Markets: A Case of Sparkling Rates?" *Journal of Political Economy*, April, 1986, 94, 345–73.

Murphy, Antoin E., *Richard Cantillon, Entrepreneur and Economist*. Oxford: Clarendon Press, 1986.

Neal, Larry, "How the South Sea Bubble Was Blown Up and Burst: A New Look at Old Data," U. of Illinois Working Paper, August, 1988.

Neal, Larry, and E. Schubert, The First Rational Bubbles: A New Look at the Mississippi and South Sea Schemes," BEBR Working Paper 1188, U. of Illinois, Urbana-Champaign, Sept. 1985.

Palgrave, R. H., Dictionary of Political Economy. London: MacMillan & Co., 1926.

Eatwell, John, Murray Milgate, and Peter Newman, eds., The New Palgrave Dictionary of Economics. London: MacMillan Press, 1987.

Posthumus, Nicolaas W., "The Tulip Mania in Holland in the Years 1636 and 1637," Journal of Economic and Business History, May 1929, 1, 434–55.

Posthumus, Nicolaas W., "Die Speculatie in Tulpen in de Jaren 1636–37," Economisch Historisch Jaarboek, 1926, 1927, and 1934.

Samuelson, Paul A., "Intertemporal Price Equilibrium: A Prologue to the Theory of Speculation," Weltwirtschaftlishes Archiv, 1957 Band 79, Heft 2, 181–219. Reproduced in Stiglitz, Joseph E., ed., The Collected Scientific Papers of Paul A. Samuelson, Vol. 2. Cambridge: The M.I.T. Press, 1966.

Samuelson, Paul A., "Indeterminacy of Development in a Heterogeneous-Capital Model with Constant Saving Propensity," In Shell, K., ed., Essays on the theory of Optimal Economic Growth, Cambridge: The M.I.T. Press, 1967.

Schumpeter, Joseph, History of Economic Analysis. New York: Oxford University Press, 1954.

Scott, William, The Constitution and Finance of English, Scottish, and Irish Joint Stock Companies to 1720, Vols, I, II, III. Cambridge: Cambridge University Press, 1910–12.

Shell, Karl and Joseph Stiglitz, "The Allocation of Investment in a Dynamic Economy," Quarterly Journal of Economics, November 1967, 81, 592–609.

Shiller, Robert, "Stock Prices and Social Dynamics," Brookings Papers, 1984, 2, 457–98.

Shiller, Robert, "Fashions, Fads and Bubbles in Financial Markets," paper prepared for Conference on Takeovers and Contests for Corporate Control, Feb. 1986.

Spooner, Frank, The International Economy and Monetary Movements in France, 1493–1725. Cambridge: Harvard University Press, 1972.

van Horne, J., "Of Financial Innovations and Excesses," Journal of Finance, No. 3, July, 1985, 40, 621–31.

3   Tulipmania

Peter M. Garber

I   Introduction

Gathered around the campfires early in their training, fledgling economists hear the legend of the Dutch tulip speculation from their elders, priming them with a skeptical attitude toward speculative markets. That prices of "intrinsically useless" bulbs could rise so high and collapse so rapidly seems to provide a decisive example of the instability and irrationality that may materialize in asset markets. The Dutch tulipmania of 1634–37 always appears as a favorite case of speculative excess, even providing a synonym in our jargon for a speculative mania.[1] As a nonessential agricultural commodity, the tulip could be reproduced rapidly and without limit, should its relative price have increased. Since market fundamental prices under any reasonable explanation should not have attained recorded levels, the tulipmania phenomenon has made it more likely that a sizable body of economists will occasionally embrace a rational or irrational "bubble hypothesis" in debates about whether bubbles have emerged in other episodes.[2]

In this chapter, I shall describe the tulip spot and futures markets that emerged during the speculation and compile price data for several varieties of bulbs. I shall conclude that the most famous aspect of the mania, the extremely high prices reported for rare bulbs and their rapid decline, reflects normal pricing behavior in bulb markets and cannot be interpreted as evidence of market irrationality. Nevertheless, a less emphasized aspect of the mania, the speculation in common bulbs, does defy explanation.

The paper is divided into seven sections. Section II presents the traditional version of the tulipmania. Section III traces the sources of the traditional version and studies its influence on the recent economics and financial literature. Section IV describes the nature of tulip markets, focusing on how the reproductive cycle of the tulip itself determined behavior.

Section V contains an analysis of seventeenth-century tulip prices. Since the data are too limited to construct "market fundamentals," I simply characterize the movement of prices for a variety of bulbs during and after the mania. I compare the pattern of price declines for initially rare eighteenth-century bulbs with that of seventeenth-century bulbs. In Section VI, I use the evidence to address the question whether the seventeenth-century tulip speculation clearly exhibits the existence of a speculative mania. Section VII contains concluding remarks.

II   The Traditional Image of Tulipmania

Descriptions of the tulip speculation are always framed in a context of doubt about how the Dutch, usually so astute in their speculations, could be caught in such an obvious blunder. Modern references to the episode depend on the brief description in Mackay (1852), which I summarize in this section.[3] The tulip originated in Turkey but diffused into Western Europe only in the middle of the sixteenth century, carried first to Austria by a fancier of the flower. The tulip was immediately accepted by the wealthy as a beautiful and rare flower, appropriate for the most stylish gardens. The market was for durable bulbs, not flowers. As in so many other markets, the Dutch dominated that for tulips, initiating the development of methods to create new flower varieties. The bulbs that commanded high prices produced unique, beautifully patterned flowers; common tulips were sold at much lower prices.

Beginning in 1634, nonprofessionals entered the tulip trade in large numbers. According to Mackay, prices of individual bulbs reached enormous levels; for example, a single Semper Augustus bulb was sold at the height of the speculation for 5,500 guilders, a weight of gold equal to $50,000 evaluated at $450 per ounce.[4] Mackay provided neither the sources of these bulb prices nor the dates on which they were observed, however,

Mackay emphasized the lunacy of the event through a pair of anecdotes about a sailor's mistakenly eating valuable bulbs and an unsuspecting English traveler's experimenting with them by peeling off their layers.[5] He also described some barter transactions for acquiring rare bulbs so that the monetary expenditure may be translated into units of goods more meaningful to the modern reader.

Mackay then shifted to the final speculative frenzy, stating that large amounts of foreign funds entered the country to add to the speculation and people from all classes hurriedly liquidated other assets to participate in the tulip market.[6] Finally and inexplicably, the frenzy terminated; and, over-night, even rare bulbs could find no buyers at 10 percent of their previous prices, creating a long-term economic distress. No evidence of postcollapse transactions prices of the rare bulbs was produced, however. Mackay cited prices from bulb sales from 60 years, 130 years, or 200 years after the collapse as indicators of the magnitude of the collapse and of the obvious misalignment of prices at the peak of the speculation. Also, no evidence was provided of the general economic context from which the speculation emerged.

III   Some *Dogmengeschichte*

Chroniclers of the tulip speculation and modern writers who invoke it take for granted that it was a mania, selecting and organizing the evidence to emphasize the irrationality of the market outcome. In the twentieth cen-tury, a strong intellectual influence on participants and observers of the financial markets has been exerted by Mackay's version of the tulipmania, although he devoted to it only seven pages of text.[7] The pre-1950s aca-demic literature written by major professional economists contains little direct reference to the tulipmania.[8] The tulipmania made its first appearance in serious economics journals with the development of capital theory in the 1950s and the discovery of the potential existence of multiple, dynamically unstable asset price paths.[9] The advent of the "sunspot" literature has generated a revival of references to tulips as a motivation for the line of research.[10] In the finance literature, the emergence of empirical anomalies has also generated references to tulipmania as bubble and fad explanations have regained respectability.[11]

Given its strategic position in current views of tulipmania, it is vital to investigate from which sources Mackay constructed his version of the speculation. While at one point he includes a minor citation to Beckmann (1846), he plagiarized most of his description from Beckmann with a little literary embellishment.[12] Beckmann carefully reported his sources of infor-mation about the functioning of the markets and bulb sales prices, using notably the dialogues between Gaergoedt and Waermondt (Anonymous, 1637, 1643a, 1643b) and Munting's (1672, 1696) discussions of this epi-sode. Gaergoedt and Waermondt is a series of three pamphlets in dialogue form that provides details about the markets and numerous prices of vari-ous bulbs, taken mostly from the final day of the speculation.[13] Munting was a botanist who wrote a 1,000-folio volume on numerous flowers. Though Mackay claims that the volume was devoted to the tulipmania, only the six pages allocated to tulips discuss the episode.[14] All the price data described in Munting can be found in the dialogues, so we must conclude that they are Munting's primary source. Thus the current version of the tulipmania, to the extent that it is based on scholarly work, follows a lattice of hearsay fanning out from the Gaergoedt and Waermondt dialogues.

A more careful line of research has had little impact on our current interpretation of the tulip speculation. Solms-Laubach's (1899) history of tulips in Europe provides an extensive description of the available literature on tulips, including the dialogues. Most of the his price data originate in Gaergoedt and Waermondt, but he also explores records left by notaries of tulip contracts written during the mania.

Van Damme (1976) documented the tulipmania in a series of short articles written from 1899 to 1903.[15] This series consists of reprints of the dialogues, reproductions of some precollapse pricing contracts, and details of bulb auctions from just before the collapse and from six years after the end of the speculation.[16]

Posthumus (1926, 1927, 1929, 1934), the only economist in this literature, extended the available data by compiling and reproducing more of the notaries' contracts. Most of his discussion, however, again depends on price information in the dialogues and information compiled by van Damme.

Finally, Krelage (1942, 1946) provides an extensive description of the markets, though his prices for the speculation period also seem to come from Gaergoedt and Waermondt. Krelage (1946) does provide tulip price lists from sales in 1708 and 1709 and a 1739 bulb catalog. In addition, he compiles a time series of prices for a large variety of hyacinth bulbs during the eighteenth and nineteenth centuries.

Even this line of research accomplishes little more than gathering additional price data, and those data that we have are not organized in a systematic time series. Posthumus does attempt to analyze the functioning of the futures markets that materialized at the end of the speculation; but in spite of his efforts, we have inherited the concept of the tulipmania as the most famous of bubbles accompanied by no serious attempt to describe what might constitute the market fundamentals of the bulb market.

IV   The Tulip and the Tulip Markets

An understanding of the tulip markets requires some information about the nature of the tulip. A bulb flower, the tulip can propagate either through seeds or through buds that form on the mother bulb. Properly cultivated, the buds can directly reproduce another bulb. Each bulb, after planting, eventually disappears during the growing season. By the end of the season, the original bulb is replaced by a clone, the primary bud that is now a functioning bulb, and by a few seondary buds. Asexual reproduction through buds, the principal propagation method, produces an increase in bulbs at a maximum annual rate of from 100 percent to 150 percent in normal bulbs (see Mather 1961, p. 44).

A bulb produced directly from seed requires 7–12 years before it flowers. The flowers appear in April or May and last for about a week. The amount of time required before the secondary buds flower depends on the size of the bulb produced from the bub.[17] In June, bulbs can be removed from their beds but must be replanted by September. To verify the delivery of a specific variety, spot trading in bulbs had to occur immediately after the flowering period, usually in June.

Tulips are subject to invasion by a mosaic virus whose important effect, called "breaking," is to produce remarkable patterns on the flower, some of which are considered beautiful. The pattern imposed on a particular flower cannot be reproduced through seed propagation: seeds will produce bulbs that yield a common flower since they are unaffected by the virus. These bulbs may themselves eventually "break" at some unknown date but into a pattern that may not be remarkable. A specific pattern can be reproduced by cultivating the buds into new bulbs.

As another effect, the mosaic virus makes the bulb sickly and reduces its rate of reproduction.[18] Smith (1937, p. 413) states that broken bulbs do not "proliferate as freely" as undiseased plants but that this weakening need not cause broken bulbs to succumb, giving as an example the broken Zomerschoon, which has been actively cultivated since 1620.[19] Van Slogteren (1960) claims that the mosaic virus may cause total loss of a plant or a 10–20 percent reduction in propagation rates.

The high market prices for tulips to which the current version of the tulipmania refers were prices for particularly beautiful broken bulbs. Single-colored breeder bulbs, except to the extent that they could potentially break, were not valued, and all the important tulip varieties in the first two centuries of European cultivation were diseased. Broken bulbs fell from fashion only in the nineteenth century (see Doorenbos 1954). Indeed, since breaking was unpredictable, some have characterized tulipmania among growers as a gamble, with growers "vying to produce better and more bizarre variegations and feathering" (Mather 1961, pp. 100–101).[20]

The Bulb Market, 1634—37

The market for bulbs was limited to professional growers until 1634, but participation encompassed a more general class of speculators by the end of 1634.[21] A rising demand for bulbs in France apparently drove the speculation.[22]

Market participants could make many types of deals. The rare flowers were called "piece" goods, and particular bulbs were sold by their weight. The heavier bulbs had more outgrowths and therefore represented a collection of future bulbs. The weight standard was the *aas*, about one-twentieth of a gram. For example, if a Gouda of 57 *azen* (plural of aas) were sold for a given price, the sale contract would refer to a particular bulb planted at a given location. Once markets developed in common bulbs, they were sold in standardized units of 1,000 azen or 1 pound (9,728 azen in Haarlem, 10,240 azen in Amsterdam). Purchase contracts for "pound" goods would not refer to particular bulbs.

A purchase between September and June was necessarily a contract for future delivery. Also, markets materialized for the outgrowths of the rarer bulbs. The outgrowths could not be delivered immediately since they had to attain some minimum size before they could be separated from the parent bulb to assure the viability of the new bulb. Hence, the contracts for outgrowths were also for future delivery.

Formal futures markets developed in 1636 and were the primary focus of trading before the collapse in February 1637. Earlier deals had employed written contracts entered into before a notary. Trading became extensive enough in the summer of 1636 that traders began meeting in numerous taverns in groups called "colleges," where trades were regulated by a few rules governing the method of bidding and fees. Buyers were required to pay $\frac{1}{2}$ stuiver (1 stuiver = $\frac{1}{20}$ guilder) out of each contracted guilder to sellers up to a maximum of 3 guilders for each deal for "wine money."[23] To the extent that a trader ran a balanced book over any length of time, these payments would cancel out. No margin was required from either party, so bankruptcy constraints did not restrict the magnitude of an individual's position.

Typically, the buyer did not currently possess the cash to be delivered on the settlement date and the seller did not currently possess the bulb. Neither party intended a delivery on the settlement date; only a payment of the difference between the contract and settlement price was expected. Thus, as a bet on the price of the bulbs on the settlement date, this market was not different in function from currently operating futures markets.[24]

The operational differences were that the contracts were not continuously marked to market, required no margin deposits to guarantee compliance, and consisted of commitments of individuals rather than an exchange so that a collapse would require the untangling of gross, rather than net, positions.

It is unclear which date was designated as the settlement date in the college contracts. No bulbs were delivered under the deals struck in the new futures markets in 1636–37 prior to the collapse because of the necessity of waiting until June to exhume the bulbs. It is also unclear how the settlement price was determined. Beckmann (1846, p. 29) states that the settlement price was "determined by that at which most bargains were made," presumably at the time of expiration of a given contract. Again, this is the standard practice in current futures markets.

Serious and wealthy tulip fanciers who traded regularly in rare varieties did not participate in the new speculative markets. Even after the collapse of the speculation, they continued to trade rare bulbs for "large amounts" (see Posthumus 1929, p. 442). To the extent that rare bulbs also traded on the futures markets, this implies that no one arbitraged the spot and futures markets. To take a long position in spot bulbs required substantial capital resources or access to the financial credit markets. To hedge this position with a short sale in the futures market would have required the future purchaser to have substantial capital or access to sound credit; substantial risk of noncompliance with the deal in the futures market would have undermined the hedge. Since participants in the futures markets faced no capital requirements, there was no basis for an arbitrage.

During most of the period of the tulip speculation, high prices and recorded trading occurred only for the rare bulbs. Common bulbs did not figure in the speculation until November 1636.

Posthumus (1929, p. 444) hypothesizes the following timing of events:

I think the sequence of events may be seen as follows. At the end of 1634, the new non-professional buyers came into action. Towards the middle of 1635 prices rose rapidly, while people could buy on credit, generally delivering at once some article of value; at the same time the sale per aas was introduced. About the middle of 1636 the colleges appeared; and soon thereafter the trade in non-available bulbs was started, while in November of the same year the trade was extended to the common varieties, and bulbs were sold by the thousand azen and per pound.

V   Some Characterization of the Data

In figures 3.1–3.8, I depict the "time series" for guilders per bulb or guilders per aas that I have been able to reconstruct for various bulbs.[25] The

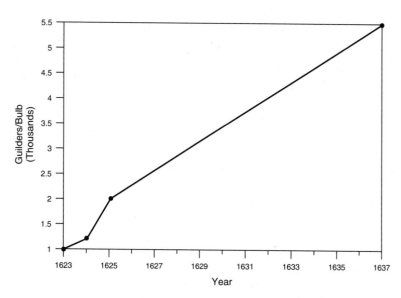

Figure 3.1
Semper Augustus

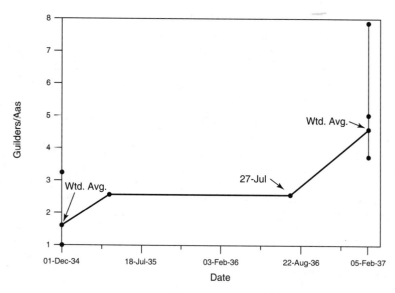

Figure 3.2
Admirael van der Eyck

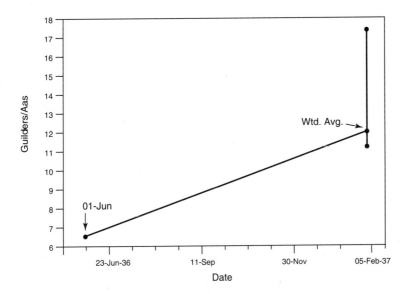

Figure 3.3
Admirael Liefkens

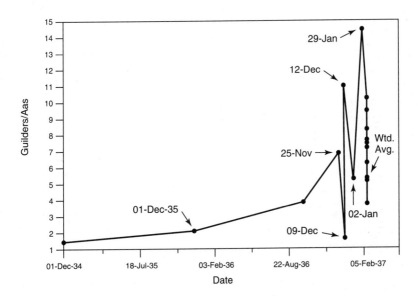

Figure 3.4
Gouda

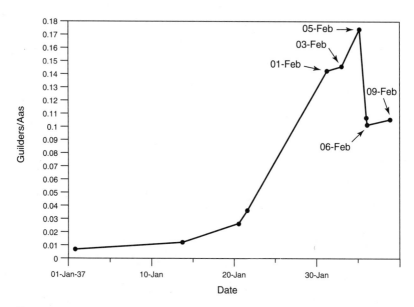

Figure 3.5
Switsers

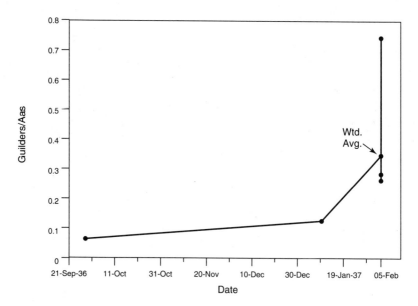

Figure 3.6
Groote Geplumiceerde

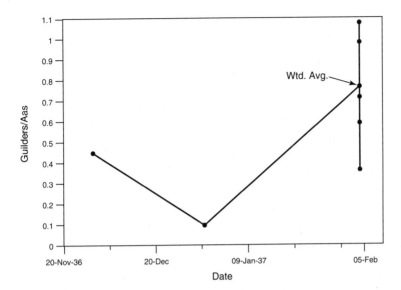

Figure 3.7
Gheele ende roote van leyden

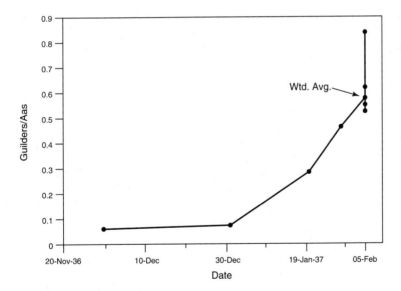

Figure 3.8
Oudenaerden

last observations for each series (except for the Switsers) were recorded on February 5, 1637, apparently the peak of the mania. For that date there are usually several price observations for each flower, but their order of appearance in the figures has no meaning. Specifically, the figures do not indicate a price explosion at an infinite rate on February 5. I have connected the price lines to the weighted average of prices for February 5.

A natural way to separate categories is to split the sample between piece goods and pound goods. Posthumus claims that there was a class difference between those who traded in piece goods and those who traded in pound goods, even in the colleges. Members of the middle classes and capitalized workers such as the weavers disdained the pound goods and traded only in the rarer bulbs.

The bulbs that can be included among piece goods are Semper Augustus, Admirael Liefkens, Admirael van der Eyck, and Gouda. Among these, the Gouda can be considered a standard since we have the most detailed price series for this bulb, starting at the beginning of the speculation. The bulbs that can be included among the pound goods, that is, bulbs trading in 1,000-aas or 1-pound lots, are Gheele ende Roote van Leyden, Groote Geplumiceerde, Oudenaerden, Switsers, and Witte Croonen.[26] The pound goods sold at much lower prices per aas than the piece goods. In the last month of the speculation, however, their prices increased much more rapidly than those of the piece goods, rising up to twentyfold. Over a much longer period, the prices of the piece goods doubled or perhaps tripled.

Postcollapse Tulip Prices

The tulip speculation collapsed after the first week of February 1637. Apparently, a general suspension of settlement occurred on contracts coming due. On February 24, 1637, delegates of florists meeting in Amsterdam proposed that sales of tulips contracted on or before November 30, 1636, should be executed and that for later contracts, the buyer would be given the right to reject the deal on payment of 10 percent of the sale price to the seller. The authorities did not adopt this suggestion. On April 27, 1637, the states of Holland decided to suspend all contracts, giving the seller the right to sell contracted bulbs at market prices during the suspension. The buyer would be responsible for the difference between this market price and whatever price the authorities eventually determined for contract settlement. This decision released the growers to market the bulbs that would emerge in June. After this decision, the disposition of further settlement becomes murky, though Posthumus (1929, pp. 446–47) states that many cities followed the example of Haarlem, where in May 1638 the city council passed a regulation permitting buyers to terminate a contract on payment of 3.5 percent of the contract price.[27]

With the end of large-scale bulb trading after February 1637, records of transaction prices virtually disappeared. Prices no longer were publicly recorded, and only an occasional estate auction of an important florist would reveal the magnitude of prices.[28] Fortunately, van Damme (1976, pp. 109–13) reports prices from a postcollapse estate auction in 1643. In the estate auction of the bulb dealer J. van Damme (no relation), fl 42,013 were raised through the sale of bulbs.[29] This amount reflects a bulb value comparable to the fl 68,553 derived from the February 1637 estate auction from which we have received most of the tulipmania peak price data. Details from this latter auction are reported in "Liste van eenige tulpaen" (1926).

Individual bulbs could still command high prices six years after the collapse. Four bulbs whose prices were listed individually also appear among the bulbs traded in 1636–37: Witte Croonen, English Admiral, Admirael van der Eyck, and General Rotgans (Rotgansen). Witte Croonen bulbs were pound goods, and the others were piece goods. Table 3.1 presents a comparison of 1637 and 1642 or 1643 prices. Even from the peaks of February 1637, the price declines of the rarer bullbs—English Admiral, Admirael van der Eyck, and General Rotgans—over the course of six years are not unusually rapid. We shall see that they fit the pattern of decline typical of a prized variety.

Table 3.1
Postcollapse bulb prices in guilders

Bulb	January 1637	February 5, 1637	1642 or 1643	Annual depreciation (%)*
Witt Croonen ($\frac{1}{2}$ lb)	64	1,668 (avg.)	37.5	76
English Admiral (bulb)	...	700 (25-aas bulb)	210	24
Admirael van der Eyck (bulb)	...	1,345 (wtd. avg.)	220[†]	36
General Rotgans (Rotgansen)	...	805 (1,000 azen)	138	35

*From February 1637 peak.
† Adjusted downward fl 5 to account for the English Admiral outgrowth.

Eighteenth-Century Tulip Prices

Though a few prices are available from the years immediately after the collapse, a gap of about 70 years arises in detailed tulip price data.[30] High prices are available only for much later periods, and these are of an order of magnitude lower than these quoted during the speculation.[31]

In table 3.2, I report prices for bulbs from January 2, 1637; February 5, 1637; 1722; and 1739.[32] Even starting in January 1637, before the peak of the speculation, the price decline is remarkable. Prices fall to levels of 1 percent, 0.5 percent, 0.1 percent, or 0.005 percent of their January 1637 values in a century. Also noteworthy is the convergence of prices of all individually sold bulbs to a common value, regardless of the initial bulb values.

In table 3.3, I have compiled the prices of bulbs common to the 1707 auction and either the 1722 or the 1739 price lists. While this was not a period known for a tulip speculation or crash, prices display the same pattern of decline. Bulbs appeared on an auction list if they were recently developed rare varieties that commanded relatively high prices.[33] By the time they appeared on a general catalog, they had diffused sufficently to become relatively common. Again, in 32 years prices declined to 3 percent, 0.25 percent, 0.35 percent, or 0.04 percent of their original values, repeat-

Table 3.2
Guilder prices to tulip bulbs common to 1637, 1722, and 1739 price lists

Bulb	January 2, 1637	February 5, 1637	1722	1739
Admirael de Man	18	209	....	.1
Gheele Croonen	.41	20.5	...	.025*
Witte Croonen	2.2	57	...	.02*
Gheele ende Roote van Leyden	17.5	136.5	.1	.2
Switsers	1	30	.05	...
Semper Augustus	2,000†	6,290	...	.1
Zomerschoon	...	480	.15	.15
Admirael van Enchuysen	...	4,900	.2	...
Fama	...	776	.03*	...
Admirael van Hoorn	...	65.5	.1	...
Admirael Liefkens	...	2,968	.2	...

Note: To construct this table I have assumed a standard bulb size of 175 azen. All sales by the bulb are assumed to be in the standard weight, and prices are adjusted proportionally from reported prices. When more than one bulb price is available on a given day, I report the average of adjusted prices.
*Sold in lots of 100 bulbs.
†This was the price of the Semper Augustus bulb on July 1, 1625.

ing the pattern of decline of the bulbs from the tulipmania. Indeed, the valuable bulbs of 1707 even converged approximately to the same prices as the valuable bulbs of 1637.

We now have a pattern in the evolution of prices of newly developed, fashionable tulip bulbs. The first bulbs, unique or in small supply, carry high prices. With time, the price declines rapidly either because of rapid reproduction of the new variety or because of the increasing introduction of new varieties. Anyone who acquired a rare bulb would have understood this standard pattern of anticipated capital depreciation, at least by the eighteenth century.

To apply this pattern to the postcollapse period, we treat as rare all eighteenth-century bulbs selling for at least 100 guilders (Premier Noble, Aigle Noir, Roi de Fleurs, and Superintendant).[34] Prices for these bulbs declined at an average annual percentage rate of 28.5 percent. From table 3.1, the three costly bulbs of February 1637 (English Admiral, Admirael van der Eyck, and General Rotgans) had an average annual price decline of 32 percent from the peak of the speculation through 1642. Using the eighteenth-century price depreciation rate as a benchmark also followed by expensive bulbs after the mania, we can infer that any price collapse for rare bulbs in February 1637 could not have exceeded 16 percent of peak prices. Thus the crash of February 1637 for rare bulbs was not of extraordinary magnitude and did not greatly affect the normal time-series pattern of rare bulb prices.

Table 3.3
Guilder prices of tulip bulbs, 1707, 1722, and 1739

Bulb	1707	1722	1739	Annual depreciation (%)	
				1707–22	1722–39
Triomphe d'Europe	6.75	.3	.2	...	...
Premier Noble	409	...	1.0	19*	...
Aigle Noir	110	.75	.3	33	...
Roi de Fleurs	251	10.0	.1	22	27
Diamant	71	2.5	2.0	22	...
Superintendant	...	100	.12	...	40
Keyzer Kazel de VI	...	40	.5	...	26
Goude Zon, bontlof	...	15	10.0	...	2
Roy de Mouritaine	...	15	2.0	...	12
Triomphe Royal	...	10	1.0	...	14

Source: Krelage (1946): Bradley (1728).
* 1707–39.

Eighteenth-Century Hyacinth Prices

As further evidence of this standard pattern in bulb prices, I now turn to
the market for hyacinths. Krelage (1946) supplies prices of hyacinths during
the eighteenth and nineteenth centuries. Hyacinths replaced tulips at the
start of the eighteenth century as the fashionable flower, and once again a
large effort arose to innovate beautiful varieties.[35]

Krelage provides long price series for many hyacinths after their introduction. In table 3.4, I have mainly selected the price patterns for bulbs
carrying particularly high prices at the time of introduction. Note that the
pattern is similar to that for prized tulips in the seventeenth and eighteenth
centuries. Within three decades, prices of even the highest-priced bulbs
usually fell to 1–2 percent of the original price. Both originally highly
priced and inexpensive bulbs converged to a price of from 0.5 to 1 guilder.
The average annual rate of price depreciation for bulbs valued at more than
100 guilders (eight observations) was 38 percent, somewhat faster than the
depreciation rate for tulip bulbs. For bulbs valued at 10–80 guilders, the
annual price depreciation averaged 20 percent.

Table 3.4
Hyacinth price patterns (Guilders)

Bulb	1716	1735	1739	1788	1802	1808
Coralijn*	100	12.75	2	.6	...	...
L'Admirable	100	...	1	1	...	...
Starrekroon	200	...	1	.3	...	.3
Vredenrijck	...	80	16	1.5	...	...
Koning Sesostris	...	100	8	1	1	...
Staaten Generaal	...	210	20	1.5	2	...
Robijn	...	12	4	1	1	5
Struijsvogel	...	161	20	...	...	...
Miroir	...	141	10	...	...	...

Bulb	1788	1802	1815	1830	1845	1875
Comte de la Coste	200	50	1	.75	.5	.15
Henri Quatre	50	30	1	3	5	1
Van Doeveren	50	...	1	2	1.2	.75
Flos Niger	60	20	10	...	.25[†]	...
Rex rubrorum	3	1.5	.3	1	.35	.24

Source.—Krelage (1946), pp. 645–55.
*Krelage (p. 645) notes that the Coralijn bulb originally sold for 1,000 guilders, though he
does not include a year.
[†] 1860.

Modern Bulb Prices

Currently, new flower bulb varieties are also highly valuable. Typically, however, new varieties are reproduced in mass by the bulb's developer and marketed at relatively low prices only when a large quantity of bulbs has been produced. Hence, prices for prototype bulbs are usually unavailable. In the few cases in which a prototype bulb does change hands, transactions prices are not announced. Information provided by officials at the Bloembollencentrum in Haarlem indicates, however, that new varieties of "very special" tulip bulbs currently sell for about 5,000 guilders ($2,400 at 1987 exchange rates) per kilogram. A small quantity of prototype lily bulbs recently was sold for 1 million guilders ($480,000 at 1987 exchange rates). Such bulbs can now be reproduced rapidly with tissue growth techniques, so they also would be marketed at relatively low prices.

VI Was This Episode a "Tulipmania"?

I now examine whether the evidence demands a mania interpretation for the tulip price movements. First, I will dispose of two nagging issues: (1) the absence of descriptions of economic distress in accounts of the period not engaged in antispeculative moralizing.[36] and (2) the claims that the disappearance of renowned bulbs or their extreme price declines over long time periods signal the lunacy of the event. Next, I will isolate the aspect of the speculation for which the evidence provides no compelling explanation, the trading in common bulbs in the period from January 2, 1637, to February 5, 1637.

It is not difficult to understand why general economic studies of this period take little notice of "economic distress" arising from the speculation. Since the longer-term price rise occurred only in the rare bulbs, no significant agricultural resources were devoted to expand their cultivation.[37] Also, since the spectacular price rise in the common bulbs occurred only after the bulbs were in the ground in September 1636, rises in these prices could also have had little effect on the allocation of resources during 1636–37. To the extent that the speculation had any impact, it can have had an effect only through the distribution of wealth. Little wealth was actually transferred, howverer; the fees paid out by buyers in the colleges must have evened out over the course of many transactions. Also, after the collapse, only small settlements were required, and of these few were made. Even the period of uncertainty about the percentage of settlement required could have had little impact: people with little credit to begin with would not have been affected by a cutoff of credit until the contracts were straightened out.

That the valuable tulips of 1634–37 later either disappeared or became common is typical of the market dynamics for newly developed bulb varieties, as indicated by price pattern for eighteenth-century tulip and hyacinth bulbs and for modern bulbs. As the bulbs propagate, their prices naturally fall with expanding supply; however, the original bulb owner's bulb stock increases. The discounted value of bulb sales can easily justify extremely high prices for the unique bulb of a new variety. Even the magnitudes of prices for valuable bulbs and their patterns of decline are not out of line with later prices for new varieties of rare bulbs. Single bulbs in the eighteenth century commanded prices as high as 1,000 guilders. In this context, the 1,000–2,000-guilder price of Semper Augustus from 1623 to 1625 or even the 5,500-guilder price of 1637 does not appear obviously overvalued.

The only facet of the speculation for which an explanation does not emerge from the evidence is the 1-month price surge for common bulbs in Janaury 1637, when prices rose up to twentyfold. After February 9, 1637, the first price observation for a common bulb, the Witte Croonen, is available only in 1642.[38] Table 3.1 contains the price data for $\frac{1}{2}$ pound of this bulb. From February 1637 to 1642, the price depreciated at an annual rate of 76 percent. As an eighteenth-century benchmark rate, I have used 17 percent per year, the average rate of depreciation of all bulbs priced between fl 10 and fl 71 in table 3. Under the assumption that, after February 1637, Witte Croonen depreciated at this benchmark rate, the price must have collapsed in the crash to 5 percent of its peak price to have attained a 1642 price of fl 37.5. Thus Witte Croonnen prices rose by about 26 times in January 1637 and fell to one-twentieth of their peak value in the first week of February. The eighteenth-century benchmark pattern of price depreciation, however, would have justified a peak price of fl 84, so the January price is not out of line.

That a precipitous price decline for common bulbs occurred is confirmed by observations on Switsers in figure 3.5. The peak price for this bulb of 0.17 guilders per aas was attained on February 5, the apparent peak of the market. Data from notarized contracts on February 6 and 9 indicate a sudden decline to 0.11 guilders per aas. This represents a substantial decline from prices in the first five days of February, but it still substantially exceeds the prices attained on January 23 and is not of the same order of magnitude as the collapse indicated above for Witte Croonen.

Since already valuable bulbs rose by no more than 200–300 percent over a longer duration, the increase and collapse of the relative price of common bulbs are the remarkable feature of this phase of the speculation. Even if detailed, day-to-day information about market events for this period were available, we would be hard-pressed to find a market fundamental explanation for these relative price movements. It is clear that the colleges generated these prices, although they are echoed in some written contracts. As noted earlier, the college futures markets suffered from a lack of internal control over the nature of contracts, which might have encouraged a speculation of this sort. These markets consisted of a collection of people without net worth making ever-increasing numbers of "million-dollar bets" with each other with some knowledge that the state would not enforce the contracts.

VII   Conclusion

An observation that the tulipmania predisposes economists to advance bubble theories of asset pricing provides the point of departure of this study. If small strata of particular episodes underpin the belief that bubbles may exist, it is desirable to undertake a detailed study of these events, most of which have not been examined from the perspective of market fundamental theories of asset pricing, to assure that other reasonable explanations have not been overlooked.

Probably, economists will never form a consensus that a bubble has affected prices in a particular modern market because of the overwhelming clutter of available data and alternative theories. Flood and Garber (1980), Hamilton and Whiteman (1985), and Hamilton (1986) have demonstrated the impossibility of distinguishing empirically between hypotheses that asset price dynamics are driven by a rational speculative bubble and that researchers have not adequately measured the future market fundamentals anticipated by market participants. More generally, data will not distinguish between a claim that market participants suffer from some mania because behavior does not conform to the prediction of some researcher's theory and a claim that the theory is flawed or misspecified. Because of this observational equivalence, economists who take a position in the debate over the existence of bubbles are making a commitment that cannot be based on the analysis of experience.

I have aimed to investigate the nature of the market and of the environment during the tulipmania. While lack of data precludes a solid conclusion, the results of the study indicate that the bulb speculation was not obvious madness, at least for most of the 1634–37 "mania." Only the last month of the speculation for common bulbs remains as a potential bubble, although the nature of the market, the contractual commitments, and the surrounding events are unclear enough that one could seriously embrace one side of the fundamentals versus bubble dispute only on the basis of strong prior beliefs.

I suspect that careful study of other purported bubbles will lead to similar conclusions. Ironically, theories of rational asset pricing do not generally preclude bubbles. A precondition for the existence of a rational bubble is the belief that a bubble can exist. The ancient examples usually cited may not themselves have been bubbles. Yet if market participants now believe that these historical events prove the existence of bubbles, rational bubbles can emerge in asset markets.

Notes

I am grateful to Herschel Grossman, Robert Hodrick, Susan Gentleman, Salih Neftci, David Ribar, Rudiger Dornbusch, and James Peck for useful discussions; to Guido Imbens for resourceful research assistance; and to Marina van Dongen for helpful translations. Librarians at Harvard's Houghton, Kress, Arnold Arboretum, and Grey Herbarium Libraries and at the Massachusetts Horticultural Society provided valuable guidance. I have benefited from the comments of three anonymous referees and from participants in workshops at Brown University, the Board of Governors of the Federal Reserve, City University of New York, Columbia University, Queen's University, University of California, Los Angeles, Massachusetts Institute of Technology, and Northwestern. I have received support for this research from National Science Foundation grant SES-8606425.

1. The Mississippi and South Sea bubbles are the other two examples that appear on everyone's short list; these provide yet another synonym for speculative mania. Samuelson (1957) uses "tulipmania" interchangeably with "Ponzi scheme," "chain letter," and "bubble."

2. Economists have placed numerous historical and contemporary episodes in the "bubble" category. For example, Kindleberger (1978) catalogs a long sequence of financial panics and manias and provides a descriptive pathology of their dynamics. Blanchard and Watson (1982) found evidence that can be interpreted as an indication of a bubble in gold markets. Recently, West (1984) and Shiller (1987) have interpreted stock market behavior as potential bubbles or fads, and Mankiw, Romer, and Shapiro (1985) and Summers (1986) have questioned hypotheses either that asset prices reflect fundamental values or that markets price assets efficiently. Shiller and Pound (1986) have proposed a contagion model of psychological forces in determining asset prices. Economists studying exchange rate determination such as Dornbusch (1982), Woo (1984), Krugman (1985), Evans (1986), Frankel and Froot (1986), and Meese (1986) have argued that recent market values of the dollar may have been driven by a speculative bubble. Major conferences and journal volumes are now devoted to the study of how crowd psychology affects asset prices. Other researchers, however, have found no evidence of bubbles in a variety of asset markets. For an extensive review of this burgeoning literature, see Camerer (1987).

3. Mackay's first edition appeared in 1841. Wirth (1858) adds little that was not presented in Mackay. P. T. Barnum (1865) plagiarized his description of the episode from Mackay without attribution.

4. The guilder was the unit of account. It was denoted by the sign fl (florin) and was divided into 20 stuivers. The stuiver was further subdivided into 16 pennings. The guilder was a bimetallic unit, equivalent to 10.75 g of fine silver from 1610 to 1614, 10.28 g from 1620 to 1659, and 9.74 g thereafter (see Posthumus 1964, p. cxv; Rich and Wilson 1975, p. 458). Its gold content was 0.867 g of fine gold in 1612, 0.856 g in 1622, 0.77 g in 1638, and 0.73 g in 1645 (see Posthumus 1964, p. cxix). Prices of foodstuffs, metals, and fibers did not display significant secular movements from 1600 through 1750; so given the orders of magnitude of bulb price changes that we will observe, we can take the price level as approximately constant in interpreting nominal prices during this 150-year period.

5. Note the implausibility of a Dutch businessman's leaving a highly valuable bulb lying about for a loutish sailor to eat for lunch or for a presumptuous English experimenter to dissect.

6. He presents no evidence of the sources and quantity of these foreign funds.

7. Bernard Baruch wrote an introduction to Mackay's book, whose reprinting he had encouraged, emphasizing the importance of crowd psychology in all economic movements. Dreman (1977), who also stresses psychological forces in asset price determination, uses the tulipmania as a prototype of market mania. Relating the same anecdotes as Mackay, he invokes the tulipmania as a constant metaphor in discussions of succeeding major speculative collapses. He states that "if, for example, my neighbor tried to sell me a tulip bulb for $5,000, I'd simply laugh at him.... The tulip craze, like the manias we shall see shortly, created its own reality as it went along. It is ludicrous to pay as much for a flower as one pays for a house" (p. 52). Whenever large and rapid fluctuations of asset prices occur, the popular media recall the tulipmania. For example, when gold prices jumped in 1979, a *Wall Street Journal* (September 26, 1979) article stated that "the ongoing frenzy in the gold market may be only an illusion of crowds, a modern repetition of the tulip-bulb craze or the South Sea Bubble." The October 19, 1987, stock market crash brought forth similar comparisons from the *Wall Street Journal* (December 11, 1987), and the *Economist* (Octobe 24, 1987) explained the event as follows: "The crash suffered by the world's stockmarkets has provided a beginning and middle for a new chapter updating Charles Mackay's 1841 book 'Extraordinary Popular Delusions and the Madness of Crowds' which chronicled Dutch tulip bulbs, the South Sea bubble.... It was the madness of crowds that sent the bull market ever upward.... It is mob psychology that has now sent investors so rapidly for the exits" (p. 75). Malkiel (1985) extensively cites Mackay in his chapter "The Madness of Crowds," including the anecdote about the sailor and the claim that the collapse led to a prolonged depression in Holland. In reference to other speculative episodes, he asks, "Why do such speculative crazes seem so isolated from the lessons of history? I have no apt answer to offer, but I am convinced that Bernard Baruch was correct in suggesting that a study of these events can help equip investors for survival. The consistent losers in the market, from my personal experience, are those who are unable to resist being swept up in some kind of tulip-bulb craze" (pp. 44–45).

8. *Palgrave's Dictionary* (1926, p. 182) includes a paragraph on tulips in its section on bubbles, citing Mackay. In his well-known study of manias, Kindleberger (1978) does not include the tulipmania among those episodes examined in detail because "manias such as ... the tulip mania of 1634 are too isolated and lack the characteristic monetary features that

come with the spread of banking" (p. 6). In his article on "bubbles" in the *New Palgrave* (1987), however, Kindleberger includes the tulipmania as one of the two most famous manias.

9. Samuelson (1957, 1967) presents the tulipmania metaphor and associates it with "the purely financial dream world of indefinite group self-fulfillment" (1967, p. 230). Students of Samuelson, in a flurry of research activity concerning the "Hahn problem," employ the tulipmania as an empirical motivation. Shell and Stiglitz (1967, p. 593) state that "the instability of the Hahn model is suggestive of the economic forces operating during 'speculative booms' like the Tulip Bulb mania." Burmeister (1980, pp. 264–86) summarizes these models.

10. For example, Azariadis (1981, p. 380) argues that "the evidence on the influence of subjective factors is ample and dates back several centuries; the Dutch 'tulip mania,' the South Sea bubble in England, and the collapse of the Mississippi Company in France are three well-documented cases of speculative price movements which historians consider unwarranted by 'objective' conditions." More recently, Azariadis and Guesnerie (1986, p. 725) state that "the reading of economic historians may suggest that these factors (sunspots) have some pertinence for the explanation of phenomena like the Dutch tulipmania in the seventeenth century and the Great Depression in our own." Under the topic "tulipmania" in the *New Palgrave* (1987), Calvo does not refer to the seventeenth-century Dutch speculative episode at all. Rather, he defines tulipmania as a situation in which asset prices do not behave in ways explainable by economic fundamentals. He develops examples of rational bubbles, of both the explosive and "sunspot" varieties.

11. In his presidential address to the American Finance Association, Van Horne (1985) embraces the possibility of bubbles and manias and as an example refers explicitly to the tulipmania, in which a "single bulb sold for many years' salary" (p. 627). In a series of papers, Shiller (1984, 1987) and Shiller and Pound (1986) have promoted the hypothesis that asset prices are driven by crowd behavior or fads. Shiller (1987) argues that the standard and accurate view, until the last few decades, has been that asset markets are driven by capricious investors acting on the basis of fads and bubbles. As one example, he provides a quotation of one of Mackay's descriptions of the high prices paid for tulips during the mania.

12. Beckmann wrote originally in German at the end of the eighteenth century; only the fourth English edition (1846) of his book was available to me. Beckmann, the original source of the two anecdotes referred to in the previous section, cites Blainville (1743) as his source for the story of the Englishman. A careful reading of Blainville turns up only a one-sentence report that a tulip speculation occurred from 1634 to 1637 in what is otherwise a baroque travelogue of Haarlem. Indeed, Blainville's description of his travels through Holland was a diary of a tour made in 1705, 70 years after the speculation. For the sailor story, Beckmann mentions that the incident occurred while John Balthasar Schuppe (1610–61) was in Holland, without other reference. However, the context of the paragraph in which the story appears seems to indicate that it happened after the tulip speculation. Mackay, who greatly dramatizes both stories, cites Blainville as the source for both, obviously without having researched beyond Beckmann.

13. These pamphlets were motivated by a moralistic attack against speculation by the authorities, as were all of the numerous pamphlets that appeared immediately after the end of the episode. For a list of these pamphlets, see the references in Krelage (1942, 1946).

14. Mackay must have recorded Beckman's reference to Munting without examining the Munting text.

15. These were published in the *Weekblad voor bloembollencultur* and are reprinted in van Damme (1976).

16. Since many of the prices in Gaergoedt and Waermondt are also on the earlier auction list, it provides a key confirmation of the validity of the prices in the dialogues.

17. Hartmann and Kester (1983, p. 499) state that the time before flowering of a bulb less than 5 cm in diameter is three years, of a bulb from 5 to 7 cm is two years, and of a bulb greater than 8 cm is one year.

18. Although seventeenth-century florists thought that breaking was a normal stage in the maturing process of breeder bulbs (the stock of bulbs vulnerable to attack by the virus), theories arose that broken tulips were diseased. For example, la Chesnee Monstereul (1654), contrasting the theory of breaking as "self-perfection" with a disease theory, noted that broken bulbs had smaller bulb and stem sizes and that they never produced more than three buds.

19. Almost all bulbs traded in the tulipmania have by now completely disappeared. For example, the Royal General Bulbgrowers Society's (1969) classification of thousands of actively grown tulips mentions such important bulbs of the tulip speculation as Admirael Liefkens, Admirael van der Eyck, Paragon Liefkens, Semper Augustus, and Viceroy only as historically important names. The only bulbs still grown were the Gheele Croonen and Lack van Rijn, despised in the 1630s as common flowers except at the height of the speculation. Even these bulbs are currently grown only by collectors.

20. Though it is now known that the mosaic virus is spread by aphids, methods of encouraging breaking were not well understood in the seventeenth century. Gaergoedt and Waermondt suggested grafting half a bulb of a broken tulip to half a bulb of an unbroken tulip to cause breaking (van Slogteren 1960, p. 27). La Chesnee Monstereul (1654, p. 163) states that the art of "speeding transformation" was controversial among florists. D'Ardène (1759, pp. 198–217) devotes a chapter to breaking in tulips, shedding little light on methods to encourage breaking.

21. Most of the remainder of this section is reconstructed from the discussions in Posthumus 91929) and Krelage (1942, 1946).

22. In France, it became fashionable for women to array quantities of fresh tulips at the tops of their gowns. Wealthy men competed to present the most bizarre flowers to eligible women, thereby driving up the demand for rare flowers. Munting (1696, p. 911) claims that at the time of the speculation a single *flower* of a particular broken tulip was sold for 1,000 guilders in Paris.

23. Posthumus (1929) translates the stuiver as a "penny," but it is clear from the context that he means stuivers and not pennings ($= 1/16$ stuiver).

24. See Munting (1672, p. 636) for a description of the types of bets undertaken by his father. All discussions of the tulipmania openly criticize the activity of buying or selling for future delivery without current possession of the commodity sold or an intention to effect delivery. They attack futures markets as a means of creating artificial risk and do not consider their role in marketing existing risks.

25. Data for a large number of observed prices for many varieties of bulbs plus descriptions of the data are compiled in a data appendix available on request from the author. These figures consist of data gathered from auctions, contracts recorded with notaries, and the Gaergoedt and Waermondt dialogues. Data in figures 3.5–3.8 are in terms of guilders per

aas for standardized weights of pound goods, but data in figures 3.2–3.4 are for individual bulbs, which vary in weight from 3 to many hundred azen. Particularly, figure 3.4 is a combination of prices for buds and for mature bulbs.

26. Others are more difficult to classify, encompassing different deals in which either odd weights or standard weights appear.

27. Even the precollapse legal status of the futures contracts was unclear. Early price manipulation and bear raids in East India Co. shares led to legal bans on short sales on the Amsterdam exchange in 1610. Future sales were permitted only to individuals already holding the shares to be delivered. In edicts of 1621, 1630, and 1636, the ban was reiterated and buyers of a short contract could legally repudiate the agreement. Whether the ban applied to traders on the new tulip futures market is unclear. Ultimately the courts did not uphold any contracts for tulips, but local attempts at settlement were made. See Penso de la Vega (1688) on the effects of this ban on short sales of stock.

28. This was a return to the pre-1634 situation. Prior to 1634 only a handful of prices are available from recorded sales contracts: a pair of bulbs from 1612 reported by Posthumus (1929) in his contract nos. 3 and 4; a 1625 sale of three bulbs; and a 1633 sale of a pair of bulbs, both reported in Posthumus (1934). Even the series in fig. I for the Semper Augustus is based on undocumented stories emanating from the historical authority Wassenaer in the 1620s, as reported by Solms-Laubach (1899, p. 77). among others.

29. This total was not broken down into individual bulb prices. For those few bulbs sold in which the estate held a fractional interest, however, the sales prices were reported (p. 111); one Tulpa Meerman, fl 430; one Vrouge Brantson, fl 25; one Verspreijt, one Vroege Brantson, and one-quarter interest in an English Admiral, fl 582; and one General Rotgans fl 138. In addition, in the records detailing the settling of the estate's accounts, there is a list of 1643 cash expenditures for bulbs purchased in 1642: $\frac{1}{2}$ pound Witte Croonen, fl 37 st 10; one Admirael van der Eyck and one outgrowth of an English Admiral, fl 225; and one English Admiral, fl 210.

30. While price data disappeared, at least the names of the important tulips from the speculation remained current thirty-two years after the collapse. Van der Groen (1669) mentions the important tulips that a fashionable garden might hold. Among them were Vroege Bleyenberger, Parragon Grebber, Gheel ende Roote van Leyden, Admirael van Enchuysen, Brabanson, Senecours, Admirael de Man, Coorenaerts, Jan Gerritz, Gouda, Saeyblom, Switsers, Parragon Liefkens, and Semper Augustus.

31. Van Damme (1976) reproduces numerous announcements of bulb sales and auctions printed in such periodicals as the *Haarlemscher courant* in the latter half of the seventeenth century, but there is no record of prices generated in the auctions.

32. These prices come from several sources. Krelage (1946) reproduces tulip lists from auctions on May 17, 1707, in the Hague (p. 542) and on May 16, 1708, in Rotterdam (p. 541), on which a participant fortuitously annotated the final sales prices. While the 1707 auction list contains 84 different bulb names and that of 1708 contains 12, no bulb name of the hundreds commonly traded in 1637 appears in the lists. Krelage reproduces only the first page of the 1708 price list. The entire list was sold to British buyers with the breakup of Krelage's library, and I have been unable to examine it as yet. Bradley (1728) reproduces the 1722 bulb catalog of a Haarlem florist. The majority of the hundreds of bulbs in this catalog were offered at prices of less than one guilder, and only one, Superintendant Roman, sold for 100 guilders. The list, however, does contain prices for twenty-five bulbs that appeared in the 1637 tulip speculation. Krelage (1946) also reproduces a 1739 Haarlem price

catalog of hyacinth and tulip bulbs. Of its several hundred different bulbs, only six names match those of bulbs traded in 1637. Interestingly, it offers Semper Augustus bulbs for 0.1 guilders.

33. None of the bulbs on the 1739 list carried a price greater than 8 guilders, while most prices were much lower. Rare and valuable bulbs would not appear on a standard dealer's list. Conversely, auctions would not likely bother with common, inexpensive bulbs. Since the 1637 rare bulbs had become common by 1707, it is not surprising that their names disappeared from auction lists.

34. For example, Roi de Fleurs would be counted as rare when its price was fl 251 in 1707. By 1722, its price was fl 10, so it would no longer be considered rare. The price declined between 1707 and 1722 by 96 percent, and the average annual decline was 21.5 percent. This 21.5 percent annual decline was averaged with similarly computed declines for other rare bulbs to produce an overall average.

35. A speculation similar to that for tulips occurred from 1734 to 1739, leading to the production of reprints of Gaergoedt and Waermondt as a warning against unconstrained financial contracting. Table 3.4 indicates the magnitude of the price declines for a few of the more expensive bulbs during the hyacinth mania. The price declined to as low as 10 percent of 1735 prices in some cases was of similar magnitude to the 1637 crash for common tulip bulbs.

36. Economic histories of the important events and institutions in the Netherlands during this period are detailed, but they hardly mention the tulip speculation. For example, *The Cambridge Economic History of Europe*, vols. 4 and 5 (Rich and Wilson 1975, 1977), does not mention tulips, though the seventeenth-century Dutch are the leading players in these narratives. The period is characterized as a sequence of Dutch commercial and financial triumphs, and economic distress seems not to have materialized in the Netherlands until after the Thirty Years' War ended in 1648. Cooper (1970, p. 100) does mention the tulip speculation in one sentence as an example of the speculative proclivity of the Dutch during this period. Schama (1987) provides a detailed discussion of the events based primarily on Posthumus and Krelage, but he does not depart from the standard interpretation of the mania.

37. Krelage (1946, p. 498) states that all florists in Haarlem maintained their gardens within the city walls until the second half of the eighteenth century. Gardens could be small since concentrations of large numbers of identical flowers were not valued highly, unlike current fashion.

38. Claims that prices dropped to less than 10 percent of peak values after the crash must have originated in the officially proposed 3.5 percent contract settlement fee. This did not necessarily reflect the true price decline but simply provided a means of relieving buyers of most of their losses. Since they never cite a specific transaction price (none exists from trades immediately after the crash), I presume that authors citing massive price falls inferred them from the percentages proposed for contract buy-outs.

References

Anonymous. *Samen-spraeck tusschen Waermondt ende Gaergoedt: Flora*. Haarlem, 1637. Reprinted in *Economisch-historisch jaarboek* 12 (1926): 20–43.

———. *Tweede samen-spraeck tusschen Waermondt ende Gaergoedt*. Amsterdam, 1643. (a) Reprinted in Economisch-historisch jaarboek 12 (1926): 44–69.

————. *Register den de prijsen der bloemen ... derde samen-spraeck....* Amsterdam, 1643. *(b)* Reprinted in *Economisch-historisch jaarboek* 12 (1926): 70–95.

Azariadis, Costas. "Self-fulfilling Prophecies," *J. Econ. Theory* 25 (December 1981): 380–96.

Azariadis, Costas, and Guesnerie, Roger. "Sunspots and Cycles." *Rev. Econ. Studies* 53 (October 1986): 725–37.

Barnum, P. T. *The Humbugs of the World.* New York: Carleton, 1865. Reprint. Detroit: Singing Tree Press, 1970.

Beckmann, Johann. *A History of Inventions, Discoveries, and Origins.* 4th ed. 2 vols. London: Bohn, 1846.

Blainville, J. de. *Travels through Holland, Germany, Switzerland, and Other Parts of Europe, but Especially Italy.* London: Straham, 1743.

Blanchard, Olivier J., and Watson, Mark W. "Bubbles, Rational Expectations, and Financial Markets." In *Crises in the Economic and Financial Structure,* edited by Paul Wachtel. Lexington, Mass.: Lexington, 1982.

Bradley, Richard R. *Dictionarium Botanicum; or a Botanical Dictionary for the Use of the Curious in Husbandry and Gardening.* London: Woodward and Peel, 1728.

Burmeister, Edwin. *Capital Theory and Dynamics.* Cambridge: Cambridge Univ. Press, 1980.

Camerer, Colin. "Bubbles and Fads in Asset Prices: A Review of Theory and Evidence." Manuscript. Philadelphia: Univ. Pennsylvania, Wharton School, April 1987.

La Chesnee Monstereul. *Le Floriste François.* Caen: Mangeant, 1654.

Cooper, J. P. *New Cambridge Modern History.* Vol. 4. *The Decline of Spain and the Thirty Years War, 1609–48/59.* Cambridge: Cambridge Univ. Press, 1970.

d'Ardène, Jean-Paul. *Traité des tulipes.* Avignon: Chambeau, 1759.

Doorenbos, J. "Notes on the History of Bulb Breeding in the Netherlands." *Euphytica* 3 (February 1954): 1–11.

Dornbusch, Rudiger. "Equilibrium and Disequilibrium Exchange Rates." *Zeitschrift für Wirtschafts- und Sozialwissenschaften* 102, no. 6 (1982): 573–99.

Dreman, David N. *Psychology and the Stock Market: Investment Strategy beyond Random Walk.* New York: AMACOM, 1977.

Evans, George W. "A Test for Speculative Bubbles in the Sterling-Dollar Exchange Rate: 1981–84." *A.E.R.* 76 (September 1986): 621–36.

Flood, Robert P., and Garber, Peter M. "Market Fundamentals versus Price-Level Bubbles: The First Tests." *J.P.E.* 88 (August 1980): 745–70.

Frankel, Jeffrey A., and Froot, Kenneth A. "The Dollar as a Speculative Bubble: A Tale of Fundamentalists and Chartists." Working Paper no. 1854. Cambridge, Mass.: NBER, 1986.

Hamilton, James D. "On Testing for Self-fulfilling Speculative Price Bubbles." *Internat. Econ. Rev.* 27 (October 1986): 545–52.

Hamilton, James D., and Whiteman, Charles H. "The Observable Implications of Self-fulfilling Expectations." *J. Monetary Econ.* 16 (November 1985): 353–73.

Hartmann, H. T., and Kester, Dale E. *Plant Propagation: Principles and Practices*. 4th ed. Englewood Cliffs, N.J.: Prentice-Hall, 1983.

Kindleberger, Charles P. *Manias, Panics, and Crashes: A History of Financial Crises*. New York: Basic Books, 1978.

Krelage, Ernst H. *Bloemenspeculatie in Nederland*. Amsterdam: van kampen, 1942.

————. *Drie eeuwen bloembollenexport*. The Hague: Rijksuitgeverij, 1946.

Krugman, Paul R. "Is the Strong Dollar Sustainable?" Working Paper no. 1644. Cambridge, Mass.: NBER, 1985.

"Liste van einige tulpaen." *Economisch-historisch jaarboek* 12 (1926): 96–99.

Mackay, Charles. *Memoirs of Extraordinary Popular Delusions and the Madness of Crowds*. 2d ed. 2 vols. London: Office Nat. Illustrated Library, 1852.

Malkiel, Burton G. *A Random Walk down Wall Street*. 4th ed. New York: Norton, 1985.

Mankiw, N. Gregory; Romer, David; and Shapiro, Matthew D. "An Unbiased Reexamination of Stock Market Volatility." *J. Finance* 40 (July 1985): 677–87.

Mather, John C. *Commercial Production of Tulips and Daffodils*. London: Collingridge, 1961.

Meese, Richard A. "Testing for Bubbles in exchange Markets: The Case of Sparkling Rates?" *J.P.E.* 94 (April 1986): 345–73.

Munting, Abraham. *Waare oeffening der planten*. Amsterdam: Rieuwertsz, 1672.

————. *Naauwkeurige beschryving der aardgewassen*. Leiden: Vander Aa, 1696.

The New Palgrave: A Dictionary of Economics, edited by John Eatwell, Murray Milgate, and Peter Newman. 4 vols. London: Macmillan, 1987.

Palgrave's Dictionary of Political Economy, edited by Henry Higgs. 3 vols. London: Macmillan, 1926.

Penso de la Vega, Josef. *Confusion de confusiones*. Amsterdam, 1688.

Posthumus, Nicolaas W. "Die speculatie in tulpen in de jaren 1636 en 1637." Parts 1–3. *Economisch-historisch jaarboek* 12 (1926): 3–19; 13 (1927): 1–85; 18(1934): 229–40.

————. "The Tulip Mania in Holland in the Years 1636 and 1637." *J. Econ. and Bus. Hist.* 1 (May 1929): 434–55.

————. *Inquiry into the History of Prices in Holland*. Leiden: Brill, 1964.

Rich, E. E., and Wilson, C. H., eds. *The Cambridge Economic History of Europe*. Vol. 4. *The Economy of Expanding Europe in the Sixteenth and Seventeenth Centuries*. Vol. 5. *The Economic Organization of Early Modern Europe*. Cambridge: Cambridge Univ. Press, 1975, 1977.

The Royal General Bulbgrowers Society. *Classified List and International Register of Tulip Names*. Haarlem: Royal General Bulbgrowers Soc., 1969.

Samuelson, Paul A. "Intertemporal Price Equilibrium: A Prologue to the Theory of Speculation." *Weltwirtschaftliches Archiv* 79, no. 2 (1957): 181–219. Reprinted in *The Collected Scientific Papers of Paul A. Samuelson*, vol. 2, edited by Joseph E. Stiglitz. Cambridge, Mass.: MIT Press, 1966.

————. "Indeterminacy of Development in a Heterogeneous-Capital Model with Constant Saving Propensity," In *Essays on the Theory of Optimal Economic Growth*, edited by Karl Shell. Cambridge, Mass.: MIT Press, 1967.

Schama, Simon. *The Embarrassment of Riches: An Interpretation of Dutch Culture in the Golden Age*. New York: Knopf, 1987.

Shell, Karl, and Stiglitz, Joseph E. "The Allocation of Investment in a Dynamic Economy." *Q.J.E.* 81 (November 1967): 592–609.

Shiller, Robert J., "Stock Prices and Social Dynamics." *Brookings Papers Econ. Activity*, no. 2 (1984), pp. 457–98.

————. "Fashions, Fads and Bubbles in Financial Markets." In *Knights, Raiders and Targets: The Impact of Hostile Takeover*, edited by Jack Coffee. Oxford: Oxford Univ. Press, 1987.

Shiller, Robert J., and Pound, John. "Survey Evidence on Diffusion of Interest among Institutional Investors." Discussion Paper no. 794. New Haven, Conn.: Yale Univ., Cowles Found., May 1986.

Smith, Kenneth M. *Textbook of Plant Virus Diseases*. London: Churchill, 1937.

Solms-Laubach, Hermann. *Weizen und Tulpe und deren Geschichte*. Leipzig: Felix, 1899.

Summers, Lawrence H. "Do We Really Know That Financial Markets Are Efficient?" Discussion Paper no. 1237. Cambridge, Mass.: Harvard Univ., Inst. Econ. Res., May 1986.

van Damme, A. *Aanteekeningen betreffende de geschiedenis der bloembollen, Haarlem 1899–1903*. Leiden: Boerhaave, 1976.

van der Groen, J. *Le jardinier Hollandais*. Amsterdam: Doornick, 1669.

Van Horne, J. C. "Of Financial Innovations and Excesses." *J. Finance* 40 (July 1985): 621–31.

van Slogteren, E. "Broken Tulips." In *The Daffodil and Tulip Yearbook*. London: Royal Horticultural Soc., 1960.

West, Kenneth D. "Speculative Bubbles and Stock Price Volatility." Financial Research Memorandum no. 54. Princeton, N.J.: Princeton Univ., December 1984.

Wirth, Max *Geschichte des Handelskrisen*. Frankfurt, 1858.

Woo, W. "Speculative Bubbles in the Foreign Exchange Markets." Discussion Paper in International Economics no. 13. Washington: Brookings Inst., 1984.

4   On Testing for Speculative Bubbles

Robert P. Flood and
Robert J. Hodrick

The possibility that movements in prices could be due to the self-fulfilling prophecies of market participants has long intrigued observers of free markets. Such self-fulfilling prophecies are often called "bubbles" or "sunspots" to denote their dependence on events that are extraneous to the market. The folklore of such episodes includes the tulip bubble, the South Sea bubble and the Mississippi bubble and the increase in equity prices during the "Roaring '20s" followed by the 1929 crash. More recently, the rise and crash of stock prices from 1982 to 1987, the appreciation of the dollar on foreign exchange markets that peaked in 1985, and sudden housing price increases in California and Massachusetts have been attributed to speculative bubbles. The idea that bubbles might exist is often traced to John Maynard Keynes's (1936) description of an equity market as an environment in which speculators anticipate "what average opinion expects average opinion to be," rather than focusing on things fundamental to the market.

If bubbles exist in asset markets, market prices of assets will differ from their fundamental values. Markets would not necessarily be allocating the savings of individuals to the best possible investment uses. Public policies might be designed to attempt to rid the markets of bubbles. Although these problems have been discussed for a long time, academic economists conducted relatively little formal empirical analysis of actual markets until recently, probably because economists' analytical and statistical tools were inadequate. Since economic theory placed essentially no restrictions on how agents formed expectations of future prices, empirical analysts had little direction for studying the possibility of self-fulfilling prophecy. The widespread adoption of the rational expectations hypothesis provided the required underpinning for theoretical and empirical study of the issues.[1]

This chapter surveys the current state of the empirically oriented literature concerning rational dynamic indeterminacies, by which we mean a situation of self-fulfilling prophecy within a rational expectations model. Empirical work in this area concentrates primarily on indeterminacies in price levels, exchange rates and equity prices.[2] To provide a common ground for later analysis, we first examine a particular type of explosive indeterminacy, usually called a rational bubble, in an example of the market for equities. Then, we consider empirical work relating to price-level and exchange-rate indeterminacies and empirical studies of indeterminacies in stock prices. Finally, we take up some interpretive issues.

Some Intuition about Rational Bubbles

Many rational expectations models have an indeterminate aspect, as explained by William Brock (1974), John Taylor (1977), and Robert Shiller (1978). Usually, this indeterminacy arises when the current decisions of agents depend both on the current market price and on their expectation of future prices. For example, consider a simple economic model in which investors' demands for an equity depend on the expected return on the equity. If a fixed amount of the equity is outstanding, the current price is determined by the intersection of investor demands with the existing supply. But, equilibrium demand depends upon the current equity price and the beliefs of agents about equity prices in the future, since realized returns depend on the cost of the equity today, on its resale value in the future and on any intermediate dividends paid to holders of the stock. Since the current price depends on the expectation of the future price and the expectation of the future price depends on the current price, the simple theory cannot determine the market price. It only determines sequences of prices. Only one sequence is the market fundamental price path, and the others will have price bubbles.

In such circumstances, economic models require additional restrictions if they are to make firm predictions about the current market price. If plausible theoretical restrictions are added to the model, it is possible for a researcher to exclude a large number of price paths, narrowing the field to a unique path. For example, Jean Tirole (1985) demonstrates that real asset prices will be unique and will depend only on market fundamentals in an economy with a finite number of rational infinitely lived traders.[3] Since the assumption of infinitely-lived agents is controversial, some economists find this antibubble logic uncompelling. Tirole (1985) also explores an overlapping generations model of real asset pricing that does not exclude explosive indeterminacies as equilibrium phenomena, but he finds that they occur only if the rate of growth of the economy is higher than the steady state rate of return on capital. Price-level models that are consistent with many researchers' prior beliefs but that still fail to exclude explosive indeterminacies are discussed by William Brock (1974) and subsequently by Maurice Obstfeld and Kenneth Rogoff (1983, 1986). Interestingly, explosive price level indeterminacies are much harder to rule out with a priori theoretical arguments than are indeterminacies concerning real asset prices. Nonexplosive indeterminacies in rational expectations models, which we call sunspots, are even harder to rule out with theoretical arguments than are explosive indeterminacies.

Many researchers argue that empirical tests for bubbles and sunspots are uninteresting because they can be ruled out by certain types of rational economic theories. Should these researchers still be interested in empirical tests of bubbles? We answer yes, primarily because bubble tests are an interesting specification test of the model. Since bubbles and sunspots arise in economic models that incorporate market fundamentals, tests for these indeterminacies require correct specification of market fundamentals. Bubble tests examine a composite null hypothesis of no bubbles and correctly specified market fundamentals, which must be construed broadly to be both the data series and the equations that constitute the economic model. Since bubble tests can only legitimately be done on models that are not rejected by the data, researchers must first conduct a battery of diagnostic tests. Bubble tests may be powerful at detecting misspecifications of the model, even if it has passed other specification tests.

It is our contention that no econometric test has yet demonstrated that bubbles are present in the data. In each case, misspecification of the model or alternative market fundamentals seems the likely explanation of the findings.

A Common Theoretical Framework for Analyzing Bubbles

If people in the economy are not averse to risk, and if they discount future utility at a constant rate r, all assets would have the same constant expected real return in equilibrium. The price of one equity share, q_t, which is the sacrifice that is made to purchase the asset, would be equal to the expected discounted present value of the dividend accruing to ownership of the equity share during the ownership period, d_{t+1}, plus the price at which the share can be sold at the end of the ownership period, q_{t+1}. These are the benefits from owning the asset. Hence,

$$q_t = E_t(d_{t+1} + q_{t+1})/(1 + r), \tag{1}$$

where $E_t(d_{t+1} + q_{t+1})$ denotes the expected value of the future dividend and the future price conditional on information available to people at time t. A typical asset pricing formula can be derived from equation (1) by a recursive process. Update equation (1) by one time period and substitute the resulting expression for q_{t+1} into the original equation. This gives

$$q_t = E_t[d_{t+1} + E_{t+1}(d_{t+2} + q_{t+2})/(1 + r)]/(1 + r). \qquad (2)$$

Then, update equation (1) again, and substitute for q_{t+2} into equation (2). Do this repeatedly. Next, use the law of iterated expectations, $E_t(E_{t+1}(d_{t+2})) = E_t(d_{t+2})$, which recognizes that the expected value today of what we will expect about the future when we have more information tomorrow is simply what we expect about the future today with less information. The eventual result with an infinite number of substitutions is that the current price equals the expected present value of all future dividends:

$$q_t^f = \sum_{i=1}^{\infty} [1/(1 + r)]^i E_t(d_{t+i}). \qquad (3)$$

We attach a superscript f to this price because we define it to be the *market fundamentals price* for this model since we assumed in its derivation that the discounted value of the expected price infinitely far in the future is zero.

Equation (3), however, does not give the only mathematical solution to equation (1). To characterize other solutions let the market price be the fundamentals price plus something else that we will call a bubble, which we denote with B_t:

$$q_t = q_t^f + B_t. \qquad (4)$$

A bubble thus represents a deviation of the current market price of the asset from the value implied by market fundamentals. If the market price in equation (4) is to satisfy equation (1), the current value of the bubble must be the expected discounted value of the future bubble next period. That is,

$$B_t = E_t(B_{t+1})/(1 + r). \qquad (5)$$

This shows that a bubble can be a possible outcome of this model, as long as the bubble represents an expectation that the bubble will continue. Apparently, market prices can be sternly sensible or very silly indeed. The definition of a bubble is sometimes rewritten as:

$$B_{t+1} = B_t(1 + r) + b_{t+1} \qquad (6)$$

where $b_{t+1} = B_{t+1} - E_t(B_{t+1})$. According to the terminology adopted by Olivier Blanchard (1979), Robert Flood and Peter Garber (1980b) and Blanchard and Mark Watson (1982), B_t is a bubble in the equity price, and b_{t+1} is the innovation in the bubble at time $t + 1$ which has mean zero. Hence, if bubbles exist, they must be expected to grow at the real rate of interest.[4]

Theory is helpful in thinking about whether terms like B_t can exist in rational markets. For example, William Brock (1982) notes that if the researcher thinks that the market can be analyzed by considering the maximization problem of a competitive, representative, infinitely-lived investor, there is a terminal condition (known as a transversality condition) that allows the analyst to deduce that rational bubbles are absent.[5]

To understand why this prevents bubbles from occurring, consider the consequences of several investment strategies available to a competitive agent. First, since the representative agent lives forever, one possible investment is the buy and hold forever strategy. This produces a marginal gain at time t equal to the expected discounted value of all future dividends, which is the market fundamentals price. If the actual price of the asset were less than the fundamentals price, the representative agent could increase utility by buying the asset and planning to hold it forever. This increased demand would raise the market price, eliminating the bubble. On the other hand, if an asset's price exceeded the market fundamentals price, rational competitive agents would sell the asset because the utility gain would exceed the utility lost from expecting to hold it forever. The decrease in demand would cause the market price to fall.

Thus, if one is willing to argue for a representative investor model, then a test for bubbles is a test of the underlying model; and a rejection of the hypothesis that no bubbles exist is a rejection of the representative investor model, including the transversality condition.

Another theoretical argument against bubbles is provided by Behzad Diba and Herschel Grossman (1987, 1988) who note that bubbles in real stock prices can never be negative. From equation (5), which provides the time path of a bubble, a negative bubble at time t would be expected to grow more negative over time. From equation (4), this implies that the market stock price would be expected to be negative within finite time, since the market fundamentals price cannot grow that fast. Since you can always walk away from your investment in the stock market, the stock price cannot be negative. Hence, negative bubbles are inconsistent with rational expectations. Ruling out negative bubbles is important since it implies that if a bubble ever is zero it cannot start again because the innovation in the bubble, b_{t+1}, which must have mean zero, would not be mean zero since there would only be one way to go. Hence, any bubbles currently present would have had to start at the initiation of the market.

Most of the empirical work on bubbles is concerned with the theoretical indeterminacy introduced above. The next two sections explore the empirical implications of this type of indeterminacy in two settings: models of price levels and exchange rates and of equity pricing.

Price-Level Bubble Tests

We now turn our attention to price-level bubble tests because they were the first empirical tests, and methodological advances were built upon them. Indeterminacies in theoretical models of the price level usually result when the demand for nominal assets depends on the expected rate of inflation. Robert Flood and Peter Garber (1980b) developed an empirical test for such bubbles in a monetary model of the German hyperinflation first studied by Phillip Cagan (1956). Their model consists of a money demand equation that is linear in natural logarithms, a money supply rule, and money market equilibrium. The equation for money market equilibrium that combines supply and demand is

$$m_t - p_t = \beta - \alpha[E_t(p_{t+1}) - p_t] + v_t, \qquad \alpha > 0. \tag{7}$$

The left-hand side of this equation represents the logarithm of actual real money supply with m_t equal to the logarithm of the nominal money supply at time t and p_t equal to the logarithm of the price level at time t. The right-hand side of the equation states that the demand for real money balances deviates from a constant level β when there is expected inflation, which decreases the demand for money, or when other determinants given by the random error term v_t change. The parameter α measures the sensitivity of the demand for money with respect to expectations of inflation. The equation is simple because the determinants of money demand other than expected inflation are thought to be effectively constant in a hyperinflation.

The "market fundamentals" solution for the price level can be found by analogy to the previous example of equity prices. In this case, the general price level p_t plays the role previously held by the equity price q_t. To find the market fundamentals solution, solve equation (7) for p_t and think of $k_t = (m_t - \beta - v_t)/(1 + \alpha)$ as playing the role of dividends paid at time t. Also, think of $\alpha/(1 + \alpha)$ as the counterpart of $1/(1 + r)$. By analogy with equation (2), the market fundamentals solution to equation (7) is:

$$p_t^f = \sum_{i=0}^{\infty} [\alpha/(1 + \alpha)]^i E_t(k_{t+i}). \tag{8}$$

Equation (8) states that the price level at any given time is determined by the discounted expected values of factors affecting the supply of money, m, relative to the demand for money (as determined by demand parameter β and the factors in v_t). As before, this formulation does not give all of the possible solutions to equation (7). A self-fulfilling price level bubble can be added to the market fundamental price if the current value of the bubble depends on the discounted expectation of the future value of the bubble such that $E_t(B_{t+1}) = [1 + (1/\alpha)]B_t$, where the reciprocal of $\alpha/(1 + \alpha)$ is $[1 + (1/\alpha)]$. Instead of exploding at the real rate of interest, this model predicts that logarithmic price level bubbles must explode at the rate $(1/\alpha)$.

Although indeterminacies such as B_t had been discussed in the theoretical literature, Flood and Garber's (1980b) attempt to identify, estimate and test for a bubble process removed it from the realm of pure theory and inserted it into empirical economics. Flood and Garber assume that the nominal money supply is exogenous and investigate its time series properties which are necessary in the estimation of the reduced form equation. They also assume that v_t follows a random walk. This simplifies the forecasting problem in equation (8). They estimate a reduced form equation for the rate of inflation assuming that a nonstochastic bubble process infects the logarithm of the price. Consequently, the bubble process satisfies $B_t = B_0[1 + (1/\alpha)]^t$, and the no bubble hypothesis is the coefficient restriction that the initial bubble $B_0 = 0$. A representative reduced form equation from their study is

$$p_t - p_{t-1} = \delta_0 + \delta_1\mu_{t-1} + \cdots + \delta_k\mu_{t+k} + B_0[1 + (1/\alpha)]^t + \varepsilon_t \qquad (9)$$

where μ_t is the money growth rate and $v_t = v_{t-1} + \varepsilon_t$. Flood and Garber found no evidence to reject the hypothesis that the parameter B_0 was equal to zero, although there are problems with their empirical methodology.

Flood and Garber mention three potential methodological weaknesses of their study. First, they assume that money is exogenous which rules out feedback from previous inflation to current money supply creation as would happen when the government prints money to finance real expenditures. Second, they allow only for a deterministic bubble process. Finally, for reasons that will be explained presently, their statistical inference does not have solid foundations in asymptotic distribution theory.

Edwin Burmeister and Kent Wall (1982) use the Flood and Garber data and the Cagan model to address the first two issues. They allow money growth to depend on past money growth and past inflation, thus relaxing the exogeneity assumption, and they allow a constant nonzero variance for the innovation in the bubble b_t, which allows the bubble to be stochastic.

But, although both the Flood-Garber and the Burmeister-Wall studies develop consistent parameter estimates, they lack convincing tests of the no bubbles hypothesis because of an exploding regressor problem. Because estimation is conducted under the alternative hypothesis that bubbles are present in the economy, the reduced form regression (9) has $[1 + (1/\alpha)]^t$ as the regressor associated with the parameter B_0, the initial value of the bubble. This regressor is exploding quite fast as t increases; indeed, it explodes so fast that the information content of its most recent observation never goes to zero as a fraction of the information content of all previous observations. This situation makes it easy to prove consistency of the estimator of B_0 since convergence is quick, but it presents serious problems for testing hypotheses concerning B_0. The information structure of the exploding regressor ensures that any time series sample *no matter how large* is always a small sample, and standard central limit theorems do not apply.

The first attempt at circumventing the asymptotic distribution theory problem was made by Flood, Garber and Louis Scott (1984) who use the fact that several countries experienced simultaneous hyperinflations following World War I to test the hypothesis that no bubbles have occurred in a time series-cross section framework. An asymptotic distribution for the bubble coefficient in equation (9) is obtained by approaching the hypothetical limit in the cross-sectional dimension; that is, by thinking that the number of countries is going to infinity rather than assuming that time periods are going to infinity. Unfortunately, Flood, Garber and Scott have data for only three simultaneous hyperinflations. While they reject the hypothesis of no bubbles in the three simultaneous hyperinflations, their appeal to large sample distribution results is probably suspect.

More recently, the empirical approach to testing the no bubbles hypothesis has taken a second, indirect approach. West (1987a) developed the indirect approach in an application to the stock market, which is discussed below. Alessandra Casella (1986) applies the West-style test to the German hyperinflation data, and it is in that context that we introduce the test. The fundamental insight involves estimating the parameters of a reduced-form price equation by two different methods.

In Casella's application to the German hyperinflation, the bubble test requires two estimates of α, the sensitivity of money demand with respect to the expected rate of inflation. The first estimation method delivers consistent (but inefficient) estimates of the parameter and its standard error regardless of the presence of bubbles. This is done by instrumental variable estimation of the money demand function (7). The second approach delivers parameter estimates and standard errors that are consistent and efficient if bubbles are absent, but that are inconsistent if bubbles are present. This second approach requires simultaneous estimation of a market-fundamentals forecasting process and a reduced form equation like equation (9), but without the bubble process present. Estimation is done subject to the rational expectations cross equation restrictions, as derived by Lars Hansen and Thomas Sargent (1981). The cross equation restrictions arise because the δ parameters in equation (9) are functions of α and the parameters that describe the money supply process.

The two estimates of α and their standard errors will yield numerically different values, which motivates a Hausman (1978) specification test. This test investigates whether the differences in the estimated coefficients are due to sampling error or to a bias in the second estimates. For example, if the market price contains a bubble that is correlated with some of the market fundamentals, then the second method which leaves the bubble process out of the reduced form estimation will yield biased coefficient estimates on the included variables.[6] In this circumstance, when all other elements of the model are thought to be correct and are therefore inserted into the maintained hypothesis, the Hausman test becomes a bubble test. One of the strengths of this type of test is that the researcher does not have to specify an ad hoc restriction on the variance of b_t—The weaknesses of the test will be discussed below.

When Casella implements her version of the West bubble test on the German data, her results are consistent with the presence of price-level bubbles if the money supply is maintained to be an exogenous process relative to inflation, but they are consistent with the no bubbles hypothesis if the money supply is modeled as an endogenous process in which case there is feedback from past inflation to current money creation. Since the money supply is exploding in a hyperinflation, lack of feedback implies an odd and perhaps implausible behavior of the monetary authority.

Exchange Rate Bubble Tests

A bubble that appears in a theoretical model of the price level, which is the value of goods in terms of a particular currency, usually appears also in a model of the foreign exchange value of that currency. Consequently, many models of price level bubbles and exchange rate bubbles have points of equivalence, as Kenneth Singleton (1987) notes.

Richard Meese (1986) applies the West (1987a) bubble test to the U.S. dollar values of the deutschemark and the pound sterling exchange rates using a two-country money market equilibrium model to determine exchange rates.[7] In his framework, money demand in each country depends on real income and the interest rate, the interest rate differential depends on the expected rate of change of the exchange rate, and deviations from purchasing power parity are a random walk. These equations may be solved for an exchange rate equation in which the current exchange rate depends on current and expected future money supplies and real incomes, which provides the market fundamentals solution. The West test indicates very strong evidence of bubbles in these exchange rates during the period from October 1973 to November 1982.

Kenneth West (1987b) conducts some additional bubble tests on the deutschemark-dollar exchange rate and the associated market fundamentals from January 1974 through May 1984. West uses a different test in this paper than the one described above. He uses a construction similar to the variance bounds tests of Stephen LeRoy and Richard Porter (1981), which are discussed below, to conclude that exchange rate variability, in the absence of bubbles, is consistent with the standard monetary model assumed by Meese but augmented to include money demand errors—that is, other potential economic determinants of money demand, and deviations from purchasing power parity as additional market fundamentals. West argues that Meese's conclusion that bubbles are present is premature in the sense that these additional features are not entertained by him. Their presence provides additional market fundamentals that may explain exchange rates without the addition of bubbles to the model. There are also additional criticisms of the Meese analysis that we discuss below.

Bubbles and Stock Price Volatility

This section examines the issues of bubbles in stock prices and the relation of bubble tests to excess volatility tests. A simple model that forms the foundation of much of the asset price bubble and excess volatility literature is the constant expected real return model presented near the start of this paper.[8] Although many authors, including those of popular financial textbooks such as Richard Brealey and Stewart Myers (1981, pp. 42–45), often refer to this model as "a standard efficient markets model," it should be understood that it is quite restrictive. This is only a simple characterization of what one could mean by the concept of an efficient market.[9] Since we think that people are averse to risk, we do not think that this simple model is a correct characterization of the actual economy. With risk aversion, there are good reasons why expected returns on assets would fluctuate even in an efficient market.

Although bubbles could make asset prices more volatile than their market fundamentals, certain kinds of asset price volatility tests are not well designed to provide tests for bubbles. Gregory Mankiw, David Romer, and Matthew Shapiro (1985) note this point, and Robert Flood and Robert Hodrick (1986) elaborate upon it. The problem is that the specification of the null hypothesis underlying the tests includes bubbles, if they exist, into a composite null hypothesis. Consequently, rejection of the null hypothesis cannot be attributable to bubbles.

This point is easily understood by consideration of the construction of the volatility tests that have typically been conducted within the confines of the constant expected rate of return model. Robert Shiller (1981) proposes a comparison between the volatilities of actual prices and of what rational prices would have been with perfect foresight. He defines the perfect foresight rational price to be the discounted present value of actual dividends:

$$q_t^* = \sum_{i=1}^{\infty} [1/(1 + r)]^i d_{t+i}. \tag{10}$$

The expected value of the right-hand side of equation (10) is the market fundamental price of the asset, and the validity of the constant expected return model can be tested by examination of the null hypothesis that $q_t = E_t(q_t^*)$. Since the realization of a variable can be decomposed into its expectation conditional on a given information set plus an innovation that is not correlated with the information set, the validity of the model also implies the variance bound inequality $V(q_t) \leq V(q_t^*)$, if the unconditional variance is well defined.

Notice that since it is impossible to measure the right-hand side of equation (10), econometric analysis must infer measurements of the discounted future value of dividends. Sanford Grossman and Robert Shiller's (1981) measurable price, $\hat{q}_t$, truncates the infinite discounted sum of dividends in the last period of the sample, say at time T, and substitutes the discounted market price at time T for the indefinite future. With this definition, the actual market price, conditional on the validity of the model, is the expected value of measurable rational price,

$$\hat{q}_t = \sum_{i=1}^{T-t} [1/(1 + r)]^i d_{t+t} + [1/(1 + r)]^{T-t} q_T, \tag{11}$$

and the null hypothesis becomes $V(q_t) \leq V(\hat{q}_t)$. To understand why bubbles are included in this null hypothesis, notice that inclusion of $q_T = q_T^f + B_T$ on the right-hand side of equation (11) implies that $q_t = E_t(\hat{q}_t)$ even if bubbles are present because $q_t = q_t^f + B_t$, and bubbles are expected to grow each period such that $E_t(B_T) = (1 + r)^{T-t}B_t$. Hence, these variance bounds tests are not well designed to test for bubbles and statistical evidence of violation of the variance bounds inequality in these tests cannot be taken as evidence of bubbles.

Shiller's (1981) first method of measuring the perfect foresight rational prices, on the other hand, substitutes the discounted average price during the sample as the forecast of the indefinite post-sample discounted sum of dividends. Unfortunately, there is no reason why the hypothesis that market price is equal to expected perfect foresight rational price should continue to be satisfied by this construction. Furthermore, Terry Marsh and Robert Merton (1986) demonstrate that this construction could have misleading properties if dividends are smoothed by management to be an exact function of current and past prices, since, by construction, the variance bound inequality must be violated when the ex post rational price is defined this way.

Much of Shiller's (1981) and Grossman and Shiller's (1981) evidence against the constant discount rate model is due to simple plots of the time series of actual prices and of constructed ex post rational prices. The plots of the time series of constructed ex post rational prices are considerably smoother than the time series of actual prices. Allan Kleidon (1986) effectively criticizes these plots by demonstrating that simulated data, generated to satisfy the model, produce plots that look very much like the plots from actual data. Kleidon's dividend process is the lognormal random walk. One reason the plots provide confusing evidence to the eye is that the perfect foresight price is highly serially correlated, even if dividends are stationary, and the eye cannot easily estimate the unconditional variance of such a process. Also, in Kleidon's case, dividends are actually nonstationary, which implies that the unconditional variance of price does not exist.

West's Specification Test

As noted above, Kenneth West (1987a) developed an ingenious test for bubbles. We now interpret the results of West's investigation of the Standard and Poor's Composite Price Index and the Dow-Jones data that were first used by Shiller (1981).

West uses the constant expected return model in testing the null hypothesis of no bubbles. He first conducts a battery of tests to check that the return equation (1) is consistent with the data, and he concludes that the evidence is not greatly at variance with the assumption. He next estimates a dividend forecasting equation in which future dividends depend upon the past history of dividends, and he checks its consistency with the data. As noted above, the West specification test compares the parameters in the projection of stock prices onto the information set of the dividend forecasting equation to the parameter estimates constructed to satisfy the Hansen-Sargent (1981) formulas, which use the estimated $1/(1 + r)$ and the parameters of the dividend forecasting equation. Since there is a substantive difference in the two sets of estimates, West (1987a, p. 554) concludes, "The data reject the null hypothesis of no bubbles. The rejection appears to result at least in part because the coefficients in the regression of price on dividends are biased upwards."

One aspect of West's test is criticized by Flood, Hodrick and Paul Kaplan (1987). They note that estimation of $1/(1 + r)$ in the specification of the return generating model presented in equation (1) involves using only the one-period relation between current price and expected next period dividend and price, while testing the constructed relation of $1/(1 + r)$ and the parameters from the dividend forecasting model to the reduced form coefficients involves implicit iteration of the return generating model an infinite number of times as in the derivation of equations (2) and (3). Although West does not find strong evidence against the specification of the constant expected return model, when using the levels of real variables, Flood, Hodrick and Kaplan find substantive evidence of misspecification of the model when they iterate the equation for a second period. The latter authors change the specification in two other ways. They formulate the model in returns, and they use dividend-price ratios as instruments.[10]

West (1987a) acknowledges this significant evidence against his model of equilibrium expected returns when these alternative instruments are used. He also attempts to allow for time variation in expected returns within a linearized model with mixed results. The support for finding bubbles in some of his specifications increases while it decreases for others.

A second area of criticism of the West (1987a) specification test for bubbles is that he assumes the dividend forecasting equations are stationary in either the levels of real dividends or their first differences. Since most macroeconomic time series appear to be stationary in first differences of natural logarithms of the real variables, both of these specifications are somewhat suspect. In addition, the likelihood that a constant dividend process characterizes over 100 years of data seems somewhat small given what little is known about the dividend process.[11]

If we restrict attention to what West (1987a) actually estimates, for the Standard and Poor's composite dividend process from 1871 to 1980, the

superior specification of the dividend process appears to require first differencing and a second order autoregression. When variability of returns is
allowed, and the test statistics are recalculated, there is no evidence against
the null hypothesis of no bubbles.

West (1987a) also notes that a popular model of the dividend process is
the lognormal random walk. In this case a closed-form expression for the
price of the stock is available in terms of $1/(1 + r)$ and the mean and
variance of the growth rate of dividends. Since the asymptotic distribution
theory necessary to provide a distribution for the coefficient in the projection of price onto dividends is inapplicable in this case, West does no
formal tests. Although the point estimates of the model are inconsistent
with the no bubbles hypothesis, the results are sensitive to the value of r,
and the no bubbles hypothesis cannot be rejected for plausible values of r.
Since there is sensitivity of the test to the estimated parameters, West
interprets the results as mild evidence against the null of no bubbles. But
the evidence seems just as easily interpretable in the opposite way, especially in light of potential for misspecification of the model.

Recent Evidence on Stock Price Volatility

We conclude this section with a discussion of some of the current literature
on the excess variability of stock prices relative to dividends. A number of
authors including Mankiw, Romer and Shapiro (1985), West (1988a), and
Campbell and Shiller (1988a, b) test implications of the variability of stock
prices relative to dividends. All find that simple models such as the constant expected return model are inconsistent with the data. The sensitivity
of these tests to the assumed structure of the dividend process and the
model of returns is an outstanding issue for research.[12]

Examples of recent findings that intrigue us include the Campbell and
Shiller (1988a, b) studies and the West (1988a) volatility tests. Campbell
and Shiller (1988a, b) estimate a vector autoregression (VAR) of the logarithm of the dividend-price ratio, the logarithm of a long average of earnings relative to price, and the first difference of the logarithm of dividends.
The hypothesis of a constant expected rate of return then implies a restriction across the coefficients of the VAR that is easily rejected by the data. A
by-product of the estimation is a ratio of the standard deviation of calculated returns that are constructed from the coefficients of the VAR assuming that the model is true relative to the standard deviation of actual
returns. This value is 0.277 with a standard error of 0.069. Thus, the false
model's predicted returns are much less variable than actual returns. When

the expected return on the stock market is allowed to be variable but is postulated to be equal to a constant plus the expected real return on commercial paper, the model is still rejected by the data at very low levels of significance, but the ratio of the standard deviation of returns implied by the model to the standard deviation of actual returns increases to 0.478 with a standard error of 0.044.

West (1988a) develops a volatility test that is quite similar in its estimated equations to the specification test described above. The test involves a comparison of estimates, constructed using two different information sets, of the innovation variance in the expected infinite sum of current and future dividends discounted at a constant rate. One information set is taken to be current and past dividends, which is a proper subset of the market's information set. The other information set is taken to be the market price under the hypothesis that constant expected returns are correct. Forecasting with a smaller information set than the market's ought to result in a larger innovation variance, but West finds the opposite and attributes a large part of the volatility of prices to either bubbles or fads. He argues that time-varying expected returns are unlikely to overturn the results.

Whether the actual volatility of equity returns is due to time variation in the rational equity risk premium or to bubbles, fads, and market inefficiencies is an open issue.[13] Bubble tests require a well-specified model of equilibrium expected returns that has yet to be developed, and this makes inference about bubbles quite tenuous.

Some Matters of Interpretation

Flood and Garber (1980b) note that an omitted variable problem can bias bubble tests toward rejection of the no bubbles hypothesis. Consider the possibility that agents may have been expecting some future event, which is relevant to the determination of the price level, that the unwary researcher does not include in the model's market fundamentals. For example, suppose agents had information during the sample that there would be an increase in the money supply at some future date, and suppose that this information is not imbedded in the historical money supply statistics used by the researcher to generate forecasts of future money supplies. In this circumstance the dynamics of the price level will rationally have anticipated the increase in the money supply in a manner that is indistinguishable from the dynamics induced by a bubble in the market. The structure of a rational expectations model of the price level forces the dynamics of the price level in response to all omitted expected future variables to be indistinguishable from dynamic paths caused by bubbles. Flood and Hodrick (1986) demonstrate the analogous point in an equity market example in which agents are anticipating a change in taxation of dividend income.[14]

Consider the biases that could plague West's (1987a) stock price bubble test. Applications of the specification test for bubbles require a forecasting equation based on a subset of the agents' information set and an unrejected return generating process. West (1987a) uses ARIMA models of dividends and tests for changes in the structure of the dividend process with a Chow test. Since he cannot reject the hypothesis of no difference in the structure of the dividend process, he proceeds with the bubble test, but this does not mean that agents were not anticipating a change in the structure of dividends that did not materialize during the sample. Similarly, although West is unable to reject the hypothesis that his return generating process is correctly specified, we note above that extension of the model to longer horizons points strongly toward model misspecification. How this misspecification biases his tests is an open issue.

Similar problems plague the study of hyperinflations if agents think that a hyperinflation will not last indefinitely, since they consequently must be anticipating a reform of the monetary process.[15] In such an environment, the price level is changing with changes in the probability of monetary reform, and without modelling this issue, researchers may associate movements in the price level caused by changes in the probability of monetary reform with changes induced by a nonexistent bubble.

In the foreign exchange market, a large body of research initiated by Richard Meese and Kenneth Rogoff (1983) indicates that standard exchange rate models forecast quite badly. As noted above, when bubble tests are conducted on these models, they find bubbles. According to much research, though, it is very unlikely that the models are correct. If the models are false, rejection of the null hypothesis of no bubbles cannot be attributed solely to bubbles since it could equally well be caused by the misspecification of the model.

The moral of this section is that research ought to find apparent evidence of bubbles when models work poorly or when agents expect the future to be somewhat different than history. We think this point presents a serious interpretive problem for all bubble tests. The current empirical tests for bubbles do not successfully establish the case that bubbles exist in asset prices. Nevertheless, bubble tests are interesting specification tests and should continue to be an important part of the econometrician's tool kit.

Notes

This research was supported by a grant from The Lynde and Harry Bradley Foundation to whom the authors express their gratitude. The comments of John Cochrane, Mark Watson and the editor, Joseph E. Stiglitz, the co-editor, Carl Shapiro, and the managing editor, Timothy Taylor, are also gratefully acknowledged.

1. Rational expectations is the requirement that the subjective expectations of the agents in an economic model be identical to the mathematical expectations of the model that are produced by the exogenous sources of uncertainty interacting with the behavior of the agents.

2. Olivier Blanchard and Mark Watson (1982) also study the market for gold.

3. No one thinks agents actually live forever, but families can be effectively linked across generations by intergenerational transfers and bequests. See Barro (1989) for a discussion of this issue as it applies to the effects on the economy of government deficits.

4. The bubble process is the homogenous part of the solution to the difference equation (1). Edwin Burmeister, Robert Flood and Peter Garber (1983) explain several indeterminacies discussed in the literature in terms of the homogenous part of the solution. This type of indeterminacy is explosive since $(1 + r) > 1$.

5. See Maurice Obstfelf and Kenneth Rogoff (1983) for additional intuition and more formal discussion of the transversality condition and for additional references to the mathematical literature on the subject.

6. The bubble need not be correlated with market fundamentals to apply the Hausman test. While a bias may be created by correlation of the bubble innovations with innovations in any of the fundamental variables, it may also be created by the bubble's mean biasing the estimate of the constant in the reduced form or because the improperly excluded bubble has exploding variance. See Casella (1986).

7. To our knowledge, Wing Woo wrote the first exchange-rate bubble paper, which was eventually published in 1987. Woo uses a portfolio balance model to test for bubbles in the exchange rate of the U.S. dollar versus the currencies of Germany, France, Canada and Japan. An interesting aspect of his investigation is that he takes a stand on the initiation mechanism for an exchange rate bubble by looking for bubbles just after major monetary disturbances. This method, probably more than most, runs the risk of confusing bubbles with expected changes in market fundamentals. We return to this possible confusion below. Additional bubble tests involving foreign exchange markets are by Kunio Okina (1985). Jeffrey Frankel (1985) and Paul Krugman (1986) develop empirical analyses that the value of the dollar relative to foreign currencies is not "sustainable." While they motivate their analyses by the strength of the dollar, which they attribute possibly to a bubble, they do not test formally for bubbles.

8. See Robert Shiller's article in this issue and the critical survey by Christian Gilles and Stephen LeRoy (1987) for additional viewpoints.

9. See Eugene Fama (1976) for a discussion of the fact that market efficiency is always a joint hypothesis that depends on a model of appropriate expected asset returns and on an information set of investors.

10. These findings are consistent with the predictability of returns at long horizons that is documented by Eugene Fama and Kenneth French (1988), James Poterba and Lawrence Summers (1988), and John Campbell and Robert Shiller (1987, 1988a, b).

11. Terry Marsh and Robert Merton (1987) investigate the aggregate dividend process and conclude that there is support for the idea that managers smooth dividends. They argue that the only constraint on the dividend process is that its present value be equal to the present value of earnings. Campbell and Shiller (1987) question whether the findings of Marsh and Merton actually reflect dividend smoothing or simply additional ability of the market to predict future dividends from information that is in addition to the past history of dividends. Campbell and Shiller (1988a) note that a long average of the earnings of the Standard and Poor's composite relative to current price is useful in predicting dividends.

12. Joe Mattey and Richard Meese (1986) investigate Monte Carlo simulations, using six different data generating environments, one of which includes a stochastic bubble, of twenty-four test statistics that have been proposed as tests of asset pricing models. Their results indicate that some tests may have poor small sample properties.

13. See Colin Camerer (1987) and West (1988b) for further discussion of these issues.

14. James Hamilton and Charles Whiteman (1985) extend this omitted variable argument by formally demonstrating the observational equivalence of omitted state variables and stochastic bubbles.

15. Flood and Garber (1980a) derive probabilities of monetary reform during the German hyperinflation by identifying them with the probability that the process for the money supply is inconsistent with a finite price level. Inconsistency is defined to be a monetary growth rate that is too fast to be discounted at the discount rate implied by the model. Such a money supply process implies an infinite price level if agents though that it would last forever.

References

Barro, Robert J., "The Ricardian Approach to Budget Deficits," *Journal of Economic Perspectives*, 1989, 3, 37–54.

Blanchard, Olivier J., "Speculative Bubbles, Crashes and Rational Expectations," *Economics Letters*, 1979, 3, 387–89.

Blanchard, Olivier J., and Mark W. Watson, "Bubbles, Rational Expectations and Financial Markets." In Wachtel, Paul, ed., *Crisis in the Economic and Financial System*. Lexington, MA: Lexington Books, 1982, pp. 295–315.

Brealey, Richard, and Stewart Myers, *Principles of Corporate Finance*. New York: McGraw-Hill, 1981.

Brock, William A., "Money and Growth: The Case of Long-run Perfect Foresight," *International Economic Review*, October 1974, 15, 750–777.

Brock, William A., "Asset Prices in a Production Economy." In McCall, John, ed., *The Economics of Information and Uncertainty*. Chicago: University of Chicago Press, 1982, pp. 1–43.

Burmeister, Edwin, Robert P. Flood, and Peter M. Garber, "On the Equivalence of Solutions in Rational Expectations Models," *Journal of Economic Dynamics and Control*, May 1983, 5, 224–234.

Burmeister, Edwin, and Kent Wall, "Kalman Filtering Estimation of Unobserved Rational Expectations with an Application to the German Hyperinflation," *Journal of Econometrics*, November 1982, 20, 255–84.

Cagan, Phillip, "The Monetary Dynamics of Hyperinflation." In Friedman, Milton, ed., *Studies in the Quantity Theory of Money*. Chicago: University of Chicago Press, 1956.

Camerer, Colin, "Bubbles and Fads in Asset Prices: A Review of Theory and Evidence," unpublished paper, University of Pennsylvania, 1987.

Campbell, John Y., and Robert J. Shiller, "Cointegration and Tests of Present Value Models," *Journal of Political Economy*, October 1987, 95, 1062–1088.

Campbell, John Y., and Robert J. Shiller, "Stock Prices, Earnings and Expected Dividends," *Journal of Finance*, July 1988a, 43, 661–676.

Campbell, John Y., and Robert J. Shiller, "The Dividend-Price Ratio and Expectations of Future Dividends and Discount Factors," *Review of Financial Studies*, Fall 1988b, 1, 195–228.

Casella, Alessandra, "Testing for Price Level Bubbles: The German Hyperinflation Once More," unpublished paper, University of California, Berkeley, December 1986.

Diba, Behzad T., and Herschel I. Grossman, "On the Inception of Rational Bubbles," *Quarterly Journal of Economics*, August 1987, 102, 697–700.

Diba, Behzad T., and Herschel I. Grossman, "Rational Inflationary Bubbles," *Journal of Monetary Economics*, May 1988, 21, 35–46.

Fama, Eugene F., *Foundations of Finance*. New York: Basic Books, 1976.

Fama, Eugene F., and Kenneth R. French, "Permanent and Temporary Components of Stock Prices," *Journal of Political Economy*, April 1988, 96, 246–273.

Flood, Robert P., and Peter M. Garber, "An Economic Theory of Monetary Reform," *Journal of Political Economy*, February 1980a, 88, 24–58.

Flood, Robert P., and Peter M. Garber, "Market Fundamentals Versus Price Level Bubbles: The First Tests," *Journal of Political Economy*, August 1980b, 88, 745–70.

Flood, Robert P., Peter M. Garber, and Louis Scott, "Mulit-Country Tests for Price Level Bubbles," *Journal of Economic Dynamics and Control*, December 1984, 8, 329–40.

Flood, Robert P., and Robert J. Hodrick, "Asset Price Volatility, Bubbles and Process Switching," *Journal of Finance*, September 1986, 41, 831–842.

Flood, Robert P., Robert J. Hodrick, and Paul Kaplan, "An Evaluation of Recent Evidence on Stock Market Bubbles," unpublished paper, Northwestern University, revised May 1987.

Frankel, Jeffrey A., "The Dazzling Dollar," *Brookings Papers on Economic Activity*, 1985, 1, 199–217.

Garber, Peter M., "Tulipmania," *Journal of Political Economy*, June 1989, 97, 535–560.

Gilles, Christian, and Stephen F. LeRoy, "The Variance-Bounds Tests: A critical Survey," unpublished paper, University of California, Santa Barbara, August 1987.

Grossman, Sanford, and Robert J. Shiller, "The Determinants of the Variability of Stock Market Prices," *American Economic Review*, May 1981, 71, 222–27.

Hamilton, James D., and Charles H. Whiteman, "The Observable Implications of Self-fulfilling Expectations," *Journal of Monetary Economics*, November 1985, 16, 353–74.

Hansen, Lars Peter, and Thomas J. Sargent, "Formulating and Estimating Dynamic Linear Rational Expectations Models." In Lucas, Robert E. Jr., and Thomas J. Sargent, eds., *Rational Expectations and Econometric Practice*. Minneapolis: University of Minnesota Press, 1981, pp. 91–126.

Hausman, Jerry A., "Specification Tests in Econometrics," *Econometrica*, November 1978, 46, 1251–71.

Keynes, John Maynard, *The General Theory of Employment, Interest and Money*. London: Macmillan, 1936.

Kindleberger, Charles, *Manias, Panics and Crashes*. New York: Basic Books, 1978.

Kleidon, Allan W., "Variance Bounds Tests and Stock Price Valuation Models," *Journal of Political Economy*, October 1986, 94, 953–1001.

Krugman, Paul R., "Is the Strong Dollar Sustainable?" In *The U.S. Dollar-Recent Developments, Outlook, and Policy Options*. Federal Reserve Bank of Kansas City, 1986, pp. 103–132.

LeRoy, Stephen F., and Richard D. Porter, "The Present Value Relation: Tests Based on Implied Variance Bounds," *Econometrica*, May 1981, 49, 555–74.

Mankiw, N. Gregory, David Romer, and Matthew Shapiro, "An Unbiased Reexamination of Stock Market Volatility," *The Journal of Finance*, July 1985, 40, 677–89.

Marsh, Terry A., and Robert C. Merton, "Dividend Variability and Variance Bounds Tests for the Rationality of Stock Market Prices," *American Economic Review*, June 1986, 76, 483–498.

Marsh, Terry A., and Robert C. Merton, "Dividend Behavior for the Aggregate Stock Market," *Journal of Business*, January 1987, 60, 1–40.

Mattey, Joe, and Richard A. Meese, "Empirical Assessment of Present Value Relations," *Econometric Reviews*, 1986, 5, 171–234.

Meese, Richard A., "Testing for Bubbles in Exchange Markets: The Case of Sparkling Rates," *Journal of Political Economy*, April 1986, 94, 345–73.

Meese, Richard A., and Kenneth Rogoff, "Empirical Exchange Rate Models of the Seventies: Do They Fit Out of Sample?" *Journal of International Economics*, February 1983, 14, 3–24.

Obstfeld, Maurice, and Kenneth Rogoff, "Speculative Hyperinflations in Maximizing Models: Can We Rule Them Out?" *Journal of Political Economy*, August 1983, 91, 675–87.

Obstfeld, Maurice, and Kenneth Rogoff, "Ruling Out Divergent Speculative Bubbles," *Journal of Monetary Economics*, May 1986, 17, 349–62.

Okina, Kunio, "Empirical Tests of 'Bubbles' in the Foreign Exchange Market," *Bank of Japan Monetary and Economic Studies*, May 1985, 3, 1–45.

Poterba, James M., and Lawrence H. Summers, "Mean Reversion in Stock Prices: Evidence and Implications," *Journal of Financial Economics*, October 1988, 22, 27–59.

Shiller, Robert J., "Rational Expectations and the Dynamic Structure of Macroeconomic Models: A Critical Review," *Journal of Monetary Economics*, January 1978, 4, 1–44.

Shiller, Robert J., "Do Stock Prices Move By Too Much to be Justified by Subsequent Changes in Dividends?" *American Economic Review*, June 1981, 71, 421–36.

Singleton, Kenneth J., "Speculation and the Volatility of Foreign Currency Exchange Rates." In Brunner, Karl, and Allan H. Meltzer, eds., *Bubbles and Other Essays, Carnegie-Rochester Conference on Public Policy*, Spring 1987, 26, 9–56.

Taylor, John, "Conditions for Unique Solutions in Stochastic Macroeconomic Models with Rational Expectations," *Econometrica*, November 1977, 45, 1377–1385.

Tirole, Jean, "On the Possibility of Speculation Under Rational Expectations," *Econometrica*, September 1982, 50, 1163–1181.

Tirole, Jean, "Asset Bubbles and Overlapping Generations," *Econometrica*, November 1985, 53, 1499–1528.

West, Kenneth D., "A Specification Test for Speculative Bubbles," *Quarterly Journal of Economics*, August 1987a, 102, 553–580.

West, Kenneth D., "A Standard Monetary Model and the Variability of the Deutschemark-Dollar Exchange Rate," *Journal of International Economics*, August 1987b, 23, 57–76.

West, Kenneth, D., "Dividend Innovations and Stock Price Volatility," *Econometrica*, January 1988a, 56, 37–61.

West, Kenneth D., "Bubbles, Fads and Stock Price Volatility Tests: A Partial Evaluation," *Journal of Finance*, July 1988b, 43, 639–656.

Woo, Wing T., "Some Evidence of Speculative Bubbles in the Foreign Exchange Markets," *Journal of Money, Credit and Banking*, November 1987, 19, 499–514.

5   An Evaluation of Recent Evidence on Stock Market Bubbles

Robert P. Flood,
Robert J. Hodrick, and
Paul Kaplan

I   Introduction

The topic of asset price bubbles has received a large amount of professional attention. The theoretical work is exemplified by that of Obstfeld and Rogoff (1983), Tirole (1985), Diba and Grossman (1985a), and Hamilton and Whiteman (1985), while the empirical work is exemplified by that of Burmeister and Wall (1982), Flood, Garber and Scott (1984), Quah (1985), Meese (1986), West (1984, 1985a, 1985b), Diba and Grossman (1985b), Woo (1984), Scott (1985b), and Okina (1985).

The asset price bubbles we discuss are the asset market counterparts of the price-level bubbles studied by Flood and Garber (1980). The definition of a bubble depends on the model at hand, so precise definitions will have to wait until precise models have been presented. Without being very precise, though, we can say that in what follows we decompose an asset price into two components. The first is due to current and expected future *market fundamentals*, in which we list the typical set of exogenous and predetermined variables usually thought important for market price. The second is the *bubble*, which is defined to be what is left after market fundamentals have been removed from price. Bubbles may be thought of as the part of price due to self-fulfilling prophecy.

Two general types of empirical work have been interpreted as being useful in addressing the question of whether bubbles are important for asset price determination. The first follows the bubbles test of Flood and Garber (1980) and the variance bounds work of Leroy and Porter (1981) in attempting to forecast the indefinite future of market fundamentals. The second follows some of the variance bounds work of Shiller (1982) and Grossman and Shiller (1981) by examining market fundamentals only up to a fixed terminal market price. In section III of this chapter we argue that the latter method, which was not designed explicitly for bubble research, gives no information about bubbles. The results of such tests do, however, provide pertinent information regarding model specification.[1]

In the remaining sections of the chapter we discuss and extend some of the recent empirical work that is theoretically well designed to give information about asset price bubbles in aggregate stock markets. This includes some recent work by West (1984, 1985a), Diba and Grossman (1985b), and Quah (1985).

The data sets used by Quah (1985) and by Diba and Grossman (1985b) are either identical to or are subsets of the data used by West (1984, 1985a), which is the same as that used by Shiller (1981a). Further, all of these studies use an equilibrium condition to price assets that is based on the Euler equations of a risk-neutral agent. Our empirical results address the adequacy of the risk-neutral specification in empirical bubble tests, and, therefore, our results reflect on all of the studies.

After duplicating West's work, we extended it in two directions. First, because of our concern about the time series stationarity of his data, we performed his estimation using returns on stock portfolios. West used the levels of real stock prices and dividends or their first differences in his study. We found that the differences in inference between using our specification and West's were actually quite minor. This was puzzling for two reasons. West's specification requires the expected real rate of return on the stock market to be constant. Since variance bounds tests based on that specification seem to us to indicate some form of model misspecification, this representation was suspect. Also, there is a large and growing body of evidence indicating that expected rates of return on a variety of assets move through time.[2] Why, then, was West's specification indicating such a different result?

One difference between the variance bounds tests and West's Euler equation tests involves the fact that the Euler equation methods consider only temporally adjacent periods, while the variance bounds tests consider widely separated periods. If the Euler equation is incorrect, it may be that its specification error is swamped in estimation by the rational-expectations prediction error. Although the one-period specification error does not imply strong rejection of the Euler equation, it is possible that the compounded one-period specification errors that appear in variance bounds tests could lead to a rejection of the model.

In order to investigate this issue we iterated the Euler equation to equate margins across two nonadjacent periods, and we used West's data and his methods to estimate the iterated Euler equation. The iterated Euler equation was resoundingly rejected by the data, calling into question

West's interpretation of his results as indicating evidence of stock market bubbles.

An obvious potential problem with West's model was his use of a risk-neutral utility function that induces his linear estimating equations. In response to our misgivings about the assumption of risk neutrality, we estimated Euler equations for all of the utility functions in the HARA (hyperbolic absolute risk aversion) class. Our results are similar to the results we find for risk neutrality—the models seem to work marginally well only when margins for adjacent periods are explicitly equated. There is more substantial evidence against the models when the iterated Euler equations equating margins for nonadjacent periods are employed.[3]

We investigated the data in two additional ways. First, because the theory deals with after-tax returns while the data we use contain only before-tax returns, we tried to allow the estimation to tell us if differential tax treatment of dividends and capital gains might be responsible for the model's failure. The results of this part of the investigation are inconclusive. There is some evidence that agents treat dividends and capital gains differently. We also looked explicitly at return forecasting equations. The risk-neutral model implies that forecasted one-period returns should be a constant equal to the inverse of the subjective discount rate. We find that past (time-varying) dividend-asset price ratios almost surely forecast returns, which we interpret as strong evidence that the risk-neutral model is inappropriate.

Our research is reported in the following five sections. In section II we present a theoretical discussion of asset pricing in a utility-maximizing framework. In this section we are explicit about our definition of asset price bubbles. In section III we show why studies of stock-price variance bounds, which use a terminal stock market price in the way suggested in much of the variance bounds literature, give information about the adequacy of the underlying specification, but they do not give information about asset price bubbles. In section IV we discuss potential problems with interpretations of bubbles tests, and we lay out West's proposed methodology. In section V we report results concerning the usefulness of the risk-neutral utility function in developing bubbles test. We also report some additional results on nonlinear utility functions, on specifications that allow differential tax treatment of dividends and capital gains, and on the ability of past data to forecast future stock market returns. In section VI we present a summary of our views of current empirical work on bubbles in stock prices, the relation of that work to the variance bounds studies, and some suggestions about directions for future research.

II   Utility Maximizing Models of Asset Prices

The purpose of this section is to set forth a simple representative agent model that is the foundation of our asset-pricing discussion. Consider a representative agent who maximizes an intertemporal utility function subject to a sequence of budget constraints. The formal problem is

$$\max_{\{c_{t+i}\}_{i=0}^{\infty}} E_t \left[\sum_{i=0}^{\infty} \rho^i U(c_{t+i}) \right], \qquad 0 < \rho < 1, \tag{1}$$

subject to the sequence of budget constraints

$$c_{t+i} + p_{t+i}k_{t+i} = y + (p_{t+i} + d_{t+i})k_{t+i-1}, \qquad i = 0, 1, 2, \ldots \tag{2}$$

where c_t is consumption in period t, $U(\cdot)$ is the period utility function, ρ is the subjective discount factor, y is exogenous real endowment, k_t is the number of units of the asset purchased at time t, and the mathematical expectation operator is given by $E_t(\cdot)$.

The first order conditions for this problem can be written as

$$E_t(z_{t+i}) = \rho E_t(z_{t+i+1} + a_{t+i+1}), \qquad i = 0, 1, 2, \ldots \tag{3}$$

where $z_t \equiv U'(c_t)p_t$, the marginal utility of a unit of the asset at time t and $a_t \equiv U'(c_t)d_t$, the marginal utility of the dividend on a unit of the asset at time t.

Notice that the Euler equation generated in the example is a linear difference equation in the variable $E_t(z_{t+i})$. The equation may be interpreted as having the forcing process $E_t(a_{t+i})$ and having a root of the equation equal to ρ^{-1}. Since ρ is by assumption between zero and one, (3) is, in the conventional sense, an unstable equation. The work of Sargent and Wallace (1973) made us aware of this issue, which arises in many rational-expectations models. Sargent and Wallace proposed that researchers generally adopt a solution to models like (3) that allows a stable time path for the endogenous variable when the exogenous variables are stable. In the present model this is the solution that sets the marginal utility of current price equal to the present value of expected future dividends. We denote this solution f_t to represent the part of asset price that depends only on market fundamentals. Formally, the proposed solution to (3) is

$$f_t = \sum_{i=1}^{\infty} \rho^i E_t(a_{t+i}). \tag{4}$$

If (3) were the entire model, the solution given in (4) would be only one of an infinite number of solutions. Other solutions can be obtained by adding an arbitrary term to (4) that is the solution to the homogenous part of (3). We denote the arbitrary element at time t by b_t. Equation (3) requires that such arbitrary elements obey

$$E_t(b_{t+i}) = \rho^{-i}b_t, \qquad i = 1, 2, 3, \ldots. \tag{5}$$

In the model at hand the elements of the sequence, $b_t, b_{t+1} \ldots$, denoted $\{b_t\}$, are elements of a bubble in the market for asset k. If the innovation in the bubble at time t is denoted v_t, it follows that

$$b_T = \rho^{-(T-t)}b_t + \sum_{i=1}^{T-t} \rho^{-i}v_{t+i}. \tag{6}$$

The actual observation of z_t may therefore consist of two elements, the market fundamentals part, f_t, plus the bubble, b_t, so that

$$z_t = f_t + b_t. \tag{7}$$

A bubble in z_t produces a related bubble in market price of the asset since $z_t = p_t U'(c_t)$, and $U'(c_t)$ need not be related to the asset market bubble. in this model, the agent's maximization problem helps the researcher formulate the hypothesis that bubbles are absent from market prices. This point was stated clearly by Obstfeld and Rogoff (1983). Their argument is as follows.

The single period Euler equation given in (3) may be iterated to equate margins for any two nonadjacent periods. For instance, the margin of substitution for period t and period $t + n$ can by equated by substituting $n - 1$ future Euler equations into the current period Euler equation and appealing to the law of iterated expectations. The n-period Euler equation is

$$z_t = \rho^n E_t(z_{t+n}) + \sum_{i=1}^{n} \rho^i E_t(a_{t+i}), \tag{8}$$

and it ensures that a maximizing agent cannot increase his expected utility by rearranging his consumption between periods t and $t + n$. When n is driven to infinity in (8), the agent's optimization implies

$$z_t = \lim_{n \to \infty} \left[\rho^n E_t(z_{t+n}) + \sum_{i=1}^{n} \rho^i E_t(a_{t+i}) \right]. \tag{9}$$

The first term on the right-hand side of (9) gives the agent's current evaluation of the expected marginal utility attached to the sale of a unit of asset k indefinitely far in the future. The second term on the right-hand side of (9) is the expected utility gain attached to the strategy of holding a unit of the asset indefinitely and consuming only the stream of dividends accruing to ownership of the asset. The current utility cost of purchasing the asset is given by z_t. Therefore, an agent can be at a maximum with a buy-and-hold (forever) strategy only if the first term on the right-hand side of (9) is zero.

This example of an infinitely lived representative agent provides a special case in which bubbles are not possible in equilibrium. The agent knows that he will live forever, and he knows that everyone in the economy is identical to him. In equilibrium the asset must be priced to be held by the infinitely lived representative agent who must follow the buy-and-hold strategy. The agent can be at an equilibrium only when the marginal utility of what he gives up to buy the asset, z_t, is equal to the expected value of what he gets from holding the asset, $\sum_{i=1}^{\infty} \rho^i E_t(a_{t+i})$. Therefore, in this model, the combination of the agent's maximization and market equilibrium give the implication that the first term in (9) must be zero. This transversality condition arises as a necessary condition of the model, and one way to test this model is to test the transversality condition.

The bubble process defined by (5) and (6) is consistent with the model's Euler equation, but it is not consistent with the transversality condition. The present value of the future marginal utility of the asset price must go to zero as the discounting period goes to infinity as long as the utility value of the asset payoffs is bounded above. The present value of the expected future bubble, however, will not go to zero, since the bubble is expected to grow at the inverse of the discount factor.

Some models imply a transversality condition that is inconsistent with the presence of bubbles in asset prices. In contrast, the theoretical analysis of Tirole (1985) indicates that other models incorporating rational expectations can be perfectly consistent with asset price bubbles in some circumstances.[4] In our view, bubble tests are analogous to tests for downward sloping demand curves—not all models imply downward sloping demand curves, but some do. Many economists like to think that asset prices are determined strictly by market fundamentals, and empirical research is necessary to verify or refute this idea.

III   Bubbles and Variance Bounds Tests

The purpose of this section is to show that failure of an asset-pricing model in certain variance bounds tests gives no information about bubbles. Such results are correctly interpreted as providing information about the adequacy of the underlying model. We conduct the argument using the model developed in the previous section. For this part of the argument we adopt the Euler equation, (3), and the pricing function, (7), which allows asset price bubbles. The bubble, if present, must follow the time series process described in (5). In the rest of this section, for brevity, we refer to the marginal utility of the asset price, z_t, simply as the asset price, and we refer to the marginal utility derived from the dividend paid to owners of the asset, a_t, as the dividend on the asset. This convention is not invoked in later sections.

The basic insights of the variance bounds literature are that the variance of an actual variable must be greater than or equal to the variance of its conditional expectation and that this latter variance must be greater than or equal to the variance of a forecast based on a subset of the information used by agents. To see how the existence of bubbles could lead in theory to a violation of variance bounds, consider the *ex post rational price*, which is defined as the price that would prevail if agents knew future market fundamentals with certainty and there were no bubbles. The ex post rational price is

$$z_t^* = \sum_{i=1}^{\infty} \rho^i a_{t+i}. \tag{10}$$

Notice that ex post rational price is a theoretical construct, and although it is subscripted with a t, it is neither in an agent's information set nor is it in an econometrician's information set.

The theoretical relation that is the foundation of many variance bounds tests is obtained by subtracting (7) from (10) and rearranging terms:

$$z_t^* = z_t + u_t - b_t, \tag{11}$$

where $u_t \equiv \sum_{i=1}^{\infty} \rho^i [a_{t+i} - E_t(a_{t+i})]$ is the deviation of the present value of dividends from its expected value based on time t information. By construction, u_t is uncorrelated with z_t and b_t, but z_t and b_t may be correlated with each other.

The innovation in x_t from time $t - n$ is $[x_t - E_{t-n}(x_t)]$. Then, the innovation variance and covariance operators are defined by

$$V_n(x_t) = E\{[x_t - E_{t-n}(x_t)]^2\}$$

and

$$C_n(x_t, y_t) = E\{[x_t - E_{t-n}(x_t)][y_t - E_{t-n}(y_t)]\}$$

where $E(\cdot)$ denotes the unconditional mathematical expectation. In what follows we treat n as a finite positive integer.

Applying the innovation variance operator to both sides of (11) yields

$$V_n(z_t^*) = V_n(z_t) + V_n(u_t) + V_n(b_t) - 2C_n(z_t, b_t), \tag{12}$$

which follows from the conditional orthogonality of u_t to z_t and b_t.

Suppose that somehow a researcher could develop very good measurements of the variance of the ex post rational price, z_t^*, and of the variance of market price, z_t. Suppose further that it was found that ex post rational price had a smaller variance than market price. Since the variance of both u_t and b_t must be nonnegative, such a finding could only be rationalized, within the framework of the model, by a positive conditional covariance between the bubble and z_t. Therefore, as long as the model is correct, and as long as the variance of ex post rational price and the variance of market price are measured appropriately, a finding of $V_n(z_t) > V_n(z_t^*)$ can be interpreted as evidence of bubbles.

The difference between the theoretical exercise described above and its practical implementation arises in the construction of an observable counterpart to z_t^*. Because it is impossible to measure ex post rational price since it depends on the infinite future, researchers typically measure a related variable that we call $\hat{z}_t$. Since actual price and dividend data are available for a sample of observations on $t = 0, 1, \ldots T$, researchers use

$$\hat{z}_t \equiv \sum_{i=1}^{T-t} \rho^i a_{t+i} + \rho^{T-t} z_T, \qquad t = 0, 1, \ldots, T - 1, \tag{13}$$

in place of z_t^*. Notice from (10) and (13) that

$$\hat{z}_t = z_t^* - \rho^{T-t} z_T^* + \rho^{T-t} z_T, \tag{14}$$

which implies from (11) that

$$\hat{z}_t = z_t^* + \rho^{T-t}(b_T - u_T). \tag{15}$$

Since u_T is the innovation in the present value of dividends between time T and the infinite future, it is uncorrelated with all elements of the time T information set, which includes the time t information set. Since b_T depends on the evolution of the stochastic bubble between t and T from (6), it is not orthogonal to time t information.

Notice what happens when (15) is solved for z_t^*, and the result is substituted into (11). After slight rearrangement, one obtains

$$\hat{z}_t = z_t + w_t \tag{16}$$

where

$$w_t = (u_t - \rho^{T-t}u_T) + (\rho^{T-t}b_T - b_t). \tag{17}$$

Equation (16) is the empirical counterpart of (11) and forms the basis of the usual variance bounds tests. The only important difference between our version of (16) and that of previous researchers is that we have allowed explicitly for rational stochastic bubbles in our derivation.

Application of the innovation variance operator to (16) gives

$$V_n(\hat{z}_t) = V_n(z_t) + V_n(w_t) + 2C_n(z_t, w_t). \tag{18}$$

The important point concerning (18) is that the innovation covariance between z_t and w_t is zero. To understand why, consider the nature of the composite disturbance W_t. First, as noted above, both u_t and u_T are uncorrelated with z_t since z_t is in the time t information set, which is a subset of the T information set. Second, and most important, the combined term $\rho^{T-t}b_T - b_t$ is uncorrelated with the time t information set, even though each term separately is not orthogonal to time t information. This follows from (6) because $\rho^{(T-t)}b_T - b_t = \sum_{i=1}^{T-t} \rho^{-i}v_{t+i}$, which is orthogonal to all time t information including z_t. Hence, $C_n(z_t, w_t) = 0$.

Therefore, (18) takes the form

$$V_n(\hat{z}_t) = V_n(z_t) + V_n(w_t), \tag{19}$$

from which it follows that

$$V_n(\hat{z}_t) \geq V_n(z_t), \tag{20}$$

by the nonnegativity of $V_n(w_t)$. Recall that (20) is derived in the presence of rational stochastic bubbles.

In a study of actual data, an assumption must be made about the form of the marginal utility of consumption foregone when purchasing an asset and the marginal utility realized from consuming the the dividends and capital value of the asset. A popular assumption in some applied work is that the marginal utility of consumption is a positive constant whose value is immaterial to agents' decisions. A finding, in applied work, that an asset-pricing model violates inequality (20) is evidence of model misspecification. Many mistakes can arise in the choice of utility function, the choice of observation period, the treatment of taxes, or some other misspecification, but the violation of (20) cannot be due to rational asset price bubbles since (20) was derived in a model that allowed bubbles.

Research that does not use the terminal price as above in variance bounds tests of stock price volatility, such as Leroy and Porter (1981), could, in principle, find variance bounds violations attributable to rational stock price bubbles. Of course, these models could also violate variance bounds if misspecified in any of the ways mentioned above.

IV   Testing for Bubbles

In the previous section we demonstrated that some volatility tests, which were not originally proposed as bubble tests, are not well-designed tests of bubbles. In this section we discuss some tests that were conceived explicitly to test for bubbles. We also provide a warning about the interpretation of such tests.

A Warning about Bubble Tests

In virtually all modern economic models, expectations of agents about the future play an important role in decision making. Empirical implementation of these models is complicated by the fact that expectations are not observable directly. The investigator must model agents' expectations in terms of observable variables; he substitutes his model of expectations for the unobservable true expectations. Once the final model of actual data is estimated, with the restrictions from expectations imposed, inference can be carried out conditionally on having modeled expectations correctly. If the model of expectations is flawed, incorrect inference can result. This problem is particularly serious in bubble tests, but it is not just in these tests that the problem arises.

The typical rational-expectations econometric methodology involves using the assumption of rational expectations and an assumed time series model for the exogenous driving processes. These assumptions allow the researcher to use historical data to substitute for the unobserved expectations variables. Suppose that the assumed time series model is incorrect and that historical time series data on market fundamentals are a poor reflection of agents' beliefs about the future evolution of data. For example, if in order to finance expansion a profitable firm has been paying no dividends and retaining all profits throughout its finite history, the firm's nonexistent dividend history gives no information about the dividends that the firm is capable of paying in the future. Consequently, the dividend history provides no information about the value of a share in that firm to an investor.

If the market knows that the firm will not be paying dividends for some time, market equilibrium requires that the expected real value of the firm rise at a rate equal to the expected real rate of interest appropriate for the riskiness of that firm. This circumstance creates a debilitating problem for a researcher interested in testing for bubbles. If the investigator assumes that it is appropriate to infer the market fundamentals price from historical dividends, he would infer that the fundamental value of the firm is zero. He would also ascribe all movements in the firm's value to a bubble, since bubbles, in the type of model presented above, are characterized by arbitrary price movements whose expected rate of change is equal to the real rate of interest.

This is an obvious, simple example of a problem in testing for bubbles that may assume a much more complex form. Stated more generally, the issue is that it seems very difficult to disentangle bubbles from the possibility that agents may be anticipating, with some finite probability, some eventual change in the underlying economic environment. Flood and Garber (1980) discussed this problem in their original bubble tests, and Hamilton and Whiteman (1985) have recently also addressed the problem. In later work, Flood and Garber (1983) referred to agents' beliefs in possible future alterations of the economic environment as *process switching*. We adopt that terminology here.

Since dividend policy is arbitrary in simple models of the firm, the problem of process switching seems particularly devastating here. By working with over one hundred years of data from the Standard and Poor's data set, Shiller and West tried to circumvent the problem in two ways. First, they used a data set with a long intertemporal dimension. Second, the data set is for a large aggregate of firms rather than for an individual firm. Intuitively, both features of the data seem useful in avoiding the process-switching pitfall in interpreting the data, but at a formal level neither seems to help very much. Having a long intertemporal dimension does not guarantee that the sample includes either a large sample of process switches or that the stochastic process governing such switches is modeled appropriately. Further, if dividend policy for one firm is arbitrary, then dividend policy for a large aggregate of firms will generally also be arbitrary. Hence, aggregation of dividends does not provide much formal help in avoiding problems of interpretation induced by process switching.

For these reasons, we interpret tests of the no bubbles hypothesis as actually being tests of the hypothesis of no bubbles *and* no process switching. Of course, conditional on no process switching, the tests may be interpreted as tests of the no bubbles hypothesis.

Tests under the Alternative Hypothesis of Bubbles

Early tests for bubbles were conducted on data from European hyperinflations following World War I. Flood and Garber (1980), Burmeister and

Wall (1984), and Flood, Garber, and Scott (1984) estimate an equation of money market equilibrium while simultaneously estimating a money-supply forcing process.

There is a close relation between these early price-level models, which allow bubbles, and the asset-pricing models discussed above. In the early models the log of the price level played the role currently being played by the marginal utility value of the asset, the log of the money supply played the role currently taken by the utility value of dividend payments, and a transformation of the semielasticity of money demand with respect to expected inflation played the role currently taken by the constant discount rate, ρ.

There are some important differences among the early studies in empirical implementation of bubble tests. Flood and Garber (1980) did a time series estimation of a nonstochastic bubble; Burmeister and Wall (1984) did a time series estimation of a specific stochastic bubble while relaxing some strong identifying restrictions Flood and Garber made about the nature of the forcing process; and Flood, Garber, and Scott (1984) combined time series and cross section data to test for a nonstochastic bubble simultaneously inhabiting a number of post—World War I hyperinflations.

There is also an important similarity in these studies. In each case the researchers desired to test the hypothesis that bubbles are absent from the data while estimating under the alternative hypothesis that bubbles are present. The Flood and Garber and the Burmeister and Wall studies both attempt time series asymptotic tests of the null hypothesis that bubbles are absent from the data. They desired to test the statistical significance of the parameters associated with the bubble against the null hypothesis that these parameters are zero. The difficulty with such tests is that the statistics used to test for bubbles must be derived under the alternative hypothesis that allows for bubbles. It is well known that the asymptotic distribution of test statistics in situations such as the presence of bubbles (exploding regressors) is difficult to derive and that standard tests are almost certainly not applicable.[5]

Flood, Garber, and Scott (1984) try to avoid the time series problem by estimating with panel data. The conceptual experiment yielding the asymptotic distributions involves letting the size of the cross section in the panel become very large, and this would produce well-behaved asymptotic parameter distributions in large samples if the cross-sectional errors satisfy the appropriate orthogonality conditions. The problem in applying this methodology is that the number of simultaneous hyperinflations was not actually very large. The size of the cross section in Flood, Garber, and Scott was only three.

West's Bubble Tests

Prompted by some ideas presented in Blanchard and Watson (1982), West (1984, 1985a, 1985b) developed bubble tests that circumvent the problems associated with obtaining limiting distributions described above. West's insight was to conduct all estimation under the null hypothesis of no bubbles. Under the null, standard asymptotic distribution theory applies for all parameter estimates, and tests of the no bubbles hypothesis may be conducted in large samples using these distributions. The nonstationarity of bubbles affects West's tests only because asymptotic distributions of the parameter estimates are not well behaved under the alternative hypothesis. Consequently, the power of his tests is unknown. This problem, though, appears in all econometric work that allows for a variety of unspecified alternative hypotheses and is not specific to West's tests.

West's first application of his bubble tests was to annual aggregate stock prices, and he interpreted his results as providing overwhelming evidence of the presence of economically important stochastic bubbles in the stocks comprising Shiller's (1981) modified Dow-Jones data and the Standard and Poor's index.

Since a large portion of our empirical work involves extensions and modifications of West's work, we now present a stylized version of his methods. Also, since our research as well as West's involves data from the stock market, we discuss the issues in the context of the example examined above. The goal of West's research is to test the hypothesis that every element in the series $\{b_t\}$ is zero, where the series $\{b_t\}$ contains the bubble elements from a specific model of an asset price series.

The first step in West's methodology is to estimate and test the specification given in (3), the Euler equation for adjacent periods. West's methods require the investigator to specify the agent's utility function, and in most of his work he assumed a risk-neutral representative agent. With risk neutrality an agent's marginal utility of consumption is constant across time and is known to all agents. Hence, the marginal utility terms divide out of each side of (3) to yield

$$p_t = \rho E_t(p_{t+1} + d_{t+1}) \tag{3a}$$

where p_{t+i} is the real price of the asset at time $t + i$ and d_{t+i} is the real dividend paid by the asset at time $t + i$ to purchasers of the asset at $t + i - 1$. The model provides no guidance to the researcher in determining the appropriate deflator to convert nominal asset prices and nominal dividends into real terms. West followed Shiller (1981) and deflated nominal stock prices and nominal dividends by a producer price index.[6]

West examines four aspects of (3a) to determine its consistency with the data. The first involves a specification test of the overidentifying restrictions. West estimated (3a) using Hansen's (1982) generalized method of moments (GMM), which is an instrumental variable technique that delivers overidentifying restrictions when the number of instrumental variables exceeds the number of parameters to be estimated. The specification test of the overidentifying restrictions involves examination of a chi-square statistic. The second specification test involves examining serial correlation of the residuals using the procedures described in Pagan and Hall (1983). The third test checks the stability of estimated coefficients by testing for midsample shifts in the coefficients. The fourth way the specification was examined involved checking the quality and reasonableness of the estimated parameters. Are the standard errors relatively small and do the point estimates correspond to reasonable economic values? Do the estimates change with changes in the instruments?

Step two of the methodology involves estimating a prediction equation for real dividends as a function of past dividends and possibly a linear trend. One of the nice aspects of West's work is that he is able to test for bubbles without taking a stand on the econometric exogeneity of any variables. He is able to carry out the tests as long as he has correctly identified the order of the lagged dividends required to forecast future dividends with a white noise error. Real dividends may depend on many contemporaneous and lagged variables not explicitly included in the forecasting equation. The methodology simply requires that the dividend forecasting equation be taken to be the projection of current dividends onto lagged dividends, which are assumed to be contained in the information set used by agents in making their predictions of future dividends. Other variables that might have entered a more primitive dividend equation have implicitly been solved out in the projection process.

The dividend forecasting equation is also subjected to a battery of tests. These include testing for midsample coefficient shifts, testing for first-order serial correlation following the Pagan and Hall procedures, and calculating the Box-Pierce Q statistic testing simultaneously for first- and higher-order serial correlation. If process switching is important, it could be manifest in the stability of the coefficients of the forecasting equation.

The third step in the methodology involves modeling the asset price in two ways. The two should be equivalent if there are no asset price bubbles. The first asset price model involves parameters estimated in the first two steps. From the work of Hansen and Sargent (1980, 1982), a closed-form expression for the market fundamentals portion of asset price is available once the econometrician takes a stand on the information set conditioning the expectation operator in (3a), the parameters entering the forecasting equation for future dividends, and the discount parameter in the agent's utility function. In West's method these parameters and their distributions are obtained in the first two steps. The second asset price equation involves estimating an unconstrained regression of asset price on the information used to form the dividend forecasts. As long as there are no bubbles, the parameters constructed from (3a) and the dividend forecasting equation ought not to be significantly different from the parameters estimated in the unconstrained regression. If a bubble is present in asset price, however, and as long as the bubble has a nonzero mean or is correlated with past dividends, the parameters calculated in the unconstrained regression will not be unbiased estimates of the parameters constructed from (3a). A Hausman (1978) test is appropriate to test the significance of the measured differences between the two asset price models.

The steps in West's methodology contain an important sequential aspect. Only if the first two steps deliver correct equations does the third step test for bubbles. Formally, the bubbles test is conditional on having correct specifications for the Euler equation and the dividend forecasting equation. If either the Euler equation or the dividend forecasting equation is incorrect, there is no reason to expect an asset-pricing function constructed from incorrect elements to be close to the unconstrained pricing function.

This methodology is applied by West (1984, 1985a) to a stock market model of a long data series of aggregated stock prices and dividends. His finding is that there is strong evidence of bubbles in aggregate stock prices. These findings intrigued us for several reasons. First, if the findings held up under additional scrutiny, they would be strong evidence of either expected process switching or of asset price bubbles, and neither possibility is particularly attractive. Second, we suspected that this linear Euler equation featuring a constant rate of return is not appropriate. Although West works with a long time series of annual data, which are considerable different from the quarterly or monthly post–World War II data in Hansen and Singleton (1982, 1983), the strength of the evidence against the constant real rate of return model in postwar data seems overwhelming. Third, we suspected that his data do not satisfy the assumption of time series stationarity necessary to conduct inference in the manner he proposed.

In the next section we use data provided to us by West to demonstrate that his interpretation of his results is almost surely incorrect.[7] We show that the data indicate it is very likely that his basic model is misspecified. His test for no bubbles is actually a test of a joint hypothesis that includes correct model specification and absence of bubbles. Since it is likely that the model is misspecified, failure of a test of this joint hypothesis does not give much evidence that bubbles are present. Of course, failure of the test is not inconsistent with bubbles; it simply does not give much information about bubbles.

V   New Empirical Analyses

The data we use consist of annual real stock price indices and associated real dividend payments for two time series. The first set of series is for the Standard and Poor's data for the years 1871–1980, and the second is for a modified Dow-Jones index for the years 1928–1978. Nominal magnitudes are deflated by the Bureau of Labor Statistics wholesale price index. The stock price data are the daily averages for each January, and the dividends are those that accrue during a year.[8]

We first replicated the results in West's table IA. Since we were concerned that first differencing the levels of the data would not be sufficient to provide a stationary time series process, we estimated the Euler equation in return form using a set of instruments that ought to be stationary in a growing real economy. The first equation estimated was

$$1 = \rho E_t(R_{t+1}) \tag{21}$$

where $R_{t+1} \equiv (p_{t+1} + d_{t+1})/p_t$, the return at time $t + 1$.

We also employed a GMM estimation using a constant and three lags of the dividend-price ratio, d_t/p_t, as instruments. The results are reported in table 5.1. The usefulness of the instrument set, as measured by its ability to predict the returns, is discussed later in this section. Equations 1 and 5 in table 5.1 report the results of estimating the Euler equation of the risk-neutral utility function. Our results are very similar to those of West even though our instruments are different and we estimated the Euler equation in return form while he estimated either in levels or in first differences.

The discount rate, ρ, is very precisely and very plausibly estimated. The estimated value using the Standard and Poor's data (specification 5) with lagged dividend-price ratios as instruments is 0.9155 with a standard error of 0.0138. The estimate using the modified Dow-Jones data (specification 1) is 0.9171 with a standard error of 0.0268. As West mentions, the discount rate estimates are quite close to the inverse of the average return on the stock market over the estimation period. That the discount rate is precisely and plausibly estimated, however, is only part of the story. The chi-square statistic that tests the overidentifying restrictions indicates

Table 5.1
GMM estimation of Euler equation

$1 = E_t \rho \{ [U'(c_{t+1})/U'(c_t)][(p_{t+1} + d_{t+1})/p_t] \}$

Instruments: $(1, d_t/p_t, d_{t-1}/p_{t-1}, d_{t-2}/p_{t-2})$
Data set (equations 1–4): modified Dow-Jones (1931–1978)

1. Utility function $\quad U(c_t) = c_t \quad$ (risk neutral)
$\hat{\rho} = 0.9171$; S.E. $= 0.0268$; M.L.S. $= 0.000$; $\chi^2(3) = 6.6461$; M.L.S. $= 0.084$

2. Utility function $\quad U(c_t) = ln(c_t) \quad$ (log utility)
$\hat{\rho} = 0.9446$; S.E. $= 0.0278$; M.L.S. $= 0.000$; $\chi^2(3) = 8.8779$; M.L.S. $= 0.031$

3. Utility function $\quad U(c_t) = [1/(1 - \alpha)]c_t^{1-\alpha} \quad$ (CRRA)
$\hat{\rho} = 0.8622$; S.E. $= 0.0470$; M.L.S. $= 0.000$; $\hat{\alpha} = -1.8663$; S.E. $= 2.0173$; M.L.S. $= 0.355$;
$\chi^2(2) = 6.7852$; M.L.S. $= 0.034$

4. Utility function $\quad U(c_t) = 1 - (1 - \alpha)\exp(-\alpha c_t) \quad$ (CARA)
$\hat{\rho} = 0.8639$; S.E. $= 0.0423$; M.L.S. $= 0.000$; $\hat{\alpha} = -0.5064$; S.E. $= 0.4791$; M.L.S. $= 0.291$;
$\chi^2(2) = 6.4260$; M.L.S. $= 0.040$

Data set (equation 5): Standard and Poor's (1874–1980)
5. Utility function $\quad U(c_t) = c_t \quad$ (risk neutral)
$\hat{\rho} = 0.9155$; S.E. $= 0.0138$; M.L.S. $= 0.000$; $\chi^2(3) = 8.8499$; M.L.S. $= 0.034$

Note: Standard errors are denoted S.E. and marginal levels of significance are denoted M.L.S. Standard errors are calculated under the null hypothesis with allowance for conditional heteroscedasticity as in Hansen and Singleton (1982).

mixed evidence concerning the model. The test statistic is $\chi^2(3) = 8.8499$ with an associated marginal level of significance of 0.034 for the Standard and Poor's data and $\chi^2(3) = 6.6461$ with an associated marginal level of significance of 0.084 for the modified Dow-Jones data.

These results are not very different from those reported by West in his table IA, when he estimated his model in levels. He found that the model performed poorly in levels for the Standard and Poor's data, and he attributed this to possible nonstationarity in prices and dividends. Consequently, he reestimated the model with some of the equations in first differenced form and other equations remaining in levels. The chi-square statistics in this instance are much more favorable to the model. We simply do not follow the logic of West's procedure. Prices and dividends were differenced to allow for possible nonstationarity in levels due to linear growth. The Euler equation, however, is estimated in level form. If prices and dividends are indeed nonstationary, the Euler equation ought also to be estimated in a form that takes satisfactory account of this nonstationarity. This is a problem that has been confronted in the literature previously, for example, Hansen and Singleton (1982, 1983), and we have adopted the typical solution—estimation of the Euler equation in return form.

We see no reason to difference our instruments or to difference the returns on the stock market. Even in an exponentially growing economy, stock market returns and dividend price ratios are stationary. Consequently, our interpretation of the data indicates that the risk-neutral specification does not work at all well for the Standard and Poor's data and works only marginally better for the modified Dow-Jones data. On the basis of these results and the tests in West's paper, there are grounds for proceeding cautiously with bubble tests based on the linear Euler equation.

Nonlinear Euler Equations

A number of recent studies have estimated nonlinear Euler equations, and a natural question is how well do some popular nonlinear period utility functions explain the current data? In table 5.1 we report our results for three nonlinear period utility functions: $U(c_t) = ln(c_t)$ (logarithmic utility), $U(c_t) = (1 - \alpha)^{-1}c_t^{(1-\alpha)}$ (constant relative risk aversion), and $U(c_t) = 1 - (1/\alpha)\exp(-\alpha c_t)$ (constant absolute risk aversion). Since we want to compare the performance of these utility functions against the performance of the linear alternative, while giving the linear alternative the benefit of the doubt, we conduct the comparison using the Modified Dow-Jones data in which the risk-neutral model performed best.

The results of this investigation are presented in table 5.1 specifications 2—4. The data set is the Modified Dow-Jones data 1931—1978 along with real per capita consumption figures for the United States.[9]

Three points about the results are noteworthy. First, the discount rate is estimated approximately as precisely and reasonably in all three specifications of nonlinear utility functions as in the case of the linear utility function. All of the estimates of the discount rate are within two standard errors of the estimate for the constant relative risk aversion utility function. Second, the tests of the overidentifying restrictions for the nonlinear utility functions are all above the chi-square statistic for the linear utility function. In fact, for the nonlinear utility functions, the Euler equation model would be rejected at standard confidence levels. Third, for the nonlinear utility functions of the constant relative risk aversion and constant absolute risk aversion types, the free parameter in the utility function is very imprecisely estimated.

Iterated Euler Equation Estimation

These results seem to us to point in the direction of the linear utility function as providing the most nearly adequate description of the data in

this class of utility functions. Of course, the utility function could be complicated in a wide variety of ways, but an investigation of such complications is beyond the scope defined for this study.

While the results thus far, on the Dow-Jones data set, point in the
direction of not rejecting the linear utility function at traditional levels of
significance, there remains one problem: Even if the linear Euler equation is
fairly close to the true Euler equation, is it close enough to the true Euler
equation to use in bubble tests? The potential problem arises because bubble tests do not simply use the Euler equation once; they use the Euler
equation iterated an indefinite number of times. Suppose, for example, that
using the linear utility function in place of the true utility function induces
a small specification error into the Euler equation that is difficult to detect.
Bubble tests require iteration of the Euler equation over and over with
future Euler equations projected onto the current information set. It might
be that this minor specification error, when summed over indefinitely many
periods, becomes a quite formidable mistake. Certainly, we have no formal
proof of such a proposition in mind, for it may also be true that the
summation of the specification errors causes cancellation such that the sum
over lots of specification errors is less formidable than any single error.[10]

One way to proceed empirically to investigate the importance of this
issue is to iterate the Euler equation a second period as in the derivation of
(8). The iterated Euler equation was subjected to the same type of testing
procedure used for the noniterated equation. Since the modified Dow-Jones
data set previously was the most favorable environment for the risk-neutral
utility function, we started our investigation using the Dow-Jones data.
Table 5.2 reports the results. We estimated the Euler equation for the four
period utility functions used above. In all cases the $\chi^2(3)$ statistic rose as
compared with the noniterated equation, and in all cases the chi-square
statistic indicates dramatic rejection of the equation. Most interesting is the
large increase in the chi-square statistic for the risk-neutral utility function.
Recall that previously, with these data, the noniterated risk-neutral utility
function appeared to provide the best explanation of the functions we
investigated. Now, with one iteration of the Euler equation, the chi-square
statistic with three degrees of freedom jumps dramatically from 6.6461 to
35.5453, indicating almost sure rejection of the risk-neutral model in these
data.

Different Discount Rates for Dividends and Capital Gains

One possibly important objection to the way we have used the data is that
we, like most other investigators, have used pre-tax returns to estimate

Table 5.2
GMM estimation of once iterated Euler equation

$1 = E_t\rho\{\rho[U'(c_{t+2})/U'(c_t)][(p_{t+2} + d_{t+2})/p_t] + [U'(c_{t+1})/U'(c_t)](d_{t+1}/p_t)\}$
Instruments: $(1, d_t/p_t, d_{t-1}/p_{t-1}, d_{t-2}/p_{t-2})$
Data set (equations 1–4): modified Dow-Jones (1931–1978)

1. Utility function $U(c_t) = c_t$ (risk neutral)
$\rho = 0.8429$; S.E. $= 0.0102$; M.L.S. $= 0.000$; $\chi^2(3) = 35.5453$; M.L.S. $= 0.000$

2. Utility function $U(c_t) = ln(c_t)$ (log utility)
$\rho = 0.9460$; S.E. $= 0.0235$; M.L.S. $= 0.000$; $\chi^2(3) = 13.7362$; M.L.S. $= 0.003$

3. Utility function $U(c_t) = [1/(1 - \alpha)]c_t^{1-\alpha}$ (CRRA)
$\rho = 0.8743$; S.E. $= 0.0811$; M.L.S. $= 0.000$; $\hat{\alpha} = -0.8023$; S.E. $= 3.4361$; M.L.S. $= 0.815$;
$\chi^2(2) = 8.2965$; M.L.S. $= 0.016$

4. Utility function $U(c_t) = 1 - (1 - \alpha)\exp(-\alpha c_t)$ (CARA)
$\rho = 0.8691$; S.E. $= 0.0716$; M.L.S. $= 0.000$; $\hat{\alpha} = -0.0195$; S.E. $= 0.7640$; M.L.S. $= 0.980$;
$\chi^2(2) = 9.3902$; M.L.S. $= 0.009$

Data set (equation 5): Standard and Poor's (1874–1980)
5. Utility function $U(c_t) = c_t$ (risk neutral)
$\rho = 0.9361$; S.E. $= 0.0115$; M.L.S. $= 0.000$; $\chi^2(3) = 10.787$; M.L.S. $= 0.013$

Note: See table 5.1.

behavior which depends on after-tax returns. If dividends and capital gains were taxed at equal constant uniform rates, the estimated discount rates could simply be interpreted as after-tax discount rates, equal to the primitive discount rate times one minus the tax rate. There are three problems though. First, tax rates are not constant; second, dividends are not subject to a flat tax rate; and third, dividends and capital gains are not taxed in the same way.

We do not treat the first two problems. We tried, however, to make a crude correction for the unequal taxation of dividends and capital gains. Our idea was simply to split the return into its capital gain component and its dividend yield component and to estimate separate discount rates for the two elements of the return. We estimated only the Euler equation for the risk-neutral utility function, and we estimated only in the Standard and Poor's data set. Table 5.3 gives the results for both the noniterated and the iterated versions of the Euler equation. The discount rates are now not very precisely estimated for discounting the dividend yield, but they continue to be quite precisely estimated for the capital gain component of the return. The hypothesis that the two discount rates are equal is not strongly supported for either estimation. In fact, the point estimate of the discount rate attached to the dividend yield is negative.

Table 5.3
GMM estimation of unequal discount rates Euler equation

Noniterated Euler equation
$1 = E_t\{[\rho_1(d_{t+1}/p_t) + \rho_2(p_{t+1}/p_t)][U'(c_{t+1})/U'(c_t)]\}$
Instruments: $(1, d_t/p_t, d_{t-1}/p_{t-1}, d_{t-2}/p_{t-2})$
Data set: Standard and Poor's (1974–1980)
1. Utility function $U(c_t) = c_t$ (risk neutral)
$\rho_1 = -1.9597$; S.E. $= 1.4844$; M.L.S. $= 0.187$
$\rho_2 = 1.0565$; S.E. $= 0.0745$; M.L.S. $= 0.000$
$\chi^2(2) = 3.4813$; M.L.S. $= 0.175$
Hypothesis test: H_0: $\rho_1 = \rho_2$ vs. H_1: $\rho_1 \neq \rho_2$
Wald statistic* $= 3.7512$; M.L.S. $= 0.053$
Once iterated Euler equation risk neutrality
$1 = E_t\{\rho_1(d_{t+1}/p_t) + \rho_1\rho_2(d_{t+2}/p_t) + \rho_2^2(p_{t+2}/p_t)\}$
(106 observations)
$\rho_1 = -2.4349$; S.E. $= 1.6234$; M.L.S. $= 0.134$
$\rho_2 = 1.1047$; S.E. $= 0.0846$; M.L.S. $= 0.000$
$\chi^2(2) = 2.2313$; M.L.S. $= 0.328$
Hypothesis test: H_0: $\rho_1 = \rho_2$ vs. H_1: $\rho_1 \neq \rho_2$
Wald statistic* $= 4.3002$; M.L.S. $= 0.038$
*Wald statistic $= (\hat{\rho}_1 - \hat{\rho}_2)^2/[V(\hat{\rho}_1) + V(\hat{\rho}_2) - 2C(\hat{\rho}_1, \hat{\rho}_2)] = \chi^2(1)$

Note: See table 5.1.

Return Forecasting Equations

Underlying all of our empirical work is the first stage forecasting equation for returns. If the risk-neutral utility function describes the data, then expected returns should be a constant equal to the inverse of the discount factor. Our estimation procedure requires that past information is useful in forecasting returns. No element of that past information set, other than a constant, should be helpful in predicting returns if the risk-neutral model is correct. In table 5.4 we present estimates of some linear regressions of stock market returns on some predetermined variables and constants. The GMM estimates we reported above implicitly used forecasting equations based on lagged dividend-price ratios, and here we present both those forecasting equations and some forecasting equations based on lagged dividend-price ratios and on lagged returns. These regressions are reported for both the Standard and Poor's and modified Dow-Jones data sets.

The interesting statistic obtained in all of these regressions is the $\chi^2(3)$ statistic that tests the hypothesis that the estimated coefficients on all of the

Table 5.4
Estimation of return forecasting equations

Data set: Standard and Poor's (1874–1980)

Equation 1. $R_t = a_0 + a_1 d_{t-1}/p_{t-1} + a_2 d_{t-2}/p_{t-2} + a_3 d_{t-3}/p_{t-3} + e_{1t}$

Coefficient	Estimate	S.E.	z	M.L.S.
a_0	0.9428	0.0606	15.5654	0.0000
a_1	−0.2746	1.3626	−0.2015	0.8403
a_2	3.2704	1.6222	2.0160	0.0438
a_3	−0.2943	1.5804	−0.1862	0.8523

$H_0: a_1 = a_2 = a_3 = 0; \chi^2(3) = 9.418;$ M.L.S. $= 0.024; R^2 = 0.032;$ D.W. $= 1.953$

Equation 2. $R_t = b_0 + b_1 R_{t-1} + b_2 d_{t-1}/p_{t-1} + b_3 d_{t-2}/p_{t-2} + e_{2t}$

Coefficient	Estimate	S.E.	z	M.L.S.
b_0	0.9030	0.1936	4.6633	0.0000
b_1	0.0292	0.1538	0.1903	0.8491
b_2	0.0725	1.9222	0.0377	0.9699
b_3	2.7903	1.7239	1.6187	0.1055

$H_0: b_1 = b_2 = b_3 = 0; \chi^2(3) = 9.263;$ M.L.S. $= 0.026; R^2 = 0.032;$ D.W. $= 1.987$

Data set: modified Dow-Jones (1931–1978)

Equation 3. $R_t = c_0 + c_1 d_{t-1}/p_{t-1} + c_2 d_{t-2}/p_{t-2} + c_3 d_{t-3}/p_{t-3} + e_{3t}$

Coefficient	Estimate	S.E.	z	M.L.S.
c_0	0.8171	0.1133	7.214	0.0000
c_1	0.7896	1.9022	0.4151	0.6800
c_2	5.0456	2.0796	2.4260	0.0094
c_3	−0.6237	2.0888	−0.2986	0.7667

$H_0: c_1 = c_2 = c_3 = 0; \chi^2(3) = 11.917;$ M.L.S. $= 0.008; R^2 = 0.076;$ D.W. $= 2.153$

Equation 4. $R_t = f_0 + f_1 R_{t-1} + f_2 d_{t-1}/p_{t-1} + f_3 d_{t-2}/p_{t-2} + e_{4t}$

Coefficient	Estimate	S.E.	z	M.L.S.
f_0	1.1142	0.2908	3.8316	0.0004
f_1	−0.2636	.2222	−1.1861	0.2419
f_2	−2.3591	2.9354	−0.8036	0.4259
f_3	7.2999	2.3440	3.1142	0.0032

$H_0: f_1 = f_2 = f_3 = 0; \chi^2(3) = 17.578;$ M.L.S. $= 0.005; R^2 = 0.1032;$ D.W. $= 1.942$

Note: See table 5.1. All standard errors are estimated using the Hansen-White correction for conditional heteroscedasticity. The z statistic, the ratio of an estimated coefficient to its standard error, is distributed as a standard normal in large samples. The R^2 is adjusted for degrees of freedom.

Table 5.5
Estimation of compound return forecasting equations

Data set: Standard and Poor's (1874–1980)

Equation 1. $R_{t+1,2} = a_0 + a_1 d_{t-1}/p_{t-1} + a_2 d_{t-2}/p_{t-2} + a_3 d_{t-3}/p_{t-3} + e_{t+1,2}$

Coefficient	Estimate	S.E.	z	M.L.S.
a_0	0.7716	0.1116	6.9144	0.0000
a_1	3.2430	2.2468	1.4430	0.1489
a_2	−0.5367	2.1492	−0.2497	0.8028
a_3	5.0880	1.9029	2.6739	0.0075

H_0: $a_1 = a_2 = a_3 = 0$; $\chi^2(3) = 13.462$; M.L.S. = 0.004; $R^2 = 0.101$;

Equation 2. $R_{t+2,3} = a_0 + a_1 d_{t-1}/p_{t-1} + a_2 d_{t-2}/p_{t-2} + a_3 d_{t-3}/p_{t-3} + e_{t+2,3}$

Coefficient	Estimate	S.E.	z	M.L.S.
a_0	0.6295	0.1513	4.1587	0.0000
a_1	1.3261	2.5997	0.5101	0.6100
a_2	6.6862	1.7869	3.7417	0.0002
a_3	4.3317	2.8192	1.5365	0.1244

H_0: $a_1 = a_2 = a_3 = 0$; $\chi^2(3) = 24.568$; M.L.S. = 0.000; $R^2 = 0.186$;

Equation 3. $R_{t+3,4} = a_0 + a_1 d_{t-1}/p_{t-1} + a_2 d_{t-2}/p_{t-2} + a_3 d_{t-3}/p_{t-3} + e_{t+3,4}$

Coefficient	Estimate	S.E.	z	M.L.S.
a_0	0.4433	0.2436	1.8198	0.0718
a_1	7.5549	3.2868	2.2985	0.0236
a_2	6.9082	0.8026	8.6072	0.0000
a_3	3.5789	3.4461	1.0385	0.3015

H_0: $a_1 = a_2 = a_3 = 0$; $\chi^2(3) =$ * M.L.S. = *; $R^2 = 0.232$;

Note: A * indicates that the matrix was not positive definite.

time-varying regressors are zero. These chi-square statistics have small marginal levels of significance ranging from the largest of 0.032 for Standard and Poor's data with a lagged return included to 0.0005 for the Dow-Jones data with a lagged return included. In our view these simple linear regressions give overwhelming evidence that the risk-neutral model does not adequately describe the data.

Since the iterated Euler equation specification gave the strongest evidence against the null hypothesis of constant expected real returns, we investigated whether the same instruments used in the specification tests in table 5.4 were useful in predicting the compound return across several periods into the future. Table 5.5 reports regressions of the compound return $R_{t+j,j+1}$, for $j = 1, 2, 3$, on a constant and the lagged dividend price ratios. The notation for the compound returns indicates that they are the product of the $j + 1$ one-period returns from time t to time $t + j$. Notice that the value of the chi-square statistic with three degrees of freedom testing the hypothesis of a constant expected two-period compound return is 13.462, which is larger than its analogue in table 5.4, equation (1). Similarly, the chi-square statistic testing the same hypothesis for the compound three-period return has a value of 24.568, which is even larger.

Unfortunately, the algorithm for computing the optimal weighting matrix needed in the calculation of the estimated GMM covariance matrix of the parameters does not constrain the estimated variance-covariance matrix of the estimated coefficients to be positive definite; and in computing the four-period compound return, the matrix was not positive definite. Since the effective degrees of freedom in 107 observations with an overlap of four is quite small, we did not choose to use one of the proposed procedures that does impose a positive definite construction. Since all of the estimation relies on asymptotic distribution theory, the results may be sensitive to sample size.

Summary and Conclusions

Some researchers have concluded that aggregate stock prices in the United States are too volatile to be explained rationally by movements in market fundamentals. Some have also concluded that stock prices may contain rational bubbles. In section III we show that failure of certain variance bounds tests conveys no information about rational bubbles. An incorrectly specified model, however, will generally fail a typical variance bounds test. In section V we examine the specification of the model usually used in variance bounds tests and in bubble tests. We find that the model used in the previous studies is inadequate to explain the data. As noted in section IV, the formal tests that have been carried out on these data are actually tests of the joint hypothesis of (i) the adequacy of the model, (ii) no process switching, and (iii) no bubbles. The joint hypothesis is rejected very strongly, and conditional on having the correct model and no process switching, the rejection has been taken to be evidence of bubbles. Since we find the model to be inadequate, we conclude that the bubble tests do not give much information about bubbles—since the model is inadequate, the null hypothesis should be rejected even if bubbles are not present.

Testing for bubbles requires an unrejected asset-pricing model that explains expected rates of return. Our results, as well as other empirical analyses such as Hansen and Singleton (1983) for example, present what we think is a convincing case that conditional expected returns on stock prices fluctuate through time. The profession is now attempting to reconcile such empirical results with theory and is searching in a number of different directions for the right model. Eichenbaum and Hansen (1985) and Dunn and Singleton (1985) try to save the representative agent Euler equation by adding the service flow from durable goods to the utility function. Garber and King (1984) argue that preference shocks may be necessary before we will be able to have an unrejected model. Grossman, Melino, and Shiller (1985) incorporate taxes and, along with Christiano (1984), explore the estimation of continuous-time models with discrete-time data. Others, such as Mehra and Prescott (1985), argue that the representative agent paradigm must be abandoned in favor of models with differential information sets across agents in order to explain the expected return premium that equity commands over bills.

To this list of research areas and problems we must add the standard caveat that the data may not be generated by ergodic processes that render invalid standard asymptotic inference. In such an environment, learning, possibly about government policies, may be an important contributing factor to time variation in expected returns. Whatever the eventual resolution of the problem, it is worth remembering that tests for bubbles are joint tests of no bubbles and no process switching and that bubble tests require an unrejected asset-pricing model.

Data Appendix

1. Stock market data were provided to us by Kenneth West who obtained the data from Robert Shiller. Two data series were used:

(a) The Standard and Poor's data for 1871–1981 with p_t defined to be the January price divided by the wholesale price index for January. Dividends paid during the year are assumed to accrue to the January holder of the stock. The sum of dividends paid during the year is deflated by the average of that year's wholesale price index and was available from 1871 to 1980.

(b) The (Shiller) Modified Dow-Jones index 1928–1979 with prices and dividends constructed and dated as in (a) above.

Both of these data sets are discussed in more detail in Shiller (1981a).

In our tables we report results for returns labeled Standard and Poor's 1874–1980 and Modified Dow-Jones 1931–1978. The year of a return is denoted by the dividend used in its construction. Estimation begins three years after the beginning of the data sets since we used three lags of the dividend price ratio as instruments.

2. The nonlinear utility functions all required a real per capita consumption measure. We used U.S. real per capita consumption of nondurables and

services. Aggregate consumption of nondurables and services were obtained from the *Economic Report of the President 1984* and were put into per capita terms by dividing by U.S. population taken from the same source. These data were then put into real terms by dividing by the wholesale price index (1967 = 100), which was taken from various issues of the *Handbook of Cyclical Indicators*.

Notes

Flood and Hodrick thank the National Science Foundation for its support of their research. We thank Vinaya Swaroop for efficient research assistance. We also thank Olivier Blanchard, John Cochrane, Lars Hansen, John Huizinga, and seminar participants at Brown University, Duke University, the International Monetary Fund, Princeton University, the University of Chicago, and Washington State University for some useful suggestions.

This paper was presented in the Business School at the University of Chicago during the 1986–87 academic year.

1. Mankiw, Romer and Shapiro (1985) mention this point in their derivation of an unbiased volatility tests. Some of section II incorporates material from Flood and Hodrick (1986), which discusses the issue in depth.

2. Huizinga and Mishkin (1984) is just one example that investigates movement in expected returns on a variety of risky assets over various time periods.

3. Our results match well with those of other researchers such as Hansen and Singleton (1982, 1983), Eichenbaum and Hansen (1985), and Scott (1985a) who report difficulty in finding an adequate representative-agent utility function to use in asset pricing.

4. Tirole (1985) explores the existence of speculative bubbles in an overlapping generations economy, which is an alternative dynamic model to the representative agent paradigm discussed in this chapter.

5. Domowitz and Muus (1985) have some new results concerning asymptotic distribution theory for exploding regressors, which may prove useful in future work on this subject.

6. Shiller (1984) finds similar results when deflating by the consumption deflator for services and nondurables.

7. West provided us with the data that he had obtained from Shiller. The data were partially constructed by Shiller, and they are described in Shiller (1981a).

8. The data are described in more detail in the Data Appendix. Estimation was done with a GMM program supplied by Kenneth Singleton. The standard errors of the statistics are calculated as in Hansen and Singleton (1982, pp. 1276–1277), and they allow for conditional heteroscedasticity.

9. The consumption data were obtained from the *Economic Report of the President, 1984* and are described in the Data Appendix.

10. Without specifying the true utility function, we could make no formal progress on this issue, and if we knew the true utility function, we would have used it in the first place.

References

Blanchard, O., 1979. "Speculative Bubbles, Crashes and Rational Expectations," *Economics Letters* 3, 387–89.

Blanchard, O. and M. Watson, 1982. "Bubbles, Rational Expectations and Financial Markets" in Paul Wachtel (ed.) *Crisis in the Economic and Financial System*, Lexington Books, Lexington, MA.

Burmeister, E. and K. Wall, 1982. "Kalman Filtering Estimation of Unobserved Rational Expectations with an Application to the German Hyperinflation," *Journal of Econometrics* 20, 255–84.

Christiano, L., 1984. "The Effects of Aggregation Over Time on Tests of the Representative Agent Model of Consumption," manuscript, University of Chicago.

Council of Economic Advisors, 1984. *Economic Report of the President*, U.S. Government Printing Office, Washington, D.C.

Diba, B. and H. Grossman, 1985. "The Impossibility of Rational Bubbles," manuscript, Brown University, August.

———, 1988. "Explosive Rational Bubbles in Stock Prices," *American Economic Review* 78, June, 520–530.

Domowitz, I. and L. Muus, 1985. "Inference in the First Order Explosive Linear Regression Model," mnauscript, Northwestern University.

Dunn, K. and K. Singleton, 1986. "Modeling the Term Structure of Interest Rates Under Nonseparable Utility and Durability of Goods," *Journal of Financial Economics* 41, 333–355.

Eichenbaum, M. and L. Hansen, 1990. "Estimating Models with Intertemporal Substitution Using Aggregate Time Series Data," *Journal of Business and Economics Statistics* 8, January, 53–69.

Flood, R. and P. Garber, 1980. "Market Fundamentals Versus Price Level Bubbles: The First Tests," *Journal of Political Economy*, August, 745–70.

———, 1983. "A Model of Stochastic Process Switching," *Econometrica*, May.

Flood R., P. Garber and L. Scott, 1984. "Multi-Country Tests for Price Level Bubbles," *Journal of Economic Dynamics and Control* 8, December, 329–40.

Flood, R. and R. Hodrick, 1986. "Asset Price Volatility, Bubbles and Process Switching", *Journal of Finance*, forthcoming.

Garber, P. and R. King, 1983. "Deep Structural Excavation? A Critique of Euler Equation Methods," NBER. Technical Paper No. 31.

Grossman, S., A. Melino and R. Shiller, 1985. "Estimating the Continuous Time Consumption Based Asset Pricing Model," NBER. Working Paper No. 1643.

Grossman, S. and R. Shiller, 1981. "The Determinants of the Variability of Stock Market Prices," *American Economic Review*, May, 222–27.

Hamilton, J. and C. Whiteman, 1985. "The Observable Implications of Self-fulfilling Expectations," *Journal of Monetary Economics* 16, November, 353–74.

Hansen, L., 1982. "Large Sample Properties of Generalized Method of Moments Estimators," *Econometrica*, July, 1029–54.

Hansen, L. and K. Singleton, 1982. "Generalized Instrumental Variables Estimation of Nonlinear Rational Expectations Models," *Econometrica*, September, 1269–86 and "Errata", January 1984, 267–268.

———, 1983. "Stochastic Consumption, Risk Aversion, and the Temporal Behavior of Asset Returns," *Journal of Political Economy* 88, October, 829–53.

Hausman, J., 1978. "Specification Tests in Econometrics," *Econometrica* 46, November, 1251–71.

Huizinga, J. and R. Mishkin, 1984. "The Measurement of Ex-Ante Real Interest Rates on Assets with Different Risk Characteristics," manuscript, University of Chicago, June.

Kleidon, A., 1986a. "Variance Bounds Tests and Stock Price Valuation Models," *Journal of Political Economy* 94, October, 953–1001.

———, 1986b. "Bias in Small Sample Tests of Stock Price Rationality," *Journal of Business*, April, 237–62.

Leroy, S. and M. Porter, 1981. "The Present Value Relation: Tests Based on Implied Variance Bounds," *Econometrica*, May, 555–74.

Mankiw, G., D. Romer and M. Shapiro, 1985. "An Unbiased Reexamination of Stock Market Volatility, "*The Journal of Finance*, July, 677–89.

Marsh, T., and R. Merton, 1987. "Dividend Variability and Variance Bounds Tests," *Journal of Business*, January, 60, 1–40.

Meese, R., 1986. "Testing for Bubbles in Exchange Markets: The Case of Sparkling Rates," *Journal of Political Economy*, April, 345–73.

Mehra, R. and E. Prescott, 1985. "The Equity Puzzle," *Journal of Monetary Economics*, March, 145–62.

Obstfeld, M. and K. Rogoff, 1983. "Speculative Hyperinflations in Maximizing Models: Can We Rule Them Out?" *Journal of Political Economy*, August, 675–87.

Okina, K., 1985. "Empirical Tests of Bubbles in the Foreign Exchange Market," *Bank of Japan Monetary and Economic Studies* 3, May, 1–45.

Quah, D., 1985, "Estimation of a Nonfundamentals Model for Stock Price and Dividend Dynamics," manuscript, MIT.

Sargent, T. and N. Wallace, 1973. "Rational Expectations and the Dynamics of Hyperinflation," *International Economic Review*, June, 328–50.

Scott, L., 1985. "The Present Value Model of Stock Prices: Regression Tests and Monte Carlo Results," *Review of Economics and Statistics* 67, 4, 599–605.

———, 1991. "Stock Prices and Market Fandamentals in a consumption-Based Capital-Asset-Pricing Model," in L. Scott, ed, *Advances in Quantative Analysis of Finance and Accounting*, Vol. 1, Part A, JAI Press.

Shiller, R., 1981a. "Do Stock Prices Move By Too Much to be Justified by Subsequent Changes in Dividends?" *American Economic Review*, June, 421–36.

————, 1981b. "The Use of Volatility Measures in Assessing Stock Market Efficiency," *Journal of Finance*, June, 291–304.

————, 1982. "Consumption, Asset Markets and Macroeconomic Fluctuations," *Carnegie Rochester Conference Series on Public Policy* 17, 203–250.

————, 1984. "Stock Price and Social Dynamics," *Brookings Papers on Economic Activity* 2, 457–510.

Singleton, K., 1986. "Testing Specifications of Economic Agents Intertemporal Problems Against Non-Nested Alternatives," Carnegie-Mellon University, *Journal of Econometrics* 30, November, 391–413.

Tirole, J., 1985. "Asset Bubbles and Overlapping Generations," *Econometrica*, 53, November, 1499–1528.

U.S. Department of Commerce, Bureau of Economic Analysis, various issues, *Handbook of Cyclical Indicators: A Supplement to Business Conditions Digest*, U.S. Department of Commerce, Washington D.C.

West, K., 1984. "Speculative Bubbles and Stock Price Volatility," Financial Research Memorandum, No. 54, Princeton University, December.

————, 1985. "A Specification Test for Speculative Bubbles," Financial Research Memorandum, No. 58, Princeton University, revised July.

————, 1987. "A Standard Monetary Model and the Variability of the Deutschemark-Dollar Exchange Rate," *Journal of International Economics* 23, August, 57–76.

Woo, W., 1987. "Some Evidence of Speculative Bubbles in the Foreign Exchange Markets," *Journal of Money, Credit, and Banking* 19, November, 499–514.

6   Asset Price Volatility, Bubbles, and Process Switching

Robert P. Flood and Robert J. Hodrick

The introduction and use of variance bounds tests by financial economists interested in asset pricing and market efficiency have generated considerable controversy. The first tests postulated a simple model in which market efficiency required assets to have a constant expected real rate of return. The rejection of this hypothesis in the work of Shiller (22, 23) and particularly Grossman and Shiller (12) was followed quickly by a number of different responses. The statistical properties of the tests in small samples and the time series assumptions of the data were criticized.[1] Substantial resources have also been devoted to complications of the model that allow time variation in discount rates and risk premiums, while remaining within the representative agent paradigm.[2] Others have taken the performance of the simple model and the excess volatility of asset prices described in the tests to be indicative of market inefficiency.

One particular type of market inefficiency that receives much attention in these discussions is that asset markets may be characterized by speculative bubbles. Representative of these statements is Ackley's (1, p. 13) discussion of Shiller's (22, 23) findings, in which he states, "But, surely, it is possible that speculative price bubbles, upward or downward, ... supply part of the explanation." Similarly, in Fischer's (7, p. 500) discussion of Shiller (25), he states, "Backing up that empirical evidence was the development, by Shiller and others, of the theory of speculative bubbles, providing a reason that prices could fluctuate excessively without smart investors being able to profit from knowing they were living in a bubble." Similar statements have been made by others in discussions of stock price volatility and in discussions of the volatility of foreign exchange rates.[3]

In this chapter we examine whether some of the variance bounds tests reported to date provide evidence for the hypothesis that asset prices contain speculative bubbles. The speculative bubbles discussed here are the type studied by Flood and Garber (9) and Blanchard and Watson (3). The variance bounds tests we discuss are of the types that were conducted by Shiller (22, 23, 24, 25) and Mankiw, Romer, and Shapiro (19) and that were discussed by Grossman and Shiller (12). We demonstrate the sense in which the existence of bubbles can in theory lead to excess volatility of asset prices relative to the volatility of market fundamentals, but we explain why certain variants of variance bounds tests preclude bubbles as a reason that asset price might violate such bounds. This result, without its formal demonstration, is mentioned by Mankiw, Romer, and Shapiro (19, p. 681), who state, "The inequalities ... hold even if there are bubbles." Since many researchers have mentioned bubbles as a possible reason for the failure of the simple rational expectations model in variance bounds tests, we thought it worthwhile to elaborate on the remark in Mankiw, Romer, and Shapiro (19).

The issue turns on how one measures the inherently unobservable construct that Shiller (22) denoted the ex post rational price. If one uses the sample's terminal market price to construct a measurable counterpart to the ex post rational price, as is done by Shiller (24, 25), Grossman and Shiller (12), and Mankiw, Romer, and Shapiro (19), failure of a variance bounds test cannot be attributed to the existence of speculative bubbles.[4] The reason is that use of the sample market price effectively builds bubbles into the null hypothesis. Rejection of the null must consequently be due to other sources. Potential explanations include general misspecification of the model, unknown small sample properties of the tests, and failure of the data to satisfy the ergodicity assumption implicit in the use of the statistics.

In bubble research one particularly important misspecification of the model occurs when the researcher incorrectly specifies agents' beliefs about the time series properties of market fundamentals. The second purpose of this paper is to explain, in terms of a simple model economy, how anticipated changes in market fundamentals may produce asset price paths that would appear, to an empirical researcher who is unaware of the potential change, to be characterized by bubbles, even though the economy is bubble free. The example economy is described by a potential change in government policies that we label a process switch.

Our presentation is in the next two sections. In section I we describe a common asset pricing model and show how it responds to variance bounds tests when bubbles are present. In section II we develop our example economy and explore possible process switches as explanations of bubble-type phenomena. Section III contains some concluding remarks.

I Variance Bounds Tests of an Asset-Pricing Model

Most variance bounds tests examine present value relations that are derived from a representative consumer's optimization problem. If a_t is the real dividend of an asset at time t and z_t is the real price ex-dividend of the asset at time t, a typical first order condition of a representative agent requires

$$p_t = \rho E_t(p_{t+1} + d_{t+1}) \tag{1}$$

where $p_t \equiv U'(c_t)z_t$, $d_t \equiv U'(c_t)a_t$, $U'(c_t)$ is the marginal utility of consumption at time t, ρ is the fixed discount factor of the agent, and $E_t(\cdot)$ is the conditional expectation operator based on all time t information. The representative agent structure presumes homogeneous information across agents at each point in time. Equation (1) requires that the utility of the real value sacrificed by the individual in purchasing the asset be equal to the conditional expectation of the utility of the real value of the benefit from holding and selling the asset.

Equation (1) has the form of a linear difference equation that arises in many rational expectations models. Hence, a solution that depends only on *market fundamentals* can be written as

$$p_t^f = \sum_{i=1}^{\infty} \lambda_i E_t(d_{t+i}), \tag{2}$$

and substitution of (2) into (1) with equality of p_t^f and p_t requires $\lambda_i = \rho^i$.

Notice that if (1) is postulated as the entire model, an additional arbitrary element, b_t, can be added to the market fundamentals solution to provide an alternative solution,

$$p_t = \sum_{i=1}^{\infty} \rho^i E_t(d_{t+i}) + b_t. \tag{3}$$

The model requires only that the sequence of b_t's possesses the property that

$$E_t(b_{t+i}) = \rho^{-i}b_t, \qquad i = 1, 2, \ldots, \tag{4}$$

since with this property the solution (3) satisfies (1). The times series $\{b_t\}$ is termed a rational bubble according to Flood and Garber (9), since it satisfies the Euler equation (1). Absence of bubbles requires that each element of the sequence is zero.[5] The time series property of bubbles described by (4) ensures that bubbles cannot be a reason for the Euler equation (1) to be deemed misspecified in an econometric investigation such as that of Hansen and Singleton (14).

Since we are interested in how various variance bounds tests perform in the presence of speculative bubbles, we take (3) as our representation of equilibrium asset price with no additional restrictions placed on the b_t sequence other than those imposed by (4).[6]

The basic insights of the variance bounds tests are that the variance of an actual variable must be greater than or equal to the variance of its conditional expectation and that this latter variance must be greater than or equal to the variance of a forecast based on a subset of the information used by agents. In order to see how the existence of bubbles could lead in theory to a violation of variance bounds, consider the ex post rational price. The variance bounds literature defines the theoretical ex post rational price to be the price that would prevail if everyone knew the future market fundamentals with certainty and there were no bubbles. Therefore, the ex post rational price is

$$p_t^* = \sum_{i=1}^{\infty} \rho^i d_{t+i}. \tag{5}$$

The theoretical relation that is the foundation of many variance bounds tests is obtained by subtracting (3) from (5) and rearranging terms:

$$p_t^* = p_t + u_t - b_t, \tag{6}$$

where $u_t \equiv \sum_{i=1}^{\infty} \rho^i [d_{t+i} - E_t(d_{t+i})]$ is the deviation of the present value of dividends from its expected value based on time t information. By construction, u_t is uncorrelated with p_t and b_t, but p_t and b_t may be correlated with each other.

Notice in (4) that, since $\rho^{-1} > 1$, a rational stochastic bubble is nonstationary. Consequently, its unconditional moments are undefined. For this reason we address our arguments to variances and covariances of the innovations of processes, which are well defined.

Let the innovation in X_t from time $t - n$ be $[X_t - E_{t-n}(X_t)]$. Then the innovation variance and covariance operators are defined by

$$V_n(X_t) = E\{[X_t - E_{t-n}(X_t)]^2\}$$

and

$$C_n(X_t, Y_t) = E\{[X_t - E_{t-n}(X_t)][Y_t - E_{t-n}(Y_t)]\}$$

where $E(\cdot)$ denotes the unconditional mathematical expectation. In what follows we treat n as a finite positive integer.

Applying the innovation variance operator to both sides of (6) yields

$$V_n(p_t^*) = V_n(p_t) + V_n(u_t) + V_n(b_t) - 2C_n(p_t, b_t), \tag{7}$$

which follows from the conditional orthogonality of u_t to p_t and b_t.

Suppose that a researcher had errorless measurements of p_t^* and p_t over a long time series and could develop very good estimates of $V_n(p_t^*)$ and $V_n(p_t)$.[7] Assume also that the researcher knew that (1) was not rejected by the data. Since the innovation variances of u_t and b_t in (7) are strictly nonnegative, a finding of $V_n(p_t) > V_n(p_t^*)$ could be rationalized, within the framework of the model, by $C_n(p_t, b_t) \geq 0$.

In typical presentations of variance bounds tests, the stochastic bubble is excluded from (6) because absence of bubbles is intended to be part of the joint null hypothesis. A theoretical variance bound derived in (7) in the absence of bubbles is $V_n(p_t^*) > V_n(p_t)$. It is easy to construct examples in which a sufficiently large innovation variance in b_t causes this variance bound to be violated. Consider the situation in which the innovations in b_t are orthogonal to the innovations in market fundamentals. In this case, $C_n(p_t, b_t) = V_n(b_t)$. Therefore, the right-hand side of (7) reduces to $V_n(p_t) + V_n(u_t) - V_n(b_t)$, and a sufficiently large innovation variance in the bubble could cause $V(p_t^*) < V(p_t)$.[8]

We imagine that theoretical exercises similar to the above have spawned the popular argument that the failure of variance bounds tests can be due to speculative bubbles. Analogously, it has been argued that failure to reject the variance bounds inequalities is due to exclusion from the sample of time periods containing bubbles.[9] We now demonstrate that this theoretical intuition is not always correct. The practical implementation of many variance bounds tests precludes rational stochastic bubbles, per se, as the explanation for the failure of the test.

The difference between the theoretical exercise described above and its practical implementation arises, of course, in the construction of an observable counterpart to p_t^*. In practice it is impossible to measure the ex post rational price because it depends on the infinite future. Researchers therefore typically measure a related variable denoted $\hat{p}_t$. Since actual price and dividend data are available for a sample of observations on $t = 0, 1, \ldots, T$, researchers use

$$\hat{p}_t \equiv \sum_{i=1}^{T-t} \rho^i d_{t+i} + \rho^{T-t} p_T, \qquad t = 0, \ldots, T-1, \tag{8}$$

in place of p_t^*.[10] Notice from (5) and (6) that

$$\hat{p}_t = p_t^* - \rho^{T-t} p_T^* + \rho^{T-t} p_T, \tag{9a}$$

which implies from (6) that

$$\hat{p}_t = p_t^* + \rho^{T-t}(b_T - u_T). \tag{9b}$$

Since u_T is the innovation in the present value of dividends between time T and the infinite future, it is uncorrelated with all elements of the time T information set which includes time t information. Since b_T depends on the evolution of the stochastic bubble between t and T, it is not orthogonal to time t information.

Notice what happens when (9b) is solved for p_t^* and the result is substituted into (6). After slight rearrangement, one obtains

$$\hat{p}_t = p_t + w_t, \tag{10}$$

where

$$w_t \equiv (u_t - \rho^{T-t}u_T) + (\rho^{T-t}b_T - b_t). \tag{11}$$

Equation (10) is the empirical counterpart of (6) and forms the basis of the usual variance bounds tests. The only substantive difference between our version of (10) and that of previous researchers is that we have explicitly allowed for rational stochastic bubbles in our derivation.

Application of the innovation variance operator to (10) gives

$$V_n(\hat{p}_t) = V_n(p_t) + V_n(w_t) + 2C_n(p_t, w_t). \tag{12}$$

The important point concerning (12) is that the innovation covariance between p_t and w_t is zero. To understand why, consider the nature of the composite disturbance term w_t. First, as noted above, both u_t and u_T are uncorrelated with p_t since p_t is in the time t information set, which is a subset of the time T information set. Second, the combined term $\rho^{T-t}b_T - b_t$ is uncorrelated with the time t information set even though each term separately is not orthogonal to time t information. This is true because $E_t(b_T) = \rho^{-(T-t)}b_t$, which follows from (4). Hence, $E_t(\rho^{T-t}b_T - b_t) = 0$, and $C_n(p_t, w_t) = 0$.

Therefore, (12) takes the form

$$V_n(\hat{p}_t) = V_n(p_t) + V_n(w_t), \tag{13}$$

from which it follows that

$$V_n(\hat{p}_t) \geq V_n(p_t), \tag{14}$$

by the nonnegativity of $V_n(w_t)$. Condition (14) was derived in the presence of rational stochastic bubbles. If the variables $\hat{p}_t$ and p_t are actually used, as they have been in several tests, and the inequality in (14) is found to be violated, one cannot conclude that stochastic bubbles are an explanation of model misspecification.

Mankiw, Romer, and Shapiro (19) conduct unbiased variance bounds tests using a terminal market price to construct their counterpart to ex post rational price. They note that their variance bounds would not be rejected because of bubbles in asset prices. In his comments on their paper, Shiller (26) mentioned that their exclusion of certain periods that may contain bubbles could be a reason that they fail to reject excess volatility in certain tests. As they noted and as our analysis indicates, their tests should continue to satisfy the variance bounds inequalities even in the presence of bubbles.[11] Since the Mankiw, Romer, and Shapiro framework is slightly different than the one we have used, we have included an appendix showing that bubbles cannot cause violations of their variance bounds.

Research that does not use the terminal price p_T to construct $\hat{p}_t$ does not discriminate among possible reasons for rejection of the null hypothesis. The research which does use the actual terminal market price therefore incorporates one of the alternative hypotheses into the null hypothesis. While this may make it more difficult to reject the null hypothesis, a reversal of the inequality in (14) cannot be attributed to rational stochastic bubbles.

II   A Cautionary Note in Tests for Bubbles

The discussion above assumes that bubbles could be present in the data and examines whether certain variance bounds tests could detect them. In this section we present a cautionary note to those who are interested in testing for bubbles. We develop an example economy that is bubble-free, but it is characterized by a potential switch in government policy that is known to agents but may not be known to the researcher. The asset price paths in the example economy could be taken to be bubbles by an unwary researcher. Consequently, we stress that all bubbles tests are conditional on the researcher having the correct specification of the model, including agents' beliefs about the nature of market fundamentals. Flood and Garber (9), Blanchard (2), and Tirole (27) all define the bubble as what is left over after market fundamentals have been removed from the price. Since neither bubbles nor market fundamentals are directly observable, one can never be sure that market fundamentals have been specified appropriately.[12] The example serves to illustrate the point in the context of the model of the previous section.

The Euler equation (1) may be rewritten as

$$U'(c_t)z_t = E_t[\rho U'(c_{t+1})(z_{t+1} + a_{t+1})]. \tag{15}$$

Consider an economy with a_{t+i} *constant at* $\bar{a}$, and for simplicity assume that aggregate output is not storable and is constant at $\bar{y}$. With population normalized to one, per capita consumption is simply $c_t = \bar{y}$ in equilibrium. We first solve the model without uncertainty, assuming the absence of bubbles. The solution for price is

$$z_t = \rho\bar{a}/(1 - \rho), \qquad t = 0, 1, \ldots. \tag{16}$$

Now consider the solution if the agents know that a government will come into existence at T. Assume that the government will institute a tax system to finance its expenditures and that the service flow of government goods enters the utility function separably from the utility of private goods. Assume also that the government will take g units of the consumption goods each period, which lowers equilibrium consumption to $c = \bar{y} - g$ in each period from T onwards.

The advent of the government sector raises the marginal utility of private consumption in period T and thereafter. We parameterize this change by writing $U'(\bar{y} - g) = (1 + \alpha)U'(\bar{y})$. Suppose further that the government finance system taxes all incomes flows but not capital gains at the rate θ, so that $g = \theta\bar{y}$. After-tax income from owning an asset is therefore $(1 - \theta)\bar{a}$.

To determine the price of the asset in periods before T, consider first what price must hold after the advent of the government. The first order condition at T is

$$U'(\bar{y} - g)z_T = \rho U'(\bar{y} - g)[z_{T+1} + (1 - \theta)\bar{a}], \tag{17}$$

which has the no-bubbles solution

$$z_t = \rho(1 - \theta)\bar{a}/(1 - \rho), \qquad t = T, T+1, \ldots. \tag{18}$$

The price of the asset before T can now be determined by recognizing that agents know at $T - 1$ that dividends will be taxed and that the marginal utility of private consumption will rise at T. Price must obey

$$U'(\bar{y})z_{T-1} = \rho U'(\bar{y} - g)(z_T + (1 - \theta)\bar{a}), \tag{19}$$

which, from (18), implies $z_{T-1} = (1 + \alpha)z_T$. Price falls from $T - 1$ to T to offset the increase in marginal utility and the incidence of taxation. Treating z_{T-1} as a terminal price, we solve for asset prices in periods before time $T - 1$.

The solution for asset price is

$$z_t = A\rho^{-t} + \rho\bar{a}/(1 - \rho), \qquad t = 0, 1, \ldots, T - 1, \tag{20}$$

where

$$A = [(1 - \theta)(1 + \alpha) - 1][\rho\bar{a}/(1 - \rho)]\rho^{(T-1)}. \tag{21}$$

The price path prior to $T - 1$ will rise, fall, or remain constant depending on the sign of A, which is governed by whether $(1 - \theta)(1 + \alpha)$ is greater than, less than, or equal to one.[13]

Now suppose agents are not sure that a government will be installed at T. Assume that their uncertainty can be represented by a time-invariant probability π that the government will begin operation at T, with corresponding probability $(1 - \pi)$ that the government will not begin operation then or at any other time in the future.

With this change the constant term (21) becomes

$$A' = [\pi + (1 - \pi)(1 + \alpha)(1 - \theta) - 1][\rho\bar{a}/(1 - \rho)]\rho^{(T-1)}. \tag{22}$$

If the transition probability is not constant but moves through time, a solution for the price path is

$$z_t = [\pi_t + (1 - \pi_t)(1 + \alpha)(1 - \theta) - 1][\rho\bar{a}/(1 - \rho)]\rho^{T-t-1} + \rho\bar{a}/(1 - \rho),$$

$$t = 0, 1, \ldots, T - 1, \tag{23}$$

which may vary stochastically through time in addition to its deterministic movements.

These simple examples illustrate situations in which an expected future event produces a price path which, if compared to the path of market fundamentals prior to the future event, appears to be characterized by a bubble. Examination of (20) and (23) indicates that asset prices correspond to the no-bubbles system with constant fundamentals price in (18) plus something else. The additional element must fulfill the bubble property given in equation (4) since it is in the homogenous part of the solution. The homogenous part will be present in price either if there are bubbles or if the no-bubbles system needs to position itself in advance of a future switch in forcing processes. The last example as well as more complex versions would generate stochastic price paths that would appear to contain stochastic bubbles that satisfy (4) even though the examples are bubble-free.

The econometric problem arises because the investigator never knows precisely what information is used by economic agents. Consider a naive investigator who examined data from periods surrounding the possible institution of the above government policies in a situation in which the policies were not instituted. If A' in (22) is nonzero, the unwary researcher who treated data for a_t as market fundamentals would conclude that the price path prior to T contained a bubble that burst. The example, of course, was bubble-free. The problem is that a_t does not capture all of the market fundamentals. The potential taxation and government spending programs also are part of fundamentals. If agents receive periodic information about potential changes in policies as in (23), those sources of information are also part of market fundamentals. Given the complexity of political processes, it may be that such misspecification occurs frequently.

The point of this section was to provide a cautionary note to the interpretation of bubbles research. Empirical bubbles tests must be interpreted either conditionally, assuming an investigator has correctly modeled both market fundamentals and agents' beliefs about future market fundamentals, or as joint tests for bubbles and possibilities of misspecification of market fundamentals. Perhaps the latter interpretation is more attractive to some researchers. It is interesting, nevertheless, to inquire whether bubble-type processes characterize the data, and, if so, what might be the misspecification of market fundamentals behind such a finding.

III Concluding Remarks

Some models imply that rational speculative bubbles should be absent from asset prices. For these models, well-designed tests for speculative bubbles are tests of the specification of the model. Other models are consistent with speculative bubbles inhabiting the data. Whether tests for rational speculative bubbles are viewed as specification tests or as tests for underlying indeterminacy of asset prices, the questions raised by considering rational bubbles are susceptible to scientific investigation.

The purpose of this paper was twofold. The first purpose was to demonstrate that failure of some variance bounds tests should not be taken as evidence of rational speculative bubbles, because design of the tests precludes bubbles as a reason for failure of the tests. The second purpose was to argue that bubble tests are hard to design since the path of a bubble in the data would look like some forms of incorrect modeling of agents' expectations.

The problem with interpreting some variance bounds tests as bubble tests lies in the construction of the observable benchmark counterpart to the unmeasurable theoretical concept of ex post rational price. In some tests researchers use a terminal market price in the construction. If bubbles processes are present in the data, they will be in the terminal market price and will therefore be built into the observable benchmark. Since the bubble is both in market price and in the constructed benchmark, the bubble does not give a reason that the volatility of actual market price is greater than the volatility of the benchmark.

With bubbles precluded as a reason for failure of some variance bounds tests, alternative explanations of the results must be found. Recall that the typical variance bounds tests conducted to date are tests of a joint hypothesis with many parts, including the following: (i) rational expectations, (ii) identical risk-neutral asset holders, (iii) annual portfolio decisions, (iv) identical tax treatment of dividends and capital gains, and (v) ergodicity of the data. Although there are other parts of the joint hypothesis, a violation of any combination of the five listed above would result in rejection of the hypothesis.

The second point of the paper is to provide a cautionary note to those who would test for bubbles. Flood and Garber (9) noted the problem that arises in development of convincing bubble tests because bubble processes can look like an investigator's misspecification of agents' unobservable expectations. We reiterated this point in an optimizing example of the stock market. Bubble tests require that the investigator correctly identify the processes used by agents in forming their expectations. In this sense bubble tests are open to the same criticism as is any test conditioned on correct modeling of agents' beliefs—the researcher must in fact conduct a test of a joint hypothesis that correctly models expectations.[14]

In our view, recent empirical research on the volatility of asset prices suggests that relaxation of the strong assumptions listed above will be necessary to develop a positive theory of asset pricing. In this regard, research is being done on a wide variety of fronts to disentangle the joint hypothesis. For example, researchers are relaxing the assumption of risk neutrality, including taxes in the analysis, developing models of agents with heterogeneous information sets, and obtaining direct observations on agents' expectations.

Appendix

In this appendix we demontrate that bubbles cannot be a reason for violation of the variance bounds tests derived in Mankiw, Romer, ad Shapiro (19). Their tests were developed in response to Flavin (8) and Kleidon (16), who argued that estimation of the sample variance by subtraction of the sample mean rather than the population mean produces small sample bias in variance bounds tests. To develop an unbiased test, Mankiw, Romer, and Shapiro (19) consider a "naive forecast" of stock price defined by

$$p_t^0 = \sum_{i=1}^{\infty} \rho^i F_t(d_{t+i}) \tag{A1}$$

where $F_t(d_{t+i})$ is the naive forecast of dividends at time $t + i$ based on some information available at time t.

Consider the following identity:

$$p_t^* - p_t^0 = (p_t^* - p_t) + (p_t - p_t^0). \tag{A2}$$

In order to avoid sample means, Mankiw, Romer, and Shapiro (19) work with the conditional second moments of (A2). Substitute from (6) into (A2) and take conditional second moments to derive

$$E_{t-n}(p_t^* - p_t^0)^2 = E_{t-n}(p_t^* - p_t)^2 + E_{t-n}(p_t - p_t^0)^2 - 2E_{t-n}[b_t(p_t - p_t^0)]. \tag{A3}$$

The last term in (A3) appears because $p_t^* - p_t = u_t - b_t$, and, although u_t is orthogonal to $(p_t - p_t^0)$, b_t is not. Notice, therefore, that the two inequalities derived by Mankiw, Romer, and Shapiro (19) in the absence of bubbles,

$$E_{t-n}(p_t^* - p_t^0) \geq E_{t-n}(p_t^* - p_t)^2 \tag{A4a}$$

and

$$E_{t-n}(p_t^* - p_t^0)^2 \geq E_{t-n}(p_t - p_t^0)^2, \tag{A4b}$$

need not hold in theory in the presence of bubbles. From (A3), notice that, if $E_{t-n}[b_t(p_t - p_t^0)]^2 > 0$, bubbles would be one of the reasons that the theoretical construct p_t^* could fail a second moment test.

Now consider substitution for p_t^* in (A2) from (9b):

$$\hat{p}_t - p_t^0 = (\hat{p}_t - p_t) + (p_t - p_t^0). \tag{A5}$$

Since p_t^* appears on both sides of (A2), the term $\rho^{T-t}(b_T - u_T)$ in (9b) does not appear in (A5). From (10), notice that $\hat{p}_t - p_t$ on the right-hand side of (A5) is uncorrelated with information at time t. Therefore, since $p_t - p_t^0$ is in the time t information set,

$$E_{t-n}(\hat{p}_t - p_t^0)^2 = E_{t-n}(\hat{p}_t - p_t)^2 + E_{t-n}(p_t - p_t^0)^2, \tag{A6}$$

which provides two empirical counterparts to (A4a) and (A4b):

$$E_{t-n}(\hat{p}_t - p_t^0)^2 \geq E_{t-n}(\hat{p}_t - p_t)^2 \tag{A7a}$$

and

$$E_{t-n}(\hat{p}_t - p_t^0)^2 \geq E_{t-n}(p_t - p_t^0)^2. \tag{A7b}$$

Since (A7a) and (A7b) were derived under the hypothesis that rational stochastic bubbles are present in the data, rejection of either hypothesis cannot be attributed to the presence of stochastic bubbles.

Notes

The authors thank the National Science Foundation for its support of their research. They also thank Paul Kaplan for helpful discussions.

1. See, in particular, Flavin (8), Kleidon (15, 16) and Marsh and Merton (20).

2. Eichenbaum and Hansen (6) and Dunn and Singleton (5) explore alternatives that allow considerable variation in the representative agent's intertemporal marginal rate of substitution.

3. Dornbusch (4) argues that the flexible exchange rate system has not worked well and suggests that speculative bubbles may be one of the culprits. See Meese (21) for a test of speculative bubbles in the foreign exhange market.

4. Marsh and Merton (20) follow Shiller (22, 23) and use the sample average price as the terminal price in constructing their counterexample to Shiller's derived variance bounds.

5. Satisfaction of a transversality condition such as $\lim_{h\to\infty} \rho^h E_t(\rho_{t+h}) = 0$ requires the absence of bubbles. Tests for speculative bubbles can consequently be thought of as tests of this model's transversality condition.

6. The restrictions that (4) places on the b_t process are not very severe. The time series process can take many possible forms, including bubble innovations that are conditionally heteroscedastic.

7. In order to simplify our argument we abstract from the sampling distribution of the sample statistics and regard them as precise estimates of their population counterparts.

8. Geweke (11) notes that in linear environments a variance bounds test is not always powerful at detecting deviations from the theory. Since $p_t = p_t^f + b_t$ from (2) and (3), and because $p_t^* = p_t^f + u_t$ from (5) and the definition of u_t, $V_n(p_t^f) - V_n(p_t) = V_n(u_t) - V_n(b_t) - 2C_n(p_t^f, b_t)$. When $V_n(u_t) > V_n(b_t) + 2C_n(p_t^f, b_t)$, the variance bounds test is unable to detect bubbles even though they are present in the data. Geweke demonstrates that an alternative regression test is more powerful. Frankel and Stock (10) reach a similar conclusion but argue that variance bounds test may be more powerful against nonlinearities in the misspecification.

9. Shiller (26, p. 689), in his discussion of Mankiw, Romer, and Shapiro (19), argues that one reason one of their tests does not find excess volatility is "that the major 'speculative bubbles' in this century of data, that of the 1920s and that of the 1950s, are given less weight."

10. The variable $\hat{p}_t$ is used by Shiller (24), Grossman and Shiller (12), and Mankiw, Romer, and Shapiro (19). Earlier, Shiller (22, 23) used the average market price over the sample period as the terminal price in (8). See note 4. Kleidon (15) and LeRoy (17) demonstrate that

use of $\hat{p}_t$ produces a smooth series compared to p_t even in situations in which the data are constructed to satisfy (1). The series look smooth because, for small k, $V(p_t^* - p_{t-k}^*) < V(p_t - p_{t-k})$ with the results being quite dramatic for highly autocorrelated dividend series. Hence, the graphs in Grossman and Shiller (12) are quite misleading.

11. In fairness to Shiller, his statements in (25) clearly indicate that he rejects the notion of rational speculative bubbles discussed in this paper, although Fischer (7) argues that Shiller's fads and fashions may ultimately prove to be the same thing as speculative bubbles when quantified empirically.

12. This point was emphasized by Flood and Garber (9, pp. 749–50) and has been reiterated by Hamilton and Whiteman (13).

13. If $U(c_t) = c_t^{1-\beta}/(1 - \beta)$, $\beta > 0$, then $(1 + \alpha)(1 - \theta)^\beta = 1$ and the type of price path followed until date $T - 1$ depends on the relationship of β to unity. If $\beta > 1$, prices rise prior to T, whereas they fall if $\beta < 1$. For quadratic utility the relationship of $(1 + \alpha)(1 - \theta)$ to unity will depend on the scale of the economy and ratios of the utility function parameters.

14. The variance bounds test described by LeRoy and Porter (18) and the methodology for testing for bubbles proposed by West (28, 29) are also sensitive to the issue of modeling gents' expectations and the potential failure of the data to satisfy the ergodicity assumption.

References

1. Gardner Ackley. "Commodities and Capital: Prices and Quantities." *American Economic Review* 73 (March 1983), 1–16.

2. Olivier Blanchard. "Speculative Bubbles, Crashes, and Rational Expectations." *Economic Letters* 3 (1979), 387–89.

3. Olivier Blanchard and Mark Watson. "Bubbles, Rational Expectations and Financial Markets." In Paul Wachtel (ed.), *Crisis in the Economic and Financial Structure*. Lexington, MA: Lexington Books, 1982.

4. Rudiger Dornbusch. "Equilibrium and Disequilibrium Exchange Rates." *Zeitschift fur Wirtschafts und Sozialwissenshaften* 102 (1982), 573–99.

5. Kenneth Dunn and Kenneth J. Singleton. "Modeling the Term Structure of Interest Rates Under Nonseparable Utility and Durability of Goods." *Journal of Financial Economics.* 41 (1986), 333–355.

6. Martin Eichenbaum and Lars Peter Hansen. "Uncertainty, Aggregation, and the Dynamic Demand for Consumption Goods." Carnegie-Mellon University, manuscript, 1984.

7. Stanley Fischer. "Comments and Discussion." *Brookings Papers on Economic Activity* 2 (1984), 499–504.

8. Marjorie Flavin. "Excess Volatility in the Financial Markets: A Reassessment of the Empirical Evidence." *Journal of Political Economy* 91 (December 1983), 929–56.

9. Robert P. Flood and Peter M. Garber. "Market Fundamentals Versus Price Level Bubbles: The First Tests." *Journal of Political Economy* 88 (August 1980), 745–70.

10. Jeffrey Frankel and James Stock. "A Relationship Between Regression Tests and Volatility Tests of Market Efficiency." National Bureau of Economic Research, Working Paper No. 1105, 1983.

11. John Geweke. "A Note on Testable Implications of Expectation Models." University of Wisconsin, Social Science Research Institute, Working Paper No. 8024, November 1980.

12. Sanford Grossman and Robert J. Shiller. "The Determinants of the Variability of Stock Market Prices." *American Economic Review* 71 (May 1981), 222–27.

13. James Hamilton and Charles Whiteman. "The Observable Implications of Self-Fulfilling Expectations." *Journal of Monetary Economics* 16 (November 1985), 353–74.

14. Lars Peter Hansen and Kenneth J. Singleton. "Generalized Instrumental Variables Estimation of Nonlinear Rational Expectations Models." *Econometrica* 50 (September 1982), 1269–86.

15. Allan W. Kleidon. "Variance Bounds Tests and Stock Price Valuation Models." *Journal of Political Economy* 94 (October, 1986), 953–1001.

16. ———. "Bias in Small Sample Tests of Stock Price Rationality." *Journal of Business* 59 (April 1986), 237–62.

17. Stephen F. LeRoy. "Efficiency and Variability of Asset Price." *American Economic Review* 74 (May 1984), 183–87.

18. Stephen F. LeRoy and Richard D. Porter. "The Present-Value Relation: Tests Based on Implied Variance Bounds." *Econometrica* 49 (May 1981), 555–74.

19. N. Gregory Mankiw, David Romer, and Matthew D. Shapiro. "An Unbiased Reexamination of Stock Market Volatility." *Journal of Finance* 40 (July 1985), 677–89.

20. Terry A. Marsh and Robert C. Merton. "Dividend Variability and Variance Bounds Tests for Rationality of Stock Market Prices." *American Economic Review* 76 (June 1986), 483–98.

21. Richard Meese. "Testing for Bubbles in Exchange Markets: The Case of Sparkling Rates." *Journal of Political Economy* 94 (April 1986), 345–73.

22. Robert J. Shiller. "Do Stock Prices Move Too Much to Be Justified by Subsequent Changes in Dividends?" *American Economic Review* 71 (June 1981), 421–36.

23. ———. "The Use of Volatility Measures in Assessing Market Efficiency." *Journal of Finance* 36 (June 1981), 291–304.

24. ———. "Consumption, Asset Markets and Macroeconomic Fluctuations." *Carnegie Rochester Conference Series on Public Policy* 17 (1982), 203–50.

25. ———. "Stock Prices and Social Dynamics." *Brookings Papers on Economic Activity* 2 (1984), 457–510.

26. ———. "Discussion." *Journal of Finance* 40 (July 1985), 688–89.

27. Jean Tirole. "Asset Bubbles and Overlapping Generations." *Econometrica* 53 (November 1985), 1499–1528.

28. Kenneth West, "Speculative Bubbles and Stock Price Volatility." Princeton University, Financial Research Center Memorandum No. 54, December 1984.

29. ———. "A Specification Test for Speculative Bubbles." Princeton University, Financial Research Center Memorandum No. 58, April 1985.

7 On the Equivalence of Solutions in Rational Expectations Models

Edwin Burmeister,
Robert P. Flood, and
Peter M. Garber

I Introduction

In recent literature four types of solutions have been proposed to macroeconomic models with rational expectations. These solutions are the widely used *market fundamentals* solution, the *market fundamental plus bubble* solution studied by Flood and Garber (1980) and Burmeister and Wall (1981), the *forward-backward* solution studied by Blanchard (1979), and the *spurious indicator* solution studied by Taylor (1977).[1] The purpose of this paper is to demonstrate that the forward-backward solution is a special case of the market fundamentals plus bubble solution and that the *spurious indicator* solution is equivalent to the market fundamentals plus bubble solution. Hence, instead of four types of solutions to macroeconomic models with rational expectations there are really only two.[2]

The appearance of two types of solutions to macroeconomic models with rational expectations is a manifestation of the well-known property of linear difference and differential equation systems that the general solution consists of a homogeneous solution plus a particular solution. For the model we will study, the market fundamentals solution is one which excludes the homogeneous solution. All other solutions combine a particular solution with the homogeneous solution.

In section II we develop the model and solve it for the solution we will refer to as market fundamentals. In section III we develop the three other solutions mentioned above and show the relationships among them. In section 4 we discuss the problem of isolating the solution actually chosen by an economy.

II The Model

The model we use for our discussion is the familiar Cagan-type money market. It consists of

$$m_t - p_t = -\alpha[E_t p_{t+1} - p_t] + \varepsilon_t, \tag{1}$$

where

m_t logarithm of money supply at time t,

p_{t+i} logarithm of price level at time $t + i$,

E_t mathematical expectation operator, conditional on information available at time t, I_t,

ε_t disturbance term having zero mean, finite variance and distributed independently of its own past values and current or past values of other disturbances.

Equation (1) portrays money market equilibrium, but it may also be thought of as a semi-reduced form arising in a wide variety of macroeconomic models. The parameter α is a constant and we assume $\alpha \neq 0$, $\alpha \neq -1$. The information set I_t includes current and past values of p_t, m_t, ε_t plus all relevant struture. By relevant structure we mean that agents know equation (1), the properties of the process generating ε_t, and the properties of the process generating m_t. At this stage we assume only that money is exogenous to price. Below we will make more specific assumptions about the money-supply process. The model's structure also includes the solution form chosen by agents.

Market fundamentals is the set of current and expected future values of money and the disturbance, ε_t. We conjecture that current price is a linear function of market fundamentals,

$$p_t = \sum_{i=0}^{\infty} \beta_i E_t m_{t+i} + \sum_{i=0}^{\infty} \gamma_i E_t \varepsilon_{t+i}. \tag{2}$$

Since $E_t m_t = m_t$, $E_t \varepsilon_t = \varepsilon_t$, $E_t \varepsilon_{t+i} = 0$ $(i = 1, 2, \ldots)$, substitute (2) into (1) and obtain the following:

$$\beta_0 = 1/(1 + \alpha), \tag{3a}$$

$$\beta_{i+1} = [\alpha/(1 + \alpha)]\beta_i, \qquad i = 0, 1, 2 \ldots, \tag{3b}$$

$$\gamma_0 = -1/(1 + \alpha). \tag{3c}$$

Thus, (2) with the restrictions imposed in (3a)-(3c) is the market fundamentals solution.

III   Other Solutions

In this section we develop the three solutions other than the market fundamentals solution and show the relationships among them.

Market Fundamentals plus Bubble

The solution proposed in equation (2) may be augmented by an arbitrary term,

$$p_t = \sum_{i=0}^{\infty} \beta_i E_t m_{t+i} + \sum_{i=0}^{\infty} \gamma_i E \varepsilon_{t+i} + A_t, \tag{4}$$

where A_t is arbitrary and the information set used by agents includes the current value of A_t. When (4) is substituted into (1) we find that (3a)–(3c) continue to hold, and in addition,

$$E_t A_{t+1} = [(1 + \alpha)/\alpha] A_t, \tag{5}$$

which is the general condition on a bubble reported by Flood and Garber (1980). Condition (5) may be fulfilled by a nonstochastic bubble as in Flood and Garber (1980) or Flood, Garber and Scott (1981) or, more generally, it may be fulfilled by a stochastic bubble as in Burmeister and Wall (1981) or Blanchard and Watson (1981). The model gives no guidance on this issue.

A possible objection to the bubble portion of (4) is that if an equation like (4) has governed price since time immemorial, then condition (5) would imply that A_t would already have approached infinity. To avoid this objection we assume that the bubble term appears in the price solution at some finite date, $t - T$. Prior to $t - T$ agents may have expected the possible emergence of a bubble at $t - T$ but their expected value of A_{t-T} must have been zero. Alternatively, $t - T$ may be any finite date before which there were no agents.

The Forward–Backward Solution

The forward–backward solution was studied by Blanchard, who used a model like our equation. (1) except he set $\varepsilon_t = 0$ for all t. Since ε_t is immaterial to the issue of equivalence, in this subsection we will also specialize the model by setting $\varepsilon_t = 0$ for all t. The solution to (1) proposed by Blanchard was

$$p_t = \lambda p_t^{(B)} + (1 - \lambda) p_t^{(F)}, \tag{6a}$$

where

$$p_t^{(B)} = \sum_{i=1}^{\infty} a_i m_{t-i}, \tag{6b}$$

$$p_t^{(F)} = b m_t + \sum_{i=1}^{\infty} c_i E_t m_{t+1}. \tag{6c}$$

Equation (6b) gives the *backward* solution, equation (6c) gives the *forward* solution, and equation (6a) gives the *foward–backward* solution.

When we substitute (6b) into (1) we find

$$a_i = -(1/\alpha)[(1 + \alpha)/\alpha]^{i-1}, \tag{7a}$$

and when we substitute (6c) into (1) we find

$$b = 1/(1 + \alpha), \tag{7c}$$

$$c_i = [\alpha/(1 + \alpha)]^i b, \qquad i = 1, 2, \ldots, \tag{7c}$$

which is the market fundamentals solution reported in (3a) and (3b).

While both the backward and the forward solutions are individually determinate, any convex combination of the two solutions is also a soluton. Hence (6a) is a solution for any value of λ. Thus the forward–backward solution contains a degree of indeterminancy which is parameterized by λ.

To see the relationship between the forward–backward solution and the market fundamentals plus bubble solution, rewrite (6a) as

$$p_t = p_t^{(F)} + \lambda(p_t^{(B)} - p_t^{(F)}). \tag{8}$$

Now let $B_t \equiv \lambda(p_t^{(B)} - p_t^{(F)})$, so

$$B_t = \lambda \left\{ -\sum_{i=1}^{\infty} (1/\alpha)[(1 + \alpha)/\alpha]^{i-1} m_{t-i} \right.$$
$$\left. -\sum_{i=0}^{\infty} [1/(1 + \alpha)][\alpha/(1 + \alpha)]^i E_t m_{t+i} \right\}, \tag{9}$$

and

$$B_{t+1} = \lambda \left\{ -\sum_{i=1}^{\infty} (1/\alpha)(1 + \alpha/\alpha)^{i-1} m_{t+1-i} \right.$$
$$\left. -\sum_{i=0}^{\infty} [(1/(1 + \alpha)][\alpha/(1 + \alpha)]^i E_t m_{t+1+i} \right\}, \tag{10}$$

Since $E_t E_{t+1} = E_t$, by the law of iterated expectations, we have $E_t B_{t+1} = [(1 + \alpha)/\alpha]B_t$, which duplicates the bubble constraint given in (5). Hence, the forward–backward solution is market fundamentals plus a term which fulfills the bubble constraint.

The forward–backward solution is a special case of the bubble because it specifies some aspects of the stochastic nature of the B_t series. In particular, use the definition of B_{t+1} to derive

$$B_{t+1} = [(1 + \alpha)/\alpha]B_t + u_{t+1}, \tag{11}$$

where

$$u_{t+1} = -\lambda \sum_{i=0}^{\infty} [1/(1 + \alpha)][\alpha/(1 + \alpha)]^i [E_{t+1}m_{t+1+i} - E_t m_{t+1+i}].$$

Notice that $E_t u_{t+1} = 0$ and that, if money is generated by a stationary time series, u_{t+1} will have a constant variance proportional to λ^2. In constrast to the bubble term implied by the forward–backward solution, equation (5) implies only

$$A_{t+1} = [(1 + \alpha)/\alpha]A_t + Z_{t+1}, \tag{12}$$

where

$$Z_{t+1} = A_{t+1} - E_t A_{t+1}. \tag{13}$$

Hence, Z_{t+1} must have zero conditional mean, but it need not have constant conditional variance as is implied by the more specialized forward–backward solution.

Spurious Indicator Solution

Taylor (1977) investigated a model like (1), except that Taylor's model had a specialized money supply process and his expectations operator in his equation like (1) used the $t - 1$ information set. Our strategy in studying Taylor's model is to impose his specialized money supply process and to solve his model with a spurious indicator—first under our information set assumption, and second under his information set assumption.

Taylor's specialized money supply process was

$$m_t = m \quad \text{(a constant)}. \tag{14}$$

In what follows we will assume $m = 0$. Thus Taylor's model, with our information set assumption, is

$$-p_t = -\alpha(_t E p_{t+1} - p_t) + \varepsilon_t. \tag{15}$$

For this specialized version of (1) the market fundamentals solution is indicated by (3c), which is

$$p_t = -\varepsilon_t/(1 + \alpha). \tag{16}$$

Alternatively, the solution form suggested by Taylor's treatment of his model is

$$p_t = \phi_1 p_{t-1} + \phi_2 \varepsilon_t + \phi_3 \varepsilon_{t-1} + \phi_4 v_t, \tag{17}$$

Where v_t is a spurious variable which has zero mean and is distributed independently of past values of itself and independently of past and current ε_t. If (17) is a solution, then the model implies

$$\phi_1 = (1 + \alpha)/\alpha, \tag{18a}$$

$$\phi_2 = \text{indeterminate}, \tag{18b}$$

$$\phi_3 = 1/\alpha, \tag{18c}$$

$$\phi_4 = \text{indeterminate}. \tag{18d}$$

To relate (17) to the bubble, note that (17) may be rewritten as

$$p_t = -[\varepsilon_t/(1 + \alpha)] + T_t, \tag{19}$$

where

$$T_t \equiv \phi_1 p_{t-1} + (\phi_2 + [1/1 + \alpha])\varepsilon_t + \phi_3 \varepsilon_{t-1} + \phi_4 v_t. \tag{20}$$

Iterating (20) forward one period and using (19), we obtain

$$T_{t+1} = \phi_1 T_t + (\phi_2 + [1/(1 + \alpha)])\varepsilon_{t+1} + \phi_4 v_{t+1}. \tag{21}$$

Since $\phi_1 = (1 + \alpha)/\alpha$, we have $E_t T_{t+1} = [(1 + \alpha)/\alpha] T_t$, and we also know $T_{t+1} - {}_t E T_{t+1} = w_{t+1}$, where $w_{t+1} = (\phi_2 + [1/(1 + \alpha)])\varepsilon_{t+1} + \phi_4 v_{t+1}$. Hence, the Taylor-type solution to our model obeys the bubble constraint and contains a stochastic bubble of the form

$$T_{t+1} = [(1 + \alpha)/\alpha] T_t + w_{t+1}, \tag{22}$$

with w_{t+1} having zero mean and unknown and possibly nonconstant conditional variance.[3] Thus, the Taylor-type spurious indicator solution is equivalent to the market fundamentals plus bubble solution.

Note that unlike Taylor's development of the model, the spurious indicator we included in (17) was not a leading indicator in the sense of being known at $t - 1$. With expectations dated at time t and the assumptions on what is included in the information set, it is impossible to include a spurious leading indicator of the type used by Taylor. If we were to attempt to include a leading indicator, then v_t would be replaced in (17) with v_{t-1}. In this case v_t would appear in $E_t p_{t+1}$ and nowhere else. A stochastic variable appearing only in $E_t p_{t+1}$ must have a zero coefficient and this coefficient is the one attached to v_{t-1} in the p_t solution.

To complete our investigation of solutions we must study the model using Taylor's information assumption. Thus the model becomes

$$-p_t = -\alpha(E_{t-1}p_{t+1} - E_{t-1}p_t) + \varepsilon_t, \tag{23}$$

where E_{t-1} is the expectation operator conditional on $t-1$ information and we continue to assume $m_t = m = 0$.

The market fundamentals solution to (23) is

$$p_t = -\varepsilon_t. \tag{24}$$

Appending a bubble term onto market fundamentals we obtain

$$p_t = -\varepsilon_t + A_t, \tag{25}$$

with the model requiring

$$E_{t-1}A_{t+1} = (1/\alpha)(A_t + \alpha E_{t-1}A_t). \tag{26}$$

Equation (26) implies $A_t = E_{t-1}[A_{t+1} - A_t]$. It follows that A_t is perfectly predictable based on $t-1$ information, or $A_t = E_{t-1}A_t$. Thus we have

$$A_{t+1} = [(1 + \alpha)/\alpha]A_t + Z_t, \tag{27}$$

where $Z_t = E_t A_{t+1} - E_{t-1}A_{t+1}$. Taylor's solution to (23) was

$$p_t = \eta_1 p_{t-1} + \eta_2 \varepsilon_t + \eta_3 \varepsilon_{t-1} + \eta_4 v_{t-1}, \tag{28}$$

with v_{t-1} now a spurious leading indicator. The model requires

$$\eta_1 = (1 + \alpha)/\alpha, \tag{29a}$$

$$\eta_2 = -1, \tag{29c}$$

$$\eta_3 = \text{indeterminate}, \tag{29c}$$

$$\eta_4 = \text{indeterminate}. \tag{29d}$$

Equation (28) may be rewritten as

$$p_t = -\varepsilon_t + T_t', \tag{30}$$

where

$$T_t' = \eta_1 p_{t-1} + \eta_3 \varepsilon_{t-1} + \eta_4 v_{t-1}. \tag{31}$$

Update (31) and use (30) to obtain

$$T_{t+1}' = [(1 + \alpha)/\alpha]T_t' + (\eta_3 - 1)\varepsilon_t + \eta_4 v_t. \tag{32}$$

Equation (32) corresponds exactly to equation (27) with Z_t in (27) corresponding to $(\eta_3 - 1)\varepsilon_t + \eta_4 v_t$ in (32). Hence, for this model the spurious indicator solution is equivalent to the market fundamentals plus bubble solution.

Existence of Solutions

We have discussed two models, one given by equation (1) and the other given by equation (23). In both of these models price is a freely determined variable at time t, with market fundamentals consisting of current and expected future values of the money supply and of the disturbance ε_t. In setting up the models we constrained α such that $\alpha \neq 0$ and $\alpha \neq -1$. However, since we are modeling a finite price level we must also constrain α so that the market fundamentals solution yields a finite price level.

For many stationary processes generating market fundamentals, forcing a finite market fundamentals solution requires $|\alpha/(1 + \alpha)| < 1$, and this is an additional constraint we impose.

In the Blanchard foward–backward solution the imposition of $|\alpha/(1 + \alpha)| < 1$ requires that we restrict attention for the backward solution to money supply processes for which the backward solution is finite. Blanchard (1979) gives an example of such a process.

In Taylor's work he discusses the possibility that a negative value of α, which might arise as a reduced-form coefficient from a model with real balances in the production function, apparently may yield finite asymptotic price variance. This apparent finite asymptotic variance would only arise for $-2 < 1/\alpha < 0$, which requires $\alpha < -\frac{1}{2}$. However if $\alpha < -\frac{1}{2}$, then $\alpha/(1 + \alpha) < -1$, so finite market fundamentals solution does not generally exist. That Taylor is able to produce a solution for $-2 < 1/\alpha < 0$ is a quirk of the undetermined coefficients algorithm he used to find his solution.

IV   Bubbles and Data

Conditional on a rational expectations model of an asset market, there are a multiplicity of solutions for asset price which may be chosen by the agents in an economy. Some investigators have argued though that only the market fundamentals solution is relevant to explaining data. These investigators often base their arguments on theoretical models, such as that of Brock (1974, 1975), which exclude price-level bubbles as being inconsistent with the maximizing behavior of individual agents. Typical research methodology then involves estimating the parameters of a proposed model conditional on the market fundamentals solution being chosen by agents. Other solutions are ruled out a priori by an appeal to Brock's work.

Several recent papers have clarified considerably the nature of the behavioral assumptions required for a logical appeal to Brock's work.[4] The problem studied by Brock (1975) was that of an economy consisting of identical individuals maximizing an infinite horizon utility function, with the one-period flow of utility of the form

$$u(c_t) + v(M_t/P_t), \tag{33}$$

where $u(\cdot)$ and $v(\cdot)$ are concave functions, c_t is a consumption at time t, M_t is nominal money balances at t (level), and P_t is the price level at t. In such a set up explosive bubble price paths can be ruled out as equilibria, if and only if

$$\lim_{(M/P)\to 0} [(M/P)v'(M/P)] > 0, \tag{34}$$

(see Brock (1978)). Hence, investigators appealing to Brock's work to rule out bubbles are assuming condition (34) to hold.

Obstfeld and Rogoff (1981) have studied condition (34) and found it to imply

$$v(0) = -\infty. \tag{35}$$

Thus, appeal to Brock's work for ruling out bubbles requires the adoption of (35). Note though that (35) implies that an agent cannot function without money, or more provocatively, according to (35) no finite stock of consumption goods could compensate an agent for his complete stock of money balances. It is hard to imagine any circumstance when an investigator would feel comfortable assuming a money to be essential to the degree implied by (35).

Investigators who have estimated rational expectations models conditional on no bubbles were exercising strong prior beliefs about the existence of bubbles. These beliefs apparently have been formed in part by reliance on Brock's results and in part by experience with data. Since the implication of the assumption which underlies Brock's work is unpalatable, the exclusion of bubbles must rest on posterior beliefs formed entirely from experience with data.

Fortunately a bubble, if present, places very strong restrictions on data. These restrictions have begun to be explored empirically in studies such as

Flood and Garber (1980), Flood, Garber and Scott (1981), Burmeister and Wall (1981), and Blanchard and Watson (1981).

Notes

We are grateful to the National Science Foundation for support and to Kenneth Rogoff, Robert Hodrick and Olivier Blanchard for comments. The views expressed herein are those of the authors and do not necessarily reflect those of the Governors of the Federal Reserve System or other members of their staff.

1. The existing terminology is unfortunate insofar as it prejudges an unresolved scientific issue by implying that "fundamental" solutions are "good," "spurious" solutions are "unimportant," etc. We emphasize that no such value judgments are intended here.

2. The issues illustrated here are not limited to either the special model we use for expository purposes or to macroeconomic models. Similar problems arise in all rational expectations models where agents look forward in time; see Burmeister (1981) and Gray (1981) for discussions of some more general but closely related stability and uniqueness issues.

3. Although Taylor assumed his spurious indicator to have constant variance there is no requirement imposed by the model that v_t have constant variance.

4. In addition to the papers mentioned below, see Brock and Scheinkman (1980), Gray (1981), and Scheinkman (1980).

References

Blanchard, O., 1979, Backward and forward solutions for economies with rational expectations, *American Economic Review* 69, May, 114–118.

Blanchard, O. and M. Watson, 1981, Bubbles, rational expectations and financial markets, Working paper (Harvard University, Cambridge, MA).

Brock, W., 1974, Money and growth: The case of long run perfect foresight, *International Economic Review* 15, Oct., 750–777.

Brock, W., 1975, A simple perfect foresight monetary model, *Journal of Monetary Economics* 1, April, 133–150.

Brock, W., 1978, A note on hyper-inflationary equilibria in long run perfect foresight monetary models: A correction, Working paper (University of Chicago, Chicago, IL).

Brock, W. and J. Scheinkman, 1980, Some remarks on monetary policy in an overlapping generations model, in: J. Karaken and N. Wallace, eds., Models of monetary economies (Federal Reserve Bank, Minneapolis, MN).

Burmeister, E., 1981, Indeterminacy and the dynamic properties of both rational expectations and perfect foresight models, Working paper (University of Virginia, Charlottesville, VA).

Burmeister, E. and K. Wall, 1981, Kalman filtering estimation of unobserved rational expectations with an application to the German hyperinflation, Working paper (University of Virginia, Charlottesville, VA).

Flood, R. and P. Garber, 1980, Market fundamentals versus price level bubbles: The first tests, *Journal of Political Economy* 88, Aug., 745–770.

Flood R., P. Garber and L. Scott, 1981, Market fundamentals versus price level bubbles: Further evidence, Working paper (University of Rochester, Rochester, NY).

Gray, J., 1981, Dynamic instability in rational expectations models: An attempt to clarify, Working paper (Board of Governors of the Federal Reserve System, Washington, DC).

Obstfeld, M. and K. Rogoff, 1981, Speculative hyperinflations in maximizing models: Can we rule them out?, Working paper (Board of Governors of the Federal Reserve System, Washington, DC).

Scheinkman, J., 1980, Discussion, in: J. Kareken and N. Wallace, eds., Models of monetary economies (Federal Reserve Bank, Minneapolis, MN).

Taylor, J., 1977, On the conditions for unique solutions in stochastic macroeconomic models with rational expectations, *Econometrica* 45, Sept., 1377–1385.

8   Multi-Country Tests for Price-Level Bubbles

Robert P. Flood,
Peter M. Garber, and
Louis O. Scott

I   Introduction

Price solutions in dynamic models which assume rational expectations often contain an arbitrary, time-dependent element in addition to the exogenous forcing variables of the model. The arbitrary element, which enters the solution through self-generating expectations, is often explosive; and the number of such possible arbitrary elements in a solution is infinite. Many attempts have been made to preclude the market selection of such solutions through a priori reasoning.[1] However, Flood and Garber (1980), hereafter F&G, have shown that the question of the existence of these "bubble" solutions is an empirical problem, subject to the usual methods of hypothesis testing. Using data from the German hyperinflation, they could not reject the hypothesis that bubbles of the type generated in a particular rational expectations model were not a factor in the determination of the German price level.

However, the German episode is only one example; to establish confidence that bubbles are merely technical artifacts of rational-expectations models, it is necessary to test for their existence in other cases. In this chapter, we extend in a number of ways the methods used by F&G to test for bubbles.[2] First, we examine data from a number of other hyperinflationary experiences in the same manner as F&G. Second, we use likelihood ratio tests in addition to the t-tests originally employed. Finally, we test whether a bubble simultaneously existed across the countries which experienced hyperinflation in the early 1920s; this test is a means of implementing the conceptual experiment proposed by F&G in deriving asymptotic distributions for their test statistics. The results which we report are mixed: the standard t-tests lead to the acceptance of the hypothesis that bubbles did not exist while in most cases the likelihood ratio tests and alternative t-tests lead to the rejection of the hypothesis. In section II we report our results from tests for individual countries. In section III we describe our test for the simultaneous existence of a bubble across countries. In section IV we comment on the properties of our maximum likelihood estimators if the disturbances are not normally distributed.

II Individual Country Tests

The model used here to test for the presence of a bubble is identical to that used by F&G. A Cagan-type money demand function is combined with an exogenous process determining money growth rates to produce a solution for the inflation rate. The parameters of this solution and the money demand function are then estimated simultaneously with nonlinear, cross-equation restrictions. Explicitly, the system of equations to be estimated is

Money demand

$$m_t - p_t = \gamma + \theta \cdot t + \alpha \pi_t^e + \varepsilon_t, \qquad \alpha < 0, \tag{1}$$

Inflation solution

$$\pi_t = \delta + \beta_1 \mu_{t-1} + \beta_2 \mu_{t-2} + \cdots + \beta_k \mu_{t-k} + A_0 \Psi^t + v_t, \tag{2}$$

where m_t is the logarithm of the money stock, p_t is the logarithm of the price level, $\pi_t \equiv p_{t+1} - p_t$ is the actual inflation rate between time t and time $t + 1$, and $\mu_{t-1} \equiv m_t - m_{t-1}$ is the percentage growth in the money stock between time $t - 1$ and t. π_t^e is the expected inflation rate between t and $t + 1$ based on time t information. All variables realized at or before time t are included in the time t information set. Equation (1) contains a time trend term, $\theta \cdot t$. Equation (2) is a rational expectations solution for the inflation rate if it is assumed that the growth rate of money is a kth-order autoregressive process. The random disturbances are ε_t, assumed to be a random walk, and v_t, a white noise disturbance. Finally, for (2) to be a rational expectations solution it is necessary that the constant root $\Psi \equiv (a - 1)/\alpha > 1$. The term $A_0 \Psi^t$ in equation (2) is the arbitrary term associated with rational expectations solutions; if $A_0 = 0$ then there is no bubble in the solution. Since $\pi_t^e = \delta + \beta_1 \mu_{t-1} + \beta_2 \mu_{t-2} + \cdots + \beta_k \mu_{t-k} + A_0 \Psi^t$, we have a system of two equations with non-linear cross-equation restrictions. We assume that v_t and the random disturbance of the first-differenced version of equation (1) are normally distributed, and we estimate the model's parameters by the method of maximum likelihood.

The episodes which we examine are the Hungarian, Polish, and German cases.[3] The sample periods are July 1921 to February 1924 for Hungary,

July 1921 to November 1923 for Poland, and July 1920 to June 1923 for Germany.[4] For each country, the parameters of money demand and of the inflation solution are estimated first with A_0 restricted to equal zero and then with $A_0 \neq 0$. Four lags on the growth rate of money are used in equation (2). Equation (1) is differenced as follows: $(m_{t+1} - p_{t+1}) - (m_t - p_t) = \mu_t - \pi_t$. We then eliminate π_t from the equation and estimate it in the following form:

$$\mu_t = \theta' + \left[\frac{1}{1 - \alpha\beta_1}\right][(\beta_1 - \alpha\beta_1 + \alpha\beta_2)\mu_{t-1} + (\beta_2 - \alpha\beta_2 + \alpha\beta_3)\mu_{t-2}$$

$$+ (\beta_3 - \alpha\beta_3 + \alpha\beta_4)\mu_{t-3} + (\beta_4 - \alpha\beta_4)\mu_{t-4}] + e_t, \qquad (1')$$

where $e_t = \varepsilon_{t+1} - \varepsilon_t$. Equation. (1') is the money supply process which is consistent with the inflation solution in equation. (2) for $k = 4$. The maximum likelihood estimates are computed by using the Davidon-Fletcher-Powell method to minimize the negative of the concentrated likelihood function. The variance-covariance matrix for the parameter estimates is computed by inverting the information matrix evaluated at the point of the parameter estimates.[5] The results for these two types of estimates are reported in tables 8.1 and 8.2, respectively. From table 8.2, the t-statistics constructed from ratios of the estimates of A_0 to their standard errors indicate that the null hypothesis that $A_0 = 0$ would be accepted for each country at standard significance levels. However, if likelihood ratio tests are used this result is reversed. The values of $-2 \cdot \log \lambda$, where λ is the ratio of the maximized restricted likelihood function to the maximized unrestricted likelihood function, are 8.11, 0.26, and 6.49 for the German, Polish, and Hungarian cases, respectively. For the german case, this leads to rejection of the null hypothesis that $A_0 = 0$ at the 0.5 percent significance level. For the Hungarian case, the null hypothesis is rejected at the 2.5 percent significance level. In the Polish case, the hypothesis can still be accepted for standard significance levels.

It would appear that we have a conflict between the standard t-tests and the likelihood ratio tests for Germany and Hungary.[6] The standard errors reported in table 8.2 are taken from the variance estimates that are computed by inverting the information matrix evaluated at the point of the parameter estimates. It is well-known that the asymptotic variances for maximum likelihood estimators generally depend on the true values of the parameters.[7] We normally use consistent estimates in place of true parameter values to compute asymptotic standard errors. In the test of the hypothesis $A_0 = 0$, we are expressing some a priori knowledge about the

Table 8.1
Restricted individual country estimates: $A_0 = 0$[a]

Parameter	Germany	Poland	Hungary
θ'	0.0193	−0.00539	0.0658
	(0.0176)	(0.0349)	(0.0226)
α	−9.890	−0.8466	−2.599
	(21.38)	(1.686)	(2.284)
δ	0.1119	0.00261	0.1761
	(0.0525)	(0.0750)	(0.0377)
β_1	0.5518	1.155	0.3770
	(0.2368)	(0.3037)	(0.2509)
β_2	0.0511	0.1011	−0.0722
	(0.0967)	(0.2400)	(0.0761)
β_3	0.0378	0.1276	−0.0944
	(0.1020)	(0.2468)	(0.0833)
β_4	0.0924	−0.0147	−0.0565
	(0.1004)	(0.2528)	(0.0673)
LL[b]	147.8839	116.5812	142.9015
DW[c]	2.021	2.092	1.367
Eq. (1′) R^2	0.8270	0.7589	0.9244
σ^2	0.00645	0.00805	0.00667
DW	1.239	1.791	1.067
Eq. (2) R^2	0.1871	0.4422	0.0702
σ^2	0.0572	0.0490	0.0272
Sample period	July '20–June '23	July '21–Nov. '23	July '21–Feb. '24

a. Standard errors in parentheses.
b. LL = log likelihood.
c. DW = Durbin-Watson.

parameter A_0. An alternative construction of the t-test would be to evaluate the information matrix using zero for A_0 and the consistent estimates for the other parameters. The resulting standard errors produce a very different set of t-tests for A_0. These alternative t-statistics for Germany, Poland, and Hungary are, respectively, 2.75, 0.33, and 2.97. The alternative t-tests are consistent with the results of the likelihood ratio tests. The low t-statistics associated with A_0 in table 2 indicate that the log-likelihood functions are relatively flat with respect to A_0 in a neighborhood around the parameter estimates, but the likelihood ratio tests indicate that there are significant increases in the log-likelihood functions for Germany and Hungary as we move away from $A_0 = 0$.[8] These results suggest that the log-likelihood function jumps as we move away from $A_0 = 0$, and then it remains relatively flat around the maximum likelihood estimates. We

Table 8.2
Unrestricted individual country estimates: $A_0 \neq 0^a$

Parameter	Germany	Poland	Hungary
θ'	0.0236	−0.00142	0.0672
	(0.0176)	(0.0349)	(0.0231)
α	−31.40	−0.7280	−1.101
	(18.35)	(1.561)	(0.7626)
δ	0.0307	0.0101	0.1403
	(0.0549)	(0.0810)	(0.0374)
β_1	0.2363	1.127	0.6039
	(0.1821)	(0.3385)	(0.2062)
β_2	0.0174	0.0782	−0.1192
	(0.0413)	(0.2486)	(0.1005)
β_3	0.00113	0.1194	−0.1373
	(0.0426)	(0.2470)	(0.0989)
β_4	0.0164	−0.0331	−0.0723
	(0.0492)	(0.2509)	(0.0879)
A_0	0.08185	1.579×10^{-14}	1.222×10^{-11}
	(0.06126)	(6.342×10^{-13})	(1.479×10^{-10})
LL	151.9369	116.7098	146.1448
DW	1.999	2.089	1.424
Eq. (1') R^2	0.8253	0.7581	0.9241
σ^2	0.00651	0.00808	0.00669
DW	1.408	1.852	1.301
Eq. (2) R^2	0.3772	0.4541	0.2198
σ^2	0.04382	0.0480	0.0229

a. Standard errors in parentheses.

pursue this point further in the next section by investigating the behavior of the log-likelihood function for the simultaneous bubble specification.

III A Test for a Simultaneous Bubble

In this section we describe a test for whether a bubble existed simultaneously in Germany, Poland, and Hungary.[9] We perform such a test in order to implement the conceptual experiment of observing parallel bubbles suggested by F&G in their footnote 18. A large sample of such parallel bubbles is sufficient to produce well-behaved asymptotic distributions for our test statistics, whereas the usual conceptual experiment of letting time go to infinity produces degenerate asymptotic distributions due to the explosive term in (2).

Associated with each country in our sample is a money supply equation (1') and an inflation equation (2). The parameters of these equations are allowed to differ across countries. The hypothesis is that at the same time ($t = 0$) a bubble of the same magnitude arose in the inflation solutions of each country. Since the α parameter is not restricted to be equal across countries, the exploding term, $A_0 \Psi^t$, may be different across countries for $t \neq 0$. Hence, the magnitude of the "mass hysteria" which produced these explosive terms is assumed to be the same across countries only at one moment of time. We set $t = 0$ on July 1921, because this is the point at which we begin the sample periods for Poland and Hungary. We start the bubble for Germany at this same point in time and assume that there was no exploding term during the preceeding year (first 12 observations for German). Thus, the hypothesis is that in July 1921, an arbitrary element of equal magnitude, A_0, entered the inflation rate solutions for Germany, Poland, and Hungary, and continued to explode throughout the remainder of the data set.

We estimate six equations simultaneously by the method of maximum likelihood. We assume for purposes of this estimation that the random disturbances in equations (1′) and (2) have a nonzero contemporaneous covariance for a given country but have zero covariances across countries and across time.[10] Then the only gain in efficiency to the simultaneous estimation method arises through the restrictions which make the parameter A_0 common to each country.

We report our results in table 8.3. Again, using a standard t-statistic, we accept the hypothesis that there was no bubble common to the three countries. Based on our assumptions for the covariances of the disturbances, the logarithm of the maximized likelihood function estimated with A_0 restricted to zero is the sum of the logarithms of the restricted likelihood functions for the individual countries reported in table 8.1. The logarithm of the restricted likelihood function is 407.3666, while that for the unrestricted likelihood function is 410.7103. Since in this case $-2 \cdot \log \lambda = 6.69$, we reject at standard significance levels the hypothesis that there was no bubble common to these episodes.

Again, we have an apparent contradiction between the standard t-test and the likelihood ratio test. When the information matrix is evaluated with $A_0 = 0$, we get a t-statistic for A_0 of 3.03, which is significant at the 0.5% significance level; the alternative t-test is consistent with the results of the likelihood ratio test. As we have noted in the previous section, the low t-statistic in table 8.3 suggests that the likelihood function is relatively flat with respect to A_0 around the parameter estimates, but the likelihood ratio statistic suggests that there is a significant increase in the value of the log-likelihood function as we move away from $A_0 = 0$. To confirm our

Table 8.3

Joint parameter estimates: A_0 restricted to be equal across countries[a]

Parameter	Germany	Poland	Hungary
θ'	0.0193	0.00198	0.0675
	(0.0176)	(0.0335)	(0.0231)
α	-9.890	-0.9560	-1.019
	(21.38)	(0.7225)	(0.6556)
δ	0.1119	0.00871	0.1392
	(0.0525)	(0.0769)	(0.0373)
β_1	0.5518	1.1403	0.6189
	(0.2368)	(0.2813)	(0.1963)
β_2	0.0511	0.0643	-0.1209
	(0.0967)	(0.2479)	(0.1022)
β_3	0.0378	0.1152	-0.1392
	(0.1020)	(0.2463)	(0.1001)
β_4	0.0924	-0.0252	-0.0727
	(0.1004)	(0.2515)	(0.0898)
A_0	3.708×10^{-10}		
	(3.516×10^{-9})		
LL	410.7103		
DW	2.021	2.087	1.424
Eq. (1') R^2	0.8270	0.7574	0.9241
σ^2	0.00645	0.00810	0.00669
DW	1.239	1.863	1.307
Eq. (2) R^2	0.1871	0.4573	0.2189
σ^2	0.0572	0.0477	0.0229

a. Standard errors in parentheses.

conjecture that there is a jump in the log-likelihood function, we have examined the behavior of this function for a range of values around and between $A_0 = 0$ and the maximum likelihood estimate of 3.708×10^{-10}. For each value of A_0, we have used the Davidon-Fletcher-Powell method to maximize the log-likelihood function over the remaining twenty-one parameters. Thus for each value of A_0, we have a corresponding value of the maximized log- likelihood function. In figure 8.1, we present a graph of these calculations. As A_0 increases from 2.897×10^{-21} to 5.794×10^{-20}, the log-likelihood function jumps from 407.3666 to 409.4181; it then increases slowly up to the maximum likelihood estimate and remains relatively flat but decreases for subsequent increases in A_0. The low value for the standard t-statistic is a result of the log-likelihood function being relatively flat with respect to A_0 in a small region around the maximum likelihood estimate. The likelihood ratio statistic and the alternative t-statistic,

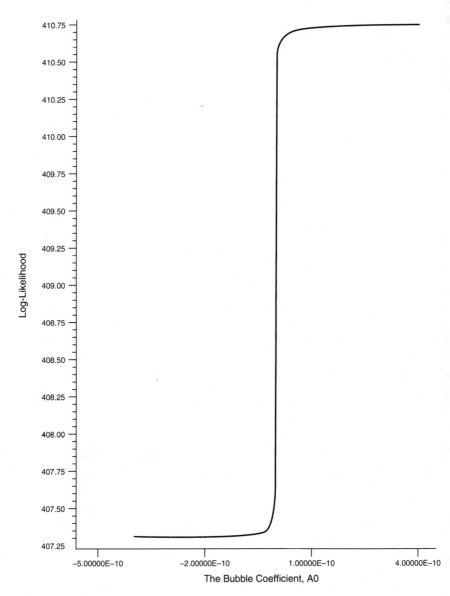

Figure 8.1
The maximized log-likelihood function

however, indicate that there is significant improvement in the fit of the equations if we relax the restriction that $A_0 = 0$. The conflict between the two test statistics in this application is more apparent than real.

Another indication of the improvement in the fit of the equations can be seen by comparing the values for the determinants of the variance-covariance matrices (Σ) for the disturbance terms of the different countries. The maximum likelihood estimator minimizes the determinants of these matrices. For each of the three countries, we compared the estimated $|\Sigma|$'s in the simultaneous bubble specification with those in which A_0 is restricted to be zero. For Hungary, the restricted $|\Sigma|$ is 0.00009909 and the unrestricted $|\Sigma|$ is 0.00008042, a reduction of 18.8 percent. For Poland, the unrestricted $|\Sigma|$ is lower than the restricted $|\Sigma|$ by only 0.78 percent, which is consistent with the insignificant bubble we found in section 2. For Germany, the unrestricted $|\Sigma|$ is the same as the restricted $|\Sigma|$ in the simultaneous bubble test because this bubble parameter is quite different from the separate estimate for Germany.

IV Properties of the Maximum Likelihood Estimators without the Normality Assumptions

The maximum likelihood estimation and the various test statistics discussed in this paper are all based on the assumption that the disturbance terms are normally distributed. Because the maximum likelihood estimators in this application are equivalent to minimum-distance estimators, the normality assumptions are not absolutely necessary. Malinvaud (1970, ch. 9, sec. 3) has shown for a more general class of models with additive error terms that maximum likelihood under the assumption of normality is equivalent to his minimum-distance estimator and the inverse of the information matrix is equivalent to the variance–covariance matrix for the minimum-distance estimators. Therefore, the t-tests which we construct here are valid even if we must relax the normality assumptions. This property has led Malinvaud (1970, pp. 675–678) and other researchers to refer to these estimators as quasi maximum likelihood estimators. We are not aware of any corresponding results for the likelihood ratio tests, but we suspect that there is a corresponding test statistic which incorporates a similar goodness-of-fit measure. In summary, the t-tests do not depend on the normality assumptions, but we have some doubts about the robustness of the likelihood ratio tests. We did find, however, that the alternative t-tests are consistent with the results of the likelihood ratio tests.[11]

Table 8.4
Shapiro-Wilk W-test for normality of disturbances

	Germany	Poland	Hungary
Eq. (1')	0.9109[a]	0.9386	0.9634
Eq. (2)	0.9253[b]	0.9600	0.9321

a. Significant at the 2% level.
b. Significant at the 5% level.

As a check on the data, we have computed the Shapiro-Wilk W-statistic to test the normality of the six disturbances in the simultaneous bubble specification. Judge et al. (1980, p. 301) have noted that the Shapiro-Wilk statistic has become the most popular normality test because of its performance in Monte Carlo simulations. The results are contained in table 8.4: the normality assumption is accepted for both equations in Poland and Hungary, but the assumption is rejected at standard significance levels for both equations in Germany. Although the normality assumption is rejected for Germany, we can invoke Malinvaud's results to justify the use of the maximum likelihood estimators and both the standard and alternative t-tests.

V Concluding Remarks

Although our results are somewhat mixed, we interpret them more as a contradiction than as a confirmation of the results in F&G (1980).[12] Thus, the technical issue of indeterminacy in rational expectations models remains in an unresolved state. Many theoretical maximizing models of money demand, particularly those of the overlapping generations variety, are fully consistent with price-level bubbles. Empirical work designed to evaluate the hypothesis of no bubbles is inconclusive. Yet, virtually all current research involving macroeconomic rational expectations models invokes the attractive assumption of the absence of speculative bubbles. We conclude that the empirical foundation for this assumption is not yet firmly laid.

Notes

This research was supported by NSF Grant #SES-7926807.

1. See for instance Brock (1973), Brock and Scheinkman (1980), Lucas (1980), or Starr (1980).

2. Burmeister and Wall (1980) have extended the F&G exercise for Germany to the case of a stochastic bubble.

3. Attempts to estimate the model for Russia and Austria were unsuccessful. When the value of A_0 is restricted to equal zero, the estimate of α for Russia is a positive value between zero and one and the estimate for Austria is a large negative number that is not statistically significant. For Austria, the likelihood function is relatively flat with respect to α, as observed previously by Salemi and Sargent (1978). For these reasons the results are not reported.

4. The sources for Germany money and price data are the same as those listed in F&G (1980). For the Hungarian data, we used Young (1925, pp. 321–322) for money and prices. Polish data are also taken from Young (1925, pp. 349, 353). For Russia, we employed data reported in Katzenellenbaum (1925, pp. 57–58). Finally, we used Walres de Bordes (1924, pp. 48–50, 88) for Austrian data.

5. For a discussion of methods of non-linear optimization, see Judge, Griffiths, Hill and Lee (1980, pp. 727–745). The Davidon-Fletcher-Powell (D-F-P) method uses analytical first partial derivatives (gradient vector) and computes and approximation to the inverse of the Hessian matrix in order to locate the minimum of a function. The non-linear optimization routine in TSP uses numerical approximations for first partial derivatives. Optimization methods that use analytical first partial derivatives generally outperform methods that do not. The α-estimate for Germany in table 2 differs from the corresponding α-estimate of -1.615 in F&G (1980). This difference is the result of different optimization techniques and different convergence criteria. To compute the maximum likelihood estimates, we experimented with different starting values and different convergence criteria, and we found that the D-F-P routine converged prematurely in some cases. We found that the D-F-P method with analytical partial derivatives works much better for the models in this paper. All of the computations were performed in CDC Fortran on Cyber computers at University of Illinois and University of Virginia. Kent Wall provided a version of the D-F-P routine.

6. Maddala (1977, pp. 179–181) discusses hypothesis testing with maximum likelihood estimation and notes that the different test statistics can produce contradictory results in actual practice. For an example, see Berndt and Savin (1977).

7. See Theil (1971, ch. 8, particularly p. 395).

8. If the log-likelihood function is relatively flat with respect to A_0 at the point of the maximum likelihood estimate, then the second partial derivative with respect to A_0 will be relatively small. When we invert the information matrix, which is the expected value of the negative of the Hessian matrix, we get a relatively large value for the variance of A_0, and hence a large standard error and a low t-statistic.

9. We excluded Russia and Austria for the same reasons cited in note 2. We added Russia and Austria separately to the simultaneous bubble model with Germany, Hungary, and Poland; but the D-F-P routine never converged.

10. By assuming zero covariances across countries, we are able to simplify the likelihood function and the computation of the maximum likelihood estimates. The sample periods are different for each of the three countries, and because of these differences we are not able to concentrate the likelihood function in the usual manner if the covariances are nonzero. With nonzero covariances across countries, we have a full 6×6 variance-covariance matrix for the disturbances in the likelihood function, and the elements in this matrix are all estimated with different numbers of observations. By assuming zero covariances across countries, we can rewrite the determinant of this variance-covariance matriix as the product of the determinants of three 2×2 matrices and we can concentrate the liklihood function to eliminate

the variances and covariances of the disturbances. The resulting concentrated likelihood function contains determinants of three 2 × 2 matrices. Computing and differentiating determinants is much easier for 2 × 2 matrices than it is for 6 × 6 matrices. With the concentrated likelihood function, we iterate on the parameters of interest to find the ML estimates and when the algorithm converges we estimate the variances and covariances for the disturbances from simple functions of the parameter estimates and the data. In the case with nonzero covariances across countries, one must iterate on both the parameters and the elements of the variance-covariance matrix.

11. Our previous comment about evaluating the information matrix at the point of the true parameter values also applies to the variance-covariance matrix for the minimum distance estimators.

12. Burmeister and Wall (1982) reject the no bubbles hypothesis using the German data, while Hamiltonian and Whiteman (1984) are unable to reject the no bubbles hypothesis using the same data.

References

Berndt, E. and E. Savin, 1977, Conflict among criteria for testing hypothesis in the multivariate linear regression model, Econometrica 45, 1263–1277.

Brock, W., 1973, Money and growth: The case of long-run perfect foresight, International Economic Review 15, 750–777.

Brock, W. and J. Scheinkman, 1980, Some remarks on monetary policy in overlapping generation models, in: J. Kareken and N. Wallace, eds., Models of monetary economics (Federal Reserve Bank of Minneapolis, MN).

Burmeister, E. and K. Wall, 1982, Kalman filtering estimation of unobserved rational expectations with an application to the German hyperinflation, Journal of Econometrics 20, 255–284.

Flood, R. and P. Garber, 1980, Market fundamentals vs. price level bubbles: The first tests, Journal of Political Economy 88, 745–770.

Hamilton, J. and C. Whiteman, 1984, The observable implications of self-fulfilling expectations, Working paper (University of Virginia, Charlottesville, VA).

Judge, G., W. Griffiths, C. Hill and T. Lee, 1980, The theory and practice of econometrics (Wiley, New York).

Katzenellenbaum, S., 1925, Russian currency and banking, 1914–1924 (P.S. King & Son, London).

Lucas, R., 1980, Equilibrium in a pure currency economy, Economic Inquiry 18, 203–220.

Maddala, G., 1977, Econometrics (McGraw-Hill, New York).

Malinvaud, E., 1970, Statistical methods of econometrics, 2nd rev. ed. (North-Holland, Amsterdam).

Salemi, M. and T. Sargent, 1979, The demand for money during hyperinflations under rational expectations: II, International Economic Review 20, 741–758.

Shapiro, S.S. and M.B. Wilk, 1965, An analysis of variance test for normality (complete samples), *Biometrika* 52, parts 3 and 4, 591–611.

Starr, R., 1980, General equilibrium approaches to the study of monetary economics: Comments on recent developments, in: J. Kareken and N. Wallace, eds., *Models of monetary economics* (Federal Reserve Bank of Minneapolis, MN).

Theil, Henri, 1971, *Principles of econometrics* (Wiley, New York).

Walres de Bordes, J., 1924, *The Austrian crown* (P.S. King & Son, London).

Young, J., 1925, *European currency and finance*, Vol. II (Commission of Gold and Silver Inquiry, U.S. Senate, Serial 9, Government Printing Office, Washington, DC).

II

Speculative Attacks

9 Collapsing Exchange-Rate Regimes: Some Linear Examples

Robert P. Flood and Peter M. Garber

I Introduction

In this chapter we construct a pair of simple linear examples to study the collapse of a fixed exchange-rate regime. Introduced by Salant and Henderson (1978), the concepts we employ were extended to the foreign exchange market by Krugman (1979) and to gold standards by Flood and Garber (1984).

Our first example, a continuous-time, perfect-foresight model, allows explicit calculation of the collapse time while preserving essential elements of Krugman's monlinear analysis. However, to perform the analysis we develop the concept of a "shadow floating exchange rate," which allows easy extensions to stochastic environments. We examine the timing of regime collapses either based entirely on market fundamentals or based in part on arbitrary speculative behavior.

A discrete time model, our second example, contains stochastic market fundamentals that force the regime collapse. Hence, agents lack perfect foresight about the collapse time. The stochastic framework removes an unsatisfactory aspect of the perfect foresight example: under perfect foresight, a fixed exchange rate regime can collapse without ever producing a forward discount on the collapsing currency.[1] In a stochastic model with a random collapse time, agents' behavior will produce a forward discount on a weak currency even when the exchange rate remains fixed.[2]

In section II we develop the continuous-time, perfect-foresight example; in section III we develop the discrete-time, stochastic model. Section IV contains some concluding remarks.

II The Continuous-time Model with Perfect Foresight

Our first example employs a small country model with purchasing power parity. We assume that agents have perfect foresight and that the assets available to domestic residents are domestic money, domestic bonds, foreign money, and foreign bonds. The domestic government holds a stock of foreign currency for use in fixing the exchange rate. Domestic money and domestic and foreign bonds dominate foreign money which yields no monetary services to domestic residents; therefore, private domestic residents will hold no foreign money. Domestic and foreign bonds are perfect substitutes.

We build the model around five equations:

$$M(t)/P(t) = a_0 - a_1 i(t), \qquad a_1 > 0, \tag{1}$$

$$M(t) = R(t) + D(t), \tag{2}$$

$$\dot{D}(t) = \mu, \qquad \mu > 0, \tag{3}$$

$$P(t) = P^*(t)S(t), \tag{4}$$

$$i(t) = i^*(t) + [\dot{S}(t)/S(t)], \tag{5}$$

where $M(t)$, $P(t)$, and $i(t)$ are the domestic money stock, price level, and interest rate, respectively. $R(t)$ and $D(t)$ represent the domestic government book value of foreign money holdings and domestic credit, respectively. $S(t)$ is the spot exchange rate, i.e. the domestic money price of foreign money. An asterisk (*) attached to a variable indicates "foreign," and a dot over a variable ($\cdot$) indicates the time derivative.

Equation (1) reflects a money market equilibrium condition, the right-hand side representing the demand for real balances.[3] Equation (2) states that the money supply equals the book value of international reserves plus domestic credit. Equation (3) states that domestic credit always grows at the positive, constant rate μ. Equations, (4) and (5) impose purchasing power parity and uncovered interest parity, respectively.

We use (4) and (5) in (1) to obtain:

$$M(t) = \beta S(t) - \alpha \dot{S}(t), \tag{6}$$

where $\beta \equiv (a_0 P^* - a_1 P^* i^*)$, which we assume is positive, and $\alpha = a_1 P^*$. Both β and α are constants since we assume that P^* and i^* are constant.

If the exchange rate is fixed at $\bar{S}$, reserves adjust to maintain money market equilibrium. The quantity of reserves at any time t is

$$R(t) = \beta \bar{S} - D(t). \tag{7}$$

The rate of change of reserves, i.e. the balance of payments deficit is

$$\dot{R}(t) = -\dot{D}(t) = -\mu. \tag{8}$$

With a lower bound on net reserves and $\mu > 0$, the fixed-rate regime cannot survive forever; any finite reserve stock earmarked to support the fixed rate would be exhausted in finite time. We assume that the government will support the fixed rate while its net reserves remain positive. After the fixed-rate regime's collapse the exchange rate floats freely forever.

The central problem in finding the collapse time lies in connecting the fixed-rate regime to the post-collapse floating regime. As our strategy we first determine the floating exchange rate conditional on a collapse at an arbitrary time z, referring to it as the "shadow floating exchange rate." Next we investigate the transition from fixed rates to the post-collapse flexible-rate system.

If the fixed-rate regime collapses at any time z, the government will have exhausted its reserve stock at z.[4] In general, agents extinguish the reserve stock in a final speculative attack, yielding a discrete downward jump in the money stock.

Immediately following the attack, money market equilibrium requires, from equation (6):

$$M(z_+) = \beta S(z_+) - \alpha \dot{S}(z_+),\qquad (9)$$

where z_+ indicates the instant after the attack and $M(z_+) = D(z_+)$, since $R(z_+) = 0$. Since the government does not intervene in exchange markets under the new regime, the exchange rate floats. To find a floating exchange rate solution, we use the method of undetermined coefficients, conjecturing the solution form $S(t) = \lambda_0 + \lambda_1 M(t)$. Remembering that $\dot{M}(t) = \dot{D}(t) = \mu$ and substituting the trial solution into equation (6), we find $\lambda_0 = \alpha\mu/\beta^2$ and $\lambda_1 = 1/\beta$. Therefore,

$$S(t) = [\alpha\mu/\beta^2] + M(t)/\beta,\qquad t \geq z. \qquad (10)$$

Since agents foresee the collapse, predictable exchange-rate jumps at time z are precluded. Since this point is crucial to the analysis, we will discuss it in some detail. Suppose first that agents expect a collapse at z and anticipate $S(z_+) > \bar{S}$. At time z speculators who attack government reserves will profit by an amount $[S(z_+) - \bar{S}]R(z_-)$, where z_- indicates the moment before the collapse. While finite in magnitude, these profits accrue at an infinite rate; and speculators compete to capture them. An individual speculator, expecting an attack at z, has incentives to pre-empt his competitors by purchasing all the reserves an instant before z. Therefore, the attack will occur prior to z. Indeed, whenever agents expect a discrete exchange rate increase they will precipitate an attack on reserves prior to the increase. We

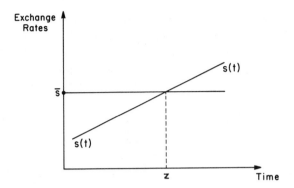

Figure 9.1

conclude that our supposition of an attack at z and a discrete exchange rate increase at z involves a contradiction.

Now suppose that agents expect both an attack at time z and a discrete currency appreciation, $S(z_+) < \bar{S}$. The profits accruing to speculators will then be $[S(z_+) - \bar{S}]R(z_-) < 0$. Agents would have no incentive to attack the government's reserves; and the fixed exchange-rate regime would survive.

We conclude that $S(z_+) = \bar{S}$ at the moment of an anticipated attack on foreign exchange reserves. We now use this condition to determine both the timing of the attack and the extent of government reserve holdings at the time of the attack. Substituting $D(t) = D(0) + \mu t$ for $M(t)$ in (10) produces the shadow floating exchange rate, the floating rate that would materialize if the fixed exchange rate collapsed at any given time t. Plotting the shadow floating rate and $\bar{S}$ against time in figure 9.1, we note that the time z of the collapse occurs when the two curves intersect. A little algebra yields:

$$z = [\beta\bar{S} - D(0)]/\mu - \alpha/\beta = R(0)/\mu - \alpha/\beta. \tag{11}$$

Equation (11) is intuitively reasonable because an increase in initial reserves delays the collapse, while an increase in μ, the rate of domestic credit growth, hastens the collapse. As $\mu \to 0$, the collapse is delayed indefinitely.

Prior to the collapse, equation (7) governs reserves, and it implies:

$$\bar{S} = [R(z_-) + D(z_-)]/\beta. \tag{12}$$

Given the expression for z from (11) and our knowledge that $D(z_-) = D(0) + \mu z$, we determine from (12) that

$$R(z_-) = \alpha\mu/\beta. \tag{13}$$

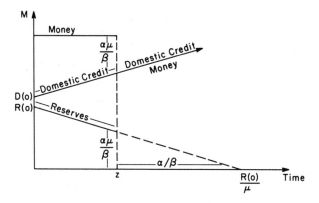

Figure 9.2

In figure 9.2 we have portrayed the time paths of reserves, domestic credit, and the money supply during the period surrounding the collapse. Prior to the collapse at z, money remains constant, but its components vary. $D(t)$ rises at the rate μ and reserves decline at the same rate. At time z, both money and reserves fall by $\alpha\mu/\beta$. Since reserves fall to zero, money equals domestic credit after z.[5] On the horizontal axis in figure 9.2 we have recorded the time $R(0)/\mu$, the time when reserves would be exhausted in the absence of a speculative attack. The time length α/β represents a correction that hastens the collapse to ensure that the exchange rate will not jump.

We have based our results on an assumption that the solution for the floating exchange rate depends only on market fundamentals. In general, however, the floating rate obeys the dynamic law:

$$S(t) = A\exp[(t - z)\beta/\alpha] + \alpha\mu/\beta^2 + M(t)/\beta, \tag{14}$$

where A, previously set to zero, is an arbitrary constant determined at time z.[6] The shadow floating exchange rate is now:

$$S(t) = A + \alpha\mu/\beta^2 + D(t)/\beta. \tag{15}$$

To find z, we again equate the shadow rate to $\bar{S}$:

$$z = [R(0)/\mu - \alpha/\beta] - A\beta/\alpha. \tag{16}$$

From (12) and (16) we determine the reserves at the time of the attack:

$$R(z_-) = \beta A + \alpha\mu/\beta. \tag{17}$$

Equation (16) reveals that the collapse time depends on both market fundamentals, $[R(0)/\mu - \alpha/\beta]$, and on the arbitrary constant A. The constant A

captures the behavior which may cause an indeterminacy in the path of the post-collapse floating rate.[7] An increase in A will hasten the collapse, causing it to occur at a higher value of $R(z_-)$, which magnifies the amplitude of the attack on the currency.

As a special case, we suppose that $\mu = 0$, a situation in which the fixed-rate regime need never collapse in the absence of arbitrary speculative behavior. In this case, equation (17) yields $R(z_-) = \beta A$. If $\mu = 0$, then $R(t)$ remains constant at $R(0)$. Therefore, a collapse may occur at any time that agents' speculative behavior sets $A \geq R(0)/\beta$.

The possibility that arbitrary speculative behavior can cause the collapse of a fixed exchange-rate regime bears on a traditional argument favoring fixed exchange rates. The argument is that since a flexible exchange rate may be subject to arbitrary speculative fluctuations, the exchange rate should be fixed in order to protect the real sectors of an economy. Our analysis indicates that arbitrary speculative behavior identical in nature to that which may manifest itself under floating rates can also render arbitrary and indeterminate the time of a fixed exchange-rate regime collapse. Hence, arbitrary speculative behavior, if present, is an economic force that is masked, not purged, by the fixing of exchange rates.

III The Discrete-time Model with Uncertainty

Our analysis has required that agents know the collapse time of the fixed-rate regime. While the regime operates, the instantaneous expected rate of change of the exchange rate, $S(t)$, must always equal zero. However, that a weak currency's forward exchange rate may exceed the fixed rate for long periods of time, a generally encountered empirical phenomenon, does not fit into the previous analysis. In this section we incorporate uncertainty into a discrete time model to study the forward exchange rate for a currency that may experience a regime collapse.

The model's principal equations are:

$$M(t)/P(t) = a_0 - a_1 i(t), \tag{18}$$

$$M(t) = R(t) + D(t), \tag{19}$$

$$D(t) = D(t-1) + \mu + \varepsilon(t), \tag{20}$$

$$P(t) = P^*(t)S(t), \tag{21}$$

$$i(t) = i^*(t) + [E(S(t+1)|I(t)) - S(t)]/S(t), \tag{22}$$

Variables common to equations (18)–(22) and (2)–(6) are defined as before, except that we now interpret t as an integer. In equation (20), $\varepsilon(t)$ represents a random disturbance with zero mean that obeys:

$$\varepsilon(t) = -1/\lambda + v(t). \tag{23}$$

The random variable $v(t)$ is distributed exponentially with an unconditional probability density function:[8]

$$f[v(t)] = \begin{cases} \lambda \exp[-\lambda v(t)], & v(t) > 0, \\ 0, & v(t) \leq 0. \end{cases} \tag{24}$$

We adopt this distribution to allow easy manipulations. To ensure that domestic credit remains positive, we specialize the distribution with the assumption $\mu > 1/\lambda$. This assumption ensures non-negative growth of $D(t)$ and permits a simple stochastic extension of the certainty model of the previous section.[9] Equation (22) introduces the notation $E(\cdot | I(t))$, the mathematical expectation operator conditional on the information set $I(t)$. $I(t)$ includes complete information about all variables dated t or earlier and the structure of the model.

Suppose that $\bar{S}$ is the fixed exchange rate and define $\tilde{S}(t)$ as the shadow floating rate, the flexible exchange rate that would prevail if agents were to purchase all the government's reserves at t. Alternatively, $\tilde{S}(t)$ is the flexible rate conditional on a collapse of the fixed-rate regime at t. A fixed-rate regime will collapse at t if and only if $\tilde{S}(t) \geq \bar{S}$. If $\tilde{S}(t) \geq \bar{S}$, agents may purchase reserves from the central bank at a price $\bar{S}$, reselling inmediately on the post-collapse market at price $\tilde{S}(t)$ and earning a profit per unit of reserves of $[\tilde{S}(t) - \bar{S}] \geq 0$. If such a profit were available, agents would purchase all the government's reserves. If $\tilde{S}(t) < \bar{S}$, agents certainly would not purchase the government's reserves at $\bar{S}$ for resale at $\tilde{S}(t)$. Thus, for an attack to occur at any t we require $\tilde{S}(t) \geq \bar{S}$, i.e. the shadow floating rate must equal or exceed the fixed rate.

Our analysis of the discrete-time uncertainty model will proceed first by examining the unconditional expected exchange rate, $E[S(t + 1)|I(t)]$. Next, we study the stochastic path of reserves. We may express $E[S(t + 1)|I(t)]$ as:

$$E[S(t + 1)|I(t)] = [1 - \pi(t)]\bar{S} + \pi(t)E[\tilde{S}(t + 1)|I(t)]. \tag{25}$$

In (25), $\pi(t)$ is the probability evaluated at t that a collapse will occur at time $t + 1$. The unconditional expected future exchange rate is a probability weighted average of the fixed rate, $\bar{S}$, which will prevail if there is no collapse at $t + 1$, and the rate expected to prevail if there is a collapse at $t + 1$.

If a collapse occurs at $t + 1$, then $R(t + 1) = 0$; and the exchange rate conditional on a collapse is:

$$\tilde{S}(t + 1) = \alpha\mu/\beta^2 + D(t + 1)/\beta, \tag{26}$$

with α and β given in the previous section. The probability of a collapse at $t + 1$ is the probability that $\tilde{S}(t + 1) \geqq \bar{S}$. Formally:

$$\pi(t) = \Pr[\alpha\mu/\beta^2 + D(t + 1)/\beta - \bar{S} > 0]. \tag{27}$$

Since from (20) and (23), $D(t + 1) = D(t) + \mu - 1/\lambda + v(t + 1)$, we write (27) as:

$$\pi(t) = \Pr[v(t + 1) > K(t)], \tag{28}$$

with $K(t) \equiv \beta\bar{S} - \alpha\mu/\beta - D(t) - \mu + 1/\lambda$. Use the probability density function (24) to obtain:

$$\pi(t) = \int_{K(t)}^{\infty} \lambda \exp[-\lambda v(t + 1)]\, dv(t + 1), \qquad K(t) \geqq 0. \tag{29}$$

Integrating (29) yields:

$$\pi(t) = \begin{cases} \exp[-\lambda K(t)], & K(t) \geqq 0 \\ 1, & K(t) < 0. \end{cases} \tag{30}$$

To obtain an analytic expression for $E[S(t + 1)|I(t)]$, we must use (26) to find:

$$E[\tilde{S}(t + 1)|I(t)] = \alpha\mu/\beta^2 + E[D(t + 1)|I(t), C(t + 1)]/\beta, \tag{31}$$

where $C(t + 1)$ indicates that the expectation is conditional on a collapse at $t + 1$. The conditional expectation of $t + 1$ domestic credit is:

$$E[D(t + 1)|I(t), C(t + 1)] = D(t) + \mu - 1/\lambda + E[v(t + 1)|I(t), C(t + 1)]. \tag{32}$$

To find $E[v(t + 1)|I(t), C(t + 1)]$, we must form the conditional p.d.f. over $v(t + 1)$, where the conditioning information is $v(t + 1) > K(t)$. This conditional p.d.f. is:[10]

$$g[v(t + 1)] = \begin{cases} \lambda \exp[\lambda(K(t) - v(t + 1))], & K(t) \geqq 0, \\ \lambda \exp[-\lambda v(t + 1)], & K(t) < 0. \end{cases} \tag{33}$$

Hence, for $K(t) \geqq 0$:

$E[v(t + 1)|I(t), C(t + 1)]$

$$= \int_{K(t)}^{\infty} \lambda v(t + 1) \exp[\lambda(K(t) - v(t + 1))] \, dv(t + 1). \tag{34}$$

Carrying out the integration in (34), we obtain:

$E[v(t + 1)|I(t), C(t + 1)] = K(t) + 1/\lambda. \tag{35}$

Substituting from (32) into (31) and the result into (30) yields:

$E[\tilde{S}(t + 1)|I(t)] = \alpha\mu/\beta^2 + [D(t) + \mu + K(t)]/\beta. \tag{36}$

Using the definition of $K(t)$ in (36), we find:

$E[\tilde{S}(t + 1)|I(t)] = \bar{S} + 1/\beta\lambda. \tag{37}$

Combining (37) and (25) yields:

$E[S(t + 1)|I(t)] = \bar{S} + \pi(t)/\beta\lambda, \tag{38}$

which implies

$E[S(t + 1)|I(t)] - \bar{S} = \pi(t)/\beta\lambda, \qquad K(t) \geqq 0. \tag{39}$

When $K(t) < 0$, we find from (32) that $E[v(t + 1)|I(t), C(t + 1)] = 1/\lambda$. For this case, we obtain:

$E[S(t + 1)|I(t)] - \bar{S} = \alpha\mu/\beta^2 - [D(t) + \mu]/\alpha - \bar{S}. \tag{40}$

In figure 9.3 we plot the forward discount, $E[S(t + 1)|I(t)] - \bar{S}$, against the level of $D(t)$. In this figure, D^* is the level of $D(t)$ for which $S(t) = \bar{S}$. Hence, $D^* = \beta\bar{S} - [\alpha\mu/\beta]$. In this figure, we assume that $D^* - \mu + 1/\lambda > 0$. Then, when $D(t) = 0$, the forward discount is $\exp[-\lambda(D^* - \mu + 1/\lambda)]$. As $D(t)$ rises from zero, the forward discount rises exponentially in accord with (38) until $D(t)$ reaches $D^* - \mu + 1/\lambda$, where the discount is $1/\beta\lambda$. When $D(t)$ exceeds $D^* - \mu + 1/\lambda$, $K(t) = D^* - D(t) - \mu + 1/\lambda < 0$. Equation (40) then governs the discount, which rises linearly with $D(t)$ at the rate $1/\beta$. When $D(t) = D^*$, the premium reaches μ/β. Further increases in $D(t)$ collapse the fixed-rate regime and under floating rates the discount μ/β.

In addition to explaining the forward-rate, spot-rate spread, our model implies that reserves are lower under fixed rates than the reserve level implied in our nonstochastic model. This results from the positive forward discount which reduces money demand relative to the certainty case.[11] The country's reserve stock absorbs the entire reduction.

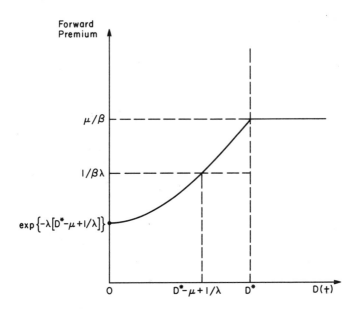

Figure 9.3

In our analysis we have ignored the possibility that the country may devalue its currency when a crisis seems imminent. While our model does not directly address this issue, it does imply a lower bound on the forward discount for a currency which will be devalued in a crisis. The variable $\bar{S}(t)$ always serves as a lower bound for a viable fixed exchange rate. If a monetary authority decides to devalue when $\bar{S}(t)$ approaches $\bar{S}$, it cannot support a fixed rate which lies below $\bar{S}(t)$. Hence, with devaluations possible, the expected rate of exchange-rate change must always equal or exceed that predicted by our model. A more complete treatment of expected devaluations would require a model of the government's decision-making process, which is not pursued here.[12]

IV   Concluding Remarks

We can imagine two alternative situations in which a fixed exchange regime can collapse. In the first, an unpredictable and cataclysmic disturbance may so change the environment that maintenance of the fixed exchange regime is not possible. Such a viewpoint has an attraction since it associates a large event—the collapse of an exchange system—with a large cause. Since the disturbance is unpredictable and its origin is outside the bounds of our theories, the only problem remaining for the economist is to determine what its minimum size must be to have such a drastic effect. In the second situation, a predictable, cumulating sequence of small events culminates in the predictable collapse of the system. Since the exchange system dies from a thousand cuts, economists need not attribute the collapse to unusually large disturbances. While this may violate some inbred intuition about the proper relationship between the magnitudes of cause and effect, it opens the attractive possibility of applying the usual economists' tools to study both the question of timing and other phenomena attendant upon the collapse.

In this chapter we have devised two workable examples of predictable collapses. We view the first, the perfect foresight case, primarily as a simple realization of Krugman's (1979) model in which an analytical solution for the collapse's timing can be readily derived. We have also shown that the fixed exchange system is subject to exactly the same type of dynamic instability problem which may affect a floating system. In the second example we have considered the problem of a foreseeable collapse in a model subject to stochastic monetary disturbances. The model produces the forward discount during the fixed-rate system which is known as the "peso problem." However, the result is not attributable to the possibility that unusual, large random disturbances may impinge on the system as in Krasker (1980). Indeed, the shocks in our model are always drawn from the same distribution; and even a small disturbance may collapse the system.

Appendix: Conditional P.D.F. for $v(t + 1)$

The random variable $v(t + 1)$ is drawn from the exponential distribution. However, if we know $v(t + 1) > K(t)$, then we know that $v(t + 1)$ must come from the right-hand tail of the $v(t + 1)$ distribution. To reflect tis knowledge, we must form a conditional p.d.f. Our p.d.f. is of the form $B\lambda \exp[-\lambda v(t + 1)]$ and must obey

$$1 = \int_{K(t)}^{\infty} B\lambda \exp[-\lambda v(t + 1)]\, dv(t + 1), \tag{A1}$$

which implies:

$$B = \exp[\lambda K(t)]. \tag{A2}$$

The p.d.f. we seek is then:

$$g(v(t + 1)) = \lambda \exp[\lambda(K(t) - v(t + 1))], \tag{A3}$$

which is the p.d.f. recorded in the text, equation (32). If $K(t) < 0$, then $\exp[\lambda K(t)]$ is replaced with $\exp[\lambda 0] = 1$.

Notes

We have received financial support for this research from NSF Grant SES-7926807. This is a slightly edited version of the original *J.I.E.* paper.

1. We are referring to the instantaneous forward discount, as in Krugman (1979). For longer maturities of forward contracts, the discount may become positive, even in the certainty case.

2. We employ a discrete-time model purely as an analytical convenience. Our results can be duplicated for some continuous-time processes.

3. We interpret eq. (1) as the linear terms of a Taylor series expansion of some nonlinear function $M^d/P(t) = l(i)$. Our linearization is appropriate for values of a_0, a_1, and $i(t)$ such that $a_0 - a_1 i(t) > 0$. We have adopted the present linearlization rather than the more standard semi-log-linearization to exploit the inherent linearity of our money supply definition.

4. While we assume that the government exhausts its reserve stock during a collapse, our analysis would change very little if we assumed that the government maintains some reserve stock, $\bar{R}$, after the collapse. On this point, see Krugman (1979). Furthermore, the analysis would remain unchanged if the lower bound on reserves were some finite negative number representing a borrowing limit.

5. $D(t)$ is a continuous variable, so $D(z_+) = D(z) = D(z_-)$.

6. As an artifact of our linearization, we must restrict $A \geqq 0$. If $A < 0$, then $S(t) < 0$ for some t.

7. Notice that if a collapse occurs due to the arbitrary element A, then the post-collapse exchange rate must be expected to follow a bubble. Such a bubble could be distinguished in the data using tests like those in Flood and Garber (1980).

8. Note that $E[v(t + 1)|I(t)] = 1/\lambda$. We choose the exponential distribution to work this example because it permits arbitrarily large realizations while allowing relatively easy analytical manipulations. We require the large realizations so that there always will exist a nonzero probability of speculative attack in the next period, which automatically produces the forward premium. Alternatively, we may assume that only two possible realizations of the domestic credit disturbance may materialize: zero or a positive number with given probabilities. While this process will provide an even simpler analysis, there will be no forward premium for small enough levels of domestic credit.

9. Owing to the linear nature of the model, the shadow spot exchange rate could be negative if negative realizations of domestic credit growth were permitted. To avoid this difficulty, we assume only positive growth. For a log-linear model of money demand, negative realizations of $\Delta D(t)$ would be permitted.

10. The conditional p.d.f. is derived in the appendix.

11. An interesting aspect of our model is that the 'offset coefficient'—the fraction of any domestic credit expansion reversed by central bank foreign reserve losses—exceeds unity. If the exchange rate were permanently fixed, our assumptions that domestic and foreign

bonds are perfect substitutes and that the foreign interest is exogenous would produce a coefficient of unity. However, in addition, a domestic credit expansion will raise the domestic interest rate through its effect on the forward premium, thus lowering domestic money demand.

12. Blanco and Garber (1982) extend a log-linear version of our model to study the problem of recurrent devaluation.

References

Blanco, Herminio and Peter Garber, 1982, Recurrent devaluation and the timing of speculative attacks, working paper, October.

Flood, Robert and Peter Garber, 1980, Market fundamentals vs. price level bubbles: The first tests, *Journal of Political Economy*, August.

Flood, Robert and Peter Garber, 1984, Gold monetization and gold discipline, *Journal of Political Economy*, February.

Krasker, William, 1980, The peso problem in testing efficiency of forward exchange markets, *Journal of Monetary Economics* 6, 269–276.

Krugman, Paul, 1979, A model of balance-of-payments crises, *Journal of Money, Credit and Banking*, August.

Salant, Stephen and Dale Henderson, 1978, Market anticipations of government gold policies and the price of gold, *Journal of Political Economy*, August.

10

Gold Monetization and Gold Discipline

Robert P. Flood and Peter M. Garber

Gold and its price have emerged as frequent topics of academic and government debate.[1] Public attention, focused on the gold market since the price of gold began fluctuating violently in 1980 and 1981, has turned to gold as a possible means of removing some discretion inherent in the current fiat money system. Since lack of adherence to monetary rules can lead to problems of dynamic policy inconsistency, academic economists have begun seriously to reconsider monetary standards based either on gold or on some other commodity as politically feasible methods of establishing rules.[2]

The political and intellectual resurrection of gold has coincided with the advent of three lines of thought concerning government gold market policy. First, Salant and Henderson (1978) have developed a partial equilibrium gold market model to analyze the interactions among rapid gold price rises, government gold auctions, and speculative attacks on government gold stocks. Salant (1983) places the possibility of a speculative attack on price stabilization schemes in a stochastic setting. Second, Barro (1979) has studied money and price dynamics under a version of the historical gold standard. Finally, others such as Laffer (1979) and Lehrman (1980, 1981) have proposed a new monetary gold standard under which the government would maintain a fixed nominal gold price while retaining the freedom to issue money without fixed gold backing.

In this chapter we intend to provide a dynamic framework suitable for analyzing various gold monetization policies. We integrate the ideas in Salant and Henderson with those in Barro to produce a model of a monetary system based on any storable commodity.

Besides analyzing a successful gold monetization, we study the possibility of an unsuccessful gold standard (i.e., a government's implementation of a gold standard destined to collapse either immediately or after a finite interval). Our results on the collapse of a gold standard draw on the work of Salant and Henderson (1978), Krugman (1979), and Salant (1983). Finally, our analytical framework operates as a systematic means of categorizing any commodity standard's dynamic evolution. Using a simple graphical technique and given the policy environment, one can determine the nature of the potential equilibria during a gold standard.

We organize the chapter into three sections. In section I we introduce our model's basic components and study the paths of the relative gold price and the price level prior to a government's announcement that gold's nominal price will be fixed. In section II we analyze the dynamics of the money and gold markets after the nominal gold price has been fixed. We find that equilibrium is not unique for some fixed gold prices. The market may determine equilibria consistent either with a permanently maintained gold standard or with a gold standard that eventually collapses. In section III we examine the significance of the "discipline of the gold standard"; we demonstrate that the notion may lack operational meaning if the alternative fiat money system is not also "disciplined." Section III is followed by some concluding remarks.

I The World prior to Gold Monetization

To study the effects of gold price fixing, we first characterize the economy before the scheme is announced. We will use concepts and methods very similar to those of Salant and Henderson (1978). However, no government gold auctions will occur, and we will modify their model to suit our problem. Specifically, we introduce a monetary sector, modify the nature of gold demand for private uses, and analyze a policy of nominal gold price pegging. Throughout the chapter we employ a continuous time model in which agents have perfect foresight.[3] We present our ideas in the form of a linearized example to make the concepts involved as concrete as possible. We divide our economy into two explicit sectors, a gold sector and a monetary sector. The real interest rate, ρ, is fixed at a constant level.[4]

The Gold Sector

Equations (1)–(3) partly describe the gold market's operation:

$$I = D(t) + G(t) + R(t), \tag{1}$$

$$\dot{D}(t) = v\left[\frac{\mu}{q(t)} - D(t)\right], \qquad \mu, v > 0, \tag{2}$$

$$\dot{q}(t) = \rho q(t), \quad \text{for } G(t) > 0, \tag{3}$$

$$= 0 \quad \text{for } G(t) = 0.$$

$I, D(t), G(t)$, and $R(t)$ are the fixed total world gold stock, the quantity of gold at time t used in consumption and industry, the quantity of gold held privately as ingots or coins in speculative hoards, and the quantity of gold in government reserves, respectively. Until gold is monetized, we will assume $R(t)$ to be the positive constant $\bar{R}$.[5]

Equation (2) describes the law of motion for the total gold stock in consumption and industrial use; $\dot{D}(t)$ equals current consumption plus industrial gold purchases. When $\dot{D}(t) > 0$, speculators reduce their hoards to accommodate the flow. The quantity $\mu/q(t)$ is a desired stock of gold used in industry and consumption, where $q(t)$ is the relative price of gold in terms of other goods at time t. Central in generating any postmonetization price-level dynamics, the form of (2) reflects a slow transformation of gold into and out of consumption and industrial uses. Equation (2) is similar to a gold sector equation set up by Barro (1979).[6] However, we ignore gold mining and the effect that capital gains on gold may have on demand for consumption and industrial use.[7] Also, we treat gold as a perfectly durable good, which allows the possibility that gold may be disgorged from other uses into hoards when the relative gold price rises sufficiently.[8]

Equation (3) requires the gold's relative price must rise at the real interest rate while private speculators hold gold. If the relative price were expected to rise faster than ρ, speculators would bid up the current price until $\dot{q}(t)/q(t)$ fell to ρ. If the price were expected to rise more slowly than ρ, then speculators would drive the current price downward.[9]

Equations (1)–(3) form a differential equation system in $D(t)$ and $q(t)$. Equation (3) yields

$$q(t) = q(0)\exp(\rho t) \tag{4}$$

when $G(t) > 0$. Substituting from (4) into (2) generates a differential equation in $D(t)$ whose solution is[10]

$$D(t) = D(0)\exp(-vt) + v\exp(-vt)\int_0^t \left[\frac{\mu}{q(0)}\right]\exp[(v-\rho)u]\,du, \tag{5}$$

where $D(0)$ is the initial value of $D(t)$.

To complete the solution we must determine $q(0)$. Since speculators hoard gold only in anticipation of future consumption and industrial uses, the speculative gold stock must be exhausted when additional gold use in these areas ceases. If T is the date when $\dot{D}(t) = 0$, then $G(T)$ must equal zero. Since $G(T) = 0$, equation (1) implies

$$I - \bar{R} = D(T). \tag{6}$$

Combining equations (6) and (2) and rearranging, we find

$$q(T) = \frac{\mu}{I - \bar{R}}. \tag{7}$$

Equation (7) indicates the "choke price" for new consumption and industrial gold use, the terminal condition required to solve for $q(0)$. To find $q(0)$, we employ (7) and (4) to yield

$$q(0) = \left(\frac{\mu}{I - \bar{R}}\right) \exp(-\rho T). \tag{8}$$

Our solution for the gold sector will be complete once we have determined the unknown choke date, T, which is a function of the initial condition $D(0)$. T is determined by substituting from (8) into (5) for $q(0)$ and setting $D(T) = I - \bar{R}$. This sequence of steps produces a single equation in T whose solution can be characterized as $T = f[D(0)/(I - \bar{R})]$ with $f' < 0$, $f(1) = 0$, and $f(0) = \log(\rho/v)/(\rho - v) \equiv k > 0$.[11]

Determining $q(0)$ completes our solution for the gold sector. Given $q(0)$, equation (4) indicates the time path of $q(t)$ from 0 to T, and $q(t) = q(T)$ for $t > T$. Given the initial condition $D(0)$, equation (5) determines the time path of $D(t)$ from 0 to T with $D(t) = D(T) = I - \bar{R}$ for $t > T$. The gold sector alone determines gold's relative price path and the quantity of gold held in speculative hoards. To find the nominal gold price, however, we must append a monetary sector.

The Monetary Sector

The operation of the monetary sector has no real effects in the model prior to gold monetization. We introduce the monetary sector now as a preliminary to the analysis of section II.

The following equations govern money market equilibrium:

$$\frac{M(t)}{P(t)} = \beta - \alpha i(t), \qquad \beta, \alpha > 0; \tag{9}$$

$$i(t) = \rho + \frac{\dot{P}(t)}{P(t)}. \tag{10}$$

$M(t)$, $P(t)$, $i(t)$, and $\dot{P}(t)/P(t)$ are the nominal quantity of money, the aggregate price level, the nominal rate of interest, and the expected and actual rate of inflation, respectively. Equation (9) is a linearization that is appropriate for $\beta - \alpha i(t) > 0$ and for $\rho + [\dot{P}(t)/P(t)] > 0$.

In this section we assume that $M(t)$ equals the quantity of fiat currency in circulation. We also assume that the government prints fiat money at a constant positive rate π to finance a fixed positive level of real expenditure g. Since $\dot{M}(t)/P(t) = g$, it follows that $\pi = gP(t)/M(t)$. Money market equilibrium then requires that $\dot{P}(t)/P(t) = \pi$, a condition used in (9) and (10) to obtain

$$P(t) = \frac{M(t)}{\phi - \alpha\pi}, \tag{11}$$

where $\phi = \beta - \alpha\rho > 0$. We define $Q(t)$ as the nominal gold price, so $q(t) = Q(t)/P(t)$.[12]

This model lacks interesting interactions between the gold and the monetary sectors. However, such interactions are introduced by a policy of gold monetization, the topic of the next section.

II Equilibrium Dynamics under a Gold Standard

We now study the price level, money market, and gold market dynamics after a government fixes gold's nominal price, committing itself to buy and sell gold at some price $\overline{Q}$. We assume the price fixing occurs immediately and completely surprises the private sector. Initially, we assume that the government does not sterilize gold market interventions in other markets. Consequently, government gold market operations affect the money stock. Through this channel a government's decision to fix gold's price links the money and gold markets. A price-fixing scheme may be permanently viable, temporarily viable, or nonviable. A temporarily viable scheme will function for some finite period, collapsing at a predictable time. A nonviable gold standard will collapse at the instant of its implementation. We will develop a general framework capable of determining the dynamics of a particular gold standard.

The Shadow Free Market Gold Price

We define the shadow free market gold price $\tilde{Q}(t)$ as the equilibrium nominal gold price that would prevail if speculators purchased all of the government's gold reserves at time t, paying $\overline{Q}$ per unit. Such an attack would force gold demonetization, allowing the market freely to determine the gold price $\tilde{Q}(t)$. A gold standard remains viable while the shadow free market gold price $\tilde{Q}(t)$ does not exceed the government's fixed price $\overline{Q}$. If $\tilde{Q}(t) > \overline{Q}$, speculators will profit by attacking the gold standard. If $\tilde{Q}(t) < \overline{Q}$, an attack on the government's gold stock would generate speculative losses. When $\tilde{Q}(t) = \overline{Q}$ an attack produces neither profit nor loss. Since our analysis depends crucially on the shadow price $\tilde{Q}(t)$, we will develop the concept in greater detail.

Determining $\tilde{Q}(t)$ requires some assumptions about government monetary policy during and after a gold standard epoch. We assume that during a gold standard the government undertakes open market operations only in the gold market. The government will back any additional monetary issue 100 percent by gold purchases and match any gold reserve contraction by an equally valued monetary contraction. If the gold standard collapses, we assume that the government immediately resumes printing money at the positive rate π. Of course, many different assumptions about monetary policy may be analyzed in our model, and below we discuss some alternatives.[13]

To determine $\tilde{Q}(t)$ we find $\tilde{P}(t)$ and $\tilde{q}(t)$, the shadow postcollapse price level and relative gold price, respectively. We define time 0 as the first moment that the gold standard functions. Under the government's monetary policy, the money supply will be $M(t) = M(0) - \overline{Q}\overline{R}$ if a collapse occurs at any time $t \geq 0$. The postcollapse price level will be

$$\tilde{P}(t) = \frac{M(0) - \overline{Q}\overline{R}}{\phi - \alpha\pi}. \qquad (12)$$

For now, we assume that $[M(0) - \overline{Q}\overline{R}] > 0$, implying that the existing money stock can purchase all the government's initial gold reserves.

To determine the postcollapse relative gold price $\tilde{q}(t)$, we use the previous section's gold market model. Following an attack that exhausts government reserves, private agents hold the entire gold supply only for productive use or in speculative hoards. When hoards are exhausted at time T, the relative gold price will attain $q(T) = \mu/I$.[14] The immediate postcollapse relative prices is $\tilde{q}(t) = (\mu/I)\exp[-\rho(T - t)]$. The amount of time $(T - t)$ until the choke date depends on the initial level of $D(t)$ and the terminal level I. In particular, $(T - t) = f[D(t)/I]$, with $f' < 0$, $f(1) = 0$, and $f(0) = k > 0$ as in section I. Combining these results, we can express $\tilde{Q}(t)$ as

$$\tilde{Q}(t) = \tilde{P}(t)\tilde{q}(t) = \frac{[M(0) - \overline{Q}\overline{R}]\mu}{(\phi - \alpha\pi)I} \exp\left\{-\rho f\left[\frac{D(t)}{I}\right]\right\}. \tag{13}$$

This expression provides an important building block used extensively below.

Gold Standard Dynamics

If the government sets $\overline{Q} > \tilde{Q}(0)$, the gold standard will function at least temporarily because no profit will arise from an immediate speculative attack. We will now analyze the dynamics of a workable standard.

The money supply provides the key element integrating the monetary and gold sectors after price fixing. After gold monetization the money supply is

$$M(t) = M(0) + \overline{Q}[R(t) - \overline{R}] + \overline{Q}G(t). \tag{14}$$

$M(0)$ is the quantity of money existing just prior to gold monetization; $\overline{Q}[R(t) - \overline{R}]$ is the nominal value of government gold purchases after the price is fixed; $\overline{Q}G(t)$ is the nominal value of gold used directly as money. Since gold's price is fixed in terms of currency, gold will yield the same nominal capital gain as currency. Gold can also serve as money, so those hoards remaining in private hands must, as perfect substitutes for currency, constitute part of the money stock. Since we cannot determine the division of monetary gold between government and private holding, it is convenient to define

$$X(t) = R(t) + G(t). \tag{15}$$

Our framework allows us to keep track of $X(t)$ but not of its components.

Using the variable $X(t)$, we can write the money supply as

$$M(t) = M(0) - \overline{Q}\overline{R} + \overline{Q}X(t). \tag{16}$$

Since we assume that the government's only open market operations occur in the gold market, only movements in $X(t)$ affect $M(t)$ after gold's price is fixed. Substituting from equation (16) for the money supply in (9), we obtain one of the equations of motion for the gold standard regime,

$$\dot{P}(t) = \left[\left(\frac{\phi}{\alpha}\right)P(t)\right] - \left[\left(\frac{\overline{Q}}{\alpha}\right)X(t)\right] - \frac{M(0) - \overline{Q}\overline{R}}{\alpha}. \tag{17}$$

The dynamics of the variable $X(t)$ are determined from those of $D(t)$. Since $D(t) = [I - X(t)]$ and $\dot{X}(t) = -\dot{D}(t)$, we substitute for $D(t)$ and $\dot{D}(t)$ in (2) to derive

$$\dot{X}(t) = -\left(\frac{v\mu}{\overline{Q}}\right)P(t) - vX(t) + vI. \tag{18}$$

Equations (17) and (18) are the laws of motion of $P(t)$ and $X(t)$ under the gold standard.

Setting $\dot{X}(t) = \dot{P}(t) = 0$ in (17) and (18), we find the steady state $(\hat{P}, \hat{X})$ of the gold standard:

$$\hat{P} = \frac{\overline{Q}(I - \overline{R}) + M(0)}{\phi + \mu} \tag{19}$$

$$\hat{X} = \frac{\phi I + \mu\{\overline{R} - [M(0)/\overline{Q}]\}}{\phi + \mu}. \tag{20}$$

$\hat{P}$ and $\hat{X}$ serve as terminal values for $P(t)$ and $X(t)$ if $\tilde{Q}(t) < \overline{Q}$ for all t. However, $\tilde{Q}(t) > \overline{Q}$ for some t, another terminal condition will prevail. We next examine jointly the dynamics of the gold standard and of $\tilde{Q}(t)$ to determine equilibrium paths for different values of $\overline{Q}$.

Terminal Conditions and Equilibrium Paths

Figure 10.1 provides a systematic means of categorizing equilibrium paths and terminal conditions under a gold standard. We plot values of $\overline{Q}$ and $X(t)/I$ on the vertical and horizontal axes, respectively. The line $\tilde{Q}\tilde{Q}$ is a locus of points $(X, \overline{Q})$ derived from equation (13) by setting $\tilde{Q}(t) = \overline{Q}$ and using $D(t)/I = 1 - [X(t)/I]$. For points above the line, $\overline{Q} > \tilde{Q}(t)$, while for points below the line $\overline{Q} < \tilde{Q}(t)$. $\tilde{Q}\tilde{Q}$ slopes negatively with vertical intercept $\tilde{Q}_{max} = M(0)\mu/[(\phi - \alpha\pi)I + \overline{R}\mu]$. When $X/I = 1$, the height of $\tilde{Q}\tilde{Q}$ is $\tilde{Q}_{min} = \tilde{Q}_{max}\exp(-\rho k)$.

We also plot the line $\hat{X}\hat{X}$ from equation (20), which produces steady-state $\hat{X}$ values as a function of $\overline{Q}$. $\hat{X}\hat{X}$ slopes positively with a vertical intercept at $\mu M(0)/(\phi I + \mu\overline{R})$. As $\overline{Q}$ approaches infinity, $\hat{X}/I$ approaches $[\phi + (\mu\overline{R}/I)]/(\phi + \mu) \leq 1$.

The $\tilde{Q}\tilde{Q}$ locus divides figure 10.1 into the regions: (i) $\overline{Q} < \tilde{Q}_{min}$, (ii) $\tilde{Q}_{max} \geq \overline{Q} \geq \tilde{Q}_{min}$, and (iii) $\overline{Q} > \tilde{Q}_{max}$. We will initially examine the first and third.

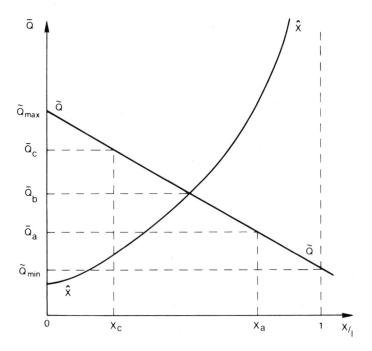

Figure 10.1

A Nonviable Gold Standard

If a government tries to establish a $\overline{Q}$ less than $\tilde{Q}_{min}$, then $\overline{Q} < \tilde{Q}(t)$ for all X. An attack will occur immediately, and the gold standard will be stillborn.

A Permanently Viable Gold Standard

If the government establishes a $\overline{Q}$ greater than $\tilde{Q}_{max}$, then $\overline{Q} > \tilde{Q}(t)$ for all X and speculators will never attack the gold standard. In this region the appropriate terminal value of $X(t)$ is $\hat{X}$. The particular path followed to $\hat{X}$ depends on the initial $X(0)$ value.

In figure 10.2 we depict the dynamic implicit in (17) and (18) for a permanent gold standard. The lines PP and XX are the loci of points $[P(t), X(t)]$ such that $\dot{P}(t) = 0$ and $\dot{X}(t) = 0$, respectively. PP and XX intersect at the dynamic system's steady-state price level and monetary gold stock, $\hat{P}$ and $\hat{X}$. We construct figure 2 for a particular value of $\overline{Q}$; an increase in $\overline{Q}$ would push the associated $(\hat{P}, \hat{X})$ to the northeast. The dynamics imply that the steady state is a saddle point with a unique stable branch, indicated by the line SS.[15] For a permanently viable gold standard we assume that economic forces determine $P(t)$, given $X(t)$, such that $P(t)$

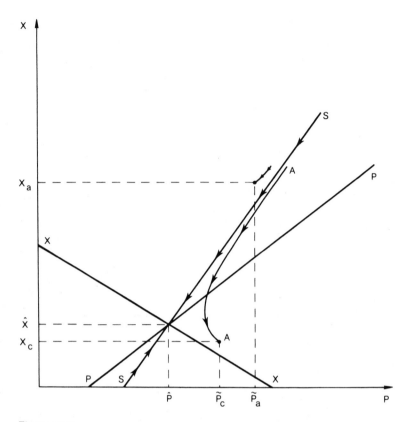

Figure 10.2

and $X(t)$ lie on the line SS.[16] For example, if $X(0) > \hat{X}$, then $P(0) > \hat{P}$ and both $P(t)$ and $X(t)$ will move along SS approaching the steady state.

Transient Gold Standards and Multiple Equilibria
We now examine the dynamics associated with different values of $\overline{Q}$ such that $\tilde{Q}_{min} \le \overline{Q} \le \tilde{Q}_{max}$. We define the pair $(X_b, \overline{Q}_b)$ as the intersection point of $\hat{X}\hat{X}$ and $\tilde{Q}\tilde{Q}$ in figure 10.1 and consider $\overline{Q}$ values less than, equal to, and greater than $\overline{Q}_b$.

A transient gold standard If $\tilde{Q}_{min} \le \overline{Q} < \overline{Q}_b$, then the gold standard's steady state is not attainable since $\tilde{Q}(t)$ exceeds $\overline{Q}$ at the steady state. In figure 1, $\overline{Q}_a$ represents such a $\overline{Q}$ setting. If the pair $[X(0), \overline{Q}]$ lies on or below $\tilde{Q}\tilde{Q}$, speculators will attack the gold standard immediately. If $[X(0), \overline{Q}]$ lies above $\tilde{Q}\tilde{Q}$, the gold standard will survive temporarily, but it must eventually collapse at a predictable time z.

The notion of a transient gold standard, implying a predictable collapse, may seem alien to the economist who senses foreseeable profit opportunities arising from discrete gold price and price-level movements. However, Salant and Henderson (1978), Krugman (1979), and Salant (1983) have shown that an anticipated collapse of a price-fixing scheme is barren of profit opportunities. In a gold standard collapse, the price level and gold accumulation rate will adjust immediately to preclude predictable speculative profit opportunities. Though it is an important development, the Salant and Henderson (1978) result has received scant attention; hence, we will spend some effort to present the concept in the context of our model.

It is possible to derive a method for determining z, the time of the collapse. However, since we were unable to construct a closed-form solution for z, we will present only a general analysis of the price continuity results necessary to approach a solution, leaving the complete discussion of the determination of z to the appendix. $\tilde{Q}(z)$ and $\tilde{P}(z)$ are the postcollapse gold price and price level, respectively. If $\overline{Q}_a$ is the fixed gold price, the collapse will occur only if $\tilde{Q}(z) \geq \overline{Q}_a$. If agents foresee $\tilde{Q}(z) > \overline{Q}_a$, then they anticipate a profit opportunity at z. Competition among agents planning to gain when the gold standard collapses will lead some agents to purchase the government's gold stock just prior to z to reap the entire speculative profit. Since the collapse would then occur before z, a foreseeable collapse at z can occur only if $\tilde{Q}(z) = \overline{Q}_a$.

Since goods are storable, no anticipated price-level jumps can coincide with the gold standard's collapse, although the money stock will discretely decline. Foreseeable price-level discontinuities would open profitable speculative opportunities involving the storable good. The equilibrium price level will be determined currently such that at time z its path is continuous.

We can graphically analyze the dynamics of a temporarily viable gold standard using figure 10.2. $\tilde{P}_a$ represents the postcollapse price level associated with $\overline{Q}_a$;[17] X_a is the quantity of monetary gold when $\tilde{Q}(z) = \overline{Q}_a$. Recognizing the coming collapse, agents foresee that afterward the price level and relative gold price will be driven by the dynamic laws established in section I. Since $(\tilde{P}_a, X_a)$ rather than $(\hat{P}, \hat{X})$ serves as the terminal condition for the gold standard dynamics, the price level and monetary gold stock will not generally move along the saddle path during the gold standard's temporary existence.[18] Instead, the system will follow an ostensibly unstable path and collapse when the monetary gold stock reaches X_a, the gold hoard that agents are just willing to hold in the pure fiat system of section I. In the appendix we show how to compute $\tilde{P}_a$, $\tilde{Q}(z)$, X_a, and z.

Multiple equilibrium paths   We now study the possible equilibria that arise when the fixed gold price equals $\overline{Q}_c \geq \overline{Q}_b$ in figure 10.1. If $X(0) < X_c$, the gold standard again will be immediately attacked. However, if the initial monetary gold stock exceeds or equals X_c, multiple equilibrium paths will arise.

The multiplicity depends purely on agents' expectations about the viability of the gold standard. If agents believe that the gold standard will function permanently, equilibrium will occur along the stable path SS associated with $\overline{Q}_c$ in figure 10.2, and $P(t)$ and $X(t)$ will decline toward the steady state $(\hat{P}, \hat{X})$. However, if agents believe that the gold standard will survive only temporarily, their behavior will establish the equilibrium along the path AA in figure 10.2. The terminal point for AA is $(\tilde{P}_c, X_c)$, where $\tilde{P}_c$ is the shadow price level associated with $\overline{Q}_c$. When the system attains this terminal point, $\tilde{Q} = \overline{Q}_c$ and the gold standard will be attacked.[19]

In our model the potential for multiple equilibria arises whenever the government extracts resources through money creation in a postcollapse fiat regime. Such a policy ensures that the $\hat{Q}\hat{Q}$ and $\hat{X}\hat{X}$ loci of figure 10.1 intersect in the positive quadrant. As g and π decline, the $\hat{Q}\hat{Q}$ locus shifts downward, intersecting the $\hat{X}\hat{X}$ locus on the vertical axis when $\pi = 0$. When $\pi = 0$, multiple equilibria will occur only for a fixed gold price given by the height of this intersection point.

Price-Level Effects of Gold Monetization

Since gold monetization is intended to provide a more stable price level than that of the current fiat system, we study the response of the price level to a newly implemented gold standard.

When the gold standard is immediately nonviable, the attack on the government's gold stock causes the money supply to fall discretely by an amount $\overline{Q}\overline{R}$. If the government does not otherwise alter its previous money growth plans, the price-level path is displaced downward by $\overline{Q}\overline{R}/[\phi - \alpha\pi]$.

If the gold standard is permanently or temporarily viable, its price-level effects depend on the specific monetary growth path followed before the gold standard is announced, the price of gold, and the model's initial conditions and parameters.

For example, we may consider the price-level effects of a permanently viable system. Prior to the implementation of the gold standard at time 0, agents had expected a growing money supply. When gold's price is fixed at $\overline{Q}$, the monetary aggregate immediately jumps from $M(0)$ to $M(0) +$

$\overline{Q}G(0-)$, where $G(0-) > 0$ is the private gold hoard just before monetization. Once the gold standard is implemented, movements of $X(t)$ drive the money stock. Depending on the choice of $\overline{Q}$, the money stock may rise, decline, or remain static through time.

Since the price level is a weighted average of future money stocks, the gold standard need not stabilize prices relative to the fiat system.[20] In order to determine the price-level effects of the monetary system change, we must know the future money stock paths. Evidently, the money stock can evolve many different ways, generating gold inflation, gold deflation, or price stability. The gold standard may be more or less stabilizing than the fiat system, depending on the initial speculative gold stocks, the parameters of gold and money demand, and the fixed gold price. In practice, the price level can be stabilized by sterilizing the shift in the money growth path at the instant of monetization and choosing a gold price placing the system at its steady state.

Some Extensions of the Analysis

At this point we wish to consider relaxing three important assumptions: (i) $\overline{Q}\overline{R} < M(0)$; (ii) the only open market operations undertaken while the gold standard functions are gold market operations; and (iii) the money growth path after a collapse is the pre–gold standard expected growth path.

If open market operations occur only in the gold market during the gold standard era, the assumption that $\overline{Q}\overline{R} < M(0)$ implies that $\overline{Q}R(t) < M(t)$ for all t. Enough currency to purchase all the government's gold at the fixed price $\overline{Q}$ always will exist, a necessary condition for a collapse. Alternatively, if we assume $\overline{Q}\overline{R} > M(0)$, the gold standard cannot collapse. When open market operations are allowed only in the gold market, further currency creation corresponds to additions to government gold stocks. Because the government's reserves, always maintaining a greater value than outstanding claims, will never be attacked, the analysis for a permanently functioning gold standard is applicable.

We may also relax the assumption that open market operations occur only in the gold market during the gold standard era. If gold's price exceeds the minimum, permanently viable price, the government, though continually maintaining the fixed gold price, possesses some discretion to increase the money stock through channels other than gold purchases. Unless it is expected that they will be transitory, such monetary expansions raise the shadow free market price, $\tilde{Q}(t)$. However, if the government limits the monetary expansion so that $\bar{Q}$ always exceeds $\tilde{Q}_{max}$, it can still ensure a permanently functioning gold standard.

Finally, we have assumed that the money growth path following the collapse is identical to the pre–gold standard path, $\dot{M}(t)/M(t) = \pi$. This assumption is applicable if the government extracts a constant resource flow through money creation in a postcollapse economy. However, the government's postattack, shadow revenue requirements may continually rise during the gold standard's operation, so that the postattack shadow inflation rate also rises. Under such circumstances, the $\tilde{Q}\tilde{Q}$ locus in figure 10.1 would continually shift upward through time, forcing the eventual collapse of an otherwise well-functioning gold standard.

III   The Discipline of the Gold Standard

Any pressure to reestablish a commodity base for the monetary system rests on a conviction that "discipline" generated by such constraining rules yields beneficial price-level stability or predictability. However, viewed in a dynamic context of periodic movements from commodity to fiat monetary systems, the discipline of commodity systems is a mask obscuring the forces that drive the global dynamic money creation process. Since all commodity standard interludes eventually are superseded by fiat systems, the notion of discipline can characterize only the underlying forces generating the entire dynamic monetary process. The application of this concept to only one facet of a general policy sequence, overlooking the empirical realization that all previous commodity standards have collapsed into fiat systems, may lead to misplaced confidence in prescriptions to return to a commodity base

Behind the sequential transitions from one monetary scheme to another that we have analyzed must lie a political economy that we have ignored. Such political economic forces determine the complete dynamic panorama of the monetary process. Their nature can be gauged only by the entire sequence of monetary bases, not by the ephemeral monetary base that currently may operate. If the fiat segments of the money creation process are inflationary enough, then a currently existing commodity standard may not be viable, even though if it continued the money stock would grow according to the commodity standard's dynamic laws. A commodity system can be interpreted as a discipline-imposing rule only if the commodity standard's permanence is somehow guaranteed. As there is no means to secure such permanence, the notion of a commodity standard as a stabilizing rule is a chimera. The monetary system is stable only if the global money generation scheme and agents' confidence in it produce stability, not if money is temporarily created according to some transitional rule.

If conditions arise that indicate the imminence of highly inflationary monetary policies contingent on a gold standard's collapse, the gold standard, though maintained by a government conditionally and scrupulously obeying its rules, may not survive. The gold standard is but one phase of an overall policy; lack of stability of the entire constellation of conditional monetary standards precludes the stability of any one of its commodity standard phases. In contrast, current policy discussions prescribe the adoption of some commodity standard *because* conditional fiat systems are too unstable. However, simply comparing the price-level dynamics of two permanent money generation schemes yields misleading results. The central political economic problem, that fiat systems are unstable, can override any stabilizing properties of permanently viable commodity standards. Unless a political system somehow ensures stability of the conditional fiat epochs of its money generation process, implementing a commodity standard may be a provisional, if not momentary, exercise. To conduct an analysis of changes in monetary systems requires the recognition that all monetary generation rules are temporary, predictably to be replaced under some circumstances.

IV   Conclusion

Many possible commodities can serve as monetary standards. However, the sequence of items on which the monetary system has been based in modern times has been so limited that it can readily be characterized as a "gold-paper-gold" cycle. Since the current paper phase of the cycle has allowed price-level instability, there has been some agitation to return to the gold standard. Proponents of such a return presume that simply allowing the market to determine the price at which gold will be fixed is sufficient to produce an "appropriate" price, imposing discipline on the money generation process. A result of this paper is that such policies will lead to price-level stability only in the presence of very specific, coincident monetary actions. To determine the nature of such policies requires detailed knowledge of gold and money market structure, the nature of expectations, and price-level and private gold accumulation dynamics. Without such monetary actions, implementing a policy to set the gold price according to a given day's market price may lead to a situation even more inflationary than that produced by the current system.

Appendix

An anticipation of an attack on government gold reserves, which will occur at time z, precludes gold price and prive-level jumps at time z. Formally, this implies $\tilde{P}(z) = \tilde{P}(z_+) = P(z)$ and $\overline{Q} = \tilde{Q}(z_+)$, where z_+ is the instant after the run. With our money growth assumption, $\tilde{P}(z) = P(0) - [\overline{QR}/(\phi - \alpha\pi)]$. Since we know $\overline{Q} = \tilde{Q}(z)$, the relative price of gold at time z is $\tilde{q}(z) = \overline{Q}/\{P(0) - [\overline{QR}/(\phi - \alpha\pi)]\}$. This will serve as an initial condition for the relative gold price at time z. Furthermore, since the gold market model of Section II governs the gold price after the collapse, we also obtain the terminal condition $q(T) = \mu/I$. Since $\dot{q}(t) = \rho q(t)$, we combine the initial and terminal conditions to find

$$T - z = \left(\frac{1}{\rho}\right)\ln\left[\frac{\mu}{q(z)I}\right]. \tag{A1}$$

According to (A1), gold will be held in speculative hoards for a period $\theta = (1/\rho)\ln[\mu/q(z)I]$ after the collapse.

Knowing θ allows us to determine $D(z)$ at the instant of the collapse. The accumulation requirement is

$$I = D(z)\exp(-v\theta) + \exp(-v\theta)\int_z^T \left[\frac{v\mu\rho}{q(z)}\right]\exp[-\rho(u - z) + vu]\,du \tag{A2}$$

or

$$I = D(z)\exp(-v\theta) + \left[\frac{v\mu\rho}{q(z)(v - \rho)}\right][\exp(-\rho\theta) - \exp(-v\theta)]. \tag{A2a}$$

Equation (A2a) determines $D(z)$ as a function of $q(z)$, and since $I = D(z) + X(z)$ we can determine $X(z)$.

Armed with the values $P(z)$ and $X(z)$, we can compute z by reference to the general solution for the price level and monetary gold given by the gold standards dynamics. That solution is

$$P(t) = c_1 A\exp(\lambda_1 t) + c_2 B\exp(\lambda_2 t) + \hat{P}, \qquad t < z, \tag{A3}$$

$$X(t) = c_1\exp(\lambda_1 t) + c_2\exp(\lambda_2 t) + \hat{X}, \qquad t < z, \tag{A4}$$

where $A = \overline{Q}/(\phi - \alpha\lambda_1)$, $B = \overline{Q}/(\phi - \alpha\lambda_2)$, λ_1 is the system's negative root, and λ_2 is the positive root.

To find z we first must solve for the constants c_1 and c_2 using our knowledge that (i) $P(z)$ in (A3) is $P(0) - [\overline{QR}/(\phi - \alpha\pi)]$ and (ii) $X(0)$ is some value given by an initial condition as in the text. These constants will be functions of z and the parameters of the model. Next, since we know $X(z)$, we set $X(t)$ in (A4) equal to $X(z)$. This will produce a single nonlinear equation in the unknown time of collapse z, which, in principle, can be solved.

Notes

Stephen Salant's extensive comments proved enormously useful in developing this chapter. Helpful comments also were given by Dale Henderson, Jeff Frankel, Ken Rogoff, and various participants in seminars at Rice University, the University of Florida, the University of Chicago, the University of Pennsylvania, M.I.T., the University of California, Berkeley, the Board of Governors of the Federal Reserve, the University of South Carolina, the Wingspread Conference, Harvard University, and Northwestern University. The chapter was partly developed while Flood was a staff member of the Board of Governors of the Federal Reserve. The views presented here are our own and do not necessarily represent the views of the governors of the Federal Reserve or other members of their staff. We would like to thank the National Science Foundation for financial support.

1. Congress decided to assess gold's monetary role by establishing a Gold Commission. While the commission was generally hostile to monetization of gold, its existence indicates that a return to a commodity base is a serious possibility.

2. For discussions of the time inconsistency problem, see Kydland and Prescott (1977) or Barro and Gordon (1983).

3. However, the switch to the gold standard itself will be treated as a complete surprise. The perfect-foresight assumption applies to the dynamics of prices *after* the advent of the gold standard.

4. Allowing the real interest rate to vary would complicate our analysis. We presume that the real side of our model consists of gold and a storable good that can be either consumed or stored to produce more goods. One unit of the stored consumable produces more consumables at the rate ρ, given exogenously as in Salant and Henderson (1978). Barro (1979) assumes that demand and supply functions are explicitly dependent on ρ; however, he exogenously fixes ρ to develop his gold standard's dynamics.

5. These assumptions preclude any gold-mining activity, a specification similar to that of Salant and Henderson (1978).

6. Surprisingly, Barro (1979) worked out the dynamics of his gold standard model using a static expectations assumption. This produced a stable dynamic system that is comparable only in its steady state to the system developed below.

7. In an early version of this paper, we solved the model for a case in which capital gains enter into desired gold use. Because no substantive result depends on this assumption, we exclude it here to simplify our report.

8. While our methods are similar to those of Salant and Henderson (1978), our gold market model differs from theirs in some important respects. Salant and Henderson interpret the variable that, in the context of their paper, is analogous to our $\dot{D}(t)$ as a demand for a perishable good. Since this gold demand must always be nonnegative in their paper, we

have avoided using their form here. Otherwise, we would preclude the possibility of a postmonentization gold inflation and the disgorging of consumer gold that occurred in 1980 and 1981. Also, we assume that the flow gold demand depends negatively on $D(t)$, the existing gold stock already used in consumption and industrial forms. This may reflect diminishing marginal productivity associated with additional industrial gold uses.

9. Salant and Henderson (1978) discuss the speculative pricing of such resources in more detail.

10. The differential equation is $\dot{D}(t) = -vD(t) + [v\mu/q(0)]\exp(-\rho t)$, when $G(t) > 0$.

11. The function determining T at time zero is $1 = D(0)\exp(-vT)/(I - \bar{R}) + v\{1 - \exp[-(\rho - v)T]\}/(v - \rho)$. For the special case of $D(0) = 0$, the solution for T is $T = \log(\rho/v)/(\rho - v)$, for $\rho \neq v$.

12. Since $P(t)$ contains the rental price of gold in consumption form, our relative price $q(t) = Q(t)/P(t)$ is not equal to the price of gold divided by the price of goods other than gold. However, we may assume that gold's consumption rental price is proportional to gold's price and that $P(t)$ is a geometric average of gold's rental price and the price of other goods. Then our $q(t)$ is proportional to the price of gold divided by the price of goods other than gold raised to the power $(1 + \Omega)$, where Ω is gold's share in the price index. In our analysis we assume that Ω is sufficiently small that it may be ignored without consequence. However, if Ω were large then our eq. (3) would become $\dot{q}(t) = \rho(1 - \Omega)q(t)$. This change would not alter our results substantively.

13. Our assumption about the gold standard monetary policy requires that the government either develop a nonmonetary method of financing g or reduce spending by g. In section II we discuss the implications of an alternative assumption about postcollapse money growth.

14. The postcollapse choke date T is not the same as the choke date discussed in section I since the total gold stock available for consumption increases by the government's reserves. However, the logic used in section I to determine T is also applicable in this case.

15. The equation of SS is $P(t) = AX(t) + \hat{P} + A\hat{X}$, where $A = \bar{Q}/(\phi - \alpha\lambda_1) > 0$ and λ_1 is the negative root of the equation system (17) and (18). To be precise, $\lambda_1 = \frac{1}{2}(-[\phi/(\alpha - v)] - \{[\phi/(\alpha - v)]^2 + 4(v/\alpha)(\phi + \mu)\}^{1/2}) < 0$. For later use we also record the positive root of the system, $\lambda_2 = [(-v/\alpha)(\phi + \mu)]/\lambda_1 > 0$.

16. This assumption requires the absence of speculative bubbles, by which we mean that prices are determined entirely by market fundamentals. We impose this requirement throughout the paper.

17. It can be shown that $\tilde{P}_a$ exceeds $\hat{P}$ when $\bar{Q} \leq \bar{Q}_{\max}$. We realize that $\hat{P}$ and $\hat{X}$ are both positive functions of $\bar{Q}$. However, we have used fig. 2 to analyze dynamics for several $\bar{Q}$ values to preserve simplicity of presentation. The reader should be reminded that the steady state will actually move as we examine different $\bar{Q}$ values.

18. Since $\tilde{P}_a > \hat{P}$ and $X_a > \hat{X}$, the gold standard will terminate northeast of $(\hat{P}, \hat{X})$ in figure 10.2. However, without precise parameter values, we do not know where $(\tilde{P}_a, X_a)$ lies with respect to SS.

19. Since $\tilde{P}_c > \hat{P}$ and $X_c > \hat{X}$, the path approaching $(\tilde{P}_c, X_c)$ must lie to the right to SS.

20. For an arbitrary money growth path, money market equilibrium will generate $P(t) = \exp(\phi t/\alpha)\int_t^\infty [M(u)/\alpha]\exp(-\phi u/\alpha)\,du$.

References

Barro, Robert J. "Money and the Price Level under the Gold Standard." *Econ. J.* 89 (March 1979): 13–33.

Barro, Robert J., and Gordon, David B. "A Positive Theory of Monetary Policy in a Natural Rate Model," *J.P.E.* 91 (August 1983): 589–610.

Krugman, Paul. "A Model of Balance-of-Payments Crises." *J. Money, Credit and Banking* 11 (August 1979): 311–25.

Kydland, Finn E., and Prescott, Edward C. "Rules Rather than Discretion: The Inconsistency of Optimal Plans." *J.P.E.* 85 (June 1977): 473–91.

Laffer, Arthur B. "Making the Dollar as Good as Gold." *Los Angeles Times* (October 30, 1979).

Lehrman, Lewis E. "Monetary Policy, the Federal Reserve System, and Gold." Working Paper. New York: Lehrman Inst., 1980.

Lehrman, Lewis E. "The Case for the Gold Standard." Working Paper. New York: Lehrman Inst., 1981.

Salant, Stephen W. "The Vulnerability of Price Stabilization Schemes to Speculative Attack." *J.P.E.* 91 (February 1983): 1–38.

Salant, Stephen W., and Henderson, Dale W. "Market anticipations of Government Policies and the Price of Gold." *J.P.E.* 86 (August 1978): 627–48.

11

Recurrent Devaluation and Speculative Attacks on the Mexican Peso

Herminio Blanco and Peter M. Garber

Recently several researchers have developed the concept of endogenously timed speculative attacks on asset price-fixing regimes.[1] This literature has demonstrated that the timing and magnitude of attacks can be determined by studying agents' rational speculative behavior. However, no effort has been made to implement these models empirically. In this paper we generate an empirical method aimed at predicting the timing and magnitude of devaluations forced by speculative attacks on fixed exchange rate systems. To illustrate the applicability of the method, we analyze the Mexican exchange rate experience during the 1973–82 period.

After almost twenty years (1954–72) of conservative monetary policy that successfully maintained a stable exchange rate, the Banco de Mexico became a major source of public sector finance beginning in 1973. Subsequently, Mexico experienced a series of balance of payments crises.[2] Major exchange rate changes occurred in August 1976 and in February and August 1982. The Banco de Mexico also implemented a series of minidevaluations during 1981 and imposed exchange controls in August 1982.

Using the Mexican experience as an example, we will produce time-series estimates of the one-period-ahead probability of devaluation. The probability series attains peak values for the observations during the 1976 and 1982 devaluations. We will also construct a time series of the expected next-period exchange rate conditional on the occurrence of a devaluation.

The paper is divided into two sections. In section I we develop a devaluation model that is an extension of some of the results in the speculative attack literature. The building blocks of the model are a domestic money market, a policy rule for devaluation, and a policy rule for domestic credit creation. From these components we derive expressions for the probability that a fixed exchange rate regime will collapse one period ahead, the expected value of the new fixed exchange rate, the variance, and the confidence interval of the forecasted exchange rate. In section II we present the estimates of the model for the Mexican sample.

I   The Devaluation Model

Since a fixed exchange rate regime involves the control of a nominal price, a government can maintain a given exchange rate by controlling domestic credit. The recurrence of devaluations must imply that the fixed exchange rate is a secondary goal of the government, maintained conditional on fulfillment of other primary policies. In this chapter we will assume that the government's fiscal policy and its implied deficits are the primary goals, unaffected by events in the exchange market. For many countries (e.g., Mexico) this assumption implies that the central bank's domestic credit creation policy is an exogenous force in the exchange market. When the requirements both to finance the government's deficit and to support the fixed exchange rate exceed some limit on the central bank's resources, the current fixed exchange rate will be relinquished.

The Money Market

A money market provides the central component of our model:

$$m_t - p_t = \beta + \Omega y_t - \alpha i_t + w_t, \tag{1}$$

Where m_t, p_t, and y_t are the logarithms of the money stock, the domestic price level, and the aggregate output level, respectively; i_t is the domestic interest rate; and w_t is a stochastic disturbance to the money demand. We further assume that the price level and the interest rate are determined by

$$i_t = i_t^* + E e_{t+1} - e_t, \tag{2}$$

$$p_t = p_t^* + e_t + u_t, \tag{3}$$

where an asterisk signifies an exogenous foreign variable and e_t and u_t are the logarithms of the nominal and the real exchange rate, respectively.[3] The operator E represents expectations conditional on information through time t.

The Devaluation Policy

Changes in the variables of equation (1) and movements of domestic credit determine the evolution of net foreign reserves. The central bank, having fixed the exchange rate at $\bar{e}$, stops intervening in the foreign exchange market when net reserves reach a critical level $\bar{R}$, measured in foreign currency units.[4] If such an event materializes at time t, the central bank establishes a new fixed exchange rate $\hat{e}_t$ using a time-invariant policy rule. We assume that the government does not impose exchange controls.

As usual for a policy rule, $\hat{e}_t$ will be a function of the model's stochastic state variables. While a given fixed exchange rate remains viable, $\hat{e}_t$ remains in the background as a "shadow" exchange rate unobservable to the researcher. It attains visibility only at the moment of a devaluation. As the new fixed exchange rate that would be set after an attack, $\hat{e}_t$ must always be a viable exchange rate. This requires that $\hat{e}_t$ exceed some minimum value, which we will derive below.

The *current* fixed rate's viability depends on the relation between the fixed exchange rate and $\hat{e}_t$. Specifically, there is an equivalence between $\hat{e}_t$'s exceeding the current fixed exchange rate and the reserve level's attaining its lower bound at time t. Sufficiency follows since, if this event occurs, agents would profit from a speculative attack that forces a currency devaluation to $\hat{e}_t$. According to its policy, the central bank will sell international reserves until they reach the lower bound $\bar{R}$. At this point the bank will establish the new exchange rate $\hat{e}_t$, thereby providing an instantaneous capital gain to those who attacked the reserves. Conversely, to demonstrate necessity, assume that net reserves have fallen to their lower bound but that there still remains an excess money supply at the current fixed exchange rate. If the policy rule sets some $\hat{e}_t$ less than the current fixed exchange rate, it would worsen the excess supply. Therefore such a policy rule would be inconsistent with the assumption of money market equilibrium.

A Viable Devaluation Policy and the Floating Exchange Rate

We will now argue that to produce a viable new exchange rate, the policy rule must prescribe an exchange rate greater than or equal to the rate that would prevail in a postattack, permanently floating exchange rate regime. In a regime with no central bank exchange market intervention, net foreign reserves would remain permanently at the minimum $\bar{R}$, and the permanently floating exchange rate would be the one that supports money market equilibrium. However, if the central bank is forced to devalue and yet attempts to establish a fixed rate below the floating rate associated with a permanent reserve level $\bar{R}$, it would face a demand for reserves that it could not satisfy because reserves would already have reached $\bar{R}$. Therefore, the permanently floating exchange rate, although unobservable in a regime with exchange rate pegging, places a lower bound on the value of a new fixed exchange rate. Since the underlying permanent flexible exchange rate constitutes an important building block in our model, we proceed to derive it.[5]

Using the money-market-clearing condition, we can determine the flexible exchange rate. Substituting (2) and (3) into (1), we obtain for any time t during the floating regime

$$\tilde{h}_t = -\alpha E\tilde{e}_{t+1} + (1 + \alpha)\tilde{e}_t, \tag{4}$$

Where $\tilde{h}_t \equiv \log[D_t + \bar{R}\exp(\tilde{e})] - \beta - \Omega y_t + \alpha i_t^* - p_t^* - u_t - w_t$, D_t is the domestic credit component of the monetary base at time t, and $\tilde{e}_t$ represents the permanently floating exchange rate. We convert $\bar{R}$ into domestic currency using the fixed exchange rate $\bar{e}$ prevailing at the time of the switch to floating rates. This follows from our assumption that the government does not repudiate its fixed exchange rate until reserves reach $\bar{R}$.[6]

We denote by h_t the initial value of $\tilde{h}_t$ that would prevail at time t if the floating rate began at t. In principle it is important to distinguish between the stochastic process that drives future values of the $\tilde{h}_t$ variable *after* the floating rate begins and the process that drives h_t. Variable h_t is determined period after period during the operation of the fixed exchange rate system. In particular, the reserve limit $\bar{R}$ may evolve during the fixed rate regime, thereby affecting the development of h_t. However, during a pure float the reserves entering into $\tilde{h}_t$ would not change. In addition, variables like D_t entering into $\tilde{h}_t$ may behave differently under a fixed rate environment than under a permanent float. However, since the $\tilde{h}_t$ process is unobservable by the researcher, we will assume that the $\tilde{h}_t$ and h_t processes are identical.[7]

The stochastic process that drives the h_t (and $\tilde{h}_t$) variable is assumed to be a first-order autoregressive process exogenous to the exchange rate.[8] Specifically, the h_t process is

$$h_t = \theta_1 + \theta_2 h_{t-1} + v_t, \tag{5}$$

where v_t is a white-noise process with a normal density function $g(v)$, with zero mean and standard deviation σ.[9]

Since in actual economies domestic credit may respond to movements in actual or shadow exchange rates, the exogeneity of the h_t process and the implicit exogeneity of domestic credit from the exchange rate are strong assumptions. Note, however, that we do not assume exogeneity among the component variables of h_t; in particular, y_t and D_t may be simultaneously determined. Relaxing the exogeneity assumption for the exchange market would require the addition of a feedback relation from the exchange rate to h_t. This would complicate the dynamics, but the solution for the floating rate would be similar to that below providing that the feedback relation can be linearized.

We obtain the flexible exchange rate $\tilde{e}_t$ by solving the difference equations in (4) and (5). The solution

$$\tilde{e}_t = \mu\alpha\theta_1 + \mu h_t, \tag{6}$$

where $\mu = 1/[(1 + \alpha) - \alpha\theta_2]$, follows from assuming that $\alpha\theta_2/(1 + \alpha) < 1$ and ruling out the existence of "bubbles."

The central bank's determination of the policy rule for the new exchange rate should involve some optimization problem.[10] However, we will assume that the new fixed rate is a simple linear function

$$\hat{e}_t = \tilde{e}_t + \delta v_t, \tag{7}$$

where δ is a nonnegative parameter,[11] and $\hat{e}_t$ is the new fixed exchange rate that will be established if the level of reserves attains the value $\bar{R}$ at time t.

Note from (6) and (7) that $\hat{e}_t$ is a function of the only state variables in the model, h_t and v_t. Also observe that, since $\delta \geq 0$, $\hat{e}_t$ exceeds the minimum viable value for a new exchange rate when reserves run out.[12] The rule (7) states that after an attack the central bank will select a new rate equal to the minimum viable rate plus a nonnegative quantity dependent on the magnitude of the disturbance that forced the collapse.

Furthermore, given (6) and (7), notice that a nonstationary process for h_t would imply an expectation that the current fixed exchange rate is transitory. For instance, priority public finance requirements may dictate rapid future domestic credit creation that will eventually collapse the current fixed rate. A stationary process for h_t would indicate a degree of commitment to the current fixed rate. While there may be disturbances that jeopardize the current fixed rate, public policy will eventually remove their impact, provided that their magnitude is not enough to trigger a devaluation contemporaneously.

The Probability of Attack and the Conditional Exchange Rate

In section I.A we demonstrated that $\hat{e}_t$'s exceeding the current fixed rate is equivalent to a devaluation at time t. Therefore, the probability of devaluation at time $t + 1$ based on information available at t is

$$\text{pr}(\mu\alpha\theta_1 + \mu h_{t+1} + \delta v_{t+1} > \bar{e}),$$

where $\bar{e}$ is the time t value of the fixed rate. Alternatively, the devaluation probability is

$$1 - F(k_t) \equiv \mathrm{pr}(v_{t+1} > k_t), \tag{8}$$

where $k_t \equiv [1/(\mu + \delta)][\bar{e} - \mu\alpha\theta_1 - \mu(\theta_1 + \theta_2 h_t)]$, and $F(k_t)$ is the cumulative distribution function associated with $g(v)$.

Knowing this density function, agents can form expectations of future exchanges rates from the average of the current fixed exchange rate and the rate expected to materialize conditional on a devaluation, both weighted by the respective probabilities of occurrence:[13]

$$Ee_{t+1} = F(k_t)\bar{e} + [1 - F(k_t)]E(\hat{e}_{t+1}|v_{t+1} > k_t).$$

Using (7), we can express the conditional expectation as

$$E(\hat{e}_{t+1}|v_{t+1} > k_t) = \mu\theta_1(1 + \alpha) + \mu\theta_2 h_t + (\mu + \delta)E(v_{t+1}|v_{t+1} > k_t), \tag{9}$$

where

$$E(v_{t+1}|v_{t+1} > k_t) = \int_{k_t}^{\infty} \frac{vg(v)}{1 - F(k_t)} dv.$$

Since $g(v)$ is a normal density function, the unconditional forecast of the exchange rate for $t + 1$ is

$$Ee_{t+1} = F(k_t)\bar{e} + [1 - F(k_t)][\mu\theta_1(1 + \alpha) + \mu\theta_2 h_t]$$

$$+ \frac{\sigma(\mu + \delta)\exp[-.5(k_t/\sigma)^2]}{\sqrt{2\pi}}. \tag{10}$$

The one-step-ahead devaluation probability (8) and the conditional and unconditional exchange rate forecasts (9) and (10) are the main products of our model. We would expect $[1 - F(k_t)]$ to peak immediately before a devaluation; Ee_{t+1} should be closely correlated with the appropriate forward or future rates.[14] Finally, the conditional forecast should approximate the exchange rate set when a devaluation occurs. The statistical significance of the difference between the conditional forecasts and the realized devaluations can be determined by using the confidence intervals associated with the probability density function (p.d.f.) $g(v)/[1 - F(k_t)]$.

II   The Mexican Devaluations

Section I extends speculative attack models to the problem of recurring devaluations. Since none of the existing models have been empirically oriented, we have constructed our theory in a manner that permits its empirical implementation. In particular, we will now compute conditional expected exchange rates and a time series of the one-step-ahead devaluation probabilities $[1 - F(k_t)]$ for the recent Mexican experience. Since devaluation probabilities are endogenous in our model, our method of computation of the probabilities allows us to use observations from the fixed exchange rate periods as well as from the periods in which devaluations occur. The information to compute the probabilities arises from the entire time series of money market and exchange rate variables and not only from the few episodes of devaluation.

At the outset the reader should be warned against interpreting our empirical results as formal tests of this model. Before such interpretation is appropriate, a considerable amount of effort needs to be invested in improving the specification of the different functional forms of the model and the estimation procedures. In this paper we intend to consider only how data may be brought to bear on the speculative attack problem. We regard our results as indicative of the usefulness of this mode of theorizing.

General Description of the Estimation Procedure

The unconditional expected exchange rate (10) is the keystone of the estimation procedure. Interpreting future or forward exchange rates as unconditional expected rates, we can estimate the unknown parameters in (10). We assume that the future rates for the Mexican peso f_t are generated by

$$f_t = Ee_{t+1} + \varepsilon_t, \tag{11}$$

where ε_t is a disturbance. Since we have assumed no risk premium in equation (2) and since Ee_{t+1} is the unconditional expectation of the next period's exchange rate, the disturbance ε_t can arise only from specification error. The existence of risk premia and the incorrect functional forms are possible misspecifications. Another is the measurement error that appears from our inability to observe w_t and its exclusion from our computed h_t below. Notwithstanding the obscure nature of ε_t, we assume that it is a well-behaved disturbance with zero expected value and is orthogonal to the variables in the expression for Ee_{t+1}.[15]

We first estimated the money demand parameters by a method described below. We then utilized a multistep, iterative estimation procedure to estimate $\bar{R}$ and δ.[16] Initial values of $\bar{R}$ and δ were assumed and used with the estimated money demand parameters to compute the h_t series. We then estimated θ_1, θ_2, and σ by minimizing the sum of squared residuals of equation (5), the AR(1) process of h_t. Substituting the AR(1) process estimates, the money demand parameter estimates, and the initial values of $\bar{R}$ and δ in equation (10), we reestimated $\bar{R}$ and δ by minimizing the sum of squared residuals of the nonlinear equation (11), the futures exchange rate equation. We iterated this procedure until the parameter estimates for $\bar{R}$ and δ converged.

Data Problems in the Mexican Case

To estimate the model's parameters, we employed quarterly data from the fourth quarter of 1973 to the fourth quarter of 1981.[17] We were limited to quarterly data because the peso futures market had only four delivery dates per year. The forward market in pesos did not develop until after the 1976 devaluation. Although the data used for parameter estimation purposes did not include the 1982 devaluations, we did substitute realized h_t values from 1982 into our estimated probability formula to examine how well our model "predicts" the 1982 episodes.

The money stock variable is the end-of-quarter monetary base. Alternative monetary concepts, such as M1, appeared unsuitable. Before the 1976 episode, the meaning of MI was blurred since the banking system's long-term liabilities could be costlessly converted to currency. Additionally, a sizable stock of domestic liabilities was denominated in dollars (mexdollars) during the sample period.[18] The level of domestic credit D_t is represented only by the Banco de Mexico's loans to the federal government because data for the bank's financing of the remainder of the economy are not readily available. For y_t and p_t we used the quarterly series of logarithms of the real gross domestic product and the gross domestic product deflator, respectively.[19] To represent the product of the foreign price level and the deviation from purchasing power parity we divided the domestic price level by the current fixed exchange rate.

During most of the period, Mexican capital markets were underdeveloped and the interest rates for bank liabilities were controlled. Therefore, as a measure of i_t, we used the U.S. three-month Treasury bill rate plus the corresponding percentage discount of the peso in the futures market. For f_t in (11), we used the logarithm of the end-of-quarter peso rate for delivery three months forward.

Finally, the Mexican episode presents a difficulty with our assumptions about $\bar{R}$, the minimum allowable net reserve value. We assumed in our theoretical development that $\bar{R}$ remains constant, regardless of the evolution of the other variables of the model. In the Mexican case, such an assumption is not tenable. First, the Mexican economy exhibited rapid growth for much of the sample period, so a minimum net reserve level that the central bank might have considered excessive in 1973 could easily have been established in 1979. Second, the real value of the dollar declined throughout the period. Maintaining any given level of net dollar reserves would have been less burdensome in real terms at the end of the period than at the beginning.

To account for this possible evolution of the reserve limit,[20] we have assumed that the reserve limit equals a constant $\bar{R}$ multiplied by an index of U.S. import prices. Accordingly, we replaced $\bar{R}$ in the h_t definition with $\bar{R}$ multiplied by this index. This alteration accounts in part for the declining real value of the dollar. Furthermore, since U.S. import prices were greatly affected by oil price changes during this period, these movements can reflect greater Mexican borrowing and repayment capacity, which may have increased the central bank's willingness to continue supporting the fixed exchange rate.

Estimation Results

In estimating the base money demand parameters in equation (1), we emplyed a two-stage technique with two alternative sets of instrumental variables. The first set contained three lags of interest rates while the other also included four lags of real income. In addition, we used dummy variables to account for possible seasonal effects on money demand. Table 11.1 contains the resulting parameter estimates.[21] The estimates of $\bar{R}$, δ, θ_1, θ_2, and σ are reported in table 11.2.[22] In computing h_t we ignored the presence of the money demand disturbance w_t since we could not observe its value. This is an added source of measurement error in our construct for h_t.[23]

Before examining the devaluation probability series, we wish to comment on the nature of the model when it assumes the parameter values above. The δ estimate implies that the new fixed exchange rate, which materializes after an attack, will exceed the permanently floating rate, which would clear the money market at the moment of the attack. Since the point estimate of the θ_2 parameter implies that the h_t process is stationary, a newly established exchange rate is expected to be permanent.[24] Only a large enough accumulation of positive v_t realizations will cause a new attack. Finally, the $\bar{R}$ parameter value implies that the minimum net reserve limit in millions of dollars was $-4,454$ in 1973:4 (U.S. import price index $= 1.476$), $-6,642$ in 1976:3, $-9,707$ in 1982:1, and $-9,667$ in 1982:3.[25]

Table 11.1
Estimates of the demand for base money parameters

Parameter	Estimate
Ω	1.196
	(.051)
α	1.310
	(.627)
March	−5.729
	(.599)
June	−5.765
	(.598)
September	−5.786
	(.601)
December	−5.656
	(.599)
$Q(15)$	27.021
R^2	.962

Source: See App.
Note: The set of instrumental variables consists of the second, third, and fourth lags of the interest rates. $Q(n)$ is the Box-Pierce statistic. The numbers in parentheses are standard errors.

Table 11.2
Estimates of the future exchange rate parameters

Parameter	Estimate
$\bar{R}$	−3,018.068
	(657.942)
δ	1.956
	(.547)
θ_1	.181
	(.438)
θ_2	.929
	(.438)
σ	.195

Source: See App.
Note: The standard errors are in parentheses. Those for $\bar{R}$ and δ are conditional on the values of θ_1, θ_2, and σ. The standard erorrs for θ_1, θ_2, and σ are derived from ordinary-least-squares estimation of the h_t equation, conditional on the estimated $\bar{R}$.

The Exchange Rate Conditional on Devaluation

One of the main building blocks of our model is the policy rule used to set the exchange rate when a devaluation occurs. It is interesting to notice in figure 11.1 and in table 11.3 that a devaluation occurred whenever $\hat{e}_t$, the exchange rate set by the policy rule, exceeded the fixed exchange rate in effect at the end of period $t - 1$. However, there are noticeable differences between $\hat{e}_t$ and the exchange rates that materialized during devaluations. For the 1976 devaluation, the exchange rate set by the Banco de Mexico (19.880) was much lower than $\hat{e}_t$ (36.232). This last finding is an indication of the potential to improve the specification of the model and the estimation procedures.[26]

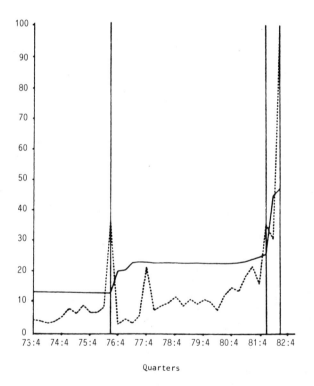

Quarters

Figure 11.1
Actual and conditional exchange rates. Source: See appendix. The solid line is $\bar{e}$, the fixed exchange rate in effect at the end of $t - 1$, and the dashed lines is $\hat{e}_t$, the exchange rate conditional on devaluation. Vertical lines indicate the quarters when devaluations occurred.

Table 11.3
Actual and conditional exchange rates

Quarter	$\bar{e}$	$\hat{e}_t$
1973:4	12.500	3.300
1974:1	12.500	3.020
1974:2	12.500	2.336
1974:3	12.500	2.895
1974:4	12.500	4.394
1975:1	12.500	7.250
1975:2	12.500	5.629
1975:3	12.500	8.407
1975:4	12.500	6.036
1976:1	12.500	6.122
1976:2	12.500	7.906
1976:3*	12.500	36.232
1976:4	19.880	2.337
1977:1	20.200	4.123
1977:2	22.700	2.732
1977:3	22.900	5.283
1977:4	22.840	21.279
1978:1	22.650	7.108
1978:2	22.750	8.590
1978:3	22.810	9.652
1978:4	22.780	11.721
1979:1	22.740	8.730
1979:2	22.800	10.978
1979:3	22.850	9.433
1979:4	22.810	10.944
1980:1	22.820	10.095
1980:2	22.860	7.397
1980:3	22.885	12.469
1980:4	23.030	15.041
1981:1	23.220	13.798
1981:2	23.610	18.863
1981:3	24.340	22.028
1981:4	25.055	16.267
1982:1*	25.980	35.821
1982:2	45.300	30.942
1982:3*	47.651	98.127

Source: See App.
Note: $\bar{e}$ is the fixed exchange rate in effect at the end of period $t - 1$, and $\hat{e}_t$ is the new fixed exchange rate at t conditional on a devaluation.
*Devaluations occurred in these quarters. In 1982:3 the Banco de Mexico also imposed exchange controls.

One-Step-Ahead Devaluation Probabilities

The series of one-step-ahead devaluation probabilities is one of the most interesting results of this exercise. We computed the series from equation (8) after substituting the parameter estimates above and the data associated with each observation.[27]

The series presented in figure 11.2 indicates that the probability of devaluation one period ahead was relatively low through the second quarter of 1975. In 1975:3 it jumped to a value of .149, reaching .188 in 1976:2, the quarter before the August devaluation, and .207 in 1976:3. The probability then declined precipitously after the 1976:3 and 1976:4 devaluations, remaining at low levels until 1978:4. The probabilities then began to rise, attaining high levels in the 3 quarters preceding the February 1982 devaluation. Even after this devaluation of almost 100 percent, the probability attained its highest level of .294 in 1982:1, 4 months before the August 1982 devaluation. In addition to the major devaluations, minidevaluations

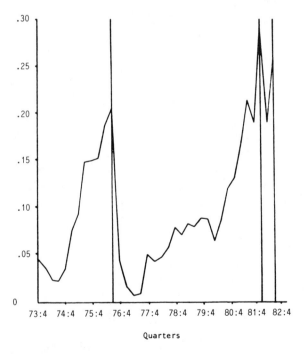

Figure 11.2
Probability of devaluation next period. Source: See appendix. Vertical lines indicate the quarters when a devaluation occurred.

occurred throughout 1981. The August 1982 devaluation was different from the others in that the Banco de Mexico resorted to exchange controls in this episode. We emphasize here that the 1982 devaluation probabilities are "out of sample" since we estimated all parameters using data only through 1981. We then employed the results to form one-step-ahead probabilities of the 1982 devaluations.

The Expected Exchange Rate Conditional on Devaluation

For several different quarters we have computed the expected current quarter exchange rate conditional on a devaluation, where the expectation is based on data from the preceding quarter. Taking the antilog of equation (7), we calculated the conditional expectation of the result in a manner analogous to the development of equation (9). Also we have constructed the conditional standard error and the confidence interval of the antilog of the expression in equation (7). We concentrate our report of results on the quarters around the major devaluations.

In table 11.4 we present the realized exchange rates, their conditional forecasts, 95 percent central confidence intervals, and standard errors for

Table 11.4
Actual exchange rates and conditional forecasts

| Quarter | Exchange rates | | Confidence interval limits | | Standard error |
	Realized	Conditional forecast	Lower	Upper	
1976:1	12.500	17.403	12.165	22.641	3.976
1976:2	12.500	17.429	12.096	22.763	4.032
1976:3	19.880	17.775	14.807	20.743	4.778
1976:4	20.200	28.544	20.152	36.937	8.204
1981:1	23.610	31.769	22.873	40.665	6.226
1981:2	24.340	32.526	23.321	41.731	6.789
1981:3	25.055	34.268	23.919	44.617	8.557
1981:4	25.980	36.150	25.088	47.211	10.726
1982:1	45.300	37.013	29.537	44.490	10.080
1982:2	47.651	68.078	46.361	89.790	25.520
1982:3	...	67.896	54.724	81.068	18.511

Source: See App.
Note: The exchange rate reached as high as 29.00 in November 1976. In 1982:3 the Banco de Mexico imposed a dual exchange rate regime with a rate of 49.50 for preferential transactions and a rate of 75.00 for all other transactions. Additionally, the exchange rate in the U.S. border (black) market was 121.99.

the forecasts. Since the relevant p.d.f. is a truncated lognormal conditional on devaluation, the asymmetry of this p.d.f. implies that central confidene intervals in terms of distance are different from central intervals in terms of probabilities.

For the 1976:3 and 1976:4 devaluations, the realized exchange rate falls within the 95 percent confidence interval. For the 1982:1 devaluation, the realized exchange rate is not contained within the 95 percent equidistant confidence interval. However, the rate does fall within the 90 percent central interval in terms of probabilities. The relatively high conditional exchange rates and probabilities of devaluation during the 1981 quarters seem to be predicting the large devaluation of February 1982 rather than the series of minidevaluations of 1981.

After the August 1982 devaluation, the Mexican government imposed exchange controls for the first time. The Banco de Mexico operated a dual exchange rate regime. For some favored transactions the exchange rate was 49.50; for the remainder the exchange rate was 75.00. The predicted rate of 67.896, made for a new fixed exchange rate with no capital controls, lies between these two values. However, the predicted rate is much lower than the 121.996 exchange rate that materialized in the U.S. border ("black") market.

III Conclusion

Countries maintaining fixed exchange rates occasionally are beset by crises that force them to devalue their currencies. If such episodes recur and future or forward rates exist, it is possible to construct a probability density function over the time of a future crisis. The key piece of information in such a derivation is the expected future exchange rate, composed of a combination of the probability of future devaluation, the exchange rate conditional on devaluation, and the current fixed rate.

To identify the probability of devaluation requires a theoretical model of the expected exchange rate that includes a distinct formulation of the probability. In this paper we have provided a sequence of steps with which the probabilities of devaluation can be indentified and estimated. Also, the method allows us to compute expected exchange rates, conditional on a devaluation in the next period.

The results of the empirical exercise are encouraging. Our model seems to replicate some aspects of the recent Mexican financial history. Devaluations, both in and out of sample, did occur when the conditional exchange rate set by the central bank's policy rule exceeded the fixed exchange rate.

The probabilities of devaluation reach relatively high values prior to actual devaluations, two of which occurred for out-of-sample observations. Furthermore, the expected exchange rates conditional on devaluation are close to the values that actually materialized in the major episodes.

Appendix

We derived our data from the following sources.

D Net financing of the federal government by the Banco de Mexico in millions of pesos. This series is a proxy for the domestic component of the monetary base. Financing of financial intermediaries by the Banco de Mexico and the "net position: other concepts" figures were not available for the whole sample period. Source: Banco de Mexico.

f Logarithm of the end-of-quarter rate of pesos for delivery three months forward. Source: *International Money Market Yearbook*, Chicago Mercantile Exchange, various issues.

m Logarithm of the end-of-quarter monetary base in millions of pesos. Source: Banco de Mexico.

i^* Interest rate on three-month Treasury bills in percentage per quarter. Source: *Federal Reserve Bulletin*, Board of Governors of the Federal Reserve System, various issues.

p Logarithm of the implicit price deflator of the gross domestic product (GDP) for Mexico. Quarterly data generated by the interpolation method of Ginsburgh (1973).

Logarithm of the implicit price deflator of the U.S. imports of goods and services. Source: Business Statistics, Bureau of Economic Analysis, Department of Commerce.

y Logarithm of GDP of Mexico in real terms. Quarterly data generated by the interpolation method of Ginsburgh (1973).

Notes

We are grateful to Robert Flood, Robert Hodrick, Robert Barro, several anonymous referees, and participants in seminars at the University of Rochester, Rice University, Queen's University, the International Monetary Fund, the International Finance Division of the Board of Governors of the Federal Reserve System, and el Colegio de Mexico for helpful comments. Financial assistance was provided by the National Science Foundation. The ideas contained in this paper are our responsibility and do not represent the views of the Committee of Economic Advisors to the President of Mexico.

1. The first paper in this literature was Salant and Henderson's (1978) study of gold price-fixing schemes. Krugman (1979) applied Salant and Henderson's idea to a perfect-foresight switch from a fixed to a floating exchange rate. Flood and Garber (1984a, 1984b) studied a stochastic version of the attack on a fixed exchange rate and the foreseeable collapse of a gold standard. Obstfeld (1984) applied a perfect-foresight version of these models to study devaluation, and Connolly and Taylor (1984) studied attacks on crawling peg systems. Salant (1983) has produced general results on the collapse of asset price-fixing schemes in a stochastic setting.

2. See Ortiz and Solis (1979) for a description of the change in monetary policy that led to the 1976 devaluation.

3. We included u_t to account for deviations from purchasing power parity.

4. A more complete version of the model would also consider an upper limit on net foreign reserves. See Grilli (1986) for the theoretical development of our model when both devaluations and revaluations are possible.

5. Flood and Garber (1984a) argued that the postattack floating rate should provide a lower bound to a new fixed exchange rate. However, concerned with studying the collapse of a fixed exchange rate regime into a permanently floating regime in a stochastic framework, they did not make further use of this observation.

6. The foreign reserve component of the money stock is the amount of reserves entered at the *book* value. The expression for $\bar{h}_t$ depends on all of the foreign exchange assets and liabilities' having been acquired during the period when $\bar{e}$ was the fixed exchange rate.

7. We could derive theoretical results similar to those in the text assuming that $\bar{h}_t$ and h_t follow different stochastic processes.

8. The h_t process can be specified as a higher-order autoregressive process without basically altering the theoretical development. In our empirical work we implemented a model with an AR(2) process for h_t and found that the coefficient on h_{t-2} was not significantly different from zero. Therefore, we simplify this chapter by analyzing only an AR(1) process.

9. The specific functional form of this density function is irrelevant for our basic results. The appropriateness of the normality assumption will be checked in the empirical section.

,010. Ideally, the exchange rate policy should result from maximizing some government objective function over the range of viable fixed rates. However, even when we posed very simple criterion functions for the government, we found that the problem was intractable. No closed-form solutions for the exchange rate policy were obtained. Therefore, we have fallen back on the assumption that in a stationary environment a government would act according to a parameterized policy rule, dependent on the current state variables.

11. More generally, the rule for fixing a new exchange rate could be expressed as $\hat{e}_t = \delta_0 + \delta_1 \bar{e}_t + \delta_2 v_t$. The theory can then be developed as in the text. However, in using this rule for our empirical work, we found that δ_0 and δ_1 were not statistically different from zero and one, respectively. Therefore, we use (7) in our theoretical and empirical development to simplify our report.

12. A negative value for v_t would mean that $\bar{e}_t > \hat{e}_t$. However, if reserves were also at their minimum in the presence of a negative v_t, the equivalence result in section. IB would imply that $\hat{e}_{t-1}$ exceeded the fixed exchange rate. Therefore, the system would have been attacked one period earlier. We then conclude that only a positive v_t realization will coincide with an attack.

13. This equation is similar to some developed by Krasker (1980) and Lizondo (1983) in modeling the persistent bias in forward rates for weak fixed exchange rate currencies. However, in Krasker and Lizondo the probability of devaluation is given exogenously. They argue that the existence of persistent bias is a small-sample problem. Only after many "devaluations" will a large enough sample accumulate to wash out this effect. While confined to a small sample, however, a researcher would infer that this excessively discounted forward rate contains a risk premium. These estimated "risk premia" would vary through time with the probability of devaluation and with the exchange rate conditional on devalution.

14. Probabilities of devaluation and conditional expected exchange rates for more than one period into the future are developed in an earlier version of this paper (Blanco and Garber 1982). From these probabilities and expectations, it is possible to construct unconditional expectations of the exchange rate for several periods into the future. These results are extended in Blanco (1984) to model the term structure of the future exchange rates for the Mexican peso.

15. To check this assumption, we estimated $f_t = \gamma_0 + \gamma_1 Ee_{t+1} + \varepsilon_t$. We were not able to reject the joint hypothesis that $\gamma_0 = 0.0$ and $\gamma_1 = 1.0$.

16. An alternative estimation procedure is to minimize the sum of squared residuals of (11) over the entire parameter vector. The estimates obtained in this fashion were not very appealing (e.g., the estimate of θ_2 is much larger than one, and the estimate of σ is several magnitudes larger than the least-squares standard error of v_t conditional on the estimate of $\bar{R}$). Additionally, substituting these etimates into (8) and (9), we obtained a flat and extremely low series of one-period-ahead devaluation probabilities. Furthermore, the expected exchange rates conditional on devaluations were extremely different from those that actually materialized in 1976 and 1982.

17. We would like to thank Armando Baqueiro of the Banco de Mexico for providing most of the data.

18. See Ortiz and Solis (1981) and Ortiz (1983) for a description of the dollarization phenomenon.

19. These two series were computed by Fernando Clavijo of the Ministry of Budget and Planning using the method developed by Ginsburgh (1973).

20. More generally, one could assume that the critical level of reserves is a function of variables such as output, domestic credit, and the price level of the country's trading partners. Then one would estimate the parameters of such a function jointly with δ, θ_1, θ_2, and σ.

21. Of all the estimation methods that we tried, only two produced negative estimates of the interest rate semielasticity: the method of instrumental variables and least squares on a partial adjustment version of equation (1). Assuming partial adjustment would require keeping track of two initial conditions to derive the floating rate solution. To avoid further complicating the dynamics of the model, we proceeded to use the instrumental variables estimates. As the Box-Pierce statistic indicates, further efforts should be made to specify the money demand function. When we additionally included four lags on real income as instrumental variables, the demand parameter estimates, as well as the estimates of the other parameters of the model, did not change significantly. Likewise, all the main empirical results of our paper were invariant to the choice between these two sets of instrumental variables.

22. These estimates were computed using the Davidon-Fletcher-Powell algorithms in Quandt's GQOPT package. For a description of the algorithm, see Powell (1971). Initial estimates were produced by a grid search procedure. The global nature of the minimum was checked by employing several sets of initial estimates.

23. The density function of v_t appears to be somewhat skewed to the right. In fact, the Jarque-Bera Lagrangian multiplier test leads to the rejection of the normality hypothesis. At this point of our research it is difficult to assess the impact that this departure from normality has on the estimators. Further research should use a more flexible density function that will allow the degree of skewness of the density function to be determined by the data.

24. One must be cautious with this assertion since the θ_2 parameter estimator would be biased downward if the h_t process were nonstationary, e.g., $\theta_2 = 1$.

25. As is well known in the international finance literature, negative net reserves imply that the liabilities of the central bank with the rest of the world are larger than its foreign assets.

26. However, it is worthwhile to notice that in November 1976 the exchange rate went as high as 29.00, a rate much closer to the conditional rate of 36.23 obtained from our model.

27. As a referee rightly noticed, we do not provide a statistical criterion to evaluate this series; i.e., when could we say that a probability is "high" enough to forecast a devaluation next period? However, in principle, we could use the probabilities of devaluation for several periods ahead to compute the expected time of collapse and the confidence interval around it.

References

Blanco, Herminio. "The Term Structure of Future Exchange Rates: The Case of the Mexican Peso." Working paper. Houston: Rice Univ., December 1984.

Blanco, Herminio, and Garber, Peter M. "Recurrent Devaluation and the Timing of Speculative Attacks." Working paper. Rochester, N.Y.: Univ. Rochester, October 1982.

Connolly, Michael B., and Taylor Dean. "The Exact Timing of the Collapse of an Exchange Rate Regime and Its Impact on the Relative Price of Traded Goods." *J. Money, Credit and Banking* 16 (May 1984): 194–207.

Flood, Robert P., and Garber, Peter M. "Collapsing Exchange-Rate Regimes: Some Linear Examples." *J. Internat. Econ.* 17 (August 1984): 1–13. (a)

———. "Gold Monetization and Gold Discipline." *J. P. E.* 92 (February 1984): 90–107. (b)

Ginsburgh, Victor A. "A Further Note on the Derivation of Quarterly Figures Consistent with Annual Data." *Appl. Statis.* 22 (Fall 1973): 368–74.

Grilli, Vittorio. "Buying and Selling Attacks on Fixed Exchange Rate Systems." *J. Internat. Econ.* 20 (1986): 143–56.

Krasker, William S. "The 'Peso Problem' in Testing the Efficiency of Forward Exchange Markets." *J. Monetary Econ.* 6 (April 1980): 269–76.

Krugman, Paul R. "A Model of Balance-of-Payments Crises." *J. Money, Credit and Banking* 11 (August 1979): 311–25.

Lizondo, Jose J. "Foreign Exchange Futures Prices under Fixed Exchange Rates." *J. Internal. Econ.* 14 (February 1983): 69–84.

Obstfeld, Maurice. "Balance-of-Payments Crises and Devaluation." *J. Money, Credit and Banking* 16 (May 1984): 208–17.

Ortiz, Guillermo. "Dollarization in Mexico: Causes and Consequences." In *Financial Policies and the World Capital Market: The Problem of Latin American Countries,* edited by Pedro Aspe Armella, Rudiger Dornbusch, and Maurice Obstfeld. Chicago: Univ. Chicago Press (for N.B.E.R.), 1983.

Ortiz, Guillermo, and Solis, Leopoldo. "Financial Structure and Exchange Rate Experience: Mexico, 1954–1977." *J. Development Econ.* 6 (December 1979): 515–48.

———. "Substitución de monedas e independencia monetaria: El caso de México." Working paper. Mexico City: Banco de Mexico, 1981.

Powell, M. J. D. "Recent Advances in Unconstrained Optimization." *Math. Programming* 1 (October 1971): 26–57.

Salant, Stephen W. "The Vulnerability of Price Stabilization Schemes to Speculative Attack." *J.P.E.* 91 (February 1983): 1–38.

Salant, Stephen W., and Henderson, Dale W. "Market Anticipations of Government Policies and the Price of Gold." *J.P.E.* 86 (August 1978): 627–48.

12

The Belmont-Morgan Syndicate as an Optimal Investment Banking Contract

Peter M. Garber and Vittorio U. Grilli

I Introduction

The Belmont-Morgan Syndicate provided the temporary institutional arrangement to preserve U.S. adherence to the gold standard in 1895. From February to September, 1895, the syndicate underwrote a large issue of U.S. bonds, delivered the proceeds in gold coin to the Treasury, part of which was imported from Europe, and guaranteed the Treasury against gold withdrawals by massive intervention in the exchange markets.

The deal between the syndicate and the Treasury has been treated as a curious episode in the long transition to a complete U.S. commitment to a permanent gold standard. However, the Belmont-Morgan contract presents the researcher with a rich blend of several concepts, each of which represents an important line of current research.

First, the episode occurred in an environment of imminent collapse of the U.S. gold standard; the triggering mechanism for the contract was the massive speculative attack on U.S. gold stocks in January, 1895. Since the attacks themselves were generated by the monetization of silver under the Sherman Silver Purchase Act of 1890, the analysis of the timing of the attacks fits naturally into current models which study the timing of speculative attacks against fixed exchange rates systems and of monetary regime switches.

Second, since the government bonds were payable either in gold or in silver coin, a collapse of the gold standard,which would entail further payments in silver rather than in gold coin, would have represented a partial repudiation of the foreign (and domestic) debt. Much recent literature has considered the problem of contractual constraints on the debt instruments of a government which may default on its debt.[1] The Belmont-Morgan contract, whose provisions were aimed at preventing such a default, provides an explicit example of the optimal contracting considerations that may arise in the presence of possible default.

Third, recent finance literature on the behavior of investment bankers underwriting risky securities issues has derived implications for the institutional features required of an optimal underwriting contract.[2] However, application of these results has been hampered because of the difficulties in specifying the stochastic environments facing particular issuers of securities and because the source of the objective functions of the risk averse firms and investment bankers is not transparent. The Belmont-Morgan contract provides an example in which the provisions of the contract, the objectives of at least one contracting party, and the stochastic environment are observable.

This chapter represents an application of theories of speculative attacks on fixed exchange rate regimes and of optimal investment banking contracts to this piece of history. Our purpose is to determine the extent to which such simple theories can elucidate both the events of that period and the features of the Belmont-Morgan contract. We will provide a uniform explanation consistent with current theories.

In the chapter, we outline the laws restricting the behavior of the Treasury, define its objectives and the historical context of the Belmont-Morgan Syndicate, and describe the provisions of the contract. We provide a theory of government and syndicate behavior which implies that the qualitative features of the contract were optimal given the constraints on the Treasury and the stochastic environment. We show how to derive the magnitude of the spread, the size of the issue, the fixed price guaranteed to the government for the bond issue, and the gold imports which the nature of the environment requires in an optimal contract.

II An Outline of the Politics and Economics behind the Belmont-Morgan Contract

The Belmont-Morgan contract was the outcome of a set of restrictions and requirements on the Secretary of the Treasury. It reflected a deadlocked Congress which imposed a continuing deficit. The nexus of previous laws restricting the actions of the Treasurer transformed the deficit into expansions of the fiat component of the money stock, thereby threatening the continuation of the gold standard. Since the Secretary of the Treasury also was charged with maintaining specie payments on national debt and currency conversions, the end of the gold standard implied an ultimate shift to a silver standard and a partial "default" on the national debt.[3] These results

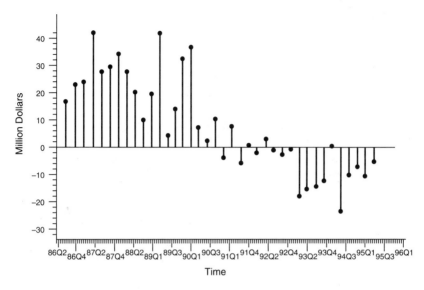

Figure 12.1
Quarterly government surplus. Source: *Commerical & Financial Chronicle.*

were the goal of the silver faction which controlled a powerful block of
senators and continually sought to corner the Treasury into abandoning
the gold standard.[4]

These are familiar elements in international finance. Priority is given to a
set of domestic policies which imply a deficit which must be financed
through dometic credit creation. The creation of domestic credit threatens
the continued existence of a fixed exchange rate regime; and the priority of
financing the expenditure and revenue policies of the government perhaps
threatens the allocation of resources to service previously incurred debt.

In this section we will present a brief history of the political and economic
events of this episode. Readers seeking more details can consult Noyes
(1909), Friedman and Schwartz (1963), Laughlin (1968), or Simons (1968).

The U.S. monetary instability of 1890–1896 began with attempts to end
the large government budget surpluses of 1886–1890. Figure 12.1 contains
a time series of the U.S. surpluses and deficits for this period. Because of the
nature of the monetary system, these surpluses led to the destruction of
much of the fiat component of the money stock and to an increase in the
gold basis of money. In particular, in managing its surplus funds, the Treasury could either absorb legal tender in its vaults, thereby directly reducing
the stock of circulating paper money, or recall or purchase at market prices
the outstanding stock of U.S. debt.[5]

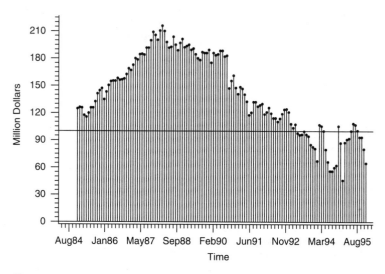

Figure 12.2a
Net gold reserves in the Treasury. Source: National Monetary Commission.

Figures 12.2a, 12.2b and 12.3 contain series of Treasury holdings of gold and legal tender currency by category for this period. Figures 12.4a, 12.4b and 12.4c contain series of the various forms of money circulating outside the Treasury. The Treasury resorted to large scale bond redemptions. Since these were simultaneous with a contraction in the stock of bank notes, the contraction of the bank notes was associated with the surplus and it was thought that the continuation of the surpluses would soon generate monetary disturbances.[6]

While the government also increased its bank deposits, banks were somewhat reluctant to accept them. They were required to hold government bonds with a face value of 1.1 times the amount of the deposit at a time when the bonds sold at high prices. Since the deposits were subject to sudden withdrawals, the returns from this transaction did not generate sufficient revenues for the risk.[7]

Political pressures in several forms arose to end the surpluses. First, there was the fear, whether valid or not, of the monetary contraction. Second, there was a coalition pressing for a protectionist tariff. Third, the silver interests wanted to maintain a large percentage of fiat in the money stock. While the Democrats sought to end the surplus simply through tariff and revenue reduction, the Republicans, who controlled the Congress and the Presidency, passed a program to end the surplus by raising a prohibitive

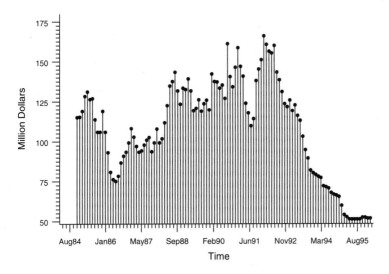

Figure 12.2b
Gold in the Treasury held against certificates outstanding. Source: National Monetary Commission.

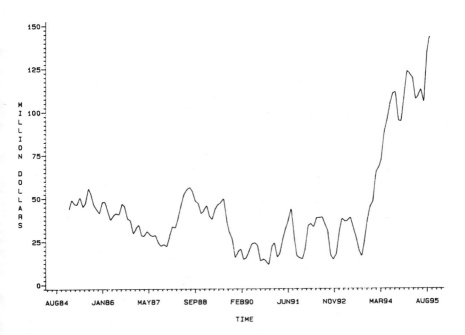

Figure 12.3
Legal tender in the Treasury. Source: Annual reports of the Secretary of the Treasury.

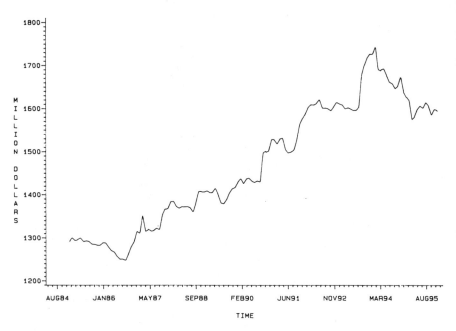

Figure 12.4a
Total money in circulation. Source: National Monetary Commission.

tariff and increasing expenditure on the military, on Civil War pensions, and on public works in 1890. However, recognizing its strategic importance in the Senate, the silver block extracted the Sherman Silver Purchase Act as its price for supporting the Republican fiscal plan.

The Sherman Silver Purchase Act of July 14, 1890 created yet another paper currency, the Treasury Notes of 1890, to be used in the required purchase at market pries of 4.5 million ounces per month of silver. Such purchases and money creation were to continue as long as the market price of pure silver remained less than $1 for 371.25 grains, the content of the standard silver dollar. The notes were legal tender and redeemable on demand in coin; the Secretary of the Treasury had the option to redeem the notes in gold or silver coin. The face value of the notes outstanding had to equal the cost of silver bullion in the Treasury purchased by the notes plus the standard silver dollars in the Treasury minted from bullion bought with the notes. Such minted silver dollars were to be produced only to redeem the notes.

Now there were two legal tender paper currencies partly backed by gold, the U.S. Notes and the Treasury Notes of 1890. The U.S. Notes were strictly

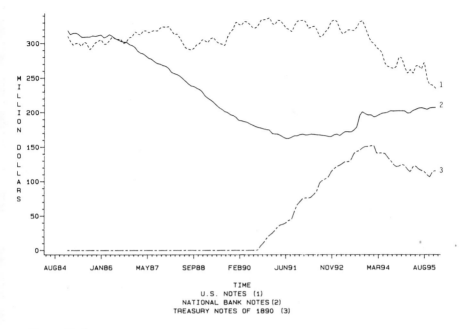

Figure 12.4b
Money in circulation. Source: National Monetary Commission.

limited in quantity, and the Treasury Notes were scheduled to grow at monthly rates which depended on the market price of silver. The Treasury had no option to cancel previously issued Treasury notes which it received in payments; it could hold them as part of its surplus funds, but it had to recirculate them in periods of budgetary deficit.

This combination of policies immediately converted the surplus to a continuing deficit, as indicated in Figure 12.1. The coalition did not collapse until the Silver Purchase Act was repealed in the midst of the Panic of 1893. An attempt was made to end the deficit in the Tariff of 1894, but protectionist interests remained powerful enough to thwart serious tariff reductions. In the environment of depressed trade of 1894–1895, the tariff still yielded insufficient revenue to end the deficit. The expenditure programs, particularly the pension increases, of course remained sacrosanct.

While the gold exports that one would expect with the domestic credit creation implied by the issuing of Treasury Notes were temporarily reversed by the unusual U.S. agricultural market successes in 1890 and 1891, continual gold exports began in 1892 along with a decline in Treasury gold holdings, as indicated in figures 12.2a and 12.2b. In 1893, there were large

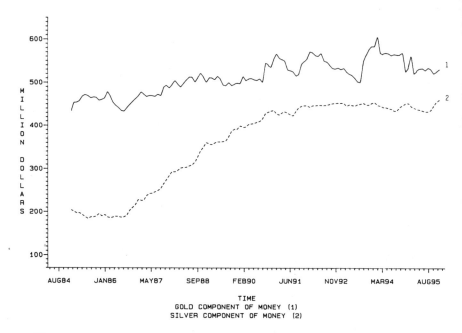

Figure 12.4c
Money in circulation. Source: National Monetary Commission.

demands on Treasury gold in exchange for legal tender notes, driving the gold stock backing the U.S. Notes below $100 million and forcing a suspension of the issue of new gold certificates.[8] Effectively, the Treasury, prevented by the Congressional deadlock from financing the deficit by new bond issues, was financing the deficits by running down its cumulated stocks of legal tender and finally gold.

While the repeal of the Silver Purchase Act terminated the steady increase in legal tender paper money, it did not reduce the outstanding stock. The sum of Treasury Notes of 1890 and U.S. Notes remaining was of a sufficient magnitude such that small changes in the variables affecting money demand threatened the Treasury with a run on its remaining gold stock. For instance, the depression following the Panic of 1893 reduced money demand and led to a continued gold outflow from the Treasury in exchange for legal tenders. See figures 12.2a, 12.2b and 12.3 for the changes in the gold stock and legal tender holdings of the Treasury at this time. Since the Treasury deficits continued, these legal tenders had to be recirculated to finance the deficit, further threatening the gold standard.

In December, 1893, the Treasury Secretary proposed that he be authorized to issue bonds to finance the continuing deficits. Alternatively, he proposed that he be authorized to issue Treasury bills to finance the deficit on a short term basis. The deadlock in the Congress blocked the enactment of either of these measures. Faced with the requirement that he finance the continuing deficit, the Treasury Secretary could only draw down the remaining surplus funds, including gold, in the Treasury.

The steady decline of Treasury gold holdings and occasional runs on its stock led the secretary to invoke the provisions of the Resumption Act and offer a $50 million issue of ten-year, 5 percent bonds intended to restore the Treasury gold stocks in January, 1894.[9] The issue was offered for public subscription with payment in gold coin at a price of 117.23, equivalent to a 3 percent bond at par. Since small quantities of these bonds were taken up, the Treasury pressured the New York banks to form a syndicate to buy the issue. However, though they paid for the bonds directly in gold, the banks quickly turned in legal tenders to the Treasury for coin. Thus, the loan, intended to expand the gold reserve, actually succeeded in removing legal tenders temporarily from circulation. As the Treasury deficits continued, the legal tenders from the bond issue were recirculated to finance them, thereby eventually threatening the gold standard once more. Thus, the bond sale provisions of the Resumption Act, intended for accumulating gold reserves to back a paper money, were used as the only means allowed to the Treasury to finance the deficit. Also, they served as a means of temporally relaxing pressure on the gold standard by briefly removing legal tenders from circulation.

By November, 1894, the Treasury's gold stock and legal tender holdings had reached levels comparable to those of February, 1894, forcing it to invoke the Resumption Act once more by offering an issue of $50 million in ten-year, five percent bonds for public subscription. Again, the gold payments for the bonds were quickly exchanged for legal tenders, so the loan simply reduced the circulation of legal tenders temporarily. Almost immediately, a run on the remaining gold reserve began, and in January, 1895, $45 million in gold was withdrawn from the Treasury in exchange for legal tenders.

Realizing that the finance methods authorized in the Resumption Act were not sufficient to preserve the gold standard against sudden attacks of this magnitude, the Secretary of the Treasury invoked Section 3700 of the Revised Statutes and contracted with the Belmont-Morgan Syndicate to market the next issue of bonds aimed at preserving the gold standard.[10]

III The Belmont-Morgan Contract and the Syndicate Operations

Through use of the Belmont-Morgan Syndicate, the Secretary of the Treasury attempted to fulfill his responsibility of preserving coin convertibility and the parity of the gold and silver dollar while satisfying all the legal constraints that hampered his actions.[11] In effect, the Treasury agreed to a large spread for the syndicate in marketing a bond issue in return for a six month line of short-term, interest-free gold credit to guarantee the maintenance of its gold reserve. The Treasury was not legally authorized directly to issue short-term credit instruments. However, to circumvent this restriction, it used its power under Section 3700 of the Revised Statutes to contract the purchase of coin with bonds under general terms.

We include the text of the contract (see table 12.1), negotiated in late January and early February, 1895. Rather than a sale of bonds for gold as in the earlier two issues, the contract was written in terms of a purchase of gold coin in exchange for bonds to conform with Section 3700.

The bonds were the thirty-year, 4 percent bonds authorized by the Resumption Act. The purchase price established for the coin implied a price of $104.5 in gold paid for the issue by the syndicate for $100 par value bonds. The yield on these bonds was 3.75 percent. The par value of the bonds to be delivered for the gold was $62.3 million, so the government was to receive $65.1 million in coin. Alternatively, the syndicate agreed to receive 3 percent gold bonds at par at the Treasury's option if Congress passed an authorization to issue such bonds. Since Congress refused, the option was not exercised. The difference in yields provides a measure, however, of the anticipated depreciation of the dollar relative to gold.

The conditions of the contract specified that one half of the coin delivered would be shipped from Europe at a rate not exceeding 300,000 ounces per month. Therefore, the syndicate had six months to complete the contract. The syndicate was given the right of first refusal of any additional government bond issues until October, 1895.

Most importantly, the syndicate agreed that "so far as lies within their power, will exert all financial influence and will make all legitimate efforts to protect the Treasury of the United States against withdrawals of gold, pending the complete performance of this contract." By this clause, the syndicate eventually undertook several operations to protect the government gold reserve.

First, when anyone delivered legal tender in return for gold to the government, the syndicate replaced the lost gold, assuming possession of the legal tender. Since the legal tenders paid no interest, the syndicate

Table 12.1

Contract

This agreement entered into this eighth day of February, 1895, between the Secretary of the Treasury of the United States, of the first part, and Messrs. August Belmont and Company, of New York, on behalf of Messrs. N. M. Rothschild and Sons, of London, England, and themselves, and Messrs. J. P. Morgan and Company, of New York, on behalf of Messrs, J. S. Morgan and Company, of London, and themselves, parties of the second part,

Witnesseth: Whereas it is provided by the Revised Statutes of the United States (section 3700) that the Secretary of the Treasury may purchase coin with any of the bonds or notes of the United States authorized by law, at such rates and upon such terms as he may deem most advantageous to the public interests; and the Secretary of the Treasury now deems that an emergency exists in which the public interests require that, as hereinafter provided, coin shall be purchased with the bonds of the United States, of the description hereinafter mentioned, authorized to be issued under the act entitled "An act to provide for the resumption of specie payments," approved January 14, 1875, being bonds of the United States described in an act of Congress approved July 14, 1870, entitled "An act to authorize the refunding of the national debt."

Now, therefore, the said parties of the second part hereby agree to sell and deliver to the United States three million five hundred thousand ounces of standard gold coin of the United States, at the rate of $17.80441 per ounce, payable in United States four per cent thirty-year coupon or registered bonds, said bonds to be dated February 1, 1895, and payable at the pleasure of the United States after thirty years from date, issued under the acts of Congress of July 14, 1870, January 20, 1871, and January 14, 1875, bearing interest at the rate of four per cent per annum, payable quarterly.

First.—Such purchase and sale of gold coin being made on the following conditions:

(1) At least one-half of all coin deliverable hereinunder shall be obtained in and shipped from Europe, but the shipments shall not be required to exceed three hundred thousand ounces per month, unless the parties of second part shall consent thereto.

(2) All deliveries shall be made at any of the subtreasuries or at any other legal depository of the United States.

(3) All gold coins delivered shall be received on the basis of twenty-five and eight-tenths grains of standard gold per dollar, if within limit of tolerance.

(4) Bonds delivered under this contract are to be delivered free of accrued interest, which is to be assumed and paid by the parties of the second part at the time of their delivery to them.

Second.—Should the Secretary of the Treasury desire to offer or sell any bonds of the United States on or before the first day of October, 1985, he shall first offer the same to the parties of the second part; but thereafter he shall be free from every such obligation to the parties of the second part.

Third.—The Secretary of the Treasury hereby reserves the right, within ten days from the date hereof, in case he shall receive authority from Congress therefor, to substitute any bonds of the United States, bearing three per cent interest, of which the principal and interest shall be specifically payable in United States gold coin of the present weight and fineness for the bonds herein alluded to; such three per cent bonds to be accepted by the parties of the second part at par, i.e.: at $18.60465 per ounce of standard gold.

Fourth.—No bonds shall be delivered to the parties of the second part, or either of them, except in payment for coin from time to time received hereunder; whereupon the Secretary of the Treasury of the United States shall and will deliver the bonds as herein provided, at such places as shall be designated by the parties of the second part. Any expense of delivery out of the United States shall be assumed and paid by the parties of the second part.

Table 12.1 (continued)

Fifth.—In consideration of the purchase of such coin, the parties of the second part, and their associates hereunder, assume and will bear all the expense and inevitable loss of bringing gold from Europe hereunder; and, as far as lies in their power, will exert all financial influence and will make all legitimate efforts to protect the Treasury of the United States against the withdrawals of gold pending the complete performance of this contract.

In witness whereof the parties hereto have hereunto set their hands in five parts this 8th day of February, 1895.

J. G. Carlisle,
Secretary of the Treasury.
August Belmont & Co.,
On behalf of Messrs. N. M. Rothschild & Sons, London, and themselves.
J. P. Morgan & Co.,
On behalf of Messrs. J. S. Morgan & Co., London, and themselves.

Attest:
W. E. Curtis
Francis Lynde Stetson.

would suffer an interest loss on this operation. Ultimately, under this clause the syndicate delivered an additional $25 million in gold to the Treasury in exchange for legal tenders.

Second, the syndicate protected the Treasury against direct withdrawals by borrowing exchange on London and selling it in New York, effectively controlling the exchange market. To the extent that individuals sold legal tenders to obtain exchange, the syndicate again had to absorb the legal tenders and suffer an interest loss. For the details of this and other syndicate operations in fulfilling the contract, see Simons (1968).

If the credit line had been unlimited, there would have been no risk of capital loss from this asset position. However, the credit line was limited to "so far as lies within their power," so some maximum extent of these additional interventions implicitly existed. Indeed, the requirement to import gold from Europe must have been a device imposed by the Treasury to guarantee the extent of the credit line immediately available for use. Presumably, the Treasury, already protected by the bond sale and the credit line, would not otherwise have worried about the source of the coin it received.

Since the credit line was limited, there was still some risk that the gold standard could collapse before the completion of the contact. Having taken an asset position in paper dollars and a liability position in gold, the syndicate then took a risk of capital loss in the event that the operation failed and the Treasury was forced to devalue the dollar.

The syndicate immediately marketed the bonds received from the Treasury at 110.46 for a total of $68.8 million. The response to the offer was large, and the syndicate distributed them to all players in the foreign exchange market to enlist them as participants in the effort to protect the government against gold withdrawals. Since the market prices of these bonds quickly rose to 124, it seems that the syndicate distributed part of the overall spread to line up other institutions in providing the credit line to the government.

IV Modeling a Speculative Attack on a Gold Standard

We will interpret the problem of defending the gold standard as that of defending a fixed exchange rate between dollars and pounds. The fixed parity is the ratio of the gold content of each of the two currencies. We can thus employ the theories of speculative attacks on fixed exchange rate systems to describe how the probability of the viability of the gold standard evolved during the first half of the 1890s and to explain the timing of the runs on the gold reserves of the Treasury.

Underlying the analysis is the following monetary model of the exchange rate for a small economy:[12]

$$m_t - p_t = \beta + \gamma y_t - \alpha i_t + w_t, \tag{1}$$

$$i_t - i_t^* = E_t e_{t+1} - e_t, \tag{2}$$

$$p_t - p_t^* = e_t, \tag{3}$$

where m, p, e and y are the logarithms of the money stock, price level, exchange rate in dollars per pound, and real income, respectively. i is the nominal interest rate, and w is a stochastic disturbance. The parameters β, α, γ are all positive and E_t is the expectation operator conditional on time t information. British variables are marked with asterisks, and all variables are assumed exogenous to the exchange rate.

The model can be solved to produce the following first order difference equation in the exchange rate:

$$(1 + \alpha)e_t - \alpha E_t e_{t+1} = h_t, \quad \text{where} \tag{4}$$

$$h_t = m_t - \beta - \gamma y_t + \alpha i_t^* - w_t - p_t^*. \tag{5}$$

In a freely floating exchange rate regime, the equilibrium exchange rate will be given by

$$e_t = \left(\frac{1}{1+\alpha}\right) \sum_{j=0}^{\infty} \left(\frac{\alpha}{1+\alpha}\right)^j E_t h_{t+j}. \qquad (6)$$

On the other hand, in a viable fixed exchange rate system, we have $E_t e_{t+1} = e_t = e$ so that the difference equation reduces to

$$e = h_t = m_t - \beta - \gamma y_t + \alpha i_t^* - w_t - p_t^*. \qquad (7)$$

In a fixed exchange rate regime, the total money supply becomes endogenous and must move to compensate the fluctuations in the other exogenous variables. The fixed parity will be viable until it becomes profitable to attack it, which will happen as soon as the post-attack exchange rate is expected to exceed the given parity. It is thus crucial to calculate the shadow exchange rate, defined as the hypothetical level of the exchange rate that would prevail at time t given that a speculative attack strikes at that time. To compute this variable, it is necessary to assume the nature of the regime which will prevail after the attack. We will assume that a paper money convertible to silver is expected to be introduced after the collapse of the gold standard, though there will not be free coinage of silver. Our next step is to analyze the behavior of the money supply before and after the attack.

V   The Probability of a Speculative Attack

The Money Stock before and after a Gold Standard Collapse

During the operation of the gold standard, the circulating money stock consisted of gold coins, silver coins, gold and silver certificates, bank notes, and legal tender which were composed of U.S. Notes and Treasury Notes of the 1890. We define G_t^P as the total of gold coins and gold certificates in circulation at time t and G_t^T as the gold in the Treasury not backing gold certificates. Then the money stock M_t equaled a "domestic credit" component DC_t plus a gold component, that is, $M_t = DC_t + G_t^P + G_t^T$. Though DC_t was that part of the money stock unbacked by gold, it did have some silver backing so it was not pure fiat. In particular, DC_t contained the legal tenders and was driven primarily by changes in those notes.

We assume that the Treasury will defend the gold standard until its net gold reserves reach a predetermined minimum level, G^m, which may be negative. If an attack occurs at time t driving the Treasury to its minimum reserve level of gold, the post attack money supply backed by silver will then be $M_t = DC_t + G^m$.[13] Since the Treasury no longer undertakes open market operation in the gold market after the gold standard's collapse, the money stock at time $t + j$, $j > 0$, will be $M_{t+j} = DC_{t+j} + G^m$. In a silver standard, gold is no longer part of the money supply, so G_t^P disappears. Moreover, G^m represents that portion of bank notes and legal tender backed by gold which could not be redeemed in the collapse of the system at time t.

The Probability of Attack

We define

$$h_t^A = \log(DC_t + G^m) - \beta - \gamma y_t + \alpha i_t^* - w_t - p_t^* \tag{8}$$

as the time t realization of the exogenous stochastic process driving the post attack exchange rate for the pre-1893 period under the Sherman Act. If an attack occurs at time $(t + 1)$, the post attack exchange rate will be given by[14]

$$e_{t+1}^A = \left(\frac{1}{1 + \alpha}\right) \sum_{j=0}^{\infty} \left(\frac{\alpha}{1 + \alpha}\right)^j E_t h_{t+j}^A. \tag{9}$$

The necessary and sufficient condition for an attack to occur at time $(t + 1)$ is[15]

$$e_{t+1}^A \geqq e. \tag{10}$$

Then the probability of an attack next period is given by

$$\Pr(e_{t+1}^A \geqq e) = \Pr\left[\left(\frac{1}{1 + \alpha}\right) \sum_{j=0}^{\infty} \left(\frac{\alpha}{1 + \alpha}\right)^j E_t h_{t+j} \geqq e\right]. \tag{11}$$

The Attack of 1893

After 1890, the Sherman Act generated a rapid growth in the domestic credit component of the money supply. This increment consisted of the sum of the nominal value of the silver purchases and the nominal deficit. Since the government could not directly issue bonds to finance the deficit because of the Congressional impasse, the nominal deficit represented an increase in legal tender because of the drawing down of surplus government funds. This growth in domestic credit implied an upward trend in h_t^A, thus making inevitable an eventual collapse of the system, unless the other variables in h_t^A moved in an offsetting direction or the policy changed.[16]

The probability of an attack on the gold standard, if agents anticipated no possibility that the Sherman Act would be repealed, is

$$\Pr\{e_{t+1}^A \geq e\} = \Pr\left\{\left(\frac{1}{1+\alpha}\right) \sum_{j=0}^{\infty} \left(\frac{\alpha}{1+\alpha}\right)^j E_t\right.$$

$$\left. \times \log(DC_{t+j} + G^m) - E_t x_{t+j}] \geq e\right\}. \tag{13}$$

where $x_t = \beta + \gamma y_t - \alpha i_t^* + p_t^* + w_t$.

Since we expect a high probability of attack when runs actually occur, the shadow exchange rate should approach the fixed rate at the time of an attack, such as in the spring of 1893 when the first major run occurred. These runs were halted by the repeal of the Sherman Act. This entailed a change in the process generating h_t, that is, downward revision of the expected value of future h_{t+j} and therefore a decrease in e_t^A.

From June 1893 to February 1895

With the repeal of the Sherman Act on November 1, 1893, the speculative buying attack temporarily halted. However, further deficit finance implied further increases in domestic credit due to the recirculation of legal tenders and a decrease in gold reserves once the legal tender paper money holdings of the Treasury had been exhausted.

The repeal of the Sherman Act, by changing the process generating the money supply, implied a change in the expectation formation about the h_t variable through the m_t term. Therefore, the probability distribution function of the shadow exchange rate and the probability of an attack on the gold standard also must have shifted. However, once we account for the switch in expectation formation, we can represent the probability of an attack for the period after 1893 exactly as in the previous section, that is, as $\Pr\{e_{t+1}^B \geq e\}$ where e_{t+1}^B is the new shadow exchange rate implied by the revised expectations about the money supply process. As in the previous case, we can reproduce the evolution of the probability of an attack and track the runs on Treasury reserves which occurred in January and December, 1894 and January and November, 1895.

VI   The Bond Issue as a Signal

Starting with the attack on January, 1894, the Treasury regularly used a strategy of issuing bonds to maintain the gold standard. We will inquire why a bond issue should decrease the probability of an attack.

Recall that the probability of the gold standard's survival into the next period is given by $[1 - \Pr\{e_{t+1}^B \geqq e\}]$. Since e_{t+1}^B is increasing in $E_t h_{t+j}^B$, the system's survival is a decreasing function of $E_t h_{t+j}^B$. To reduce the probability of an attack, it is sufficient to reduce $E_t h_{t+j}^B = E_t\{\log(DC_{t+j} + G^m) - x_{t+j}\}$ for all j. For a given patter of x_t, this implies a reduction in $E_t \log(DC_{t+j} + G^m)$ for all j. This can be achieved by an unexpected reduction in either DC_t or G^m.[17]

The Treasury could reduce these variables only through bond issues. If a bond issue were subscribed in legal tenders, it would reduce DC_t and thereby the probably of an attack. We interpret subscriptions in gold as a signal of a lower G^m. Suppose that the public initially believes that the defence of the gold standard will continue until the exhaustion of the Treasury's gross gold reserves, i.e., until $G_t^T = 0$.[18] Then before any bond issue occurs, $G^m = 0$. A bond issue of G dollars subscribed in gold reduces G^m to $G^m = -G$. From this perspective, bond issues subscribed either in gold or in legal tenders have identical impacts on the probability of attack.

That the Treasury insisted on subscription in gold coin stemmed from the legal restrictions imposed on its power to issue bonds. In particular, the Treasury was allowed to issue bonds only to 'provide for redemption' of legal tenders. Thus, it would issue bonds only to replenish gold reserves once they fell below $100 million.

This bond issue strategy was used repeatedly by the Treasury from 1894 to 1896. Each new issue generated an instantaneous drop in the probability of an attack due to a reduction in DC_t or G^m. Deficit financing, however, implied an eventual rise in the probability of an attack back to the original value (ignoring movements in x_t). The probability rose by the same magnitude if deficits were paid either by recirculating legal tenders or by expending gold reserves. Use of legal tenders to finance the deficit increased domestic credit; use of gold reserves increased the minimum level of net reserves G^m, since G^m would have remained unchanged only if the Treasury had employed gold exclusively for the redemption of legal tenders.

VII The Belmont-Morgan Contract

Whenever the probability of an attack reached high levels, the Treasury decided to issue bonds, thus signalling either a reduction of G^m or a decrease in DC_t. This happened in January, 1894, November, 1894, February, 1895, and January, 1896. Because it was formally underwritten by an investment banking syndicate and because the Treasury contracted the defence of its gold reserve to the syndicate, the issue of February, 1895 was unique among these bond issues. In the remainder of the paper we will examine the meaning of this clause, proposing a theory which interprets the contract as the result of Treasury optimizing behavior.

As is usual in the investment banking literature, we will formalize the Principal's (Treasury) objective function and the agent's (syndicate) profit function. In this setup, we will ignore possible problems of incentive incompatibility in the contract, assuming a Treasury ability to monitor the agent's activity and to retaliate in case of deviation from the contract.

The Treasury's Objective Function

We assume that the Treasury aims to minimize the probability of an attack, that is, $\min \Pr\{e_{t+1}^{B} > e\}$. From the discussion of the previous sections, this minimum is attained by choosing DC_t and G^m to minimize $\log(DC_t + G^m)$. Becaue of the requirements of Section 3700 of the Revised Statutes, the bond could have been subscribed only in gold, so we express this minimization problem only in terms of the net reserve minimum or

$$\min G^m,$$

subject to the bond's being sold above some minimum acceptable price and to the Treasury's gross reserves' exceeding $100 million.

It is useful to express the optimization problem in terms of the bond issue size G plus other shoft-term debt G^c the government is willing to incur instead of in terms of G^m. The relationship between them is

$$G^m = -G - G^c,$$

where we assume that the minimum level of gold reserves before the bond issue was zero. This assumption is reasonable since the previous two issues had been subscribed in legal tenders and since any gold added to reserves by these issues had been expended in deficit finance. G is the amount in dollars of the subscription, and G^c is the extent of the government's potential short-term borrowing. While the Congress blocked the use of short-term credit, the financial breakthrough made by invoking Section 3700 involved the Treasury's sudden ability to tap the syndicate's line of credit in gold. The contract then signalled Treasury access to more gold than that directly generated by the bond sale. That the Treasury, in case of necessity, would use this line of credit to defend the parity reduced the perceived G^m to the extent of the line of credit.

We interpret the clause concerning the defence of the Treasury reserves as a syndicate commitment to open a line of credit to the Treasury for the duration of the contract. It is important to note that the effect of this type of operation would only temporarily to note that the effect of this type of operation would only temporaily reduce G^m, since the credit line would vanish with the expiration of the contract. However, this withdrawal of credit would not adversely affect the gold standard if adverse movement in the state variables generating the demand for money had been expected to be important only for the duration of the contact, so that an unusually low G^m would be needed only for a limited amount of time.[19]

That the syndicate turned over $25 million in gold in exchange for legal tenders in excess of the amount specifically contracted indicates the existence of the line of credit. Moreover, the syndicate's direct intervention in the exchange market can be interpreted as indirect short-term lending of international reserves to the Treasury to the extent that the syndicate absorbed legal tenders in this operation. Finally, after the conclusion of the contract, the Treasury was forced to another issue of bonds, revealing the increase in the probability of an attack due to the expiration of the line of credit.

These two different methods of affecting G^m, long-term borrowing or short-term lines of credit, can be represented in figure 12.5. G^c is the maximum amount in dollars of the line of credit. The lines $FI1$, $FI2$, $FI3$ are iso-probability loci where $FI3 > FI2 > FI1$. The iso- probability loci have slopes of -1, indicating that G and G^c have the same effect on the probability that the system remains viable.

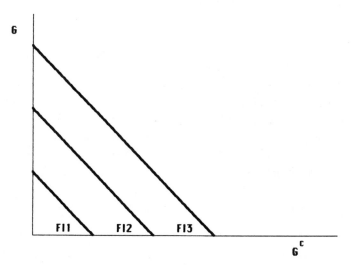

Figure 12.5

The Behavior of the Syndicate

We can study the behavior of the syndicate through the following profit function:

$$\pi = [P(N) - \bar{P}]N - I(G^c) \geqq K, \tag{14}$$

where $\bar{P}$ is the price which the syndicate pays to the government for the issue, N is the number of \$100 par value bonds in the issue, $P(N)$ is the expected prie at which it will sell the issue to the public, and $P'(N) < 0$; $I(G^c)$ is the expected cost connected with the provision of a line of credit with a maximum G^c with $I'(G^c) > 0$.[20] The constant K represents the minimum level of profit that the sydinicate will find acceptable for the operation, determined exogenously to the model. From (14) we can determine the price of the issue $\bar{P}$ as a function of N and G^c:

$$\bar{P} = P(N) - [I(G^c) + K]/N$$

so that we can write

$$\bar{P} = F(N, G^c),$$

$$\partial \bar{P}/\partial N = P'(N) + [I(G^c) + K]/N^2 ? 0,$$

$$\partial \bar{P}/\partial G^c = -I(G^c)/N < 0.$$

The derivative of $\bar{P}$ with respect to N is ambiguous due to the opposite effects of an increase in N on the total revenue of the syndicate. An increase in N, given P, will increase total revenue. However, an increase in N will also decrease $P(N)$, thus tending to decrease total revenue. We can expect a revenue maximum, so that the increase in N will increase total revenue until a critical value N^* and decrease total revenue for $N > N^*$. However, we are also concerned with the costs arising from the line of credit. $\bar{P}$ must respond to changes in N to keep profits constant. Thus, the effect of change in N on $\bar{P}$ will depend also on the level of G^c and K. The higher is G^c, the higher will be the critical point at which the derivative changes sign. On the other hand, the derivative of $\bar{P}$ with respect to G^c is always negative since an increase in G^c increases cost, so that P must decrease to maintain constant profits.

We can represent the price schedule for payments to the government as

$$\bar{P} = F(N, G^c),$$

$$F_1 > 0 \quad \text{if} \quad N < N^*(G^c), \qquad F_2 < 0.$$

In order to express the syndicate profit as a function of the same variables that appear in the Treasury objective function, we will use the identity $N = G/\bar{P}$. This allows us to rewrite the underwriting price as a function of G and G^c. It can be shown that the derivative with respect to G is:

$$\partial\bar{P}/\partial G = \{P'(N) + [[I(G^c) + K]/N^2]\}/\{\bar{P} + P'(N)N + [[I(G^c) + K]/N]\} \gtrless 0.$$

The sign of the derivative remains ambiguous. However, if we substitute $G/\bar{P}$ for N and define G^* analogously to N^*, the above analysis is still valid. The above price schedule, now a function of G and G^c, is given by the syndicate to the Treasury, which chooses the combination of G and G^c to maximize the probability of the gold standard's survival, given the legal constraints.

It is more appealing to transform the price schedule into a yield cost schedule. Once we take as given the kind of bond to be issued, a thirty-year, 4 percent bond, there is a one-to-one relationship between $\bar{P}$ and r, the yield to maturity indicated by $r = r(\bar{P})$, $r'(\bar{P}) < 0$.[21] Finally, we can write r as a function of G and G^c:

$$r = r(G, G^c),$$

$$r_1 < 0 \quad \text{if} \quad G < G^*(G^c), \qquad r_2 > 0.$$

The schedule $r(G, G^c)$ represents the cost, in terms of yield to maturity, of various combinations of G and G^c.

The Feasible Contracts Curve

In figure 12.6, we depict in (G^c, G) space the yield cost function to the government as a mapping of iso-yield cost curves. A given curve represents all (G^c, G) combinations which imply a given yield for the bond issue. Here $r_1 < r_2 < r_3$.[22]

In figure 12.7, we combine the iso-probability loci in figure 12.5 with the iso-yield cost loci in figure 12.6. The curve C represents the curve of feasible contracts, the combinations of G and G^c that achieve a given FI at the minimum yield cost.

The Optimal Contract

To find the optimal contract on the curve C, we must introduce the constraints faced by the Treasury, a maximum yield constraint and a minimum

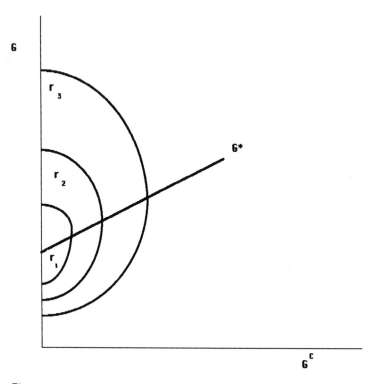

Figure 12.6

gross reserves constraint. The yield cost constraint assumes the simple form, $r < \tilde{r} < 4$ percent, since the bonds could not be sold under par.[23] In figure 12.8, the shaded area represents the points that satisfy this constraint. Point A would be the optimal combination (G_A, G_A^c) chosen by the Treasury, barring other restrictions. However, at a minimum, \$100 million of gross gold reserves was required of the Treasury, or $G_t^T >$ \$100 million. Expressed in terms of the magnitude of the bond issue, $G >$ [\$100 million $- G_t^T] = G_{min}$. If $G_{min} > G_A$, we will have a corner solution, as depicted in figure 12.9. The amount of the issue will be G_{min}, the line of credit maximum G_B^c, and the probability of survival FI_B. Note that the minimum gross reserve constraint, imposed to sustain the viability of the gold standard, has the effect, when binding, of reducing the probability of viability fromFI_A to FI_B. That the Treasury actually chose a level $G \cong G_{min}$ suggests that the legal constraint was binding.

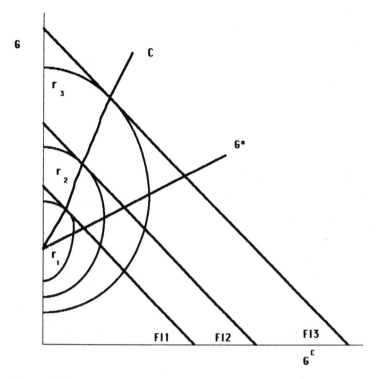

Figure 12.7

Other Features of the Contract

In the previous section, we provided an explanation of how the optimal size of the issue, the price at which the syndicate was willing to undertake the issue, and the optimal size of the line of credit can be determined. However, we have not explained the other features of the contract. We can summarize them as:

(1) The alternative underwriting by the syndicate of 3 percent thirty-year gold bonds at par at the option of the government and the choice among the coin bonds of the 4 percent, thirty-year bond instead of the five percent, ten-year bond or the 4.5 percent, fifteen-year bond. We can imagine that the syndicate computed the different price functions. $P(N)$, associated with the different characteristics of the potential bonds, following an analysis identical to that for the 4 percent, thirty-year bond. The syndicate then offered to the Treasury these four different price functions; and the

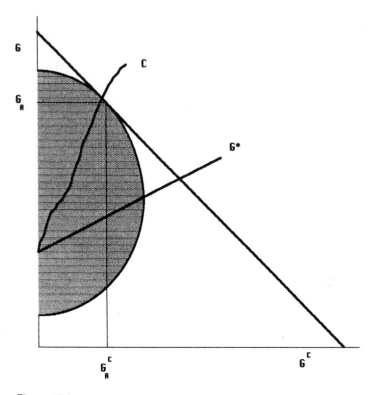

Figure 12.8

Treasury, faced with four different iso-yield cost maps, solved its optimization problem by selecting the bond characteristics that maximized the probability of the gold standard's viability given the legal constraints. The optimal solution was presumably the three percent, thirty-year gold bond, while the 3.75 percent, thirty-year coin bond was a second best solution forced by the lack of Congressional approval of the gold bond.

(2) Half of the gold for the subscription had to originate in Europe. As we said before, the requirement to import gold from Europe must have been a device imposed by the Treasury to guarantee the extent of the credit line immediately available for use. Presumably, the Treasury, already protected by the bond sale and the credit line, would not otherwise have worried about the source of the coin it received.

(3) The duration of the contract was six months. We have explained the duration of the contract by suggesting that the adverse conditions in the balance of payments were considered temporary, with an improvement

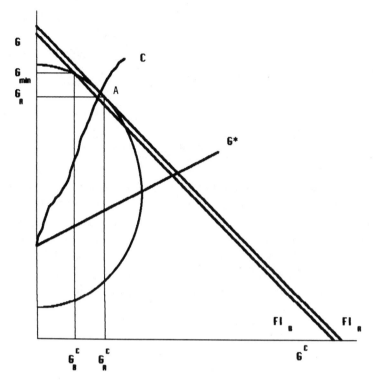

Figure 12.9

expected with the harvest season. Six months of the additional line of credit until September would have been optimal if the balance of payment perturbations had actually stopped. Presumably, the syndicate would have extracted a higher spread for a commitment of longer duration, and the six months balanced these two considerations.

VIII   Summary and Conclusions

In this chapter we wanted to study how theories of specualtive attacks on fixed exchange rate systems and of optimal investment banking contract, could be used to produce a coherent explanation of the contract of 1895 between the U.S. Treasury and the Belmont-Morgan Syndicate. We think that the experiment is interesting because it allows us to combine economic theory and legal structure into a uniform and consistent story.

We showed how the economic environment of the early 1890s can be sensibly analyzed by using speculative attack models. This, in turn, allowed us to specify objective functions for both the U.S. Treasury and the Syndicate.

In the final step, we demonstrated how the features of the contract could be reproduced by solving a Principal-Agent optimization problem, subject to the legal and political constraints faced by the parts involved in the transaction.

Appendix: The Syndicate Profit Function

In the chapter, we assumed that $P(\cdot)$, the price of the bond issue to the public, was a function only of the size of the issue G and that $I(\cdot)$, the cost of the credit line, was a function only of the size of the line of credit G^c. In a rational expectations environment, however, $P(\cdot)$ and $I(\cdot)$ should depend on both G and G^c. Both the price at which the public will absorb the issue and the cost of the line of credit depend on whether and when the gold standard will collapse; and the probability and magnitude of a collapse will depend on the sizes of the issue and the line of credit. In this appendix we will produce the price and cost function $P(\cdot)$ and $I(\cdot)$ consistent with the speculative attack environment.

The Price Function

In general, the price at which the public will subscribe the issue is given by

$$P(G, G^c) = [1 - PV_1(G, G^c)]P(G, G^c|C_1) + PV_1(G, G^c)P(G, G^c|V_1), \quad (\text{A}.1)$$

where PV_1 is the probability that the system will be viable in period 1, $P(\cdot|C_1)$ is the price that investors would pay for the issue, given that the system collapses in period one, and $P(\cdot|V_1)$ is the price that individuals would pay if the system is viable in period one. C_i indicates the event of a collapse at time i; V_i indicates the event of a viable gold standard at time i. However, $P(G, G^c|V_1)$ will itself be a convex combination of the price that the public would pay if the system is viable in period two, and the price it would pay if the system collapses in period 2, conditional on its viability in period one:

$$P(G, G^c|V_1) = [1 - PV_2(G, G^c|V_1)]P(G, G^c|C_2 \cap V_1)$$

$$+ PV_2(G, G^c|V_1)P(G, G^c|V_2 \cap V_1), \quad (\text{A}.2)$$

where $\cap$ is the intersection operator. By repeating the same reasoning for $P(G, G^c|V_1 \cap V_2), P(G, G^c|V_1 \cap V_2 \cap V_3)$, etc., until the last period of the loan, and by substituting back into (A.1), we find the formula for the bond price

$$P(G, G^c) = \left\{ \sum_{i=1}^{360} \left[\prod_{j=0}^{i-1} PV_j\left(G, G^c \middle| \bigcap_{k=1}^{j-1} V_k \right) \right] \left[1 - PV_1\left(G, G^c \middle| \bigcap_{k=1}^{i-1} V_k \right) \right] \right.$$

$$\left. \times P\left(G, G^c \middle| G_i \cap \left(\bigcap_{k=1}^{i-1} V_k \right) \right) \right\}$$

$$+ \left\{ \prod_{j=1}^{360} PV_j\left(G, G^c \middle| \bigcap_{k=1}^{j-1} V_k \right) P\left(G, G^c \middle| \bigcap_{k=1}^{360} V_k \right) \right\}, \qquad (A.3)$$

where 360 is the number of periods (months) in the 30 year duration of the contract.

The Cost Function

The cost of the credit line is composed of two parts, an interest cost and a capital loss. We assume here that the syndicate always has on hand at the insistence of the Treasury the total amount of the line of credit, so that the interest cost is computed on the maximum G^c either for the duration of the contract or until the collapse of the system if it occurs before the expiration of the contract. Thus the interest cost component will depend on the size of the line of credit, the probability of an attack, and the timing of an attack.

The capital loss is incurred only in the case of a collapse. All the credit line G^c be used in this event, and the attack itself will produce an instantaneous jump in the price of gold. Since the syndicate holds legal tenders as assets and gold liabilities, the capital loss will be given by the jump in the price of gold, multiplied by the amount of the credit line. The expected capital loss is then a function of the probability and timing of an attack and of the size of the devaluation produced by the attack itself.

We can write the expected cost function as

$$I_1(G, G^c) = (1/1 + r_1)\{[1 - PV_1(G, G^c)]$$

$$\times [G^c[\exp[E_t(e_{t+1}|C_1) - e] - 1] + r_1 G^c]$$

$$+ PV_1(G, G^c)[r_1 G^c + I_2(G, G^c)]\}. \qquad (A.4)$$

We can apply the same reasoning to $I_2(G, G^c)$:

$$I_2(G, G^c) = (1/1 + r_2)\{[1 - PV_2(G, G^c|V_1)]$$

$$\times [G^c[\exp[E_t(e_{t+2}|C_2 \cap V_1) - e] - 1] + r_2 G^c]$$

$$+ PV_2(G, G^c|V_1)[r_2 G^c + I_3(G, G^c)], \qquad (A.5)$$

solving for I_3, I_4, I_5, and I_6, and substituting back into (A.4), we find

$$I_1(G, G^c) = \sum_{i=1}^{6} \rho_i \left\{ \left[\prod_{j=0}^{i-1} PV_j\left(G, G^c \middle| \bigcap_{k=1}^{j-1} V_k\right) \right] \left[1 - PV_i\left(G, G^c \middle| \bigcap_{k=1}^{i-1} V_k\right) \right] \right.$$

$$\times G^c \left[\exp\left[E_t\left(e_{t+i}|C_i \cap \left(\bigcap_{k=1}^{i-1} V_k\right)\right) - e \right] - 1 \right] \right\}$$

$$+ \sum_{i=1}^{6} \rho^i r_i G^c \left[\prod_{j=1}^{i-1} PV_j\left(G, G^c \middle| \bigcap_{k=1}^{j-1} V_k\right) \right]. \qquad (A.6)$$

Both the price function $P(G, G^c)$ and the cost function (G, G^c) are complicated, and the derivation of an explicit solution would require a large effort,
out of proportion to the benefit we expect from it. We decided to assume
an ad hoc specification for both price and cost function, which are sensible
and simple enough to generate interesting answers from the model.
Though it permits a consistent, simple specification of the Treasury's side
of the contract, the rational expectations, speculative attack modelling
approach produces an intractable specification for the syndicate's side.
Nevertheless, we consider our result as an improvement over the existing
literature on investment bank contracts, where both the Principal's and
the Agent's objective functions are usually ad hoc specifications.

Notes

We have received financial support from the National Science Foundation and from a
Chemical Bank grant for the Rochester Financial History Workshop.

1. See Sachs and Cohen (1982), or Eaton and Gersovitz (1984).

2. See Mandelker and Raviv (1977), Baron (1979), and Baron and Holmstrom (1980).

3. Under the Public Credit Act of March 18, 1869, the Treasury was committed to pay the
interest and principal of all U.S. debt in coin of the current standard metallic content. Since
"coin" meant either legal tender gold or silver coin, U.S. bonds contained a government
option to pay in either metal at the discretion of the Treasury. Such bonds were referred to
as "coin" bonds; and by the 1870s all outstanding bonds were coin bonds. The U.S.
government never circulated bonds payable only in gold in the nineteenth century. The text
of this and other laws described in the present paper can be found in Dunbar (1893). The
laws regulating the convertibility of U.S. paper money began with the Resumption Act of
January 14, 1875. The law prescribed that the Treasury would redeem the legal tender paper

money called U.S. Notes (greenbacks) in coin after January 1, 1879. At the time, "coin" meant standard U.S. gold coins, since the standard silver dollar was removed from the list of coins with unlimited legal tender by the Act of February 12, 1873, Section 15. By 1878, the Bland-Allison Act had restored the coinage and the unlimited legal tender status of the standard silver dollar. Since "coin" then meant either gold or silver coins at the time of the resumption of convertibility, the Treasury had the legal option to redeem U.S. Notes and bonds either in gold or in silver.

4. In addition to restoring the unlimited legal tender status and coining of the silver dollar, the Bland-Allison Act of February 28, 1878 provided for the circulation of silver certificates backed by silver coin deposits. Though the coin deposits were themselves legal tender, the certificates were not, though they were receivable at face value for customs and taxes. In addition, the Bland-Allison Act forced the Treasury to purchase each month from $2 million to $4 million in silver at market prices to be coined into silver dollars. However, this was not sufficient to threaten the de facto gold standard.

5. In an Act of May 31, 1878, the Treasury was forbidden from cancelling or retiring any of the U.S. Notes (greenbacks) then outstanding. The notes, after receipt, had to be reissued and maintained in circulation. Since the reissuing of the notes could occur only through normal expenditures, in times of budget surplus, the Treasury might legally accumulate a stock of U.S. Notes if it did not redeem outstanding bonds or deposit the notes in banks. By this law the stock of U.S. Notes, including the part held by the Treasury, was frozen at $346.7 million for the remainder of the century.

6. See Noyes (1909, pp. 123–126). It is not clear why the debt reduction caused the banknote reduction. While national banks were required to deposit Treasury bonds to back their note circulation, the magnitude of the bonds outstanding never served as a binding constraint on note circulation. [See Champ (1984).] A rise in the price of the bonds associated with the purchases would make note circulation less profitable and thereby cause banks to contract the note supply. However, in an international market with freely mobile capital, it is not clear how these purchases themselves would raise prices. Alternatively, the surpluses themselves, regardless of how they were managed would signal a lower probability of a termination of gold payments, thereby raising bond prices. Thus, ending the surplus would make the Treasury bonds riskier in gold, thereby lowering their prices and ending the banknote contraction.

7. See Noyes (1909, pp. 124–125) and Annual Treasury Report (1887, p. xviii, 1888, p. 19, 453, 457).

8. In an Act of July 12, 1882, Section 12, the Treasury was authorized to issue gold deposits in return for gold certificates. All the deposited coin was to be retained as full backing for the certificates and paid on demand to the certificate holders. Though not legal tender, the certificates were receivable in payment of customs and taxes and associations of national banks were required to receive them in the clearing of clearinghouse balances. By this act, the Treasury was required to suspend the issue of new gold certificates whenever the coin and bullion reserve available for the redemption of U.S. Notes fell below $100 million. This is the only legal prescription of a minimum gold reserve to back U.S. Notes. Though it legally triggered only a suspension of gold certificate issue, subsequent Secretaries of the Treasury interpreted it as a reserve limit below which some action must be taken to restore the gold backing of U.S. Notes.

9. To guarantee coin convertibility, the Treasury was empowered by the Resumption Act to use surplus government funds for note redemption or to issue at not less than par in coin "to the extent necessary for the provision of the act" any of the classes of bonds

authorized in the Refuncing Act of July 14, 1870. The principal and interest of all of these bonds were payable in coin "at the present, (1870) standard." The bonds prescribed in the 1870 act were a ten-year, 5 percent coupon bond, a fifteen-year, 4.5 percent coupon bond, and a thirty-year, four percent coupon bond, all with interest payable semi-annually. Payments on these bonds were exempt from all taxes.

10. The law which granted the Treasury the power to contract the complicated investment banking services of the Belmont-Morgan syndicate without Congressional approval was the Act to Authorize the Purchase of Coin of March 17, 1862, also contained in Section 3700 of the Revised Statutes. To purchase coin, the Secretary of the Treasury was authorized to exchange any of the previously authorized bonds of the United States, at rates and terms that he deemed most advantageous to the public interest. Such issues were considered purchases of coin and not sales of bonds, and the Secretary had the power to require whatever additional services he wanted of the seller of the coin without Congressional approval.

11. The syndicate consisted at least of Drexel, Morgan & Co., A. Belmont & Co., J. S. Morgan & Co. of London, and N. M. Rothschild & Sons of London. The identity of other members, if any, remained secret.

12. This model has been widely used in the speculative attack literature. See Flood and Garber (1984), Blanco and Garber (1983), Obstfeld (1984a,b) and Grilli (1985).

13. This assumes that gold money goes out of circulation at the time of the collapse. For some cases where this does not hold, see Rolnick and Weber (1985).

14. The process generating the silver backed money may not be expected to be viable forever. In the case of the Treasury Notes of 1890 there was a trigger mechanism to terminate the production of additional notes when the market price of silver first reached $1 per 371.25 grains, the silver content of the standard silver dollar. Thus, the system contained an endogenously timed stochastic regime switch triggered by a first passage through a prearranged price. To see the extent of the complexities generated by an equivalent problem, see Flood and Garber (1983).

15. We assume that there are not restrictions on the credit market, or that speculators are able to organize themselves when confronted with a profit opportunity, so that the above condition is always sufficient, independently of the process driving the overall state variable. For a discussion, see Grilli (1985).

16. This would have implied an increase in domestic output or inflation in Great Britain. However, as Friedman and Schwartz (1963, p. 104) point out, there was a deflation in Great Britain at this time.

17. We are assuming that these unexpected reductions do not alter the process driving the state variables. There is no process switching in the domestic credit creation, or equivalently, no change in the deficit financing policy. Then the reduction in DC_t or G implies an equal reduction in all future post-attack money supplies.

18. $G^T = 0$ is not crucial and is assumed for expositional convenience only.

19. Recall that during this period adverse seasonal conditions in the balance of payments were expected to disappear in the harvest season.

20. We assume that the syndicate exchanges gold in return for legal tender through the credit line but that it holds the legal tenders in its vaults until completion of the contract. If

it did not withdraw the money from circulation, the loan would be useless since the recirculated legal tenders would immediately be presented to the Treasury for gold. $I(G^c)$ represents the expected opportunity cost deriving from the commitment to lend to the Treasury; it includes expected interest costs, expected capital losses from possible devaluations, and possible profits from dealing in the exchange markets. The above expected price and cost functions are not formally derived from the behavior of markets consistent with the assumed speculative attack model. In the appendix, we provide specifications of the price and cost functions consistent with the rational expectations assumption. However, such functions are too complicated to be fruitfully used in the analysis. We therefore opted for simpler, though ad hoc, functions which are reasonably consistent with the environment we specify.

21. $\bar{P} = [\sum(1/1 + r^*)^j] + 100/1(1 + r^*)^{60}$, where r^* is the three month implicit interest rate. (Recall that the cupons were paid four times a year). There exists an inverse relationship between $\bar{P}$ and r as in the text where $r = (1 + r^*)^4 - 1$, the annual yield.

22. The vertical intercept of an isocost curve must be positive since it is necessary that $G > 0$ for the syndicate to earn any profit.

23. The size of $\bar{r}$ is given by political constraints imposed on the Secretary of the Treasury. In any case it cannot surpass the legal limit of four percent.

References

Baron, David P., 1979, The incentive problem and the design of investment banking contracts, *Journal of Banking and Finance* 3, 157–175.

Baron, David P., 1982, A model of the demand for investment banking advising and distribution services for new issues, *Journal of Finance* 37, no. 4, 955–976.

Baron, David P. and Bengt Holmstrom, 1980, The investment banking contract for new issues under asymmetric information: Delegation and the incentive problem, *Journal of Finance* 35, no. 5, 1115–1137.

Blanco, Herminio and Peter M. Garber, 1983, Recurrent devaluation and speculative attacks on the Mexican peso, *Journal of Political Economy*, Feb. 1986.

Champ, Bruce A., 1984, The underissuance of national bank notes during the period 1875–1913, V.P.I. working papers.

Commercial and Financial Chronicle, 1890–1896.

Committee on Finance, 1896, Investigation of the sale of bonds during the years 1894, 1895, and 1896 (Government Printing Office, Washington, DC).

Dunbar, Charles F., 1893, Laws of the United States relative to currency, finance and banking, from 1789 to 1891 (Ginn & Company, Boston, MA).

Eaton, Jonathan and Mark Gersovitz, 1984, A theory of expropriation and deviations from perfect capital mobility, *Economic Journal* 94, 16–40.

Flood, Robert and Peter M. Garber, 1983, A model of stochastic process switching, *Econometrica* 51, 537–551.

Flood, Robert and Peter M. Garber, 1984, Collapsing exchange rate regimes: Some linear examples, *Journal of International Economics* 17, 1–13.

Friedman, Milton and Anna Schwartz, 1963, A monetary history of the United States 1867–1960 (Princeton University Press, Princeton, NJ).

Grilli, Vittorio U., 1985, Buying and selling attacks on fixed exchange rate systems, *Journal of International Economics* 20, 143–56.

Laughlin, Laurence J., 1968, The history of bimetallism in the United States (Greenwood Press, New York, NY).

Mandelker, Gershon and Artur Raviv, 1977, Investment banking: An economic analysis of optimal underwriting contracts, *Journal of Finance*, 683–694.

Noyes, Alexander D., 1909, Forty years of American finance (Putnam's Sons, The Knickerbocker Press, New York, NY).

Obstfeld, Maurice, 1984a, Balance of payments crises and devaluation, *Journal of Money Credit and Banking* 16, 208–217.

Obstfeld, Maurice, 1984b, Rational and self-fulfilling balance of payments crises, Working paper (Columbia University, New York, NY).

Rolnick, Arthur and Warren Weber, 1985, Gresham's law or Gresham's fallacy? *Journal of Political Economics* 94, no. 1, 185–199.

Sachs, Jeffrey and Danial Cohen, 1982, LDC borrowing with default risk, NBER working paper no. 925.

Simons, Matthew, 1968, The Morgan-Belmont syndicate of 1895 and the intervention in the Foreign Exchange Market, *Business History Review*, 385–417.

U.S. National Monetary Commission, 1910, Statistics for the United States 1867–1909 (Government Printing Office, Washington, DC).

U.S. Treasury, Annual Report, 1885–1895.

13   Real Aspects of
Exchange-Rate Regime
Choice with Collapsing
Fixed Rates

Robert P. Flood and
Robert J. Hodrick

I   Introduction

Typical evaluations of the performance of an economy under alternative
exchange-rate regimes proceed under the assumption that exchange rate
regimes last forever.[1] This assumption is a gross contradiction of the fact
that exchange-rate regimes are actually quite transitory. Countries never
really followed the "rules of the game" under the gold standard, and it
evolved into the gold exchange standard. During the Great Depression
currencies became inconvertible. The Bretton Woods system was planned
as a system of fixed exchange rates, but it was recognized that countries
would devalue and revalue their currencies when in "fundamental disequilibrium." Although this term was never formally defined, countries did
devalue and revalue their currencies, often by large amounts, during the
two decades preceding the breakdown of the system in 1971.

The purpose of this paper is to reexamine the determination of real
output in two popular models of the open economy accounting explicitly
for the transitory nature of fixed exchange-rate regimes. Rational agents
understand that an exchange-rate regime may be temporary, and they
incorporate expectations of the collapse of the regime and its associated
capital gains or losses into their behavior. The models we examine are
simple stochastic versions of the Dornbusch (1976) model of exchange-rate
dynamics with flexible output and the Flood and Marion (1982) model of
wage indexation in an open economy. We work with simplified versions of
these models since our point is that some of the implications of the models
are drastically altered when we allow agents to act on their understanding
of regime impermanence. These alterations are robust to more complex
versions of the models, but since we are presenting some counterexamples,
model complexity only obscures our points. Our work builds on previous
research on the temporary nature of government policies including Salant

and Henderson (1978), Krugman (1979), Flood and Garber (1983, 1984) and Flood and Marion (1983).

In section II of the chapter we develop our version of the Dornbusch model. We provide an example of the model in which the regime of permanently floating exchange rates always produces a higher unconditional variance of output than does a regime of permanently fixed exchange rates. This result is confirmed when we consider a temporary fixed-rate regime, although we find the disadvantage of a floating-rate regime diminishes as the possibility of an attack on a fixed-rate regime rises. This result is an unsurprising extension of the original comparison between fixed and flexible exchange rates. What is surprising to us, however, is that output variance conditional on maintaining a fixed-rate regime which may collapse can be higher than output variance under floating rates. Intuitively, this measure of the conditional variance of real output corresponds to the sample or measured output variance during a fixed exchange-rate regime that has not collapsed.

Our examination of the wage indexing model begins in section V. It is well known that optimal wage indexation depends on the stochastic structure of the underlying economy, and a contribution of Flood and Marion (1982) was to demonstrate that the degree of wage indexation would not be invariant to the country's choice of exchange rate regime. In their analysis, different permanent exchange-rate regimes lead to different optimal wage indexing policies, and each policy is a fixed function of the time invariant stochastic structure of the economy. In this paper we discuss fixed exchange-rate regimes which may collapse, and we find that the optimal degree of wage indexation is state dependent and thus time varying even though the stochastic structure of the economy is time invariant.

Our results are presented in the next seven sections. For each type of model we first examine permanent exchange-rate regimes turning then to a characterization of the economy when a fixed exchange-rate regime may possibly collapse. In each model we take the domestic credit component of the money supply to be an exogenous process. This creates an inherent tension between the two government policies, the domestic credit process and the fixed exchange-rate regime, which is resolved by the collapse of the regime. This appears to capture the actual priorities of governments without modeling the objective function of the monetary and fiscal authorities. The literature on the monetary approach to the balance of payments, for example, Frenkel and Johnson (1975), was quite clear that a policy of fixing the exchange rate made the total money supply backed by reserves and domestic credit an endogenous variable. If the governments do not use their policies to prevent losses of reserves, attacks are possible. Our exogenous domestic credit policy is merely one example of such a situation.

Because algebraic complexity quickly renders complex versions of each type of model analytically intractable, we worked with simple stripped down versions of each type of model while attempting to retain the essential economic aspects of the problems.[2]

II A Dornbusch-type Model

The original Dornbusch (1976) model depicted a medium-size open economy that was large in the market for goods produced at home and small in world asset markets. The crucial feature of the model was that domestic currency prices of domestic goods were predetermined while the country's exchange rate and other asset prices were currently determined and free to respond to all current shocks. This feature gave rise to the famous overshooting result. Since home goods prices were predetermined, the immediate response of the exchange rate to a money-market disturbance had to be larger than that response would have been had all prices been free to adjust. We use a version of the model that makes output demand determined. It consists of the following relations.

Glossary of Variables for Model I

m_t logarithm of the money supply

h_t logarithm of the domestic currency price of the domestic good

i_t level of the domestic interest rate

i_t^* level of the foreign interest rate

s_t logarithm of the spot exchange rate

d_t logarithm of the demand for domestic output

h_t^* logarithm of the foreign currency price of the foreign good

b_t logarithm of domestic credit

r_t logarithm of international reserves

$\bar{y}$ logarithm of the natural level of domestic output

u_t white noise goods market disturbance with variance σ_u^2

v_t white noise money supply distrubance with variance σ_v^2

Equations of Model I

Money market equilibrium:

$$m_t - h_t = -\alpha i_t + \gamma d_t, \qquad \alpha > 0, \gamma \geqq 0. \tag{1}$$

Capital market equilibrium:

$$i_t = i_t^* + E_t s_{t+1} - s_t. \tag{2}$$

Goods market demand:

$$d_t = \beta(h_t^* + s_t - h_t) + u_t. \tag{3}$$

Domestic price determination:

$$\beta(h_t^* + E_{t-1}s_t - h_t) + E_{t-1}u_t = \bar{y}. \tag{4}$$

Money supply definition:

$$m_t = \omega b_t + (1 - \omega)r_t, \qquad 0 < \omega < 1. \tag{5}$$

Domestic credit process:

$$b_t = \mu + b_{t-1} + v_t. \tag{6}$$

Equation (1) is money market equilibrium. The logarithm of the real money supply, $m_t - h_t$, equals the demand for real money balances, $-\alpha i_t + \gamma d_t$.[3] The demand for money depends negatively on the opportunity cost of holding money, the nominal interest rate, and it depends positively on the real demand for home goods, d_t. The equilibrium condition for the world capital market is given in equation (2) by the uncovered interest rate parity condition. The demand for domestic output is specified in equation (3). Demand for home goods depends negatively on the logarithm of the relative price of home goods in terms of foreign goods, $h_t - (h_t^* + s_t)$ and u_t is a stochastic demand disturbance. Equation (4) states that h_t is set at time $t - 1$ at the level that is expected to clear the market for domestic goods by equating expected demand to full employment output, $\bar{y}$. Actual output in period t is determined by the demand for it given the predetermined variables h_t and h_t^*. The composition of the money supply is given by equation (5). The nominal money supply is composed of a domestic credit component and an international reserves component.[4] Equation (6) states that the rate of growth of domestic credit, $b_t - b_{t-1}$, is a constant, μ, plus a stochastic term, v_t.

$E_{t-j} x_t$ is the mathematical expectation of x_t conditional on information from date $t - j$, $j = 0, 1$. It is assumed that u_t and v_t are mutually and serially uncorrelated with $E_{t-1} u_t = E_{t-1} v_t = 0$ and with constant variances σ_u^2 and σ_v^2. The foreign price and foreign interest rate are also exogenous stochastic processes. We assume that $h_t^* = h_{t-1}^* + z_{t-1}^*$, where z_{t-1}^* is serially uncorrelated and uncorrelated with the model's other disturbances. Its variance is σ_z^2, and it is an element of the time $t - 1$ information set. This dating convention recognizes that foreign price setters are also setting prices for period t at time $t - 1$. The foreign nominal interest rate, $i_t^* = i^* + x_t^*$ is assumed to be serially uncorrelated with mean i^*. The innovation in the foreign interest rate, x_t^*, is assumed to be orthogonal to the other stochastic processes and to have a constant variance σ_x^2.

Our comparison of alternative exchange-rate regimes focuses on the variability of real output. For the permanent regimes we measure variability with the conditional variance $V_{t-1}(y_t) = E_{t-1}(y_t - E_{t-1} y_t)^2$. For the collapsing fixed-rate regime we use this measure as well as an alternative. In all regimes $\bar{y} = E_{t-1} d_t$, and in order to simplify the presentation, we normalized $\bar{y} = E_{t-1} d_t = 0$. Consequently, the conditional variance of output is

$$E_{t-1}(d_t^2) = \beta^2 V_{t-1}(s_t) + \sigma_u^2 + 2\beta C_{t-1}(s_t; u_t), \tag{7}$$

where $C_{t-1}(\cdot; \cdot)$ denotes the conditional covariance operator.

III Solutions for Permanent Exchange-Rate Regimes

When exchange rates are perfectly flexible, there is no intervention in the foreign exchange market implying that r_t is the constant $\bar{r}$. A solution for the exchange rate can be found by recognizing that the variables on the right-hand side of (8) completely describe the current state of the system. Consequently, the linearity of the model allows us to apply the method of undetermined coefficients, and we find

$$s_t = \lambda_0 + \lambda_1 h_t^* + \lambda_2 b_{t-1} + \lambda_3 x_t^* + \lambda_4 z_t^* + \lambda_5 v_t + \lambda_6 u_t, \tag{8}$$

where

$\lambda_0 = (1 + \alpha)\omega\mu + (1 - \omega)\bar{r} + \alpha i^*$,

$\lambda_1 = 1$,

$\lambda_2 = \omega$,

$\lambda_3 = \alpha/(\alpha + \gamma\beta),$

$\lambda_4 = -\alpha/(\alpha + \gamma\beta),$

$\lambda_5 = (1 + \alpha)\omega/(\alpha + \gamma\beta),$

$\lambda_6 = -\gamma/(\alpha + \gamma\beta).$

From (7) and (8), the conditional variance of real output under a pure flexible exchange-rate regime is

$$V_{t-1}(y_t)|_{\text{Flex}} = \beta^2(\lambda_3^2\sigma_x^2 + \lambda_4^2\sigma_z^2 + \lambda_5^2\sigma_v^2 + \lambda_6^2\sigma_u^2) + \sigma_u^2 + 2\beta\lambda_6\sigma_u^2. \quad (9)$$

If the exchange rate is permanently fixed at a level $\bar{s}$ and the government runs an exogenous domestic credit process, the r_t becomes endogenous. International reserves adjust during the period to equate the demand for money and the supply of money. Under a permanently fixed exchange-rate regime, $s_t = \bar{s}$ for all t, and the conditional variance of output is simply

$$V_{t-1}(y_t)|_{\text{Fix}} = \sigma_u^2. \quad (10)$$

By comparing (9) and (10) we see that the conditional variance of real output under a flexible exchange-rate regime exceeds the conditional variance of real output under a fixed-rate regime whenever

$$\beta[\alpha^2(\sigma_x^2 + \sigma_z^2) + (1 + \alpha)^2\omega^2\sigma_v^2] > (2\alpha + \gamma\beta)\gamma\sigma_u^2. \quad (11)$$

Because the flexible exchange-rate regime allows foreign price and interest rate disturbances and the domestic money supply disturbance to affect the exchange rate thereby altering the terms of trade, these disturbances add additional variance to the demand for and supply of real output under such a regime. A counterbalancing effect that tends to reduce the volatility of real output under flexible rates when compared to fixed rates is that positive real demand shocks appreciate the domestic currency thereby improving the terms of trade, and this change in relative prices reduces the demand for real output. The appreciation of the currency arises because the increase in real demand increases the demand for money. The smaller is the elasticity of the demand for money with respect to real output, γ, the more likely is the volatility of real output to be greater under flexible exchange rates than under fixed rates. In order to provide a striking comparison in what follows, we assume that $\gamma = 0$. With this change, permanently flexible rates produce an unambiguously larger volatility of real output than permanently fixed exchange rates.

IV   Solution for a Temporary Fixed Exchange-Rate Regime

Our fixed exchange-rate solution from the previous section ignored the possibility that the economy may evolve into a state where it is worthwhile for agents to attack the government's foreign exchange reserves and end the fixed-rate regime.[5] We assume that the monetary authority will defend the fixed-rate regime only until its reserves hit some known lower bound, $\bar{r}$. After reserves hit this bound, the monetary authority is assumed to abandon the fixed-rate regime forever. If agents successfully attack the fixed-rate regime, they produce the floating rate whose level is given by

$$\tilde{s}_t = \tilde{\lambda}_0 + \lambda_1 h_t^* + \lambda_2 b_{t-1} + \lambda_3 x_t^* + \lambda_4 z_t^* + \lambda_5 v_t, \tag{12}$$

where $\tilde{\lambda}_0 \equiv [(1 - \omega)\bar{r} + \alpha i^* + (1 + \alpha)\omega\mu]$, and λ_1 through λ_5 are as above except with $\gamma = 0$. If $\tilde{s}_t > \bar{s}$, risk-free profits can be had at the expense of the monetary authority. If $\tilde{s}_t < \bar{s}$, attackers would make losses and consequently would not attack. If an attack took place when $\tilde{s}_t = \bar{s}$, no profits would be realized, and the post-attack exchange rate would be $\bar{s}$. Thus, we treat this case as part of the no attack situation without loss of generality, and an attack takes place if and only if $\tilde{s}_t > \bar{s}$.[6]

At time $t - 1$, when setting nominal prices for period t, agents realize that the fixed exchange-rate regime could collapse next period. Therefore, the conditional expectation of the exchange rate in period t is not simply $\bar{s}$, but it is the probability weighted average of the conditional expectations under the two possible regimes:

$$E_{t-1} s_t = (1 - \pi_{t-1})\bar{s} + \pi_{t-1} E_{t-1}(\tilde{s}_t | C_t), \tag{13}$$

where π_{t-1} is the probability at time $t - 1$ of an attack at time t and $E_{t-1}(\tilde{s}_t | C_t)$ is the expectation at $t - 1$ of $\tilde{s}_t$ conditional on a collapse at time t.

The probability of an attack next period, is $\pi_{t-1} = \text{pr}_{t-1}\{\tilde{s}_t - \bar{s} > 0\}$, where $\text{pr}_{t-1}\{x\}$ is the probability of event x given the $t - 1$ information set Examination of the solution for the flexible exchange rate in (12) indicates that the probability of an attack can be stated as $\pi_{t-1} = \text{pr}_{t-1}\{\varepsilon_t > \delta_{t-1}\}$, where $\varepsilon_t = \lambda_3 x_t^* + \lambda_4 z_t^* + \lambda_5 v_t$ is the innovation in the shadow flexible exchange rate that becomes the actual flexible rate if there is a collapse of the fixed rate regime at time t, and $\delta_{t-1} = \bar{s} - \tilde{\lambda}_0 - \lambda_1 h_t^* - \lambda_2 b_{t-1}$ is the amount by which the fixed exchange rate exceeds the conditional expectation of $\tilde{s}_t$ based on time $t - 1$ information. As δ_{t-1} falls, the probability of collapse increases monotonically since a larger part of the distribution of ε_t can induce a collapse.

The volatility of real output under a fixed exchange-rate regime that may collapse is

$$V_{t-1}(y_t)|_{C.Fix} = \beta^2 E_{t-1}(s_t - E_{t-1}s_t)^2 + \sigma_u^2, \tag{14}$$

which is clearly larger than $V_{t-1}(y_t)|_{Fix}$. It is also true that $V_{t-1}(y_t)|_{C.Fix}$ is less that $V_{t-1}(y)|_{Flex}$. In order to determine this result, consider the following decomposition of the conditional variance of the exchange rate under the two regimes:

$$V_{t-1}(s_t)|_{C.Fix} = (1 - \pi_{t-1})\bar{s}^2 + \pi_{t-1}E_{t-1}(\tilde{s}_t^2|C_t)$$
$$- [(1 - \pi_{t-1})\bar{s} + \pi_{t-1}E_{t-1}(\tilde{s}_t|C_t)]^2, \tag{15a}$$

$$V_{t-1}(s_t)|_{Flex} = (1 - \pi_{t-1})E_{t-1}(\tilde{s}_t^2|NC_t) + \pi_{t-1}E_{t-1}(\tilde{s}_t^2|C_t)$$
$$- [(1 - \pi_{t-1})E_{t-1}(\tilde{s}_t|NC_t) + \pi_{t-1}E_{t-1}(\tilde{s}_t|C_t)]^2. \tag{15b}$$

Expressions (15a) and (15b) utilize the facts that the unconditional moment of a distribution is the probability weighted sum of the conditional moments and that the exchange rate does not collapse (NC_t) when $\varepsilon_t \leqq \delta_{t-1}$. Subtracting (15a) from (15b) and rearranging terms gives

$$(1 - \pi_{t-1})V_{t-1}(s_t|NC_t) + \pi_{t-1}(1 - \pi_{t-1})\{[\bar{s} - E_{t-1}(\tilde{s}_t|NC_t)]^2$$
$$+ 2[\bar{s} - E_{t-1}(\tilde{s}_t|NC_t)][E_{t-1}(\tilde{s}_t|C_t) - \bar{s}]\}, \tag{16}$$

which is unambiguously positive since $E_{t-1}(\tilde{s}_t|C_t) > \bar{s} > E_{t-1}(\tilde{s}_t|NC_t)$. This demonstrates that a regime of collapsing fixed rates has a more volatile real output than a regime of permanently fixed rates, but the volatility is not larger than under a pure flexible-rate regime.

These results are not particularly surprising since as δ_{t-1} increases, the probability of an attack decreases, and the conditional variance of output approaches that under a fixed exchange-rate regime. Similarly, as δ_{t-1} decreases, the probability of an attack increases, and the conditional variance of real output approaches that under a flexible exchange-rate regime. For intermediate values of δ_{t-1}, the conditional variance is between the two extreme regimes.

The conditional variance used in the above comparisons takes into account the forecast errors that arise from both parts of the distributions of ε_t which we have denoted C_t $(\varepsilon_t > \delta_{t-1})$ and NC_t $(\varepsilon_t \leqq \delta_{t-1})$. Development of a sample counterpart to (15a) obviously requires data from multiple collapses. An alternative way to examine the volatility of output under a potentially collapsing fixed exchange-rate regime is to estimate the variance of output by examining only the realizations of output under a regime that could collapse but had not collapsed during the sample. This corresponds to the sample variance that one would measure by using all the data during a regime of fixed rates up to the point of a collapse. Clearly, this is a biased estimate of (15a). We find it interesting because it is the type of calculation that a naive statistician might do in comparing the performance of the economy under alternative exchange-rate regimes.

The volatility of real output in this case is denoted

$$V_{t-1}(y_t)|_{\text{C. Fix. 2}} = \beta^2(\bar{s} - E_{t-1}s_t)^2 + \sigma_u^2. \tag{17}$$

In order to conduct an analytical comparison of (17) and (15b), it is necessary to consider an actual probability distribution for ε_t. The point of the analysis is to demonstrate that the squared exchange-rate forecast error in (17) can be greater than the one in (15b). To make the point simply, we examined the model under the hypothesis that ε_t had a uniform distribution.

When ε_t is uniformly distributed, we have

$$f(\varepsilon_t) = 1/2\eta, \qquad -\eta \leqq \varepsilon_t \leqq \eta,$$
$$f(\varepsilon_t) = 0, \qquad \text{elsewhere,} \tag{18}$$

where $f(\varepsilon_t)$ is the probability density function for the random variable ε_t. The unconditional expected value of ε is zero and its unconditional variance is $\eta^2/3$. It also follows that

$$\pi_{t-1} = (\eta - \delta_{t-1})/2\eta, \qquad -\eta \leqq \delta_{t-1} \leqq \eta. \tag{19}$$

In the following discussion we will assume $-\eta \leqq \delta_{t-1} \leqq \eta$, since this is the region of interest. If $\delta_{t-1} > \eta$, $\pi_{t-1} = 0$, and δ_{t-1} cannot be less than $-\eta$, since this would make $\pi_{t-1} = 1$ and would casue the collapse in period $t - 1$.

We use (7) and (18) to find the conditional variance of output during a fixed-rate regime which may collapse. The expression is

$$V_{t-1}(y_t)|_{\text{C. Fix}} = \beta^2[-(\eta - \delta_{t-1})^4/16\eta^2 + (\eta^3 - \delta_{t-1}^3)/6\eta]$$
$$- \beta^2[\delta_{t-1}(\eta - \delta_{t-1})/2] + \sigma_u^2. \tag{20a}$$

We also use (7) and (18) to find the conditional variance of output during a permanently floating exchange-rate regime. This expression is

$$V_{t-1}(y_t)|_{\text{Flex}} = \beta^2\eta^2/3 + \sigma_u^2. \tag{20b}$$

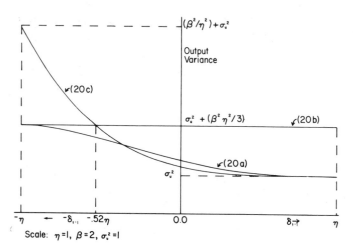

Figure 13.1

In figure 13.1, equations (20a) and (20b) are plotted against δ_{t-1}. Expression (20b) is independent of δ_{t-1}, and it is the upper limit of (20a) as $\delta_{t-1} \to -\eta$. The lower limit of (20b) as $\delta_{t-1} \to \eta$ is σ_u^2, which is output variance for a fixed-rate regime without collapse. These results confirm what was found earlier for arbitrary probability distributions. When $\delta_{t-1} = \eta$, and attack next period is unprofitable with probability one, so output variance is σ_u^2. When $\delta_{t-1} = -\eta$, an attack next period happens with probability one, so output variance is $[\beta^2\eta^2/3] + \sigma_u^2$. For values of δ_{t-1} between η and $-\eta$, output variance is a convex combination of the two extremes with weights that vary nonlinearly with δ_{t-1}.

In our examination of these results, however, we asked what would happen to measured output variance during the fixed-rate regime as δ changed but the regime did not collapse. Output variance during the fixed-rate regime would be given by

$$V_{t-1}(y_t)|_{\text{C.Fix.2}} = \beta^2(\eta - \delta_{t-1})^4/16\eta^2 + \sigma_u^2. \tag{20c}$$

This quantity also depends on δ_{t-1} and is plotted in figure 13.1. The interesting feature of this line is that the maximum variance for output is *above* output variance for a permanent float. Indeed, the volatilities in (20b) and (20c) are equal when $\delta_{t-1} = -[(16/3)^{1/4} - 1]\eta = -0.52\eta$. The implication of this relationship is that while δ_{t-1} is in the range below -0.52η, measured output variance under the fixed exchange-rate regime is *larger* than output variance would be under a floating exchange-rate regime.

This result is due entirely to the fact that exchange-rate prediction errors can be larger, for some rages of δ, for fixed-rate regime which might collapse but does not than for a floating-rate regime. In our example with exchange-rate innovations drawn from a uniform distribution, this occurs whenever $\delta_{t-1} < -0.52\eta$. The lower is δ_{t-1}, the more likely is a collapse of the regime, but if actual draws of ε are not greater than δ_{t-1}, the regime remains viable and output variance is larger than under flexible rates.

V   A Flood–Marion-type Model

One version of the Flood-Marion (1982) model depicted an open economy that was small both in the market for goods and in the market for assets. Wage contracts were set one period in advance of the realizations of disturbances. Wages, however, were indexed to the price level in a manner to minimize the deadweight loss from wages being different than their level in a frictionless (no contract) economy.[7] An important result of Flood and Marion was that the degree of wage indexation depended on the choice of exchange-rate regime. They found that a small open economy would index wages fully under a regime of permanently fixed exchange rates, but wages would only be indexed partially under a regime of floating exchange rates. Their results indicated that the degree of wage indexing would remain constant under any single regime as long as the underlying stochastic structure of the economy was constant. Their results were consistent with Lucas's (1976) demonstration that behavioral functions depend on the policy regime when agents are rational optimizers.

In our version of the Flood-Marion model, the fixed exchange-rate regime may collapse. Hence, wages are not fully indexed for such a regime, and the degree of indexation is time varying even though the underlying exogenous stochastic structure is time invariant. Optimizing agents examine the probabilities associated with changes in government policies when making decisions that will affect them in the future.

We demonstrate this result in a stripped-down version of the Flood-Marion model consisting of the following relations.

Glossary of Variables for Model II

m_t logarithm of the money supply

p_t logarithm of the price level

b_t logarithm of domestic credit (assumed constant)

r_t logarithm of international reserves

p_t^* logarithm of the foreign price level

s_t logarithm of the exchange rate

y_t logarithm of domestic output

$\hat{y}_t$ logarithm of the benchmark level of domestic output

u_t domestic real disturbance with variance σ_u^2

v_t^* foreign price disturbance with variance σ_v^{2*}

Equations of Model II

Money market equilibrium:

$$m_t - p_t = \alpha + u_t. \tag{21}$$

Law of one price:

$$p_t = p_t^* + s_t. \tag{22}$$

Aggregate supply:

$$y_t = \bar{y} + z(p_t - E_{t-1}p_t) + u_t. \tag{23}$$

Benchmark output:

$$\hat{y}_t = \bar{y} + \rho u_t, \quad 0 < \rho < 1. \tag{24}$$

Money supply definition:

$$m_t = \omega \bar{b} + (1 - \omega)r_t. \tag{25}$$

Foreign price process:

$$p_t^* = p_{t-1}^* + v_t^*. \tag{26}$$

Equation (21) states that the supply of real money balances, $m_t - p_t$, is equal to the demand for them, $\alpha + u_t$. To make the model analytically tractable, we simplified the money demand function, removing from the Flood-Marion model the opportunity cost of holding money as well as the portion of output that is responsive to prices. Money demand thus depends only on a constant, α, and the productivity disturbance, u_t. The qualitative properties of our results do not depend on these simplifications, but they enormously simplify some later calculations. Equation (22) gives the goods arbitrage condition, which is equivalent to purchasing power parity in this one-good model. Equation (23), which is derived in the appendix of Flood and Marion, is the aggregate supply function. The variable z is proportional to one minus the optimal degree to which the nominal wage is indexed to the price level. Since z is a deterministic linear function of the degree of indexing, the optimal wage contract may be found by minimizing the loss function (given below) with respect to z. Equation (24), which is also derived in the appendix of Flood and Marion, gives the frictionless benchmark (no indexing) level of output, $\hat{y}_t$. Equation (25) specifies that the money supply is composed of domestic credit, which we hold constant, and international reserves. As specified in equation (26), the foreign price follows a random walk. The disturbance terms, u_t and v_t^*, have zero unconditional means and are mutually and serially uncorrelated.

As in Flood and Marion, it is assumed that wage contracts are set according to

$$\min_z E_{t-1}(y_t - \hat{y}_t)^2, \tag{27}$$

where $E_{t-1}x_t$ is the mathematical expectation of x_t conditional on information from time $t - 1$, which includes all variables dated $t - 1$ and earlier as well as the structure of the model. The problem posed in (27) is to minimize a quadratic measure of deadweight loss by an appropriate choice of z.

By substituting from (23) and (24), the optimal indexing problem (27) may be rewritten as

$$\min_z E_{t-1}[z(p_t - E_{t-1}p_t) + \lambda u_t]^2, \tag{28}$$

where $0 \leqq \lambda = 1 - \rho \leqq 1$. The solution to (28), denoted z_{t-1} to reflect the possibility that it may depend on time $t - 1$ information, is

$$z_{t-1} = -\lambda C_{t-1}(p_t; u_t)/V_{t-1}(p_t), \tag{29}$$

where $C_{t-1}(\cdot; \cdot)$ denotes the conditional covariance and $V_{t-1}(\cdot)$ denotes the conditional variance.

VI Solutions for Permanent Exchange-Rate Regimes

When the exchange rate is flexible, there is no intervention in the foreign exchange market. Thus, international reserves, r_t, are constant at the level $\bar{r}$, and the exchange rate is $s_t = \bar{m} - \alpha - u_t - p_t^*$, where $\bar{m} \equiv \omega \bar{b} + (1 - \omega)\bar{r}$. The domestic price prediction error, $p_t - E_{t-1}p_t$, equals $v_t^* + s_t - E_{t-1}s_t$, which is equal to $-u_t$. Hence, the optimal value of z is $z|_{\text{Flex}} = \lambda$, and this value of z will set the loss function to zero. This special result is due to the assumed absence of independent disturbances to the money supply or to money demand in this simplified version of the model. In general, the optimal z will depend on the relative sizes of the variances of the various shocks [see Flood and Marion (1982, p.54)]. Presently, the important point is that $z|_{\text{Flex}}$ is positive and time invariant.

When the exchange rate is permanently fixed, r_t becomes demand determined, and the domestic price is given by $p_t = p_t^* + \bar{s}$, where $\bar{s}$ is the fixed exchange rate. In this circumstance the domestic price prediction error, $p_t - E_{t-1} p_t$, is simply the prediction error of foreign prices, v_t^*. Consequently, since v_t^* and u_t are uncorrelated, the solution to (29) is to set $z|_{\text{Fix}} = 0$ to screen foreign price disturbances out of the domestic loss function. This is exactly the result in Flood and Marion.

VII Solution for a Temporary Fixed Exchange-Rate Regime

The fixed-rate solution in the previous section presumed that the fixed-rate regime would last forever. As before, however, for some configurations of the state variables of the economy it may be profitable for agents to attack the government's stock of foreign exchange reserves and end the fixed-rate regime. We continue to assume that the monetary authority will defend the fixed rate only until international reserves hit some known lower bound, $\bar{r}$, and that after hitting this bound, the fixed-rate regime will be abandoned forever in favor of a flexible exchange-rate regime. In this model, if agents attack the fixed rate, they will produce the floating rate given by

$$\tilde{s}_t = \tilde{m} - p_t^* - \alpha - u_t, \tag{30}$$

where $\tilde{m} \equiv \omega \bar{b} + (1 - \omega)\bar{r}$. Thus, when forming wage contracts based on information available at time $t - 1$, the contracting parties must plan for the possibility that the fixed-rate regime will be attacked successfully at time t. The probability of an attack at t, based on $t - 1$ information, is $\pi_{t-1} = \text{pr}_{t-1}\{\tilde{s}_t - \bar{s} > 0\}$, or $\pi_{t-1} = \text{pr}_{t-1}\{(u_t + v_t^*) < \gamma_{t-1}\}$, where $\gamma_{t-1} \equiv (\tilde{m} - p_t^* - \alpha - \bar{s})$.

As before, when there is a possibility that the exchange rate regime will collapse, the agents take account of the possiblity in determining their contractual relations. In this case, the optimal degree of indexing depends on the probability of the collapse because this affects the unconditional time $t - 1$ covariance and variance in (29).

The solution to (29) for this case is to set z_{t-1} equal to

$$\frac{-\pi_{t-1}\lambda E_{t-1}[u_t(s_t - \bar{s})|C_t]}{\sigma_v^2 + \pi_{t-1}E_{t-1}[(\tilde{s}_t - \bar{s})^2|C_t] + \pi_{t-1}^2[\bar{s} - E_{t-1}(\tilde{s}_t|C_t)]^2 + 2\pi_{t-1}E_{t-1}[(\tilde{s}_t - \bar{s})v_t^*|C_t]}, \tag{31}$$

where $\sigma_{v^*}^2$ is the unconditional variance of v_t^*, and $E_{t-1}(\cdot|C_t)$ is the expectation operator based on time $t-1$ information but conditional on a collapse taking place at t. The expression on the right-hand side of (31), although complicated, is simply the covariance of λu_t and p_t conditional only on $t-1$ information divided by the variance of p_t conditional only on $t-1$ information.

In typical wage indexing models the optimal z is a time invariant function of the variances and covariances of the underlying disturbances. Our main point in this section is that it will not in general be time invariant when stochastic process switching is possible. This point can be seen at an intuitive level by examining (31) and noticing that z_{t-1} depends on π_{t-1}, the state dependent probability at $t-1$ of an attack at t.

To make additional progress concerning z_{t-1}, we again make specific assumptions about the probability distribution functions for v_t^* and u_t. We assume that the orthogonal disturbances v_t^* and u_t are each uniformly distributed on the interval $[-\eta, \eta]$. This assumption leads to a closed form but complicated expression for z_{t-1}. Since the final expression for z_{t-1} is so complicated, we simulated it for a few values of γ_{t-1} in the interval $[-2\eta, 0]$, and we set $\eta = 1$.[8] In this situation we found

$$\lim_{\gamma_{t-1} \to -2} z_{t-1} = 0, \tag{32a}$$

$$\gamma_{t-1} = -1 \Rightarrow z_{t-1} = (0.107)\lambda, \tag{32b}$$

$$\gamma_{t-1} = 0 \Rightarrow z_{t-1} = (3/8)\lambda. \tag{32c}$$

Example (32a) is the Flood-Marion result; when $\gamma_{t-1} \to -2$, it is impossible for $v_t^* + u_t$ to be less than γ_{t-1}. Consequently, $\pi_{t-1} \to 0$, and an attack on the fixed-rate regime at time t is impossible because it cannot be profitable. It is thus optimal to set $z_{t-1} = 0$ (index wages fully), thereby screening all foreign disturbances out of the loss function. For larger values of γ_{t-1}, such as -1 and 0 in examples (32b) and (32c), an attack is possible and contracts written at $t-1$ allow for this contingency by setting z_{t-1} at optimal values between 0, the optimal value for a fixed exchange rate with no attack possible, and λ, the optimal value for a permanently floating exchange rate.

The point of this simple example is to note that an economy's optimal choice of wage indexation to the price level may not depend simply on the policy currently being pursued by the government and the constant covariance structure of exogenous disturbances. It may also depend on agents' rational beliefs about the possibility of switches in government policies in the future. Consequently, the observation that indexing in wage contracts is time varying need not necessarily be associated with variation in the conditional covariance matrix of the underlying exogenous disturbances, it may instead be associated with the variation in agents' beliefs concerning the permanence of currently implemented policies.[9]

VIII   Conclusions

The purpose of this chapter was to examine how some aspects of the real economy, such as the determination of output, relative prices and real wages, are influenced by the potential collapse of a fixed exchange-rate regime. We examined the implications of the potential switch in government policies in simple versions of two popular international macroeconomic models. In both models, agents must take an action that predetermines some nominal variable. Consequently, monetary policy and the choice of exchange-rate regime have real effects. In both models the monetary authority is only willing to defend its exchange rate until its reserves hit a known lower bound. In each case the monetary authority also conducts an exogenous domestic credit policy. If the authorities were willing to conduct an endogenous domestic credit policy, there would be no need for international reserves, and the probability of collapse of the fixed exchange-rate regime would be zero.

Clearly, one interesting area for future work is the linkage of the domestic credit policy and the constraints imposed by the government budget constraint with the choice of exchange-rate regime. Eaton (1985) has investigated this problem in a neo-classical context with exogenous real output.

Another interesting area for future work is to focus on devaluations as opposed to the switch from fixed to flexible rates investigated here. What determines the timing and magnitude of a devaluation? Blanco and Garber (1984) have begun such an investigation.

Notes

Early versions of this chapter were presented at the Econometric Society Meeting in December 1983 and at a National Bureau of Economic Research Mini-Conference held at the University of Chicago in May 1984. We thank the discussant, Joshua Aizenman, and the other participants for their comments. We also thank participants in workshops at Columbia University, University of Illinois, and Ohio State University. This work was supported by a grant from the National Science Foundation.

1. Early contributions to the debate on fixed versus flexible exchange rates are surveyed by Ishiyama (1975) and Tower and Willett (1976). Some of the more recent analytical contributions to this area that are based on rational expectations include Flood (1979), Lapan and Enders (1980), Helpman (1981), Weber (1981), Kimbrough (1983), Turnovsky (1983), Aizenman and Frenkel (1985) and Eaton (1985).

2. A technical appendix presenting derivations of some of the results is available in our National Bureau of Economic Research Working Paper No. 1603 of the same title as this paper.

3. The Dornbusch model deflates nominal money balances by the domestic price of the domestic good instead of deflating them by a price index composed of the domestic price of domestic goods and the domestic price of foreign goods. For our purposes this is a harmless simplification which we also adopt.

4. We treat ω as a constant in our log-linear solution. This approximation does no harm to the theory, but it ought to be relaxed in empirical implementation of the model.

5. Although we examine only fixed and freely floating exchange rates, our methods could easily encompass "crawling pegs" or any rule that makes the fixed exchange rate a deterministic function of the previous state. Our methods could also be extended to analyze a "dirty float" of the form $m_t - m_{t-1} = \psi s_t + v_t$, such as that studied by Aizenman and Frenkel (1985). In such a circumstance, while the private sector could not attack the moeny printing rule, the fiscal authority might require a change in the monetary rule if the real resources obtained by seignorage were smaller than were required for deficit finance. The inability of Southern Cone countries to stay on preannounced crawling peg schedules seems to us to be an example of the change in monetary rules described above. In such countries an exchange rate policy seems not to be permanently viable unless it accommodates the fiscal authority's revenue requirements.

6. The conditions we use for an attack are those in Flood and Garber (1984). An alternative view, where the agents who would attack the price fixing scheme are small and disorganized is proposed by Obstfeld (1984). According to the Obstfeld view, $\bar{s}_t > \bar{s}$ is necessary for an attack but not always sufficient. The condition is necessary and sufficient in the present model though, as Obstfeld (1984) has shown.

7. Indexing wages to prices is motivated only by the larger number of such contracts actually implemented. The value of the loss function can generally be made smaller if contracts include more complex indexing to the state as in Karni (1983) or Aizenman and Frenkel (1985). Our intent, however, is not to specify an ideal contract, but rather to indicate how actual contracts affect the economy in a second best environment.

8. The precise expression for z_{t-1} is available in our NBER paper.

9. Cecchetti (1984) derives and documents changes in an implied indexing parameter for union wage changes from 1964 to 1978 for U.S. unionized manufacturing. The movement in the parameter may be due to movement in the conditional variance of the exogenous monetary and real processes of the economy, but the analysis in this paper suggests that such movement might also arise from agents' perceptions of the likelihood of switches in government policies. Since the contracting paradigm also leads to the aggregate supply curve studied by Lucas (1973), the perceived impermanence of existing exchange-rate regimes is an additional reason why the slope parameters would differ across countries.

References

Aizenman, Joshua and Jacob A. Frenkel, 1985, Optimal wage indexation, foreign-exchange intervention, and monetary policy, *American Economic Review* 75, June, 402–423.

Blanco, Herminio and Peter Garber, 1984, Recurrent devaluation and speculative attacks on the Mexican peso, University of Rochester manuscript, Feb.

Cecchetti, Steven, 1984, Indexation and incomes policy: A study of wage adjustment in unionized manufacturing, Working Paper, Solomon Center, New York University.

Dornbusch, Rudiger, 1976, Expectations and exchange rate dynamics, *Journal of Political Economy* 84, December, 1161–1176.

Eaton, Jonathan, 1985, Optimal and time consistent exchange rate management in an over-lapping generations economy, *Journal of International Money and Finance* 4, Mar., 83–100.

Flood, Robert P., 1979, Capital mobility and choice of exchange rate system, *International Economic Review* 20, June, 405–416.

Flood, Robert P. and Peter Garber, 1983, A model of stochastic process switching, *Econometrica* 51, May, 537–552.

Flood, Robert P. and Peter Garber, 1984, Collapsing exchange rate regimes: Some linear examples, *Journal of International Economics* 17, Aug., 1–14.

Flood, Robert P. and Nancy Peregrim Marion, 1982, The transmission of disturbances under alternative exchange-rate regimes with optimal indexing, *Quarterly Journal of Economics* 96, Feb., 43–66.

Flood, Robert P. and Nancy Peregrim Marion, 1983, Exchange rate regimes in transition: Italy 1974, *Journal of International Money and Finance*, Dec., 279–297.

Frenkel, Jacob A. and Harry G. Johnson, 1975, The monetary approach to the balance of payments (George, Allen and Unwin, London).

Helpman, Elhanan, 1981, An exploration in the theory of exchange-rate regimes, *Journal of Political Economy* 89, Oct., 865–890.

Ishiyama, Yoshihide, 1975, The theory of optimum currency areas: A survey, International Monetary Fund Staff Papers, July, 344–383.

Karni, Edi, 1983, On optimal wage indexation, *Journal of Political Economy* 91, April, 282–292.

Kimbrough, Kent, 1983, The information content of the exchange rate and the stability of real output under alternative exchange-rate regimes, *Journal of International Money and Finance* 2, April, 27–38.

Krugman, Paul, 1979, A model of balance of payments crises, *Journal of Money Credit and Banking* 11, Aug., 311–325.

Lapan, Harvey E. and Walter Enders, 1980, Random disturbances and the choice of exchange regimes in an intergenerational model, *Journal of International Economics* 10, May, 263–283.

Lucas, Robert E. Jr., 1973, Some international evidence on output-inflation tradeoffs, *American Economic Review* 63, June, 326–334.

Lucas, Robert E. Jr., 1976, Econometric policy evaluation: A critique, in: Karl Brunner and Allan H. Meltzer, eds., The Phillips Curve and Labor Markets Vol. I, Carnegie-Rochester Conference on Publc Policy, supplement to the *Journal of Monetary Economics*.

Obstfeld, Maurice, 1984, Rational and self-fulfilling balance-of-payments crises, National Bureau of Economic Research Working paper, No. 1486.

Salant, Stephen W. and Dale W. Henderson, 1978, Market anticipation of government gold policies and the price of gold, *Journal of Political Economy* 86, Aug., 627–648.

Tower, Edward and Thomas D. Willett, 1976, The theory of optimum currency areas and exchange-rate flexibility, Special paper in International Economics No. 11, May, International Finance Section, Princeton University.

Turnovsky, Stephen J., 1983, Wage indexation and exchange market intervention in a small open economy, *Canadian Journal of Economics* 16, Nov., 574–592.

Weber, Warren, 1981, Output variability under monetary policy and exchange-rate rules, *Journal of Political Economy* 89, Aug., 733–751.

14

Exchange-Rate Regimes in Transition: Italy 1974

Robert P. Flood and Nancy P. Marion

From August 1971, when the United States suspended dollar convertibility, until February 1973, when the dollar was devalued another 10 percent, the Bretton Woods System was in the final stage of collapse. During the transition period from fixed but adjustable exchange rates to managed floating, some major European countries adopted a middle-ground position, instituting some sort of two-tier exchange market, with separate exchange rates for current-account and capital-account transactions. The authorities generally pegged the commercial exchange rate and allowed the financial exchange rate to be determined by market forces. It was hoped that the two-tier exchange market would relieve pressure on official reserves caused by massive shifts in capital flows. At the same time, it would insulate commercial transactions from exchange-rate fluctuations and eliminate the need for discretionary restrictions on capital transactions. Insulation of foreign trade from exchange-rate fluctuations seems to have been a less pressing objective for some countries during this period, since they pursued a two-tier float where the commercial rate was allowed to float in its own tier.

Italy, France, the Belgium-Luxembourg Economic Union (BLEU), the United Kingddom, and the Netherlands were the major European practitioners of two-tier exchange markets in the early 1970s, although the BLEU has operated such a system continuously since 1957 and France adopted a modified version again in the spring of 1981.

Existing studies of two-tier exchange markets (e.g., Fleming, 1971, 1974; Barattieri and Ragazzi, 1971; Argy and Porter, 1972; Lanyi, 1975; Decaluwe and Steinherr, 1976; Flood, 1978; Marion, 1982; and Flood and Marion, 1982) have focussed on the operation of a two-tier exchange market, with special emphasis on such topics as the ability of the system to insulate an economy from foreign disturbances and the formulation of expectations under such a regime. Neglected in all these studies is the fact that the two-tier markets of the early 1970s represented an intermediate step in the transition from fixed (but adjustable) exchange rates to flexible (but managed) exchange rates. The transitional nature of these regimes— their perceived temporariness—may help to explain the behavior of exchange rates under such regimes which cannot be otherwise explained by standard market fundamentals.

A case in point is the strange behavior of Italian exchange rates during the transition from a two-tier float to a uniform flexible exchange rate on 22 March 1974. Table 14.1 illustrates the behavior of Italian exchange rates during the December 1973–March 1974 period. The table shows the percentage premia of the financial lira over the commercial lira.

The Italian data pose an interesting puzzle. If rational agents had expected the exchange markets to be unified on a fixed future date, then the bidding away of expected speculative profits would have driven the financial and commercial exchange rates together, with any gap between the two rates vanishing the instant before market unification.

This was not the case. The spread between the financial and commercial lira did not narrow steadily.[1] In fact, it grew from around 2 percent at the beginning of 1974 to 9 percent on 4 March 1974. The two rates then moved together somewhat during the period 4–21 March but on 21 March, the final day of the Italian two-tier float, a 2.7 percent discount in the financial lira remained. Figure 14.1 shows that Italian exchange rates were also quite volatile prior to the 22 March transition date.

The purpose of this chapter is to present a model of an exchange-rate regime in transition which is consistent with the Italian data. We hypothesize that forward-looking agents believed the Italian two-tier float to be temporary, but they were uncertain about the type of exchange-rate regime the authorities would next adopt. Our model shows that expectations of a transition in regime, combined with uncertainty about the nature of the post-transition regime, can cause a jump in the exchange rates at the moment of transition as well as extreme volatility in exchange rates prior to the transition. Moreover, the presence of a discrete jump in the exchange rates at the time of transition implies only that speculative profits were made ex-post, not that they were expected ex-ante.

Several items illustrate the nature of the confusion surrounding Italy's exchange-rate regime transition. First, agents in the lira markets had seen the French abandon their two-tier float and move to a unified flexible rate on 21 March. Undoubtedly agents believed the same sort of move could be imminent in Italy. Second, agents apparently believed that a return to a

Table 14.1
Dual market premia

				Italy			
Dates[a]	S[b]	X[c]	ln(S/X)[d]	Dates	S	X	ln(S/X)
731203	606.75	628.75	−0.0356	740130	663	694.69	−0.0467
731204	610.8	633.73	−0.0369	740131	662.5	694.2	−0.0467
731205	611.75	630.72	−0.0305	740201	658.5	691.56	−0.0490
731206	608.5	630.72	−0.0359	740204	657	691.56	−0.0513
731207	608	628.73	−0.0335	740205	654	689.66	−0.0531
731210	610	628.73	−0.0302	740206	659.5	693.48	−0.0502
731211	608	627.35	−0.0313	740207	661.25	698.25	−0.0542
731212	605.2	624.22	−0.0309	740208	660.5	697.59	−0.0546
731213	605.125	624.02	−0.0307	740211	660.5	696.86	−0.0536
731214	606.125	618.43	−0.0201	740212	657.25	695	−0.0558
731217	605.85	623.05	−0.0280	740213	657.75	697.11	−0.0581
731218	606.75	616.33	−0.0157	740214	657.5	698.08	−0.0599
731219	605.25	608.83	−0.0059	740215	656	696.86	−0.0604
731220	604.5	604.41	0.0001	740219	650	691.56	−0.0620
731221	604.38	605.69	−0.0022	740220	649.88	690.85	−0.0611
731226	—	—	—	740221	650.25	690.85	−0.0606
731227	606	610.87	−0.0080	740222	649.05	687.29	−0.0572
731228	608	616.14	−0.0133	740225	649.5	693.24	−0.0652
740102	612.5	623.05	−0.0171	740226	648	694.69	−0.0696
740103	619.5	632.91	−0.0214	740227	648.25	696.14	−0.0713
740104	620	630.12	−0.0162	740228	647.75	700.04	−0.0776
740107	630	636.54	−0.0103	740301	654.5	708.72	−0.0796
740108	636.5	642.67	−0.0096	740304	652.75	715.82	−0.0922
740109	628.75	636.74	−0.0126	740305	650	710.48	−0.0890
740110	630	636.54	−0.0103	740306	648.125	703.23	−0.0816
740111	628.5	—	—	740307	650	701.51	−0.0763
740114	630.75	637.15	−0.0101	740308	648	681.43	−0.0503
740115	637.5	643.09	−0.0087	740311	645	670.02	−0.0381
740116	639.5	644.12	−0.0072	740312	641	660.72	−0.0303
740117	641.5	652.1	−0.0164	740313	640.75	668	−0.0416
740118	650	663.35	−0.0203	740314	640.75	673.63	−0.0500
740121	653	677.51	−0.0368	740315	639.75	674.08	−0.0523
740122	671	694.68	−0.0347	740318	639	674.54	−0.0541
740123	675	696.62	−0.0315	740319	635	670.47	−0.0544
740124	674.5	702.49	−0.0407	740320	633.375	670.69	−0.0572
740125	673.5	708.47	−0.0506	740321	625.5	642.67	−0.0271
740128	664.5	702.99	−0.0563	740322	623.75	—	—
740129	668.25	698.81	−0.0447				

Date source: IMF Desk Sheets.
Notes: a. year, month, day; b. commercial exchange rate, lira/dollar; c. financial exchange rate, lira/dollar; d. ln(S/X) is approximately equal to the percentage difference between S and X divided by 100.

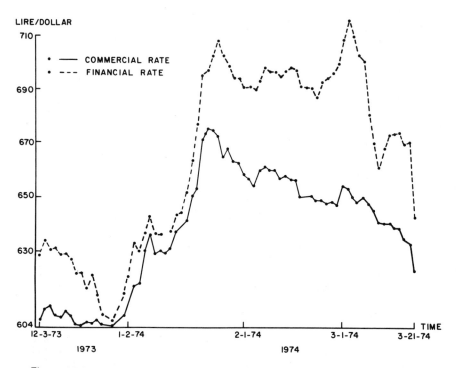

Figure 14.1

standard two-tier exchange market with a pegged commercial rate was possible. Rushing (1974), for example, wrote at the time:

> In February 1973, Italy adopted a two-tier exchange-rate structure ... Currently [March 1974], however, both rates are floating against all currencies. Presumably, the rationale for maintaining the two-tier structure even though both rates are floating is the expectation of an eventual return to a fixed rate for noncapital (i.e., current-account) transactions. (p. 13)

Confusion was also generated by the Italian authorities. For example, in early March 1974, the Italian Treasury Ministry made public a letter of intent backing an Italian request for a $1.2 billion International Monetary Fund (IMF) stand-by credit. In that letter, the Ministry reaffirmed its intention to maintain controls on capital movements "for a certain period," and this included keeping some sort of two-tier exchange market mechanism.

With agents confused about the nature of the post-transition regime, political events in early 1974 could only heighten their confusion. OPEC's fourfold increase in oil prices in early 1974 was expected to cause severe balance-of-payments difficulties for Italy, and agents were unsure of how the authorities would respond. Then in March 1974, a new center-left coalition government was established in Italy whose specific foreign-exchange market policies could hardly have been known to agents in the foreign-exchange markets.

Our strategy in modeling Italy's exchange-rate regime transition is first to develop a general model capable of describing the relevant exchange-rate regime alternatives for Italy. This general model is presented in section I. In section II we provide exchange-rate solutions for each type of exchange-rate regime. In section III we parameterize the "confusion" surrounding the Italian transition. We then examine Italy's actual transition from a two-tier float to a unified flexible exchange rate given that agents thought a transition to either a two-tier regime with a fixed commercial rate or to a uniform float was possible. Section IV provides some concluding remarks and highlights an important conclusion of the analysis: the "temporariness" of an exchange-rate regime should be treated as a market fundamental, and agents' subjective probabilities about the nature of a transition may be a key explanatory variable of exchange-rate movements prior to the transition.

I   The General Model

Italy adopted a two-tier exchange market with a fixed commercial rate in January 1973, after substantial outflows of private capital, coupled with expectations of a devaluation of the lira, led to mounting pressure on official reserves. From February 1973 until March 1974, when the two-tier regime was abolished, the commercial rate was allowed to float in its own tier. In this section, we present a macro model general enough to incorporate the three exchange-rate regime alternatives for Italy:

1. The two-tier float (TTF), which was the regime in effect prior to the transition.

2. The two-tier exchange market with a fixed commercial rate (TT), which the Italians operated in January 1973, and which agents believed could become the post-transition regime.

3. The uniform flexible exchange-rate regime (FLEX), which agents believed was a possible post-transition regime and which, in fact, was adopted on 22 March 1974.

Because of turmoil in the foreign-exchange markets, including the pressures of massive interest-sensitive and speculative capital flows, the

Table 14.2
Notation

d	Domestic component of monetary base
g	International reserve component of monetary base
i	Domestic interest rate (level)
k	Domestic stock of traded securities
m	Monetary base
p	Domestic price level
ε	Uniform flexible exchange rate (home currency/foreign currency)
s	Commercial exchange rate
x	Financial exchange rate
w	Domestic real financial wealth
y	Domestic real output
t	Time

Note: Lowercase letters generally denote logarithms of variables; a dot over a variable indicates the time derivative; a bar over the variable indicates that it is held constant; an asterisk indicates "foreign."

uniform fixed exchange-rate regime was never a viable option for Italy during this period.

The general macro model is presented below. Notation used in the model is identified in table 14.2. In the model, the domestic economy is assumed to be small both in commodity markets and in the market for internationally traded financial assets.

The Model

Monetary Sector:

$$m(t) - p(t) = \alpha_0 - \alpha_1 i(t) + \alpha_2 y(t); \alpha_1, \alpha_2 > 0 \tag{1}$$

$$i(t) = i^*(t) + \gamma(s(t) - x(t)) + \dot{x}(t); \gamma > 0 \tag{2}$$

$$m(t) = \theta g(t) + (1 - \theta)d(t); 0 \le \theta \le 1 \tag{3}$$

$$\dot{m}(t) = \dot{d}(t) = \dot{g}(t) = 0 \qquad \text{(FLEX, TTF)} \tag{4a}$$

$$\dot{m}(t) = \theta \dot{g}(t); \dot{d}(t) = 0 \qquad \text{(TT)} \tag{4b}$$

Saving:

$$\dot{w}(t) = \Psi_0 + \Psi_1(y(t) - w(t)) + \Psi_2(i(t) - \dot{p}(t)); \Psi_1, \Psi_2 > 0 \tag{5}$$

$$w(t) = \eta m(t) + (1 - \eta)(x(t) + k(t)) - p(t); 0 \le \eta \le 1 \tag{6}$$

Foreign-Exchange Market:

$$s(t) = x(t) = \varepsilon(t) \qquad\qquad \text{(FLEX)} \qquad \text{(7a)}$$

$$s(t) = \bar{s} \qquad\qquad\qquad\qquad \text{(TT)} \qquad \text{(7b)}$$

Prices:

$$p(t) = p^*(t) + s(t) \tag{8}$$

Exogenous Variables:

$$y(t) = \bar{y} \tag{9}$$

$$d(t) = \bar{d} \tag{10}$$

$$p^*(t) = \bar{p}^* \tag{11}$$

$$i^*(t) = \bar{i}^* \tag{12}$$

$$k(t) = \bar{k} \qquad\qquad\qquad \text{(TT, TTF)} \qquad \text{(13)}$$

Equation (1) depicts money-market equilibrium. It equates the real monetary base, $m(t) - p(t)$, to money demand, which depends negatively on the opportunity cost of holding money and positively on real output.

Equation (2) specifies the opportunity cost of holding money. It is general enough to encompass the three alternative exchange-rate regimes. In the case of two-tier exchange rates, the principal on foreign bonds must be acquired and repatriated at the financial rate, X (level), but interest income, a current-account item, must be repatriated at the commercial rate S (level). To derive Equation (2), we consider the opportunity cost of holding money for a time period of length h and then let $h \to 0$ to obtain our continuous-time expression.

At the beginning of a period of length h, one unit of domestic money will buy $1/X(t)$ units of financial foreign exchange which may be repatriated at the end of the period at the rate $X(t + h)$. During the period, the $1/X(t)$ units of foreign exchange earn $hi^*(t)/X(t)$ in interest income which may be repatriated into domestic money in amount $S(t + h)hi^*(t)/X(t)$. These two elements of return can be combined to given an overall return of

$$\frac{X(t + h)}{X(t)}\left(1 + \frac{S(t + h)hi^*(t)}{X(t + h)}\right)$$

Hence, the opportunity cost of holding domestic money from time t to time $(t + h)$ is $hi(t)$ in the expression

$$1 + hi(t) = \frac{X(t + h)}{X(t)} \left(1 + \frac{S(t + h)hi^*(t)}{X(t + h)} \right) \tag{14}$$

A logarithmic approximation to (14) is

$$hi(t) = x(t + h) - x(t) + \frac{S(t + h)hi^*(t)}{X(t + h)} \tag{15}$$

Dividing each side of (15) by h and letting $h \to 0$, we obtain

$$i(x) = \dot{x}(t) + \frac{S(t)i^*(t)}{X(t)} \tag{16}$$

Finally, we approximate $S(t)i^*(t)/X(t)$ in (16) by $i^*(t) + \gamma[s(t) - x(t)]$ to get equation (2).[2]

When we analyze the two-tier float, $s(t)$ and $x(t)$ in equation (2) are simultaneously determined endogenous variables. When we examine a two-tier market with a fixed commercial rate, $s(t)$ is held fixed at $\bar{s}$ by the domestic monentary authorities. Under unified flexible exchange rates, $s(t) = x(t) = \varepsilon(t)$ and equation (2) becomes the familiar uncovered interest arbitrage condition with risk neutrality.

Equation (3) states that the nominal domestic monetary base, $m(t)$, is a weighted average of the book value of an international reserve component, $g(t)$, and a domestic component, $d(t)$. Throughout the analysis we hold $d(t)$ constant at $\bar{d}$[3]. We also assume that under the TTF and FLEX regimes, the government does not intervene in the foreign-exchange market, so $g(t)$ is constant at $\bar{g}$. Consequently, equation (4a) holds for these two regimes. Under the TT regime, the government must intervene in the foreign-exchange market to peg the commercial rate, so $g(t)$ will not be constant. Equation (4b) holds for this regime. Since the foreign-exchange markets are partitioned under the TT regime, the accumulation of reserves, $\dot{g}(t)$, is determined solely by the current-account surplus. Consequently, $g(t)$ is a continuous variable and does not make discrete jumps as it might under a uniform fixed exchange rate.

Equation (5) equates real wealth accumulation to planned saving. Planned saving depends positively on the output-wealth ratio, $y(t) - w(t)$, and positively on the real rate of interest, $i(t) - \dot{p}(t)$.

Equation (6) specifies the logarithmic linearization of real wealth, with nominal wealth being a weighted average of nominal money, $m(t)$, and the nominal domestic-currency value of traded securities, $x(t) + k(t)$. Net domestic holdings of trade securities are assumed to be nonnegative.[4]

The exchange-rate regime in effect dicates the channels through which the economy alters its real stock of wealth. Indeed, the way in which wealth is acquired is the most significant difference between the TTF, TT, and FLEX regimes.

Under the TTF regime, the flexible commercial rate keeps the current account in balance while the flexible financial rate prevents net capital flows. Since we have also assumed that there is no change in the domestic component of the money base, equations (4a), (10), and (13) are relevant and real wealth accumulation under the TTF regime is

$$\dot{w}(t) = (1 - \eta)\dot{x}(t) - \dot{p}(t) \tag{17}$$

Under the TT regime, real wealth accumulation becomes

$$\dot{w}(t) = \eta\theta\dot{g}(t) + (1 - \eta)\dot{x}(t) - \dot{p}(t) \tag{18}$$

Equation (18) differs from (17) by the term $\eta\theta\dot{g}(t)$, which gives the wealth effect of a current-account surplus or deficit and the extent of current-account intervention to peg $s(t)$ at $\bar{s}$. Under the FLEX regime, we have

$$\dot{w}(t) = (1 - \eta)(\dot{x}(t) + \dot{k}(t)) - \dot{p}(t) \tag{19}$$

where $\dot{k}(t)$ need not equal zero.

Equations (7a) and (7b) describe exchange-rate relationships under the various regimes. Equation (7a) states that for the FLEX regime, there is one uniform exchange rate; (7b) states that for the TT regime the commercial rate is pegged. Under the TTF regime, no set relation between the commercial and financial rates exists independently of private behavior. Under the TT regime, the financial rate is flexible and the model determines the relationship between $\bar{s}$ and x.

Equation (8) is the goods arbitrage condition. In logs, the price of domestic output, $p(t)$, equals the foreign output price plus the commercial exchange rate. Since commodity trade is a current-account transaction, it is appropriate to specify the arbitrage condition using the commercial exchange rate.

Equations (9)–(12) list the model's exogenous variables.

This completes the exposition of the general model. Our aim is to use the model to study the expected transition from a temporary TTF regime to either the TT or the FLEX regime. To accomplish our aim, we find in the next section the exchange-rate solutions of our model for the various regimes. In section III we model the expected transition by taking the general exchange-rate solutions of the TTF regime ($s(t)$ and $x(t)$) and using a weighted average of the TT and FLEX exchange-rate solutions as our terminal conditions. Further, since our motivation for this study comes from the Italian experience in 1974, we will indicate in our analysis any additional assumptions which limit the generality of our model in order to make it more directly applicable to the Italian case.

II Exchange-Rate Solutions

In this section we use the general model to derive exchange-rate solutions for the three regimes, TTF, TT and FLEX. We do so by solving a system of linear differential equations for each regime. In section III we model the expected regime transion.

The TTF Solution

Equations (1)–(3), (4a), (5)–(6), and (8)–(13) of the general model are used to derive the two primary equations of the TTF regime. These two equations represent semireduced forms of money market equilibrium and planned savings behavior.

$$\bar{m} - \bar{p}^* - s(t) = \alpha_0 - \alpha_1 [i^* + \gamma(s(t) - x(t)) + \dot{x}(t)] + \alpha_2 \bar{y} \tag{20}$$

$$(1 - \eta)\dot{x}(t) - \dot{s}(t) = \Psi_0 + \Psi_1(\bar{y} - \eta\bar{m} - (1 - \eta)(x(t) + \bar{k}) + \bar{p}^* + s(t))$$
$$+ \Psi_2(i^* + \gamma(s(t) - x(t)) + \dot{x}(t) - \dot{s}(t)) \tag{21}$$

Equations (20) and (21) are a pair of simultaneous linear differential equations in the exchange rates $s(t)$ and $x(t)$.

In our investigation of conditions actually prevailing in Italy in late 1973 and early 1974, we discovered that Branson and Halttunen (1979) had constructed a time series on the level of Italian net foreign assets which ecompassed the late 1973 to early 1974 period. Their data indicate that during this period, Italian net foreign assets were approximately zero. Since we are interested in the Italian case, it seems reasonable to specialize our solutions to account for the Branson-Halttunen data. Hence, we specialize our solutions by reporting the limiting case of the solutions with $(1 - \eta) \to 0$.[5]

The exchange-rate solutions for the TTF regime are:

$$x(t) = C_1 e^{\gamma t} + \frac{(1 - \alpha_1 \gamma)}{\alpha_1(\mu - \gamma)} C_2 e^{\mu t} + \hat{x} \tag{22}$$

$$s(t) = C_2 e^{\mu t} + \hat{s} \tag{23}$$

where

$$\mu = \frac{(\Psi_1 + (\Psi_2/\alpha_1))}{\Psi_2 - 1}$$

$$\hat{x} = \frac{(1 - \alpha_1\gamma)B_2}{\gamma\alpha_1\mu} - \frac{B_1}{\gamma}$$

$$\hat{s} = \frac{-B_2}{\mu}$$

$$B_1 = \frac{1}{\alpha_1}[\alpha_0 - \alpha_1\bar{i}^* - \bar{m} + \bar{p}^* + \alpha_2\bar{y}]$$

$$B_2 = \frac{\Psi_0 + \Psi_1(\bar{p}^* - \bar{m} + \bar{y}) + \Psi_2(\bar{i}^* + B_1)}{\Psi_2 - 1}$$

and we assume $(\Psi_2 - 1) \neq 0$.

In equations (22) and (23), $\hat{x}$ and $\hat{s}$ are the steady-state values of $x(t)$ and $s(t)$, respectively, μ and γ are the two distinct roots of the system, and C_1 and C_2 are as yet undetermined coefficients.

Since $x(t)$ and $s(t)$ are both simultaneously determined, "forward-looking" variables, the model of the TTF regime does not in general have the now familiar saddle-point property which often occurs when one endogenous variable is predetermined and the other is forward looking. Note the if μ is positive, then the system contains two positive roots, and the TTF model is formally an unstable node. Under these circumstances, non-zero values for C_1 and C_2 will prevent the financial and commercial exchange rates from ever reaching their steady-state values. Instead, they will both ride a speculative bubble indefinitely.

If the TTF regime were expected to be *permanent*, then the condition of no speculative bubbles would require agents to set $C_1 = 0$ and $C_2 = 0$ when $\mu > 0$. However, since agents expect the TTF regime to be *temporary*, the coefficients C_1 and C_2 need not be set at zero. As we shall see in section III, agents will set C_1 and C_2 at values where a transition to some more permanent regime—either the TT or FLEX—can be made without expected speculative profits.

The TT Solution

Equations (1)–(3), (4b), (5)–(6), (7b), and (8)–(13) from the general model are used to derive the semireduced forms of the money market equilibrium condition and planned saving behavior for the TT regime:

$$(1 - \theta)\bar{d} + \theta g(t) - \bar{p}^* - \bar{s} = \alpha_0 - \alpha_1(\bar{i}^* + \gamma(\bar{s} - x(t)) + \dot{x}(t)) + \alpha_2 \bar{y}$$

(24)

$$\eta\theta\dot{g}(t) + (1 - \eta)\dot{x}(t) = \Psi_0 + \Psi_1\{\bar{y} - \eta[(1 - \theta)\bar{d} + \theta g(t)]$$

$$- (1 - \eta)[x(t) + \bar{k}] + \bar{p}^* + \bar{s}\}$$

$$+ \Psi_2(\bar{i}^*\gamma(\bar{s} - x(t)) + \dot{x}(t))$$

(25)

Recall that under the TT regime, the financial exchange rate is flexible but the government pegs the commercial exchange rate. The government's foreign-exchange market intervention to peg $s(t)$ at $\bar{s}$ alters the international reserve component of the monetary base over time. Consequently, equations (24) and (25) represent a pair of simultaneous linear differential equations in $g(t)$ and $x(t)$.

The exchange-rate and reserves solutions for the TT regime are:

$$g(t) = (g(T) - \hat{g})e^{(\Psi_1 + (\Psi_2/\alpha_1))} + \hat{g}; \qquad t \geq T$$

(26)

$$x(t) = \lambda g(t) + \hat{x} - \lambda g; \qquad t \geq T$$

(27)

where

$$\lambda = \frac{\theta}{\alpha_1(\Psi_1 + (\Psi_2/\alpha_1) + \gamma)}$$

$$\hat{g} = \frac{B_3}{\Psi_1 + (\Psi_2/\alpha_1)} + \frac{\bar{s}}{\theta}$$

$$\hat{x} = \frac{\theta B_3}{\gamma\alpha_1(\Psi_1 + (\Psi_2/\alpha_1))} - \frac{B_4}{\gamma} + \bar{s}$$

$$B_3 = \frac{1}{\theta}[\Psi_0 + \Psi_1(\bar{y} + \bar{p}^* - (1 - \theta)\bar{d}) + \Psi_2(\bar{i}^* + B_4)]$$

$$B_4 = \frac{1}{\alpha_1}[\alpha_0 - \alpha_1\bar{i}^* + \alpha_2\bar{y} - (1 - \theta)\bar{d} + \bar{p}^*]$$

and where T is defined as the transition date. The terms $\hat{g}$ and $\hat{x}$ are the steady-state values of $g(t)$ and $x(t)$, respectively.

Unlike the TTF regime, the TT regime exhibits saddle-points stability. The value of $g(t)$, which represents the book value of international reserves, is given by history at an instant in time. The financial exchange rate, $x(t)$, is not predetermined; rather, it is a currently determined forward-looking variable.

Since T represents the transition date—the initial instant of the TT regime—$g(T)$ is the initial condition for our solution of the time path of $g(t)$, $t \geq T$.

The initial condition for our solution of the time path of $x(t)$ is found by invoking the requirement that the model place itself on the stable branch leading to the steady state. Equation (27) is the stable branch of the equation system (24), (25). Equation (26) traces the motion of $g(t)$. The motion of $x(t)$ is obtained by substituting (26) into (27).

The final component in our solution of the TT model is the setting of the commercial rate at $\bar{s}$. If agents believe during the operation of a TTF regime that the authorities will switch to a TT regime, then they must form beliefs about the level at which s will be set under the TT regime. These beliefs are subjective, but some guidance can be obtained from public policy announcements just prior to the transition. For example, in Italy's March 1974 letter of intent to the IMF, it firmly undertook to eliminate its nonoil current-account deficit. Hence, agents may reasonably have believed that the commercial exchange rate would be set at a level designed to achieve some current-account target, Z, at time T. Let

$$Z = \dot{g}(T) = -(\Psi_1 + \Psi_2/\alpha_1))(g(T) - \hat{g}) \tag{28}$$

where the final equality in (28) follows from differentiating (26).

To find the value of $\bar{s}$ which will yield current-account target Z, substitute the definition of $\hat{g}$ into (28) to obtain

$$Z = (\Psi_1 + \Psi_2/\alpha_1))(-g(T)) + \frac{B_3}{(\Psi_1 + \Psi_2/\alpha_1))} + \frac{\bar{s}}{\theta} \tag{29a}$$

Rearranging (29a), we get

$$\bar{s} = \theta g(T) + \frac{\theta(Z - B_3)}{(\Psi_1 + (\Psi_2/\alpha_1))} \tag{29b}$$

Equation (29b) has the sensible property that a larger current-account surplus target (a smaller current-account deficit target) requires a higher price for commercial foreign exchange, since

$$\frac{d\bar{s}}{dZ} = \frac{\theta}{(\Psi_1 + (\Psi_2/\alpha_1))} > 0$$

The complete solution of the TT model is obtained in the following manner. First, substitute (29b) into the definitions of $\hat{g}$ and $\hat{x}$. This gives:

$$\hat{g} = \frac{B_3}{(\Psi_1 + (\Psi_2/\alpha_1))} + g(T) + \frac{Z - B_3}{(\Psi_1 + (\Psi_2/\alpha_1))} \tag{30a}$$

$$\hat{x} = \frac{\theta B_3}{\gamma\alpha_1(\Psi_1 + (\Psi_2/\alpha_1))} - \frac{B_4}{\gamma} + \theta g(T) + \frac{\theta(Z - B_3)}{(\Psi_1 + (\Psi_2/\alpha_1))} \tag{30b}$$

Next, substitute (30a) and (30b) into the solutions for $g(t)$ and $x(t)$ in equations (26) and (27). We now have a complete solution to the TT regime conditional on the current-account targe Z and the model placing itself on the stable branch leading to the steady state.[6]

The FLEX Solution

Under the FLEX regime, the general model of section I decomposes, and we need only know the money-market equilibrium condition to determine the value of the exchange rate. Equations (1)–(3), (4a), (7a) and (9)–(12) of the general model can be combined to derive the semireduced form of the money market equilibrium for the FLEX regime:

$$\bar{m} - \bar{p}^* - \varepsilon(t) = \alpha_0 - \alpha_1(\bar{i}^* + \dot{\varepsilon}(t)) + \alpha_2\bar{y}; \quad t \geq T \tag{31}$$

Equation (31) is a linear differential equation in $\varepsilon(t)$. In the absence of speculative bubbles, the solution to (31) is

$$\varepsilon(t) = \bar{m} - \bar{p}^* + \alpha_1\bar{i}^* - \alpha_2\bar{y} - \alpha_0; \quad t \geq T \tag{32a}$$

Since $\varepsilon(t)$ in (32a) is a constant, it will be the exchange rate in effect at the initial instant the authorities switch to a FLEX regime. Hence,

$$\varepsilon(T) = \bar{m} - \bar{p}^* + \alpha_1\bar{i}^* - \alpha_2\bar{y} - \alpha_0 \tag{32b}$$

III The Transition from a TTF Regime

In this section we will study the expected transition from a TTF regime to either a FLEX regime or TT regime. Prior to the transition, the market will set exchange rates at levels such that speculators could not anticipate making speculative profits by entering the market the instant before the transition.

As an example of what is meant by the absence of expected speculative profits, suppose that at the instant after the regime switch financial foreign exchange would be worth 700 lire per dollar if the switch were made to the FLEX regime or 800 lire per dollar if the switch were made to the TT regime. The absence of expected speculative profits requires

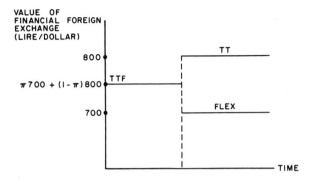

Figure 14.2

$x(T_-) = \pi 700 + (1 - \pi)800$

where T_- represents the instant before the transition and π is the subjective probability attached by speculators to an actual transition to the FLEX regime. The above expression states that financial foreign exchange just prior to the transition will be a weighted average of the price of foreign exchange under a FLEX regime at time T and the price of foreign financial exchange under the TT regime at time T.

Figure 14.2 depicts one possible time path for the value of financial foreign exchange given our example. As seen in figure 14.2, $x(T_-)$ is set at a level between 700 and 800 lire per dollar such that speculators do not expect to profit from the transition. Of course, once the actual regime switch is announced and instituted on date T, the value of financial foreign exchange will make a discrete jump. If the switch is made to a TT regime, then financial foreign exchange will jump up in value, if the switch is made to a FLEX regime, financial foreign exchange will jump down in value. Consequently, when agents are uncertain about the nature of the post-transition regime, the requirement that there be no expected speculative profits just prior to a regime switch leads to a discrete jump in exchange rates on the transition date.

The condition that speculators bid away expected profits prior to the transition date is the terminal condition which allows us to set C_1 and C_2 in our solution to the TTF regime. In particular, suppose that at time $t < T$ agents attach probability $\pi(t)$ to the event "transition to FLEX" and probability $(1 - \pi(t))$ to the event "transition to TT." The terminal conditions for the TTF model at time t are

$$x^{\text{TTF}}(T) = \pi(t)\varepsilon(T) + (1 - \pi(t))x^{\text{TT}}(T) \tag{33}$$

$$s^{\text{TTF}}(T) = \pi(t)\varepsilon(T) + (1 - \pi(t))\bar{s}^{\text{TT}} \tag{34}$$

where x^{TTF} refers to the financial exchange rate of the TTF regime, etc. The variable $\pi(t)$ is the subjective probability attached by agents at time t to an actual transition to the FLEX regime at time T.

Given the terminal conditions (33) and (34), we can now solve for the undetermined coefficients C_1 and C_2 in equations (22) and (23) and obtain complete exchange-rate solutions for the TTF regime prior to the transition.

Combining (22), (23) with (33), (34), we know that at time $t < T$, the absence of expected speculative profits at time T implies

$$\pi(t)\varepsilon(T) + (1 - \pi(t))x^{\text{TT}}(T) = C_1(t)e^{\gamma T} + \frac{(1 - \alpha_1\gamma)}{\alpha_1(\mu - \gamma)}e^{\mu T} + \hat{x}^{\text{TTF}} \tag{35}$$

$$\pi(t)\varepsilon(T) + (1 - \pi(t))\bar{s}^{\text{TT}} = C_2(t)e^{\mu T} + \hat{s}^{\text{TTF}} \tag{36}$$

Solving these equations for $C_1(t)$ and $C_2(t)$ yields

$$C_1(t) = \left\{ \pi(t)\varepsilon(T) + (1 - \pi(t))x^{\text{TT}}(T) - \hat{x}^{\text{TTF}} \right.$$

$$\left. - \frac{(1 - \alpha_1\gamma)}{\alpha_1(\mu - \gamma)}[\pi(t)\varepsilon(T) + (1 - \pi(t))\bar{s}^{\text{TT}} - \hat{s}^{\text{TTF}}] \right\}e^{-\gamma T} \tag{37}$$

$$C_2(t) = \{\pi(t)\varepsilon(T) + (1 - \pi(t))\bar{s}^{\text{TT}} - \hat{s}^{\text{TTF}}\}e^{-\mu T} \tag{38}$$

Because our terminal conditions depend on $\pi(t)$, which may vary with time, we have allowed C_1 and C_2 also to depend on time. Note that at any time t, $\pi(t)$ refers to an event in the future. Agents set $\pi(t)$ at time t at the level which optimally uses all information available. Hence, agents except $\pi(t)$ to be constant and thus expect $C_1(t)$ and $C_2(t)$ to be constant. However, as new information becomes available, agents may alter π through time.

It is through these possibly time-varying subjective probabilities that we capture another aspect of the confusion in Italy's foreign-exchange market in early 1974. Typical exchange-rate models yield exchange-rate solutions where exchange rates change only when standard market fundamentals such as money supplies, foreign interest rates, foreign prices, output or wealth change, or when agents perceive such market fundamentals will change. Our model stresses a previously neglected source of volatility in exchange rates—changes in agents' subjective probabilities about the nature of an exchange-rate regime transition. Our model recognizes the inherently temporary nature of the Italian TTF regime in 1973–74, and it demonstrates that changes in agents' subjective probabilities of a transition to either a TT or a FLEX regime may account for erratic exchange-rate movements under the TTF regime not otherwise explained by standard market fundamentals.[7]

During early 1974, the political situation in Italy was quite unsettled, and agents must have been forming beliefs about exchange-rate regime transition based on relatively little information. This situation is exactly the one where rumors and announcements can have dramatic effects on agents' probabilities over a transition. According to the complete solution of our TTF model for $t < T$, dramatic movements in $\pi(t)$ may cause dramatic movements in $C_1(t)$ and $C_2(t)$, and dramatic movements in $C_1(t)$ and $C_2(t)$, according to equations (22) and (23), may cause dramatic movements in exchange rates.

Thus, through movements in $\pi(t)$ our model is consistent with the erratic fluctuations in Italian exchange rates just prior to the transition, and because of uncertainty about which regime would be adopted after the transition, our model is consistent with the discrete jump observed in the Italian financial rate at the time of the transition.

In our discussion of the Italian case, we have focussed on just one source of uncertainty—the nature of the transition. We have assumed that agents know with certainty both the transition date, T, and the government's current-account target, Z.

It turns out that our results are completely unaffected by assuming that agents do not know the transition date. Neither the state variables nor the terminal conditions (33) and (34) depend on the transition date T; consequently the exchange-rate solutions for the TTF regime will not depend on the transition date T.[8]

However, our solutions will be altered if agents did not know for certain the government's current-account target, Z. Therefore, a more complete treatment of uncertainty in the Italian case would require more general terminal conditions than (33) and (34).

These new terminal conditions could be developed by recognizing that at any date $t < T$, agents must have formed some subjective probability density function $f(Z|t)$ over the random variable Z. The more general terminal conditions would then be obtained by integrating the terminal conditions (33) and (34) over Z. The undetermined coefficients $C_1(t)$ and $C_2(t)$, of our TTF solutions could then be calculated by applying these more general terminal conditions.

We have not pursued this extension because it merely reinforces our point that volatility in agents' subjective probabilities about the nature of a transition can result in exchange-rate volatility prior to the transition.

IV Concluding Remarks

The two-tier exchange markets of the early 1970s represented an intermediate step in the transition from fixed but adjustable exchange rates to flexible but managed exchange rates. Our attempt to explain the behavior of the lira during the operation of the Italian two-tier exchange market in 1973–74 has led us to develop a model of exchange-rate regimes in transition.

On the assumption that the market will set exchange rates so as to eliminate expected speculative profits at the time of transition, our model indicates that expectations of a transition, combined with uncertainty about the nature of the posttransition regime, can cause a jump in exchange rates at the moment of transition as well as volatile exchange-rate movements prior to the transition. The model suggests that the *perceived temporariness* of an exchange-rate regime should be treated as a market fundamental. Moreover, agents' time-varying subjective probabilities about the nature of a transition can account for exchange-rate movements not explained by standard market fundamentals.

Notes

The research reported here was accomplished in part while the authors were at the Board of Governors. The Research is also part of the National Bureau of Economic Research program in International Studies. It was partially supported by the NBER Summer Institute in International Studies and by National Science Foundation Grant SES-7926807. Any opinions expressed are those of the authors and not those of the National Bureau of Economic Research or the Board of Governors of the Federal Reserve System or other members of its staff. The authors wish to thank Julie Withers for research assistance.

1. The rates did converge in the French case, however. France made a transition from a two-tier float to a uniform flexible exchange rate on 21 March 1974, and the spread between the financial and commercial franc narrowed steadily as the 21 March transition date approached. When the French authorities instituted the two-tier float, they stated that the arrangement would last for six months and then the franc would be pegged. However, we have been unable to uncover any government announcement that indicated an intent to return to a *unified* fixed exchange rate as opposed to a two-tier exchange market with a fixed commercial franc. It remains unclear why the French and Italian experiences differed in this regard.

2. We have used two logarithmic approximations in obtaining equation (2). First, for small $hi(t)$, $ln(1 + hi(t)) \approx hi(t)$. Second, $S(t)i^*(t)/X(t) \approx i^*(t) + i^*(t)[s(t) - x(t)]$. We have used $i^*(t)[s(t) - x(t)] \approx \gamma[s(t) - x(t)] \times \chi i^*(t) + \gamma\chi$, where γ is the mean value of $i^*(t)$ and χ is the mean value $[s(t) - x(t)]$. For simplicity, we have chosen the normalization $\chi = 0$.

3. We recognize that during the 1973 to early 1974 period, the domestic component of the Italian money supply was growing rapidly. Incorporation into the model of a constant money growth path or a nonconstant but exogenous money growth path would be no more difficult than assuming the domestic component is fixed at $\bar{d}$; however, it would not substantially change any of our results. Incorporation of a nonconstant, endogenous money growth path would be much more difficult to handle, since it would require solving a higher order linear differential equation system.

4. See the evidence cited in section IIA on the Italian net foreign asset position during this period.

5. The solutions for the general case where $(1 - \eta) \not\rightarrow 0$ are available from the authors on request. The solutions reported in the text are simpler and not substantively different from the more general solutions.

6. We realize that it is unreasonable for agents to have had precise knowledge of the government's target current-account, Z. In the next section, we will not require agents to know Z exactly prior to the transition.

7. In fact, our model of the TTF regime treats standard market fundamentals as constant (equations (4a), (9)–(13)), highlighting the role of volatile subjective probabilities about a transition in generating volatile exchange-rate movements.

8. If we had not assumed our exogenous variables to be constant prior to the transition, then the exchange-rate solutions for the TTF regime would depend on the time of transition, and T would be an additional source of uncertainty.

References

Argy, V. and M. Porter, "The Forward Exchange Market and the Effects of Domestic and External Disturbances Under Alternative Exchange-Rate Systems," *IMF Staff Papers*, November 1972, 19:503–529.

Barattieri, V. and G. Ragazzi, "An analysis of the Two-Tier Foreign Exchange Market," *Banca Nazionale del Lavoro Quarterly Review*, December 1971, 24:354–372.

Branson, W.H. and H. Halttunen, "Asset-Market Determination of Exchange Rates: Initial Empirical and Policy Results," in J. P. Martin and A. Smith, eds, *Trade and Payments Adjustment under Flexible Exchange Rates*, London: Macmillan, 1979.

Decaluwe, B. and A. Steinherr, "A Portfolio Balance Model for a Two-Tier Exchange Market," *Economica*, May 1976, 43:111–125.

Fleming, J. M., "Dual Exchange Rates for Current and Capital Transactions: A Theoretical Examination," in his *Essays in International Economics*, London: Allen and Unwin, 1971.

Fleming, J. M., "Dual Exchange Markets and Other Remedies for Disruptive Capital Flows," *IMF Staff Papers*, March 1974, 21:1–27.

Flood, R., 'Exchange-Rate Expectations in Dual Exchange Markets', *J. Int. Econ.*, February 1978, 8:65–77.

Flood, R. and N. Marion, "The Transmission of Disturbances Under Alternative Exchange-Rate Regimes with Optimal Indexing," *Q. J. Econ.*, February 1982, 97:43–66.

Lanyi, A., "Separate Exchange Markets for Capital and Current Transactions," *IMF Staff Papers*, November 1975, 22:714–749.

Marion, N., "Insulation Properties of Two-Tier Exchange Rates in a Portfolio-Balance Model," *Economica*, February 1981, 48:61–70.

Rushing, P., "The Two-Tier Exchange-Rate System," *New England Econ. Rev.*, March–April 1974, pp. 13–22.

International Monetary Fund Desk Sheets.

15

The Linkage between Speculative Attack and Target Zone Models of Exchange Rates: Some Extended Results

Robert P. Flood and Peter M. Garber

I Introduction

Agents in the public or private sectors often follow one systematic set of actions when their environment lies within some prescribed boundaries and switch to another set when the boundaries are reached. Their recognition of the presence of the boundaries ties the two sets of actions together and determines the prices of assets whose payoffs are keyed to the actions. In a stochastic setting, several authors have recently investigated such an environment with a set of tools that readily generate closed-form solutions for exchange rates controlled in a target zone.[1]

In this chapter, we will generalize the target zone exchange rate model formalized by Krugman (1988, 1989) and extended by Froot and Obstfeld (1989).[2] The main contribution of these pages consists of linking the recent developments in the theory of target zones to the mirror-image theory of speculative attacks on asset price fixing regimes.[3] We also use aspects of this linkage to provide an intuitive interpretation of the "smooth pasting" condition, generally invoked as a boundary condition in this literature. We will study a system in which the exchange rate zones are either permanent or temporary.[4]

We aim to unify these two literatures by showing that the solution concepts in both are identical. Indeed, we can show that in the target zone context "speculative attacks" on reserves must generally occur as a result of a policy to defend the zone.[5] Thus, Krugman's recent (1987, 1988) work is actually a step toward coming full circle on his (1979) contribution on balance-of-payments crises.

We present our results in the four remaining sections. In section II, we present the exchange rate target zone problem in a standard exchange rate model. The target zone literature developed thus far has considered only the case of infinitesimal interventions. We extend the analysis to situations in which the policy authority may use discrete interventions. This extension provides the link between the earlier literature on discrete attacks on foreign exchange reserves and clarifies the latitude available to a policy authority while maintaining the target zone. In section III, we examine the interest rate implications of adopting a target zone in this model. Finally, in section IV, we extend the possibility of discrete interventions to Krugman's (1989) recent work on collapsing target zones.

II A Model of Target Zones

The target zone is a nonlinear compromise between fixed exchange rates and freely flexible exchange rates. In an exchange rate target zone, a country or group of countries sets explicit margins within which exchange rates will be allowed to fluctuate. While the exchange rate is within those boundaries, policy can be directed toward other goals. When the boundary is reached, the policy maker focuses resources on maintaining the boundaries. The target zone does not preclude foreign exchange interventions inside the boundaries. Indeed, the target zone studied by Krugman simply does not specify government behaviour inside the target zone boundaries. This is the point of the target zone: while the exchange rate is inside the band, policy can be directed as desired toward goals other than fixing the exchange rate.

Krugman (1988) was able to characterize the behaviour of the exchange rate within a target zone when exchange rate fundamentals are driven by regulated Brownian motion. In Krugman's case, the unregulated fundamentals follow nondrifting Brownian motion. The intervention which regulates the process is triggered by the edges of the target zone, which are symmetric about zero. Froot and Obstfeld (1989) extended Krugman's results to the case of fundamentals driven by Brownian motion with constant drift and of nonsymmetric zones.[6]

To study the behaviour of the exchange rate inside a band, Krugman and Froot and Obstfeld use a standard law of motion for a flexible price exchange model.

$$x(t) = k(t) + aE[dx(t)]/dt \qquad a > 0 \qquad (1)$$

$x(t)$ is the logarithm of the exchange rate, a can be interpreted as the Cagan interest rate semi-elasticity, and the expectation operator is conditioned on current information. Only information about the forcing variable $k(t)$ is relevant. In a standard monetary approach model, $k(t)$ is a linear combination of the logarithms of foreign and domestic money supplies, real incomes, money demand disturbances and real exchange rate movements.

$k(t)$ can be controlled by intervention of the monetary authorities. Specifically, the authorities can control $k(t)$ to ensure that

$$x^u > x > x^l \tag{2}$$

where x^u and x^l are the upper and lower bounds of the exchange rate target zone, respectively. For example, the authorities could intervene with a monetary contraction to prevent the exchange rate from exceeding x^u. Krugman and Froot and Obstfeld assume that the authorities interfere with the motion of k only when x reaches the boundaries of the target zone.[7] When the exchange rate is inside the target zone boundaries, k follows a random walk with drift that is independent of the exchange rate:[8]

$$dk = \eta dt + \sigma dz \tag{3}$$

where η and σ are constants and z is a standard Wiener process.

A Derivation of the Functional Form of the Exchange Rate Solution

We now follow Krugman and Froot and Obstfeld to develop explicitly the functional form of the exchange rate solution, $x = g(k)$. If $g(k)$ is the solution $E[dx]/dt$ can be derived by applying the Ito differential

$$dx = g'(k)\,dk + \tfrac{1}{2}g''(k)(dk)^2 \tag{4}$$

Taking the expectation of each side of equation (4), conditional on current information:

$$E[dx]/dt = g'(k)\eta + \tfrac{1}{2}g''(k)\sigma^2 \tag{5}$$

Substituting from equation (5) into equation (1), we derive

$$x = g(k) = k + a[g'(k)\eta + \tfrac{1}{2}g''(k)\sigma^2] \tag{6}$$

The general solution to (6) is

$$x = g(k) = k + a\eta + A\exp[\lambda_1 k] + B\exp[\lambda_2 k] \tag{7}$$

where $\lambda_1 = -[(\eta^2 + 2\sigma^2/a)^{1/2} + \eta]/\sigma^2$ and $\lambda_2 = [(\eta^2 + 2\sigma^2/a)^{1/2} - \eta]/\sigma^2$. The constant terms A and B are to be determined by the boundary conditions given by the upper and lower bounds on the exchange rate target zone.

To solve for A and B in equation (7), researchers have imposed the "smooth pasting condition," a requirement that $g'(k^u) = 0$ when $x^u = g(k^u)$

for some high level k^u of k at which intervention occurs. Similarly, $g'(k^l) = 0$ when $x^l = g(k^l)$ for some low value of k. These conditions provide sufficient boundary information to determine A, B, k^u and k^l; and we plot the form of the solution in figure 15.1.

In using these conditions, Krugman implicitly and Froot and Obstfeld explictly assume that such interventions are infinitesimal; they associate the attainment of x^u with the simultaneous attainment of k^u. In the generalization to discrete interventions, the events of hitting the zone limit and having an intervention will not coincide.

An Exchange Rate Solution with Discrete Intervention

Nevertheless, the functional form is invariant to the size of the intervention, since the intervention size will affect neither A nor B for a given target zone. Once the upper and lower bounds of the zone are defined, A and B are set. We have drawn figure 15.1, however, with extensions for values of k beyond the point at which the function reaches its maximum and minimum levels.

Consider a situation in which the Brownian motion process k is controlled with discrete interventions. When it is between the bounds k^u and k^l in figure 15.1, k follows the Brownian motion process of equation (3). When k hits the upper bound k^u, a monetary intervention throws k discontinuously back to the interior point Q, where $k^u - Q$ measures the magnitude of the contraction. At Q, the k process resumes the random motion given in (3). If k hits the lower bound k^l, a discrete monetary expansion throws it back to the point q.[9] These discontinuous shifts in k can be interpreted as interventions that occur to maintain the exchange rate x within its prescribed bounds.

The pair (k^u, Q) is constrained only by a requirement that the exchange rate be continuous at the time of the intervention. Hence, for the function g associated with a given zone, any pair (k^u, Q) such that $g(k^u) = g(Q)$ defines an intervention capable of maintaining the upper bound on the zone. A similar condition constrains the pair (k^l, q).[10,11]

What is the intutition behind the continuity of the exchange rate in the presence of discrete foreseen interventions? This is a natural requirement familiar from the speculative attack literature. If there were an exchange rate discontinuity in response to an anticipated intervention, that is, if $g(k^u)$ did not equal $g(Q)$, there would be a foreseeable profit at an infinite rate. Speculators would act to remove this opportunity.

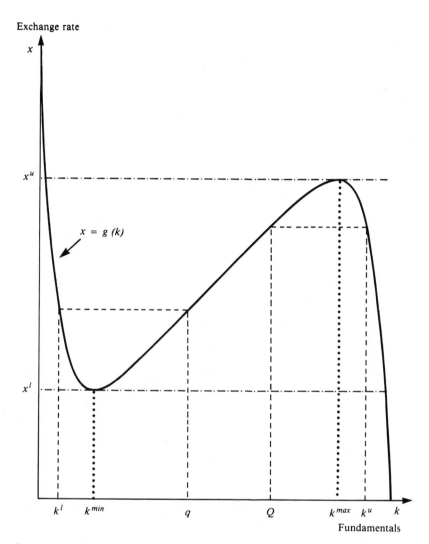

Figure 15.1
An exchange-rate target zone

Recall that in the speculative attack literature by Krugman (1979) or Flood and Garber (1984a, b), domestic credit is usually rigged with upward drift. An attack on a fixed exchange rate system is timed to prevent a discontinuity in exchange rates. In the context of equation (1), exchange rate continuity in the face of an expected attack on the fixed exchange rate regime requires the exchange rate to be the same in the instant just before and the instant just after the attack The expected rate of change of the exchange rate would jump discontinuously from zero to a positive number, driving down money demand and accommodating the sudden loss of re- serves at the moment of the attack.

The logic for a discrete intervention in a target zone is identical. When the distance from k to k^u is infinitesimally small, there will be a shift from k^u to Q with probability one. Now evaluate equation (1) at k^u and at Q, respectively, and subtract the two results. Since the exchange rate is the same at the two k values, the results is $k^u - Q = -a\{E[dx(k^u)]/dt - E[dx(Q)]/dt\}$. The discontinuous shift in k (i.e. the re- duction in foreign reserves or bondholdings of the policy authority) ex- actly offsets the discontinuous shift in expectations.

In this target zone problem, the shift in the expected depreciation adjusts to the arbitrary magnitude of the intervention. In the speculative attack literature, the magnitude of the intervention adjusts to the specified shift in expected depreciation rates rigged into the problem. Otherwise, the prob- lems are identical.

Indeed, there is even a run on reserves in the target zone model. When k reaches a high enough level, speculators will approach the policy author- ity to covert domestic currency for reserves, thereby forcing an interven- tion of the prescribed magnitude. This "run" serves to preserve the target zone, however.

Because of the many possible quadruples (k^u, Q, q, k^l) consistent with a given zone, simply announcing a specific target zone is not a fully specified policy. A particular target zone can be supported by an infinity of interven- tion strategies. This incompleteness is not an indictment of the target zone policy, which was designed as part of a broader policy. Indeed, the incom- pleteness allows policy to be directed toward other goals with only occa- sional attention to the maintenance of the target zone.

The Smooth Pasting Condition

To see that the smooth pasting condition is valid in the cases studied by Krugman and Froot and Obstfeld, again consider figure 15.1. Define k^{max}

and k^{min} as the solutions of $g'(k) = 0$. Note that $k^u > k^{max} > Q$ and $k^l < k^{min} < q$. Now let k^u and Q converge toward each other, always assuring that $g(k^u) = g(Q)$. Also, let k^l and q similarly converge. Q and k^u will then converge to k^{max} and q and k^l will converge to k^{min}. Therefore, for infinitesimal interventions, $g'(k^u) = g'(k^l) = 0$, the smooth pasting condition. Whatever the intervention policy may be, the smooth pasting condition is applicable for determining the values of A and B in solving for the exchange rate function g. Nevertheless, the assumption that the target zone boundary points are attained simultaneously with the k boundary points is true only in the case of infinitesimal intervention.

III The Volatility of Exchange Rates and Interest Rates

Krugman (1988) showed that the target zone will stabilize the exchange rate. This result occurs because the function $g(k)$ is everywhere less responsive than the functional relation between x and k in a pure floating regime. Yet, the possibility of achieving some exchange rate stability without actually having to intervene has the disturbing appearance of a free lunch. Where does the volatility go?

To address this question, let us assume that the domestic interest rate i equals the constant foreign interest rate plus the expected rate of depreciation. Since the foreign interest rate is constant, the only volatility in the domestic interest rate stems from movements in $E[dx]$. Then

$$V(i(k), t) = a^{-2}V(g(k) - k, t) \tag{8}$$

where $V(y, t)$ is the variance of the variable y over an interval of length t.

For both fixed and floating exchange rates $V(i(k), t) = 0$ in the constant drift cases that we have considered. Since $g(k) - k$ is not constant for the target zone, however, $V(i(k), t) > 0$ in the target zone. Thus the exchange rate becomes less volatile at the expense of raising interest rate volatility

IV A Collapsing Target Zone with Discrete Intervention

Krugman (1989) split the variable k into two components, m and v, where m is the logarithm of the money supply and v is an exogenous variable encompassing other factors that drive the exchange rate. The money supply $m = ln(D + R)$, where D is the level of domestic credit and R is foreign exchange reserves. The variable m and its components remain constant until an intervention occurs, taking the form of a change in R. If R falls to zero, no further intervention will occur. We assume that v is a Brownian motion process with no drift, that is, $dv = \sigma dz$.

Exchange rate

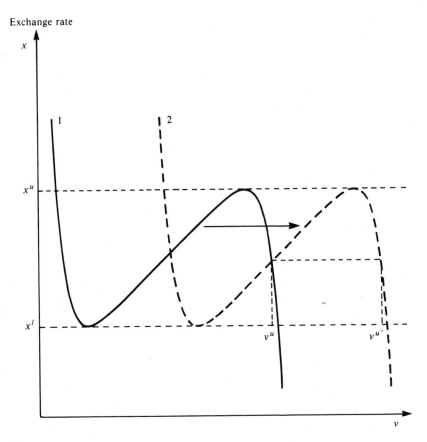

Figure 15.2
Discrete intervention with declining reserves

If x rises toward its maximum level x^u because v rises, an intervention involving a sale of reserves and a decline in the money supply will occur. This decline might be infinitesimal, aimed at offsetting infinitesimal increases in v. Alternatively, the decline in the money supply may be discrete and large. Conversely, if x tended to its minimum value x^l because v was falling, the intervention would entail an increase in the money supply through a purchase of reserves.

Figure 15.2 depicts the exchange rate solution, drawn on the basis of a discrete intervention policy. For a given money supply, the curve labelled 1 represents the exchange rate as a function of v, where v is permitted to reach an upper bound v^u before an intervention aimed at maintaining the zone occurs. Thus, as v rises, the exchange rate rises and then falls before

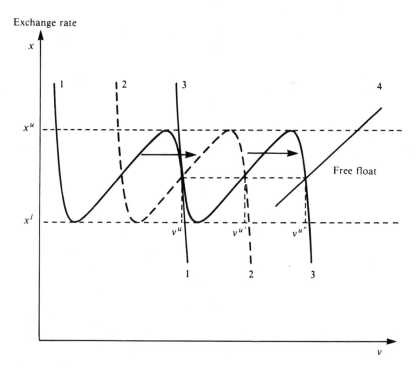

Exchange rate

Figure 15.3
Collapse with discrete intervention

the intervention occurs, as we saw earlier. The intervention in this case involves reducing reserves and the money supply discretely. Since this is a credible policy, the intervention comes as no surprise; and there is no jump in the exchange rate with the intervention. Since v is exogenous, it does not change from v^u as a result of the intervention, however. The monetary contraction has the effect of shifting the exchange rate function from the curve labeled 1 rightward to the curve labeled 2. The shift occurs by an amount which maintains exchange rate continuity when the new solution is evaluated at v^u; v then evolves freely from this starting point v^u. If it moves up to $v^{u'}$, another contractionary intervention occurs, and the process repeats.[12]

The Collapse of a Target Zone

Any lower bound on reserves, however, will be approached at some time. For example, in figure 15.3, suppose that when v reaches $v^{u'}$, reserves have declined to a level such that one more intervention of the usual size will push reserves exactly to zero, after which the authorities will expend no further reserves to maintain the zone. The intervention policy is then credible for one last time, so the exchange rate will move along the new target zone solution path indicated by curve 3. If v continues to rise to $v^{u''}$, the intervention will occur as promised, but thereafter further interventions are no longer credible. The exchange rate solution will then follow curve 4, the usual linear function of the fundamentals. Note that exchange rate continuity will be maintained at $v^{u''}$.

V Conclusions

Public and private sector agents often adopt one set of actions when some indicator is within certain bounds and switch to another set of actions when the bounds are reached. Examples of such action patterns are widespread in policymaking circles and seem to describe an important part of the policymaking process not captured by linear rules.

The purpose of the present chapter was primarily technical: to extend the literature to the possibility of finite-sized interventions in defence of a target zone. Finite interventions produce counter-intuitive policy behaviour. For example, to implement a target zone, a central bank would impose a large monetary contraction when the exchange rate is appreciating. Hence, we do not propose that such interventions be taken seriously as a description of actual policy. Nevertheless, we find that the zero-profit terminal condition required for the finite-size interventions readily provides intuition for the smooth pasting condition used to analyse infinitesimal interventions. Both problems are most easily understood by relating them to the mirror image problem of describing an anticipated speculative attack.

Notes

1. The new research, aimed at issues in exchange rate policy, has been due to Smith (1987), Krugman (1987, 1988), Smith and Smith (1990), Miller and Weller (1989), Froot and Obstfeld (1989), Svensson (1989) and Bertola and Caballero (1989). Additional work in a microeconomic setting has been carried out by Krugman (1987), Bertola (1987) and Dixit (1987, 1988). This recent work was partly stimulated by the publication of Harrison (1985), which shows how to derive closed-form solutions for a variety of problems in controlled Brownian motion. Harrison's results make it easy to implement the idea that the anticipation of "bumping into" the boundaries generates important nonlinearities that are not well modeled by linear approximations. In previous work, we have studied economic behaviour in similar situations, but we found it difficult to produce closed-form solutions. In Flood and

Garber (1980, 1983b), we studied the impact of a random future endogenous triggering of monetary reform on the current price level in the German hyperinflation. In Flood and Garber (1983a) we considered the determination of the current floating exchange rate when the regime would switch to a fixed rate system at an endogenously determined, random time.

2. The Krugman target zone is in spirit a simplified version of the target zone blueprint offered by Williamson and Miller (1987).

3. For some literature on speculative attacks, see Salant and Henderson (1978), Krugman (1979), Salant (1983), Flood and Garber (1984a, b), and Obstfeld (1984, 1986).

4. The target zone models can be integrated with models of speculative attacks either of the buying or selling varieties, if a limit is placed on the amount of reserves or bonds that the authorities are willing to buy or sell to defend the zone. Krugman (1989) has developed this result for the case of a selling attack.

5. Because of the upper and lower bounds in a target zone, these may be either buying or selling attacks as in Grilli (1986).

6. Froot and Obstfeld (1989) have also extended these results to the case of a different forcing process, the Ornstein-Uhlenbeck process, and to the case of absorbing barriers. The absorbing barriers case was studied by Flood and Garber (1983a) with closed form solutions first derived by Smith (1987).

7. Both x and k are functions of time, but we will usually suppress the time-dependence notation in the following presentation.

8. Krugman assumes a zero drift parameter. Froot and Obstfeld argue that the policy specification in Krugman is incomplete since both discrete jumps in k and infinitesimal interventions are compatible with a given target zone. They base their discussion on a similar point made in Obstfeld and Stockman's (1985) discussion of an indeterminacy in Flood and Garber (1983a). Nevertheless, they consider only the case of infinitesimal intervention. It turns out that this case implies intervention only at the boundaries of the target zone.

9. When $k^u = Q$ and $k^l = q$ and these values are the critical values of the function g, we have the case of Froot and Obstfeld: asymmetric reflecting barriers with infinitesimal interventions. When, in addition, $\eta = 0$ and $k^u = -k^l$, we have the symmetric special case of Krugman.

10. Of course, the pairs are constrained to provide exchange rate realizations within the zone. Also, Q must exceed k^l and k^u must exceed q.

11. The continuity condition requires that $g(k^u) = g(Q)$ and $g(k^l) = g(q)$. These two conditions are also sufficient to determine A and B in equation (5) as functions of the policy quadruple (k^u, Q, q, k^l). The pair (A, B) associated with a specific target zone can then be generated by an infinite number of combinations of value for the inner and outer bounds on k.

12. Alternatively, the intervention might be infinitesimal, as in Krugman. Such an intervention can be depicted in figure 15.1 by setting v^u equal to v^{max}, the argument at which the exchange rate function represented by curve 1 is flat. Repeated infinitesimal interventions then slide the solution curve continuously rightward in the zone.

References

Bertola, G. (1987), "Irreversible investment," MIT Working Paper.

Bertola, G. and R. Caballero (1989), "Target zones and realignments," Working Paper.

Dixit, A. (1987), "Intersectoral capital reallocation under price uncertainty." Mimeo, Princeton University.

——— (1988), "A simplified exposition of some results concerning regulated Brownian motion." Mimeo, Princeton University.

Flood, R. P. and P. M. Garber (1980), "An economic theory of monetary reform," *Journal of Political Economy* 88, 24–58.

——— (1983a), "A model of stochastic process switching," *Econometrica* 51, 537–52.

——— (1983b), "Process consistency and monetary reform: further evidence," *Journal of Monetary Economics* 12, 279–96.

——— (1984a), "Gold monetization and gold discipline," *Journal of Political Economy* 92, 90–107.

——— (1984b), "Collapsing exchange rate regimes: some linear examples," *Journal of International Economics* 18, 1–13.

Froot, K. A. and M. Obstfeld (1989), "Exchange rate dynamics under stochastic regime shifts: a unified approach," Working Paper.

Grilli, V. (1986), "Buying and selling attacks on fixed exchange rate systems," *Journal of International Economics* 20, 143–56.

Harrison, J. M. (1985), *Brownian Motion and Stochastic Flow Systems*, New York: John Wiley and Sons.

Krugman, P. R. (1979), "A model of balance-of-payments crises," *Journal of Money, Credit and Banking* 11, 311–25.

——— (1987), "Trigger strategies and price dynamics in equity and foreign exchange markets," NBER Working Paper No. 2459.

——— (1988), "Target zones and exchange rate dynamics," NBER Working Paper No. 2841.

——— (1989), "Target zones with limited reserves," Working Paper.

Miller, M. and P. Weller (1989), "Solving stochastic saddlepoint systems: a qualitative treatment with economic applications," CEPR Discussion Paper No. 308.

Obstfeld, M. (1984), "Balance-of-payments crises and devaluation," *Journal of Money, Credit and Banking* 16, 208–17.

——— (1986), "Rational and self-fulfilling balance of payments crises," *American Economic Review* 76, 72–81.

Obstfeld, M. and A. G. Stockman (1985), "Exchange rate dynamics," in R. W. Jones and P. B. Kenen (eds.) *Handbook of International Economics*, Vol. 2, Amsterdam: North-Holland.

Salant, S. W. and D. W. Henderson (1978), "Market anticipations of government policies and the price of gold," *Journal of Political Economy* 86, 627−48.

Smith, G. W. (1987), "Stochastic process switching," Queen's University Working Paper.

Smith, G. W. and T. Smith (1990), "Stochastic process switching and the return to gold, 1925," *Economic Journal* 100, 164−75.

Svensson, L. (1989), "Target zones and interest rate variability," Seminar Paper No. 457, Institute for International Economic Studies, University of Stockholm.

Williamson, J. and M. Miller (1987), *Targets and Indicators: a Blueprint for the International Coordination of Economic Policy,* Washington: Institute for International Economics.

III

Policy Switching

16   A Model of Stochastic Process Switching

Robert P. Flood and Peter M. Garber

Often, a policy authority such as a central bank operates by establishing a policy rule to set the variables under its control. Such a rule is allowed to operate freely as long as certain endogenous variables of interest to the authority remain within particular bounds; however, when those endogenous variables cross their bounds, the authority switches to a new policy rule which it had prepared to meet this contingency. Since variables such as prices are determined partly by agents' beliefs about future events, agents' behavior injects the probabilities that policy switches will occur at particular future times into current price determination.

In this chapter we explore in a formal model the determination of a current exchange rate when future policy regime switches are possible. In order to do this we develop a new aspect of an otherwise standard exchange-rate model; this key component is the probability density function (p.d.f.) for the first passage through a barrier of the endogenous variable (the exchange rate) which interests the policy authority.[2] Since analytical solutions for first passage p.d.f.'s are available for only a limited number of stochastic processes, we are restricted to these processes in formulating our example. However, within this class of processes, our results are generally applicable to many different kinds of macro-economic problems.

We present our ideas in the context of a model of exchange rate determination. Our choice of a specific example is intended to add concreteness to the analysis but should not be interpreted as setting limits on the applicability of the analysis. Indeed, the structure of the problem at hand virtually duplicates the structures which would be appropriate for studying problems such as a monetary authority's possible return to an interest rate rule, the possible introduction of wage and price controls, possible tax reform, the future fixing of gold's price, or virtually any other uncertain future policy switch. In addition our set-up should be useful for studying the effects of currently nonbinding regulations. For example, an economy with a Regulation Q ceiling on some interest rates may currently be below that ceiling. However, if relevant interest rates were to reach the ceiling then some of the stochastic processes in the economy would change as a result of the now binding regulation.

In the specific example we study, when agents know that at a future time the exchange rate will be fixed at a known level, then in a rational expectations world the solution for the current exchange rate assumes a form reflecting such knowledge. If the level is known while the timing is uncertain, then, though the solution technique is analogous, the actual solution for the current exchange rate will be a more complex form. As an example of the latter case, our results are particularly applicable to studying the movements of the French and British exchange rates in the early 1920s.

In section I we set up the exchange-rate model when future fixing is possible. In section II we present the major steps necessary to produce an exchange-rate solution.

I   Determining the Current Exchange Rate When Future Fixing is Likely

That the exchange rate between two currencies is allowed to float freely means that governments do not intervene currently in exchange markets to set the rate. However, it is possible that under some future contingencies a government may intervene and establish a fixed rate system; this possibility will partly determine the current floating rate through its effect on expectations.

The specific example that we have in mind is that of Britain in the 1920s. The British decision to return to the gold standard at the prewar parity of $4.86/£ was announced in the Budget Speech of April 28, 1925, and effective in the exchange market the next day (Moggridge [8, p. 9]). However, as early as 1918 the Treasury and Ministry of Reconstruction appointed a Committee on Currency under Lord Cunliffe, which reported in 1919 "in our opinion it is imperative that after the war the conditions necessary to the maintenance of an effective gold standard should be restored without delay" (Moggridge [8, p. 12]). Since the dollar was fixed to gold at that time, the British government was indicating that in the future it would fix the dollar-pound exchange rate at its pre–World War I level; the timing depended on achieving purchasing power parity at the prewar exchange rate. Adopting such a policy affects the current exchange rate. Here we present a model in which this result is explicit.

In order to highlight the novel aspects of our study we adopt the simplest exchange-rate model popular in the current literature. This is the monetary model of Bilson [1], Frenkel [2], and Mussa [9]. The model consists of semi-log linear money demand functions for the countries studied, assumptions of purchasing power parity and uncovered interest parity, and an assumption that semielasticities of money demand with respect to interest rates are identical across countries.

The model is described by the following equations:

$$m(t) - p(t) = \alpha_0 + \alpha_1 y(t) - \alpha_2 i(t) + v(t), \qquad \alpha_1, \alpha_2 > 0, \tag{1}$$

$$\overset{*}{m}(t) - \overset{*}{p}(t) = \overset{*}{\alpha}_0 + \overset{*}{\alpha}_1 \overset{*}{y}(t) - \overset{*}{\alpha}_2 \overset{*}{i}(t) + \overset{*}{v}(t), \qquad \overset{*}{\alpha}_1, \overset{*}{\alpha}_2 > 0, \tag{2}$$

$$p(t) = \overset{*}{p}(t) + x(t), \tag{3}$$

$$i(t) = \overset{*}{i}(t) + E(\dot{x}(t)|I(t)). \tag{4}$$

Lowercase letters generally denote logarithms; an asterisk (*) over a variable denotes "foreign" (U.K.). $m(t)$ is the money supply, $p(t)$ is the price level, $y(t)$ is output, $i(t)$ denotes interest rate (level), $v(t)$ is a stochastic disturbance, and $x(t)$ is the exchange rate. $E(\dot{x}(t)|I(t))$ is the expected rate of change of $x(t)$ conditional on $I(t)$, where $I(t)$ is the time t information set containing the structure of the model and all variables dated t or earlier.

The left-hand side of (1) is the real domestic money supply which must equal real money demand, the right-hand side of (1). The money demand function is the basic behavioral building block of the model, and its parameters $(\alpha_0, \alpha_1, \alpha_2)$ are assumed to be structural. For simplicity we impose $\alpha_2 = \overset{*}{\alpha}_2$.[3] Equation (3) is the assumption of purchasing power parity, which is an arbitrage condition in a one-good world. Equation (4) is the condition of uncovered interest parity, which, with risk neutrality, follows from an assumption that domestic and foreign earning assets are perfect substitutes.[4] We assume that $m(t)$, $\overset{*}{m}(t)$, $y(t)$, $\overset{*}{y}(t)$, $v(t)$, and $\overset{*}{v}(t)$ are exogenous to $x(t)$.

Combine (1)–(4) to obtain

$$m(t) - \overset{*}{m}(t) - x(t) = \alpha_0 - \overset{*}{\alpha}_0 + \alpha_1 y(t) - \overset{*}{\alpha}_1 \overset{*}{y}(t) - \alpha_2 E(\dot{x}(t)|I(t))$$
$$+ v(t) - \overset{*}{v}(t), \tag{5}$$

We define $K(t) \equiv \overset{*}{\alpha}_0 - \alpha_0 + \overset{*}{\alpha}_1 \overset{*}{y}(t) - \alpha_1 y(t) - \overset{*}{m}(t) + m(t) + \overset{*}{v}(t) - v(t)$. Hence (5) may be written as

$$x(t) = K(t) + \alpha_2 E(\dot{x}(t)|I(t)). \tag{6}$$

Equation (6) is the standard sort of equation that monetary models have produced and is a structural semireduced form consistent with a wide variety of models. To address the problem of the future fixing of an exchange rate we must specify both the stochastic nature of the exogenous forcing function $K(t)$ and the nature of the policy rule whereby the monetary authority decides the time for fixing the exchange rate. With rational expectations, the decision to fix the exchange rate implies a decision to change the stochastic nature of $K(t)$. This follows from equation (6): when $x(t)$ is fixed, with rational expectations, $E(\dot{x}(t)|I(t))$ must be zero; hence $K(t)$ must be fixed. For the purposes of this example we will assume that, as long as the monetary authority does not actively fix the exchange rate, $K(t)$ is a random walk with drift, that is, $K(t)$ can be written as

$$K(t) = K(0) + \eta t + e(t) \tag{7}$$

where η is the drift rate and $e(s)$ is a Wiener process, that is, $e(s) \sim N(0, \sigma^2 s)$. While many alternative specifications for $K(t)$ are possible, we select a process reflecting a U.K. government goal to return to a prewar parity, fixed exchange rate. Control over the process governing $K(t)$ can be exercised by control of $m^*(t)$ so that $K(t)$ will drift toward the desired fixed exchange rate.

In order to specify a policy rule for when the exchange rate will be fixed, we suppose that the monetary authorities in the foreign country will fix the exchange rate when purchasing power parity holds at some particular $\bar{x}$, that is, when $\bar{x} = p(t) - \overset{*}{p}(t)$. Since by assumption the domestic price level minus the foreign price level is too low for this to obtain currently, we expect $p(t) - \overset{*}{p}(t) = x(t)$ to make a first passage through $\bar{x}$ from below at the time of the exchange rate's fixing.[5] At any time t, the moment T in the future at which this first passage occurs is random with a p.d.f. $f(T - t|\bar{x}, K(t))$, which is conditional on $\bar{x}$ and $K(t)$.

Taking expectations of both sides of (6) conditional on the information set $I(t)$ available to agents at time t, we find

$$E(x(t)|I(t)) = E(K(t)|I(t)) + \alpha_2 E(\dot{x}(t)|I(t)). \tag{8}$$

This is a differential equation in the expected exchange rate conditional on $I(t)$; rearranging, we have

$$E(\dot{x}(t)|I(t)) = -\frac{1}{\alpha_2} E(K(t)|I(t)) + \frac{1}{\alpha_2} E(x(t)|I(t)). \tag{9}$$

Given a terminal condition we can solve (9) for the expected (and therefore actual) exchange rate at time t.

Suppose first that purchasing power parity at the exchange rate $\bar{x}$ occurs at time T; then the exchange rate is fixed at $\bar{x}$ for $\tau > T$ and $x(T) = \bar{x}$. Since $x(T)$ is fixed at T, its expected rate of change conditional on fixing at T is zero at T and hence, from (6), $\bar{x} = K(T)$. The $x(\tau)$ makes a first passage through $\bar{x}$ at T is equivalent to $K(\tau)$ making a first passage through $\bar{x}$ at T.[6]

Conditional on first passage at T, the current exchange rate (and its current expectation) can be determined as

$$E(x(t)|I(t), T) = \bar{x} \exp\left\{\frac{t - T}{\alpha_2}\right\}$$

$$+ \frac{1}{\alpha_2} \exp\left\{\frac{t}{\alpha_2}\right\} \int_t^T E(K(\tau)|I(t), T) \exp\left\{-\frac{\tau}{\alpha_2}\right\} d\tau$$

where $E(K(\tau)|I(t), T)$ indicates the expected path of $K(\tau)$, $t \leq \tau \leq T$, give $I(t)$ and $K(T) = \bar{x}$ for the first time. The unconditional exchange rate is then the integral of (10) weighted by the first passage p.d.f.:

$$x(t) = \int_t^\infty E(x(t)|I(t), T) f(T - t|\bar{x}, K(t)) dT. \tag{11}$$

Equation (11) is of the form of a typical solution to a rational expectations model. The problem which remains is to express the right-hand side of (11) in terms of a finite number of in principle observable variables. In linear rational expectations models this final step is often accomplished by conjecturing that the solution is a linear function of the state variables and then requiring the unknown coefficients in the conjectured solution to obey the model at hand. This is the method of undetermined coefficients recently popularized by Lucas [7]. Our problem, however, is substantially more difficult because the as yet unknown nonlinear form of the solution must be constructed from first principles. The solution we seek will be a non-structural relation whose parameters will depend on current and expected future government behavior.

II   The Forms of $f(T - t| \bar{x}, K(t))$ and $E(K(\tau)| I(t), T)$

To obtain the reduced form exchange-rate equation we proceed in two steps, first finding the density function $f(T - t|\bar{x}, K(t))$, and second finding $E(K(\tau)|I(t), T)$.[7] Analytical expressions for these two magnitudes may then be substituted into (10) and (11), yielding the reduced form we seek.

The solution for the first passage p.d.f. of a Wiener process with drift is available in standard texts (see Karlin and Taylor, [6, p. 363]). The p.d.f.

over the first passage of $K(\tau)$ through $\bar{x}$, given $K(t) < \bar{x}$ is

$$f(T - t|\bar{x}, K(t)) = \frac{\bar{x} - K(t)}{\sigma\sqrt{2\pi}(T - t)^{3/2}} \exp\left\{-\frac{1}{2}\frac{[\bar{x} - K(t) - \eta(T - t)]^2}{\sigma^2(T - t)}\right\}.$$

$$(12)$$

The derivation of $E(K(\tau)|I(t), T)$ is an exercise in stochastic processes. We first write out the explicit formula for this expectation and explain its components. Then we explain the determination of $E(K(\tau)|I(t), T)$.

Recall that $E(K(\tau)|I(t), T)$, $t \leq \tau \leq T$, is the expectation of $K(\tau)$ given $K(t)$ and given that at time T, $K(\underset{*}{T}) = \bar{x}$ for the first time. Let $T_1 \equiv T - t$, $\tau_1 \equiv \tau - t$, $Z \equiv \bar{x} - K(t)$, and $\overset{*}{Z} \equiv (Z/\sigma)\sqrt{((1 - \tau_1/T_1)/\tau_1)}$. Then the explicit formula for the conditional expectation is

$$E(K(\tau)|I(t), T) = \bar{x} - C_2/C_1 \tag{13}$$

where

$$C_2 \equiv \left[1 - \frac{\tau_1}{T_1}\right]\left\{\left[\left(1 - \frac{\tau_1}{T_1}\right)Z^2 + \sigma^2\tau_1\right]\Phi(\overset{*}{Z}) + \sigma Z\tau_1^{1/2}\left(1 - \frac{\tau_1}{T_1}\right)^{1/2}\right.$$

$$\times\ \phi(-\overset{*}{Z}) - \exp\left\{\left(1 - \frac{\tau_1}{T_1}\right)\frac{2\eta Z}{\sigma^2}\right\}\left[\left[\left(1 - \frac{\tau_1}{T_1}\right)Z^2 + \sigma^2\tau_1\right]\right.$$

$$\left.\left.\times\ \Phi(-\overset{*}{Z}) - \sigma Z\tau_1^{1/2}\left(1 - \frac{\tau_1}{T_1}\right)^{1/2}\phi(-\overset{*}{Z})\right]\right\} \tag{14}$$

and

$$C_1 \equiv \left[\sigma\tau_1^{1/2}\left(1 - \frac{\tau_1}{T_1}\right)^{1/2}\phi(\overset{*}{Z}) + Z\left(1 - \frac{\tau_1}{T_1}\right)\Phi(\overset{*}{Z})\right]$$

$$-\ \exp\left\{\left(1 - \frac{\tau_1}{T_1}\right)\frac{2\eta Z}{\sigma^2}\right\}$$

$$\times\ \left[\sigma\tau_1^{1/2}\left(1 - \frac{\tau_1}{T_1}\right)^{1/2}\phi(\overset{*}{Z}) - Z\left(1 - \frac{\tau_1}{T_1}\right)\Phi(-\overset{*}{Z})\right]. \tag{15}$$

In these formulas, $\phi(x) \equiv 1/\sqrt{2\pi}\exp\{-x^2/2\}$ and $\Phi(x) \equiv \int_{-\infty}^{x}\phi(y)\,dy$.

To derive formulas (13)–(15), we must find the conditional density of $K(\tau)$, given T, the time of first passage through $\bar{x}$, where $T > \tau > t$. Call this density function $h(K(\tau)|T)$. Then we need only multiply by $K(\tau)$ and integrate to determine the first moment. We can find this density function by first determining the joint density over $(K(\tau), T)$. For simplicity, let us

$$F(T|K(\tau)) = \frac{\bar{x} - K(\tau)}{\sigma\sqrt{2\pi}(T-\tau)^{3/2}} \exp\left\{-\frac{(\bar{x} - K(\tau) - \eta(T-\tau))^2}{2\sigma(T-\tau)}\right\}$$

$$= \frac{\bar{x} - K(\tau)}{\sigma(T-\tau)^{3/2}} \phi\left(\frac{\bar{x} - K(\tau) - \eta(T-\tau)}{\sigma\sqrt{T-\tau}}\right). \tag{24}$$

Finally,

$$g(K(\tau), T) = H(K(\tau))F(T|K(\tau)) \tag{25}$$

so $h(K(\tau)|T)$ is simply (25) divided by $f(T)$ and evaluated at a particular value of T.

To derive C_1 and C_2, we performed a change of variable in (25) to produce a p.d.f. over $u(\tau) \equiv \bar{x} - K(\tau)$. In the formula (13), C_1 is simply the inverse of the normalizing constant for this p.d.f. while C_2 is the unnormalized first moment of this p.d.f. Hence, $C_2/C_1 = E(u(\tau)|u(t), T)$ so that $E(K(\tau)|K(t), T) = \bar{x} - C_2/C_1$. Deriving the actual formulas (14)–(15) requires the cranking out of some horrendous integrals, which we relegate to the Appendix.

III Application

We have derived analytical expressions for $f(T - t|\bar{x}, K(t))$ and $E(K(\tau)|I(t), T)$. The next step is to substitute these results into (10) and (11) and continue the integration. However, the remaining double integral has proven intractable to us, so we simply report our solution for $x(t)$ as

$$x(t) = \int_t^\infty \left[\bar{x}\exp\left\{\frac{t-T}{\alpha_2}\right\} + \frac{1}{\alpha_2}\exp\left\{\frac{t}{\alpha_2}\right\}\int_t^T (\bar{x} - C_2(\tau)/C_1(\tau))\right.$$

$$\left. \times \exp\left\{-\frac{\tau}{\alpha_2}\right\}d\tau\right]\cdot f(T - t|\bar{x}, K(t))\, dT. \tag{26}$$

The nonlinear exchange-rate equation resulting from the above can in principle be estimated using a combination of nonlinear techniques and numerical integration subroutines.

The unfortunate feature of our result is that it implies that it is not appropriate to estimate an exchange-rate equation by typical linear methods during a period when agents are anticipating stochastic process switching. For example, Frenkel and Clements [3] estimate a US/UK exchange-rate equation over the period February 1921 to May 1925, which encompasses a large part of the period when agents may have been anticipating process switching. To allow for the endogeneity of interest rate differentials Frenkel and Clements used a linear two-stage least squares procedure. According to our results the first stage of their procedures should have been specified in accord with our nonlinear exchange-rate equation.

It seems to us that the problem encountered in Frenkel and Clements may be quite widespread. Indeed, whenever policy makers deliberate, they inject into agents' forecasting problems an element of stochastic process switching. However, it is atypical of such deliberations that they result in a stochastic process switching problem as clearly defined as the British return to prewar parity.

Appendix

Derivation of C_1 and C_2

1. Solution to Integral in Text Equation (23)
Notice that the integral part of the right-hand side of equation (23) (text) is a convolution. It is

$$\int_0^\tau w(t_1) Z(\tau - t_1)\, dt_1 \tag{A1}$$

where

$$w(t_1) \equiv \frac{\bar{r}}{\sigma t_1^{3/2}} \phi\left(\frac{\bar{r} - \eta t_1}{\sigma t_1^{1/2}}\right) \tag{A2}$$

and

$$Z(\tau - t_1) \equiv \frac{(\tau - t_1)^{-1/2}}{\sigma} \phi\left(\frac{K(\tau) - \bar{x} - \eta(\tau - t_1)}{\sigma(\tau - t_1)^{1/2}}\right). \tag{A3}$$

It is a property of the Laplace transform, $L[\ ]$, that $L[w(\tau)] \cdot L[Z(\tau)] = L[\int_0^\tau w(t_1) Z(\tau - t_1)\, dt_1]$ (see Simmons, [10, pp. 407–408]). For our problem

$$w(\tau) = \frac{\bar{x}}{\sigma \tau^{3/2}} \phi\left(\frac{\bar{x} - \eta \tau}{\sigma \tau^{1/2}}\right) \tag{A4}$$

and

$$Z(\tau) = \frac{\tau^{-1/2}}{\sigma} \phi\left(\frac{K(\tau) - \bar{x} - \eta \tau}{\sigma \tau^{1/2}}\right). \tag{A5}$$

This property is useful to us because the problem of integrating (A1) may be stated equivalently as finding $L^{-1}[L[w(\tau)]L[Z(\tau)]]$, where $L^{-1}[\ ]$ is the inverse Laplace transform. We will develop our analytic expression for (A1) using Laplace transforms.

Our first step is to note

$$L[w(\tau)] = \exp\left\{\frac{\bar{x}}{\sigma^2}(\eta - [\eta^2 + 2\sigma^2 p]^{1/2})\right\},\tag{A6}$$

where p is the parameter of the Laplace transform (see Karlin and Taylor [6, p. 362]). Further, since

$$L[\tau w(\tau)] = -\partial L[w(\tau)]/\partial p\tag{A7}$$

(see Simmons [10, p. 402]) we have

$$L[\tau w(\tau)] = \bar{x}[\eta^2 + 2\sigma^2 p]^{-1/2}\exp\left\{\frac{\bar{x}}{\sigma^2}(\eta - [\eta^2 + 2\sigma^2 p]^{1/2})\right\}.\tag{A8}$$

(A8) will prove useful in finding $L[Z(\tau)]$, to which we now turn.

Recall that $\phi(x) = \phi(-x)$ so

$$Z(\tau) = \frac{\tau^{-1/2}}{\sigma}\phi\left(\frac{\bar{x} - K(\tau) + \eta\tau}{\sigma\tau^{1/2}}\right),\tag{A9}$$

which is the form of $Z(\tau)$ we will work with subsequently. Comparing (A9) with (A4) we note that $Z(\tau)$ is $w(\tau)\tau/\bar{x}$ with the constant in the numerator of $\phi(\ )$ in $Z(\tau)$ being $\bar{x} - K(\tau)$ instead of $\bar{x}$ in the corresponding term in $w(\tau)$ and $-\eta$ in $w(\tau)$ being η in $Z(\tau)$. It follows that we obtain the Laplace transform of $Z(\tau)$ by dividing (A8) by $\bar{x}$ and then replacing $\bar{x}$ in that result with $\bar{x} - K(\tau)$ and replacing $-\eta$ with η (i.e., change the sign of η). We obtain

$$L[Z(\tau)] = [\eta^2 + 2\sigma^2 p]^{-1/2}\exp\left\{\frac{\bar{x} - K(\tau)}{\sigma^2}(-\eta - [\eta^2 + 2\sigma^2 p]^{1/2})\right\}.\tag{A10}$$

From (A6) and (A10) obtain

$$L[w(\tau)]L[Z(\tau)]$$

$$= [\eta^2 + 2\sigma^2 p]^{-1/2}\exp\left\{\frac{-2\bar{x} + K(\tau)}{\sigma^2}[\eta^2 + 2\sigma^2 p]^{1/2} + \frac{\eta K(\tau)}{\sigma^2}\right\}.\tag{A11}$$

(A11) is the Laplace transform of the integral we seek so we are now looking for the inverse Laplace transform of (A11).

Notice that if in (A10) we replae $K(\tau)$ with $K(\tau) - \bar{x}$ then we will produce the expression on the right hand side of (A11) multiplied by the factor $\exp\{-2\eta\bar{x}/\sigma^2\}$. Thus, we create the function

$$q(\tau) \equiv \exp\{2\eta\bar{x}/\sigma^2\}\,\frac{\tau^{-1/2}}{\sigma^2}\,\phi\left(\frac{K(\tau) - 2\bar{x} - \eta\tau}{\sigma\tau^{1/2}}\right) \tag{A12}$$

and by construction we know $L[q(\tau)] = L[w(\tau)]L[Z(\tau)]$. Hence

$$q(\tau) = L^{-1}[L[w(\tau)]L[Z(\tau)]] = \int_0^\tau w(t_1)Z(\tau - t_1)\,dt_1,$$

so $q(\tau)$ is the analytic integral we have sought.

We were attempting to solve the integral in text equation (23) so that we could obtain an analytic expression for $g(K(\tau), T)$. To obtain this expression we now use (A12) in text equation (23) and we use equations (23) and (24) in (25) yielding

$$g(K(\tau), T) = C\frac{\tau^{-1/2}}{\sigma}\left[\phi\left(\frac{K(\tau) - \eta\tau}{\sigma\tau^{1/2}}\right) - \exp\left\{\frac{2\eta\bar{x}}{\sigma^2}\right\}\phi\left(\frac{K(\tau) - 2\bar{x} - \eta\tau}{\sigma\tau^{1/2}}\right)\right]$$

$$\times\left[(\frac{\bar{x} - K(\tau)}{\sigma(T - \tau)^{3/2}}\right]\phi\left(\frac{\bar{x} - K(\tau) - \eta(T - \tau)}{\sigma(T - \tau)^{1/2}}\right)\right]. \tag{A13}$$

C is a normalizing constant. Given T, the first time $K(\ )$ passes through $\bar{x}$, (A13) is also the form of the conditional p.d.f. $h(K(\tau)|T)$, except that the normalizing constant $h(K(\tau)|T)$ will be different because of the need to divide (A13) through by the value of the marginal p.d.f. over T.

2. *Deriving the Normalizing Constant for* $h(K(\tau)|T)$
Defining $u \equiv \bar{x} - K(\tau)$, substituting u into (A13) and dropping all the constant coefficients, the function (A13) can be written as

$$u\left[\phi\left(\frac{\bar{x} - u - \eta\tau}{\sigma\sqrt{\tau}}\right) - \exp\left\{\frac{2\eta\bar{x}}{\sigma^2}\right\}\phi\left(\frac{-u - \bar{x} - \eta\tau}{\sigma\sqrt{\tau}}\right)\right]$$

$$\times\,\phi\left(\frac{u - \eta(T - \tau)}{\sigma\sqrt{T - \tau}}\right) \equiv u\Omega(u). \tag{A14}$$

Except for a nomalizing constant, (7) is a p.d.f. over u, We are interested in the moments

$$C_n = \int_0^\infty u^n\Omega(u)\,du. \tag{A15}$$

Here $1/C_1$ is the normalizing constant and C_2/C_1 is the conditional mean of u. The conditional mean of $K(\tau) = \bar{x} - C_2/C_1$.

By elementary algebra,

$$\phi\left(\frac{u-a}{\sigma\tau^{1/2}}\right)\phi\left(\frac{u-b}{\sigma(\tau-T)^{1/2}}\right)$$

$$= (2\pi)^{-1}\exp\left[-\frac{\{u-(1-\tau/T)a-(\tau/T)b\}^2}{2\sigma^2\tau(1-\tau/T)} - \frac{a^2+b^2}{2\sigma^2T}\right]. \tag{A16}$$

Using this result with $a = \pm\bar{x} - \eta\tau$ and $b = \eta(T - \tau)$ and remembering that $\phi(r) = \phi(-r)$, we find that C_n is proportional by a factor independent of n to

$$C_n' = \int_0^\infty u^n\left[\phi\left(\frac{u-(1-\tau/T)\bar{x}}{\sigma[\tau(1-\tau/T)]^{1/2}}\right)\right.$$

$$\left.- \exp\left\{\frac{(1-\tau/T)2\eta\bar{x}}{\sigma^2}\right\}\phi\left(\frac{u+(1-\tau/T)\bar{x}}{\sigma[\tau(1-\tau/T)]^{1/2}}\right)\right]du. \tag{A17}$$

To find the normalizing constant we set $n = 1$ in (A17) and we perform a change of variables using the following definitions

$$\varepsilon_1 \equiv \frac{u-(1-\tau/T)\bar{x}}{\sigma[\tau(1-\tau/T)]^{1/2}}, \tag{A18}$$

$$\varepsilon_2 \equiv \frac{u+(1-\tau/T)\bar{x}}{\sigma[\tau(1-\tau/T)]^{1/2}}. \tag{A19}$$

We have

$$C_1' = \int_{-x^*}^\infty [(1-\tau/T)\bar{x} + \varepsilon_1\sigma[\tau(1-\tau/T)]^{1/2}]\sigma[\tau(1-\tau/T)]^{1/2}\phi(\varepsilon_1)d\varepsilon_1$$

$$- \exp\left\{\frac{(1-\tau/T)2\eta\bar{x}}{\sigma^2}\right\}$$

$$\times \int_{x^*}^\infty [-(1-\tau/T)\bar{x} + \varepsilon_2\sigma[\tau(1-\tau/T)]^{1/2}]\sigma[\tau(1-\tau/T)]^{1/2}$$

$$\cdot\phi(\varepsilon_2)d\varepsilon_2 \tag{A20}$$

where

$$x^* \equiv \frac{\bar{x}(1-\tau/T)^{1/2}}{\sigma\tau^{1/2}}.$$

Recall that $\phi(w) = (2\pi)^{-1/2}\exp\{-1/2w^2\}$ and define $\Phi(w) \equiv \int_{-\infty}^{w} \phi(y)\,dy$ so $\Phi(w) + \Phi(-w) = 1$. (A20) reduces to

$$C_1' = \sigma\tau^{1/2}(1 - \tau/T)^{3/2}\Phi(x^*) + (2\pi)^{-1/2}\sigma^2\tau(1 - \tau/T)\exp\{-1/2x^{*2}\}$$

$$- \exp\left\{\frac{(1 - \tau/T)2\eta\bar{x}}{\sigma^2}\right\}[-\sigma\bar{x}\tau^{1/2}(1 - \tau/T)^{3/2}\Phi(-x^*)$$

$$+ (2\pi)^{-1/2}\sigma^2\tau(1 - \tau/T)\exp\{-1/2x^{*2}\}]. \tag{A21}$$

3. Deriving the C_2' Integral

Now consider

$$C_2' = \int_{-x^*}^{\infty}[(1 - \tau/T)\bar{x} + \varepsilon_1\sigma[\tau(1 - \tau/T)]^{1/2}]^2\sigma[\tau(1 - \tau/T)]^{1/2}\phi(\varepsilon_1)\,d\varepsilon_1$$

$$- \exp\left\{\frac{(1 - \tau/T)2\eta\bar{x}}{\sigma^2}\right\}\int_{x^*}^{\infty}[-(1 - \tau/T)\bar{x} + \varepsilon_2\sigma[\tau(1 - \tau/T)]^{1/2}]^2$$

$$\times \sigma[\tau(1 - \tau/T)]^{1/2}\phi(\varepsilon_2)\,d\varepsilon_2 \tag{A22}$$

which results from (A17) with $n = 2$ and ε_1, ε_2 and x^* defined as before.

The right-hand side of (A22) is now broken into two integrals and we will evaluate these in turn.

3a. First Integral

The first integral in (A22) is

$$\sigma[\tau(1 - \tau/T)]^{1/2}\int_{-x^*}^{\infty}[(1 - \tau/T)^2\bar{x}^2 + 2\sigma\bar{x}\tau^{1/2}(1 - \tau/T)^{3/2}\varepsilon_1$$

$$+ \sigma^2\tau(1 - \tau/T)\varepsilon_1^2](2\pi)^{-1/2}\exp\{-1/2\varepsilon_1^2\}\,d\varepsilon_1 \tag{A23}$$

where we have substituted $\phi(\varepsilon_1)$'s functional form and expanded the quadratic from the first part of (A22). The term in square brackets under the integral in (A23) is a sum of three elements and we will treat these in turn.

$$\int_{-x^*}^{\infty}\bar{x}^2(1 - \tau/T)^2(2\pi)^{-1/2}\exp\{-1/2\varepsilon_1^2\}\,d\varepsilon_1 = (1 - \tau/T)^2\bar{x}^2\Phi(x^*); \tag{A24}$$

$$\int_{-x^*}^{\infty}2\sigma\bar{x}\tau^{1/2}(1 - \tau/T)^{3/2}(2\pi)^{-1/2}\varepsilon_1\exp\{-1/2\varepsilon_1^2\}\,d\varepsilon_1$$

$$= 2\sigma\bar{x}\tau^{1/2}(1 - \tau/T)^{3/2}\phi(-x^*). \tag{A25}$$

The third term is

$$\int_{-x^*}^{\infty} \sigma^2 \tau (1 - \tau/T) \varepsilon_1^2 (2\pi)^{-1/2} \exp\{-1/2\varepsilon_1^2\} \, d\varepsilon_1 \tag{A26}$$

and we must integrate this by parts. Set $dF = (2\pi)^{-1/2} \varepsilon_1 \exp\{-1/2\varepsilon_1^2\} \, d\varepsilon_1$ and set $H = \varepsilon_1$. We know $\int H \, dF = HF - \int F \, dH$. Hence

$$\int H \, dF = -[(2\pi)^{-1/2} \varepsilon_1 \exp\{-1/2\varepsilon_1^2\}]_{-x^*}^{\infty}$$

$$- \int_{-x^*}^{\infty} - (2\pi)^{-1/2} \exp\{-1/2\varepsilon_1^2\} \, d\varepsilon_1 \quad \text{or}$$

$$\int H \, dF = -x^* \phi(-x^*) + \Phi(x^*).$$

Since $\int H \, dF$ is (A25) up to a constant we find that (A26) is

$$\sigma^2 \tau (1 - \tau/T) [\Phi(x^*) - x^* \phi(-x^*)]. \tag{A27}$$

Summarizing, the first integral on the right hand side of (A22), which is (A23), is

$$\sigma[\tau(1 - \tau/T)]^{1/2} [(1 - \tau/T)^2 \bar{x}^2 \Phi(x^*) + 2\sigma \bar{x} \tau^{1/2} (1 - \tau/T)^{3/2} \phi(-x^*)$$

$$+ \sigma^2 \tau (1 - \tau/T) [\Phi(x^*) - x^* \phi(x^*)]]. \tag{A28}$$

When we substitute $x^* = [\bar{x}(1 - \tau/T)^{1/2} \tau^{-1/2}]/\sigma$ for the x^* coefficient in the last term of (A28) we obtain

$$\sigma \tau^{1/2} (1 - \tau/T)^{3/2} [\{(1 - \tau/T)\bar{x}^2 + \sigma^2 \tau\} \Phi(x^*)$$

$$+ \sigma \bar{x} \tau^{1/2} (1 - \tau/T)^{1/2} \phi(-x^*)], \tag{A29}$$

and this is our expression for (A23).

3b. Second Integral
The second integral in (A22) is

$$-\exp\{(1 - \tau/T) 2\eta \bar{x} \sigma^{-2}\} \sigma \tau^{1/2} (1 - \tau/T)^{1/2}$$

$$\times \int_{x^*}^{\infty} [(1 - \tau/T)^2 \bar{x}^2 - 2\bar{x}(1 - \tau/T)\sigma \tau^{1/2} \varepsilon_2 + \sigma^2 \tau (1 - \tau/T)\varepsilon_2^2] \phi(\varepsilon_2) \, d\varepsilon_2. \tag{A30}$$

Substituting in (A30) the results in (A24), (A25), and (A28), the second integral equals

$$-\exp\{(1 - \tau/T)2\eta\bar{x}\sigma^{-2}\}\sigma\tau^{1/2}(1 - \tau/T)^{1/2}$$

$$\times [(1 - \tau/T)^2\bar{x}^2\Phi(-x^*) - 2\sigma\bar{x}\tau^{1/2}(1 - \tau/T)^{3/2}\phi(-x^*)$$

$$+ \sigma^2\tau(1 - \tau/T)(\Phi(-x^*) + x^*\phi(-x^*))].\tag{A31}$$

Terms in (A31) may be rearranged to give

$$-\exp\{(1 - \tau/T)2\eta\bar{x}\sigma^{-2}\}\sigma\tau^{1/2}(1 - \tau/T)^{1/2}$$

$$\times [(1 - \tau/T)^2\bar{x}^2\Phi(-x^*) - \bar{x}\sigma\tau^{1/2}(1 - \tau/T)^{3/2}\phi(-x^*)$$

$$+ \sigma^2\tau(1 - \tau/T)\Phi(-x^*)].\tag{A32}$$

Combining (A32) and (A29) we find

$$C_2' = \sigma\tau^{1/2}(1 - \tau/T)^{3/2}\{[(1 - \tau/T)\bar{x}^2 + \sigma^2\tau]\Phi(x^*)$$

$$+ \bar{x}\tau^{1/2}(1 - \tau/T)^{1/2}\sigma\phi(-x^*) - \exp\{(1 - \tau/T)2\eta\bar{x}\sigma^{-2}\}$$

$$\times [(1 - \tau/T)\bar{x}^2\Phi(-x^*) + \sigma^2\tau\Phi(-x^*) - \sigma\bar{x}\tau^{1/2}(1 - \tau/T)^{1/2}\phi(-x^*)]\}.$$

4. Alterations Needed to Produce the Form Reported in the Text

Since we are interested only in the ratio C_2'/C_1' we can remove all coefficients common to the terms in C_1' and C_2'. Since $\sigma\tau^{1/2}(1 - \tau/T)^{1/2}$ is common to both C_1' and C_2' it is not included in the values which we report for C_1 and C_2 in the text.

Notice also that the text uses for notation τ_1, T_1, Z, and Z^* in place of τ, T, $\bar{x}$, and x^*, respectively, which we have used in the appendix. Recall that for simplicity we assumed that the time at which this forecast is made is time zero for the derivations in the appendix. The time for which the forecast is made is called τ in the appendix. In the text the time at which the forecast is made is called t; the time for which the forecast is made is called τ. Hence the variable $\tau_1 \equiv \tau - t$, in the text notation, is substituted for τ, in the notation of the appendix. Similarly, $T_1 \equiv T - r$ in the text notation is substituted for T in the notation of the appendix. In the Appendix $K(0)$ is set at zero; in the text $K(t)$, the value of $K( )$ at the time at which the forecast is made, need not be zero. Hence, we subtract $K(t)$ from $\bar{x}$ to derive a barrier equivalent to $\bar{x}$ in the text. Defining $Z \equiv \bar{x} - K(t)$ we substitute Z for $\bar{x}$ in the notation of the appendix. Finally, letting $Z^* \equiv (Z/\sigma)((1 - \tau_1/T_1)/\tau_1)$, we substitute Z^* for x^*. This produces the formulas for C_2 and C_1 in the text.

Notes

1. We would like to thank Peter Kenyon, J. H. Kemperman, and two anonymous referees for their advice. This research was supported in part by NSF Grant SES-7926807. This paper represents the views of the authors and should not be interpreted as reflecting the views of the Board of Governors of the Federal Reserve System or other members of its staff. The research reported here is part of the NBER's research program in International Studies. Any opinions expressed are those of the authors and not those of the National Bureau of Economic Research.

2. Models of pricing for some types of options make use of first passage probability density functions. For example, Ingersoll [5] uses first passage p.d.f.'s in studying the prices of convertible securities.

3. By assuming $\alpha_2 = \overset{*}{\alpha}_2$ we are able to determine $x(t)$ without modeling the goods market. Alternatively we could allow $\alpha_2 \gtrless \overset{*}{\alpha}_2$, impose world goods market equilibrium, and produce an exchange-rate solution slightly different from that reported below.

4. Some empirical support for the assumption of open interest parity can be found in Hansen and Hodrick [4].

5. In our example we are treating the United States as the home country and the United Kingdom as the foreign country so $\bar{x} = \ln(\$4.86/\pounds)$.

6. The nature of the exchange-rate fixing policy precludes the existence of a multiple solution type bubble which would cause $x(t)$ to rise through $\bar{x}$. However, it does not preclude the existence of negative bubbles which would prevent $x(t)$ from passing through $\bar{x}$ from below even though $K(t)$ passes through $\bar{x}$. Therefore, for the stated equivalence to hold we must explicitly rule out the existence of multiple solutions to (9) of the speculative bubble variety. Hence the solution to (9) depends only on market fundamentals, as the formal expressions (10) and (11) for a solution explicitly indicate.

7. We are extremely grateful to J. H. Kemperman for showing us how to derive the conditional expectation of $K(\tau)$.

References

[1] Bilson, J.: "Rational Expectations and the Exchange Rate," Chapter 5 in *The Economics of Exchange Rates*, ed. by J. Frenkel and H. Johnson. Reading, Massachusetts: Addision-Wesley, 1978.

[2] Frenkel, J.: "A Monetary Approach to the Exchange Rate: Doctrinal Aspects and Empirical Evidence," Chapter 1 in *The Economics of Exchange Rates*, ed. by J. Frenkel and H. Johnson. Reading, Massachusetts: Addison-Wesley, 1978.

[3] Frenkel, J., and K. Clements: "Exchange Rates, Money and Relative Prices: The Dollar-Pound in the 1920's," *Journal of International Economics*, 10(1980), 249–262.

[4] Hansen, L., and R. Hodrick: "Forward Exchange Rates as Optimal Predictors of Future Spot Rates: An Econometric Analysis," *Journal of Political Economy*, 88(1980), 829–853.

[5] Ingersoll, J.: "A Contingent-Claims Valuation of Convertible Securities," *Journal of Financial Economics*, 4(1977), 289–322.

[6] Karlin, S., and H. Taylor: *A First Course In Stochastic Processes*, 2nd ed. New York: Academic Press, 1975.

[7] Lucas, R.: "Econometric Testing of the Natural Rate Hypothesis," in *Econometrics of Price Determination Conference*, ed. by O. Eckstein. Washington, D.C.: Board of Governors of the Federal Reserve System and S.S.R.C., 1972, pp. 50–59.

[8] Moggridge, D.: *The Return to Gold 1925*. Cambridge: Cambridge University Press, 1969.

[9] Mussa, M.: "The Exchange Rate, the Balance of Payments and Monetary and Fiscal Policy Under a Regime of Controlled Floating." Ch. 3 in *The Economics of Exchange Rates*, ed. by J. Frenkel and H. Johnson. Reading, Massahusetts: Addison-Wesley, 1978.

[10] Simmons, G.: *Differential Equations with Applications and Historical Notes*. New York: McGraw-Hill, 1972.

17   An Economic Theory of
        Monetary Reform

Robert P. Flood and
Peter M. Garber

In Cagan's (1956) classic study of seven hyperinflations the treatment of the German episode excluded the observations from August 1923 through November 1923: this was the period of maximum inflation and maximum rate of money creation. Subsequent investigators of the German case (e.g., Barro 1970; Frenkel 1977; Garber 1977; Sargent 1977; Evans 1978) have also been forced to truncate their time series prior to the end of the hyperinflation. Apparent to Cagan and the other researchers was the inability of the existing hypotheses concerning the nature of money demand to explain the final months of the German hyperinflation. Something qualitatively different from any previously studied money demand behavior happened in Germany in the final months of 1923; contrary to the predictions of standard theory, real money balances increased in the face of accelerating inflation.

Cagan advanced two hypotheses to account for this phenomenon:

The first one is that in a hyperinflation rumors of *currency reform* will encourage the belief that prices will not continue to rise rapidly for more than a certain number of months. This leads individuals to hold higher cash balances than they would ordinarily desire in view of the rate at which prices are expected to rise in the current month. As long as currency reform remains *improbable* for the near future individuals adjust their real balances according to the rate at which they expect prices to rise for some time. When they believe that the current rate at which they expect prices to rise will not last indefinitely they are less willing to incur certain costs involved in keeping their balances low. [Cagan 1956; italics ours]

Cagan's second hypothesis, that he had used the "wrong" functional form in fitting his money demand function, has been studied by Frenkel (1977), with the results apparently supporting the Cagan form.

The main purpose of the present paper is to investigate Cagan's first hypothesis, that agents expected a monetary reform toward the end of the German hyperinflation. In order to accomplish our goal we must first develop a theory of monetary reform which can confront the following fundamental questions: (1) Why might agents have expected a monetary reform? (2) How could agents have formed expectations of the timing of monetary reform?

In order to address these questions we define a monetary reform to be a change in the class of stochastic processes governing the supply of money to the private sector.[1] A reform may be effected by means of the introduction of a new medium of exchange, with the new currency circulating simultaneously with the old and an exchange rate arising between the two currencies. However, the introduction of a new currency is neither a necessary nor a sufficient condition to indicate that a reform has taken place because the essential aspect of a monetary reform involves the class of processes by which money is supplied to the public rather than the color or name of the currency.

The crucial barrier to our understanding the aberrations at the end of the hyperinflation is the problem of the formation of expectations of reform. In our model, agents believe that a monetary reform must take place whenever a class of processes by which money is supplied to the private sector becomes "inconsistent" with the private sector's money demand behavior. When such an "inconsistency" arises, that object which was previously used as money ceases to perform the standard functions of money. The "inconsistency" triggers the expectation of the demise of the old money supply process. Equivalently, the "inconsistency" induces the expectation of certain reform of the money supply process.

We may connect this condition of reform to the standard enumeration of the essential properties of money, for example, portability, durability, and divisibility (Jevons 1880, pp. 31–38). To this list we introduce *process consistency*, an essential characteristic of anything which pretends to serve as money. Our condition for a belief in monetary reform involves a situation in which something that previously had been serving as money no longer possesses this basic property and consequently ceases to function as money.

The remaining sections of this paper develop a theory of monetary reform with the concept of process consistency as its centerpiece. In section I we provide a general version of the theory. In section II we apply the theory to a particular class of money supply processes, consistent with the technique used by Cagan in interpolating the money supply data for the end of the German hyperinflation. We provide the empirical implementation of the theory for the German case in section III. We close with some concluding remarks and our technical and data appendices.

I   A Model of Monetary Reform

The major element of our model is a simple representation of the money market. Following Cagan, we began with

$$m_t^d - p_t = \gamma + \alpha(_t p_{t+1}^x - _t p_t^x) + v_t, \qquad \alpha < 0 \quad \text{(money demand)}, \qquad (1)$$

$$m_t^s = \overline{m}_t^s \quad \text{(exogenous money supply)}, \tag{2}$$

$$m_t^d = m_t^s \quad \text{(money market equilibrium)}. \tag{3}$$

In (1)–(3), m_t^d, m_t^s, and p_t are the natural logarithms of nominal money demand, nominal money supply, and the price level, respectively. The right-hand subscript on each of these terms indicates that they are values prevailing at time t. The terms $_t p_t^x$ and $_t p_{t+1}^x$ are the expectations formed at the time t for prices at time t and time $t + 1$, respectively. We assume that v_t is a random disturbance term with finite variance, σ_r^2, and $E(v_t|I_{t-1}) = 0$, where E is the mathematical expectation operator. I_{t-1} is an information set containing the realizations of all economic variables through time $t - 1$, as well as the structure of money demand. Our assumption concerning the process generating the v's is an expositional simplification. All of our later results hold for any stationary process generating the v's.

Following Muth (1961), we assume that expectations are formed rationally, implying that expected prices are the mathematical expectations of prices conditional on all available information used in conjunction with the given model. We assume that costless information is available only with a one-period lag, while current information is infinitely costly.[2] Thus,

$$_t p_{t+1}^x = E(p_{t+1}|I_{t-1})$$
$$_t p_t^x = E(p_t|I_{t-1}). \tag{4}$$

The above specification is familiar from the current literature which combines rational expectations with Cagan's model of hyperinflation; and we can convert it easily to analyze behavior in a situation of possible monetary reform.

In a world where monetary reform is a possibility, we construct two conditional money demands whose probability-weighted sum represents actual (unconditional) money demand at any point in time. These are:

$$(m_t - p_t)^d = \begin{cases} \gamma + \alpha[E(p_{t+1}|I_{t-1}, NR) - E(p_t|I_{t-1}, NR)] + v_t, \\ \text{conditional on no reform class of money} \\ \text{supply processes, } NR. \\ \\ \gamma + \alpha[E(p_{t+1}|I_{t-1}, R) - E(p_t|I_{t-1}, R)] + v_t, \\ \text{conditional on reform class of money} \\ \text{supply processes, } R. \end{cases} \tag{5}$$

Based on the information set I_{t-1} and assuming that monetary reform has not occurred already, the first and second branches of money demand in (5) are conditional on the money supply's being generated by a process in the no reform class (NR) and by a process in the reform class (R), respectively, over the forecasting horizon. Because we assume that the forecasting horizon of money demand stretches only one period into the future, the first branch of money demand excludes the possibility of reform only in the coming period $(t, t + 1)$, but not at any later date.

To obtain actual money demand we must take the probability-weighted sum of the two conditional money demands. This yields

$$(m_t - p_t)^d = \gamma + \alpha\{[1 - q_t|I_{t-1})][E(p_{t+1}|I_{t-1}, NR)$$

$$- E(p_t|I_{t-1}, NR)] + (q_t|I_{t-1})[E[p_{t+1}|I_{t-1}, R)$$

$$- E(p_t|I_{t-1}, R)]\} + v_t, \tag{6}$$

where $(q_t|I_{t-1})$ is the subjective probability of monetary reform at time t given information in I_{t-1}.

Note that the unconditional expected rate of inflation is

$$E(p_{t+1}|I_{t-1}) - E(p_t|I_{t-1}) = [1 - (q_t|I_{t-1})][E(p_{t+1}|I_{t-1}, NR)$$

$$- E(p_t|I_{t-1}, NR)] + (q_t|I_{t-1})[E(p_{t+1}|I_{t-1}, R)$$

$$- E(p_t|I_{t-1}, R)]. \tag{7}$$

Hence, a rising expected rate of inflation conditional on NR can be consistent with a rising demand for real balances, if $(q_t|I_{t-1})$ is rising and the expected rate of inflation conditional on R is sufficiently less than the expected rate of inflation conditional on NR. This simple result models Cagan's explanation of the anomalously rising level of real balances associated with the end of the German hyperinflation.

So far we have developed only a formal statement of Cagan's hypothesis. The interesting problem is to provide an operational theory of $(q_t|I_{t-1})$ and to apply that theory to the data from the German episode.

The Probability of Reform

In this section we derive a theory of the probability of reform by developing and integrating two strands of thought: our concept of process consistency, and our presumption that agents believe that money may be supplied according to a reformed process at some uncertain future time. We knit the two strands together by assuming that agents' beliefs about the reform of a particular class of money supply processes depend upon their assessment of the probability that the unreformed class of money supply processes is process consistent. Furthermore, we provide an example of an "amorphous political mechanism" under which agents' beliefs about monetary reform become rational expectations.

As our first step toward a useful definition of *process consistency*, we use the equilibrium condition in the money market to solve for the expected price level at time t. Money market equilibrium is

$$m_t - p_t = \gamma + \alpha[E(p_{t+1}|I_{t-1}) - E(p_t|I_{t-1})] + v_t. \tag{8}$$

Applying the operator $E(\ |I_{t-1})$ to both sides of (8) and rearranging, we obtain

$$(1 - \Psi L)E(p_{t+1}|I_{t-1}) = -\frac{E(m_t|I_{t-1}) - \gamma}{\alpha}, \tag{9}$$

where $\Psi = (\alpha - 1)/\alpha$ and L is the backward lag operator. Equation (8) is a first-order linear difference equation whose stable solution[3] requires

$$E(p_t|I_{t-1}) = \left(\frac{\Psi^{-1}}{-\alpha}\right) \sum_{i=0}^{\infty} [E(m_{t+i}|I_{t-1}) - \gamma]\Psi^{-i}. \tag{10}$$

Equation (10) is familiar from other work which assumes rational expectations in Cagan's model (e.g., Sargent 1977).

The existence of a finite value of $E(p_t|I_{t-1})$ is essential to the working of a monetary economy. If agents found that they could not calculate a finite $E(p_t|I_{t-1})$, then they would expect that their money would be worthless in the coming period.[4] According to (10) a finite value of $E(p_t|I_{t-1})$ requires the convergence of the infinite sum on the right-hand side of (10). All other researchers who have worked with Cagan's model under rational expectations have imposed the requirement that the infinite sum in (10) be finite; but, as far as we know, they have neither tested the plausibility of this assumption nor integrated it with agents' behavior. In the present paper the convergence of the infinite sum in (10) will be of central concern. Hence we will refer to the convergence of such sums as *process consistency*. We choose this name because any money supply *process* (or class of processes) for which the infinite sum in (10) does not converge is not *consistent* with money demand behavior. Hence, a "money candidate" which does not meet the condition of *process consistency* cannot serve as money, as agents do not expect that such a candidate will allow them to command real resources.

We now reconsider (10), the solution for $E(p_t|I_{t-1})$, given the possibility of monetary reform. At first we assume that agents know at time t that monetary reform will take place at $t + T$, that is, starting at time $t + T$ money will be supplied according to the reformed process.[5] Equation (10) then becomes

$$E(p_t|I_{t-1}, R_{t+T}) = -\gamma + \left(\frac{\Psi^{-1}}{-\alpha}\right)\left\{\sum_{i=0}^{T-1} E(m_{t+i}|I_{t-1}, NR)\Psi^{-i}\right.$$

$$\left. + \sum_{i=T}^{\infty} E(m_{t+i}|I_{t-1}, R_{t+T})\Psi^{-i}\right\}, \tag{11}$$

where R_{t+T} is the condition of reform's occurring at $t + T$ and where we adopt the convention

$$\sum_{i=0}^{-1} E(m_{t+i}|I_{t-1}, NR)\Psi^{-i} = 0.$$

In our model, however, agents never know with certainty when reform will take place.[6] Indeed, even when reform does occur agents require some time to learn about the event. Thus, our agents must account for a myriad of possible times for reform; and we can divide these reform times into two categories. The first category is conditional on reform having already occurred, and we denote agents' subjective probability of this condition by $[1 - \lambda(t)]$. The other category is conditional on reform occurring during the coming period or during some future period, and agents attach a probability of $\lambda(t)$ to this condition. Under the latter condition agents must account for all of the possible future dates at which reform may happen. Therefore we can specialize (10) to

$$E(p_t|I_{t-1}) = -\gamma + [1 - \lambda(t)]\left(\frac{\Psi^{-1}}{-\alpha}\right)\sum_{i=0}^{\infty} E(m_{t+i}|I_{t-1}, R_{t-})\Psi^{-i}$$

$$+ \lambda(t)\left(\frac{\Psi^{-1}}{-\alpha}\right)\sum_{T=0}^{\infty}\left\{\sum_{i=0}^{T-1} E(m_{t+i}|I_{t-1}, NR)\Psi^{-i}\right.$$

$$\left. + \sum_{i=T}^{\infty} E(m_{t+i}|I_{t-1}, R_{t+T})\Psi^{-i}\right\}(q_{t+T}|I_{t-1}), \tag{12}$$

where $(q_{t+T}|I_{t-1})$ is the subjective probability of monetary reform occurring at time $t + T$ given I_{t-1}. $E(m_{t+i}|I_{t-1}, R_{t-})$ is expected money at time $t + i$ given I_{t-1} and conditional on the occurrence of reform prior to time t. Equation (12) is a detailed version of (10), and we will assume that it fulfills the condition of process consistency.[7] Zellner (1971) provides a technique useful for determining $\lambda(t)$, which technique we describe in our appendix E. In essence, agents determine $\lambda(t)$ by measuring how well the R versus NR classes of money supply processes explain the data. The better the NR class of processes explains the data, the closer is $\lambda(t)$ to unity.

The nature of the time series data on money during the final months of the German hyperinflation is such that agents must have found implausible the notion that monetary reform had already occurred. Hence, in our investigation we will assume that $[1 - \lambda(t)]$ is so small for the final months of the hyperinflation that we can safely ignore it; and we focus our attention only on the second group of terms in (12).

The foregoing discussion demonstrates that the only type of money supply process which provides a useful money is one which is process consistent. This property of money supply processes suggests that agents' confidence in a particular class of processes may be measured by the agents' subjective probability that the class provides a money which is process consistent.

We wish to integrate this relationship between process consistency and agents' confidence in a class of money supply processes with Cagan's hypothesis about agents' expectation of monetary reform. Therefore, we make the behavioral assumption that agents' subjective probability of monetary reform taking place at time t, $(q_t|I_{t-1})$, is a monotonically increasing function of those agents' subjective probability that the NR class of processes is not process consistent. This suggests that a nation also can measure agents' confidence in its money, supplied in accord with a particular class of processes, by the agents' subjective probability of this class's process consistency.

We have not supplied a political mechanism which precipitates monetary reform. Thus we present our notion of how agents form their beliefs about reform as an assumption rather than as a rational expectation derived from a political model. However, we may expect a nation to be sensitive to its money customers' confidence in its money and to reform a class of money supply processes for which this confidence is lacking.[8]

As a concrete example of a political mechanism in which agents' beliefs are rational expectations, we can assume that there is a variable ρ_t, $0 < \rho_t < 1$, such that if the subjective probability that the NR class of processes is process consistent falls below ρ_t, the money supply process will be reformed with certainty. We assume that ρ_t is unknown to the agents in the economy and that the agents have a diffuse prior p.d.f. over ρ_t. Since ρ_t is unknown and has a uniform subjective density function, the probability of reform at time t, $(q_t|I_{t-1})$, is

$$\int_{S(t|I_{t-1})}^{1} d\rho_t = 1 - S(t|I_{t-1}), \tag{13}$$

where $S(t|I_{t-1})$ is the subjective probability that the NR class of processes is process consistent. Alternatively, $S(t|I_{t-1})$ is the probability that

$$\left(\frac{\Psi^{-1}}{\alpha}\right) \sum_{i=0}^{\infty} (m_{t+i}|NR)\Psi^{-i}$$

is finite.[9]

We chose this example because of the analytic simplicity of the resulting probability of monetary reform. If we choose a more complex reform mechanism, then agents' expectations of the probability of reform will become correspondingly more complex.

Relating the Theory to the Evidence

We wish to relate our theoretical concepts to the episode which we will study in the remainder of the paper. If, with probability 1, a money supply process is not process consistent, then agents find it impossible to quote finite prices in terms of the government-supplied money. This will drive the government entirely out of the money supply business, with barter and private and imported money taking the place of domestic government money. In the German case, government money was supplanted to some extent by other media of exchange. However, government money never fell entirely out of use, which would necessarily occur if the government-supplied money failed the process-consistency test and agents did not expect future monetary reform.

In a slightly less dramatic situation, which more closely resembles the German data, agents do not believe that the government will allow itself ever to go out of the money supply business. The rationale behind their belief stems from their comprehension of the real value of the government's right to print money. If the government were to provide a money which was totally rejected by the private sector, so that imported money would take its place, then the real value of the government's right to print money would be lost to some foreign monetary authority. Since individuals believe that the government will *always* provide a useful money,[10] their expectations of monetary reform will depend upon their belief that the current class of money supply processes is consistent.

The conditions which we propose for the expectation of monetary reform are extreme; agents may use additional information in forming the expectation of reform. Thus, our theory concerning monetary reform may understate the subjective probability of reform. The magnitude of the bias is an empirical issue which we do not know how to resolve on a theoretical level. We can evaluate our measure of the expectation of reform only by the accuracy of its predictions for a particular historic episode.

II   An Explicit Money Supply Process

Cagan's discussion of the money supply's time series properties at the end of the German hyperinflation motivates an explicit example of a money supply process for which $(q_t|I_{t-1})$ will diverge from zero. Cagan discusses (p. 101) the various interpolation methods that he used in matching the dates for which money and prices were reported. About the methods used on the 1923 data, Cagan says, "... interpolations for 1923 were linear between the logarithms of the quantity of bank notes up to June and were linear between the second logarithms thereafter."

In our empirical section we will make extensive use of the results obtained for the following example in computing a time series for $[1 - (q_t|I_{t-1})]$. A stochastic money supply process that is consistent with Cagan's interpolations for the end of the hyperinflation is[11]

$$m_t = m_{t-1} \exp\{\beta_t\} \tag{14a}$$

$$\beta_t = \theta\beta_{t-1} + \varepsilon_t; \varepsilon_t \sim N(0, \sigma^2), E(\varepsilon_i\varepsilon_j) = 0, i \neq j, \tag{14b}$$

representing a stochastic process on the growth rate of the natural logarithm of the money supply. In appendix A we show that the process-consistent parameter region for (14) is

$$-1 < \theta < 1 \tag{15a}$$

$$\frac{\sigma^2}{2(1 - \theta)^2} < \log \Psi, \tag{15b}$$

where $\Psi = (\alpha - 1)/\alpha$.

We assume that individuals know the general form of the process given by equations (14a) and (14b) but possess only subjective probability density functions for the parameters θ and σ^2. We next employ Bayesian methods in conjunction with the explicit process (14a), (14b) to derive posterior probability density functions over the parameters θ and $Z \equiv [\sigma^2/2(1 - \theta)^2]$. With the probability density function in hand, we can state explicitly the probability of being in the convergent region given by (15a) and (15b) for any point in time.

By Bayes's Theorem, the posterior density function over θ, σ^2, given previous observations on β, $\vec{\beta}$, is equal to the prior density function multiplied by the likelihood function. The maximal data information prior density function is $1/\sigma$ (see Zellner 1977). Since we have assumed that $\varepsilon_t \sim N(0, \sigma^2)$ and $E(\varepsilon_i \varepsilon_j) = 0$, $i \neq j$, we write the likelihood function as

$$L(\theta, \sigma | \vec{\beta}) \propto \frac{1}{\sigma^T} \exp\left\{ \frac{-\sum_{\tau=1}^{T} (\beta_\tau - \theta\beta_{\tau-1})^2}{2\sigma^2} \right\}.$$

Therefore, the posterior density function is

$$P(\theta, \sigma | \vec{\beta}) \propto \frac{1}{\sigma^{T+1}} \exp\left\{ \frac{-\sum_{\tau=1}^{T} (\beta_\tau - \theta\beta_{\tau-1})^2}{2\sigma^2} \right\}.$$

A transformation of variables is required to convert $P(\theta, \sigma | \vec{\beta})$ to $H(\theta, Z | \vec{\beta})$ in order to have a density function over our criterion parameters. The transformed p.d.f. over (θ, Z) is[12]

$$H(\theta, Z | \vec{\beta}) \propto \frac{1}{|1 - \theta|^T (\sqrt{2Z})^{T+2}} \exp\left\{ -\frac{1}{4Z(1 - \theta)^2} \sum_{\tau=1}^{T} (\beta_\tau - \theta\beta_{\tau-1})^2 \right\}. \tag{16}$$

The detailed steps in the transformation are performed in appendix B.[13]

Two Simplifications

To facilitate the following discussion, we wish to make some simplifying changes. First, instead of the explicit but cumbersome notation $(q_t | I_{t-1})$, which represents the subjective probability of reform's taking place at t, we will adopt the notation $q_t \equiv (q_t | I_{t-1})$. Consistent with this convention, $1 - q_t$ is the subjective probability of no reform at time t. Second, we will assume that the monotonic, decreasing function which transforms probabilities of process consistency into probabilities of reform is the simplest possible such function,

$$q_t = 1 - S(t|I_{t-1}),\qquad\qquad\qquad\qquad\qquad (17)$$

which is in accord with the mechanism we proposed previously. Thus, in the next section we will speak interchangeably of the proabability of monetary reform and the probability that the NR class of processes fails the test of process consistency.[14]

III   Empirical Implementation of the Model

We have selected the episode of the German hyperinflation for examination for three reasons: (1) The German episode lasted longer than any other hyperinflation; thus many observations exist. (2) The Statistisches Reichsamt compiled detailed and disaggregated statistics for the inflationary period, so the German data are richer and more reliable than those of other hyperinflations. (3) The German economy was the largest and most highly developed economy to pass through the hyperinflationary experience.

In the present paper our empirical goals are modest. We present results which justify the use of the double-log class of money supply processes from the last section. In addition, we present tables of the $(1 - q_t)$ estimates associated with α estimates of Cagan (1956) and Frenkel (1977). As an illustration we use these $(1 - q_t)$ estimates to alter Cagan's computation of the expected rate of inflation for the last four months of the hyperinflation and reestimate the parameters of the money demand equation in appendix F. We discuss in detail the hyperinflation data in appendix C.

The Money Supply Process

In interpolating his money data, Cagan, using Statistisches Reichsamt (1925) as a data source, employed three different methods: he used interpolations linear in levels for the data through 1922, linear in logarithms up to June 1923, and linear in the second logarithm after June 1923. To each technique there corresponds a class of money supply processes. The first technique employed interpolations in the levels of money, for example, $\overline{M}_t \equiv \delta M_{t-1/2} + (1 - \delta)M_{t+1/2}$, $0 < \delta < 1$, where M is the level of the money supply; and this method corresponds to a class of processes of the form $M_{t+1/2} = M_{t-1/2}(1 + \beta_{t+1/2})$. The second technique interpolates between the logarithms of money, for example, $\overline{m}_t \equiv \delta m_{t-1/2} + (1 - \delta)m_{t+1/2}$, and the corresponding class of processes is $M_{t+1/2} = M_{t-1/2}\exp\{\beta_{t+1/2}\}$. The third technique interpolates between the second logarithms of money, for example, $\log \bar{m}_t \equiv \delta \log m_{t-1/2} + (1 - \delta) \log m_{t+1/2}$; this method corresponds to a class of money supply processes $m_{t+1/2} = m_{t-1/2} \exp\{\beta_{t+1/2}\}$. Therefore, the unusual class of money supply processes selected as an example in section II has appeared consistently throughout the hyperinflation literature; investigators making use of Cagan's data, or of similarly transformed data, implicitly have endorsed this class.[15]

To determine agents' beliefs over the parameters in each of these classes we must have observations on the β_{t-j} at all $j = 1, 2, 3, \ldots, t$. Since, at the beginning of the learning process, we assume a diffuse prior p.d.f. over the money supply parameters, we must select a starting point reflecting such ignorance. While such a selection is arbitrary, we note that a revolution occurred in Germany in November 1918; and a revolutionary situation can obviously create extreme uncertainty about future policies. Therefore, November 1918 marks the start of our learning process both on the classes of money supply processes and also on the money supply parameters.

While Cagan lists three classes of processes which may have generated the supply of money in the hyperinflationary period, there is also an obvious fourth class which influenced the reform period. This class of processes was that which maintained a fixed exchange rate between the dollar and the mark, that is, essentially the same class of processes by which the dollar was generated. Although there are many other potential classes of money supply processes, we limit the list to four.

We wish to determine how agents decided which of the classes actually was generating the money supply. This is a problem treated formally in appendix E, where we assume that starting in 1918 individuals lacked knowledge both of the class of processes generating the money supply and of the values of the parameters which governed each particular process. We follow Zellner (1971, pp. 291–312) by assuming that in 1918 agents possessed prior probabilities $W_{C(1)}$, $W_{C(2)}$, $W_{C(3)}$, W_D over each of Cagan's three money supply process classes and over the dollar-reformed class, respectively. Since we assume that these four classes are exhaustive, $W_{C(1)} + W_{C(2)} + W_{C(3)} + W_D = 1$. Agents altered these probabilities as they received new information about the money supply; for parameters of a given class, they formed posterior density functions in the usual manner.

Presumably, in the stages of mild inflation, agents attached little weight to the double-log process class portrayed in (14). However, we concentrate our attention on the double-log class, even though Cagan's other classes also need not be process consistent. If in later stages of the inflation agents attached a high probability to the double-log class, then their subjective probability of a reform may have been quite high, presuming great weight was attached to the nonconvergent parameter values.

We have not yet attempted to implement empirically the theory described above and in appendix E. Instead, our approach is to follow Cagan in assuming that the class of processes generating the money supply beginning in the summer of 1923 was double-log with probability $\simeq 1$. Then a computation of the subjective probabilities attached to the convergent values of the double-log parameters, starting in the summer of 1923, will produce the subjective probabilities of no reform, $(1 - q_t)$, for this period.

Before investigating the validity of the double-log process, we wish to consider the problem of the number of observations that exist for this hyperinflation. As indicated above, the choice of the first observation is arbitrary; but since data on prices and some money categories are reported at decreasing time intervals during the course of the hyperinflation, the choice of any fixed-length observation interval is also arbitrary. All other researchers have used only monthly observation intervals, probably because price data are reported through 1922 at monthly intervals. From 1923 onward, data are reported at ten-day or weekly intervals. Cagan and other workers employing Cagan's data have used the weekly reports only in their interpolations; for example, money is interpolated by using the money stocks reported a few days before and a few days after the price report date. Implicit in the interpolation of 1923 money data separated by weekly intervals is an assumption that the relevant time interval for examining the money supply process is a week during 1923, while prior to 1923 the relevant interval is a month. Therefore, the use of Cagan's method is consistent with an assumption that the processes governing the inflation sped up in 1923. However, almost all of the weekly data for the most interesting part of the hyperinflation have been ignored by other researchers in the field.

One means of recovering the weekly data is to select a week as the arbitrary observation interval and to examine data only for 1923–25, thereby ignoring the events of the first two years of the hyperinflation rather than the intramonth events of the last year. We intend eventually to use only a weekly interval for 1923–25.

However, since the usual assumption is that the functioning of the monetary system continued without interruption by the hyperinflation, we wish to embed our model in the observations in such a way that the hyperinflation bridges the monetary environments that preceded and followed it. It has been customary in the literature to examine the hyperinflation disconnected from the reform era that followed it. If we begin our examination in 1923, then we will not tie the hyperinflation to the era that preceded it. We seek to link the hyperinflation to both periods without sacrificing information contained in the data, and our solution to the problem consists of using monthly and weekly data together as our observations, so that they occur at varying time periods. Thus, time intervals of one month will separate the first fifty observations through the end of 1922; after January 6, 1923, intervals of approximately one week will separate the remaining observations.[16]

In the computations presented here, past observations on money are incorporated into the posterior density function over the money supply parameters. Thus, the use of mixed monthly and weekly observations simply establishes the shape of the posterior density function over money supply parameters at the beginning of our computations of q_t in April 1923.

Since we have assumed a money supply process $m_t = m_{t-1} \exp\{\beta_t\}$ where $\beta_t = \theta\beta_{t-1} + \varepsilon_t$, we wish to determine whether the data contradict this class for the appropriate period. The constant in the equation for β_t is zero, thus avoiding a third parameter in the subjective probability density function derived in section II. A third parameter would force us to perform trivariate numerical integration in our estimation process, thereby transforming an extravagant estimation procedure into one beyond the range of our resources.

We use ordinary least squares to estimate the parameters in

$$\beta_t = \delta + \theta\beta_{t-1} + \varepsilon_t \tag{18}$$

and

$$\beta_t = \theta\beta_{t-1} + \varepsilon_t, \tag{19}$$

where β_t is the average daily growth rate of the logarithm of money between observation t and observation $t - 1$ and β_0 is based on the money supply observations in October and November 1918. Equations (18) and (19) were fitted a number of times as we added more and more observations to the sample. The interest of this sequence of regressions lies both in its portrayal of how the moments of the subjective p.d.f. on (θ, σ^2) evolved through time and in the applicability of the double-log class in the early periods of the inflation.

Tables 17.1 and 17.2 contain the results of these regressions; table 17.3 presents the dates associated with the observations. In the earlier periods,

Table 17.1

$\beta_t = \delta + \theta\beta_{t-1} + \varepsilon_t$

Observations	δ	θ	$\hat{\sigma}$	R^2	Durbin's h	Number of observations
2–20	$.7228 \times 10^{-3}$ (2.5198)	.2409 (1.0782)	$.7739 \times 10^{-3}$	.0640	−.0595	19
2–32	$.5236 \times 10^{-3}$ (2.8539)	.2718 (1.609)	$.7141 \times 10^{-3}$	.0820	−1.097	31
2–44	$.6037 \times 10^{-3}$ (3.5587)	.3101 (2.0913)	$.7157 \times 10^{-3}$	.0964	−.562	43
2–50	$.8131 \times 10^{-3}$ (.4735)	1.0372 (12.7056)	$.9258 \times 10^{-3}$	.7745	−1.857	49
2–63	$.3673 \times 10^{-3}$ (1.3067)	.8584 (12.8592)	$.1687 \times 10^{-2}$	.7338	.399	62
2–87	$.1538 \times 10^{-3}$ (1.3253)	.92076 (20.3835)	$.4468 \times 10^{-2}$	.8318	1.516	86
2–99	$.9040 \times 10^{-3}$ (1.1425)	.9018 (20.3612)	$.6655 \times 10^{-2}$	.8120	1.702	98
2–111	$.7870 \times 10^{-3}$ (1.1232)	.9051 (22.016)	$.6294 \times 10^{-2}$	.8178	1.747	110
2–135	$.6372 \times 10^{-3}$ (1.1309)	.9066 (24.6142)	$.5801 \times 10^{-2}$	.8211	1.689	134

Note: Numbers in parentheses are t-statistics, based on the assumption that the parameter is zero.

the specifications in equations (18) and (19) explain little of the variation in β_t. The R^2 does not rise to significant levels until we use fifty observations in the regression, and the last six of these observations are taken from the last half of 1922 when the growth rate of money increased dramatically. In the regressions covering earlier periods, the δ estimate in equation (18) is always significantly different from zero, while the θ estimate is not. With the constant excluded, the hypothesis that θ equals zero is always rejected at standard confidence levels.[17] However, since the R^2, computed using standard formulas, is usually negative when the constant term is excluded in the early periods, we conclude that neither of the models seems adequate for the early observations. The rise in the θ estimates as the inflation proceeds seems reasonable given the acceleration of money growth.

After the fiftieth observation, we begin to add the weekly observations, which do not seem to change significantly any of the parameter estimates in the two equations except for the σ estimate. As we continue to add the 1923 observations, the estimated coefficients in the two equations approach common values; and the assumption that $\delta = 0$ in (19) seems

Table 17.2

$\beta_t = \theta\beta_{t-1} + \varepsilon_t$

Observations	θ	$\hat{\sigma}$	R^2	Durbin's h	Number of observations
2–20	.6831 (4.337)	$.8814 \times 10^{-3}$	*	−.969	19
2–32	.6165 (4.6931)	$.7945 \times 10^{-3}$	*	−2.005	31
2–44	.7141 (6.6226)	$.8090 \times 10^{-3}$	*	−1.923	43
2–50	1.0618 (17.026)	$.9183 \times 10^{-3}$	.7734	−1.595	49
2–63	.9149 (17.876)	$.1697 \times 10^{-2}$	.7262	0.198	62
2–87	.9528 (24.7867)	$.4488 \times 10^{-2}$	.8283	1.426	86
2–99	.9284 (24.632)	$.6666 \times 10^{-2}$	.8094	1.532	98
2–111	.9282 (26.0549)	$.6301 \times 10^{-2}$	.8157	1.591	110
2–135	.9256 (28.227)	$.5807 \times 10^{-2}$	.8194	1.551	134

Note: Numbers in parentheses are t-statistics, based on the assumption that θ is zero.

*Negative R^2 computed, based on the formula $R^2 = 1 - \dfrac{\text{ESS}}{\text{TSS}}$.

Table 17.3

Dates associated with observations

Observation	Date	Observation	Date
Prereform era:		67	May 7, 1923
1	November 1918	71	June 7, 1923
3	January 1919	75	July 7, 1923
15	January 1920	79	August 7, 1923
20	June 1920	83	September 7, 1923
27	January 1921	87	October 6, 1923
39	January 1922	91	November 7, 1923
44	June 1922	Reform era:	
50	December 1922	95	December 7, 1923
51	January 6, 1923	99	January 7, 1924
55	February 7, 1923	111	April 7, 1924
59	March 7, 1923	135	October 7, 1924
63	April 7, 1923		

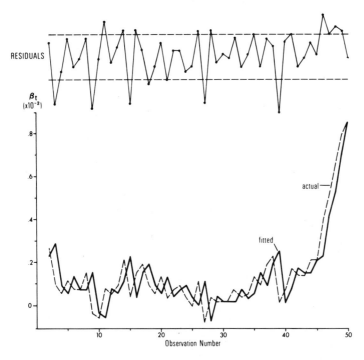

Figure 17.1
Plot of actual and fitted values; $\beta_t = \theta\beta_{t-1} + \varepsilon_t$ (November 1918–December 1922)

appropriate, since the σ and R^2 estimates are essentially identical for the two specifications. Starting in 1923, the θ estimates hover around 0.9 and never decline thereafter. The σ estimate rises dramatically with the addition of the 1923 observations and does not begin to fall until after the currency reform.

In figures 17.1, 17.2 and 17.3, we present plots of the results of the regressions for equation (19) for observations 2-50, 2-63, and 2-111. In the first plot we see that the large increase in R^2 results from the surge of activity occurring in the last half of 1922; four of the last five residuals are outliers. Apparently, the money supply process entered is explosive phase in the summer of 1922.

In figure 17.2, we have added the first twelve weekly observations in 1923 to the previous monthly observations. The 1922 observations are still outliers, and the volatility that began in 1922 seems to have continued with the addition of the weekly observations.

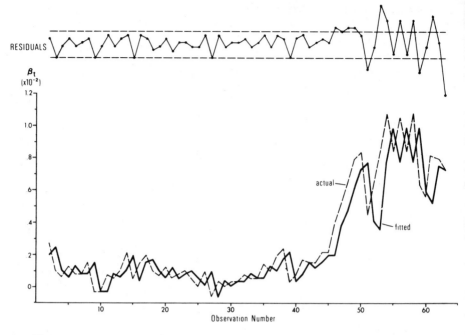

Figure 17.2
Plot of actual and fitted values; $\beta_t = \theta \beta_{t-1} + \varepsilon_t$ (November 1918–March 29, 1923)

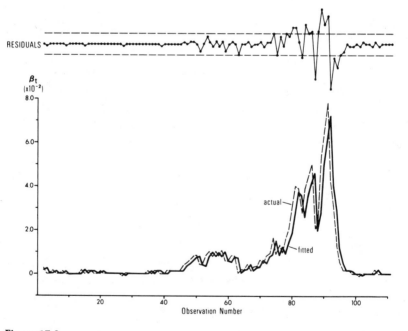

Figure 17.3
Plot of actual and fitted values; $\beta_t = \theta \beta_{t-1} + \varepsilon_t$ (November 1918–March 31, 1924)

In figure 17.3, we see the entire process of hyperinflation embedded in the earlier "normal" time and in the reform era. Observation 92 corresponds to November 15, 1923, the beginning of the currency reform. In the last three months of the hyperinflation almost all of the residuals are outliers.

A quick scan of figure 17.3 reveals that threre is heteroskedasticity in the error terms of the process estimated for the entire period. In forming posterior density functions over the parameters of the double-log class a rational agent should account for this heteroskedasticity; otherwise he would be ignoring valuable information. The possibility that processes with a number of different variances may be generating the money supply will not affect the convergence criteria established above, since only the current variance is projected into the future. However, this difficulty will affect the method by which the posterior density function over the parameters of the double-log class is calculated. Zellner (1971, pp. 98–107) provides a technique for deriving a posterior density function over all parameters of the model when heteroskedasticity is present. Using this technique, we can integrate the posterior p.d.f. over all past variance parameters to produce the relevant joint posterior p.d.f. over θ and the current variance. We may then transform variables to produce a posterior p.d.f. over (θ, Z). In appendix D we develop the posterior probability density function over the parameters of the heteroscedastic process. Since this p.d.f. has eight critical points, it is more difficult to analyze its nature than to analyze the posterior p.d.f. for the homoskedastic class; and we have not yet determined the parameter regions over which most of the weight is concentrated. Therefore, we report and analyze here only the values of $(1 - q_t)$ derived from the p.d.f. developed in section II.

We report these $(1 - q_t)$ estimates in table 17.4 and in figure 17.4. In appendix D we discuss in detail the method by which we numerically integrated the p.d.f. of section II to determine the $(1 - q_t)$. It consists simply of integrating (16) over the region (15) each time a new observation β_t is added to the sample.

Since the value of $(1 - q_t)$ depends upon log Ψ, we must select some of the values of α in equation (1) estimated by previous researchers. We have chosen the α estimates of Cagan ($\hat{\alpha} = -5.46$) and of Frenkel ($\hat{\alpha} = -3.316$) for use in computing $(1 - q_t)$.[18] The choice of Cagan's $\hat{\alpha}$ is arbitrary, since most other researchers have used essentially the same data and techniques and have produced approximately the same estimate of α. Frenkel, in using

Table 17.4
Subjective probability of no reform $(1 - q_t)$ based on Cagan's $\hat{\alpha}$ and Frenkel's $\hat{\alpha}$

Observation number	Date	Cagan's $(1 - q_t)$ $(\hat{\alpha} = -5.46)$	Frenkel's $(1 - q_t)$ $(\hat{\alpha} = -3.316)$
Prereform era:			
65	April 23, 1923	.5783	.5914
66	April 30	.5784	.5915
67	May 7	.5705	.5836
68	May 15	.5870	.6000
69	May 23	.5844	.5973
70	May 31	.5833	.5962
71	June 7	.5687	.5816
72	June 15	.5805	.5934
73	June 23	.5580	.5711
74	June 30	.5456	.5586
75	July 7	.4618	.4774
76	July 14	.5854	.6045
77	July 23	.5437	.5632
78	July 31	.5879	.6076
79	August 7	.5281	.5479
80	August 15	.4624	.4818
81	August 23	.2984	.3130
82	August 31	.1441	.1534
83	September 7	.1599	.1699
84	September 15	.4390	.4571
85	September 22	.2468	.2614
86	September 29	.1610	.1727
87	October 6	.0939	.1023
88	October 15	.7324	.7512
89	October 23	.6597	.6797
90	October 31	.3581	.3764
91	November 7	.1719	.1849
92	November 15	.0542	.0604
Reform era:			
93	November 23	.7359	.7572
94	November 30	.8219	.8405
95	December 7	.8886	.9034
96	December 15	.8979	.9120
97	December 22	.9005	.9145
98	December 31	.9015	.9154
99	January 7, 1924	.9027	.9165
100	January 15	.9039	.9176
101	January 23	.9049	.9186
102	January 31	.9060	.9195
103	February 7	.9071	.9206
104	February 15	.9081	.9215
105	February 23	.9091	.9224
106	February 29	.9101	.9233
107	March 7	.9109	.9240
108	March 15	.9121	.9252
109	March 22	.9130	.9260

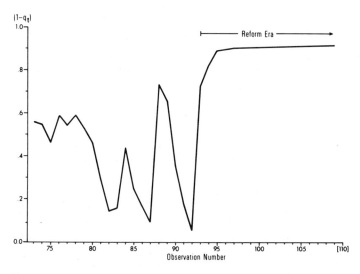

Figure 17.4
Subjective probability of no reform (Cagan's $\hat{\alpha}$)

a market indicator of the expected rate of inflation, added a new series of data to the study of the German inflation. In addition his α estimate substantially differs from Cagan's so we may determine the robustness of the $(1 - q_t)$ estimator to different values of $\hat{\alpha}$. In figure 17.4 we show only the $(1 - q_t)$ for Cagan's $\hat{\alpha}$, since those for Frenkel's $\hat{\alpha}$ yield a similar pattern.

Cagan assumes that the double-log money supply class began in July 1923, which corresponds to our observation 75. The estimates from July 7, 1923, through August 14, 1923, move erratically between 0.46 and 0.59 for both α estimates. Computations of the weights attached to the convergent parameter regions for observations prior to 75 also indicate that the weights fall consistently between 0.5 and 0.6. Thus, there seems to be little change in the weights attached to the convergent region of the double-log class through August 15, 1923.

From December 7, 1923 (observation 95) onward, the $(1 - q_t)$ estimate remains almost constant. This is the period of monetary reform, and the $(1 - q_t)$ can be interpreted as the probability that the money supply process is governed by parameters in the convergent region, given that money is supplied according to the double-log class. However, once reform has taken place we cannot retain the assumption, made in section I, that $[1 - \lambda(t)] = 0$. In fact, once reform takes place $[1 - \lambda(t)]$ will begin moving toward unity. Thus, while our interpretation of the q_t for the reform period is perfectly correct, these numbers do not give the probability of monetary reform during the reform era. This issue is treated in more depth in appendix E.

The period of greatest interest is that from August 23, 1923 (observation 81) through November 30, 1923 (observation 94), during which we observe three cycles in $(1 - q_t)$ of progressively increasing amplitude. Reference to the residuals in figure 17.3 can aid in the description of these cycles. The decreasing part of each cycle is marked by a series of residuals which are large, positive outliers as the double-log class becomes explosive. The turning point occurs in each case with an ever larger negative residual outlier, which dramatically increases the probability attached to the convergent regions in the next period. It shoud be noted that the $(1 - q_t)$ associated with the trough of each cycle (observations 81, 87, 92) is computed with data available through the previous observation (observations 80, 86, 91, respectively); that is, it is associated entirely with the series of large, positive residuals which preceded it.

In general we find the pattern of the $(1 - q_t)$'s consistent with the implications of our theory in sections I and II. Given that the double-log class generates the money supply, it is possible for the money process to be inconsistent; the greatest subjective probability that the process is inconsistent should occur when the money supply realizations are most explosive. Given that money is supplied by the double-log class, the subjective probability that the double-log class is inconsistent should permanently decline in the reform era. That the lowest value of $(1 - q_t)$, .0542 for Cagan and .0604 for Frenkel, occurs on November 15, 1923, the week of the start of the currency reform, is evidence that an expectation of currency reform based on the consistency of the money supply process was rational at the very end of the German hyperinflation.[19]

The α Estimation Problem

The next step is to compute an estimate of α. Since both $(1 - q_t)$ and $[E(p_{t+1}|I_{t-1}) - E(p_t|I_{t-1})]$ are now known functions of α, we can use a nonlinear regression routine to estimate α. Such a procedure is very costly in practice, although the expense may be reduced to some degree by assuming a more analytically tractable process on money, such as the single-log process. The benefits of such a procedure are that the entire series of data for the pre- and posthyperinflationary years can be used in estimating α.

We have not obtained an estimate of α based on our other procedures. However, the series we have generated for $(1 - q_t)$ allows us to address the interesting question of how Cagan's estimate of α would be affected by incorporating our results. Since this question is not within the central focus of our study, we report the reworked Cagan estimates in appendix F.

IV Conclusion and Extensions

The German hyperinflation has attracted an extraordinary research effort intended to unravel its unusual data. Since all previous researchers have been forced to ignore the available data from the final weeks of the hyperinflation, our purpose has been to extend standard monetary theory to a point where it is capable of encompassing these data in the context of a model equally well suited to the examination of more normal times.

The empirical section of our paper was designed to justify our use of Cagan's double-log money supply process and to provide calculations of the probability of monetary reform. The results are striking: we found that the double-log money supply process cannot be rejected for the final months of the hyperinflation and, more importantly, that our measure of the probability of monetary reform, q_t, hit its peak during the very week commonly asserted to mark the beginning of the reform.

Although we have addressed the crucial issues concerning the expectation of reform, our argument is based on some assumptions which have yet to be supported. Notable is our assumption that the subjective probability that the double-log process generated the money supply was approximately unity, which can be tested using the procedure outlined in the text. Furthermore, we have not accounted for the heteroskedasticity observable in the ε_t during the hyperinflation. Although we intend to examine both complications in future work, we believe that the first problem is the more important. Certainly, accounting for heteroskedasticity will push us closer to an understanding of the chaotic events at the hyperinflation's end. However, in constructing the money class weights, $W_{C(1)t}$, $W_{C(2)t}$, $W_{C(3)t}$, and W_{Dt}, we can produce a method by which the hyperinflation can be connected, as part of a continuous process, to the normal period which began with the currency reform. Therefore, we now have an approach through which we can study the influence of the monetary explosions in the first half of the 1920s on the equally dramatic economic phenomena at the end of the decade.

Appendix A

1. In this section we determine the convergent parameter region for the money supply process in (14).

By repeated iteration of the process (14a), (14b) obtain

$$m_t = m_{t-1} \exp\{\theta\beta_{t-1} + \varepsilon_t\}$$

$$m_{t+1} = m_{t-1} \exp\{\theta\beta_{t-1} + \varepsilon_t + \theta^2\beta_{t-1} + \theta\varepsilon_t + \varepsilon_{t+1}\}$$

$$\vdots$$

$$m_{t+k} = m_{t-1} \exp\{\theta\beta_{t-1}(1 + \theta + \theta^2 + \cdots + \theta^k)$$
$$+ \varepsilon_t(1 + \theta + \theta^2 + \cdots + \theta^k)$$
$$+ \varepsilon_{t+1}(1 + \theta + \theta^2 + \cdots + \theta^{k-1}) + \cdots + \varepsilon_{t+k-1}(1 + \theta) + \varepsilon_{t+k}\}.$$

This may be reduced to

$$m_{t+k} = m_{t-1} \exp\left\{\frac{\theta}{1-\theta}\beta_{t-1}(1 - \theta^{k+1}) + \frac{\varepsilon_t}{1-\theta}(1 - \theta^{k+1}) + \cdots\right.$$
$$\left. + \frac{\varepsilon_{t+k-1}}{1-\theta}(1 - \theta^2) + \frac{\varepsilon_{t+k}(1-\theta)}{1-\theta}\right\}.$$

Since m_{t+k} is lognormally distributed, obtain

$$E(m_{t+k}|I_{t-1}, \theta, \sigma) = m_{t-1} \exp\left\{\frac{\theta}{1-\theta}\beta_{t-1}(1 - \theta^{k+1})\right.$$
$$+ \frac{\sigma^2}{2(1-\theta)^2}(1 - \theta^{k+1})^2 + \frac{\sigma^2}{2(1-\theta)^2}(1 - \theta^k)^2$$
$$\left. + \cdots + \frac{\sigma^2}{2(1-\theta)^2}(1 - \theta^2)^2 + \frac{\sigma^2(1-\theta)^2}{2(1-\theta)^2}\right\}.$$

Combining terms yields

$$E(m_{t+k}|I_{t-1}, \theta, \sigma) = m_{t-1} \exp\left\{\frac{\theta}{1-\theta}\beta_{t-1}(1 - \theta^{k+1})\right.$$
$$+ \frac{\sigma^2}{2(1-\theta)^2}[(1 - \theta)^2 + (1 - \theta^2)^2 + \cdots$$
$$\left. + (1 - \theta^k)^2 + (1 - \theta^{k+1})^2]\right\}. \tag{A1}$$

which further reduces to

$$E(m_{t+k}|I_{t-1}, \theta, \sigma) = m_{t-1} \exp\left\{\frac{\theta}{1-\theta}\beta_{t-1}(1 - \theta^{k+1})\right.$$

$$+ \frac{\sigma^2}{2(1-\theta)^2}\left[(k+1) - \frac{2\theta}{1-\theta}(1 - \theta^{k+1})\right.$$

$$\left.\left.+ \frac{\theta^2}{1-\theta^2}(1 - \theta^{2(k+1)})\right]\right\}. \tag{A2}$$

(A2) may be rewritten as

$$E(m_{t+k}|I_{t-1}, \theta, \sigma) = m_{t-1} \exp\left\{\frac{\theta}{1-\theta}(1 - \theta^{k+1})\left[\beta_{t-1} - \frac{\sigma^2}{(1-\theta)^2}\right]\right.$$

$$+ \frac{\sigma^2\theta^2}{2(1-\theta)^2(1-\theta^2)}(1 - \theta^{2(k+1)})$$

$$\left.+ \frac{\sigma^2}{2(1-\theta)^2}(k+1)\right\}. \tag{A3}$$

Our concept of the probability of monetary reform involves the convergence of the series

$$\sum_{k=0}^{\infty} E(m_{t+k}|I_{t-1}, \theta, \sigma)\Psi^{-k}. \tag{A4}$$

A necessary condition for the convergence of (A4) is

$$\lim_{k\to\infty} E(m_{t+k}|I_{t-1}, \theta, \sigma)\Psi^{-k} = 0. \tag{A5}$$

In order to examine this condition we calculate

$$E(m_{t+k}|I_{t-1}, \theta, \sigma)\Psi^{-k} = m_{t-1} \exp\left\{\frac{\sigma^2}{2(1-\theta)^2}\right\}$$

$$\cdot \exp\left\{\frac{\theta}{1-\theta}\left[\beta_{t-1} - \frac{\sigma^2}{(1-\theta)^2}\right][1 - \theta^{(k+1)}]\right\}$$

$$\cdot \exp\left\{\frac{\sigma^2\theta^2}{2(1-\theta)^2(1-\theta^2)}[1 - \theta^{2(k+1)}]\right\}$$

$$\cdot \exp\left\{\left[\frac{\sigma^2}{2(1-\theta)^2} - \log\Psi\right]k\right\}. \tag{A6}$$

To aid in the analysis of the limit of (A6) as $k \to \infty$ we reproduce the relevant terms

$$\exp\left\{\frac{\theta}{1-\theta}\left[\beta_{t-1} - \frac{\sigma^2}{(1-\theta)^2}\right](1-\theta^{k+1})\right\} \tag{A6a}$$

$$\exp\left\{\frac{\sigma^2\theta^2}{2(1-\theta)^2(1-\theta^2)}[1-\theta^{2(k+1)}]\right\} \tag{A6b}$$

$$\exp\left\{\left[\frac{\sigma^2}{2(1-\theta)^2} - \log\Psi\right]k\right\}. \tag{A6c}$$

These terms contain the possibly explosive parts of (A6).

First note that for $-1 > \theta$ or $\theta > 1$ expression (A6b) dominates both (A6a) and (A6c) in the sense that as $k \to \infty$ (A6b) explodes much faster than (A6a) could explode or go to zero, and since (A6b) involves $\theta^{2(k+1)}$ it explodes faster than (A6c) could explode or go to zero as (A6c) is only linear in the k power. Further, the borderline cases, $\theta = 1$ and $\theta = -1$, both yield division by zero in (A6b) and give explosion of (A6b) for all k. Hence, a necessary condition for convergence is $-1 < \theta < 1$.

Now suppose $-1 < \theta < 1$. This implies that (A6a) and (A6b) converge to the finite levels

$$\exp\left\{\frac{\theta}{1-\theta}\left[\beta_{t-1} - \frac{\sigma^2}{(1-\theta)^2}\right]\right\}$$

and

$$\exp\left\{\frac{\sigma^2\theta^2}{2(1-\theta)^2(1-\theta^2)}\right\},$$

respectively. Thus, (A5) holds only if, in (A6c),

$$\frac{\sigma^2}{2(1-\theta)^2} - \log\Psi < 0. \tag{A7}$$

Since $\Psi > 1$ we know $\log\Psi > 0$, implying that (A7) is possible. We have shown that the conditions

$$-1 < \theta < 1 \tag{A8a}$$

$$\frac{\sigma^2}{2(1-\theta)^2} < \log\Psi \tag{A8b}$$

are necessary for the convergence of (A4). We will now show that (A8a), (A8b) are also sufficient for the convergence of (A4).

Suppose that $-1 < \theta < 1$. This implies that there exists some positive finite Y such that

$$Y \geq \left\{ \frac{\theta}{1-\theta}\left[\beta_{t-1} - \frac{\sigma^2}{(1-\theta)^2}(1-\theta^{k+1}) + \frac{\sigma^2\theta^2[1-\theta^{2(k+1)}]}{2(1-\theta)^2(1-\theta^2)}\right]\right\}, \text{ for all } k.$$

Thus

$$m_{t-1}\exp\left\{\frac{\sigma^2}{2(1-\theta)^2}\right\}\exp\{Y\}\exp\left\{\left[\frac{\sigma^2}{2(1-\theta)^2} - \log\Psi\right]k\right\}$$

$$\geq E(m_{t+k}|I_{t-1}, \theta, \sigma)\Psi^{-k} \tag{A9}$$

for all k.

By taking the infinite sum of each side of (A9) we see that a sufficient condition for the convergence of (A4) is the convergence of

$$\sum_{k=0}^{\infty}\exp\left\{\left[\frac{\sigma^2}{2(1-\theta)^2} - \log\Psi\right]k\right\}$$

which converges if and only if $\sigma^2/[2(1-\theta)^2] - \log\Psi < 0$. Thus the necessary conditions for convergence, (A8a), (A8b), are also sufficient.

2. If the process on β_t is $\beta_t = \delta + \theta\beta_{t-1} + \varepsilon_t$, then one can derive the criteria for the convergence as $-1 < \theta < 1$, $\delta/(1-\theta) + (\sigma^2/2)$ $[1/(1-\theta)]^2 < \log\Psi$ in a manner similar to that above.

Appendix B

The change of variables performed in the derivation of the p.d.f. $H(\theta, Z\vec{\beta})$ is based on a standard theorem which is reproduced below (from Wilks 1962, p. 57).

Suppose (x_1, x_2) is a continuous random variable with p.d.f. $f(x_1, x_2)$. Let $g_i(x_1, x_2)$, $i = 1, 2$, be single valued and have continuous first partial derivatives in some open region A in the x_1, x_2 plane. Let $y_i = g_i(x_1, x_2)$; $i = 1, 2$, have a unique inverse $x_i = g_i^{-1}(y_1, y_2)$, $i = 1, 2$, for all points in A. Let B be the image of A in the y_1, y_2 p;ane. Let J be the Jacobian defined by the determinant

$$J = \left|\frac{\partial x_i}{\partial y_i}\right| \qquad i,j = 1,2$$

having a nonzero value at all points in A. The p.d.f. $h(y_1, y_2)$ at any point $(y_1, y_2) \in B$ is given by

(2.8.10) $h(y_1, y_2) = f(x_1, x_2)\cdot|J|$

where on the right of (2.8.10), (x_1, x_2) are to be replaced by $g_1^{-1}(y_1, y_2), g_2^{-1}(y_1, y_2)$, respectively.

Furthermore,

$$\int_A f(x_1, x_2)\, dx_1 dx_2 = \int_B f(x_1, x_2)|J|\, dy_1 dy_2.$$

Consider the function

$$G(\theta, \sigma) = [g_1(\theta, \sigma), g_2(\theta, \sigma)] = \left[\theta, \frac{\sigma^2}{2(1 - \theta)^2}\right].$$

The function $g_1(\theta, \sigma) = \theta$ is single valued over the θ, σ plane with

$$\frac{\partial g_1}{\partial \theta} = 1, \frac{\partial g_1}{\partial \sigma} = 0.$$

The function $g_2(\theta, \sigma) = \sigma^2/[2(1 - \theta)^2]$ having $\partial g_2/\partial\theta = \sigma^2/(1 - \theta)^3$, $\partial g_2/\partial\sigma = \sigma/(1 - \theta)^2$ is single valued with continuous partial derivatives on the two open intervals of the θ, σ plane which are broken by the borderline case $\theta = 1$. Thus our open regions involve all σ and $\theta < 1$ and $\theta > 1$. Formally we have the open regions $A_1 = \{\sigma, \theta | \theta < 1\}$, $A_2 = \{\sigma, \theta | \theta > 1\}$. It is also simple to confirm that the inverse functions g_1^{-1} and g_2^{-2} produce unique values over these open regions since $g_1^{-1}(\theta, Z) = \theta$; $g_2^{-1}(\theta, Z) = |1 - \theta|\sqrt{2Z}$. The relevant Jacobian is

$$J = \det\begin{bmatrix} 1 & 0 \\ -2\sqrt{2Z} & |(1 - \theta)|(2Z)^{-1/2} \end{bmatrix} = |1 - \theta|(2Z)^{-1/2}.$$

Hence the transformed posterior p.d.f. becomes

$$H(\theta, Z|\vec{\beta}) \propto \frac{1}{\sigma^{T+1}} \exp\left\{-\frac{1}{2\sigma^2}\sum_{\tau=1}^{T}(\beta_\tau - \theta\beta_{\tau-1})^2\right\}|1 - \theta|(2Z)^{-1/2},$$

which may be reduced to

$$H(\theta, Z|\vec{\beta}) \propto \frac{1}{|1 - \theta|^T(\sqrt{2Z})^{T+2}} \exp\left[-\frac{1}{4Z(1 - \theta)^2}\sum_{\tau=1}^{T}(\beta_\tau - \theta\beta_{\tau-1})^2\right].$$
(B1)

To obtain the normalizing constant, N, we need to calculate

$$N = \int_0^\infty \int_1^\infty H(\theta, Z|\vec{\beta})\, d\theta dZ + \int_0^\infty \int_{-\infty}^1 H(\theta, Z|\vec{\beta})\, d\theta dZ.$$
(B2)

We may now calculate

$$(1 - q_t) = \frac{1}{N}\int_0^{\log\Psi} \int_{-\infty}^1 H(\theta, Z|\vec{\beta})\, d\theta dZ,$$

where $t = T + 1$. In the empirical section we provide numerical approximations of $(1 - q_t)$ for the German episode using (B1) for $H(\theta, Z|\vec{\beta})$.

Appendix C

The Data

The data that we use in this study, part of which are identical to those used by Cagan, consist of a time series on currency in circulation. The series on money begins in October 1918 and ends in December 1925. All data through 1923 are taken from Statistisches Reichsamt (1925). Data for nominal money (p. 46) are reported on a monthly basis as of the end of each month from October 1918 through December 1922. Money in the monthly reports consists of Reichsbanknotes, Private Bank Notes, and the notes of special issue banks (Darlehnskassenscheine, Reichskassenscheine). From January 6, 1923, through December 31, 1923, nominally valued currency is reported at weekly intervals in terms of Goldmarks (pp. 47–48); however, the daily Goldmark-Papermark exchange rate (p. 10) can be used to convert the data into nominal values. Prior to September 15, 1923, the data for nominal money in circulation consist of information on Reichsbanknotes, special currency, and officially accounted special emergency money; Reichsbanknotes represent a very large percentage of nominal money, the sum of these three categories. Starting on September 22, 1923, the railroad issued nominal emergency money in such quantities that railroad money represented more than 25 percent of the nominal money supply by the end of November. Therefore, all railroad nominal emergency money is included in the total supply from September 22.

In addition to nominally valued currencies, a number of "fixed value" currencies were issued in the last months of the hyperinflation. Although on paper these had a fixed value in terms of gold, they had no gold backing at all and so in fact were also paper monies. Apparently the public accepted them at their face value since the exchange rate between them and nominally valued currency reflected the exchange rate between the Goldmark and nominally valued currencies. Among these currencies were the gold loans, small denomination debt instruments of various governments which circulated as currency; fixed-value railroad emergency money; emergency gold loans; and the Rentenmark. Although the Rentenmark, supplied by a new bank of issue in mid-November 1923, was never legal tender, it was the currency through which the reform was effected. Fixed value currencies were first reported October 31, 1923 (p. 49), and since in real terms their quantity exceeded that of the paper currencies by November 7, we have converted them to nominal values and added them to the nominal currency totals in determining the overall money supply.

The data for the money supply for the years 1924 and 1925 were taken from the 1924 and 1925 volumes of *Statistisches Jahrbuch für das Deutsches Reich*. The data were taken from pages 324 and 325, respectively, of the 1924 and 1925 volumes. All observations are separated by weekly intervals. The monetary totals for 1924 are determined by adding the same categories used to derive the 1923 totals with the exception that emergency monies disappeared from the system by the end of 1924. The 1925 money total consists of the sum of Reichsbanknotes, Rentenmarks, private bank notes, and coins.

It should be noted at this point that the money supply variable includes neither demand deposits nor large quantities of many emergency monies that circulated by the end of 1923. This omission is due, of course, to a lack of data for the two categories; demand deposits information is available only at long intervals, and no reliable data exist at all for much of the emergency money.

Appendix D

1. Transformed P.D.F. for the Heteroskedastic Case

In figure 17.3, there appear to be four different variances determining the size of the error term, σ_1^2, σ_2^2, σ_3^2, σ_4^2; and the observations at which the variances change seem to be observations 45, 79, and 97. Using a diffuse prior p.d.f., $1/\sigma_1\sigma_2\sigma_3\sigma_4$, the posterior density function over the parameters for observations T occurring after observation 97 is

$$p(\theta, \sigma_1, \sigma_2, \sigma_3, \sigma_4, \vec{\beta}) \propto \frac{1}{\sigma_1^{45}\sigma_2^{35}\sigma_3^{19}\sigma_4^{T-96}} \exp\left\{ -\frac{1}{2\sigma_1^2} \sum_{\tau=2}^{45} (\beta_\tau - \theta\beta_{r-1})^2 \right.$$

$$-\frac{1}{2\sigma_2^2} \sum_{\tau=46}^{79} (\beta_\tau - \theta\beta_{\tau-1})^2 - \frac{1}{2\sigma_3^2} \sum_{\tau=80}^{97} (\beta_\tau - \theta\beta_{\tau-1})^2$$

$$\left. -\frac{1}{2\sigma_4^2} \sum_{\tau=98}^{T} (\beta_\tau - \theta\beta_{\tau-1})^2 \right\}.$$

Integrating over σ_1, σ_2, and σ_3, and transforming from (θ, σ_4) to (θ, Z), we have

$$H(\theta, Z | \vec{\beta}) \propto \frac{1}{|1 - \theta|^{T-97}} \frac{1}{Z^{(T-95)/2}}$$

$$\exp \left\{ -\frac{1}{4Z(1 - \theta)^2} \sum_{\tau=98}^{T} (\beta_\tau - \theta\beta_{\tau-1})^2 \right\} \cdot \left[\sum_{\tau=2}^{45} (\beta_\tau - \theta\beta_{\tau-1})^2 \right]^{-22}$$

$$\cdot \left[\sum_{\tau=46}^{79} (\beta_\tau - \theta\beta_{\tau-1})^2 \right]^{-17} \cdot \left[\sum_{\tau=80}^{97} (\beta_\tau - \theta\beta_{\tau-1})^2 \right]^{-9}.$$

$H(\theta, Z | \vec{\beta})$ can be integrated over the convergent regions of (θ, Z) to determine $(1 - q_t)$.

2. Numerical Integration of the P.D.F. in Section II

We used Simpsons's rule twice in computing the bivariate numerical integrals of the p.d.f. in section II (see Zellner 1971, appendix C). For each observation we computed the integral for each of 36 regions and added the integrals in the convergent regions to determine $(1 - q_t)$. In each of the regions the p.d.f. was evaluated at 625 values of (θ, Z). The intervals for Z were (0.0–0.006086), (0.006086–0.010002), and (0.010002–0.025). The intervals for θ were (0.6–0.8), (0.8–0.9), (0.9–0.95), (0.95–0.975), (0.975–0.9875), (0.9875–1.00), (1.00–1.009375), (1.009375–1.01875), (1.01875–1.0375), (1.0375–1.075), (1.075–1.15), and (1.15–1.3). The value 0.006086 is the log Ψ associated with Cagan's $\hat{\alpha}$ while 0.010002 is the corresponding value for Frenkel's $\hat{\alpha}$.

Appendix E

The purpose of this Appendix is to outline a method for the determination of $[1 - \lambda(t)]$, the probability that monetary reform has already taken place, given that the NR class contains only Cagan's three processes and that the R class consists only of that money supply process which maintains a fixed exchange rate with the dollar.

Let Cagan's three processes be given by

$$M_{t+1/2} = M_{t-1/2}(1 + \beta_{t+1/2}) \tag{C(1)}$$

$$M_{t+1/2} = M_{t-1/2} \exp(\beta_{t+1/2}) \tag{C(2)}$$

$$M_{t+1/2} = M_{t-1/2}^{\exp(\beta_{t+1/2})} \tag{C(3)}$$

and denote the fixed exchange rate money supply process by D. Further, let $W_{C(1)t}$, $W_{C(2)t}$, $W_{C(3)t}$, and W_{Dt}, $W_{C(1)t} + W_{C(2)t} + W_{C(3)t} + W_{Dt} = 1$, be the subjective probabilities attached to C(1), C(2), C(3), and the fixed rate process, respectively.

A technique that is useful for calculating the W's, on the basis of a given historical time series on money, is described by Zellner (1971, pp. 291–312). The probability that reform has already taken place, $[1 - \lambda(t)]$, is equal to W_{Dt} calculated via Zellner's methods.

Although we have not yet performed a technical exploration of this issue, we believe that the time series on money toward the end of the hyperinflation will produce values of $W_{Dt} = [1 - \lambda(t)]$ which are very close to zero. However, we have calculated the values of $(q_t|I_{t-1})$ in the text for periods which extend well beyond the consensus date of German monetary reform. As we indicate in the text, these postreform values of the $(q_t|I_{t-1})$ are not true subjective probabilities that the money supply will be drawn from the R class over the forecasting horizon; once reform actually takes place, agents will begin to learn about it. They will calculate

$$(q_t^*|I_{t-1}) = W_{C(1)t}(q_t^{C1}|I_{t-1}) + W_{C(2)t}(q_t^{C2}|I_{t-1}) + W_{C(3)t}(q_t^{C3}|I_{t-1}).$$

$(q_t^*|I_{t-1})$ is the probability that money at time t will be drawn from the reform process, given that reform has not yet occurred; and $(q_t^{C1}|I_{t-1})$, $(q_t^{C2}|I_{t-1})$ and $(q_t^{C3}|I_{t-1})$ are the probabilities that the money supply is not process consistent, given that it is generated by C(1), C(2), and C(3), respectively. Note that $(q_t^{C3}|I_{t-1})$ is identical to $(q_t|I_{t-1})$ in the text. Further, we have followed Cagan by assuming that for the last few months of the hyperinflation C(3) was the actual process, that is, $W_{C(3)} = 1$ and $W_{C(1)} = W_{C(2)} = W_D = 0$.

Following the event of monetary reform W_{Dt} will diverge from zero and begin climbing toward unity. Our calculated values of $(q_t|I_{t-1})$ in the text ignore W_{Dt} even after the reform. Thus, they are unreliable indicators of behavior for that period since the probability that reform occurs at time t is actually $(1 - W_{Dt})(q_t|I_{t-1})$, given that $W_{C(1)t}$ and $W_{C(2)t}$ remain equal to zero.

Appendix F

In the absence of an estimate of α which uses our other procedures, we present in figure 17.5 Cagan's plot of the curve fitted between real balances and his computed expected rates of inflation for the German hyperinflation. In addition, we include Cagan's deleted expected inflation computations, multiplied by our $(1 - q_t)$ weights. Problems with this comparison include

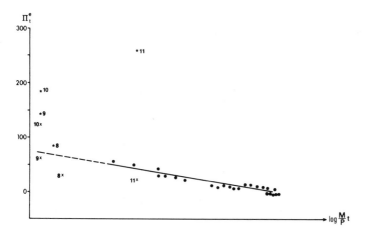

Figure 17.5
Plot of Cagan's data, his fitted money demand function, and his data revised by our $(1 - q_t)$ estimates.

the possibilities that the adaptive expectations mechanism was not rational while $(1 - q_t)$ is based on rational expectations, that some of the earlier Cagan expected inflation computations may also require $(1 - q_t)$ weights, and that the expected rate of inflation under the reform process is implicitly assumed to be zero. Therefore, we must regard the comparison between Cagan's data and our altered data as an illustration rather than as evidence for or against our technique.

The asterisks labeled 8, 9, 10, and 11 represent Cagan's expected inflation rates in the last four months of the hyperinflation, which Cagan did not use in the estimation of the money demand function. The x's labeled 8, 9, 10, and 11 are determined by multiplying Cagan's reported expected rate of inflation for the corresponding month by the weighted average of the $(1 - q_t)$ estimates which straddle the day for which Cagan reports real balances. The altered expected rates of inflation from August through November 1923 are 0.433, 0.517, 1.317, and 0.230, respectively. These data appear to be scattered about Cagan's fitted relationship, although the variance of money demand for the last months is obviously higher than for the earlier observations.

We estimated the parameters of the money demand function using ordinary least squares both for Cagan's original data through July 1923 and for the additional $(1 - q_t)$ weighted data through November 1923. The results are (standard errors in parentheses):

September 1920–July 1923 (original Cagan data):

$\hat{\gamma} = -2.362 \quad \hat{\alpha} = -5.436 \quad R^2 = .974, \text{D-W} = 0.3319, \text{SEE} = 0.1465$
$(.0361) \qquad\quad (.1561)$

September 1920–November 1923 (original Cagan data):

$\hat{\gamma} = -3.020 \quad \hat{\alpha} = -1.537 \quad R^2 = 5.186, \text{D-W} = 0.3897, \text{SEE} = 0.7939$
$(.1496) \qquad\quad (.2436)$

September 1920–November 1923 (transformed Cagan data):

$\hat{\gamma} = -2.6555 \quad \hat{\alpha} = -4.016 \quad R^2 = .768, \text{D-W} = 1.855, \text{SEE} = 0.5509.$
$(.1177) \qquad\quad (.3627)$

It is difficult to compare these results because of the autocorrelation in the residuals (the Durbin-Watson statistic for the transformed data is dominated by the large residuals for the last four observations). However, it appears that the instability of the money demand function at the end of the hyperinflation is reduced somewhat by accounting for the probability of reform. These results represent our effort to incorporate Cagan's hypothesis about monetary reform into *his* work. As such these results are open to all of the criticisms leveled at Cagan throughout the years as well as all of the caveats we have mentioned previously.

Notes

We would like to thank Robert Hodrick, Elizabeth Jaeger, Laura La Haye, Robert Lucas, Michael Mussa, John Pettengill, Kenneth Singleton, Ernest Tanner, Arnold Zellner, and an anonymous referee for helpful comments. We would also like to acknowledge our debt to the members of the Macroeconomics Workshop at the University of Virginia and the Money and Banking Workshop at the University of Chicago.

1. By *class of stochastic processes* we mean a specific functional form. An individual stochastic process on a money is then defined, within such a class, by specific parameter values. Note that our definition of monetary reform is dependent on our definition of class of stochastic processes. In appendix E we broaden our definition of class of stochastic processes; and thus, we discuss a slightly different concept of monetary reform there.

2. In section III we mention the implications of an alternative information structure for the interpretation of our empirical work.

3. If we relax the assumption that the stable solution is chosen our argument does not change. The assumption that the stable solution is chosen places restrictions on the data. In a separate paper (Flood and Garber, 1980), we tested these restrictions and were unable to refute the hypothesis that agents chose the stable solution during the German hyperinflation.

4. Money would become worthless if (10) were to fail to converge in the sense

$$\lim_{k \to \infty} \sum_{i=0}^{k} [E(m_{t+1}|I_{t-1}) - \gamma]\Psi^{-i} = +\infty.$$

However, if (10) were to fail to converge in the sense

$$\lim_{k \to \infty} \sum_{i=0}^{k} [E(m_{t+i}|I_{t-1}) - \gamma]\Psi^{-i} = -\infty,$$

then money would become infinitely valuable and velocity would go to zero. If for a class of money supply processes (10) were to fail to converge in this latter sense, then that class of processes would, ironically, provide a "money" so valuable that agents would be unwilling to exchange "money" for goods. Thus, a class of processes for which (10) fails to converge in the second sense does not provide a medium of exchange.

5. La Haye (1978) uses the assumption that agents knew the timing of monetary reform to construct an alternate test for the existence of reform expectations in the German case.

6. Since real balances must be built up to noninflationary levels, there will be a transition period in which the money supply will still grow rapidly even after a reform.

7. Note that at this point we make the same kind of process consistency assumption that is usually made in the literature. However, we will next make behavioral assumptions which allow us to incorporate information about the process consistency of a particular class of money supply processes into an explanation of agents' behavior.

8. The evidence indicates that at the end of the hyperinflation in Germany confidence in the national currency was so lacking that the nation began to disintegrate into its component states. Not only did local governments adopt their own currencies or seek to join currency areas provided by other nations but also Berlin lost political control over some of the old German states. Bavaria was virtually independent by November 1923 (the putsch attempt occurred on November 8–9); Communist regimes took power in Saxony and Thuringia and a Communist revolt broke out in Hamburg (October 26); and a movement in the Rhineland, partly under the control of the French and Belgians, sought a separate state (see Ringer 1969).

9. With the definition of $(q_t|I_{t-1})$ produced in (13), we can derive the entire p.d.f. at time t over the time of future monetary reform. In (13) all of the $(q_{t+i}|I_{t-1})$, $i = 0, 1, 2, \ldots,$ are based only on I_{t-1}. Thus, an agent's subjective probability of a reform's taking place at a future date, conditional on no reform prior to that date, must equal $(q_t|I_{t-1})$. Furthermore, since the probability of reaching a date $t + T$ without having had a reform is $[1 - (q_t|I_{t-1})]^T$, it follows that $(q_{t+T}|I_{t-1}) = (q_t|I_{t-1})[1 - (q_t|I_{t-1})]^T$.

10. The condition that agents believe that there will always exist some useful money is embodied in our assumption of process consistency with regard to the *unconditional* expectation of future money, i.e., process consistency with respect to (10) and (12).

11. Note that (14b) could be written $\beta_t = \delta + \theta\beta_{t-1} + \varepsilon_t$. We have suppressed the constant term for simplicity.

12. $H(\theta, Z|\vec{\beta})$ is a bimodal function with local maxima at $[\theta_i, Z(\theta_i)]$, $i = 1, 2$. The θ_i are the roots of the polynominal

$$\theta^2 \left(\frac{T}{T+2} \sum_{t=1}^{T} \beta_{t-1}^2 \right) + \theta \left(\frac{2-T}{T+2} \sum_{t=1}^{T} \beta_t\beta_{t-1} - \sum_{t=1}^{T} \beta_{t-1}^2 \right) + \left(\sum_{t=1}^{T} \beta_t\beta_{t-1} - \frac{2}{T+2} \sum_{t=1}^{T} \beta_t^2 \right) = 0,$$

$$\text{and } Z(\theta_i) = \frac{1}{2(T+2)} \frac{\sum_{t=1}^{T} (\beta_t - \theta_i\beta_{t-1})^2}{(1 - \theta_i)^2}.$$

13. If (16) is the posterior p.d.f. over (θ, Z), the implied prior over (θ, Z) is

$$p(\theta, Z) \propto \frac{1}{|1 - \theta|\sqrt{Z}},$$

which is not a diffuse prior. The reasons for this phenomenon are discussed in Zellner (1977). Alternatively, we may begin with a diffuse prior over the (θ, Z) parameterization, $p(\theta, Z) \propto 1/Z$ to produce a posterior p.d.f.

$$H^*(\theta, Z|\beta_t) \propto \frac{1}{|1 - \theta|^{T-1}\sqrt{Z^{T+3}}} \exp\left\{\frac{-\sum\limits_{t=1}^{T}(\beta_t - \theta\beta_{t-1})^2}{4Z(1 - \theta)^2}\right\}.$$

For moderate T, this should be close to the p.d.f. in (16). E.g., the modal values of H^*, $[\theta_i^*, Z^*(\theta_i)]$ are the roots of the quadratic equation

$$\theta^2\left(\frac{T - 1}{T + 3}\sum_{t=1}^{T}\beta_{t-1}^2\right) + \theta\left[\frac{5 - T}{T - 3}\sum_{t=1}^{T}\beta_t\beta_{t-1} - \sum_{t=1}^{T}\beta_{t-1}^2\right] + \left(\Sigma\beta_t\beta_{t-1} - \frac{4}{T + 3}\Sigma\beta_t^2\right) = 0.$$

$$Z^*(\theta_i^*) = \frac{\sum\limits_{t=1}^{T}(\beta_t - \theta_i^*\beta_{t-1})^2}{2(T + 3)(1 - \theta_i^*)^2}.$$

For $T = 65$, the smallest sample size that we use, the modal values for the two p.d.f.'s should be approximately equal.

14. Our assumption is that the probability of reform is an increasing function of the probability that the NR class of processes fails the process consistency test. Thus, when we assume that $q_t = 1 - S_t$, we impose a restriction on the nature of this function which will affect the results that we obtain in refitting Cagan's model, which we present in appendix F. An alternative methodology is to use our computations for $(1 - S_t)$ to fit simultaneously both Cagan's model and also a model of the monotonic function which converts $(1 - S_t)$ into q_t. We will not follow this methodology since, in either case, serious objections have been raised about Cagan's specifications, for example, Evans (1978).

15. While it is possible for the single-log process on money to be inconsistent, we maintain the use of the double-log process because of the common use of Cagan's data in the hyperinflation literature. A possible difficulty with the money supply process in (14) is that we assume it to be exogenous to prices, while recent results (Sargent and Wallace 1973; Frenkel 1977; Evans 1978) indicate that this assumption does not hold. However, these results are obtained with Cagan's interpolated data or with data interpolated in a way similar to those of Cagan. Evans points out that such interpolation can confound the estimated relationship between prices and money for 1-period leads and lags. This problem alone is sufficient to cast doubt on Sargent and Wallace's and Frenkel's interpolation of their empirical results. In addition, it is unclear that Sims's (1972) theorems may be applied to interpret these results because the theorems are based on the assumption of a linear, time-invariant, covariance stationary time series process while the Cagan interpolations are carried out with weights which vary through time. While such interpolation problems may not cause great difficulties for causality tests in normal times, we believe that they are important in the context of hyperinflation because of the magnitude and rapidity of changes in prices and money. A separate issue, which was raised by Salemi and Sargent (1979), is that these exogeneity results were obtained in a "model-free" setting, that is, estimation was performed without the parameterization constraints imposed by a money market model. Salemi and Sargent find that they are able to *reject*, for all methods used with the German data, the joint hypothesis: (1) Cagan's money market model, (2) rational expectations, and

(3) inflation is exogenous. Since we maintain hypotheses 1 and 2 in the present paper, the Salemi and Sargent results contradict earlier exogeneity results, which found inflation to be exogenous. Therefore we conclude that the question of whether or not money was exogenous to prices in the German hyperinflation remains an open issue; and we feel free to choose an exogenous money supply process to conduct our analysis.

16. As a justification for the use of varying time intervals, we note that the properties of the data produced by the statistical reporting industry were endogenous to the inflationary process. As the rate and variability of inflation rose, information was required at ever shorter intervals because agents desired to react more rapidly than before to disturbances; a process that previously had taken a month to work out might now take only a week. Thus, we may view the switch from monthly to shorter reporting intervals as a sign of the switch in the "time intensity" of the inflationary process. The process previously associated with the monthly reporting interval may then be identical to that associated with the weekly intervals, and we may combine monthly data with weekly data without fear of any statistical difficulties. This explanation is consistent with the methods used by Cagan to derive the interpolated money supplies in 1923. For a more detailed discussion of the issue, see Garber (1977).

17. While the parameter estimates are consistent, tests of hypotheses using standard statistics become dubious as more data are added to the sample because of the apparent heteroskedasticity.

18. Since we have converted our basic money data into average daily rates of growth of the log of money, the $\hat{a}$'s, which carry units of months, must be converted into units of days in computing Ψ.

19. Under the assumption that current information is available, the $(1 - q_t)$ estimates would all apply to the next earlier observation date.

References

Barro, Robert J. "Inflation, the Payments Period, and the Demand for Money." *J.P.E.* 78, no. 6 (November/December 1970): 1228–63.

Bartle, Robert G. *The Elements of Real Analysis.* 2d ed. New York: Wiley, 1976.

Cagan, Phillip. "The Monetary Dynamics of Hyperinflation." Reprinted in *Studies in the Quantity Theory of Money,* edited by Milton Friedman. Chicago: Univ. Chicago Press, 1956.

Evans, P. "Time-Series and Structural Analysis of the German Hyperinflation." *Internat. Econ. Rev.* 19 (February 1978): 195–209.

Flood, R., and Garber, P. "Market Fundamentals versus Price Level Bubbles: The First Test." *J.P.E.* 88, no. 41 (August 1980): 745–70.

Frenkel, Jacob A. "The Forward Exchange Rate, Expectations, and the Demand for Money: The German Hyperinflation." *A.E.R.* 67, no. 4 (September 1977): 653–70.

Garber, Peter M. "Costly Decisions and the Demand for Money." Doctoral dissertation, Univ. Chicago, 1977.

Jevons, William S. *Money and the Mechanism of Exchange.* New York: Appleton, 1880.

La Haye, Laura. "Inflation and Currency Reform: A Study of the Effects of Anticipated Policy Switching." Working paper, Univ. Chicago, November 1978.

Muth, John F. "Rational Expectations and the Theory of Price Movements." *Econometrica* 29 (July 1961): 315–35.

Ringer, Fritz K., ed. *The German Inflation of 1923.* New York: Oxford Univ. Press, 1969.

Salemi, M., and Sargent, Thomas J. "The Demand for Money during Hyperinflation under Rational Expectations: II." *Internat. Econ. Rev.* 20 (October 1979): 741–58.

Sargent, Thomas J. "The Demand for Money during Hyperinflations under Rational Expectations: I." *Internat. Econ. Rev.* 18 (February 1977): 59–82.

Sargent, Thomas J., and Wallace, Neil N. "Rational Expectations and the Dynamics of Hyperinflation." *Internat. Econ. Rev.* 14, no. 2 (June 1973): 328–50.

Sims, Christopher A. "Money, Income, and Causality." *A.E.R.* 64, no. 4 (September 1972): 540–52.

Statistisches Reichsamt. *Sonderhefte Zur Wirtschaft und Statistik.* "Zahlen Zur Geldenwertung in Deutschland 1914 bis 1923." Berlin: 1925.

———. *Jahrbuch für das Deutsches Reich 1924/1925.* Berlin: Hobbing, 1925.

———. *Jahrbuch für das Deutsches Reich 1925.* Berlin: Hobbing, 1926.

Wilks, Samuel S. *Mathematical Statistics.* New York: Wiley, 1962.

Zellner, A. A. *An Introduction to Bayesian Inference in Econometrics.* New York: Wiley, 1971.

———. "Maximal Data Information Prior Distributions." In *New Developments in the Applications of Bayesian Methods,* edited by A. Aykac and C. Brumat. Amsterdam: North-Holland, 1977.

18

Process Consistency and Monetary Reform: Some Further Evidence

Robert P. Flood and Peter M. Garber

I Introduction

This century's postwar hyperinflations have displayed rates of price and money supply increase which have isolated them almost as a separate area of monetary theory and experience. Economic researchers have treated hyperinflations primarily as intense monetary experiments, remarkable opportunities to test basic monetary and expectational theories in environments devoid of confounding real movements.[1]

In Flood and Garber (1980a) we devised a model which employed the concept of *process consistency*, the requirement that a money supply process generate a finite price level, to examine the transition from extreme hyperinflation to monetary reform. Our empirical results, based on the German case, provided evidence in favor of the model, in that the reform occurred at the moment that the probability of process consistency reached its lowest value. Our study can be interpreted, in line with the usual treatment of hyperinflation, as yet another test of abstruse monetary theory provided by the extreme of the hyperinflationary wind-tunnel.[2,3]

In this chapter we provide additional evidence that *process consistency* may have materialized as a restrictive constraint on the money generation process. In addition to recomputing the time series of process consistency probabilities using new data for the German case, we also apply our empirical technique to the data from the other hyperinflations studied by Cagan (1956). In the most extreme case, Hungary II, Germany and Greece, we find that, as in our earlier study, the probability of process consistency reached its lowest value at the initiation of the reform.

II Empirical Results

In this section we report our constructed time series for process consistency probabilities in a number of hyperinflations. The assumptions and theory

behind these computations are those employed in Flood and Garber
(1980a). In particular, we assume that the forms of the money demand
functions and the money supply processes are those which are analyzed in
our previous paper,

$$m_t^d - p_t = \gamma + \alpha[E(p_{t+1} - p_t | I_{t-1})] + v_t \quad \text{(money demand)}$$

$$\alpha < 0, \quad E(v_t | I_{t-1}) = 0, \quad E(v_t^2 | I_{t-1}) = \sigma_v^2, \tag{1}$$

$$m_t = m_{t-1} \exp\{\beta_t\} \qquad \text{(money supply)} \tag{2a}$$

$$\beta_t = \theta \beta_{t-1} + \varepsilon_t, \quad \varepsilon_t \sim N(0, \sigma^2), \quad E(\varepsilon_i \varepsilon_j) = 0, \, i \neq j, \tag{2b}$$

the variables m_t^d, m_t, and p_t are the logarithms of money demand, the
money stock and the price level, respectively; E is the mathematical expectations operator; and I_{t-1} is an information set which contains all relevant
economic data through time $t - 1$, together with the money demand
parameters.[4] ε_t and v_t are random disturbances and γ, α, σ_v^2, σ^2, and θ are
parameters. Agents do not know the parameters of money supply; they
form beliefs about θ and σ^2 by means of Bayesian posterior probability
density functions.

Application of standard methods for the solution of difference equations
to (1) yields the following solution for expected price:

$$E(p_t | I_{t-1}) = \frac{\Psi^{-1}}{\alpha} \sum_{i=0}^{\infty} [E(m_{t+i} | I_{t-1}) - \gamma] \Psi^{-i} \quad \text{where} \quad \Psi \equiv \frac{\alpha - 1}{\alpha}.$$

If the money supply is expected to grow rapidly enough relative to the
money demand parameter embodied in Ψ, the expected (and actual) price
solution will be infinite. In such a case, no agent will exchange goods for
currency; hence, the supply process will not provide a useful money.

We classify any money supply process which yields a finite price level
solution as process consistent. Conversely, any supply process which
yields an infinite expected price solution is called process inconsistent. If an
economy is to continue functioning as a monetary economy, agents must
believe that any supply process which they perceive as process inconsistent
will be overthrown in favor of a process consistent money supply process.
Therefore, if there were little likelihood that a supply process is consistent,
we would expect a monetary reform.

Since agents are unsure about the values of the parameters of the money
supply process, they are also unsure about whether the money supply
process is process consistent. However, there is a region of (θ, σ^2) values
for which the supply process is process consistent; therefore, the probabil-

ity of process consistency at any time can be determined by integrating the posterior probability density function for (θ, σ^2) over the appropriate region.

Specifically, the construction of the probability of process consistency is an exercise in the integration of the posterior p.d.f.:

$$H(\theta, Z|\vec{\beta}) \propto \frac{1}{|1 - \theta|^T (\sqrt{2Z})^{T+2}} \exp\left\{ -\frac{1}{4Z(1 - \theta)^2} \sum_{t=1}^{T} (\beta_t - \theta\beta_{t-1})^2 \right\} \quad (3)$$

over the parameter region

$$-1 < \theta < 1, \qquad Z < \log \Psi, \qquad (4a, b)$$

where $Z \equiv \sigma^2/2(1 - \theta)^2$. With the money supply data from the various hyperinflations and estimates for α, we can compute the posterior probabilities of process consistency. To insure convergence of the numerical integration we have altered our previous integration technique somewhat; in the appendix we explicitly describe our new method.

An Overview of the Hyperinflations

The seven instances which form the basis of most hyperinflation studies encompass a wide range of inflationary intensity. Table 18.1 (which is constructed from Cagan's (1956, p. 26) table 1) arranges the various episodes by the magnitude of price level change experienced during the course of the inflation.

The first three hyperinflations in table 18.1 can be categorized as particularly extreme inflationary episodes; the last three were relatively mild; and the Russian case lies somewhere between the other two groups. In

Table 18.1
Order of magnitude of hyperinflations[a]

Country	P_e/P_0[b]	Period
(1) Hungary II	3.81×10^{27}	Aug. 1945–July. 1946
(2) Germany	1.02×10^{10}	Aug. 1922–Nov. 1923
(3) Greece	4.7×10^{8}	Nov. 1943–Nov. 1944
(4) Russia	1.24×10^{5}	Dec. 1921–Jan. 1924
(5) Poland	699.0	Jan. 1923–Jan. 1924
(6) Austria	69.0	Oct. 1921–Aug. 1922
(7) Hungary I	44.0	March 1923–Feb. 1924

a. Source: Cagan (1956, table I).
b. P_e = price level at end of period. P_0 = price level at beginning of period.

studying the extreme hyperinflations, Cagan (1956) was forced to exclude observations from the final months of each episode because he observed far more real balances than predicted by money demand relationships estimated from earlier observations. Following Cagan, others who have studied these inflations have also excluded those months in which prices rose most rapidly. Of the other inflations, only the Polish case required a similar exclusion of observations; Cagan deleted the final two months of Polish data.[5]

For all the hyperinflations except the Greek case, the time of the reform is defined as the time at which the price level or exchange rate stabilized; in these cases, a new money supply process clearly was instituted. In the Greek case, the government announced a monetary reform in November 1944; the reform proved abortive in that the inflation and money creation continued, but since we pinpoint this time as a switch in a money supply process, it is a possible candidate for the time of reform.

The German Case

In our earlier examination of the German case, we employed a time series on money which, partly due to the availability of data, combined monthly observations from the inflation's first years with weekly observations from the last year. In addition, the money supply data from the last weeks of the German inflation included the newly introduced "fixed value" currencies, converted into nominal units by a market exchange rate.

We have recomputed the process consistency probabilities for Germany with two different alterations in our data series. First, we have constructed a purely weekly time series by combining the weekly Reichsbanknote series for 1919–1922 reported in Flood and Garber (1980b) with the weekly series for 1923 used in our (1980a) study.[6] Therefore, any statistical problems which may arise through the combination of weekly and monthly series are eliminated. Second, we have used a weekly money series consisting only of Reichsbanknotes; the fixed value monies which appeared in the final weeks are ignored.[7]

In table 18.2, we report the series for the probability of process consistency for each money aggregate. The two money series are identical until September 15, 1923, when nominal railroad money began to appear; upon its appearance at the end of October 1923, fixed value money was included with nominal currency to form the series for all monies. The date of the first observation on Reichsbanknotes is December 23, 1918. The $\hat{\alpha}$ used to compute $\log \Psi$ was Cagan's estimate, $\hat{\alpha} = -5.46$ months, converted to

Table 18.2
Probabilities of process consistency—Germany (weekly data)

Date	Probability: includes fixed value money	Probability: only Reichsbanknotes	Date	Probability: includes fixed value money	Probability: only Reichsbanknotes
1923					
May 15	0.9999	0.9999	Nov. 7	0.0538	0.6480
May 23	0.9999	0.9999	Nov. 15	0.0258	0.1828
May 31	0.9999	0.9999	Nov. 23	0.8922	0.8482
June 7	0.9999	0.9999	Nov. 30	0.9664	0.9888
June 15	0.9999	0.9999	Dec. 7	0.9940	0.9942
June 23	0.9999	0.9999	Dec. 15	0.9953	0.9972
June 30	0.9999	0.9999	Dec. 22	0.9955	0.9972
July 7	0.9997	0.9997	Dec. 31	0.9956	0.9972
1924					
July 14	0.9999	0.9999	Jan. 7	0.9957	0.9974
July 23	0.9999	0.9999	Jan. 15	0.9958	—
July 31	0.9999	0.9999	Jan. 23	0.9959	—
Aug. 7	0.9993	0.9993	Jan. 31	0.9960	—
Aug. 15	0.9998	0.9998	Feb. 7	0.9961	—
Aug. 23	0.7635	0.7635	Feb. 15	0.9961	—
Aug. 31	0.0655	0.0655	Feb. 23	0.9962	—
Sept. 7	0.1323	0.1323	Feb. 29	0.9963	—
Sept. 15	0.9659	0.9783	March 7	0.9964	—
Sept. 22	0.5143	0.5662	March 15	0.9965	—
Sept. 29	0.5367	0.6454	March 22	0.9965	—
Oct. 6	0.2621	0.3346	March 31	0.9966	—
Oct. 15	0.9949	0.9969	April 7	0.9967	—
Oct. 23	0.9564	0.9696			
Oct. 31	0.4378	0.7112			

weekly time units. The rates of growth of the logarithms of the money supply (the β_t's) were the rate per week.

In the last weeks of the hyperinflation, our original series and the two new series exhibit similar patterns of movement in the process consistency probabilities. The three cycles beginning on August 15, 1923 appear for all three money aggregates. For the original money series and for the all-inclusive weekly series, the probability of process consistency reaches its lowest value on November 15, 1923, the week in which the reform began. For the Reichsbanknote series, the lowest probability is reached on August 31; however, the probability of process consistency for this money series does reach a relatively low value on November 15. The major change observable in our new results is that the probability of process consistency is almost unity prior to August 15, 1923. Our earlier computations

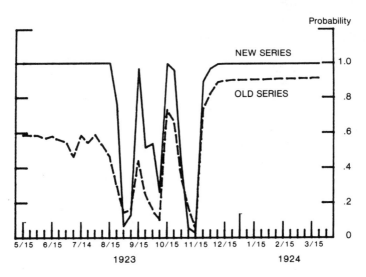

Figure 18.1
Probabilities of process consistency—Germany

indicated that the probability of process consistency moved between 0.46 and 0.58 prior to August 15. The results for the weekly series indicate that agents could be fairly confident in their money's process consistency prior to August, 1923.[8]

In figure 18.1, we reproduce figure 4 from our previous (1980a) paper; this is simply a diagram of the movement through time of the process consistency probabilities based on the original money series. Superimposed (solid lines) on figure 18.1 is the probability time series computed from the all-inclusive weekly money data. While the timing of the cycles is the same in both cases, the cycles for the all weekly data exhibit a substantially higher amplitude.

The Greek Case

We computed the probabilities of process consistency for the Greek inflation from January 1943 through August 1946. Data are available at monthly intervals and we used the end of month money series reported in Cleveland and Delivanis (1948). For the first money supply observation we selected July, 1941, the beginning of the Nazi occupation.

An attempt at monetary reform occurred on November 11, 1944; but this reform is generally considered to have been abortive since it was followed by nearly two more years of money stock and price increases. A data problem coincides with this reform attempt because the money stock is reported as of November 11, 1944, rather than as of November 30. Thus, we were forced to interpolate to derive a November 30 observation. We tried two different methods to produce a continuous time series of money observations. In the first method (series I) a linear interpolation in the double logarithm of the money supply was performed on the November 11 and December 31 observations to yield on observation for November 30. In the second method (series II) the average monthly β_t's were computed from the observations on October 31 and November 11 and from the observations on November 11 and December 31; this method is essentially the same as that used in our original German series in that observations taken at varying time intervals are connected in a time series.

We report process consistency probabilities for both series in table 18.3; of course, the two series are identical prior to November 11, 1944. The $\hat{\alpha}$ used to derive log Ψ is that reported by Cagan, $\hat{\alpha} = -4.09$ months.

The process consistency probability for the drachma fluctuates between 0.55 and 0.79 from January 1943 through April 1944. Starting in June 1944 it declines steadily, reaching a value near zero by November 30, the moment the reform started. By January 1945, the probability of process consistency reaches 0.84, the highest value to date, and begins a steady rise toward unity. Thus, the Greek case is similar to the German case in that the probability of process consistency reaches its lowest value at the moment of the reform. The reform did not succeed in halting the inflation, but apparently it was successful in restoring the public's confidence in the process consistency of the drachma.

In figure 18.2, we plot the probabilities of process consistency for the series I data. Observation 5 corresponds to May 1943; observation 22 is November 1944.

The Hungary II Case

The Hungarian II case, like the German case, is complicated by the introduction of a "fixed value" currency during the last months of the inflation. The tax pengo was a demand deposit which was indexed to a cost-of-living price index, although its units were always measured in terms of the nominal pengo. Introduced in Janory 1946, it maintained its real value until May. The inflation then became so rapid that the indexation, based on the price index on the day prior to withdrawal, was not sufficient to maintain its real value; and the tax pengo also depreciated rapidly in real terms. Thus, the "fixed value" money became a nominal money in the last

Table 18.3
Probabilities of process consistency—Greece

Date	Probability series I	Probability series II	Date	Probability series I	Probability series II
Jan. 1943	0.722	0.722	Nov.	0.937×10^{-7}	0.936×10^{-7}
Feb.	0.771	0.771	Dec.	0.498	0.921×10^{-8}
March	0.779	0.779	Jan. 1945	0.845	0.911
April	0.748	0.748	Feb.	0.859	0.916
May	0.714	0.714	March	0.887	0.929
June	0.793	0.793	April	0.893	0.933
July	0.780	0.780	May	0.895	0.935
Aug.	0.732	0.732	June	0.901	0.939
Sept.	0.732	0.732	July	0.904	0.941
Oct.	0.730	0.730	Aug.	0.908	0.944
Nov.	0.634	0.634	Sept.	0.910	0.946
Dec.	0.644	0.644	Oct.	0.913	0.949
Jan. 1944	0.583	0.583	Nov.	0.916	0.951
Feb.	0.741	0.741	Dec.	0.919	0.952
March	0.710	0.710	Jan. 1946	0.921	0.954
April	0.555	0.555	Feb.	0.923	0.956
May	0.149	0.149	March	0.924	0.957
June	0.506	0.506	April	0.928	0.959
July	0.463	0.463	May	0.930	0.961
Aug.	0.383	0.383	June	0.933	0.962
Sept.	0.044	0.044	July	0.935	0.964
Oct.	0.00022	0.00022	Aug.	0.937	0.965

months of the inflation. See Nogaro (1948) for a detailed discussion of this inflation.[9]

To account for this difficulty, we again employed two time series for money. The first (series I) is a series of nominal money only, which, prior to January 1946, is the sum of paper pengos and demand deposits. From Janaury 1946 onward, the demand deposits were indexed, so from that date series I consists only of paper pengos. The second series (series II) consists of paper pengos plus the nominal value of tax pengos throughout the hyperinflation. Series II seems to be the preferable series, since by the end of July 1946, the ratio of the nominal value of deposits to the nominal value of notes was on the order of magnitude of 10^{10} that is, notes had ceased to be money. With the reform on August 1, 1946, a new currency, the forint was introduced, and the ratio of notes to deposits resumed its pretax pengo value, approximately six to one.

In table 18.4, we report the money supply figures for the Hungarian II case so that the reader may obtain an idea of the magnitudes involved. The

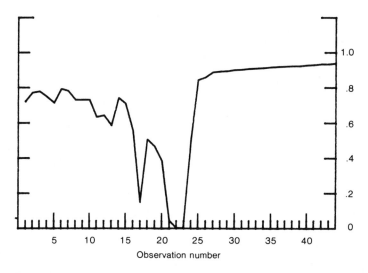

Figure 18.2
Probabilities of process consistency—Greece

data are the end of month figures. We begin our first money stock observation in June, 1945.[10] Starting in August 1946, the forint was introduced; it was exchanged with the pengo at a rate of 400 octillion (10^{27}) pengo/forint. We have converted all money totals to pengos.

In table 18.5 we report our computed probabilities of process consistency for both data series. The $\hat{\alpha}$ used to compute $\log \Psi$ is Cagan's, $\hat{\alpha} =$ -3.63 months. The probability series begins with low process consistency probabilities, which then rise somewhat. This phenomenon results from our starting our money observations in June 1945; this means that the first few β_t observations, which are increasing, have a strong influence on the posterior p.d.f., causing it to give substantial weight to the nonconvergent region. The decline in β_t for November–December 1945 produces the jump in the process consistency probability. The probabilities then decline until the reform in August 1946; the series II process consistency probability reaches its lowest value at the moment of the reform and then rises steadily. We diagram this series in figure 18.3; observation three corresponds to January 1946 while observation 10 corresponds to August 1946.

The series I probability reaches its lowest value in July 1946, rises in August, and declines again in September. This phenomenon can be interpreted from the data in table 18.4. Recalling that the process consistency probability for a given observation is computed using money data through the prior observation, we note that the ratio of pengos in June 1946 to

Table 18.4
Money supply—Hungary II[a]

Date	Notes (billion pengo)	Deposits (billion pengo)	Total (billion pengo)
Jan. 1945	11.1	—	—
Feb.	11.1	—	—
March	11.1	—	—
April	11.6	—	—
May	12.1	—	—
June	14.5	3.2	17.2
July	16.3	3.9	20.2
Aug.	24.4	4.7	29.1
Sept.	41.9	6.2	48.1
Oct.	110.0	9.6	119.6
Nov.	360.0	28.0	338.0
Dec.	770.0	64.0	834.0
Jan. 1946	1.6×10^3	151.0	1.75×10^3
Feb.	5.2×10^3	1.1×10^3	6.3×10^3
March	3.4×10^4	1.2×10^4	4.6×10^4
April	4.3×10^5	3.5×10^5	7.8×10^5
May	6.6×10^7	1.1×10^8	1.76×10^8
June	6.3×10^{12}	1.7×10^{13}	2.33×10^{13}
July	4.7×10^{16}	2.4×10^{26}	2.4×10^{26}
Aug.[b]	3.56×10^{26}	0.51×10^{26}	4.07×10^{26}
Sept.	6.07×10^{26}	1.10×10^{26}	7.17×10^{26}
Oct.	8.43×10^{26}	1.172×10^{26}	10.15×10^{26}
Nov.	9.37×10^{26}	2.45×10^{26}	11.82×10^{26}
Dec.	9.68×10^{26}	2.80×10^{26}	12.48×10^{26}
Jan. 1947	10.17×10^{26}	3.05×10^{26}	13.22×10^{26}
Feb.	10.93×10^{26}	3.56×10^{26}	14.47×10^{26}
March	11.73×10^{26}	4.04×10^{26}	15.77×10^{26}
April	12.58×10^{26}	4.48×10^{26}	17.06×10^{26}
May	14.08×10^{26}	4.89×10^{26}	18.97×10^{26}
June	14.68×10^{26}	5.15×10^{26}	19.83×10^{26}

a. Source: U.N. Monthly Bulletin of Statistics, Jan. 1947, no. 1, Dec. 1947, no. 12.
b. Data in forints converted to pengos at 400 octillion (10^{27}) pengo/forint.

Table 18.5
Probabilities of process consistency—Hungary II

Date	Probability series I	Probability series II
Nov. 1945	0.0322	0.0322
Dec.	0.0597	0.0597
Jan. 1946	0.424	0.424
Feb.	0.485	0.461
March	0.390	0.357
April	0.264	0.236
May	0.203	0.157
June	0.051	0.036
July	0.0036	0.0028
Aug.	0.277	0.000058
Sept.	0.096	0.422
Oct.	0.481	0.449
Nov.	0.502	0.474
Dec.	0.523	0.497
Jan. 1947	0.543	0.519
Feb.	0.561	0.541
March	0.579	0.561
April	0.596	0.580
May	0.612	0.599
June	0.628	0.616
July	0.642	0.633

pengos in May 1946 was an order of magnitude greater than the July–June ratio. The β_t observation for July would then be lower than that for June causing a rise in the process consistency calculation for August. The decline in the probability calculation for September can be explained by the August reform. The July 1946 money data indicate that the pengo notes had become an insubstantial part of the money stock by that date. The reform on August 1 restored a more normal ratio of notes to deposits (in terms of forints); when the forints are converted to pengos in August, notes appear to have risen by a factor of 10^{10} over July, thereby causing a fall in the process consistency probability measured for September. Obviously, the results for series I must be treated gingerly.

The Russian Case

As in the German and Hungarian II episodes, the Russian experience is complicated by the introduction of a fixed value currency, the chevronetz, prior to the monetary reform. The reform can be dated around February–

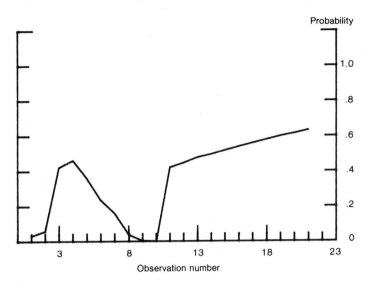

Figure 18.3
Probabilities of process consistency—Hungary II

March 1924; the chevrontsi started to circulate in Jaunary, 1923. We computed probabilities of process consistency both for the money series consisting of paper rubles alone (series I) and for the series consisting of paper rubles plus the paper value of the chevronetz circulation (series II). The data for the quantities of money in circulation and the market exchange rates are available in Katszenellenbaum (1925).

We report the results of these computations in table 18.6. The starting date for the money supply series was November 1917, the beginning of the Bolshevik revolution. The $\hat{\alpha}$ used to compute log Ψ was Cagan's $\hat{\alpha} =$ −3.06 months. The computed probabilities of process consistency do not approach the low levels reached by the more extreme inflations. The lowest level attained was 0.526 in February 1922.[11] There is a fairly substantial decline in the probabilities near the end of the inflation (to 0.777 for the paper ruble series in December, 1923), but the reform occurred two or three months later.

The Polish Case

To study the Polish case, we used a money supply series observed at ten-day intervals. The monetary aggregate (central bank notes in circulation) is the same as that usually used for this case, but the time between

Table 18.6
Probabilities of process consistency—Russia

Date	Prob.: paper rubles only	Prob.: paper rubles and chevrontsi	Date	Prob.: paper rubles only	Prob.: paper rubles and chevrontsi
April 1, 1921	0.996	—	Jan. 1, 1923	0.960	—
May 1	0.997	—	Feb.	0.947	0.942
June 1	0.997	—	March	0.952	0.946
July 1	0.997	—	April	0.961	0.956
Aug. 1	0.998	—	May	0.947	0.936
Sept. 1	0.995	—	June	0.951	0.933
Oct. 1	0.990	—	July	0.968	0.961
Nov. 1	0.985	—	Aug.	0.961	0.941
Dec. 1	0.938	—	Sept.	0.954	0.898
Jan. 1, 1922	0.869	—	Oct.	0.958	0.827
Feb. 1	0.526	—	Nov.	0.957	0.782
March 1	0.727	—	Dec.	0.777	0.865
April 1	0.797	—	Jan. 1, 1924	0.920	0.873
May 1	0.771	—	Feb.	0.926	0.850
June 1	0.859	—	March	0.920	0.749
July 1	0.806	—	April	0.804	0.793
Aug. 1	0.902	—	May	0.987	0.976
Sept. 1	0.910	—	June	0.988	0.979
Oct. 1	0.915	—			
Nov. 1	0.948	—			
Dec. 1	0.946	—			

observations has been one month. We obtained our data from weekly issues of *Economist* published contemporaneously with the Polish inflation; starting on August 31, 1922, the money stock was regularly sampled at ten-day intervals through the inflation's end in February, 1924.

Table 18.7 contains the probabilities of process consistency for Poland. Once again Cagan's $\hat{\alpha} = -2.30$ months, altered to conform to the ten-day time interval, was employed in computing log Ψ. The lowest process consistency probability, 0.927, occurs on December 10, 1923, two months prior to the reform.

The Austrian and Hungarian I Cases

For the Austrian and Hungarian I inflations, we used money supply series observed at weekly intervals instead of the monthly series used by other researchers. Weekly data for the Austrian crown are available in Walres des Bordes (1924); we chose January 7, 1920 for our first observation on the

Table 18.7
Probabilities of process consistency—Poland

Date	Prob.	Date	Prob.
July 20, 1923	0.989	Jan. 10, 1924	0.942
July 31	0.989	Jan. 20	0.989
Aug. 10	0.986	Jan. 31	0.983
Aug. 20	0.989	Feb. 10	0.940
Aug. 31	0.989	Feb. 20	0.989
Sept.10	0.975	Feb. 29	0.992
Sept. 20	0.987	March 10	0.990
Sept. 30	0.988	March 20	0.994
Oct. 10	0.974	March 31	0.994
Oct. 20	0.986	April 10	0.995
Oct. 31	0.981	April 20	0.996
Nov. 10	0.932	April 27	0.996
Nov. 20	0.980		
Nov. 30	0.965		
Dec. 10	0.927		
Dec. 20	0.983		
Dec. 31	0.969		

Austrian money supply. For Hungary, weekly data exists in *Economist's* weekly reports on central bank balance sheets in contemporary volumes; we selected December 31, 1921 as our first observation on the Hungarian money stock. For Austria, the reform occurred in September, 1922; for Hungary, the reform can be dated in February, 1924.

Cagan's $\hat{\alpha}$'s, altered to account for the weekly observation period, were employed; for Austria, $\hat{\alpha} = -8.55$ months while for Hungary, $\hat{\alpha} = -8.70$ months. The Austrian probability of process consistency was computed for each week in the period March 15, 1922 to December 15, 1922; for all observations the probability of process consistency is at least 0.9999. For Hungary, the probabilities were computed for each week in the period March 15, 1923 to March 31, 1924; for all but two observations, the probability of process consistency was at least 0.99. For two weeks August 23 and August 31, 1923, the probability fell to 0.983.

III Conclusion

In this study we have applied our technique for measuring process consistency probabilities to all the hyperinflationary episodes examined by Cagan. As in our previous work, we find that for the severe hyperinflations the process consistency probabilities attain their lowest values at the times of the monetary reforms. These results are useful in that they allow us to

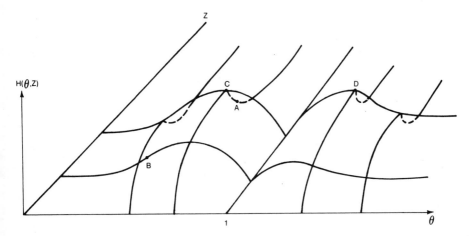

Figure 18.A.1
Diagram of $H(\theta, Z)$

make some sense of the unusual events which occur at the ends of extreme hyperinflations. With such understanding the hyperinflations can be treated as one part of an overall time series of data rather than as isolated monetary experiments.

However, results pertaining to process consistency are applicable in a different dimension. In many optimizing models of money demand, a transversality condition on preferences is imposed which forces every money supply process to be process consistent. Evidence that process inconsistency may be a factor in terminating a particular money supply process can serve as evidence against such transversality conditions. We leave the development of this possibility to another paper.

Appendix

In this appendix we describe the method which we used to integrate numerically the p.d.f. in (3) over the region in (4). The function $H(\theta, Z)$ is bimodal; one mode occurs in a region where $\theta > 1$ and one is in a region where $\theta < 1$. The function has properties such that for given $\bar{Z}$, $\lim_{\theta + \to 1} H(\theta, \bar{Z}) = 0$ and $\lim_{\theta - \to 1} H(\theta, \bar{Z}) = 0$. For given $\bar{\theta}$, $\lim_{Z + \to 0} H(\bar{\theta}, Z) = 0$. Along the Z-axis, for given $\bar{\theta}$, there is a single inflection point. In the θ-direction for $\theta < 1$ and given $\bar{Z}$, there is a single inflection point; similarly, for $\theta > 1$ and given $\bar{Z}$, there is a single inflection point. The function is diagrammed in figure 18.A.1. Point A is an

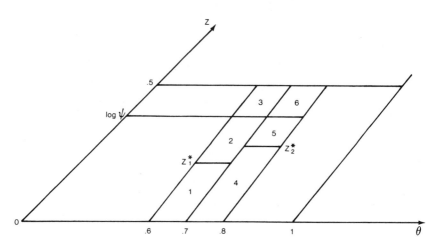

Figure 18.A.2
Regions of integration

inflection point of the function for given $\bar{\theta}$; B is an inflection point for given $\bar{Z}$; and C and D are the two modal values.

We integrated this p.d.f. over thirty-six contiguous regions in the (θ, Z) plane; the probability weights outside of those regions were never significant. The regions were determined as follows. The θ-axis between 0.6 and 1.3 was divided into twelve segments, six on either side of $\theta = 1$. The points on the θ-axis which define the division, were 0.6, 0.7, 0.8, 0.9, 0.95, 0.975, 1.00, 1.01, 1.03, 1.05, 1.075, 1.15, and 1.3. For a given segment of the θ-axis the Z-axis was divided into three segments. The position of these segments depended on the average over the θ-segment of the p.d.f.'s Z-direction inflection points. For instance, the first θ segment, between 0.6 and 0.7, was subdivided into twenty-five subsegments for the numerical integration: for the endpoint of each subsegment there is a value of Z which locates the inflection point of the p.d.f. Define Z^* as the average of these Z's across the given θ segment. Then for the θ segment between 0.6 and 0.7 the Z-axis was segmented from zero to Z^*, from Z^* to log Ψ, and from log Ψ to 0.5. If, by chance, $Z^* >$ log Ψ, then the segments were zero to log Ψ, log Ψ to Z^*, and Z^* to 0.5.

The regions of integration for a given observation in a given hyper-inflation might then appear as in figure 18.A.2. Region 1 is the rectangle defined by $[0.6 \leq \theta \leq 0.7, 0 \leq Z \leq Z_1^*]$, where Z_1^* is the average of the inflection points for the $0.6 \leq \theta \leq 0.7$ segment. Region 2 is the rectangle $[0.6 \leq \theta \leq 0.7, Z_1^* \leq Z \leq$ log $\Psi]$; Region 3 is the rectangle $[0.6 \leq \theta \leq 0.7,$

$\log \Psi \leqq Z \leqq 0.5$], region 4 is the rectangle $[0.7 \leqq \theta \leqq 0.8, 0 \leqq Z \leqq Z_2^*]$, etc. For purposes of the numerical integration, each rectangle, except the two rectangles containing the modal values of (θ, Z), was subdivided by splitting its sides into twenty-five subsegments; thus, the p.d.f. was evaluated at 625 points in each region. The sides of the modal rectangles were divided into fifty subsegments, so in these two regions the p.d.f. was evaluated at 2500 points.

We took this care in setting our regions and grid sizes because of the nature of the p.d.f. Typically, $H(\theta, Z)$ produced a very narrow ridge running in the θ direction; the probability weight was so concentrated, that it was easy to miss significant portions of it by making the mesh of our grids too large. Using the inflection points of the p.d.f. assured that we would catch most of the probability weight. The same reasoning lay behind our selecting a finer mesh in the modal regions.

To carry out the integration, we used Simpson's rule twice. See Zellner (1971, appendix C) for a description of this method.

Notes

This research was supported by NSF grant SES-7926807. Louis Scott carried out the computational work in this paper.

1. Less emphasis has been given to the role of hyperinflation as part of the continuous economic process, producing effects which may still manifest themselves long after the monetary reform.

2. In addition, our model is capable of removing the discontinuity between an extreme hyperinflation and its post-reform era.

3. Some of our previous work involving the German case has been criticized on the grounds that hyperinflation data contains massive measurement errors. We find this critique hard to take seriously. A relevant measure of the importance of measurement error in data might be the ratio of variance induced by measurement error to total variance. A measure of unity would indicate worthless data. Because total variance in the data is so astoundingly huge, we feel, as did Cagan (1956, pp. 47–51), that measurement error is not a serious problem.

4. We assumed that no current information is used by agents forming inflation expectations because we wanted a *simple* method to capture agents' inability to observe current money currently. A more complex alternative would involve agents observing prices currently and forming an estimate of current money from that price information. The imposition of this additional complication is not pursued. If we did pursue this complication our results would be a weighted average of our present results and the results assuming agents to have full current information about money and prices. The full current information results may be obtained from those presented below by pushing all of our probabilities back in time one observation interval.

5. Cagan suggested that this phenomenon may have been due to agents' anticipation of monetary reform. If this suggestion is correct, then agents in the extreme inflations must have had a reason to believe in impending reform while agents in the mild inflations had no such reason. The need to exclude the last two months of the Polish data as outliers may have arisen in Cagan's empirical technique; Barro (1970) managed to incorporate the entire Polish data set in estimating his model.

6. The Reichsbanknotes were the currency which drove the hyperinflation. While other currencies constituted a third of the money supply in 1918, they remained relatively stable during the following years, so that by the end of 1922 they represented only 1.5 percent of the money stock.

7. Cagan felt that the "fixed value" currencies should be left out of the money totals since they were not depreciating in terms of goods. However, these currencies had no backing; they were promises to pay in some asset denominated in gold which would be available at some point in the future.

8. One reason that this change may have occurred is that use of a weekly series quadruples the number of pre-1923 observations from 50 to 200; any given 1923 observation would then produce less of an alteration in the posterior p.d.f. However, beginning in August the observations on β_t deviated substantially enough from the predictable values that the posterior p.d.f.'s (at least in terms of the probabilities associated with the convergent regions) were essentially the same.

9. Bomberger and Makinen (1980) have recently reiterated Nogaro's observations in a more modern idiom.

10. The Russian invasion of Hungary occurred in the early months of 1945, so this is a reasonable time to start with diffuse priors. Before 1945, there was a substantial money creation, but with the Russian invasion Hungarian Nazis ran off with the currency reserves, so there was little money creation before June 1945.

11. There was an attempt to reform the currency in early 1922 by replacing the old ruble with a new ruble. Table 1 indicates the degree of success of this reform.

References

Barro, R. J., 1970, Inflation, the payments period and the demand for money, Journal of Political Economy 78, no. 6, Nov./Dec., 1228–1263.

Bomberger, W. and G. Makinen, 1980, Indexation, inflationary finance, and hyperinflation: The 1945–1946 Hungarian experience, Journal of Political Economy 88, no. 3, June, 550–560.

Bresciani-Turroni, C., 1968, The economics of inflation (Kelley, Northampton).

Cagan, P., 1956, The monetary dynamics of hyperinflation, in: M. Friedman, ed., Studies in the quantity theory of money (Chicago University Press, Chicago IL).

Cleveland, W. and D. Delivanis, 1949, Greek monetary developments 1939–1948 (Indiana University Press, Bloomington, IN).

Economist, 89–98 (Jan, 1919–June 1924).

Flood, R. and P. Garber, 1980a, An economic theory of monetary reform, Journal of Political Economy 88, no. 1, 24–58.

Flood, R. and P. Garber 1980b, Market fundamentals vs. price level bubbles: The first tests, *Journal of Political Economy* 88, No. 4, 745–770.

Katzenellenbaum, S., 1925, Russian currency and banking, 1914–1924 (P.S. King & Son, London).

Nogaro, B., 1948, Hungary's recent monetary crisis and its theoretical meaning, *American Economic Review* 48, Sept.

Statistisches, Reichsamt, 1925, Zahlen zur Geldentwertung in Deutschsland 1914 bis 1923, Sonderhefte zur Wirtschaft and Statistik (Hobbing, Berlin).

Walres de Bordes, J., 1924, The Austrian crown (P.S. King & Son, London).

U.N. Monthly Bulletin of Statistics Jan. 1947, no. 1, Dec. 1947, no. 2.

Zellner, A., 1971, *An introduction to Bayesian inference in econometrics* (Wiley, New York).

19

Nominal Contracts in a Bimetallic Standard

Peter M. Garber

The objective of this chapter is to determine the value of contracts to deliver dollars under a bimetallic standard, a multiple commodity standard of the sort embraced by many of the industrializing countries in the nineteenth century. Since contracting in bimetallic dollars grants the short interest an option to deliver either gold or silver, a dollar contract can be evaluated by applying results from the options literature. With such an evaluation, one can determine the magnitude of wealth transfers effected by terminating or returning to a bimetallic standard, as occurred during phases of the nineteenth-century silver agitation. Also, evaluation of the bimetallic contract provides a rationale for the high yields on dollar securities relative to sterling yields observed in the nineteenth century. While high dollar yields have been interpreted in the literature as an indicator of a higher cost of capital in the United States, they resulted merely from the difference in monetary standards.

Under a bimetallic monetary standard, the unit of account is defined as either a given weight of gold or a given weight of silver.[1] Since the market relative price between the two metals rarely equals the legally implied exchange ratio, the cheaper metallic unit or its value equivalent is delivered to satisfy contracts in the nominal unit.[2]

Most discussions of bimetallic standards focus on the necessary appearance of a sequence of monometallic epochs which alternate between deliveries of gold and silver money.[3] The observed failure of most bimetallic systems to achieve the simultaneous circulation and delivery of both metals is deemed obvious evidence of the weakness of bimetallism. Economists have proposed more sophisticated metallic or general commodity standards, such as symmetallism or tabular standards, aimed both at circumventing this monometallic circulation and at stabilizing the price level.[4] While many economists expect welfare gains from price level stabilization, it is not clear why recurrent switching from one circulating metal to another should be detrimental of itself.

Policy discussions of the US. bimetallic standard peaked in the 1890s and 1930s. Since these were periods of depression, deflation, and cheap silver, powerful coalitions of groups which would benefit from inflation organized around the reestablishment of the original bimetallic dollar standard. In such a system, cheap silver-based money would immediately become the circulating medium, driving up the price level and effecting substantial transfers to debtors.

This chapter develops a method to price actual nominal contracts under bimetallism and to address some historical issues arising from the U.S. bimetallic experience. In the development of a pricing model and of the estimates of the bimetallic option values, I follow the same strategy as Gerald Gay and Steven Manaster (1984), who constructed the option values of delivering different qualities of wheat in a futures contract. Section I presents a brief history of nineteenth-century U.S. coinage laws relating to bimetallism. Section II contains a demonstration of how to evaluate a bimetallic contract using results from the options pricing literature. In an example based on results in Robert Merton (1973), William Margrabe (1978), and René Stulz (1982), the current value of a contract to deliver dollars in the future is developed for continuous time environments. One can readily show that the price paid for a dollar contract will be less than the prices paid for otherwise identical contracts promising to pay only gold or only silver. The measured yields on dollar contracts will then be higher than yields on monometallic contracts.

In section III, I compute theoretical values of actual U.S. Treasury securities promising to deliver bimetallic dollars in varying future payment streams. I calculate the implied option value of the bimetallic bonds relative to gold bonds and compare bimetallic theoretical bond prices to actual realized prices. In section IV, I address the issue of whether capital was more costly in the nineteenth-century United States than in Great Britain, a standard debate in the historical literature. In section V, I use the computed option values to examine the potential wealth transfers from terminating the free coinage of silver in 1873 and restoring it at the end of the nineteenth century. The results indicate that the wealth transfer from debtors associated with the termination of the free coinage of silver in 1873 was small, amounting to no more than one year's interest payment on outstanding debt. Given the low price of silver in the 1890s, restoration of free coinage of silver would have far more than offset the value of the original transfer.

I   The Evolution of U.S. Bimetallism

Here I present a brief chronology of the legal development of U.S. bimetallism. Also, I describe some of the legislation implemented in the post-1873 agitation to restore the free coinage of silver. I have relied on J. Laurence Laughlin (1885), Charles Dunbar (1883), the U.S. Senate Finance Committee (1894), and Milton Friedman and Anna Schwartz (1963) as sources for this discussion.

Prior to the adoption of the Constitution, foreign coins, primarily silver Spanish dollars, comprised the specie of the United States. The first national coinage was provided under the Act of 1792 which established the mint and defined the dollar as 371.25 grains (.773 troy ounces) of silver. The law authorized the coinage of a silver dollar and half-dollars, quarter-dollars, dimes, and half-dimes containing corresponding weights of silver. In addition, the mint was authorized to issue ten-dollar gold coins (eagles) containing 247.5 grains (.515 troy ounces) of gold, as well as half-eagles and quarter-eagles. Effectively, the law defined the monetary value of a given weight of gold as fifteen times that of the same weight of silver. It provided for free coinage of both metals in that anyone delivering a given weight of a metal to the mint could receive in exchange authorized coins containing an equal weight of the same metal. This service would be provided free of charge if the delivering party were willing to allow the coinage to occur "as speedily as may be after the receipt thereof [of the bullion]" (Dunbar, p. 228). Finally, the law declared that the coins struck at the mint were lawful tender "in all payments whatsoever, those [coins] of full weight according to the respective values herein before declared" (Dunbar, p. 229).[5]

Figure 19.1 indicates the ratio of the market price of gold to that of silver from 1787 to 1884. In 1792, as the coinage act was passed, the market ratio was approximately 15/1. However, the ratio permanently rose above 15/1, making silver overvalued at the mint. Since contracting parties would then deliver only silver or its value equivalent to satisfy dollar contracts, the real value of the dollar was the value in terms of goods of 371.25 grains of silver.

In an act of 1834, the dollar was devalued in terms of gold. The ten-dollar gold coin would now contain 232. grains (.483 troy ounces) of gold, a devaluation of 6.3 percent, which changed to 16/1 the weight ratio of silver to gold in the dollar. Proprotional changes were made in the gold content of the smaller gold coins. Since the market relative price fluctuated between 15.5 and 16., this devaluation meant that gold or its value

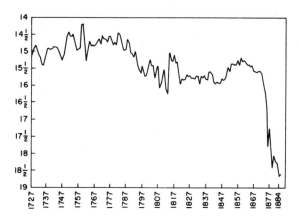

Figure 19.1
The number of ounces of silver exchangeable for one ounce of gold. Source: Laughlin,
p. 161

equivalent would now be delivered to satisfy dollar contracts. The act of
1837 slightly revalued the ten-dollar coin to 232.2 grains of gold, with
corresponding changes in the smaller gold coins.

In 1853, the full silver weight and unlimited legal tender properties of
the fractional coinage were terminated. The amount of silver in the fractional coins was reduced by 7 percent, and they were made legal tender in
quantities not exceeding five dollars. Furthermore, the free coinage of fractional coins was terminated. This change meant that the ratio of silver
contained in a dollar's worth of fractional coins to gold in the gold dollar
was less than 15/1. The law left unchanged the definition of the silver
dollar.

In 1859, the enormous Nevada Comstock Lode was discovered, a silver
strike which reversed the decline in the relative value of gold begun with
the Californian and Australian gold strikes of the 1840s. Silver prices slowly
declined until 1873 when the accelerating development of the Nevada
deposits initiated a rapid fall in the silver price.

In the act of February 12, 1873, silver was effectively demonetized. The
old silver dollar was not included among the silver coins authorized for
minting in the United States, although a "trade dollar" and fractional coins
were allowed. Only these authorized silver coins were given legal tender
status for payments not exceeding five dollars. Free coinage of legal tender
silver was eliminated. By this act the metallic dollar was effectively defined
as a given weight of gold alone.[6] Any contracts for future delivery of

dollars were redefined by this act in that only gold or greenbacks could be delivered, where before silver could have been delivered. From the point of view of the government, which delivered only specie on its debt, its contractual option to deliver silver was now removed.[7] In addition to the United States, other important countries abandoned silver simultaneously, that is, Germany which had a silver standard and the Latin Union (France, Italy, and Belgium) which had a bimetallic standard.

Some researchers have argued that the changes had little practical effect since the market ratio of the gold price to the silver price was still below 16/1 in 1873.[8] However, though the 1873 market ratio was still below 16/1, this change may have represented an important wealth transfer. If the value of the bimetallic option to pay in silver was high, anyone engaged on the short side of a dollar contract prior to 1873 would immediately feel the impact of the change in standard as a transfer from himself to his creditors. Similarly, taxpayers would recognize a transfer from themselves to the government's creditors.

Soon after the law's passage, the market ratio exceeded 16/1, reaching levels over the next twenty years which were unprecedented in the prior two centuries of data. The sudden rise in the market ratio triggered a quarter-century agitation to restore the free coinage of silver. First fruit of this movement was the Bland-Allison Act of 1878 which reauthorized the issue of the standard silver dollar with legal tender status and required limited Treasury silver purchases with silver certificates. Since government obligations required only the delivery of coin, this change restored the bimetallic option to the government. However, free coinage of silver was not restored.

The Sherman Silver Purchase Act of 1890 repealed the silver purchase provisions of the Bland-Allison Act, replacing them with a requirement to purchase silver more rapidly. Payment for the silver was made in Treasury notes of 1890, a legal tender currency redeemable on demand into gold or silver coin at the option of the government. The law required the purchase of 4.5 million ounces of silver per month at market prices until the market price reached one dollar for 371.25 grains of silver. Had this law remained in effect indefinitely, it would have increased the domestic credit (silver) component of the money base until only silver coin or notes convertible to silver would have been delivered to satisfy nominal contracts. Effectively, this would have been equivalent to a resumption of free coinage of silver, thereby threatening the continued circulation of gold. Within three years, the gold dollar was sufficiently threatened that the Sherman Silver Purchase Act was repealed in the midst of the Panic of 1893. However, the agitation for free coinage of silver was not extinguished until the presidential election of 1896.

II   Evaluating a Future Dollar Delivery

Here I produce a pricing formula for contracts promising future dollar deliveries in a bimetallic standard, emphasizing that a delivery option is the essential feature of a bimetallic standard. The dollar contract pricing solution and the extent of the discount will be developed in a continuous time environment. In this section, all prices will be denominated in terms of units of gold. Units of gold and silver are defined as the legal pure gold and silver content of the dollar, respectively. I will assume that an individual's portfolio may hold positions in contracts for future dollar deliveries, in silver or gold bonds, and in options to supply a unit of gold in exchange for a unit of silver in the future (silver option). Alternatively, it may contain an option to supply a unit of silver in exchange for a unit of gold (gold option).[9] These metal exchange options are standard call options. For example, since the holder of the silver option can require the delivery of a unit of silver for a unit of gold, he has a call option on silver with a striking price of unity.

The procedure involved in finding the time t value of a contract to deliver one dollar at time $t + \theta$ borrows directly from concepts in the option price literature. I find appropriate positions in pure discount gold bonds, silver bonds, or metal call options in the time t portfolio which perfectly duplicate the payoffs of the dollar contract in all future contingencies. The value of the dollar contract can be determined as the equity value of the bond and option positions through a simple arbitrage argument.

Specifically, the time t market value of an agreement to deliver one dollar at time $t + \theta$ can be derived by evaluating a position in pure discount silver bonds and silver call options which duplicates the $t + \theta$ payoff of the dollar contract. The silver bonds mature at $t + \theta$ and have a face value of one unit of silver, and the call option expires at $t + \theta$.

Using table 19.1, it is easy to verify that a portfolio long one silver discount bond and short one silver call option mimics the dollar contract. One silver discount bond will pay one unit of silver at $t + \theta$, with a gold value of $P_s(t + \theta)$. The short position in the silver option will entail a zero payoff if $P_s(t + \theta) < 1$ and a negative payoff $1 - P_s(t + \theta)$ if $P_s(t + \theta) > 1$. When the silver dollar is worth less than the gold dollar, the dollar contract will pay out one unit of silver with a value of $P_s(t + \theta)$. Otherwise, it will pay out a gold dollar valued at 1. The net payoff of the silver bond-

Table 19.1
Payoffs from silver bond, silver option, and dollar contract

	Contingencies at $t + \theta$	
Asset	$P_s(t + \theta) < 1$	$P_s(t + \theta) > 1$
1. Silver Bond	$P_s(t + \theta)$	$P_s(t + \theta)$
2. Silver Option	0	$1 - P_s(t + \theta)$
3. Dollar Contract	$P_s(t + \theta)$	1

silver option position is $P_s(t + \theta)$ if $P_s(t + \theta) < 1$ and 1 if $P_s(t + \theta) > 1$, which is identical to the payoff pattern of the dollar contract. Therefore, arbitrage would prevent the current gold value, $V(P_s(t), \theta)$, of the dollar contract from differing from the value of the equity in the silver bond-silver option position.

The equity value of the position depends on the assumed stochastic laws of motion for the $P_s(t)$ and for the yields on gold and silver bonds. For example, I will assume that gold and silver bonds pay continuously compounded, constant own yields π_g and π_s, respectively. Also, the relative price of silver in terms of gold is driven by the stochastic process:

$$dP_s(t)/P_s(t) = \mu \, dt + \lambda dZ(t), \tag{1}$$

where μ is the instantaneous expected percentage relative price change of silver; λ is the associated instantaneous standard error, assumed constant; $Z(t)$ is a Wiener process. The time t prices of gold, 1, and silver, $P_s(t)$, will move exogenously to the market for dollar contracts.

In this case the equity value of the silver bond-silver option position is

$$V(P_s(t), \theta) = \exp[-\pi_s \theta]P_s(t) - D_s(P_s(t), \theta), \tag{2a}$$

where $\exp(-\pi_s \theta)$ is the current value in silver of the bond, and $D_s(P_s(t), \theta)$ is the value of the silver call option expiring at $t + \theta$, given time t prices. Using a similar argument based on positions in gold discount bonds and gold options, the dollar contract's value can also be expressed as

$$V(P_s(t), \theta) = \exp[-\pi_g \theta] - D_g(P_s(t), \theta), \tag{2b}$$

where $D_g(P_s(t), \theta)$ is the value of an option to deliver a unit of silver in exchange for a unit of gold.

To derive the price $D_s(P_s(t), \theta)$, I argue that the option on silver is analogous to a call option on a stock which continuously pays a dividend equal to a constant percentage of the stock's market price. Since Merton has produced a pricing formula for such an option, I can then substitute it for D_s in (2a).[10] Since the numeraire gold will be delivered in payment by the holder in exercising the option, instantaneous gold loans are the analogs to the riskless nominal loans in the standard option pricing formulas; and the instantaneous gold yield π_g is the analog to the yield on risk-free loans.

To complete the analogy, I must consider which asset constitutes the underlying asset of the option. Since the option is a call option on one unit of silver, I must find a silver-denominated asset which delivers one silver unit at $t + \theta$. This delivery requirement is satisfied by the holding of one silver coupon bond maturing at $t + \theta$ with a par value of one unit of silver and continuous coupon rate of π_s. The silver coupon bond would deliver the one unit of silver at time $t + \theta$, so a call option on the bond exercisable at $t + \theta$ is a call on a unit of silver. Therefore, the coupon bond can represent the underlying security of the option. Also, the time t price in silver of this coupon bond is one silver dollar; so its time t price and coupon payment in gold are $P_s(t)$ and $\pi_s P_s(t)$, respectively. Since the stochastic processes driving the gold price of the silver coupon bond and its interest payments are exactly those assumed by Merton, his pricing formula is applicable:

$$D_s(P_s(t), \theta) = \exp[-\pi_s\theta]P_s(t)N(d_1) - \exp[-\pi_g\theta]N(d_2), \tag{3}$$

where

$$d_1 = [\ln(P_s(t)) + (\pi_g - \pi_s + \lambda^2/2)\theta]/\lambda\sqrt{\theta}$$

and

$$d_2 = d_1 - \lambda\sqrt{\theta}.$$

$N(x)$ is the value of the cumulative standard univariate normal distribution function evaluated at x, and λ^2 is the variance of the percentage change in the relative price between the gold and silver content of the dollar.

Substituting from (3) into (2) completes the calculation of $V(P_s(t), \theta)$. More generally, bimetallic coupon bonds which make discrete dollar payments $H(\theta)$ at $\theta = 1, 2, 3, \ldots, N$, have a current value of

$$VB(P_s(t)) = \sum_{\theta=1}^{N} V(P_s(t), \theta)H(\theta). \tag{4}$$

III   The Nominal Values of U.S. Bimetallic Securities

Here, I apply the dollar contract pricing formula derived in section II to compute the theoretical value of bonds promising to pay bimetallic dollars issued by the U.S. government in the nineteenth century. I employ formula (4) except that I compute security values in nominal rather than in gold terms. I simply multiply both sides of (4) by $\hat{P}_g$, the nominal value of the gold dollar. For P_s, the price of the silver dollar in terms of gold dollars, I substitute $\hat{P}_s/\hat{P}_g$, where $\hat{P}_s$ is the nominal value of the silver dollar. $\hat{P}_s$, $\hat{P}_g$, π_s, and π_g are obtained from actual observations. I report the steps required to compute $\hat{P}_g$ and $\hat{P}_s$ in the Appendix. For π_g, I use the beginning of January yield on British 3% Consols from 1818 to 1882 and 2.5 percent annuities from 1883 to 1896. Since Great Britain adhered to a monometallic gold standard for most of the period and paid these loans in gold throughout the period, the Consol and annuity yields represent the yield on pure gold loans. For π_s, I used the beginning of January yield on various longterm Prussian loans through 1870. Along with the rest of the German states, Prussia maintained a pure silver standard through 1873, so these yields represent the yield on pure silver loans. However, though Prussia switched to a gold standard in 1873, it had begun a transition from silver in 1871. Therefore, for 1871–96, I used the yield on rupee loans selling in London for π_s.[11]

The assumptions in the section II example of constant π_g and π_s and on the form of the process driving $P_s(t)$ are very strong. A glance at table 19.2 indicates that π_g and π_s fluctuated from 1818 to 1896. Thus, it is desirable to construct the price of the bimetallic bond in an environment of random movement of silver and gold yields to produce a proper model of the term structures for gold and silver loans. John Cox, Jonathan Ingersoll, and Stephen Ross (1985a, b) have recently provided a method of pricing discount loans and options on bonds in a one-good optimizing model. From assumptions on the stochastic process driving the productivity of capital, they derived the equilibrium stochastic process driving the yield on instantaneous riskless loans along with the equilibrium term structure on discount bonds. Cox et al. show that arbitrage methods for pricing securities may produce prices that are not supported in equilibrium because of arbitrary assumptions about the stochastic process driving the interest rate on riskless loans. For implementation in the present problem, their model must be extended to an environment of multiple, storable goods so that silver and gold can be priced along with consumption goods. Also, the empirical implementation of their methods requires the estimation of taste parameters, the identification of which is achieved by assuming that there are no taste disturbances. On this problem, see my paper with Robert King (1984). Finally empirical implementation of the Cox et al. model requires

Table 19.2
Data employed in bimetallic bond formula

Year	Dollar Price of Gold	Silver	Yield Gold	Silver	λ^{2a}
1818	1.0235	1.0000	0.0369	0.0598	0.00079
1819	0.9984	1.0000	0.0388	0.0558	0.00082
1820	1.0141	1.0000	0.0446	0.0586	0.00086
1821	1.0567	1.0000	0.0430	0.0570	0.00103
1822	1.0567	1.0000	0.0390	0.0539	0.00089
1823	1.0567	1.0000	0.0378	0.0541	0.00088
1824	1.0567	1.0000	0.0347	0.0445	0.00027
1825	1.0349	1.0000	0.0318	0.0446	0.00031
1826	1.0392	1.0000	0.0369	0.0467	0.00031
1827	1.0567	1.0000	0.0380	0.0455	0.00031
1828	1.0392	1.0000	0.0363	0.0438	0.00035
1829	1.0567	1.0000	0.0345	0.0398	0.00028
1830	1.0567	1.0000	0.0320	0.0435	0.00028
1831	1.0567	1.0000	0.0371	0.0425	0.00012
1832	1.0567	1.0000	0.0364	0.0428	0.00012
1833	1.0747	1.0000	0.0347	0.0412	0.00015
1834	1.0567	1.0000	0.0339	0.0400	0.00018
1835	1.0000	1.0095	0.0330	0.0393	0.00054
1836	1.0000	1.0116	0.0327	0.0393	0.00053
1837	1.0000	1.0180	0.0339	0.0388	0.00048
1838	1.0000	1.0086	0.0332	0.0389	0.00049

Year	Dollar Price of Gold	Silver	Yield Gold	Silver	λ^{2a}
1844	1.0000	1.0044	0.0309	0.0346	0.00043
1845	1.0000	1.0086	0.0300	0.0357	0.00005
1846	1.0000	1.0044	0.0316	0.0372	0.00005
1847	1.0000	1.0192	0.0320	0.0379	0.00007
1848	1.0000	1.0002	0.0350	0.0440	0.00010
1849	1.0000	1.0129	0.0337	0.0395	0.00009
1850	1.0000	1.0107	0.0309	0.0414	0.00009
1851	1.0000	1.0447	0.0310	0.0392	0.00019
1852	1.0000	1.0298	0.0308	0.0369	0.00020
1853	1.0000	1.0404	0.0299	0.0384	0.00020
1854	1.0000	1.0447	0.0322	0.0421	0.00020
1855	1.0000	1.0447	0.0330	0.0408	0.00020
1856	1.0000	1.0425	0.0345	0.0425	0.00020
1857	1.0000	1.0510	0.0317	0.0428	0.00019
1858	1.0000	1.0425	0.0318	0.0412	0.00015
1859	1.0000	1.0171	0.0309	0.0414	0.00021
1860	1.0000	1.0510	0.0313	0.0406	0.00030
1861	1.0000	1.0383	0.0324	0.0393	0.00022
1862	1.0299	1.0651	0.0329	0.0389	0.00021
1863	1.3362	1.3931	0.0324	0.0398	0.00020
1864	1.5162	1.5808	0.0328	0.0384	0.00020

Year					
1839	1.0000	1.0256	0.0323	0.0386	0.00045
1840	1.0000	1.0256	0.0332	0.0386	0.00045
1841	1.0000	1.0235	0.0334	0.0383	0.00045
1842	1.0000	1.0129	0.0335	0.0384	0.00048
1843	1.0000	1.0057	0.0317	0.0387	0.00044
1870	1.2187	1.2499	0.0325	0.0492	0.00004
1871	1.1087	1.1371	0.0326	0.0414	0.00003
1872	1.0974	1.1279	0.0323	0.0394	0.00003
1873	1.1212	1.1369	0.0325	0.0387	0.00003
1874	1.1049	1.0864	0.0326	0.0392	0.00010
1875	1.1237	1.0954	0.0326	0.0369	0.00009
1876	1.1274	1.0679	0.0319	0.0382	0.00013
1877	1.0687	1.0372	0.0317	0.0399	0.00023
1878	1.0000	0.9112	0.0318	0.0413	0.00052
1879	1.0000	0.8412	0.0315	0.0417	0.00089
1880	1.0000	0.8889	0.0307	0.0410	0.00139
1881	1.0000	0.8645	0.0304	0.0393	0.00138
1882	1.0000	0.8815	0.0300	0.0382	0.00148
1883	1.0000	0.8518	0.0284	0.0388	0.00151

Year					
1865	2.2599	2.3562	0.0333	0.0391	0.00020
1866	1.4324	1.4965	0.0344	0.0413	0.00020
1867	1.3437	1.3867	0.0332	0.0422	0.00021
1868	1.3349	1.3663	0.0326	0.0433	0.00021
1869	1.3512	1.3887	0.0324	0.0497	0.00015
1884	1.0000	0.8624	0.0269	0.0394	0.00156
1885	1.0000	0.8455	0.0272	0.0392	0.00156
1886	1.0000	0.7882	0.0279	0.0399	0.00183
1887	1.0000	0.7819	0.0268	0.0411	0.00165
1888	1.0000	0.7533	0.0256	0.0394	0.00150
1889	1.0000	0.7204	0.0277	0.0401	0.00118
1890	1.0000	0.7522	0.0262	0.0398	0.00102
1891	1.0000	0.8222	0.0265	0.0398	0.00199
1892	1.0000	0.7416	0.0256	0.0384	0.00274
1893	1.0000	0.6473	0.0252	0.0377	0.00402
1894	1.0000	0.5382	0.0242	0.0377	0.00594
1895	1.0000	0.5255	0.0232	0.0377	0.00592
1896	1.0000	0.5191	0.0220	0.0377	0.00596

a. Variance of percent change of relative price between gold and silver.

observations of more maturities along the term structure than are likely to be available in the present problem.

Oldrich Vasicek (1977) provides an intermediate method for addressing the stochastic natue of π_s and π_g. Using an arbitrage approach, he assumes that the instantaneous riskless interest rate follows an Ornstein-Uhlenbeck process which drifts to some long-term mean. With this assumption, he can solve explicitly for the price of discount bonds of arbitrary maturity. Empirical implementation requires time-series observations on the rate of interest on riskless loans and observations on the slope of the term structure of interest rates at the short maturities. However, there is a problem in gathering the necessary data. For example, throughout the nineteenth century, British debt consisted almost exclusively of the 3 percent Consols, a long-term debt instrument. A small percentage consisted of Exchequer bills. According to Charles Fenn (1883), Exchequer bills comprised 4.3 percent of the total debt in 1825, 3.5 percent in 1835, 2.1 percent in 1845, and 2.8 percent in 1855, part of which was always held by the Bank of England. Prices for new bills are available in British periodicals. However, since there was a thin market even for new bills, yield data on short bills and on the slope of the short end of the term structure would not be easily available. The problems are yet more difficult for yields on short-term silver loans; I have not yet found data on Prussian bill yields, though Sidney Homer (1977) does present data on short-term commercial loans.

In the absence of the necessary data for the more realistic pricing formulas, I have chosen to implement the section II pricing solution. I estimated λ^2 for each year by computing a moving sample variance of actual percentage changes in the relative value of the gold dollar to the silver dollar. In the results which I report here, the sample consists of the ten previous years' percentage changes. I have also constructed estimates for λ^2 by sampling backward fifteen years and by sampling forward ten and fifteen years. The computed theoretical values of bond prices hardly vary with these changes in the method for computing estimates of λ^2. Based on estimates of λ^2, these computed values of the bimetallic bond prices are themselves estimates of the true bimetallic bond prices. All the series substituted in formula (4) are reported in table 19.2.

Potential Problems in Applying the Bimetallic Pricing Formula

Options Excluded from the Pricing Formula
The pricing formula for the dollar contract was derived from the assumption that only the bimetallic option was available for the debtor. In practice,

several other options were available to the government in paying off its securities; and these may cause the observed market prices to deviate from the computed theoretical prices.

First, the government had the option of directly defaulting on its obligations. However, this was an unlikely step for a government as well established as that in United States in the nineteenth century. More likely, the government would default indirectly either by devaluing the legal content of the dollar in terms of one or both metals or by adding a new overvalued legal tender. The U.S. government exercised both of these options in the nineteenth century in the 1834 devaluation and the 1862–78 addition of greenbacks as an overvalued legal tender. Neither of these changes affected the payment streams of existing government debt. By 1834, the federal government had paid off the national debt, so the devaluation affected only private obligations. However, to the extent that the public anticipated future possible devaluations prior to 1834, the anticipated relative price movement of the metal content of the dollar would consist of the anticipated market movement of the relative price of pure ounces of metal *and* anticipated movements in the legal ratio of silver to gold in the dollar.

The greenbacks were made legal tender for all payments *except* interest payments on the public debt, and the government continued to pay gold coin on its debt throughout the greenback era. However, since the repayment of principal with Treasury notes was not explicitly prohibited, there was extensive fear that the government would pay the principal in paper currency. This possibility ended in the March 1869 Public Credit Act, which assured future payment of principal in coin. From 1862 to 1869, however, the possibility of repayment in greenbacks forced high nominal yields on government debt and produced wide divergence between bimetallic security values and the actual prices of government debt.

In most of its bonds, the U.S. government maintained a redemption option; typically, a contract stated that the bond was redeemable at the option of the government after a given date. Rarely was there an explicit maturity. The existence of this feature made the duration of the payments stream uncertain to the lender and may therefore have affected the price of the bond. However, since most bonds were issued at high wartime coupon rates, the government almost always redeemed them immediately after reaching the contracted earliest redemption date.

In a few issues, the government gave the lender a par convertibility option into other securities. The option could be exercised on demand or, in some cases, after a certain period of time. In addition, the government gave holders of certain securities an ex post convertibility option, although the option was not a feature of the written contract. Because of difficulties with pricing convertible securities, I have eliminated the contractually convertible bonds from the sample.

An additional option of the government was the possibility of switching to a monometallic payment policy. Thus, it might have decided to continue delivering gold to pay off its debt even if silver became the overvalued metal. While this option would add to the cost of paying off the debt, it was the option actually exercised in the 1873 removal of the free coinage and legal tender status of silver; and it continued in force even after the restoration of legal tender silver dollars in 1878.

Other Assumptions in the Pricing Formula
In deriving the pricing formula, I assumed that the yield on pure gold and silver loans is independent of the length of the loan. However, the actual rates vary across observations. Agents, accounting for this variation, would act so that realized prices would differ from the bimetallic formula's prediction, as described above. Also, for the series on pure silver loans, I have used yields on the longterm bonds of Prussia through 1870; Prussia switched from a silver to a gold standard in the 1870s. These data may not represent the interest payments on pure silver loans if anticipations of a possible switch were built into the bond prices of the silver standard era. An additional problem with the British and Prussian yields arises from the option of these governments to redeem the bonds at par. For the British 3 percent Consols of the Prussian 4 percent loans, this would cause an overstatement of the yield, especially in the 1840s.

Finally, the pricing formula is based on an assumption that the relative price between silver and gold is exogenous to which metal circulates in the bimetallic country. However, since some metal circulates as a medium of exchange, it is reasonable to presume that a switch in the circulating metal would feed back on the relative price. To avoid this problem requires a small country assumption for the bimetallic countries.

Empirical Results: Realized Prices, Theoretical Prices, and the Value of the Bimetallic Option

The period from 1818 to 1859 can be considered the heyday of the bimetallic dollar. Prior to 1818, the circulation of Treasury notes in the War of 1812 led to a suspension of specie payments and a divergence of the dollar from its metallic definition. By 1818, this divergence had terminated and the possibility that the government might default on bonds disappeared.

Also, Great Britain and Prussia were firmly attached to the gold and silver standard, respectively. From 1834 to 1841, the government either had no debt at all or the debt consisted only of short-term notes for which no meaningful price quotations are available. By 1860, the credit of the country was in question, and from 1862 to 1869, the public feared that the government would pay principal in greenbacks. The bimetallic standard free from fears of default was restored only from 1870 to 1873, but the bill to remove free coinage and legal tender status for silver was already moving through the Congress.

In table 19.3, I report actual January prices and predicted bimetallic prices in dollars for 23 different bond issues in the market from 1818 to 1896. I present the characteristics of these bonds in table 19.4. Table 19.3 reports the theoretical value in dollars which each bond would have if its promised payments were explicitly gold dollars.

Finally, I report the dollar value of the bond's bimetallic option relative to a pure gold standard, that is, the value of an option to deliver silver in exchange for gold. I compute the option value by subtracting the bimetallic bond value from that of the gold bond. The option value represents the wealth transfer from a debtor to a creditor of a sudden switch from a bimetallic standard to a gold standard. For the period 1818–34, the option value produced theoretical discounts in dollar bonds of from 6 to 18 percent from the value of the gold bond. The 6 percent minimum discount represents the amount by which the gold dollar was undervalued at the mint at the time of the 1834 devaluation. For example, the 5 percent Loan of 1821 had an option value of 6.40 dollars at the time of its expiration in 1834; this amount is the value of an "in the money" option just before its expiration date. Discounts much above 6 percent occur early in the life of a bond and represent the possibility that the value of silver may decline greatly during the remaining life of the loan.

By the 1840s, there had been a 6 percent devaluation of the gold dollar and large gold discoveries which guaranteed that gold would circulate as money. In this period, the option feature of the bimetallic contract was an "out of the money" option, so the option component produced a much lower percentage discount from the value of a gold bond relative to the earlier period.[12]

Some Regression Results

From the pricing relationships among the bimetallic bond, the gold bond, and the bimetallic option emerges a regression equation:

Table 19.3
Bond prices: Actual, predicted bimetal, option value, and gold bond

Year	Actual	Bimetal	Option	Gold	Year	Actual	Bimetal	Option	Gold
War Loan of 1812					*7% Stock of 1815*				
1819	99.5	101.6	9.4	111.0	1818	109.5	105.5	17.6	123.0
1821	106.5	100.8	11.3	112.1	1819	104.5	106.6	9.7	123.0
1822	105.5	101.5	10.4	111.9	1820	104.0	104.4	8.4	112.8
1823	102.5	101.0	9.1	110.1	1821	108.9	104.4	11.7	116.0
1824	102.3	101.5	6.8	108.3	1822	107.0	104.3	10.6	114.8
					1823	103.5	102.9	9.3	112.2
War Loan of 1813					1824	102.3	102.5	6.8	109.3
1819	99.4	101.0	6.6	107.6					
1821	107.5	100.4	8.6	109.1	*5% Loan of 1820*				
1822	106.3	100.5	7.3	107.8	1821	102.5	93.9	18.0	111.9
					1822	109.0	96.7	18.4	115.1
War Loan of 1814					1823	106.0	96.8	18.5	115.3
1821	107.5	101.2	13.8	115.0	1824	106.5	103.5	13.3	116.7
1822	108.0	102.4	13.2	115.6	1825	110.3	103.0	12.1	115.1
1823	106.0	101.9	12.3	114.3	1826	100.0	101.5	9.6	111.1
1824	105.0	104.3	8.9	113.2	1827	109.3	101.8	9.5	111.3
1825	111.5	102.9	6.2	109.1	1828	108.8	102.1	7.0	109.1
1826	102.3	101.3	5.0	106.3	1829	101.6	102.8	7.4	110.2
					1830	100.0	101.2	8.1	109.3
War Loan of 1815					1831	101.0	100.7	6.3	107.0
1819	100.3	102.2	12.0	114.2					
1821	109.0	101.2	13.8	115.0	*5% Loan of 1821*				
1822	111.5	102.4	13.2	115.6	1822	109.0	95.9	21.3	117.2
1823	108.0	101.9	12.3	114.3	1823	105.8	96.0	21.8	117.8
1824	108.0	104.3	8.9	113.2	1824	107.0	104.5	15.6	120.2
1825	106.5	102.9	6.2	109.1	1825	111.0	104.0	15.3	119.4
1826	101.3	101.3	5.0	106.3					

Year				
1826	100.0	102.1	12.0	114.2
1827	108.5	102.8	11.4	114.2
1828	107.5	103.5	9.1	112.5
1829	106.0	105.3	9.0	114.3
1830	105.0	102.8	11.6	114.4
1831	105.8	102.6	8.0	110.6
1832	103.8	102.0	7.7	109.7
1833	101.3	101.6	9.0	110.6
1834	100.0	101.0	6.4	107.3
4.5% Loan of 1824 (5/24/24)				
1825	105.5	100.2	11.9	112.0
1826	98.8	99.0	9.4	108.4
1827	102.0	99.7	9.3	109.0
1828	100.5	100.4	6.9	107.3
1829	98.5	101.5	7.3	108.8
1830	101.3	100.3	8.1	108.3
1831	102.3	100.2	6.3	106.5
Exchange 4.5% Stock of 1824				
1825	105.0	100.2	14.0	114.1
1826	97.8	98.8	11.0	109.7
1827	102.3	99.6	10.6	110.2
1828	103.0	100.5	8.3	108.8
1829	101.0	102.3	8.4	110.7
1830	102.5	100.5	10.3	110.8
1831	103.5	100.7	7.4	108.0
1832	100.3	100.4	7.0	107.4
1833	100.1	100.4	8.2	108.6

Year				
6% Loan of 1841				
1843	99.5	103.8	1.6	105.4
5.5% Loan of 1841				
1843	98.3	102.9	1.6	104.5
1844	100.0	101.6	0.8	102.4
Loan of 1842				
1843	101.0	128.8	12.2	141.0
1844	115.8	133.5	7.7	141.1
1845	114.5	132.6	8.5	141.1
1846	107.5	128.5	8.1	136.6
1847	101.0	127.9	6.5	134.4
1848	98.5	116.8	11.6	128.4
1849	107.0	122.7	6.0	128.7
1850	108.8	119.3	11.3	130.6
1851	112.5	123.5	5.0	128.5
1852	111.5	122.8	4.0	126.8
1853	114.3	121.1	4.5	125.6
1854	116.5	117.0	4.4	121.3
1855	116.0	116.2	2.4	118.6
1856	110.0	113.4	2.1	115.5
1857	110.0	113.0	2.2	115.2
1858	113.0	111.5	1.3	112.8
1859	102.5	108.0	2.8	110.8
Loan of 1843				
1844	103.6	111.1	4.2	115.4
1845	103.0	111.0	3.7	114.7
1846	98.5	108.5	3.5	112.0

Table 19.3 (continued)

Year	Actual	Bimetal	Option	Gold
1847	91.5	108.3	2.0	110.3
1848	91.5	102.6	4.6	107.2
1849	99.3	105.1	1.6	106.6
1850	100.1	103.6	2.5	106.2
1851	102.0	104.3	0.2	104.5
1852	100.9	102.6	0.1	102.8
1853	100.0	101.0	0.0	101.0
Loan of 1846				
1848	96.8	111.4	7.4	118.8
1849	104.5	114.8	3.2	118.0
1850	106.5	112.0	5.9	118.0
1851	107.0	114.0	1.5	115.6
1852	105.0	112.0	1.3	113.3
1853	108.5	110.3	0.9	111.2
1854	106.5	107.4	0.4	107.8
1855	102.0	105.0	0.1	105.1
1856	102.0	102.5	0.0	102.5
Loan of 1847				
1848	99.3	120.4	14.7	135.0
1849	108.3	128.0	8.1	136.0
1850	111.0	124.1	15.4	139.4
1851	115.3	129.6	8.0	137.6
1852	116.3	129.9	6.3	136.2
1853	119.8	128.0	7.3	135.8
1854	121.1	128.7	8.1	130.8
1855	116.0	122.8	5.1	128.0
1856	116.3	119.6	4.9	124.5

Year	Actual	Bimetal	Option	Gold
1857	116.0	119.5	6.3	125.8
1858	112.5	118.9	4.8	123.7
1859	114.0	115.2	7.3	122.0
Loan of 1848				
1849	109.0	128.4	8.4	136.8
1850	112.3	124.5	15.8	140.2
1851	115.4	130.2	8.3	138.5
1852	117.0	130.6	6.6	137.1
1853	119.5	128.6	8.1	136.7
1854	121.3	123.2	8.5	131.6
1855	116.0	123.4	5.4	128.8
1856	116.3	120.2	5.2	125.3
1857	116.0	119.6	6.7	126.8
1858	112.0	119.6	5.2	124.7
1859	111.0	115.8	7.7	123.5
Mexican Indemnity Stock				
1850	100.8	102.4	1.2	103.6
1851	98.0	101.8	0.0	101.8
Loan of 1858				
1859	104.3	110.6	11.7	122.4
1866	96.5	155.6	2.8	158.4
1867	102.5	143.7	4.4	148.1
1868	108.0	140.6	5.3	145.9
1869	115.0	138.5	7.4	145.8
1870	110.0	125.0	4.7	129.7
1871	105.0	115.8	0.5	116.3

Loan of July and August, 1861

Year				
1868	109.6	158.6	14.1	172.7
1869	112.3	151.0	21.8	172.7
1870	117.8	135.9	17.5	153.4
1871	110.9	130.8	6.6	137.4
1872	115.6	126.2	7.9	134.1
1873	119.1	130.6	3.8	134.6
1874	118.4	122.9	7.3	130.2
1875	118.3	123.8	6.2	130.0
1876	119.6	118.1	10.4	128.4
1877	114.1	112.0	7.3	119.3
1878	106.6	98.4	13.0	111.4
1879	106.4	87.6	19.1	106.7
1880	104.3	91.3	13.0	104.2
1881	101.5	87.3	14.1	101.5

5% Loan of 1881

Year				
1872	112.4	121.5	3.5	125.1
1873	115.1	122.5	3.7	126.1
1874	112.9	115.9	6.8	122.7
1875	113.8	117.4	5.9	123.2
1876	116.9	112.7	9.8	122.5
1877	112.0	107.7	6.9	114.6
1878	105.3	95.4	12.3	107.7
1879	107.0	85.6	18.4	104.0
1880	103.4	89.8	12.5	102.3
1881	101.5	86.7	13.8	100.5

4% Loan of 1907

Year				
1878	101.8	88.8	26.6	115.3
1879	99.5	81.4	34.2	115.6
1880	103.0	87.0	29.8	116.8
1881	112.5	87.1	30.1	117.2
1882	117.6	90.2	27.3	117.5
1883	119.5	86.5	33.8	120.2
1884	123.8	86.7	35.9	122.6
1885	121.8	85.3	36.0	121.3
1886	123.0	78.7	40.7	119.3
1887	127.5	76.8	43.8	120.6
1888	126.0	75.7	46.1	121.9
1889	126.0	71.8	45.8	117.6
1890	126.3	75.2	44.0	119.2
1891	121.0	84.2	33.7	117.9
1892	117.0	75.4	42.9	118.3
1893	113.5	66.2	51.6	117.8
1894	113.0	55.0	63.0	118.1
1895	113.3	53.7	64.5	118.1
1896	110.0	52.9	65.2	118.2

Loan of 1904

Year				
1895	117.0	57.4	64.3	121.7
1896	113.3	56.2	64.2	120.4

Loan of 1925

Year				
1896	116.3	53.8	84.5	138.4

Table 19.4
Characteristics of bonds in the sample

Name of bond	Coupon rate[a]	Payment period	Date redeemable
7% Stock of 1815	7	Quarterly	January 1825
War loan of 1815	6	Quarterly	January 1827
War loan of 1812 a. 6% Loan of 1812 b. Exchanged 6% stock of 1812	6	Quarterly	January 1825
War loan of 1813 a. 16 Million loan of 1813 b. 6 Million loan of 1813 c. Undesignated loan of 1813	6	Quarterly	January 1823
War loan of 1814 a. 10 Million loan of 1814 b. 6 Million loan of 1814 c. Undesignated loan of 1814	6	Quarterly	January 1827
5% Loan of 1820	5	Quarterly	January 1832
5% Loan of 1821	5	Quarterly	January 1835
4.5% Loan of 1824 (5/24/24)	4.5	Quarterly	January 1832
Exchange of 4.5% stock of 1824	4.5	Quarterly	January 1834
5.5% Loan of 1841	5.5	Quarterly	January 1845
6% Loan of 1841	6	Quarterly	January 1845
Loan of 1842	6	Semiannual	January 1863
Loan of 1843	5	Semiannual	January 1853
Loan of 1846	6	Semiannual	December 1856
Mexican indemnity stock	5	Semiannual	January 1852
Loan of 1847	6	Semiannual	January 1868
Loan of 1848	6	Semiannual	July 1868
Loan of 1858	5	Semiannual	January 1874
Loan of July and August, 1861 (includes loan of 1863)	6	Semiannual	July 1881
5% Loan of 1881	5	Quarterly	April 1881
4% Loan of 1907	4	Quarterly	July 1907
Loan of 1904	5	Quarterly	January 1904
Loan of 1925	4	Quarterly	January 1925

a. Shown in percent.

Table 19.5
Relation of bond price to gold bond and gold exchange option prices[a]

Period	ϕ_1	ϕ_2	R^2	Observations
1818–34	.45 (.23)	−.22 (.24)	.12	56
1842–59	.61 (.23)	.51 (.18)	.18	56
1818–59	.61 (.16)	.28 (.14)	.12	110

a. Standard errors are shown in parentheses.

$$B_{jt} = \phi_1 PG_{jt} - \phi_2 EG_{jt} + u_{jt}, \tag{5}$$

where B_{jt}, PG_{jt}, and EG_{jt} are the realized price, the gold bond value, and the value of the option to acquire a unit of silver in exchange for a unit of gold, respectively, of bond j at time t. If the option features other than the bimetallic option are of minor importance in determining the bond's market value, then $\phi_1 = \phi_2 = 1$. Carrying out an ordinary least squares regression for a first-differenced version of equation (5) for all bond prices observed for the periods 1818–34, 1842–59, and 1818–59, I report the results in table 19.5.

For all the gold bond-gold option estimates, the coefficients of the exchange options differ significantly from predicted values. This divergence of the parameter estimates from the theoretical predictions is not atypical of results in the empirical options pricing literature. For example, Gay and Manaster, in regressions of futures prices on current wheat prices plus storage costs and on the delivery quality option value, find that their estimates diverge significantly from the theoretical prediction. In the bimetallic case, other option features may have been important in these bonds in the pre–Civil War period. Alternatively, a bias built into the option value estimate may affect the results.[13]

Finally, since many bond observations are drawn from the same years, the disturbances in (5) will covary across bonds. To address this problem, I have isolated the observations from the 5 percent Loan of 1821 and the Loan of 1842 and repeated the estimation procedure reported in table 19.5 for these bonds alone. I have selected these loans because each provided the longest time-series of price observations for any single bond in the periods 1818–34 and 1842–59, respectively. Table 19.6 contains the parameter estimates for these bonds.

Table 19.6
Relation of bond price to gold bond and gold exchange option prices 5% Loan of 1821 and loan of 1842[a]

Period	ϕ_1	ϕ_2	R^2	Observations
1822–34	.86	.09	.17	12
	(.59)	(.53)		
1842–59	.72	.92	.33	16
	(.48)	(.42)		
1822–59	.86	.63	.24	28
	(.36)	(.32)		

a. Standard errors are shown in parentheses.

For these loans, F-tests of the parameter restrictions support the hypothesis that $\phi_1 = \phi_2 = 1$ at standard significance levels. The difference from the previous results arises primarily because of a doubling in the standard errors of the parameter estimates, though the point estimates of the parameters are closer to the theoretical value of unity.

IV   Cross-Country Comparisons of Antebellum Yields

The results of sections II and III are useful in addressing a line of research on comparative technological development whose conclusions hinge partly on cross-country comparisons of yields on antebellum securities. Following up on the work of H. J. Habakkuk (1962), Peter Temin (1966) examined the apparently greater use of labor-saving machinery in the United States relative to that in Great Britain during the 1850s. Choice of a capital-intensive technique would follow from a higher wage-rental ratio within the same technology or from a different technology in which capital was relatively more productive in the United States. Based on observations in Homer of higher yields on securities in the United States, Temin argued that the wage-rental ratio was actually higher in Great Britain. Therefore, the observed relative factor intensities conflicted with an assumption that both countries had access to the same technology.

Edward Ames and Nathan Rosenberg (1968) and Alexander Field (1983) developed this cross-country comparison by considering more refined production technologies while accepting the claim that a higher observed yield in the United States was associated with a higher cost of capital. Paul Uselding (1972) and V. Kerry Smith (1978) turned in the direction of estimating sophisticated antebellum production functions for the United States alone, but they both treated observed U.S. yields as pure interest rates.

Table 19.7
Homer's reported yields and yields corrected for option feature

Year	3% consols	Prussian loans	U.S. Loan of 1848	1848 gold	1848 silver	Value of silver option
1850	3.11	4.10	4.58	3.53	4.68	0.05
1851	3.09	3.99	4.47	3.88	4.78	1.04
1852	3.02	3.76	4.39	3.90	4.59	1.02
1853	3.07	3.82	4.02	3.43	4.33	0.89
1854	3.27	4.21	4.14	3.47	4.51	0.80
1855	3.31	4.10	4.18	3.77	4.54	1.22
1856	3.22	4.15	4.11	3.64	4.47	1.09
1857	3.27	4.23	4.30	3.65	4.81	0.87
1858	3.10	4.15	4.32	3.76	4.76	0.78
1859	3.15	4.29	4.72	3.81	4.94	0.24

Source: For the second, third, and fourth columns, Homer, tables 19, 32, and 41.

However, since dollar securities contained an option feature not contained in sterling securities, otherwise identical debt contracts in the different nominal units should have commanded different prices. For the simple case of a pure discount loan, the bimetallic pricing equation (2b) indicates that the price of the dollar loan equals the price of the sterling loan less the value of the option to pay silver instead of gold. Since the live option always has a positive value, dollar loans must command lower market price in gold than sterling loans, even if yields on pure gold loans in the two countries are identical. By the same logic, a dollar loan should command a lower price than a pure silver loan.

These implications are supported by evidence reported in table 19.7. The second, third, and fourth columns are Homer's reported yields from the 1850s on British 3 percent Consols, Prussian loans, and the U.S. Loan of 1848, respectively. Historians have interpreted these data as signals of a higher capital cost in the United States than in Great Britain. In computing the yields, Homer assumes that the foreign loans were perpetuities, but he calculates yields to maturity for the U.S. loans. The reported yields are annual averages.

A gold bond with characteristics otherwise identical to the Loan of 1848 should have a value equal to that of the bimetallic bond plus the value of the gold option. For each year, I have converted Homer's U.S. bond yields into the implied market price and added the computed values of the gold options for the Loan of 1848 from Table 3.[14] This produces an estimate of the market price of a Loan of 1848 payable in gold, assuming that U.S. and British gold yields and U.S. and Prussian silver yields are identical. Next, I converted these price estimates into yields to maturity, producing a series labelled 1848 Gold on U.S. gold yields reported in the fifth column of table 19.7.

The U.S. yields corrected for the bimetallic option are much closer to British yields than are Homer's yields. In one case, the U.S. yield falls by more than 100 basis points. For the decade of the 1850s, average British yields were 3.16 percent. The uncorrected and corrected average U.S. yields were 4.32 and 3.68 percent, respectively. The uncorrected yield differential is 116 basis points, and the corrected yield differential is 52 basis points. The bimetallic option accounts for more than one-half the yield differential.

If the Loan of 1848 had promised to pay only silver, its value could be estimated by adding the value of the silver option (in gold) to the market price implied in Homer's yields. Dividing this sum by the market price of the silver dollar, $\hat{P}_s(t)$, produces the silver price of the U.S. silver bond. Table 19.7 contains computations of the gold value of the silver options for the Loan of 1848; and the column "1848 Silver" contains the corrected yields of the Loan of 1848 payable in silver.[15] I constructed these yields in a manner analogous to that of the corrected gold yields, converting the silver price of the silver Loan of 1848 into a yield to maturity. Because of the low value of the silver option in the 1850s, the corrected silver yields, though somewhat higher, are much closer to Homer's reported yields than are the corrected gold yields. The increase in yield results mainly from the conversion from gold to silver units, since $\hat{P}_s(t)$ exceeds unity in this period. For the 1850s, Prussian bond yields averaged 4.08 percent. The corrected U.S. silver bond yield averaged 4.64 percent, an increase of 32 basis points from the uncorrected average yield. The differential between U.S. and Prussian silver yields averaged 56 basis points during the decade, compared to the 52 basis-point differential between U.S. and British gold yields.

V Option Values and the Silver Agitation

By 1873, even after a rapid depreciation of silver, the option feature of the bimetallic bond was still "out of the money." For the Loan of 1858, redeemed before the 1873 demonetization of silver, little value was attached to the silver delivery option. Even the longer-term loans, such as the Loan of July and August, 1861 and the 5 percent Loan of 1881, have bimetallic option value in the early 1870s comparable to those prevailing in the 1840s when there was little chance of exercise.

Using the bimetallic option values associated with these loans, we can estimate the magnitude of the transfer from debtors to creditors generated by the termination of free coinage of silver in 1873. For the Loan of July and August 1861, I calculated that the value of the option to deliver silver was 3.80 dollars. Using the theoretical bimetallic bond value of 130.60 dollars, the transfer from the debtor was 2.9 percent of the value of the bond. Using the actual bond value of 119.10 dollars, the transfer from the debtor was 3.2 percent of the value of the bond. This is of the order of magnitude of one year's interest payment. Repeating the computation for the 5 percent Loan of 1881 yields similar results.

This computation of the extent of the transfer may be misleading because of the wide divergence of the theoretical bimetallic bond price from the actual market price in 1873. This divergence signals that the simple pricing formula does not capture some important features of the bond. For example, doubt about the resolve of the government to avoid paying off its debt in greenback would cause the theoretical dollar price of the bimetallic bond to exceed the observed price.

From the spreads between the theoretical prices of the gold bonds and the actual prices of the dollar bonds, an alternative method of estimation of the value of the option in 1873 is available. For the Loan of July and August 1861, the spread declined from 15.50 dollars in 1873 to 11.80 dollars in 1874. Attributing this decline to the removal of the option yields an option value of 3.70 dollars in 1873. Thus, the transfer was 3.1 percent of the actual value of the bond. For the 5 percent Loan of 1881, the transfer was 1 percent.

Only by the late 1870s, with the continued decline in silver, did the option value associated with a restored bimetallic standard rise to unprecedented levels. By this time, the dollar was de facto a gold dollar, as evidenced by the near equality between the realized bond values and the gold bond values. This equality emerges for the first time in the entire sample in the late 1870s. The bimetallic option values are indicative of the magnitude of the transfer from creditor to debtor which would have occurred with the reintroduction of free coinage of silver. By the 1890s, the potential transfer reached levels exceeding 50 percent of the realized value of the bonds. Indeed, simply comparing the market price of silver to the legal silver content of the dollar would indicate the potential transfer to debtors of a return to free coinage of silver, since the option was very much in the money by 1890. The rapidly increasing potential transfer parallels the increasing intensity of the silver agitation, which reached its peak in the mid-1890s.

VI Conclusion

Having provided methods for pricing a wide variety of previously inaccessible assets, finance theory has led more or less naturally to the description of numerous contracts or institutions as essentially options. Though overlooked by modern analyses of bimetallism, the option of which metal to deliver encompasses the fundamental aspect of the bimetallic standard; and proponents of bimetallism in the nineteenth century recognized the central importance of the option to the system. The pricing of bimetallic securities provides a natural application of option pricing methods. Pricing the option feature of such contracts opens several issues to examination. First, one can easily show that antebellum international yield comparisons, used often in research on the nature of nineteenth-century production functions, are misleading because of the different nature of otherwise similar securities in bimetallic and monometallic standards. Second, the value of the option provides a measure of the magnitude of transfer from debtor to creditor of a switch from a bimetallic to a gold or silver standard.

Data Appendix

I have used several price and yield series in computing the dollar contract prices in the text. In particular, I employ series on both the market nominal prices of and the relative price between the quantities of gold and silver legally contained in the dollar. In addition, I have used yield series on bonds requiring the delivery of only gold or only silver. Here I describe the construction of these series.

The Ratio of Fine Ounces of Gold to Fine Ounces of Silver

From 1800 to 1817, I used annual average ratios of nominal gold to nominal silver prices, as reported in Laughlin (p. 290). These were market ratios gathered by Soetebeer from trading in Hamburg.

From 1818 to 1896, I used the nominal prices of standard gold and standard silver in London in early January, as reported in *The London Times* through 1844 and in *The Economist*, 1845–96. The silver prices for 1824 and 1825 were taken from Thomas Tooke (1838, p. 385). I have used London rather than New York prices because of the greater standardization of the metals which were traded in London. Throughout the century, London was the central market for silver. Weekly New York prices for American gold coin, Spanish gold doubloons, and Spanish silver dollars are available from 1817 in the *New York Commercial*. However, as discussed in government papers written by Treasury Secretary Ingham in 1830 (see U.S. Senate, Executive Document No. 58, 1879, pp. 558–84) recommending the use of London prices to gauge the market ratio between gold and silver, the weights of the coins traded in New York varied sufficiently that one can place no faith in their consistency. By the time of the Civil War, the New York gold market had become an active and accurate indicator of the market price of standard gold. Also, by the 1870s, accurate silver prices are available from New York trading. However, to maintain consistency, I use the London prices throughout. Since most government bond prices were taken from mid-January or later, I chose early January gold and silver prices to allow for the transmission of information about metal price movements to New York.

To begin the construction of the series, let p'_g and p'_s represent the nominal price in pence of an ounce of fine gold and silver, respectively. From 1822 onward, Great Britain maintained a gold standard in which one ounce of gold, 11/12 fine, had a nominal value of 934.5 pence. Since a standard ounce of silver was 37/40 fine, Laughlin (p. 295) provides a formula for producing the market ratio of the number of ounces of fine silver to an ounce of fine gold: $p'_g/p'_s = 943/x$ where x is the current price of standard silver in pence.

For 1818–21, the nominal price of gold varied, and there was no direct market quote for standard gold. However, *The London Times* provided prices for "Foreign Bar Gold." I presumed that foreign bar gold was standard gold. The price of standard gold multiplied by 12/11 is the price of fine gold, that is, $p'_g = $ [(Foreign Bar Price in Pence)] $\times$ 12/11. Then the ratio of fine silver to fine gold for 1818–21 is $p'_g/p'_s = p'_g/[x\ 40/37]$. I will refer to an element of this series as q_t.

The Nominal Values of the Gold and Silver Content of the Dollar

From the q_t series, I computed the nominal prices $\hat{P}_g$ and $\hat{P}_s$ of the legal amount of gold and silver in the dollar, respectively. For the entire sample, the legal silver content of the dollar was .7733 fine ounces. Through 1834, the legal gold content of the dollar was 24.75 grains or .0515625 fine ounces. From 1835 to 1837, the legal gold content was 23.2 grains or .048333 fine ounces; and from 1838 onward, the legal gold content of the dollar was 23.22 grains or .048375 fine ounces.

Until 1834, silver was overvalued at the mint, so silver coins circulated in payment of dollar obligations. The nominal price of the silver dollar, $\hat{P}_s$, was therefore one dollar; and the nominal value of an ounce of fine silver was 1.293 dollars. The nominal value of the gold dollar can be determined from the market relative price between gold and silver, the nominal price of silver, and the gold content of the dollar. Through 1834, $\hat{P}_g = 1.293 \times q_t \times .0515625 = 0.06667q_t$.

From 1835 to 1861, the gold dollar circulated as money, so the nominal price of the gold dollar was one dollar. From 1835 to 1837, the nominal price of a fine ounce of gold was therefore 20.689669 dollars; while from 1838 to 1861, the nominal value of a fine ounce was 20.671835 dollars. The nominal value of the silver content of the dollar was $\hat{P}_s = 20.6897(.7733)/q_t = 16./q_t$ from 1835 to 1837; and from 1838 to 1861, $\hat{P}_s = 20.67184(.7733)/q_t = 15.9855/q_t$.

From 1862 to 1878, greenbacks were delivered in payment of dollar contracts (except government debt payment and explicit gold loans). However, an active gold exchange began in January 1862, so the nominal market price of the gold dollar $\hat{P}_g$ is directly available on a daily basis for this period. I have taken price data from Wesley Mitchell (1903) and *Commercial and Financial Chronicle* to coincide with the dates for which bond prices are reported. The nominal price of the silver dollar is $\hat{P}_s = .7733\hat{P}_g/(.048375q_t) = 15.9855P_g/q_t$.

From 1879 to 1896, gold again circulated so the nominal price of the gold dollar was one dollar and that of the silver dollar was $\hat{P}_s = 15.9855/q_t$. For the period 1818–96, I report the nominal prices of the gold and silver content of the dollar in table 19.2.

Bond Prices and Characteristics

For the prices of U.S. government bonds from 1818 to 1859, I have used January price quotes from *New York Commercial* with a few exceptions. For the 1819 prices of the War Loans of 1812, 1813, and 1815, I used *Grotjan's Philadelphia Public Sale Reports'* listings for the Baltimore Stock Market for January 18,1819. I used the *Saturday Evening Post* (Philadelphia) for Philadelphia dealers' quotes for Mexican Indemnity Stock (January 19, 1851) and for 1855–57 quotes for the Loans of 1842, 1846, 1847, and 1848. From 1866 to 1896, I have used January price quotes from *Commercial and Financial Chronicle*. When quotes were listed as a bid-asked spread, I let the average represent the price. Since some outstanding securities were not listed every day, I could not always employ price quotations from the same day. Most often, I used prices in the middle of January, but for some issues in some years, I had to employ price information from the end of January or the beginning of February. In table 19.3, I list the prices of some bonds used in the sample years. In table 19.4, I list the coupon and redemption characteristics of these bonds; this information was taken from R. A. Bayley (1881) and William DeKnight (1900).

I did not include every bond issued as part of the sample. For some issues the repayment period was completely at the discretion of the government, so they were hard to price. Therefore, I did not include such loans as the 5.5 percent Stock of 1795, the 4.5 percent Stock of 1795, the Navy 6 percent Stock, the Converted 6 percent Stock of 1807, the Temporary Loan of 1812, the Mississippi Stock, the 5 percent Loan of 1816, and the Bounty-Land Scrip. For Treasury notes, the issue and redemption dates were uncertain, so I could not interpret the nature of the payment stream represented by a given price. Thus, I had to eliminate short-term debt issued in the War of 1812, the 1837–40 depression, the Mexican War, and the Civil War from the sample. Also eliminated are the 5–20's of the Civil War, the Consols of 1865, and the Consols of 1868 because of the uncertain redemption time associated with these issues. Finally, the 7–30's of 1864 and 1865 were eliminated because they contained a contractual convertibility feature and because they were payable in greenbacks. Included in the sample are 23 of the approximately 125 government securities issued between 1790 and 1895.

To derive the yield on a pure gold loan, I used the early January London ex-coupon prices of 3 percent Consols from 1818 to 1882. I found these prices in issues of *The London Times* from 1818 to 1845 and in *The Economist* from 1846 to 1882. After 1882, I used the London price of 2.5 percent annuities as reported in *The Economist* to compute the gold loan yield because the consol price was affected by an increasing probability of par redemption as the market yield declined. See Homer (pp. 192–200) or Fenn (pp. 34–30) on this issue.

To derive the yield on pure silver loans, I used the prices of Prussian bonds from 1818 to 1870, a period when Prussia was on a pure silver standard. These yields are available in Julius Kahn (1884, pp. 209–12). From 1818 to 1843, I used the end of December prices for 4 percent government bonds to derive silver yields applicable to January of the next year. From 1844 through 1868, I used end of December prices for 3.5 percent government bonds. For the 1870 yield, I used the March 30, 1870 price of 4 percent bonds because of the termination of the 3.5 percent price series.

Since India was also on a silver standard until it shifted to a gold standard in 1894, I used the yield on rupee bonds to represent the silver loan yield for 1871–93. For 1894–96 yields, I simply used the rupee yield of 1893. India shifted from a bimetallic to a silver standard in 1835. However, since India was governed by the East India Company, rupee bonds were not traded in London. The only official external borrowing was represented by the sterling denominated debt of the East India Company. With the rebellion of 1857, the East India Company was replaced by the Imperial Government as the Government of India, and immediately this government began to finance itself by selling securities in London. Since the Government of India was a creature of the British government, its debt was considered almost as secure from default as British government debt.

Indian debt was mainly denominated in sterling, but a large amount of rupee paper traded in London. A category of rupee debt called "Enfaced Paper" was the most regularly quoted in the London Markets. The rupee coupon and principal of Enfaced Paper was payable in London as a rupee draft on Calcutta. The most often quoted of the Enfaced Paper was the 4 percent Enfaced Paper. Since after 1879 this instrument was payable on three months notice, it was comparable in its option features to the British 3 percent Consols. *The Economist* contains prices of 4 percent Enfaced Paper, which I used to compute silver yields. The gold and silver yields for 1818–96 are reported in table 19.2.

Notes

I am grateful to Cliff Smith, Stan Engerman, Neil Wallace, Tony Kuprianov, J. S. Butler, Paul Romer, Bob King, Lauren Feinstone, Naomi Lamoreaux, and two referees for useful comments. I have also benefited from comments by participants in seminars at Northwestern University, Brown University, Yale University, the Wharton School, North Carolina State University, MIT, and the Federal Reserve Bank of Minneapolis. Luis Suarez provided helpful and resourceful research assistance. Research for this paper was supported by NSF grant SES-8319627.

1. More accurately, legal tender coins defined as equal to a certain number of units of account contain precisely defined weights of one or the other precious metal.

2. Arthur Rolnick and Warren Weber (1986) have recenty discussed circumstances under which Gresham's Law will not apply, using the U.S. bimetallic and greenback periods as examples. Even in such circumstances the value equivalent of the overvalued metal will be delivered to satisfy dollar contracts.

3. This is particularly true of J. Laurence Laughlin (1885) who was strongly opposed to bimetallism. However, less partisan writers such as Alfred Marshall (1887), Irving Fisher (1923), and Robert Barro (1979) also raise this issue. For a concentration on the delivery option dimension of bimetallism, see William Jevons (1899) who characterized bimetallism as an "alternating standard." The delivery option feature was recognized as the essence of bimetallism by its supporters, who also clearly understood the necessary alternation of monometallic epochs under bimetallism. See U.S. Congress (1877, pp. 11, 91–101) for a clear statement of the nature of the option feature from the pro-bimetallic camp.

4. Symmetallism prescribes the definition of the dollar in terms of a basket of metals, where a given weight of each metal is contained in the basket. There is no option associated with the short interest. In a tabular standard, the dollar is valued according to a particular price index. See, for example, Milton Friedman (1984) for a recent description of a tabular standard and Marshall (1887) on symmetallism.

5. Why a bimetallic standard was the preferred standard of the political process is not clear. Although carefully considered, the reasons for selecting the 1792 system outlined by Alexander Hamilton (1791) seem to have had their basis in the existing system of circulating coinage bequeathed to the United States.

6. The greenbacks, introduced in 1862, were also legal tender; but by 1879 they were redeemable in coin under the Resumption Act of 1875.

7. There is some evidence that silver was demonetized in anticipation of the decline in its relative price. See, for example, P. O'Leary (1960).

8. Laughlin argued that the act of 1873 simply ratified a demonetization of silver that had occurred with the 1853 removal of full legal tender status for subsidiary silver coins. Since few silver dollars had been minted through 1873, he claimed that the act of 1873 merely recognized existing conditions (p. 92). Friedman and Schwartz reiterated Laughlin's argument in their discussion of the episode (p. 114).

9. Margrabe has priced an option to exchange one asset for another. I consider this kind of option because Stulz shows that the current value of a contract to deliver the lesser valued of assets A and B in the future equals the current price of A less the current price of an option to exchange B for A in the future. Stulz developed a pricing formula for a European call option on the less valuable of two risky assets in a continuous time framework. A European call option can be exercised only on the expiration date. For the special case in which the striking price is zero, such an option is a contract to deliver one of two assets, where the short position has the option of which asset to deliver. The option will always be exercised at the expiration date, and the short side will always deliver the less valuable of the two assets. This is exactly the contractual arrangement of an agreement to deliver future dollars in a bimetallic standard. If the future delivery is simply the repayment of a previous loan, then the special case of a zero striking price materializes.

10. For a simplified discussion of this formula, see Clifford Smith (1976, p. 26).

11. In the data appendix I discuss the nature of Indian rupee bonds and their rate of return.

12. The Loans of 1842, 1847, and 1848 expired in 1863, 1868, and 1868, respectively. The relatively high value of the option for these bonds reflects their long remaining lives and an apparent anticipated depreciation of the relative price of silver. The anticipated depreciation is reflected in a positive yield differential between silver and gold loans. The shorter-term Loans of 1843 and 1846 had very low option values in this period.

13. Since they are nonlinear functions of the unbiased λ^2 estimates, the bimetallic bond estimates are generally biased, as shown by John Butler and Barry Schachter (1983a,b; undated). Typically in the options pricing literature, no correctives are applied to remove the bias. Though Butler and Schachter have provided such a corrective, I have not applied it at this stage, so the results reported in this section, though consistent with standard practice in the options pricing literature, are biased.

14. The option values were calculated based on gold and silver yields observed in January. Since Homer's yields were annual averages, some discrepancy may arise.

15. I computed the silver option value as follows. First, I discounted the remaining payments stream of the Loan of 1848 with the Prussian yield from table 19.2 and multiplied by $P_s(t)$. This produced the gold value of the Loan of 1848 as if it were a silver bond, assuming that the U.S. silver yield equalled that of Prussia. Subtracting the theoretical bimetallic bond values in gold reported in Table 3 from this silver bond value produces the gold value of the silver option implicit in the bond.

References

Ames, Edward and Rosenberg, Nathan, "The Enfield Arsenal in Theory and History," *Economic Journal*, December 1968, 78, 827–42.

Barro, Robert J., "Money and the Price Level Under the Gold Standard," *Economic Journal*, March 1979, 89, 13–33.

Bayley, R. A., *The National Loans of the United States from July 4, 1776 to June 30, 1880*, Washington: USGPO, 1881.

Butler, John S. and Schachter, Barry, (1983a) "Biased Estimation of the Black Scholes formula," Working Paper 84-W22, Vanderbilt University, May 1983.

————, (1983b) "Unbiased and Mean Square Error Estimation of the Standard Deviation in the Estimation of Option Prices: A Note," Working Paper, Vanderbilt University, November, 1983.

————, "Unbiased Estimation of the Black-Scholes Formula," Working Paper 83-W31, Vanderbilt University, undated.

Cox, John C., Ingersoll, Jonathan E. and Ross, Stephen A., (1985a) "An Intertemporal General Equilibrium Model of Asset Prices," *Econometrica*, March 1985, 53, 363–84.

————, (1985b) "A Theory of the Term Structure of Interest Rates," *Econometrica*, March 1985, 53, 385–408.

DeKnight, William F., *History of the Currency of the Country and of the Loans of the United States*, Washington: USGPO, 1900.

Dunbar, Charles F., *Laws of the United States Relating to Currency, Finance and Banking from 1789 to 1891*, Boston: Ginn and Company, 1883.

Fenn, Charles, *Fenn's Compendium of the English and Foreign Funds*, London: Effingham Wilson, Royal Exchange, 1883.

Field, Alexander, "Land Abundance, Interest/Profit Rates, and Nineteenth Century American and British Technology," *Journal of Economic History*, June 1983, 43, 405–31.

Fisher, Irving, *The Purchasing Power of Money*, New York: McMillan, 1913.

Friedman, Milton, "Financial Futures Markets and Tabular Standards," *Journal of Political Economy*, February 1984, 92, 165–67.

———— and Schwartz, Anna J., *A Monetary History of the United States*, NBER Business Cycles, No. 12, Princeton: Princeton University Press, 1963.

Garber, Peter M. and King, Robert G., "Deep Structural Excavation Identification Problems in Euler Equation Methods," Working Paper, University of Rochester, July 1984.

Gay, Gerald and Manaster, Stephen, "The Quality Option Implicit in Futures Contracts," *Journal of Financial Economics*, September 1984, 13, 353—70.

Habakkuk, H. J., *American and British Technology in the 19th Century*, Cambridge: Cambridge University Press, 1962.

Hamilton, Alexander, "Treasury Report on the Establishment of a Mint" (January 28, 1791), in H. Krooss, ed., *Documentary History of Banking and Currency in the United States*, Vol. 1, New York: Chelsea House, 1969, 162—192.

Homer, Sidney, *A History of Interest Rates*, New Brunswick: Rutgers University Press, 1963; 1977.

Jevons, William S., *Money and the Mechanism of Exchange*, New York: D. Appleton, 1899.

Kahn, Julius, *Geschichte Des Zinsfusses in Deutschland seit 1815*, Stuttgart: J. G. Cotta'schen Buchhandlung, 1884.

Laughlin, J. Laurence, *The History of Bimetallism in the United States*, New York: D. Appleton, 1885.

Margrabe, William, "The Value of an Option to Exchange One Asset for Another," *Journal of Finance*, March 1978, 23, 177—86.

Marshall, Alfred, "Remedies for Fluctuations of General Prices" (1887), in A. C. Pigou, ed., *Memorials of Alfred Marshall*, London: Macmillan, 1925.

Merton, Robert, "Theory of Rational Option Pricing," *Bell Journal of Economics*, Spring 1973, 4, 141—83.

Mitchell, Wesley C., *A History of the Greenbacks*, Chicago: University of Chicago Press, 1903.

O'Leary, P., "The Scene of the Crime of 1873 Revisited: A Note," *Journal of Political Economy*, August 1960, 68, 388—92.

Rolnick, Arthur and Weber, Warren, "Gresham's Law or Gresham's Fallacy," *Journal of Political Economy*, February 1986, 94, 185—99.

Smith, Clifford, "Option Pricing: A Review," *Journal of Financial Economics*, January/March 1976, 3, 3—51.

Smith, V. Kerry, "The Ames-Rosenberg Hypothesis and the Rule of Natural Resources in Production Technology," *Explorations in Economic History*, July 1978, 15, 257—68.

Stulz, René, "Options on the Minimum or the Maximum of Two Risky Assets," *Journal of Financial Economics*, July 1982, 10, 161—85.

Temin, Peter, "Labor Scarcity and the Problem of American Industrial Efficiency in the 1850's," *Journal of Economic History*, September 1966, 26, 277—98.

Tooke, Thomas, *A History of Prices and of the State of the Circulation from 1793 and 1837*, London: Longman, Orme, Green and Longmans, 1838.

Uselding, Paul, "Technical Progress at the Springfield Armory, 1820–1850," *Explorations in Economic History*, Spring 1972, 9, 291–316.

Vasicek, Oldrich, "An Equilibrium Characterization of the Term Structure," *Journal of Financial Economics*, November 1977, 5, 177–88.

U.S. Congress, *Report of the U.S. Monetary Commission, Washington:* USGPO, 1877.

U.S. Senate, *Report of the Proceedings of the International Monetary Conference, 1878*, Executive Document No. 58, Washington: USGPO, 1879.

————, *Coinage Laws of the United States, 1792 to 1894*, Finance Committee, Washington: USGPO, 1894.

20

Monetary Policy Strategies

Robert P. Flood and Peter Isard

This chapter addresses issues that are relevant to the design and implementation of monetary policy strategies. A simple framework is developed that can be used to analyze different types of strategies for an open economy in which social welfare depends negatively on both price level instability and deviations of output from its full employment level (section I). To set the stage for discussing different strategies, it is initially assumed—unrealistically—that the structure of the economic model is known completely and that disturbances to the economy can be characterized as having well-understood probability distributions (section II). The traditional distinction is drawn between discretion (that is, policies derived from conditional optimization) and rules (that is, policies derived from unconditional optimization); a further distinction is drawn between fully state-contingent rules and partially state-contingent rules.

The authors are grateful to Kenneth Rogoff, Elhanan Helpman, Dale Henderson, and seminar participants at the University of Michigan and the Fund for helpful comments and reactions.

The chapter then turns to the realistic case in which knowledge about the structure of the economy and the nature of economic disturbances is incomplete, and in which it may be costly for society to delay policy ractions until new events are fully understood. It is argued that such considerations make fully state-contingent rules irrelevant in practice, and it is demonstrated that partially state-contingent rules are not necessarily superior to policies derived from conditional optimization. The paper then explores the possibilities arising under a hybrid policy in which a partially state-contingent rule is mixed with discretion (section III). In addition to demonstrating that such mixed strategies can dominate both complete discretion and rigid adherence to the partially state-contingent rule, we investigate the appropriate setting of parameters in a partially state-contingent policy when it is acknowledged that the rule will not be followed on all occasions—that is, that sometimes the monetary authority will resort to discretion.

The results of this section have general applicability to the design and evaluation of policy rules. The typical design and evaluation strategy in economics involves setting an initial rule and then simulating the counterfactual path that a model economy would have taken had the proposed rule been in place and had agents expected the rule to be in place forever. In this methodology the parameters in the proposed rule are then "fine-tuned" to give desirable properties to the counterfactual path. To the extent, however, that the rule evaluated using such methodology is not fully state-contingent, it is possible that policymakers, had they actually been confronted with the counterfactual history, would have chosen to respond to contingencies not specified in the rule. In general, the possibility of such responses by the policymaker, which would have been recognized ex ante by rational market participants, renders inappropriate the parameter settings obtained by using a methodology that does not account for the nonzero probability of occasional discretionary reactions to unspecified contingencies. It thus becomes interesting to explore conditions, in a particular model environment, under which the usual policy evaluation methodology gives the "right answers" even though the evaluation problem is only partially specified. In doing so, our approach to the problem of setting optimal rules that are not fully state-contingent draws on the "process-switching" literature (for example, see Flood and Garber (1980, 1983)).

One further issue that deserves serious consideration is the question of how to design institutional arrangements for mitigating the credibility problems that could arise under a hybrid policy that left the monetary authorities with some discretion (section IV). Concluding remarks are provided in section V, which notes that the relative merits of different choices of variables for a monetary rule may depend on whether the policy strategy calls for rigid adherence to the rule or for mixing the rule without discretion.

I Analytic Framework

This section develops a simple analytic framework that illustrates several issues that arise in adopting a monetary policy strategy for an open economy. Following conventional practice, we consider an economy in which society dislikes deviations of output from its full employment level and also dislikes price level instability. In this context, it is assumed for simplification that the objective of monetary policy is to minimize the quadratic loss function:

$$\psi_t = (y_t - \bar{y})^2 + \alpha(p_t - p_{t-1})^2, \qquad \alpha > 0, \tag{1}$$

where y_t is the logarithm of output in period t, $\bar{y}$ is the logarithm of full employment output, p_t is the logarithm of the price level, and α is a strictly positive weight that society places on price level stabilization relative to output stabilization.[1]

Following Gray (1976), Canzoneri (1985), and others, we assume that output is produced by labor, that the nominal wage rate is set in a contract negotiated before the realization of the price level, and that the employment contract calls for workers to supply whatever amount of labor is demanded by firms at the negotiated wage rate. These assumptions are taken to imply that, in combination, the production function and the labor demand function yield a relationship in which output is a decreasing function of the real cost of a unit of labor:

$$y_t = d - c(w_t - p_t) + \mu_t. \tag{2}$$

Here, w_t is the logarithm of the wage rate, c and d are parameters, and μ_t is a mean-zero productivity shock.[2] It is also convenient to assume that wage setters know the output supply function and act to minimize the expected squared deviation of output (employment) from some implicit target level ($\bar{y}$) that may differ from the full employment concept that enters the social loss function.[3] Thus, the wage level is determined from the first-order condition.

$$\frac{\partial}{\partial w_t} E_{t-1}(y_t - \bar{y})^2 = 0, \tag{3}$$

which, together with equation (2), implies that

$$w_t = E_{t-1}p_t + \frac{d - \bar{y}}{c}. \tag{4}$$

Substitution of equation (4) into equation (2) yields an output supply relationship,

$$y_t = \bar{y} + c(p_t - E_{t-1}p_t) + \mu_t, \tag{5}$$

that is similar to the standard rational expectations supply function introduced by Lucas (1972). Substitution of equation (5) into equation (1) implies that

$$\psi_t = [c(p_t - E_{t-1}p_t) - \kappa + \mu_t]^2 + \alpha[p_t - p_{t-1}]^2 \tag{6}$$

or

$$\psi_t = [c(\pi_t - E_{t-1}\pi_t) - \kappa + \mu_t]^2 + \alpha\pi_t^2, \tag{7}$$

where $\pi_t = p_t - p_{t-1}$ is the rate of inflation and where

$$\kappa = \bar{y} - \tilde{y} \tag{8}$$

is the difference between the social concept of full employment output and the level of output that wage setters implicitly target when negotiating their wage contracts. The existence of "distortions" such as unemployment compensation or income taxation—or of incentives for wage setters to maximize the welfare of some subset of the labor force that is already employed (or that has seniority rights to employment)—may give rise to a situation in which k is positive.

To address monetary policy issues for an open economy, it is convenient to use the relationship

$$\pi_t = \pi_t^* + s_t + \phi_t, \tag{9}$$

where π_t^* is the foreign rate of inflation, s_t is the rate of change of the nominal exchange rate (the rate of change of the domestic currency price of foreign exchange), and ϕ_t is a shock to the purchasing power parity relation. It is assumed that monetary authorities control base-money growth and that the nominal rate of depreciation of the domestic currency can be decomposed into one component that varies systematically with the differential between the domestic base-money growth rate (b_t) and the foreign inflation rate (π_t^*), a second component (ϕ_t) corresponding to the purchasing power parity shocks, and a third part (v_t) that reflects other elements responsible for nominal exchange rate movements. This relationship is given by[4]

$$s_t = b_t - \pi_t^* - \phi_t + v_t. \tag{10}$$

To simplify the later algebra, it is assumed that $E_{t-1}v_t = 0$. Thus, under the additional assumptions that v_t is exogenous to domestic policy and uncorrelated with μ_t,[5] and that the distortion term, k, is time and policy invariant, equations (9) and (10) can be combined to yield[6]

$$\pi_t = b_t + v_t \tag{11}$$

and

$$\psi_t = [c(b_t + v_t - E_{t-1}b_t) - \kappa + \mu_t]^2 + \alpha[b_t + v_t]^2. \tag{12}$$

To simplify notation further, it is convenient to transform variables and to express the policy problem as that of minimizing the social loss function,

$$L_t = (b_t + v_t - E_{t-1}b_t - k + u_t)^2 + a(b_t + v_t)^2, \tag{13}$$

where $L_t = \psi_t/c^2$, $k = \kappa/c$, $u_t = \mu_t/c$, and $a = \alpha/c^2$.

Note that, although our primary interest lies in analyzing monetary policy for an open economy, equations (11)–(13) apply not only to an open economy with stochastic terms in the purchasing power parity relation and the nominal exchange rate equation, but also to a closed economy with white noise in the relationship between inflation and base-money growth.

II Comparisons of Alternative Strategies

The analytic framework developed in the previous section will now be used to compare social welfare—as measured by the expected value of the social loss function (13)—under a regime that allows the monetary authorities to exercise discretion and under two regimes in which monetary policy is governed by rules. One of the rules is fully state-contingent, and the other is partially state-contingent. For the discretion regime, we assume that the authorities attempt to minimize the value of the social loss function, and—consistently—under the two different rule regimes we solve for parameter values under which the expected value of the social loss function is minimized.

A central consideration in any discussion of the optimal design of monetary policy is the extent to which the structure of the macroeconomic model is known, the relevant economic variables are observable, and the disturbances to the economy can be characterized in terms of well-defined probability distributions. In this regard, we assume initially that both the monetary authorities and the private sector know the macroeconomic structure, can deduce u_t and v_t from observable variables and their knowledge of the parameters of the model ex post, and have accurate ex ante information about the probability distributions from which u_t and v_t are drawn.

In reality, of course, monetary policy strategies must be designed for an environment in which there is incomplete information ex ante about both the macroeconomic structure and the probability distributions of disturbances. Moreover, the problem of optimal policy design is complicated by the fact that it can be costly to delay policy reactions until new information is fully assimilated from those events that contain new information. Section

III will attempt to address the problem formally in such an environment. The purpose of considering a partially state-contingent rule in this section, where we adopt the assumption of "complete" ex ante information, is to provide the groundwork for section III.[7] Furthermore, to avoid semantic confusion at a later stage, we will use the term "conditional optimization" as a synonym for "discretion" and the term "unconditional optimization" as a synonym for "rules."

Discretion, or Conditional Optimization

Under a strategy of discretion or conditional optimization—henceforth denoted CO—the monetary authority sets b_t to minimize equation (13) subject to the observed values of u_t and v_t and, most important, *subject to predetermined expectations of base-money growth*, $E_{t-1}b_t$. The first-order condition for a minimum of equation (13) with respect to b_t is

$$b_t = -v_t + \frac{1}{1+a}(E_{t-1}b_t + k - u_t). \tag{14}$$

Private agents understand the monetary authority's motives, so they form their expectations of base-money growth by taking the expectation of b_t in equation (14). Combining this expectation with the expectation of equation (11) yields

$$E_{t-1}\pi_t = E_{t-1}b_t = k/a. \tag{15}$$

This expression links the inflationary bias that arises under CO to the distortion term k. If k were zero, deviations of output from its full employment level would also be zero in the absence of inflation surprises and productivity shocks (recall conditions (5) and (8), and there would be no inflationary bias.

To evaluate social welfare, substitute equation (15) into equation (14) to obtain

$$b_t|CO = -v_t - \frac{u_t}{1+a} + \frac{k}{a}, \tag{16}$$

where $b_t|CO$ is base growth under conditional optimization (discretion). Thus, from equation (5), the realized loss from CO is

$$L_t|CO = \frac{(1+a)}{a}\left(-k + \frac{a}{(1+a)}u_t\right)^2, \tag{17}$$

and the expected loss is

$$E_{t-1} L_t | CO = \frac{1+a}{a} k^2 + \frac{a}{1+a} V(u), \tag{18}$$

where $v(u)$ is the variance of u_t conditional on information from period $t-1$.[8] The first term on the right-hand side of equation (18) reflects the expected loss associated with whatever output or labor market distortions are responsible for the inflation bias, whereas the second term reflects the loss associated with fluctuations in productivity.

Rules, or Unconditional Optimization

Next consider the implications of following a rule or an unconditional optimization strategy—henceforth denoted UO. Given the functional form of a rule that is known to the public, the optimal parameter values for the rule are derived under the condition that $E_{t-1} b_t$ is not a predetermined variable.

Fully State-Contingent Unconditional Optimization (UOF)
The optimal fully state-contingent rule—UOF—can be derived by postulating that base-money growth is given by[9]

$$b_t = \lambda_0 + \lambda_1 u_t + \lambda_2 v_t \tag{19}$$

and then minimizing the expected value of the loss function with respect to λ_0, λ_1, and λ_2. The resulting optimal policy is

$$b_t | UOF = -v_t - \frac{u_t}{1+a}, \tag{20}$$

which mimics the CO policy (16) without including a response to the distortion term k.

Under the UOF policy,

$$E_{t-1} L_t | UOF = k^2 + \frac{a}{1+a} V(u). \tag{21}$$

Partially State-Contingent Unconditional Optimization (UOP)
Next consider the case of a partially state-contingent rule—UOP—in which base money reacts to the u_t disturbances but not to the v_t disturbances. The optimization problem is analogous to the UOF case, except that now we seek values of τ_0 and τ_1 that minimize the expected loss for rules having the form

$$b_t = \tau_0 + \tau_1 u_t. \tag{22}$$

The optimal policy of this form is

$$b_t | UOP = -\frac{u_t}{1 + a}. \tag{23}$$

Thus,

$$E_{t-1} L_t | UOP = \frac{a V(u)}{1 + a} + (1 + a) V(v) + k^2. \tag{24}$$

Discussion

If time-consistency issues are ignored for a moment, it is evident from equations (18), (21), and (24) that the UOF policy dominates both the CO policy and the UOP policy. It is also evident that the CO and UOP policies are not unambiguously ranked. The CO policy is advantageous relative to the UOP policy when $V(v)$ is large, whereas UOP is advantageous relative to CO when k is large.[10] This reflects the fact that discretion has the desirable consequence of allowing the monetary authority to react to shocks that are not allowed for in the partially state-contingent rule but has the undesirable consequence of generating an inflationary bias whenever there are distortions affecting the determination of output.[11]

The time-consistency issue arises in an environment in which a policy authority announces its intention to follow either the UOF or UOP policy but is tempted actually to follow the CO policy (see Kydland and Prescott (1977)). The source of temptation is that when private agents believe that the policymakers will follow either UOF or UOP, the monetary authority can achieve a welfare gain in the short run by exploiting the agents' predetermined expectations and following the CO policy instead. Accordingly, agents in the economy, understanding this point, will expect the authority to follow the CO policy no matter what policy is announced. Thus, the only time-consistent equilibrium in this example is the CO policy.

Despite widespread awareness of this time-consistency issue, many economists favor the adoption of a UOP policy (for example, see McCallum (1987, 1988)). These individuals must believe either that time-consistency problems are not likely to be important in practice or that such problems can be avoided through institutional mechanisms that precommit the authorities to adhere to the UOP rule. For example, some form of penalty —either formal or informal—could be imposed on the authority or on society to remove the incentive for the monetary authority to exploit the predetermined expectations.[12] Such institutional arrangements are discussed in section IV.

III   The Strategy of Mixing a Partially State-Contingent Rule with Discretion

If it were feasible and costless to specify and follow a fully state-contingent monetary rule, and if appropriate institutional mechanisms could be established for precommitting the authorities to follow the rule, then there would be no justification for relying on either discretion or a partially state-contingent rule in the conduct of monetary policy. As illustrated in the previous section, it is clear in theory that both discretion and partially state-contingent rules are "second-best" strategies.

As a practical matter, however, a fully state-contingent rule for monetary policy is simply not a relevant possibility in a world in which (1) knowledge about the macroeconomic structure and the nature of disturbances is incomplete, (2) it takes time and other resources to assimilate new information from those events that contain new information, and (3) it can be very costly to society to delay policy reactions until new information is fully assimilated. Consistently, the various types of "simple rules" that have actually been proposed for monetary policy are not fully state-contingent UOF policies.

When fully state-contingent rules are discarded as irrelevant alternatives, new scope emerges for advancing the analysis of rules versus discretion. Indeed, given that discretion (that is, CO policies) and partially state-contingent rules (that is, UOP policies) cannot be unambiguously ranked, it is natural to investigate strategies that optimally mix a partially state-contingent rule with discretion.

In focusing on this issue, it may be helpful to keep the semantics precise in this section by referring to CO and UOP policies rather than to discretion and partially state-contingent rules. Our intuition at the outset is that the advantage of mixing a UOP policy with a CO policy is that the CO policy allows reactions to disturbances not incorporated in the UOP policy. The disadvantage is that, under the mixed strategy, part of the inflationary consequences of the CO policy will be built into agents' inflation expectations even during periods when the monetary advantages and disadvantages appropriately in selecting the optimal degree of mixing.

The remaining parts of this section have two objectives: to derive the optimal values of the coefficients in the UOP policy, given that that the authority is actually following a mixed policy; and to show that a mixed strategy can be socially preferable to both the CO and the UOP policies. In connection with the first objective, it is important to note that the typical evaluation methodology used for UOP policies is not generally valid when a monetary authority adopting a UOP policy occasionally "bails out" of the policy to react to the realization of some state that had not been prescribed in the UOP policy. In particular, the typical methodology for evaluating proposed UOP policies, and for deriving optimal parameter values for such policies, is based on the assumption that the policies will be followed indefinitely. Accordingly, we are interested in finding conditions such that the parameters obtained through traditional methodology are also optimal when the UOP policy is recognized to be part of a mixed strategy that includes occasional reliance on CO policy.

Setting Optimal UOP Parameter Values as Part of a Mixed Strategy

Consider the problem of finding the optimal values of τ_0 and τ_1 in the policy $b_t = \tau_0 + \tau_1 u_t$ (as defined in equation (22)), where these values solve

$$\min_{\tau_0, \tau_1} E_{t-1} L_t = q E_{t-1}(L_t | UOP) + (1 - q) E_{t-1}(L_t | CO). \tag{25}$$

Here q denotes the probability that the UOP policy will be followed during period t, whereas $1 - q$ is the probability that the CO policy will be followed. For now, we will take q to be an exogenous constant ($0 \leq q \leq 1$). In the next subsection we will begin to model q.

To solve this problem it is convenient to first obtain $E_{t-1} b_t$, which enters into the loss function under both branches of the policy. If UOP is follwed, $b_t = \tau_0 + \tau_1 u_t$; if CO is followed (recall equation (14)), $b_t = (1 + a)^{-1}(E_{t-1} b_t - u_t + k) - v_t$. Accordingly, since $E_{t-1} b_t = q E_{t-1}(b_t | UOP) + (1 - q) E_{t-1}(b_t | CO)$,

$$E_{t-1} b_t = \frac{(1 + a)q}{a + q} \tau_0 + \frac{(1 + a)q}{a + q} \tau_1 E_{t-1}(u_t | UOP)$$

$$+ \frac{(1 - q)}{a + q}(k - E_{t-1}(u_t | CO)) - \frac{1 + a}{a + q} E_{t-1}(v_t | CO). \tag{26}$$

To obtain the optimal values of τ_0 and τ_1, first substitute equation (22) and equation (26) into equation (13) and obtain the appropriate expression for $E_{t-1}(L_t | UOP)$; next, substitute equation (14) and equation (26) into equation

(13) and obtain the appropriate expression for $E_{t-1}(L_t|CO)$; finally, substitute these expressions into the policy problem (25) and obtain through optimization two equations in τ_0 and τ_1. In general, the optimal values of τ_0 and τ_1 will depend on the conditional expectations of u and v. However, for the case in which the CO policy is used symmetrically in the sense that $E_{t-1}(u_t|CO) = E_{t-1}(u_t|UOP) = E_{t-1}(v_t|CO) = 0$, then the optimal parameter values are $\tau_0 = 0$ and $\tau_1 = -1/(1 + a)$, which are identical to the optimal values of the policy parameters obtained for the pure UOP policy (recall equation (23)). This "symmetric" case is of interest because it provides a plausible environment in whch the typical policy evaluation methodology delivers the correct policy rule parameterization even when the policy rule will sometimes be violated.

The Optimality of a Mixed Strategy

This section of the chapter demonstrates that rigid adherence to a simple rule may be inferior to the strategy of mixing a simple rule with discretion. We illustrate the possible gains from a mixed strategy using the above framework. Following the results of the previous subsection, the mixed strategy that we study combines the policy resulting from conditional optimization (CO) with the partially state-contingent policy (UOP) that is optimal when it is known that the CO policy will sometimes be applied.

To capture the idea that society wants the central bank to exercise discretion only when there are relatively large payoffs in terms of the social loss function, we assume that the central bank has been motivated to minimize the sum of the social loss function L (as specified by condition (13)) plus a cost that arises whenever policy settings deviate from the UOP rule.[13] For purposes of providing a simple illustration, we consider the analytic framework developed in section I under the assumption that $u_t \equiv 0$. We further assume that the distribution of v_t shocks is symmetric and that society wants the monetary authorities to follow the UOP rule $b_t = 0$ for small v_t shocks and to switch to the CO policy for shocks that exceed (in absolute value) a threshold size θ. As shown in the previous subsection, $b_t = 0$ is the optimal UOP policy under these circumstances. If society has established the appropriate incentives for the monetary authority (that is, made the cost of overriding the rule large enough but not too large), then society can expect that the rule will be overridden if and only if the shock is large in the sense that it is outside the θ boundaries. Thus, the probability of following the UOP policy is

$$q = \text{prob}\{|v_t| \leq \theta\}. \tag{27}$$

For this case, it is straightforward to show that for some parameter values the mixed strategy is preferable to (that is, results in a smaller expected loss than) both the UOP policy (the rule) and the CO policy (discretion). The first step in the demonstration is to note that

$$E_{t-1}b_t = qE_{t-1}b_t|UOP + (1 - q)E_{t-1}b_t|CO, \tag{28}$$

where $E_{t-1}b_t|UOP$ is the period $t-1$ conditional expectation of base-money growth given that UOP is being followed, and $E_{t-1}b_t|CO$ is the $t-1$ conditional expectation of b_t given that CO is being followed. Recall that a CO policy must satisfy the first-order condition (14); it therefore follows that

$$b_t|CO = \frac{1}{1 + a}(E_{t-1}b_t + k) - v_t, \tag{29}$$

where we have used $u_t \equiv 0$. Next, use equation (17) and the condition $b_t|UOP = 0$ to derive

$$E_{t-1}b_t|CO = \frac{k}{a + q}. \tag{30}$$

The probability of following UOP—that is, q—shows up in equation (30) because this scheme modifies agents' rational expectations of base-money growth. As long as q is positive, the scheme reduces expected base growth conditional on discretion and will therefore reduce the inflationary bias. Unconditional expected base-money growth, which is obtained from equations (30) and (28), is

$$E_{t-1}b_t = \frac{(1 - q)k}{a + q}. \tag{31}$$

Next, consider that the expected value of the loss function under the mixed strategy is

$$E_{t-1}L_t = qE_{t-1}(L_t|UOP) + (1 - q)E_{t-1}(L_t|CO). \tag{32}$$

From equations (13) and (32) it can be seen that

$$L_t|UOP = \left[\frac{(1 + a)}{(a + q)}k - v_t\right]^2 + av_t^2 \tag{33}$$

and

$$E_{t-1}L_t|UOP = \frac{(1 + a)^2}{(a + q)^2}k^2 + (1 + a)V(v|UOP), \tag{34}$$

where $V(v|UOP)$ is the variance of v conditional on the UOP policy, which is equivalent to being conditional on v being "small." Similarly, from equations (13), (14), and (31) it can be seen that

$$L_t|CO = E_{t-1}L_t|CO = \frac{a(1 + a)}{(a + q)^2}k^2. \tag{35}$$

Combining these two branches of the loss function yields

$$E_{t-1}L_t = (1 + a)\left[\frac{k^2}{a + q} + qV(v|UOP)\right]. \tag{36}$$

So far, our demonstration is simply a formalism. What we will show next is that under a range of parameter values the mixed strategy is superior to both the optimal UOP rule and discretion. Because we simply want to show a possibility, an example will suffice. Recall equation (27) and consider a situation in which v_t is uniformly distributed on the interval $[-\gamma, \gamma]$ such that $q = \theta/\gamma$ for any choice of θ on the relevant interval. For this distribution, $V(v) = \gamma^2/3$ and $V(v|UOP) = q^2\gamma^2/3$. Furthermore, by substituting the conditional variance into equation (36) and minimizing $E_{t-1}L_t$ with respect to q, it can be shown that the optimal value of q must satisfy the condition[14]

$$q^2 + aq - k/\gamma = 0. \tag{37}$$

The probability q need not be an object of choice—we simply want to illustrate that it is feasible for the optimal q to take on a value between zero and unity. Such a case arises when $k/\gamma < 1 + a$, which provides an example in which the mixed strategy dominates both UOP (rule) and CO (discretion).

Note that the mixed strategy is not always optimal. Indeed, if k is large or if γ is small, the rule will dominate (that is, $q = 1$ will be optimal as a corner solution). But note also that if γ is extremely large relative to k, then discretion has an advantage relative to the rule. Although a large value of γ makes CO (discretion) attractive in this example, the mixed strategy always dominates CO (that is, $q = 0$ is never optimal as long as $k > 0$) but does not always dominate UOP (the rule).

As a general point, it should be emphasized that the support that such analysis provides for strategies that combine rules and discretion requires careful interpretation. In particualr, the analysis does not support the strategy of announcing a rule but not taking the rule seriously, as has sometimes appeared to have been the practice in the past. Rather, as we interpret the analysis, the mixed strategy calls for the monetary authorities to follow a precisely defined rule in normal circumstances but to be prepared to override the rule in abnormal circumstances. In implementing such a strategy, society would have to think carefully about how it wants to define "abnormal circumstances." Our example interpreted abnormal circumstances as synonymous with large v shocks, but it might also be appropriate for the central bank to override the rule temporarily whenever the ultimate target variables have drifted too far from their intended course.

IV Institutional Arrangements for Mitigating Credibility Problems

Because we know from the literature on time consistency that even authorities concerned solely with maximizing social welfare may be tempted to deviate from the optimal rule in the presence of distortions (recall the third subsection of section II), it is important to establish mechanisms for overcoming problems of the credibility of monetary policy. In some countries the existence of independent central banks, and the practice of granting long and overlapping tenures to central bank governors, may provide an institutional framework within which an announced monetary policy strategy has more credibility than would be the case if monetary policy was controlled by elected officials with shorter terms of office. Nevertheless, even independent central banks have credibility problems in the sense that their policy announcements are not always accepted at face value.

As emphasized above, problems of monetary policy credibility can easily be resolved if the structure of the macroeconomic model is well known to all economic agents, if all relevant economic variables are observable, and if all disturbances to the economy can be characterized as having well-defined probability distributions. In that case, an optimal fully state-contingent rule would be well defined, society would derive no benefit from allowing the central bank to exercise discretion, and, conversely, society would have nothing to lose from resolving the problems of monetary policy credibility by requiring the central bank to adhere rigidly to the optimal fully state-contingent rule. By contrast, when information is incomplete, and when the central bank has the opportunity to base the settings of its policy instruments on better information about the economy than private agents have (or had) in making contracts for wages and other relevant variables, eliminating monetary policy discretion can have the undesirable consequence of preventing central banks from performing a beneficial stabilization role.

In analyzing the difficulties that can arise in resolving problems of monetary policy credibility when central banks have "private information"—that is, information different from what other economic agents can obtain or vefiy—Canzoneri (1985) has noted that "private information" includes both superior information about the economy and information about the policymaking process that the private sector cannot reconstruct. We think it is important to recognize that the poliymaker's environment includes seldom-experienced events—such as wars, commodity price shocks, asset market panics, or horizon-expanding inventions—that are not amenable to any ex ante codification of policy reactions. In our view, this environment —superimposed on a world in which private agents find it rational (based on transaction and negotiation costs) to enter into contracts for wages and other variables for fixed periods of time in forms that are not fully state-contingent or subject to continuous revision—creates the possibility that discretionary central bank responses to seoldom-experienced events might play a valuable stabilization role.

In considering the strategy of mixing a simple rule with discretion in the manner defined in the previous section, one of the important issues that arises is how to limit the exercise of central bank discretion when the very circumstances in which discretionary responses are desired cannot be defined precisely in advance. Our formal analysis relied on the assumption that the central bank was induced to minimize the sum of the social loss function plus a fixed cost that it incurred whenever it deviated from the rule. In practice, the achievement of an appropriate mix of rule and discretion seems likely to depend on (1) the selection of a clearly defined rule that can be expected to steer the economy in a direction broadly consistent with social preferences, (2) the appointment of central bankers whose preferences are closely aligned with those of society at large, and (3) the imposition of an appropriate penalty for deviating from the rule.

With regard to the first of these factors, many countries have allowed their central banks to operate with imprecisely defined rules for monetary growth. For example, most monetary targets have been specified as ranges, few countries have adopted rules that preclude "drift" between targets for successive years, some countries have shifted their targeting strategies from one measure of money to another, and other countries have specified simultaneous targets for several monetary aggregates that cannot easily be controlled independently. Thus, in the context of the political viability that would come from an explicit understanding that rules would be mixed with discretion, there is scope for all countries to define their monetary rules more precisely. There also may be scope for adopting more sensible types of simple rules—for example, rules that prescribe explicit countercyclical behavior.

For some countries, the achievement of an optimal mix of rule and discretion might also be facilitated by changes in the process for selecting central bank governors. Rogoff (1985) has emphasized that, in the context of a time-consistency problem, society can sometimes make itself better off by leaving monetary policy to the discretion of central bankers with preferences that attach more weight than the preferences of society at large to price level stabilization relative to output stabilization. By contrast, under the mixed strategy envisioned in this paper, society wants its central bankers to adhere rigidly to a rule under "normal" circumstances, and only to deviate from the rule when doing so provides a sufficient reduction in the value of the social loss function. Accordingly, in this setup it seems desirable to appoint central bankers whose preferences are similar to those of society at large.

Finally, the issue of how severely to penalize central banks for exercising discretion to override the rule may be a matter that can be decided only through experimentation. At present, some countries subject their central bankers to regular cross-examinations by elected officials, but it is difficult for such procedures to discipline central bankers effectively when announced rules for monetary policy are not precisely defined. With a precisely defined monetary rule, the costs imposed by public cross-examinations and protestations might well dissuade central bankers from overriding the rule with much frequency. Regardless of whether public cross-examination is sufficient for this purpose, however, the severity of the penalty (or the cross-examination) should be inversely related, other things being equal, to the level of confidence with which it is expected that the rule will steer the economy in a direction consistent with social preferences.

V   Concluding Remarks

During the 1980s, monetary authorities in the major industrial countries have become more tolerant of variability in monetary growth rates relative to preannounced targets or projections, while giving increasing consideration to exchane rate objectives.[15] Although these authorities have not modified their broad objective of maintaining appropriate conditions for sustained noninflationary growth, there are important unresolved questions about the appropriate strategy for pursuing that objective, particularly in the largest countries.

This paper has used a simple analytic framework to review and reconsider some of the basic issues that arise in designing and implementing a strategy for monetary policy. Among the main points made are the following.

• Under the unrealistic assumption that both the monetary authorities and the private sector know the macroeconomic structure, can observe all relevant economic variables accurately ex post, and have accurate ex ante information about the probability distributions of disturbances to the economy, the optimal strategy is a fully state-contingent rule rather than the type of non-state-contingent monetary targets that countries have adopted in the past.[16] To the extent that time-consistency problems exist in such a situation, the optimal state-contingent rule can be made credible through institutional mechanisms to insure precommitment.

• The resolution of credibility problems and the design of an optimal strategy become more complicated when there is incomplete information about the economic structure and the nature of disturbances. On the one hand, the environment generates new information that can be used to re-evaluate continuously the structure or structural parameters of the economy and the nature of economic disturbances; thus, there are important potential gains from allowing the central bank to make use of the latest available information in its attempts to stabilize the economy. On the other hand, when the environment includes seldom-experienced events that are not amenable to any ex ante codification of policy reactions, and when it takes time and other resources to assimilate the new information that such events provide, it would seem virtually impossible to formalize the policy-making process—let alone to formalize it in a way that the private sector could reconstruct and monitor. Thus, the credibility of monetary policy would be questionable if the central bank announced a complicated state-contingent procedure for setting its policy instruments and was allowed to use new information to make period-by-period revisions of the structural model, of the parameter estimates on which its instrument settings were based, or of both. In practice, a complicated state-contingent rule that included period-by-period revisions could not be adequately distinguished from discretion.

• Although the problems associated with complicated state-contingent strategies have led some economists to propose the adoption of simple policy rules, a mixed strategy of combining a simple rule with discretion may be preferable both to rigid adherence to the rule and to complete discretion. The type of mixed strategy we are referring to here is not a strategy of announcing a rule but not taking the rule seriously, as has sometimes appeared to have been the practice in the past, but rather a strategy that calls for the authorities to follow a precisely defined (but simple) rule in "normal circumstances" and to override the rule only under certain conditions.

• Institutional mechanisms that penalized central banks for exercising discretion under "normal" conditions might be important for resolving credibility problems under a mixed strategy, just as they might be for precommitting the authorities to adhere rigidly to a rule in all circumstances. In this context, existing institutional oversight arrangements (usually involving regular cross-examinations of central bankers by elected officials) might be more effective if the rule component of the mixed strategy was defined precisely.

• In the context of a mixed strategy involving a simple rule that can be overridden under certain conditions, many of the arguments against some types of monetary rules lose their force. A rule for targeting nominal gross national product, for example, becomes more attractive when the rule can be overridden in response to supply shocks.

• The typical procedure for designing and evaluating policy rules based on counterfactual historical simulations is flawed when the rules under investigation are not fully state-contingent. In particular, it is not generally valid to base counterfactual simulations on the assumption that rational market participants would have expected the authorities to adhere rigidly to a partially state-contingent rule when policymakers, had they actually been confronted with the counterfactual history, would have sometimes had incentives to deviate from the rule.

Notes

The authors are grateful to Kenneth Rogoff, Elhanan Helpman, Dale Henderson, and seminar participants at the University of Michigan and the Fund for helpful comments and reactions.

1. This single-period optimization framework abstracts from issues involving the "reputation" of the policymaker. See Rogoff (1987) for a survey of issues concerning reputation. See also Barro and Gordon (1983).

2. If it is assumed that the logarithm of the production function is $y_t = \lambda + \theta l_t + x_t$, where l_t is the logarithm of labor input, x_t is the shock to the production function, and $0 < \theta < 1$, then $\mu_t = x_t/(1 - \theta)$.

3. See Rogoff (1985) for one possible elaboration of this approach. Rogoff defined $\bar{y}$ as the level of output (employment) that would arise if contracts could be negotiated after observing the productivity shock and all other period-t information.

4. The formulation is intended to be a stripped-down version of a flex-price model.

5. Allowing correlations of the various shocks would introduce covariances into the later analysis but would not change any of the basic conclusions. We have refrained from analyzing exchange rate regimes in this setup because of the key role played in the literature on the choice of exchange rate regime by the covariances we are assuming away.

6. Although the main points are robust to many relaxations of the white noise and independence assumptions about the shocks, things would be much more complicated in the realistic setting where the coefficient attached to b_t in equation (10) is not known with certainty.

7. In our view much of the attraction of partially state-contingent rules—such as constant money growth rules, or nominal income targeting rules—stems from economists' (apparently invincible) ignorance about many aspects of the relevant economic environment. In earlier versions of this paper we attempted to discuss such ignorance in terms of Knight's (1985) classic distinction between risk and uncertainty. These attempts reflected our conviction that it is important to emphasize the existence of Knightian uncertainty—or, as Fischer (1987) puts it, of contingencies that cannot be foreseen or described when formulating a rule—but also convinced us of the difficulty of incorporating such a concept, in a satisfactory way, into a formal economic model.

8. It is assumed that policy strategies in this uncertain environment are evaluated by using the expectation of the loss function.

9. From the structure of the model and the assumption of uncorrelated disturbances, it is intuitively clear that the optimal fully state-contingent rule must have a linear form.

10. The two policies provide the same expected loss when $k^2 = a(1 + a)V(v)$.

11. We are ignoring additional "accountability" considerations that would arise if the central bank had different preferences than society at large and thus would not seek to minimize the social loss function if left to its own discretion.

12. Formally, imposing the penalty on the private sector would work as well as imposing costs on the monetary authority, since the monetary authority is assumed to care about the well-being of the private sector.

13. From the point of view of this example, it makes little difference whether society imposes the cost on itself (perhaps in the form of a costly insitutional adjustment) or imposes the costs directly on the central bank (perhaps in the form of reduced bonuses or endless congressional testimony). We adopt the simplest structure by assuming that the cost is imposed on the monetary authority, and we assume that the cost is not a deadweight loss to society as a whole. Other examples can be constructed with alternative cost assumptions.

14. To obtain this condition, substitute the conditional variance into equation (36) and set the derivative of this expression with respect to q equal to zero. Rearrange the resulting expression so that it becomes

$$k^2 = (a + q)^2 q^2 \gamma^2.$$

Equation (37) then follows from taking the square root of each side of the above and rearranging.

15. In recent years, monetary policy strategies have involved policy coordination among countries to encourage the depreciation of the U.S. dollar during a period following the Plaza Meeting of the Group of Five countries in September 1985, and to resist further large

changes in exchange rates during the period since the Louvre Accord was announced in February 1987. See Isard and Rojas-Suarez (1986) for a review of the experience with targeting monetary aggregates.

16. It can also be shown, under this unrealistic assumption, that a fixed exchange rate strategy would not be optimal.

References

Barro, Robert J., and David B. Gordon, "Rules, Discretion and Reputation in a Model of Monetary Policy," *Journal of Monetary Economics* (Amsterdam), Vol. 12 (1983), pp. 101–21.

Canzoneri, Matthew B., "Monetary Policy Games and the Role of Private Information," *American Economic Review* (Nashville, Tennessee), Vol. 75 (1985), pp. 1056–70.

Fischer, Stanley, "Rules Versus Discretion in Monetary Policy," NBER Working Paper 2518 (Cambridge, Massachusetts: National Bureau of Economic Research, 1987).

Flood, Robert P., and Peter M. Garber, "An Economic Theory of Monetary Reform," *Journal of Political Economy* (Chicago), Vol. 88 (1980), pp. 22–58.

———, "A Model of Stochastic Process Switching," *Econometrica* (Evanston, Illinois), Vol. 51 (1983), pp. 537–51.

Gray, Jo Anna, "Wage Indexation: A Macroeconomic Approach," *Journal of Monetary Economics* (Amsterdam), Vol. 2 (1976), pp. 221–35.

Isard, Peter, and Liliana Rojas-Suarez, "Velocity of Money and the Practice of Monetary Targeting: Experience, Theory, and the Policy Debate," in International Monetary Fund, *Staff Studies for the World Economic Outlook*, (Washington, D.C., 1986), pp. 73–114.

Knight, Frank H., *Risk, Uncertainty, and Profit* (Chicago: University of Chicago Press, 1985).

Kydland, Finn E., and Edward C. Prescott, "Rules Rather Than Indiscretion: The Inconsistency of Optimal Plans," *Journal of Political Economy* (Chicago), Vol. 85 (1977), pp. 473–92.

Lucas, Robert E., Jr., "Expectations and the Neutrality of Money," *Journal of Economic Theory* (New York), Vol. 4 (1972), pp. 103–24.

McCallum, Bennett T., "The Case for Rules in the Conduct of Monetary Policy: A Concrete Example," in *Federal Reserve Bank of Richmond Economic Review*, (September–October 1987), pp. 10–18.

———, "Robustness Properties of a Rule for Monetary Policy," in *Money, Cycles, and Exchange Rates: Essays in Honor of Allan H. Meltzer*, Carnegie-Rochester Conference Series in Public Policy, Vol. 29, ed. by Karl Brunner and Bennett T. McCallum (Amsterdam and New York: North-Holland, 1988), pp. 173–203.

Rogoff, Kenneth, "The Optimal Degree of Commitment to an Intermediate Monetary Target," *Quarterly Journal of Economics* (Cambridge, massachusetts), Vol. 100 (1985), pp. 1169–89.

———, "Reputation, Coordination and Monetary Policy" in *Handbook of Modern Business Cycle Theory*, ed. by Robert J. Barro (Oxford: Basil Blackwell, 1989).

21

Transition from Inflation to Price Stability

Peter M. Garber

I   Introduction

The accelerating inflation rates of the past decade have elicited proposals to implement monetary policies which will eventually stabilize the price level. There seems to be a general agreement that the steady-state costs of the current inflation rate are high and that the rate should be reduced.[1] However, that additional substantial real costs may arise because of the transition has led some economists to prescribe monetary policies aimed at reducing such costs through a gradual reduction of the inflation rate.[2] Other economists, believing that the transition costs may be low, suggest policies designed rapidly to move to price stability.[3]

The nature of the transition costs has strong implications for the kind of research input required for policy decisions intended to reduce inflation. If transition costs are low, then one should seek to attain price stability immediately, without requiring any additional knowledge about the steady-state costs of various inflation rates. If the transition is costly, then there is a tradeoff between transitional costs and steady-state costs. Since only vague notions about the relative magnitudes of these costs exist, a large-scale, time-consuming research effort would have to precede any serious policy recommendations.[4]

Since there are many theories producing as many different predictions about the effects of transitional policies, sifting through them requires an examination of historical episodes which display transitions from inflation to price stability.[5] Of the recent empirical studies concerning the real effects of such policy shifts, Sargent's (1980) examination of the post–World War I hyperinflations is most provocative.[6] Sargent argues that these extreme inflations were brought to sudden ends without substantial negative real effects. This finding suggests that the transitional costs of a sudden change to a price-stabilizing policy may be quite low relative to the efficiency losses arising from current inflation rates. If true, this builds added confidence in a recommendation immediately to end the inflation, perhaps obviating the need to study more intensely the magnitude and nature of transition costs before making a policy recommendation.

In this chaper I will provide a detailed discussion about the real phenomena which followed the German stabilization. I reach conclusions that are different from those of Sargent; there is substantial evidence of large-scale negative real effects in the aftermath of the German hyperinflation.[7] Such effects were probably due more to the extreme nature of the inflation and its other attendant distortions than to the nature of its termination. The costs that did arise were due to a policy of subsidizing the capital goods industry through the inflation tax revenue. When this source of revenue was terminated, a major reallocation of resources among industries was required; it was the reallocation that generated the transitional costs. Thus, the allocative effects of monetary deceleration had little to do with the price or expectational stickiness that can be found in current discussions. Rather, they stemmed from a close relationship between the inflation and other governmentally imposed distortions. Regardless of their source, since the costs did rise the German case cannot serve as evidence that there may be an easy escape from the current lack of confidence in particular transitional policy recommendations.

II The German Case

In analyzing the monetary reforms of the post–World War I hyperinflations, Sargent (1980) emphasized common features which emerged in the successful price stabilizations. Basic reforms were the central banks' refusals to supply governments' credit demands and governments' changes of fiscal policy to regimes in which debt would be backed by future taxes. The implementation of these policies triggered sudden shifts from extreme inflation to price stability.[8] These cases provide dramatic evidence that economies can achieve rapid shifts to stable prices.

However, in addition, Sargent, citing data on industrial production or unemployment, suggests that these reforms were accomplished with small transitional costs. In this section I will present evidence which indicates that large transitional costs materialized in the German case, assuming the form of industrial production declines and unemployment increases. The economic decline which I will describe did not appear in the immediate aftermath of the reform, the period which Sargent examined; rather, beginning an era called the "Rationalization Period," it arose one and a half years after the November 1923 reform. Intuition suggests that transition costs should occur immediately after a reform and persist until the stable-price steady state has been attained. I will argue that this intuition should be suspended in the German case; a number of factors postponed the German transition.

The section is subdivided into two subsections. In the first I will describe the organization of industry and of output in both the inflationary period and the rationalization period. In the second I will examine the factors which postponed the transitional costs; also, I will measure both the length of time that the lack of "credibility" was important and present evidence indicating that agents fully believed in the price stabilization policy before the transitional costs materialized. In my opinion, this evidence implies that agents' correctly predicting and recognizing new policy regimes is not sufficient to prevent large transitional costs. In the second subsection I will also gauge the extent of the transitional costs and suggest that the transition was still in progress when the German economy was overwhelmed by the Great Depression.

The Organization of Output and Industry

To determine how the structure of the German economy changed in moving toward a stable-price steady state, it is necessary first to study the structure that prevailed during the inflation. The development of the German economy was molded not only by the inflationary money-creation policy but also by a portfolio of other policies which were tied intimately to the inflation.

One of the inefficiencies that arises in an inflationary period stems from the reduction in real balances; capital and labor resources must be substituted from other activities to replace money. The economy's capacity both to consume and produce is reduced. Although the reduction of real balances impinges on all transactions, I will confine the following simple discussion to its effects on production in order to focus the exposition.

In figure 21.1, the curve DAC is a production possibility frontier associated with a stable price level. A cost of inflation can be depicted as a movement from A, the efficient output combination with a zero inflation rate, to B, the efficient output combination when the inflation rate is high. Such a cost forms a component of that which is measured by the usual triangle under the real balance demand curve. In essence, the production possibility curve shifts inward with the destruction of real balances. If these production possibility frontiers were homothetic, there would be no change in the ratios of different goods produced, provided that the inflation did not

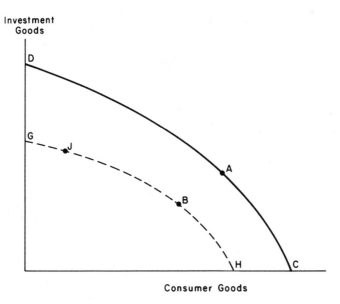

Figure 21.1

affect relative prices. However, an increasing inflation rate may automatically trigger other distortions through its association with the economy's other institutional arrangements. Fischer and Modigliani (1978) and Fischer (1980) studied these automatic distortions, suggesting that they may increase substantially the costs of steady-state inflation. Such distortions may manifest themselves through a relative price shift; in the context of figure 21.1, the relative price of investment goods may rise, moving the composition of output from B to J.

I will now argue that such automatic distortions did affect the relative prices and structure of the German economy; later, I will discuss the sources of these distortions. In table 21.1, I present evidence that substantial movements in relative prices occurred in the German inflation, causing production to shift toward investment goods.[9] The entries in the table are the ratio of the wholesale price index to the cost of living index. Included in the WPI are both investment goods and goods destined for consumption; the ratio probably understates the order of magnitude of the relative price shift between consumer goods and investment goods. In the first half of 1921, there was a very mild deflation; the relative price that prevailed from January to July can be interpreted as the relationship that might prevail with a stable-price level. The inflation resumed in August 1921,

Table 21.1
Ratio of wholesale price index to cost of living index

Date	1921[1]	1922[1]	1923[1]	1924[2]	1925[3]
Jan.	.97	1.43	1.91	.89	.94
Feb.	.95	1.34	1.62	.94	.94
Mar.	.94	1.46	1.33	.94	.93
Apr.	.94	1.43	1.38	.94	.92
May	.94	1.32	1.67	.92	.93
June	.94	1.31	1.95	.89	.92
July	.91	1.45	1.53	.93	.90
Aug.	1.14	1.92	1.24	.94	.90
Sept.	1.20	1.64	1.23	1.00	.91
Oct.	1.30	1.97	1.49	.93	.90
Nov.	1.51	1.98	.85	.94	.92
Dec.	1.41	1.67	.81	.97	.91

1. Source: Statistisches Reichsamt, *Zahlen zur Geltentwertung*, p. 21, p. 33. The CLI used in all years is that which excludes housing, which was price controlled. The index in gold was multiplied by 100 and divided into the WPI.
2. Source: Statistisches Reichsamt, *Jahrbuch für das Deutsche Reich, 1924*, p. 260, p. 265. Indexes are for end of month.
3. Source: Statistisches Reichsamt, *Jahrbuch für das Deutsche Reich, 1925*, p. 238, p. 301. A new computation method was used by the Statistisches Reichsamt to compute these indices.

continuing at increasing rates until November 1923. Immediately, the ratio of the WPI to the CLI increased substantially, more than doubling in a number of months in 1922 and 1923. When the inflation ended, the ratio immediately fell to the level which had prevailed in the first half of 1921, remaining there for the next two years.

Again, to focus the exposition, let us assume that the Stolper-Samuelson theorem is applicable. Then there should be a predictable relationship among movements in goods relative prices, outputs, relative factor prices, absolute factor incomes, and factor intensity changes in each industry. In particular, if the investment-goods industry was relatively capital intensive, this shift in the relative price of goods should have been associated not only with a rise in the rent/wage ratio but also with a decline in the absolute income of labor. There is some indication that the investment-goods industry was capital intensive.[10] Table 21.2, with data on the number of persons employed in each industry, indicates to some extent that resources flowed into investment-goods industries during the inflation and into consumer-goods industries after the reform.[11] In table 21.3, I present some evidence on the movement of real wages. During the hyperinflation these declined substantially, rising steadily after the reform. Numerical evidence on the return to capital is not as readily available as wage data.

Table 21.2
Employment in capital goods and consumer goods industries*

	Capital goods industries		Consumer goods industries	
Year	Persons employed	%	Persons employed	%
1907	5,960,973	71.5	2,315,177	28.5
1913	6,732,354	70.4	2,829,632	29.6
1919	5,628,566	73.8	1,993,907	26.2
1922	7,277,795	72.3	2,787,565	27.7
1923	6,262,079	73.5	2,253,159	26.5
1924	6,143,302	68.7	2,800,780	31.3
1925*	6,036,000	57.0	4,577,000	43.0

Source: 1907–1924, *Vierteljahrshefte zur Konjunkturforschurg*, 1926, Heft 2, p. 47.
*Source: *Vierteljahrshefte zur Konjunkturforschurg*, 1927, Heft 4, p. 18. The organization producing the 1925 data was different from that which produced the data prior to 1925. Hence, there is some discrepancy. The employment figures reported by this source are 6.7 million in the capital goods industry and 5.9 million in the consumer goods industry. The 1926 source does not account for the category "Wohnung, Kultur, Luxus." Since the 1927 source includes this category among consumer goods, I have subtracted the workers in this group (1.98 million) from the consumer goods total for 1925. In addition, the earlier source includes paper and leather goods among consumer goods, while the later source includes them among capital goods. Hence, for 1925, I have moved the workers in these categories (631 thousand) into consumer goods.

However, the accounts of the period seem to indicate that profits were very large during the inflationary period, especially in the investment-goods industries.[12] New investment flowed into the capital-goods industry along with labor. Both Bresciani-Turroni (pp. 201–2) and Graham (p. 242) discuss the expansion of plant that proceeded during the inflation. Due to the very low wage-rental ratio, the new investment congealed in plants employing labor-intensive techniques.[13]

In addition to the shifts in prices, output composition, and resource allocation, a change in the organization of industry occurred during the inflation.[14] German industry had always been somewhat horizontally integrated; cartels were common prior to the inflation. However, during the inflation industries both integrated vertically and formed enormous combines of wholly disparate firms; the combines controlled vast sectors of the economy.[15] In part, the purpose of constructing such organizations was to avoid the use of money by employing internal accounting and payments systems.[16]

The distortion which, in combination with the inflation, determined this organization of output and industry was the subsidization of the investment-goods industry with the inflation tax revenue. The subsidies derived from the money creation assumed a number of forms. First, capital-goods

Table 21.3

Index of weekly real wages, (1913 = 100)

	Skilled workers	Unskilled workers
April 1922	71.9	93.4
July	71.5	93.8
October	54.8	70.7
November	51.3	65.9
December	61.6	80.3
January 1923	48.7	63.6
February	63.5	82.2
March	78.7	102.0
April	74.1	96.0
May	65.1	84.2
June	65.1	84.0
July	48.0	62.0
August	67.2	86.4
September	61.2	78.2
October	52.0	64.8
November	53.3	66.0
December	69.9	85.0
January 1924*	81.2	95.4
February	81.7	94.0
March	83.4	91.9
April	90.4	96.9
May	96.8	104.3
June	101.2	108.1
July	101.9	108.6
August	102.5	109.3
September	102.7	109.3
October	104.2	111.3
November	106.5	114.5
December	109.8	117.7
January 1925	110.7	119.0
February	111.9	120.2
March	114.6	122.9
April	117.8	125.6
May	120.6	128.2
June	122.6	130.4
July	125.4	133.2
August	126.8	135.2
September	128.2	136.4
October	128.8	136.9
November	131.2	139.4
December	131.3	139.5

Source: 1922–23 data are from Statistisches Reichsamt, *Zahlen zur Geldentwertung in Deutschland*, p. 42.
The 1924–25 data are taken from *Vierteljahrshefte zur Konjunkturforschung*, 1 Jahrgang, 1926, p. 61. These data are reported in Reichsmarks/week. However, since the 1913 weekly goldmark wage was reported by the Statistisches Reichsamt reference, the Index can be computed by forming the ratio of the two wages because 1 Reichsmark = 1 goldmark.
*In International Labour Office (1925), the reported Indexes are lower for 1924 (p. 79) than reported here. However, the pattern of growth is similar.

industries were supported directly through the government's budget. In addition to government enterprises such as the railway, the government subsidized shipbuilding and electrical power generation.[17] Second, beginning in 1922, the Reichsbank began directly to discount the bills of private business. The annual discount rates were 6 percent in July 1922, 18 percent in April 1923, 30 percent in August 1923, and 90 percent in September 1923. The inflation rates prevailing at these dates were at such high levels that only a negligible percentage of a loan's real value was ever repaid.[18] The large combines, organized around the basic capital-goods industries, had special access to such loans for financing their commercial activities, thereby effectively receiving large subsidies for their inputs. Some idea of the relative values of the Reichsbank loans to the government and to industry can be gained from table 21.4. Finally, the Reichsbank, unable to print currency fast enough to satisfy demand, licensed a number of institutions, including private firms, to print "emergency money" in order to meet their pressing needs for cash. The large combines had an advantage in circulating such cash in payment for their inputs because of their large size.[19] This policy subsidized both the formation of large conglomerates and the production of capital goods.[20]

In summary, the combination of the inflation with other government and central bank policies caused new capital investment and labor to shift into the investment-goods industries, substantially increased the amount of fixed capital utilizing labor-intensive technology, and produced an environment in which gigantic, centralized industrial organizations could form and survive. Also, it shifted the relative prices of goods and factors of production and destroyed real balances by generating inflationary expectations. That these expectations and price distortions ended with the reform did not indicate that the transition from an inflationary environment to a steady-state, stable-price environment had also terminated. Rather, the transition continued until the technical nature of capital, the quantity of capital, and the organization of industry returned to normal.

The Rentenmark, the Dawes Loan, and the Rationalization of Industry

The Rentenmark
The monetary reform was implemented in November 1923. Since Sargent discusses the event extensively, I will review only some relevant details. A new bank, the Rentenbank, was created with the power to issue Rentenmarks in limited amounts; the Rentenmark was a new form of paper money, but its value remained close to one goldmark (4.2 goldmarks = $1). Half of the

Table 21.4
New discounts of the Reichsbank (million goldmarks)[a]

Date	New state bills discounted	New private bills discounted	Date	New state bills discounted	New private[b] bills discounted
January, 1922	−140.5	−1.46	January, 1924	—	655.0
February	170.4	5.6	February	—	380.0
March	190.4	4.6	March	—	438.0
April	129.8	3.6	April	—	163.0
May	178.5	14.3	May	—	9.4
June	247.4	18.6	June	—	−76.2
July	207.8	32.2	July	—	−146.2
August	169.2	54.8	August	—	−88.5
September	287.5	82.0	September	—	452.0
October	191.6	76.6			
November	108.9	81.5			
December	289.6	99.1			
January, 1923	150.2	97.2			
February	288.1	243.7			
March	322.7	109.2			
April	332.6	122.1			
May*	116.7	66.8			
June*	279.7	78.6			
July*	133.6	42.9			
August*	380.3	59.6			
September*	1160.1	91.7			
October*	384.4	62.1			
November*	90.9	346.3			
December	—	210.3			

Source: *Jan. 1922−Oct. 1923* Statistisches Reichsamt, *Zahlen zur Geldentwertung in Deutschland*, p. 52, p. 23. *Nov. 1923*, *Economist*, Volumes XCVIII, XCIX. From sections on Central Bank returns. *Sept. 1924*
a. 4.2 goldmarks = 1 dollar.
b. This amount is the sum of the changes in the following asset categories: Advances, Rentenmark Discounts and Advances, Bills of Exchange and Checks, and Rentenmark Bills of Exchange and Checks.
*Prior to May, 1923, new nominal discounted bills were converted to gold values using mid-month exchange rates. From May to November 1923, conversions were performed with end of month exchange rates. Thus, the gold value of these months' new bills may be severely understated.

Rentenmarks (1.2 billion) were loaned to the government to finance its deficits in transition to a balanced budget; some Rentenmarks (ultimately .8 billion) were loaned to the Reichsbank. The government drastically cut its expenditures and raised taxes. On November 16, the Reichsbank stopped discounting government bills; and the government extinguished its entire debt to the Reichsbank, using part of its Rentenmark loan to repurchase the debt. The Reichsbank announced that after November 22 it would no longer exchange paper marks for emergency money.

However, the Reichsbank, basing its actions on a real-bills doctrine, continued to discount private bills at a rapid rate. The real values of its new loans to industry and agriculture in the five months after the reform exceeded those of the loans during the inflation, as indicated in table 21.4. The Reichsbank's acquisition of these assets was reflected in an increased circulation of papermarks in addition to the Rentenmarks circulated after the reform. Since the price level and exchange rate were relatively stable after the reform, the added currency represented an increase in real balances.[21] For the period after the reform, total currency in circulation and its components are presented in table 21.5. Notice that currency in circulation more than doubled in the first six months after the reform.

The effects of this post-reform monetary policy on the price level can be determined by table 21.6. After an initial decline in prices, the inflation resumed in the spring of 1924 at a substantial annual rate. This new inflation so alarmed the Reichsbank that it suddenly stopped its discounting of new private bills after the first week in April, 1924.[22]

Expectations and "Credibility"
The effect of this policy shift on inflationary expectations can be determined by examining the interest rates for day money, month money, and gold bonds in table 21.7. The rates for day money and month money were nominal; those for the gold bonds were real, since the bonds and their coupons were denominated in gold.[23] Although there were differences with the term and risk associated with these assets, the difference between the nominal and real rates should reflect at least the order of magnitude of the anticipated inflation rate. In the spring of 1924, the differential in interest rates indicates an anticipated annual inflation rate of 20–30 percent. Within eight months after the Reichsbank imposed its credit restrictions, the difference fell to a level reflecting a negligible anticipated inflation rate.

These interest-rate differences can also be used to address the question of the "credibility" of the central bank's new policy. Even in the winter of

Table 21.5
Currency in Ciculation* (in million Rentenmarks)[1]

Date (end of month)	Total[2]	Reichsbank notes	Railroad emergency money	Rentenmarks	Gold loans	Fixed value railroad emergency money	Emergency gold loans	Coins
November 1923	1484.1	400.3	114.8	501.0	216.4	35.4	216.2	—
December	2271.2	496.5	109.0	1049.1	240.0	141.9	234.7	—
January 1924	2275.7	483.6	64.6	1196.3	140.0	144.2	146.0	1.0
February	2632.1	587.9	51.1	1563.8	207.9	144.2	71.4	5.8
March	2823.3	689.9	26.6	1760.3	146.6	123.6	50.4	25.9
April	2817.6	777.0	8.0	1708.8	111.0	93.2	41.4	85.2
May	2917.0	926.9	3.5	1728.5	24.0	70.6	25.0	138.5
June	3128.6	1097.3	—	1771.6	—	55.5	9.5	194.7
July	3299.7	1211.0	—	1803.4	—	37.1	1.0	247.2
August	3534.7	1391.9	—	1832.4	—	19.9	—	290.5
September	3707.6	1520.5	—	1853.1	—	7.2	—	326.8
October	3823.8	1780.9	—	1715.1	—	—	—	327.8
November	3897.4	1863.2	—	1677.4	—	—	—	356.8
December	4159.1	1941.4	—	1835.1	—	—	—	383.0
January 1925	4077.3	1901.3	—	1780.4	—	—	—	395.7
February	4250.1	2106.2	—	1736.1	—	—	—	407.7
March	4337.2	2308.0	—	1611.2	—	—	—	418.0
April	4358.1	2447.2	—	1480.2	—	—	—	430.8
May	4606.3	2601.7	—	1551.4	—	—	—	453.3
June	4608.1	2464.4	—	1671.7	—	—	—	472.1
July	4715.9	2522.5	—	1701.3	—	—	—	492.1
August	4808.2	2585.4	—	1712.6	—	—	—	510.2
September	4878.2	2637.1	—	1713.2	—	—	—	528.0

Table 21.5 (continued)

Date (end of month)	Total[2]	Reichsbank notes	Railroad emergency money	Rentenmarks	Gold loans	Fixed value railroad emergency money	Emergency gold loans	Coins
October	4883.7	2794.2	—	1542.6	—	—	—	546.9
November	4799.3	2756.9	—	1480.3	—	—	—	562.1
December	5001.8	2944.4	—	1475.7	—	—	—	584.8
January 1926	4675.1	2640.1	—	1450.2	—	—	—	584.8
February	4749.2	2814.6	—	1335.4	—	—	—	599.2
March	4874.4	3150.0	—	1156.8	—	—	—	626.2
April	4859.2	3076.8	—	1156.8	—	—	—	626.2
May	4880.6	2868.9	—	1373.1	—	—	—	638.6
June	4997.6	2963.2	—	1387.8	—	—	—	646.6
July 1926	5118.7	3096.4	—	1363.4	—	—	—	658.9
August	5144.4	3218.2	—	1260.0	—	—	—	666.2
September	5294.1	3240.5	—	1369.2	—	—	—	684.4
October	5325.4	3313.1	—	1317.6	—	—	—	694.7
November	5257.2	3366.2	—	1199.0	—	—	—	692.0
December	5623.4	3710.1	—	1164.0	—	—	—	749.3

1. 1 Rentenmark = 1 goldmark = 1 Reichsmark = 1 trillion paper marks
2. Total excludes private bank notes.
*Source: November, 1923–December, 1924, Statistisches Reichsamt, *Jahrbuch für das Deutsche Reich, 1924/25*, p. 313. January–December, 1925.
———, *Jahrbuch für das Deutsche Reich*, 1925, p. 325. January–December, 1926. ——— , *Jahrbuch für das Deutsche Reich*, 1926, p. 358.

Table 21.6
Price indexes, 1924–1925[1] (1913 = 100)

Date[2]	Wholesale price index	Cost of living[3] index
December 1923	120.0	142.8
January 1924	114.8	129.0
February	118.0	126.0
March	120.8	128.0
April	124.6	133.0
May	120.2	131.0
June	112.6	127.0
July	118.5	128.0
August	120.9	128.0
September	131.5	132.0
October	128.5	138.0
November	129.0	136.9
December	134.5	137.8
January 1925	143.5	152.0
February	142.7	151.9
March	141.3	152.2
April	138.6	151.4
May	139.0	149.7
June	140.9	153.2
July	142.8	158.9
August	144.3	159.5
September	144.4	159.1
October	143.1	157.3
November	141.6	154.7
December	139.8	154.4

1. The jump in the indices between December 1924 and January 1925 is due to the introduction of a new computation method for both indices.
2. End of month for 1924, Monthly average for 1925.
3. Excludes housing.
Source: Statistisches Reichsamt, *Jahrbuch für das Deutsche Reich, 1924/25*, p. 260, p. 265.
———, *Jahrbuch für das Deutsche Reich, 1925*, p. 259, p. 301.

1924, agents apparently believed that prices would rise at low annual percentage rates relative to those that had prevailed in the hyperinflation. Given that prices had risen at rates of 500 percent per week in October 1923, the 1924 interest rates indicate a dramatic and rapid shift in agents' beliefs about monetary policy.[24] Agents also learned rapidly about the final shift to the stable-price policy. It seems reasonable to claim that agents in the German economy believed in a stable-price policy regime by April 1925. Thus, the length of time during which credibility may have been an issue was at most one and a half years, starting in November 1923.

Table 21.7
Interest rates[1]

Date	Day money	Month money	5% gold bonds	Date	Day money	Month money	5% gold bonds
January 1924	87.6	28.3	7.8	January 1926	7.1	9.0	7.5
February	34.9	22.6	7.8	February	6.0	7.4	7.0
March	33.1	30.0	9.2	March	5.7	6.8	6.6
April	45.5	44.5	10.5	April	4.6	6.0	6.1
May	27.8	44.3	12.8	May	4.8	5.9	6.1
June	22.6	32.6	13.3	June	4.8	5.8	6.2
July	16.8	22.9	11.2	July	5.0	5.8	6.1
August	17.1	18.8	9.3	August	5.0	5.9	6.0
September	15.0	16.8	8.3	September	5.1	6.2	6.0
October	14.1	14.4	8.4	October	5.0	6.3	5.9
November	13.0	13.8	8.3	November	4.8	6.4	5.8
December	11.1	12.6	8.3	December	6.0	7.4	5.5
January 1925	10.0	11.3	7.4	January 1927	4.3	6.3	5.4
February	10.6	11.9	7.4	February	5.4	5.9	5.3
March	9.0	11.3	7.2	March	5.1	7.3	5.4
April	8.5	10.1	7.3	April	5.8	7.1	5.5
May	8.8	10.5	7.4	May	6.3	7.6	5.6
June	8.8	10.7	7.8	June	6.0	8.2	5.8
July	9.5	10.9	8.0				
August	9.0	10.8	8.3				
September	8.9	10.8	8.2				
October	9.4	10.8	8.0				
November	8.5	10.7	8.2				
December	8.2	10.3	8.2				

1. Annual percentage rates.
Source: *Vierteljahreshefte zur Konjunkturforschung 1926/27*, Heft 2, p. 92 and *1927*, Heft 3, p. 112.

Real effects of reform and credit stringency

While 1922 was by all accounts a boom year, industrial production in 1923 was depressed, as shown in table 21.8. In the last half of 1923, unemployment grew substantially as indicated in table 21.10. It is difficult to isolate the cause of this depression in output. In January 1923, the French and Belgians occupied the Ruhr, the industrial heartland of Germany; the "passive resistance" that ensued disrupted production both in the Ruhr and in the rest of the country. Simultaneously with the advent of the reform, the passive resistance ended. Therefore, the revival of output in early 1924 can be attributed either to the end of the inflation or to the end of the Ruhr struggle.

Industrial production rapidly approached its 1922 levels until the stable-price regime began in earnest in April 1924. At that point output collapsed

Table 21.8a
Index of industrial production (1913 = 100)

Year	Index of production
1920	61
1921	77
1922	86
1923	54
1924	77
1925	90
1926	86
1927	111

Table 21.8b
(1928 = 100)

	1924	1925	1926	1927	1928	1929
January	51.2	83.1	71.8	91.4	98.8	95.2
February	58.3	85.4	72.2	92.0	102.0	90.9
March	64.0	86.5	72.5	96.0	105.0	99.0
April	76.0	86.8	72.3	98.8	104.7	108.3
May	59.1	86.9	75.0	103.2	103.0	109.1
June	70.6	85.3	77.0	101.9	103.0	109.8
July	69.3	83.4	76.1	101.2	104.4	104.7
August	68.2	81.6	80.2	102.4	102.3	103.3
September	72.7	82.7	83.0	104.4	102.2	101.8
October	76.1	80.4	85.9	104.4	98.1	101.3
November	81.0	81.2	90.4	105.9	84.6	101.1
December	82.0	75.6	90.7	100.0	91.9	95.5

Sources: Annual data are taken from Graham, p. 287. Graham took the data from *Bulletin de la Statistique Generale de la France*. Monthly data are from *Vierteljahreshefte zur Konjunkturforschung*, 1929, 4 Jahrgang, Heft 4, Teil A. p. 43.

Table 21.9
German population statistics, 1925

Total Population	62,349,000
Employed	31,113,000
Farming and Forestry	9,762,000
Industry	12,598,000
Business & Transport	5,384,000
Service	3,369,000
Union Members	3,635,000

Source: *Vierteljahrshefte zur Konjunkturforschung*, (1927, Heft 4, p. 20, p. 128), (1926, Heft 2, p. 56).

Table 21.10
Union members fully unemployed (percent)

	1923	1924	1925	1926	1927	1928	1929
January	4.2	26.5	8.1	22.6	16.5	11.2	19.4
February	5.2	25.1	7.3	22.0	15.5	10.4	22.3
March	5.6	16.6	5.8	21.4	11.5	9.2	16.9
April	7.0	10.4	4.3	18.6	8.9	6.9	11.1
May	6.2	8.6	3.6	18.1	7.0	6.3	9.1
June	4.1	10.5	3.5	18.1	6.3	6.2	8.5
July	3.5	12.5	3.7	17.7	5.5	6.3	8.6
August	6.3	12.4	4.3	16.7	5.0	6.5	8.9
September	9.9	10.5	4.5	15.2	4.6	6.6	9.6
October	19.1	8.4	5.8	14.2	4.5	7.8	10.9
November	23.4	7.3	10.7	14.2	7.4	9.5	13.7
December	28.2	8.1	19.4	16.7	12.9	16.7	20.1

Note: Yearly average: 1912, 2.0; 1913, 2.9; 1914 (first half), 3.2; 1920, 3.8; 1921, 2.5; 1922, 1.5.

Sources: 1912–1923: *The Workers Standard of Life in Countries with Depreciated Currency*, p. 21. *Vierteljahrshefte zur Konjunkturforschung*, (1926, Heft 1, p. 60), (1927, Heft 4, p. 123), (1928, Heft 1, Teil B, p. 73), (1928, Heft 4, Teil B, p. 71).

Table 21.11
Persons collecting unemployment compensation (thousands)

	1924	1925	1926	1927	1928	1929
January	—	593	2031	1827	1333	2246
February	—	540	2056	1696	1238	2461
March	—	466	1942	1121	1011	1899
April	572	320	1781	870	729	1126
May	402	233	1744	649	629	808
June	426	195	1741	540	611	723
July	526	197	1652	453	564	710
August	588	231	1548	404	574	726
September	513	266	1394	355	577	749
October	435	364	1308	340	671	889
November	437	673	1370	605	1030	1200
December	536	1499	1749	1188	1702	1774

Source: *Vierteljahrshefte zur Konjunkturforschung*, (1926/7, Heft 2, p. 99), (1927, Heft 2, p. 122), (1928, Heft 2, Teil B, p. 85), (1929, Heft 4, Teil B, p. 71). *Statistisches Jahrbuch für das Deutsche Reich*, 1927.

Table 21.12a
Number of bankruptcies

Year	Monthly average
1913	815
1919	83
1920	109
1921	257
1922	84
1923	22

Table 21.12b
Bankruptcies by month and year

	1922	1923	1924	1925	1926	1927	1928
January	140	24	31	760	2013	473	753
February	123	17	41	700	1920	457	706
March	151	30	68	744	1871	537	778
April	107	45	138	660	1302	403	619
May	95	32	322	755	1046	451	702
June	91	35	579	709	913	407	765
July	81	18	1173	797	701	418	663
August	59	13	855	718	493	395	547
September	45	9	817	887	467	355	551
October	43	15	520	1139	485	455	691
November	34	8	599	1320	453	582	687
December	39	17	572	1598	427	605	

Source: Annual data and monthly data for 1922–23, Graham, p. 280. Monthly data, 1924–28: Flink, p. 122, p. 165, p. 169, p. 173, p. 197.

to the rate prevailing early in the year and unemployment increased. Also, large numbers of firms went bankrupt in the summer of 1924, as shown in table 21.12a,b.

The first cycle after the monetary reform had a period of eight months and a fairly large amplitude. During the cycle, agents' expectations of inflation seem to have been correct, and the composition of output began to shift with the relative price shift. Real wages rose steadily, attaining their 1913 level by the summer of 1924. However, the technical nature of capital and the organization of industry did not substantially change in this cycle. The labor-intensive machinery and the industrial structure spawned by the inflation survived through the continued financing of the Reichsbank; and the months of credit restriction in the spring and summer of 1924 were not sufficient to remove them.[25]

The Dawes Loan
The revival from the Reichsbank's credit restrictions began in the fall of 1924 with the influx of foreign credits made available by the Dawes Loan. At that time the Reichsmark replaced the papermark as the legal-tender money and the Reichsbank resumed new discounts of private bills.[26] The Dawes Plan required Germany to place legal restrictions on the Reichsbank to insure the stability of the new currency and fixed a schedule and method for reparations payments.[27] Also, an official loan of 800 million gold marks was made to Germany in 1924; and substantial private foreign loans and direct investment flowed into the country.[28]

These foreign loans stimulated a reduction in unemployment and a recovery of production that peaked in May 1925, an expansion of nine months. Writers on this period share the common opinion that the loans served once again to postpone the reorganization of capital and industry to states consistent with a steady-state, stable-price environment, although the mechanism through which this delay occurred is not clear.[29] For a period of six months in this interregnum, unemployment reached much lower levels than at any time during the next ten years.

The Rationalization of Industry
The transition to the economic structure associated with a stable-price regime began finally in the summer of 1925. A number of huge combines constructed during the inflation collapsed at this time; the most notable liquidation was that in June 1925 of the enormous organization formed by Stinnes. The industrial reorganization was not confined only to the large combines; vast numbers of firms formed in the inflation were forced into bankruptcy at this time, as shown in table 21.12.[30]

From peak to trough, industrial production declined by 20 percent in less than a year as shown in figure 21.2. Unemployment reached 22 percent of union members by 1926 and did not fall below 10 percent until the second quarter of 1927.

However, output did not decline as much as employment, and it recovered much more rapidly. This resulted from the second aspect of rationalization, the transformation of plant and equipment to techniques reflecting a greater capital intensity. With the rise in real wages, much of the vast labor-intensive physical investment installed in the inflation proved to be inefficient. Large amounts of recently constructed capital which had negative marginal productivity were scrapped, especially in the mining, steel, shipbuilding, cement, and machinery industries.[31] The closing of inefficient plant and reorganization of methods within the remaining plant

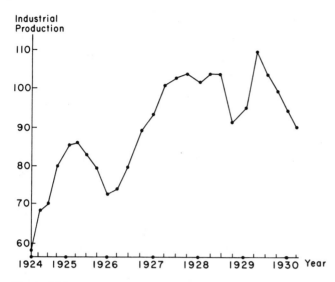

Figure 21.2
Quarterly index of industrial production

rapidly increased labor productivity, allowing output to increase faster than the fall in unemployment during the recovery. The rationalization movement continued for a number of years beyond 1925, during which unemployment was always high by previous standards.[32]

III   Conclusion: Interpreting the German Episode

The German evidence can be interpreted in two different ways. One may conclude that the 1925–26 downturn and the subsequent high unemployment were intimately connected to the inflation and reform, embodying the economy's transition process to a stable-price steady state. On the other hand, one may treat these later events as phenomena unconnected to the transition process, presuming that the transition was completed in the first one and a half years after the reform.

While most authors writing about this period agree with the first interpretation, this viewpoint generates the task of explaining why there was a one and a half year delay in observing the transition's negative real effects.[33] Explaining the lag by the credits granted to industry by the Reichsbank and foreign lenders leaves unanswered the question of why industry used these credits to maintain plants and organizations which were inefficient in a stable-price environment. In addition to the lag problem, the first interpretation also creates the usual question of whether the transitional monetary policy was optimal. Could some other policy have utilized more of the unemployed resources during the transition? The mere appearance of unemployed resources does not imply that the Reichsbank's policy was suboptimal.[34] Indeed, it appears to me that the inflation was sailing so fast out of control in the fall of 1923 that the Reichsbank's only choice was to throw out as heavy an anchor as possible, hoping it would catch hold of something solid. The object to which the mark attached itself was the dollar.

Maintaining the second interpretation of the German data leaves one with the problem of why the organization of industry and of production spawned by the inflation collapsed at this time. Also, the downturn was confined to Germany; none of the other industrialized countries experienced a similar cycle in these years.

In general, I consider that the results of this analysis imply that a large burden is involved in studying optimal transitional policies.[35] If the costs of both steady-state inflation and the transition to stable prices are high, then detailed study of the nature of each cost is necessary before reliable policy recommendations can be made. This is a discouraging prospect, filled with the potential for endless disputes. Sargent attempted to cut through this impasse with an observation that a sudden, resolute shift to a stable-price monetary regime can shift an economy at once to a stable-price steady state at small cost. If it is true that the transition costs are low, then one need not worry about studying the trade-off between transition costs and inflation costs. However, the evidence that I have presented indicates that there may have been large transition costs in the German case.

The German evidence also illuminates another aspect of this cost-trade-off issue. As a basis for arguing that the costs of steady-state inflation may be quite high, Fischer and Modigliani (1978) and Fischer (1980) have added distortions in capital markets which worsen as the inflation rate rises. Such distortions may alter the nature of the capital stock from its stable-price state, thereby also making the transition costs higher. Therefore, although the steady-state inflation costs may be higher because of these distortions, it may be desirable to implement a slower transition process.

Finally, on a more positive note, it appears from the German evidence that the credibility problem was not an important factor in the transition. Inflationary expectations seem to have been consistently correct prior to the realization of the large transitional costs.

Notes

I am indebted to Robert Barro, Robert Hodrick, Robert King, and Michael Schmid for useful comments. Support for this research was supplied through NSF Grant #SES-7926807.

1. More accurately, a general direction of research has been toward determining the least painful method to reduce the current inflation rates. See, for example, Okun (1978), Taylor (1979), Sargent (1980), Fellner (1979, 1980), McCallum (1980), Gordon (1981).

2. Working from entirely different frameworks these include Okun (1978), Perry (1978), Fellner (1979), Taylor (1980), Cagan (1980).

3. Such suggestions are not readily found in the writings of academic economists. They seem confined to some economists in the policy recommendation and forecasting business.

4. See Lucas (1980) for discussion of this gap in knowledge.

5. Even very similar theories yield different conclusions about the effect of sudden shifts to noninflationary policies. For instance, a flexible-price model with a Lucas-type supply function would respond to such a change differently in the case of purely rational expectations from the case of Bayesian learning about the new policy.

6. Gordon (1981) has studied fourteen different episodes, including the United States, Great Britain, Germany, France, and Switzerland, in which policies having the effect of reducing the inflation rate were implemented. Examining subsequent movements in prices and real income, he has found fairly large negative real effects, especially for the United States cases.

7. The bulk of Sargent's paper concerns the steps followed to bring about a sudden, successful stabilization rather than the real effects of such steps. With this analysis I have little disagreement.

8. With this shift in the rate of return on money, there was an increased demand for real balances which was satisfied in each case by continued rapid money creation on the part of central banks. These once and for all gains in revenue were used to finance the governments until they could shift the public-finance regime.

9. Graham (pp. 197–202) discusses the differential movements in the wholesale and cost of living price indices. The Statistisches Reichsamt (1925, p. 21) also broke the WPI into "Industry Inputs" and "Foods" through 1923. Data for these categories in 1924 are available in Statistisches reichsamt, Jahrbuch fur das Deutsche Reich, 1924, p. 265. The pattern of the ratio of the "Industry Inputs" price to the CLI price is identical to that in table 1. The pattern of the ratio of the "Industry Inputs" price to the "Foods" price is erratic. High in 1920, this price ratio fell in 1921 and did not begin to rise until the end of 1922. The ratio reached its highest level in 1923 and declined throughout 1924.

10. The industries to which I refer as "Capital-Goods Industries" are listed in the references as "Produktionsmittel industrien." They consist primarily of heavy industries: coal, electricity generation, steel and metals, chemical products, construction materials, construction industries, machine construction, and electrical installations. The consumer-goods industries, listed as "Verbrauchsguterindustrien," consist of producers of food, drink, clothing, cleaning, and tobacco. Due to data inconsistencies furniture, glassware, kitchen utensils, and luxury goods are excluded.

Some crude evidence that the investment-goods industry was capital intensive is provided in Vierteljahrshefte zur Konjunturforschung, 1927, Heft 4, p. 18. An attempt was made to measure the amount of capital in each industry in 1925 by measuring the total horsepower associated with it. For the investment-goods industry, labor employed was 6.7 million persons and avaiable horsepower was 13.6 million. For the consumption-goods industry, employment was 5.9 million persons while horsepower was 4.5 million. Interpreting horsepower as capital implies that the investment-goods industry was relatively capital-intensive, at least in 1925.

11. Bresciani-Turroni (1937, p. 371) cites the same source to make a similar point. He does not include the data for 1919, information which destroys the monotonic rise of labor in the capital-goods industry during the inflation. However, there was a large inflation in 1919. Bresciani-Turroni (pp. 198–199) also describes the flow of labor into particular heavy industries, mentioning an opinion at the time that the shift in output composition was without historical precedent.

12. See Bresciani-Turroni (pp. 196–98) or Graham (p. 11, p. 181, p. 281).

13. See Angell (1929, pp. 46–7).

14. In addition to being a monetary experiment, the German inflation was an experiment in the organization of industry. In the course of four years the economy shifted from a rather decentralized to a very centralized organization and back in the absence of underlying technological change. The driving factors were the monetary and subsidy policies of the central bank and government. For some discussion of the the details of German industrial organization, see National Industrial Conference Board (1931), Brady (1933), or Feldman (1977).

15. See Angell (pp. 45–54) or Bresciani-Turroni (pp. 203–212).

16. The structure of management and the nature of entrepreneurship also changed substantially. Production and marketing became secondary activities relative to finance. Financial personnel, with the ability to be creatively short on money during inflation, seem to earn large rents during such periods. See Bresciani-Turroni (pp. 295–298).

17. Bresciani-Turroni (p. 196); Graham (pp. 306–310).

18. Bresciani-Turroni (pp. 75–78); Graham (pp. 61–66). By August, 1923, a constant-value clause was added to the loans made by he Reichsbank to private individuals. A borrower had to repay the nominal principal of a loan plus an additional 80 percent of the depreciation of the principal in terms of sterling. If the depreciation rate of the mark were great enough and the discount rate were low enough, as in the fall of 1923, the loans would still represent a substantial subsidy. However, the borrower did take some risk with these loans; if the exchange rate depreciated faster than the price level rose, a borrower could have paid a large real-rate.

19. Bresciani-Turroni (p. 343, p. 209). The Reichsbank exchanged such legally authorized emergency money at a rate of 1 papermark of 1 mark of emergency money. Schacht (1927, p. 106) estimates that the total amount of emergency money in circulation at the end of 1923 equalled the entire Reichsbank note issue.

20. Why this combination of subsidies should have affected output, relative prices, and wage-rental ratios exactly in this way is unclear. To the extent that the demand for capital goods was subsidized directly, the measured relative market-price for capital goods should have risen as in Table 1. The shift in demand to capital goods should have raised the rental rate on existing capital. However, the subsidy should have lowered the rental rate relevant to entrepreneurs as the new capital entered production. The ultimate effect of this policy on the wage-rental ratio is unclear. Also, to the extent that supply of capital goods was subsidized, the measured relative market-price should have fallen.

21. However, real balances were reduced by the gradual withdrawal from circulation of the emergency money, the gold loans, and the foreign currency which had constituted part of the media of exchange during the inflation. See Bresciani-Turroni (pp. 348–9).

22. For the Reichsbank's viewpoint in making this policy change, see Schacht (pp. 152–162). Schacht states, "Not only the currency, but also the belief in the currency was made stable by this action on the part of the Reichsbank; and the belief was not evoked by long argument and persuasion, but imposed by the act." (p. 157).

23. For a description of the day-money and month-money markets, see Northrop (p. 126).

24. In Flood and Garber (1980) we presented evidence that agents must have been almost certain that a reform would take place just prior to the actual reform in November, 1923. We assumed that the reformed monetary process was noninflationary for the purpose of our analysis; but the new process could also have been inflationary, as long as it was process consistent.

25. This is the opinion of Bresciani-Turroni (p. 406) and Schacht (pp. 152–3). See also Flink (p. 124).

26. The Rentenmarks were phased out during the next 10 years and replaced by Reichsmarks.

27. Northop (pp. 28–38) describes in detail the law regulating the Reichsbank. Angell (pp. 61–81) describes the Dawes Plan. See also Flink (pp. 126–49).

28. The total foreign lending by the end of 1924 was about 1200–1500 million Reichsmarks. See Schmidt (p. 32) or Northrop (p. 176). The official loan was used to pay most of the reparations due for the year 1924–5; see Angell (p. 69).

29. Among the mechanisms mentioned are positive "psychological factors" (Northrop, p. 176), (Schmidt, p. 32), sales of interests in business firms to foreigners (Schmidt, p. 32), irrational employment of foreign credits, and a continued speculative spirit on the part of entrepreneurs (Bresciani-Turroni, p. 309, p. 406), disorganization of the German capital markets, and a resulting continuation of the financing of unproductive investment (Flink, p. 153). Flink (pp. 150–171) devotes a chapter to the question. However, the exact mechanism for this postponement remains sketchy.

30. Bresciani-Turroni (p. 406) contends that most of the bankruptcies occurred in firms formed during the inflation.

31. Bresciani-Turroni (pp. 388–90); Angell (pp. 82–189).

32. I do not know if changes in unemployment compensation encouraged this increase, as in the British case.

33. Bresciani-Turroni quotes from the *Report* of the Deutsche Bank for 1926: "This crisis is not due to a change in circumstances, but is essentially a phase in the process of deflation which German economic condition is undergoing after the monetary stabilization."
Graham (pp. 290–91) is not sure whether the 1925–26 downturn should be attributed to the stabilization. Graham is of the opinion that, aside from questions of income distribution, Germany gained on net from the hyperinflation; thus, he tends to minimize the connection of this downturn to the inflation. For Bresciani-Turroni's opinion of Graham, see Bresciani-Turroni, (p. 401, note).

34. Nor does it imply that these costs arose from the reform itself. In Flood and Garber (1980) we argue that the reform was endogenous. The inflation had become so extreme in autumn, 1923 that failure to end it immediately would have caused the collapse either of the state or of the monetary economy.

35. Because of its extreme rates of inflation, there is some doubt that the German episode can greatly illuminate current discussions aimed at reducing a 10–20 percent/year inflation rate. First, the current inflation is not proceeding at such a high rate that it threatens the continued existence of the state or of the moneary economy. Since it is not absolutely imperative that the Fed put an end to the inflation, agents' beliefs about the nature of the money-supply process can lag far behind an anti-inflationary shift in policy. Second, there is a different set of institutional arrangements under mild inflation. As an example, the over-lapping contract literature is irrelevant for analyzing the real effect of a switch to stable prices from hyperinflation; wage contracts, which had a very short life, were almost continuously renegotiated. See International Labour Office (pp. 44–73) for a detailed description of such contracts in the German case. The sudden end of the inflation could have had real effects through this channel only for a week or two.

References

Angell, J. (1929) *The Recovery of Germany*. New Haven: Yale University Press.

Brady, R. (1933) *The Rationalization Movement in German Industry*. Berkeley: University of California Press.

Bresciani-Turroni, C. (1968) *The Economics of Inflation*. Northampton: Augustus M. Kelley.

Cagan, P. (1980) Reflections to Rational Expectations, *Journal of Money, Credit and Banking*, 12:826–832.

Economist, volumes XCVIII, XCIX.

Feldman, G. (1977) *Iron and Steel in the German Inflation 1916–1923*. Princeton: Princeton University Press.

Fellner, W. (1980) The Valid Core of Rationality Hypotheses in the Theory of Expectations, *Journal of Money, Credit and Banking*, XII:763–787.

Fischer, S. (1980) Towards an Understanding of the Costs of Inflation: II. Amsterdam: North Holland, *Carnegie-Rochester Conference Series 15*, eds. K. Brunner and A. Meltzer.

Fischer, S. and Modigliani, F. (1978) Towards an Understanding of the Real Effects and Costs of Inflation. *Weltwirtschafliches Archiv*, 114:810–833.

Flink, S. (1930) *The German Reichsbank and Economic Germany*, New York: Harper.

Flood, R. and Garber, P. (1980) An Economic Theory of Monetary Reform, *Journal of Political Economy*, 88:24–58.

Gordon, R. J. (1981) Why Stopping Inflation May be Costly: Evidence from Fourteen Historical Episodes. Paper presented at Conference of NBER Project on Inflation.

Graham, F. (1930) *Exchange Prices, and Production in Hyperinflation: Germany, 1920–1923*. Princeton: Princeton University Press.

Institute für Konjunkturforschung. (1926–1930) *Vierteljahrshefte zur Konjunkturforschung*.

International Labour Office (1925) *The Workers Standard of Life in Countries with Depreciated Currency*. Studies and Reports, Series D, No. 15.

Lucas, R. E. (1978) Unemployment Policy, *American Economic Review*, Papers and Proceedings, 68:353–357.

Lucas, R.E., (1980) Rules, Discretion, and the Role of the Economic Adviser, *Rational Expectations and Economic Policy*, S. Fischer, ed. Chicago: University of Chicago Press.

McCallum, B. (1980) Rational Expectations and Macroeconomic Stabilization Policy; An Overview, *Journal of Money, Credit and Banking*, XII:716–746.

Meyer, L. and Rasche, R. (1980) On the Costs and Benefits of Anti-Inflation Policies, Federal Reserve Bank of St. Louis monthly *Review*, 62:3–14.

National Industrial Conference Board (1931) *Rationalization of German Industry*. New York: National Industrial Conference Board.

Northrop, M. (1938) *Control Policies of the Reichsbank, 1924–1933* New York: Columbia University Press.

Okun, A. (1978) Efficient Disinflationary Policies, *American Economic Review*, Papers and Proceedings, 68:348–352.

Perry, G. (1978) Slowing the Wage-Price Spiral: the Macroeconomic View, *Brookings Papers on Economic Activity*, 259–291.

Sargent, T. (1980) The Ends of Four Big Inflations Working Paper 158, Federal Reserve Bank of Minneapolis.

Schacht, H. (1927) *The Stabilization of the Mark*. New York: Adelphi Company.

Schmidt, C. (1934) *German Business Cycles, 1924–1933* New York: NBER.

Statistisches Reichsamt (1925) *Zahlen zur Geldentwertung in Deutschland, 1914 bis 1923* Berlin: Hobbing.

Statistisches Reichsamt (1927) *Statistisches Jahrbuch für das Deutsche Reich*, 46. Jahrgang, Berlin.

Taylor, J. (1975) Monetary Policy during a Transition to Rational Expectations, *Journal of Political Economy*, 83:1009–1021.

Taylor, J. (1979) An Econometric Business Cycle Model with Rational Expectations: Some Estimation Results Discussion Paper, Columbia University.

Taylor, J. (1979) Recent Developments in the Theory of Stabilization Policy. Working Paper, prepared for Federal Reserve Bank of St. Louis Conference on Stabilization Policy.

22

Comment on the Output Cost of Bringing Down Inflation

Robert P. Flood

The NBER Conference on Exchange Rates and International Macro-economics has presented me with the welcome opportunity to comment formally, for the second time, on the work of Buiter and Miller (B-M)[1] concerning the output cost of disinflation. In my first comment[2] I discussed some technical aspects of the sticky-price rule adopted by B-M. Presently, however, I will discuss some deeper aspects of the B-M methodology, which are typical in modern macroeconomics. In particular, B-M assume that an elected policy authority may reduce drastically a country's rate of monetary growth without opposition from other important political groups in the country. This assumption manifests itself when B-M solve their model conditional on agents' believing that the current policy regime will last indefinitely

An alternative methodology is to model agents' beliefs concerning the possibility that the current political regime will not last indefinitely. In particular, if a regime's policies are perceived to be too costly, then the regime may be ousted at the next election or the regime may disavow its former policies in order to be reelected. In either case, a policy which is perceived to be too costly is reversed at the next election.

When a political regime comes to power and attempts to lower the inflation rate by lowering the money growth rate, the effectiveness of their policy will depend on two elements: first, their ability actually to lower the money growth rate, and second, their ability to convince agents that the lowering of money growth is permanent. Since a regime can be ousted, a fine line must be tread: the lower the money growth rate, the higher the probability agents attach to the demise of the current regime at the next election. If the opposing political group favors a higher money growth rate than does the current regime, then raising the probability of the current regime's demise will raise the expected long-term rate of money growth. Thus, a lower current rate of money growth may raise the expected long-term rate of money growth and may not have the desired effect of lowering the inflation rate.

Sargent (1981) has discussed the importance of a country's political climate as a precondition for a successful low-cost transition from high inflation to low inflation. My intention in this comment is to provide a formal model of the political-economic interaction determining the success or failure of a political regime's attempt to reduce a country's inflation rate. The methods I use are drawn from a series of papers I have written with Peter Garber; especially relevant is Flood and Garber (1982).

A Model with Political Stochastic Process Switching

The framework for analysis is a stripped-down version of the B-M model. Its primary equations are:

$$m_t - p_t = -\lambda(E_t e_{t+1} - e_t), \qquad \lambda > 0, \tag{1}$$

$$p_{t+1} - p_t = \phi y_t + E_t \bar{p}_{t+1} - \bar{p}_t, \qquad \phi > 0, \tag{2}$$

$$y_t = \delta(e_t - p_t), \qquad \delta > 0, \tag{3}$$

where, in logarithms, m_t = money stock; p_t = home goods price level; e_t = exchange rate; y_t = demand for home goods; $\bar{p}_t$ = the value of p_t such that $y_t = 0$; and E_t = mathematical expectation operator conditioned by full information at time t, which includes all variables dated t or earlier. Equation (1) gives money market equilibrium; the supply of real money balances $(m_t - p_t)$ equals the demand for them $[-\lambda(E_t e_{t+1} - e_t)]$.[3] Equation (2) is a price adjustment function stating that inflation $(p_{t+1} - p_t)$ equals a function of excess demand for goods (ϕy_t) plus a "core" inflation rate, $E_t \bar{p}_{t+1} - \bar{p}$. The variable y_t is the excess demand for home goods, since the natural rate of output is normalized to zero; p_t is a predetermined variable, and output is assumed to be equal to the demand for it, y_t. Equation (3) specifies that output demand depends on the relative price of the home goods. The foreign price of foreign goods is constant and normalized to zero.

Since my version of the model appears to be quite different from that of B-M, I will describe it in more detail. First, I have used a discrete-time model, while B-M use a continuous-time one. This alteration is intended only to facilitate the stochastic analysis which follows. Second, I have ignored the foreign interest rate and a scale variable in the money demand function and the real rate of interest in the demand function for home goods; these are first-pass analytical simplifications. Third, the "core inflation" term in (2), $E_t \bar{p}_{t+1} - \bar{p}_t$, reflects my own preferred specification rather than that of B-M. In the present setup, $\bar{p}_t = e_t$.[4]

In this model, e_t is a "jumping" variable and p_t is a predetermined variable. Since $\bar{p}_t = e_t$, $\bar{p}_t$ also is a "jumping" variable.

The only exogenous variable in the model is the money supply. Thus, an exchange rate solution for the model is an expression giving e_t as a function of the predetermined variable p_t and all expected future values of m_t. Such a solution is

$$e_t = \beta p_t + \sum_{i=0}^{\infty} \gamma_i E_t m_{t+i}, \tag{4}$$

where

$$\beta = \frac{-1}{\delta \phi \lambda} < 0,$$

$$\gamma_0 = \frac{1 + (1/\delta \phi \lambda)}{1 + \lambda},$$

$$\gamma_1 = \gamma_0 \left(\frac{\lambda}{1 + \lambda} \right)^i; \qquad i = 0, 1, 2, \dots.$$

Note that $\sum_{i=0}^{\infty} \gamma_i = 1 + (1/\delta \phi \lambda) > 1$, as in Dornbusch (1976).

I assume that two money supply processes are relevant to agents' calculations of the infinite sum in (4). The current regime expands money according to

$$m_{t+i} = \mu_1 + m_{t+i-1} + v_{t+i}, \qquad i = 1, 2, 3, \dots, \tag{5}$$

where v_{t+i} is a zero mean disturbance which is not serially correlated. The opposition regime, if in power, would expand money according to

$$m_{t+i} = \mu_2 + m_{t+i-1} + v_{t+i}; \qquad i = 1, 2, 3, \dots, \mu_2 \geq \mu_1. \tag{6}$$

The current regime, though, is definitely in power from t to $t + 1$. However, at $t + 1$ there will be an election and the current regime will be deposed with probability π, where π is the probability agents at t attach to the current regime's being defeated in the $t + 1$ election. For simplicity, I assume that the $t + 1$ election is the only future election.[5] The probability π is determined by a simple model of the political process. In particular,

$$\pi = pr\{[y_{t+1}|OR] < \bar{y}\}, \tag{7}$$

where $pr\{x < y\}$ is the probability that x is less than y for any x and y. Thus, π is the probability that y_{t+1}, conditional on the continuation of the old regime, $[y_{t+1}|OR]$, is less than the minimum level required to maintain the current regime's majority, $\bar{y}$. Intuitively, (7) formalizes a political process which works as follows. The electorate at $t + 1$ examines the state of the world at $t + 1$ and calculates the level of y_{t+1} which would prevail if the old regime were left in power. If this conditional y_{t+1} is below the minimum $(y, \bar{y})$ required to preserve the current regime's majority, then the electorate ousts the old regime and elects a new regime. By assumption, the new regime will follow a monetary policy no more restrictive than that of the old regime.

To complete the solution of the model, we must calculate π and use π in the infinite sum in (4) to find e_t. Once e_t is found as a function of the current state, we may use the expression for e_t in (2) to find the inflation rate. The first task then is to determine π.

Forwarding equation (3) and using the definition of π from equation (7), obtain

$$\pi = pr\{\delta([e_{t+1}|OR] - p_{t+1}) < \bar{y}\}, \tag{8}$$

where $[e_{t+1}|OR]$ is the value of e_{t+1} conditional on the old regime's continuing in power at $t + 1$; p_{t+1} is determined at t and is an unconditional realization. To find $[e_{t+1}|OR]$, use (5) in (4), both forwarded appropriately, to obtain

$$[e_{t+1}|OR] = \beta p_{t+1} + (1 - \beta)m_{t+1} + (1 - \beta)\mu_1 \lambda. \tag{9}$$

Since m_{t+1} is generated by equation (5), we may use (9) and (5) in (8) to obtain

$$\pi = pr[v_{t+1} < Z + p_{t+1} - m_t - \mu_1(1 + \lambda)], \tag{10}$$

where $Z \equiv \bar{y}/\delta(1 - \beta)$.

To make more progress, a specific assumption must be made about the probability density function (p.d.f.) governing v_{t+1}. In particular, I assume that $v_{t+i}(i = 0, 1, 2, \ldots)$ has a uniform p.d.f., which is

$$f(v_{t+i}) = 1/(2\eta); \qquad -\eta \le v_{t+i} \le \eta, i = 1, 2, 3, \ldots,$$

$$f(v_{t+i}) = 0; \qquad v_{t+i} > \eta, i = 1, 2, 3, \ldots,$$

$$v_{t+i} < -\eta, i = 1, 2, 3, \ldots. \tag{11}$$

It follows that the probability that v_{t+1} is less than any number x is given by

$$pr(v_{t+1} < x) = \int_{-\eta}^{x} \frac{1}{2\eta} dv_{t+1} = \frac{x + \eta}{2\eta}, \tag{12}$$

when $-\eta \le x \le \eta$. If x lies outside the $[-\eta, \eta]$ bounds, then $pr(v_{t+1} < x)$ becomes either 0 or 1 depending on which bound is violated. In what follows I assume that η is large enough that the formula given in (12) is applicable.

Combine (12) and (10) to obtain

$$\pi = \frac{1}{2\eta}[\eta + Z + p_{t+1} - m_t - \mu_1(1 + \lambda)]. \tag{13}$$

The terms m_t, η, Z, and $\mu_1(1 + \lambda)$ are either state variables at t or parameters; however, p_{t+1} is an endogenous variable at t which may be expressed in terms of the state variables and parameters.

Using equations (2), (3), and the definition of $\bar{p}_{t+i}$, obtain

$$p_{t+1} = (1 - \theta)p_t + (\theta - 1)e_t + E_t e_{t+1}, \tag{14}$$

where $\theta \equiv \phi\delta$ and the stability of the model requires $\theta < 2$, which I assume.[6] Equation (4) allows us to express e_t and $E_t e_{t+1}$ as functions of p_t, p_{t+1} and expected future values of money. These expressions are

$$e_t = \beta p_t + \gamma_0 m_t + \gamma_1 E_t m_{t+1} + (1 - \pi) \sum_{i=2}^{\infty} \gamma_i E_t(m_{t+i}|OR)$$

$$+ \pi \sum_{i=2}^{\infty} \gamma_i E_t(m_{t+i}|NR), \tag{15}$$

and

$$E_t e_{t+1} = \beta p_{t+1} + \gamma_0 E_t m_{t+1} + (1 - \pi)\frac{(1 + \lambda)}{\lambda} \sum_{i=2}^{\infty} \gamma_i E_t(m_{t+i}|OR)$$

$$+ \pi \frac{(1 + \lambda)}{\lambda} \sum_{i=2}^{\infty} \gamma_i E_t(m_{t+i}|NR), \tag{16}$$

where $E_t(m_{t+1}|OR)$ and $E_t(m_{t+i}|NR)$ are expectations of m_{t+i} conditioned on time t information and on the old regime (OR) and new regime (NR), respectively. The law of iterated expectations allows us to convert the $t + 1$ expectations in the expression for e_{t+1} into t expectations in (16).

Under condition (OR), equation (5) governs m_{t+i}, and under (NR) equation (6) governs m_{t+i}. Use this information in (15) and (16) and combine those results in (14) to obtain

$$p_{t+1} = (1 - \theta)p_t + \theta m_t + \theta(1 - \beta)\lambda\mu_1 + \frac{\theta(1 - \beta)\lambda^2\pi(\mu_2 - \mu_1)}{1 + \lambda}. \tag{17}$$

To determine π, substitute (17) into (13) and rearrange to yield

$$\pi = \frac{(1 + \lambda)[\eta + Z + (1 - \theta)(p_t - m_t - \lambda\mu_1)]}{2\eta(1 + \lambda) + \lambda^2\theta(1 - \beta)(\mu_1 - \mu_2)}. \tag{18}$$

In interpreting (18), recall that η must be large enough to ensure $-\eta \leq Z + p_{t \neq 1} - m_t - \mu_1(1 + \lambda) \leq \eta$. This condition, along with the stability condition $\theta < 1$, allows $\partial\pi/\partial\mu_1 < 0$, which says that a reduction in the current money growth rate increases the chance that the old regime will be voted out at the next election.

The current inflation rate is $p_{t+1} - p_t$. Since p_t is predetermined at t, we may use (17) to obtain

$$\frac{\partial(p_{t+1} - p_t)}{\partial\mu_1} = \theta(1 - \beta)\lambda\left[\left(1 - \frac{\pi\lambda}{1 + \lambda}\right) + \frac{(\mu_2 - \mu_1)\lambda}{1 + \lambda}\left(\frac{\partial\pi}{\partial\mu_1}\right)\right]. \tag{19}$$

From (19), when $\mu_1 = \mu_2$, a reduction in current money growth (μ_1) must reduce inflation as $\pi\lambda/(1 + \lambda) < 1$. However, when μ_1 is less than μ_2, then a further reduction in μ_1 may *increase* inflation as $\partial\pi/\partial\mu_1 < 0$. Indeed, by setting (19) equal to zero, we find that value of μ_1 which minimizes the current inflation rate. This value is obtained by substituting the derivative of (18) into (19) and equating the result to zero to yield

$$\hat{\mu}_1 = \mu_2 - \frac{2\eta[1 + (1 - \hat{\pi})\lambda]}{\lambda(1 + \lambda)}. \tag{20}$$

where $\hat{\mu}_1$ is the inflation minimizing value of μ_1 and $\hat{\pi} = \pi(\hat{\mu}_1)$.

Final Remarks

This comment is not an appropriate place to draw out the nonstandard implications and interpretations of the type of political-based stochastic process switching model presented here. However, this simple model does serve to point out the importance of such considerations. Few propositions in monetary economics are as widely accepted as the proposition that decreasing the money growth rate will lower the inflation rate. However, it has been shown presently, in a simple example, that when an opposition party is lurking in the background with a policy more expansionary than that of the current regime, reducing the money growth rate need not reduce inflation.

Notes

This chapter appeared originally as Comment to Buiter and Miller (1983).

The views expressed here are those of the author and do not necessarily reflect the views of the Government of the Federal Reserve System or other members of their staff. The author would like to thank the National Science Foundation for support and Robert Hodrick for comments.

1. This comment is intended to apply equally to Buiter and Miller (1982) and Buiter and Miller (1983).

2. My first comment is Flood (1982).

3. I have followed B-M, section 10.2, in deflating nominal money balances by the domestic price of home goods. Apparently, B-M follow Dornbusch (1976) in adopting this simplification. Using this deflator leads to the B-M, section 10.2, definition of inflation, $p_{t+1} - p_t$, which I also use. The algebra of the model would be more difficult if a consumer price index deflated money balances and defined inflation. However, such complications do not reverse B-M's results or mine; thus they are avoided.

4. The price adjustment rule I use is based largely on the work of Michael Mussa and is applied to the open economy in his 1982 paper.

5. Allowing a single election makes the present setup a special case of Flood and Garber (1982). My paper with Garber is more general than the present model in that our joint work allows calculation of an equilibrium when the endogenous stocahstic variable (y_{t+i}) may pass a critical barrier $(\bar{y})$ at *any* future data.

6. This is not a stability condition in the sense of assuming away "bubbles." It is a condition for the stability of "market fundamentals" in the sense of Flood and Garber (1980). To see this point clearly, examine equation (17) with $\mu_1 = \mu_2 = 0$.

References

Buiter, W., and M. Miller. 1982. Real exchange rate overshooting and the output cost of bringing down inflation. *European Economic Review* 18:85–123.

Buiter, W., and M. Miller. 1983. Real exchange rate overshooting and the output cost of bringing down inflation: Some further results. In J. E. Frenkel, ed. *Exchange Rates and International Macroeconomics*. (Chicago: University of Chicago Press).

Dornbusch, R. 1976. Expectations and exchange rate dynamics. *Journal of Political Economy* 84 (December): 1161–76.

Flood, R. 1982. Comment on the Buiter and Miller paper. *European Economic Review* 18:125–27.

Flood, R., and P. Garber. 1980. Market fundamentals versus price level bubbles: The first tests. *Journal of Political Economy* 88, no. 1:24–58.

Flood, R., and P. Garber. 1982. A model of stochastic process switching. Board of Governors of the Federal Reserve, Washington, D.C. Working paper.

Mussa, M. 1982. A model of exchange rate dynamics. *Journal of Political Economy* 90, no. 1:74–104.

Sargent, T. 1981. Stopping moderate inflations: The methods of Poincaré and Thatcher. University of Minnesota. Working paper.

Index